COMMONWEALTH
CATHOLICISM

COMMONWEALTH CATHOLICISM

CATHOLICISM

*A History of the
Catholic Church in Virginia*

GERALD P. FOGARTY, S.J.

UNIVERSITY OF NOTRE DAME PRESS
Notre Dame, Indiana

Designed by Wendy McMillen
Set in 10.8/13.2 Stempel Garamond by Stanton Publication Services, Inc.
Printed in the U.S.A. by Sheridan Books, Inc.

Manufactured in the United States of America

Library of Congress Cataloging-in-Publication Data
Fogarty, Gerald P.
Commonwealth Catholicism : a history of the Catholic Church in
Virginia / Gerald P. Fogarty.
p.   cm.
Includes bibliographical references and index.
ISBN 0-268-02264-x (cloth : alk. paper)
1. Catholic Church. Diocese of Richmond (Va.)—History.
2. Richmond (Va.)—Church history.   I. Title.
BX1417.R5 F64 2001
282'.755—dc21
00-011711

∞ This book was printed on acid-free paper.

To the Catholics of Virginia who,
from colonial times,
have handed on the faith

The University of Notre Dame Press
gratefully acknowledges the
generous support of

WALTER F. SULLIVAN
Bishop of Richmond

CONTENTS

Writing the history of a diocese is a difficult task at best. Writing one that will please everyone is virtually impossible. In the case of a southern diocese, the problem is made greater because historians have focused their attention on the Northeast and Midwest. In the specific case of the Church in Virginia, the task was made more complicated by the fact that there has never been one geographical focus for the Church in that state. When our story begins in the colonial period, Catholics had clustered in Stafford County on the Potomac River. By the time the diocese was established in 1820, Catholics were gathered in small communities as far removed as Norfolk and Martinsburg, now in West Virginia. The diocese covered the entire original state of Virginia, until the establishment of the diocese of Wheeling in 1850. The Civil War divided the state, but left the original boundaries of the dioceses as they had been before hostilities broke out. Part of West Virginia remained in the diocese of Richmond, and part of Virginia was retained by the diocese of Wheeling. This situation prevailed until 1974, when the new diocese of Arlington was established and diocesan lines were made to coincide with state lines.

Since the diocese had no geographical focal point, I found myself with the task of telling several, often divergent, stories of the Catholic people in the diocese, who had in common only that they lived at the same time in the same state, whether they were entrepreneurs and priests in Norfolk or merchants and politicians in Richmond or railroad workers in Harpers Ferry. My strategy was to attempt to narrate the beginnings of each of these disparate communities with as much attention as documentary evidence would permit to the laypeople who kept the faith even before they had a resident priest. Laypeople, in general, left few documents about their involvement in the church, except for those important indications of their sacramental life: baptismal and marriage records retained in the parishes. I had transcribed onto a computer file all the records of the parishes before the Civil War and initially intended to analyze those records and compare them with census and tax rolls to give some flesh to the dry bones of the parish records. Unfortunately, I was unable to recruit any assistance for that task. Although I could do only limited work on those data myself, the sacramental records provide an important source for our understanding of the stability, or the mobility, and the social status of Virginia's Catholics—and perhaps illuminate the question as to how many Catholic immigrants were lost to the Church because of the lack of a priest. They would be a key to creating a social profile of the Catholic community, but the effort involved would be time-consuming.

If the laity left few records, the same is true for priests, except for the letters they may have written to the bishop that were preserved. Some of the prominent priests mentioned in this history may have merited a study in themselves, but for the fact that there is simply no correspondence to or from them, aside from disputes they may have had with the bishop. Richmond, moreover, was a diocese that never produced 50 percent of its priests and had to recruit them from elsewhere. All Hallows College, Drumcondra, Ireland, and the American College, Louvain, were two principal sources. Some early European recruits, fortunately, wrote back lively accounts of their missionary experiences.

Richmond's first bishops fared little better in terms of leaving a paper trail. The first bishop, Patrick Kelly, left after a short time. My efforts to find material in the diocese of Waterford and Lismore, to which he was transferred, yielded nothing, despite the generous efforts of the present bishop of that see, William Russell. Richmond's second bishop, Richard V. Whelan, was an itinerant, who soon moved to Wheeling, where he became the first bishop. In the diocese of Wheeling, rumors persist that correspondence was thrown away with the construction of the new cathedral in the 1920s. For whatever reason, there are no Whelan papers. Whelan's successor in Richmond, John McGill, was highly selective in what he preserved, but at least he seems to have been later persuaded by Francis Janssens to record what he considered to be the important events of his episcopate. The papers of McGill, James Gibbons, John J. Keane, Augustine van de Vyver, and Denis J. O'Connell were calendared and microfilmed at the University of Notre Dame, which maintains an index to the collection on its archives' web page. Since the O'Connell collection is already well indexed, I have assessed all other documents from the episcopate of McGill to that of Peter L. Ireton with ZYIndex, enabling any document to be retrieved in a matter of seconds. At the present writing, Bishop Walter F. Sullivan of Richmond is in the process of establishing an archive center and reorganizing the material. Since the present order of documents will be retained, however, I have cited them without their present box numbers, which will shortly be changed.

While primarily narrating the story of Catholicism in the diocese of Richmond, I was also concerned with portraying the activities of the bishops in relation to other bishops. A diocese, after all, is part of the national and universal Church. Until 1916, American bishops had the right to nominate other bishops within their metropolitan province. The records for Richmond's bishops in these matters are largely to be found in other dioceses or in the archives of the Congregation of Propaganda Fide in Rome. They reveal the vision of Richmond's bishops for the broader church. As I introduce each bishop, therefore, I have included a section on his interaction with his colleagues in neighboring dioceses. In the case of the appointment of Augustine van de Vyver as bishop, these records also indicate the opposition he met from his two predecessors, Cardinal James Gibbons of Baltimore and John J. Keane, the first rector of the Catholic University of America, as well as from his successor, Denis J. O'Connell, then rector of the American College in Rome. The demise of the system of American bishops nominating other bishops, incidentally, meant in the case of Richmond's bishops that they seldom corresponded with even their metropolitan, the archbishop of Baltimore. In short, the strong tradition of collegiality came to an end in the American Church.

This history, then, is one in a traditional mode, derived almost exclusively from archival sources, supplemented by newspapers or other contemporary records. Catholics in Virginia were a tiny minority for much of their history. After 1840, they were primarily Irish immigrants, some of whom were well-to-do merchants. Germans and Italians also came, but in smaller numbers. All accommodated to the prevailing culture and, with the exceptions of the Know-Nothing campaign of the 1850s and the Ku Klux Klan opposition in the 1920s, they got along with their neighbors. But they also kept a low profile, proving their loyalty by marching to war behind the Stars and Bars. Only during Reconstruction did some of them emerge to political prominence, but then primarily in Richmond. This quest to blend in may also account for the lack of any correspondence between the bishops and political leaders. In this regard, it is unfortunate that the governors' papers in the Virginia State Library are not indexed but are arranged only in chronological order. In the absence of a precise issue and date, it is difficult to find any letters from the bishops of Richmond, nor are there any extant letters from governors in the bishops' files.

I actually end this history with the implementation of Vatican II. And, there I derive my information almost exclusively from published material. The reason is simple. As any historian knows, once one gets that close to the present, there is danger of losing objectivity in trying to evaluate people who are still alive. My final chapter on the division of the diocese of Richmond is actually the conclusion, recounting the population growth in northern Virginia but omitting the financial, ideological, or personal tensions that may have existed.

This book has been ten years in the making. In the course of my research, I have met numerous people who have helped me on my way. First, I am grateful to Bishop Sullivan, who supported me for a year to initiate my research and manifested great patience as he eagerly awaited, in vain, the completion of the work in time for the one hundred and seventy-fifth anniversary of the diocese in 1995. I wish also to thank the University of Virginia for granting me another sabbatical year to continue my work. Archivists, as every historian knows, can help or hinder research. I have been fortunate. First of all in the archdiocese of Baltimore, I want to thank Sister Felicitas Power, R.S.M., and her successor, Father Paul Thomas; in the diocese of Charleston, Sister Anne Francis Campbell, O.L.M.; in the diocese of Wheeling, Miss Margaret Brennan and Dr. Tricia Pyne; and in the diocese of Arlington, the late Bishop John R. Keating. Of those who helped me in the archives of religious communities and institutions in the United States, I am grateful to Sister Margaret O'Rourke, S.B.S, archivist of the Blessed Sacrament Sisters, Father Peter Hogan, S.S.J., archivist of the Josephite Fathers, Sister M. Aloysia, D.C., archivist of the Daughters of Charity, Sister St. Michel Mullany, I.H.M., archivist of the Sisters, Servants of the Immaculate Heart of Mary, and Dr. Kelly Fitzpatrick of Mount Saint Mary's Seminary and College. Anyone who has used the Sulpician archives in Baltimore is well aware of the friendly reception to which one looks forward from Father John Bowen, S.S., now retired.

For providing me with material on other aspects of Virginia history, I want to thank Michael Holt, professor of history at the University of Virginia, and Michael Plunkett, director of special collections of the Alderman Library. Linda McGubbins, then a graduate student at Old Dominion University, provided me with information on Virginia women converts and Mrs. Julia Woodbridge Oxrieder furnished me with newspaper clippings and other material for the Catholic community in Williamsburg.

In Rome, I wish to express my gratitude to Sean Brady, then Rector of the Irish College and now archbishop of Armagh, for so graciously opening the archives on a Saturday and then acting as my research assistant; to Josef Metzer, O.M.I., former archivist of the Vatican Secret Archives; to the staff of the archives of the Congregation of Propaganda Fide; and to Brother Randall Riede, C.F.X., librarian of the North American College. At the American College, Louvain, Dr. Jack Dick not only gave me easy assess to the archives, but proved to be a valuable source of information. At All Hallows College, Drumcondra, Father Brian Rafferty, C.M., was generous with his time not only in giving me full run of the archives but in providing me with the history of the college.

Within the diocese of Richmond, I want to express my gratitude first to Dr. James Henry Bailey, whose earlier *History of the Diocese of Richmond* up to 1872 became a starting point for this study and whose unpublished manuscript on the later period proved especially valuable in providing me with a guide to articles in *The Catholic Virginian*. I benefited from an early critique from the late Brother Philip Dougherty, C.F.X., and have also depended on the advice of several priests who graciously plowed through the first draft of the manuscript, especially Monsignor Raymond Barton, Monsignor William Sullivan, and Monsignor Thomas Shreve. In addition, several priests of both Richmond and Arlington were generous with their time in granting me interviews or in reading excerpts from my manuscript, especially Monsignor John Hannan, Father Vernon Bowers, Monsignor Chester Michael, Monsignor Thomas Scannell, and Monsignor Francis Bradigan. All of them helped me not only by providing a context within which to place my archival material but by warning me not to venture into waters that for the present had best be left uncharted.

I would not think of publishing anything of any moment without the careful scrutiny of my friend and former professor, James Hennesey, S.J., then at Lemoyne College, who diligently read an overly lengthy and, in hindsight, very tedious early draft of this work. For the painstaking work of helping me put the bibliography together, I want to thank Sara Weaver, one of the best undergraduate students I have taught here at the University of Virginia.

Having acknowledged my gratitude to so many, it remains only for me to say that I am alone responsible for what I have written.

Bishop Walter F. Sullivan

Father Gerald Fogarty has fashioned for us from the past a gift for the future. It is a useful and essential gift. As we journey into the new millennium, it is a gift we can carry along, consult with often, and turn to for wisdom and inspiration for many years to come.

A full decade in the making, Father Fogarty's work builds upon our first diocesan history published by Dr. James Bailey in 1956. Father Fogarty conducts us through those decades which forged our character as a missionary diocese. He introduces us to our forebears in faith whose determined and practical ways of being Catholic helped mold us into the people with a mission that we are today.

Like any good history should, Father Fogarty's chronicle ends where things are just beginning. He brings us to that moment of transition when our diocese looks toward receiving, under the wise and visionary leadership of my beloved predecessor Bishop John J. Russell, the decrees of the Second Vatican Council. Someday another history will tell of Bishop Russell's initiatives to implement those decrees and will recount the living out of those decrees—a process that I have followed throughout my twenty-six years as Bishop of Richmond.

This book is in no way a tedious compilation of dry facts and forgotten dates. It is a wealth of tales woven together into an ongoing story of faith. The story chronicles the evolution of a church constantly alive in the hearts of its people. It parallels the secular history of those people—in our nation's struggles for independence in the eighteenth century, during the times of civil strife in the nineteenth century, and all through the progressive movement toward world prominence in the twentieth century. The story tells of the ventures and adventures of a missionary people who carried their faith to the far corners of Virginia and West Virginia and who spread their faith over every mile of those vast territories. It is the story of a diocese whose borders once extended from the Atlantic Ocean to the Ohio River and whose vitality gave birth to two other dioceses—the Diocese of Wheeling in that section of Virginia that became West Virginia and the Diocese of Arlington in Northern Virginia.

Father Fogarty's history is indeed a gift for which I am most grateful. It blesses us with the legacy of conviction and dedication in faith that is our inheritance from so many Catholic women and men of the past. Their lives are our history. That history reassures us of the lasting value of our own daily endeavors in faith. The faith we live today, because of the faith of those who came before us, will be our gift of encouragement to the generations of Catholics who will follow us.

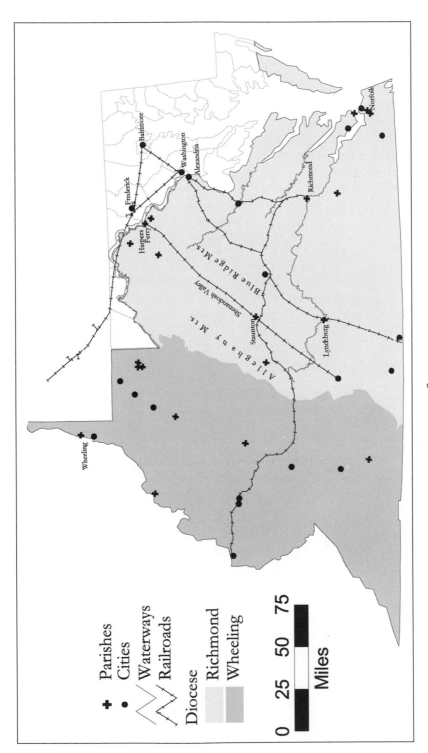

Parishes +
Cities ●
Waterways
Railroads

Diocese
　Richmond
　Wheeling

Miles
0　25　50　75

Baltimore
Washington
Alexandria
Frederick
Harpers Ferry
Blue Ridge Mts.
Shenandoah Valley
Allegheny Mts.
Staunton
Lynchburg
Richmond
Norfolk
Wheeling

— 1850 —

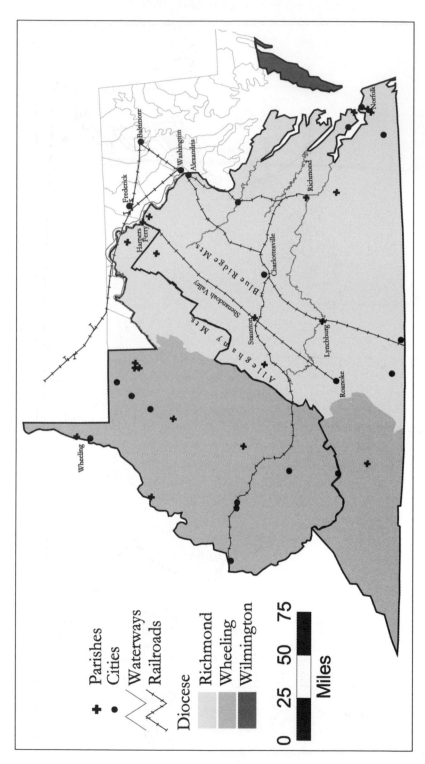

— 1866–1974 —

Parishes +
Cities ●
Waterways
Railroads

Diocese
Richmond
Wheeling
Wilmington

Miles
0 25 50 75

Baltimore
Frederick
Washington
Alexandria
Harpers Ferry
Wheeling
Blue Ridge Mts.
Shenandoah Valley
Allegheny Mts.
Charlottesville
Richmond
Staunton
Lynchburg
Roanoke
Norfolk

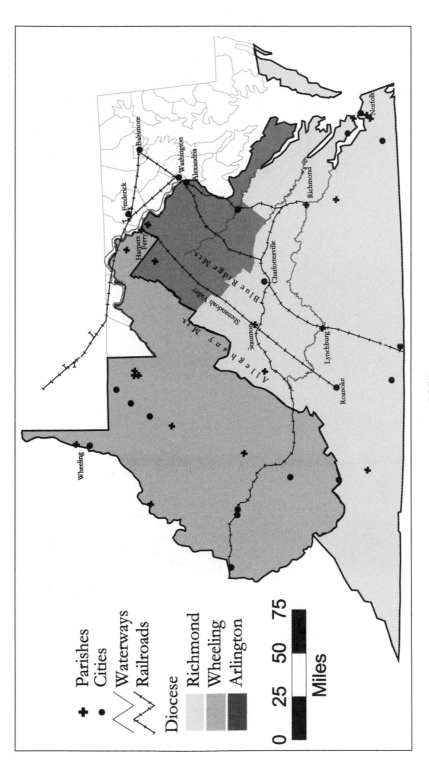

— 1974 —

COMMONWEALTH
CATHOLICISM

PART I

Creating Catholic Space
in a Protestant Wilderness

Virginia was not a hospitable place for Catholics. During the colonial period, Virginians sent out a clear message that to be Virginian meant to be Protestant. Yet, even then, they could be pragmatic, if Catholics were willing to accommodate themselves to the culture. The Brents were the only known Catholic family in colonial Virginia. They thrived and remained devout, but unostentatious, in their religion; their service to the community as outstanding members of the legal profession and the militia led most of their neighbors not to apply to them the otherwise harsh anti-Catholic laws of the colony.

The Revolution brought a respite in anti-Catholicism, especially since Americans had won their independence with the assistance of Catholic France—a point later Virginia Catholics would remember. But life in the early republic was still not easy for Catholics. Many of Virginia's leaders openly embraced the Enlightenment and the French Revolution, with its persecution of the Church. As Catholics trickled into the state, they had to contend with not only rationalist attacks on any supernatural religion but also opposition to Catholicism because of its "foreign" allegiance to the pope. But some Catholics also embraced the Enlightenment, especially some of the lay trustees in Norfolk who adopted many of Virginia's democratic mores and went into schism. While many of their demands were extreme, such as the right to elect their pastor, and some of their arguments dishonest, such as the claim that they had no priest, historians have too often failed to note that some Norfolk trustees remained faithful members of the

Church and that trustees elsewhere never sought to intrude into the legitimate exercise of ecclesiastical authority. The Norfolk dispute, however, illustrated how little Roman officials understood about the new nation. In 1820, relying on erroneous information, they established the diocese of Richmond, with Patrick Kelly as the first bishop. Two years later, they had to return it to the administration of the archbishop of Baltimore who retained it until 1840.

Until 1863, Virginia included the present state of West Virginia. Richmond's second bishop, Richard V. Whelan, preferred the rugged western part of the state and ultimately moved there to become the first bishop of Wheeling. He personified the itinerant missionary priest and bishop willing to travel long distances in search of a scattered flock living in a hostile environment. When he recruited priests, he painted a stark portrait of missionary life. Although there were a few well-to-do Catholics in the state, most were Irish and, later, German immigrants who worked in the shipyards around Norfolk and on the canals and railroads that gradually linked the disparate parts of the state together. Because of the vastness of Virginia, in 1849 Whelan succeeded in having the state split into two dioceses, with himself in Wheeling and John McGill appointed third bishop of Richmond.

Cities presented a different challenge than the one Whelan seemed to prefer, for in the urban setting Catholics associated more closely with their Protestant neighbors and their actions fell under closer scrutiny. For this reason, Father Timothy O'Brien in Richmond and later Father Matthew O'Keefe in Norfolk insisted that their churches be architectural statements of Catholic presence. To gain acceptance, Catholics, laity and clergy, were only too eager to show they were loyal Virginians. On the one, hand this meant defense of slavery. On the other, it meant the heroic service of O'Keefe and the Daughters of Charity in Norfolk during the Yellow Fever epidemic of 1855 that resulted in the founding of St. Vincent's Hospital, now the De Paul Medical Center. Yet, some Virginians still challenged the right of Catholics to be Americans. In the gubernatorial campaign of 1855, in the midst of the Yellow Fever epidemic, the Know-Nothings conducted a spirited, but unsuccessful, bid for the office. While they were successful in gaining some local offices, they were thwarted statewide, in part because Virginia by this time had several prominent converts to Catholicism.

Virginia's Catholics, like their coreligionists in other parts of the country, solidified their position in society by serving in the Civil War. Richmond's Irish elite provided a company that served for the duration of the war, while other units enlisted for shorter periods. McGill and Whelan both remained staunch supporters of the Confederacy, as did most of their priests. Daughters of Charity from Emmitsburg and Sisters of Charity of Our Lady of Mercy from Charleston nursed in Virginia's military hospitals. At the war's end, service in the military or in hospitals had done more than McGill's efforts, in an apologetical work, to win Catholic acceptance in Virginia.

The period that ended with Reconstruction coincided with the beginning of the end of an ecclesiastical era. Part of the "job description" for a bishop in Whelan and McGill's day was concern for other dioceses within the metropolitan province of Baltimore, which, until 1850, encompassed the entire nation. Though Richmond was far from an important see, McGill's recommendations for vacant dioceses are informative for revealing not only his concern for the national church but also the type of prelate he thought qualified to govern a diocese. After the First Vatican Council (1869–70), this expression of episcopal collegiality gradually declined until the Vatican removed it in the twentieth century.

CHAPTER I

Catholicism in Colonial Virginia

Bahía de Santa María. This was the name the Spanish, on their maps of the 1520s, gave the large bay opening into the Atlantic Ocean. The English would later call it by its Indian name of Chesapeake. But the Spanish failed to explore it. For one thing it was elusive. Depending on the weather and time of year, a ship could mistake its entrance for a cove. In 1526, Lucas Vásquez de Ayllón had received a license from the king to settle the Atlantic coast. With 600 colonists, he had established a short-lived settlement on the shores of what he believed to be St. Mary's Bay, but which more recent research indicates was probably Sapelo Sound in Georgia.[1] The Spanish made no further effort to establish settlements in the future United States until the French began making incursions into Florida and threatening the return voyages of treasure-laden galleons. In 1565, Pedro Menéndez de Avilés took over the proprietorship of Florida and established the first permanent European settlement at St. Augustine. From thence would come missionaries to a land the natives called Ajacán. The English later named it Virginia, after Elizabeth, their virgin queen.

Virginia's Catholic history began when Spanish Jesuits attempted to establish a mission, but they were all massacred within a short time. A generation later, Virginia's English settlers were no more hospitable to Catholics, although the Brent family managed to thrive in the Northern Neck. Only the Revolution brought full religious toleration, but the colonial period had shaped the ethos within which later Catholics would have to preserve their religion.

The Spanish Jesuit Mission in Virginia

In 1565, after the settlement of St. Augustine, Menéndez wished to fortify this northern region against French and English encroachments and, perhaps, find the fabled passage to the western ocean. Missionaries of the new religious order, the Society of Jesus, founded only in 1540, envisioned it as a site for yet another in a series of evangelization successes, for Francis Xavier had already established the Jesuits' reputation in the mission fields of India and Japan. The story had all the makings of a television adventure—a Spanish governor out for the glory of Spain, dedicated Jesuit missionaries, and a native Algonquin cacique, a convert to Christianity, eager, or so he said, to bring the cross of Christianity to his people.

This cacique, Don Luis de Velasco, named after his baptismal sponsor, the viceroy of Mexico, fell into Spanish hands around 1559. He was probably a youth at the time, for all the colonizing powers captured young Indians who could learn a European language and later act as interpreters. Taken to Spain, he befriended King Philip, and then went to Havana. At some point, he met Pedro Menéndez de Avilés. He was only too eager to guide Menéndez' expedition to establish a defensive line in Ajacán.

Menéndez originally entrusted the missionary work to two Dominican friars in 1566, but the expedition was aborted when Don Luis failed to recognize his homeland. Their ship was blown out to sea and returned to Spain, where the friars bitterly complained of Menéndez' administration of Florida.[2] The governor then turned to the Jesuits, whom he had been trying to recruit since 1565. In 1566, the first contingent of two priests and one brother arrived in Florida. In 1568, Father Baptista de Segura, two other priests, three brothers, and five catechists arrived. Within a year, Segura, the vice-provincial, had travelled enough through Florida to be convinced that he and his companions should seek a more fruitful mission field elsewhere. His dream coincided with the plans of Menéndez and Don Luis. On August 5, 1570, Segura, with Don Luis as guide, set out from St. Elena on the Florida coast. Other members of the missionary band were Father Luis Quirós, Brothers Gabriel Gómez, Sancho de Zaballos, still a novice, Juan Baptista Méndez, Pedro de Linares, Cristóbal Redondo, Gabriel de Solís, and a young boy, Alonso de Olmos, son of a settler. Taking with them chalices, vestments, and other items needed for the new mission, they refused a military escort, for they had already discovered that the disedifying conduct of the soldiers and their cruelty to the natives only impeded the work of evangelization. On September 10, they reached the "land of Don Luis" and were warmly welcomed by his brother caciques.[3]

According to the available evidence, the expedition rounded Cape Henry and sailed some forty miles up the James River to what is now College Creek. They then moved overland, probably to Chiskiak on Queens Creek, off the York River, more accessible to a supply ship. Both Segura and Quirós wrote back to Cuba and King Philip asking for further supplies, especially seeds for spring planting. Like missionaries elsewhere, the Jesuits intended to teach the natives agricultural techniques, both to stave off the famine then raging and to make them more sedentary and, therefore, more easily evangelized.

All seemed to go well in the beginning. Don Luis asked to have his dying three-year-old brother baptized. He then rejected his younger brother's surrender to him of the leadership of the clan, for, he stated, he came on a spiritual mission. Within a week, however, he abandoned the missionaries to live in the territory of his uncle, an important cacique, a journey of a day and a half away. He claimed that he was gathering students for the mission and searching for food, but his real reason was less virtuous—as a chief he could take several wives. Twice, Segura sent a novice to reprimand him. In the meantime, the missionaries had consumed their meager supplies and were bartering with the local villages for corn. Their only hope was the arrival of the supply ship.

In January, 1571, Segura made a final overture to Don Luis. This time he sent Father Quirós and Brothers Solís and Méndez. Don Luis agreed to follow them back to the mission. Instead, on February 4, he and a party intercepted them, probably near Jamestown, killed Quirós and Solís, and wounded Méndez, who fled into the woods, where he was slain the next morning. Don Luis burned the bodies and stole their clothing. On February 9, he and his party arrived at the mission, asked for all the axes on the pretense of cutting wood, but then killed the Jesuits. After burying the bodies, the natives adorned themselves with the Jesuits' clothing, vestments, and patens, which they hung around their necks. Only Alonso, the young boy, was spared, apparently protected by a friendly chief. Virginia had received its first martyrs.[4]

In the spring of 1571, the relief expedition finally arrived. Instead of the prearranged signal fires on the shoreline, the sailors saw men on shore wearing the Jesuits' cassocks and gesturing to them to come ashore. As the ship drew closer, several boats of natives attacked it. The Spanish drove them off and captured two chiefs, from whom they learned of the Jesuits' massacre and of Alonso's survival. A year later, Menéndez led a punitive expedition back to the site, rescued Alonso, killed several Indians, and captured several more. Of the captives, he hanged eight or nine for implication in the killings and released five, but Don Luis eluded Menéndez' wrath.[5]

The recovery of the young Alonso ended any Spanish effort to found a mission in Virginia. The martyrdom of Virginia's first missionaries led Father Francis Borgia, S.J., their general, to direct future Jesuit efforts away from Florida and its adjacent territory to Mexico. A decade later, Sir Walter Raleigh made the first English incursions into this territory claimed by the Spanish. The Spanish were not to settle Virginia, but the memory of their presence lingered, as did legends about Don Luis.

Virginia as an English Colony

When the English framed a treaty with the Chickahominies, one settler reported they were more than willing to furnish armed men "against the Spaniards, whose name is odious among them, for Powhatan's father was driven by them from the west-Indies [a generic term for Spanish territory] into these parts." "Powhatan's father" may have been, in fact, his older brother, Opechancanough, reputed to have been "a Prince of a Foreign Nation," who came from "the South-West." This has led to conjecture that Opechancanough may have been Don Luis, especially because John Smith found the chief surprisingly curious about European affairs. What is certain is that the Indians the English encountered seemed to retain some memory of a Spanish presence.[6] Virginia's permanent European settlers would join the natives in hostility to the Spanish and all things Catholic.

The settlement of Jamestown in 1607 marked the beginning not only of English but also of Protestant presence in America. James I's grant of land to the Virginia Company brought conflict with the competing claims of the Spanish to the south and the French to the north.

But this colonial competition was inseparable from religious hostility. The Church of England had been independent of Rome for seventy-five years, and almost two decades had passed since the defeat of the Spanish Armada in 1588. As recently as November 5, 1605, England had been in upheaval over the discovery of the Gunpowder Plot, the scheme supposedly designed by the Catholic Guy Fawkes to blow up the Parliament buildings. The English settlers of Jamestown inherited long-standing suspicions of anyone with Catholic loyalties. The first expedition carried with it sealed instructions from the Virginia Company appointing the members of the governing council. Among them was Edward Maria Wingfield, who was elected president of the council for the first year. From an old Catholic family—his father was the godson of Mary Tudor and Cardinal Reginald Pole—Wingfield had taken the oath of supremacy, renouncing his Catholicism and conforming to the Church of England. Imperious by nature, he had imprisoned John Smith for plotting mutiny during the voyage over. Once at Jamestown, his first act as president was to have Smith excluded from the governing council to which the company had appointed him. The two never resolved their differences, and, in September, 1607, Wingfield was deposed.[7] Whether Wingfield's problem was the suspicion that he was a crypto-Catholic is difficult to determine. In view of James I's charters to the Virginia Company, it is unlikely that a known "Papist" would be allowed to go to Virginia, much less hold office.

King James's first charter on November 20, 1606, decreed that the Church of England was to be established in Virginia. On May 13, 1609, he issued a second charter that stated:

> We should be loath that any person should be permitted to pass, that we suspected to affect the superstitions of the Church of Rome; we do hereby declare that it is our will and pleasure that none be permitted to pass in any voyage . . . but such as first shall have taken the oath of supremacy.[8]

The Virginia Company reinforced this royal policy. In 1610, it appointed Thomas West, the third Lord De la Warr, as its first governor. At his departure from England, he listened to the words of William Crashaw, an Anglican divine: "Suffer no Papists, let them not nestle there; nay, let the name of Pope and Poperie be never heard in

Virginia."[9] West took these words to heart when a Jesuit, Father Pierre Biard, came as a captive to Jamestown.

James I's charter to the Virginia Company gave it all the territory north to Canada. In 1613, Biard and several other Jesuits had established a mission on Mount Desert Island in what is now Maine. In September, Captain Samuel Argall from Virginia raided the mission and adjacent settlement. Although France and England were then at peace, Argall claimed the territory for Virginia and even stole from the French commander his commission from King Henry IV authorizing the settlement. In the initial attack, one of the Jesuits was wounded and subsequently died in the care of Argall's doctor, whom Biard described as "a Catholic, and known as such." Unfortunately, no record can be found of this supposedly Catholic physician.[10] Biard and Father Enemond Massé revealed their identity as Jesuits to Argall and asked for the release of his French captives. Instead, Argall cast Massé and others adrift, while he took Biard and fourteen others to Virginia.

As Biard recalled his Virginia sojourn, "this charming Marshal [de la Warr]..., when he heard an account of us, talked about nothing but ropes and gallows, and of having every one of us hanged." Only after Argall "published our commissions and Royal patents, . . . which he had surreptitiously removed," did De la Warr back down.[11]

While Biard's party was thus spared, Argall, under the council's orders, returned to New France and burned Port Royal after erecting crosses and claiming the territory for England. Biard eventually made his way back to France to resume his earlier teaching post at Lyons. Unfortunately, he mentioned no one at Jamestown, other than De la Warr and Argall, nor is there any documented reaction of the English settlers to these French captives.

Despite the presence of Argall's unnamed surgeon, Virginia was not a friendly place for Catholics. In 1625, Father Gregorio de Bolivar, O.F.M., a veteran of Mexican missions, submitted a report on Virginia to the Congregation de Propaganda Fide, the branch of the Roman Curia founded in 1622 to supervise missionary activities. The oldest document in the Propaganda archives pertaining to the United States, the report was a response to Pope Urban VIII's request about the feasibility of sending missionaries to the Indians in Virginia. De Bolivar, then in Rome, gave an overview of the "land and situation of Virginia where English Lutherans [as the Spanish generically desig-

nated Protestants] have settled and have begun to spread their pestilential sect among the simple miserable Indians there." He was optimistic that Virginia's natives could be readily converted to Christianity, once they were won over from polygamy and cannibalism,
practices that "the heretics tolerate." He suggested that any missionary who went to Virginia could be Spanish but should speak English.
Apparently ignorant of the earlier Jesuit mission, he recommended
that missionaries could come from Florida. If the pope wanted, he
was even willing to undertake the mission himself.[12] Whatever the
pope's intentions, no missionaries were to come to Virginia's Indians.
Virginia remained closed to Catholics, even those who were members
of the Virginia Company.

In 1627, George Calvert, the first Lord Baltimore, who had converted to Catholicism around 1624, attempted to establish a colony at
Ferryland, Newfoundland. He had innovative ideas about religious
toleration, and his expedition consisted of both Catholics and
Protestants, including two priests and a Protestant preacher. After
harsh winters and French attacks, however, Calvert abandoned his
colony in 1629.[13] As a member of the Virginia Company, he decided
to settle in Virginia, where he arrived early in October to a chilly
reception. As the Virginia council explained to the English Privy
Council: "We were readily inclined to render unto his Lordship all
those respects which were due unto the honor of his person." But
when he substituted an oath of his own for the oaths of supremacy
and allegiance, Virginia's leaders "could not imagine that so much lati-
tude was left for us to decline from the prescribed form, so strictly
exacted and so well justified and defended by the pen of our late
Soveraigne Lord, King James, of happy memory." So wise and beneficial did the council consider James' oath to be that "among the many
blessings and favors for which . . . this Colony hath received from his
most gracious majesty, there is none whereby it hath been made more
happy than in the freedom of our Religion which we have enjoyed,
and that no papists have been suffered to settle . . . amongst us."[14]

Calvert, nevertheless, seems to have remained in Virginia for two
years, before he sailed for England, leaving his wife and some of his
children behind. One of the priests who came with him from Newfoundland may also have remained to administer to Lady Baltimore
and her children and possibly to some Irish exiles. Lady Baltimore was
subsequently lost at sea while returning to England.[15]

Back in England, Charles I granted Baltimore land north of the Potomac. Before the charter could pass the great seal, however, George Calvert died. In 1632, his son, Cecil, the second Lord Baltimore, received the charter for the new colony that was to be named Maryland after Queen Henrietta Maria. Cecil shared his father's ideas on religious toleration. The first expedition to set out from England in November 1633 consisted of both Protestants and Catholics. The English province of the Jesuits had also contributed to the enterprise, so the two priests and one brother who were in the first group came not as clergymen, but as settlers. Like other colonists, they took up land in their own name, not in the name of the Catholic Church or their religious order. It was a pragmatic way of keeping church and state separate.[16]

Father Andrew White, one of the original Maryland missionaries, recorded the voyage to Maryland and the early months of the colony in his *Relatio Itineris in Marylandiam.* On January 26, 1634, they came to the island of Montserrat, whose "inhabitants . . . are Irishmen, who were expelled by the English of Virginia for the profession of the Catholic faith."[17] In 1622, Irish laborers had been brought to Virginia and settled near Newport News.[18] These may have been the Irishmen to whom Lady Baltimore's priest ministered in 1629 and who had now settled on Montserrat.

On February 27, 1634, the Maryland colonists reached Point Comfort, "full of fear," as White recorded, "for whatever evil the English inhabitants were planning against us, for to them our plantation was somewhat displeasing." But Leonard Calvert, Cecil's brother and governor of the colony, carried with him the royal charter and letters from the king and chief judge of England. These assuaged the Virginia officials.[19] Cecil had, moreover, instructed his brother and his commissioners to make sure that "all Acts of Romane Catholique Religion . . . be done as privately as may be," lest there be any cause of complaint in Virginia or England. As soon as they reached Maryland, they were to send an Anglican colonist to Governor John Harvey of Virginia bearing Lord Baltimore's personal respects. They were to do the same with Captain William Clayborne, a Virginian who had established a settlement on Kent Island just off the eastern shore of the Chesapeake.[20] Baltimore's instructions were merely part of his pragmatic approach to keeping religious peace. But the fact that Maryland was now carved out of territory Virginia had claimed as its own simply added a further source of friction. For the time, however, Harvey displayed benevolence toward the new colony.

Once in Maryland, the Jesuits ministered primarily to the colonists and the Indians, but they also looked for opportunities in Virginia. In 1638, they reported they had bought the freedom of two Catholics, "who had sold themselves into servitude in Virginia." Other Maryland colonists followed their example by "buying from there Catholic servants, of whom there is a large number in that place; for every year many sell themselves as servants; living among men of the worst possible example and destitute of every spiritual aid, they generally achieve the loss of their souls."[21] From time to time, the Jesuits themselves also made direct incursions into Virginia.[22]

Despite the relatively amicable relations between Virginia and Maryland in the beginning, as England became wracked by the Civil War Virginia passed harsh anti-Catholic laws. In 1642, the assembly enacted a law "that no popish recusants should at any time hereafter exercise the place or places of secret counsellors . . . that it should be unlawful under the penalties aforesaid for any popish priest that shall hereafter arrive to remain five days after warning given for departure."[23]

With such legal restrictions on Catholics in Virginia, few ventured to settle there. In November 1643, Isaac Jogues, the Jesuit missionary to the Hurons in the present state of New York who was canonized with seven others in 1930, had just been released from a year's captivity among the Iroquois. During a brief sojourn at "Manate," as he called New Amsterdam, on his way back to France, he recorded that an Irishman from Virginia came to him to confession and reported that Jesuits were working in Virginia, where one was killed while laboring among the Indians.[24] Jesuits, of course, were not formally working in Virginia, and perhaps Jogues's unidentified penitent thought the priest might be more familiar with Virginia than with Maryland. As for the Jesuit being killed, this might have been Father Ferdinand Poulton who was accidentally shot near St. Mary's City in 1641.

Ironically, despite its laws against Catholics, Virginia became a temporary haven for Jesuits when Maryland went through an anti-Catholic revolution. Lord Baltimore was so optimistic about his experiment in religious liberty that he even invited Massachusetts Puritans to settle in his colony. This open-door policy created internal problems in his colony. In 1645, Protestants overthrew Baltimore's government. Andrew White and Thomas Copley were taken in chains to England. Three others, Bernard Hartwell, Roger Rigby, and John Cooper, took refuge in Virginia, where they died in a place unknown probably in 1646. No priests remained in English-speaking America. In 1647, Baltimore regained his rule, and the Jesuits returned. Late that year, the Jesuit general in Rome instructed the English provincial to follow his advisers "in regard to Virginia what is necessary for the care of those Catholics."[25] Unfortunately, there is no further designation of who "those Catholics" were.

Shortly after Baltimore's restoration, Virginia became the home of its first known permanent Catholic family. Giles Brent had originally settled in Maryland, where he married an Indian "princess" and was later joined by his sisters, Margaret and Mary. Margaret was a pioneer of women's rights, who had earlier claimed the right to two votes in the Maryland assembly. Though denied a vote, she did gain a seat, the first woman legislator in the nation's history. In 1651, Giles had a falling out with the Calvert proprietary government of Maryland and moved across the Potomac to Aquia Creek in Stafford County in the Northern Neck, where his sisters later joined him.[26] He and his descendants held several public offices, including that of sheriff, for Virginians could be pragmatic. The Brents were Catholics, but what was more useful than to have Catholics hostile to Maryland guarding the frontier?

Shortly after the Brents settled in Virginia, revolution again broke out in Maryland and the Jesuits again sought refuge across the Potomac. In 1650, Oliver Cromwell established the Commonwealth in England. Two years later, Virginia commissioners of the Commonwealth used a border dispute with Maryland to invade the colony and overthrow Baltimore's government. In 1654, the Protestant-dominated assembly declared that Catholics no longer enjoyed the protection of the law. The Jesuits saw their missions and residences plundered. Their annual letter to Rome reported that some of their number, "having secretly fled to Virginia, barely live their lives in pain amid the total lack of necessities."[27] Again, there was, unfortunately, no reference to where these Jesuits were in Virginia. In 1656, Cromwell restored Baltimore's government, and, in 1660, Charles II returned from exile in France to assume the throne of England. Virginia's Catholic neighbors settled in for a temporary respite from persecution.

Simultaneously, however, Virginia passed yet more restrictive laws against its few Catholic inhabitants. In 1661, recusants, those who refused to take the oath of supremacy, were to be fined for not attending church.[28] The fine of £20 a month was sufficient to destroy even the wealthiest person. Yet Giles Brent and his sisters continued to accumulate thousands of acres of land and never seem to have paid any fines. Furthermore, Anglican services were few and far between on Virginia's Northern Neck, so the Brents' absence from church could well go unnoticed. Religion in Virginia, moreover, was not the pervasive obsession it was in New England. Virginia's Anglicans, for example, were never pious enough to petition to have a bishop. In Tidewater, the Anglican Church was under the secular influence of wealthy planters.[29] This laissez-faire attitude toward religion contributed to the acceptance and prosperity of Giles Brent. At his death, probably during the winter of 1671–72, he made provision in his will for masses, but with such a circumlocution as not to arouse any suspicion about his religion. He stipulated that "three thousand pounds of good tobacco with cask [are] to be given by them my Executors unto pious uses where and to whom they shall see fitt for which doing and how and to whom I Will that to none else but God they shall be accountable." He may have intended this legacy to be transferred to his three other sisters in the convent in Cambrai.[30]

Giles Brent's son, Giles II, was likewise accepted in the society of Virginia's Northern Neck, but his family life disintegrated and he died in 1679 at the age of twenty-seven. The family leadership then shifted to George Brent, a nephew of Giles I, who had settled at Woodstock plantation in Virginia in 1673. He soon took up the practice of law as a partner of William Fitzhugh, an Anglican and committed Tory, and was joined in his lucrative practice by his brother, Robert. It seemed to matter little to the Stafford County judges that the lawyers practicing before them were supposed to be subject to fines. George Brent also served as the captain of the Stafford Rangers, although on one occasion in 1681 the troop refused to ride under its recusant commander. Even the royal governor, Thomas Lord Culpepper, overlooked Brent's religion and named him his receiver-general in the Northern Neck in 1683.

With the succession to the English throne of the Catholic James II, in 1685, Brent arrived at the pinnacle of his public career. Culpepper's successor, Francis, Lord Howard of Effingham, named him the king's attorney-general in Virginia for 1686 and 1687. The same year, James II suspended the penal laws and the requirement of the oath of supremacy. In 1688, Brent was elected as one of Stafford County's representatives to the assembly. The Glorious Revolution of 1688, however, endangered Brent's standing in the community. In England, James II was overthrown, to be replaced by William and Mary, his son-in-law and daughter. In Maryland, Baltimore's rule was again ended. In the Northern Neck, Brent became the victim of a long-standing political feud. Rumors abounded that he would lead an attack of Maryland Catholics and Seneca Indians on Stafford County. He took refuge in the home of his law partner and fellow Tory, Fitzhugh, and the governor's council ordered the arrest of Brent's attackers.[31]

The Brents remained prominent in Stafford County but none held elected office after 1688. George and his brother Robert continued to practice law, despite occasional attempts to have them take the required oaths. Like his uncle before him, George was circumspect in his will in providing for masses for the repose of his soul. Occasionally, too, mass was said at his estate, if the word of Colonel John Coode, leader of the Maryland rebellion against Baltimore's proprietary government, is to be believed. In 1690, Coode wrote to Nathaniel Bacon, president of the Virginia council, demanding the surrender of William and Mary's "professed enemyes," who had fled from Maryland to Virginia. He specified in particular "one Cannon and Hubbard [sic], Popish priests." He also mentioned "one Gulick, a Jesuit, fled for treasonable words against their Majesties (as I am informed)."[32] Cannon is unknown, but Basil Hobart was one of several English Franciscans who served the Maryland mission from 1672 to 1720. Nicholas Gulick, who left the Jesuits and died in 1694, may have been the priest to whom the Jesuits' annual report alluded in 1696. It stated that, "under the pretext of teaching the sons of a very wealthy merchant, not unfriendly to the Catholic religion," a Jesuit had begun working in Virginia, but "was compelled to withdraw under pressure from all the English colonists."[33] Coode informed Bacon that Hobart could be found "at his Popish patrons, Mr. Brents in Stafford Co." But Bacon never replied to Coode's request.[34] As will be seen, the Brents provided the nucleus for a Catholic presence in Virginia at the time of the American Revolution. They married fellow Catholics either among their extended family in Virginia or in Maryland and remained major figures in Stafford County society.

One other priest crossed the pages of Virginia history prior to England's Glorious Revolution. On September 15, 1687, Hugh

Campbell appeared before the judges of Norfolk County to give "information against one Edmonds, who pretends himself a Papist Priest and goeth by the name of Father Edmonds." The priest was charged with having witnessed the marriage of John Brockwell and Mary Bustian, a widow. All were ordered to appear in court the following day. Edmonds acknowledged that he had married the couple, but only after the banns had been published in the Elizabeth River parish. The court referred the case to the governor and demanded that both Campbell and Edmonds post security. This the priest refused to do, but he did appear before the general court, where he argued that, according to James II's "Proclamation of liberty of conscience ... he intended [sic] the house of Mrs. Charles Egerton, the house of Capt. Robert Jordan and the house of Henry Asdick to meet at and there celebrate the Mass and other Rights of their Church."[35] Edmonds, whose name was also given as Raymond, does not appear on the lists of either the Jesuits or Franciscans who were on the Maryland mission at that time. It is possible that, like many of the Jesuits of the time, he adopted an alias to protect his family in England. Whoever he was, his brief appearance in Norfolk indicates that in 1687 a tiny Catholic community had settled there.

After the Glorious Revolution, Virginia and Maryland passed a series a laws against Catholics. Maryland, which had more of a "Catholic problem," had become a royal colony after the overthrow of Lord Baltimore. In September 1704 the assembly prohibited priests from celebrating mass, but then amended its act to allow priests to say mass in private homes.[36] Not having any known resident priests, Virginia simply sought to restrict the activities of Catholic laity. In 1705, the assembly legislated "That Popish recusants convict, negroes, mulattoes and Indian servants, not being Christians, shall be deemed and taken to be persons incapable in law, to be witnesses, in any case whatsoever."[37] It also declared that all freeholders, with the exception of recusants, were obliged to vote under penalty of a fine.[38] But the operative phrase here was "Popish recusants convict." In 1762, George Brent III of Woodstock cast a vote for Henry Lee for the House of Burgesses. When his vote was challenged on the basis that he was "a Roman Catholick," the Committee of Privileges and Elections allowed Brent's vote to stand, for it did not appear to the committee "that the said George Brent is a Recusant convict."[39] It was a technicality. Brent had never been convicted of being a "Recusant" or "Roman Catholick," because apparently no one had ever brought the charges against him.

During the decades preceding the Revolution, Virginia reflected the hysteria of the other colonies faced with upheaval at home and abroad. In 1745, Bonnie Prince Charlie's abortive invasion of England ended any attempts to restore the Catholic Stuarts, but the aftermath in England and the colonies caused loyal Englishmen to look for plotters, especially Catholics, everywhere. On April 24, 1746, William Gooch, lieutenant governor of Virginia, heard priests from Maryland were coming to Fairfax County and were "endeavouring by crafty Insinuations, to seduce his Majesty's good subjects from their Fidelity and Loyalty to his Majesty, King George, and his Royal House." He, therefore, ordered "all Magistrates, Sheriffs, Constables, and other His Majesty's Liege People, within this colony, to be diligent in apprehending and bringing to Justice the said Romish Priests, or any of them, so that they may be prosecuted according to law."[40] From some other scattered evidence, it appears that a few Catholics may have taken up residence in other sections of Virginia, but they were still not welcome.

In 1752, the Virginia assembly repealed the statute forbidding Catholics from being witnesses, only to reenact a similar law the next year.[41] The French and Indian Wars were closer to home than an uprising in favor of the Stuarts. The French were Catholic and were allied with the Indians; both were threatening the frontier of English America. Were English-speaking Catholics a fifth column ready to ally with their fellow Catholics in New France? The colonial assemblies of Pennsylvania, Maryland, and Virginia answered in the affirmative. Beginning in 1754, Virginia enacted a series of laws prohibiting Catholics from bearing arms. In 1756, the assembly legislated that no Papist or reputed Papist was to possess any arms, without taking the prescribed oath, nor was any Papist to own a horse valued at more than £5.[42] It was during this period, however, that George Brent III was challenged for casting a vote. The laws were harsh, but their enforcement depended on the attitude of the local magistrate and how well he knew the Catholics brought before him. Virginia simply did not have many Catholics, but the laws passed on the eve of the American Revolution illustrated that Virginians, like colonists elsewhere, were doubtful whether Catholics could be good citizens. But, if American colonists suspected the loyalties of

Catholics, Church officials abroad were not really certain where the Catholics were.

Catholics in Virginia and the other English colonies at that time were subject to the vicar apostolic of the London District. In 1756, Bishop Richard Challoner, the vicar apostolic, wrote to a friend in Rome that there were Catholic missionaries only in Maryland and Pennsylvania. While these were subject to him, he knew "not the origin of this" and presumed that he and his predecessors received jurisdiction over the colonies by analogy to the Anglican bishop of London having authority over the Anglican Church in the colonies. He noted further that the Jesuits received faculties (permission to exercise the ministry) from him, but previously received only approbation.[43] Ecclesiastical jurisdiction was vague at best and would create problems in the years after the American Revolution.

THE AMERICAN REVOLUTION AND VIRGINIA'S CATHOLICS

The American Revolution set in motion a series of events that gained not only American independence but also toleration for Catholics and the establishment of ordinary Church government. One of the first signs of a new wind blowing was George Washington's proclamation on November 5, 1775, banning the celebration by the Continental Army of Guy Fawkes Day, which he termed the "ridiculous and childish custom of burning the Effigy of the pope." The practice was, furthermore, insensitive to the Catholicism of the French Canadians, whom Washington and the Continental Congress hoped would join the American cause. He made no mention of sensitivity to Catholics serving in the Continental Army.[44]

Virginia's only contact with Catholics during the Revolution was indirect but symbolically significant. On July 4, 1778, Colonel George Rogers Clark, leading a force of Virginia militia, captured Kaskaskia in the Illinois territory. Virginia had been given this territory in its original charter, but it was then occupied by the French and was subject to the extension of toleration for Catholics granted by the Quebec Act, one of the causes of the Revolution. The resident priest was Father Pierre Gibault, who was impressed with Clark's treatment of the French settlers. As Clark's expedition advanced on Vincennes, Jeane Baptiste Laffont, Kaskaskia's doctor, was its guide, but Gibault

received both blame and praise. Henry Hamilton, the British lieutenant governor, informed Lord George Germain three weeks after
the capture of Kaskaskia that he heard "a French Priest named
Gibault had his horse already saddled to proceed" to Vincennes from
Kaskaskia, "with design to act as an agent for the Rebels. This
Ecclesiastic is a fellow of infamous morals, and I believe very capable
of acting such a part."[45]

Gibault's "infamous morals" meant his lack of British loyalties.
In 1780, they won him Governor Patrick Henry's commendation and
a resolution of gratitude from the legislature.[46] His support of the new
government and of Clark's military expedition made him a patriot. As
he informed Clark from Vincennes in May 1780, "we are of good
courage and are so good Americans that we are ready to defend ourselves to the death against any who attack us."[47] Not for the last time
were Catholics accepted as Americans by proving themselves patriotic in the nation's wars.

Anti-Catholicism also declined with the alliance between the
United States and Catholic France. On the one hundred and fiftieth
anniversary of Cornwallis's surrender at Yorktown, as will be seen, a
monument was erected to those Frenchmen, presumably Catholic,
who had died fighting for American independence. These French
forces brought with them Catholic priests as chaplains, some of whom
played a role in Catholic Virginia's later history. A military chaplain
may also have said the first Mass in Charlottesville. With the surrender of Burgoyne at Saratoga in October 1777, Hessian soldiers were
taken prisoner. After being detained in Cambridge, Massachusetts,
for a year, they marched to camps in Charlottesville, Staunton, and
Winchester. In Charlottesville, their chaplain was a priest whose name
is given only as Theobald. In 1779, he wrote to George Washington
complaining of the treatment he was receiving and asking permission
to accept a pastoral charge in Albany.[48]

The end of the American Revolution meant also the end of the ec-
clesiastical jurisdiction of Bishop Challoner over the former colonies.
In 1773, Pope Clement XIV had suppressed the Society of Jesus,
members of which were the only priests in English-speaking America.
Theoretically, these priests then became secular priests under the
London bishop. The Declaration of Independence and the Revolution
that followed made the maintenance of such authority impossible.
During the war, the former Jesuits remained on their missions and,

for the most part, operated under the authority of their former superior, named vicar general by Bishop Challoner. One priest, however, refused to accept this twice-delegated authority of a vicar general of a vicar apostolic.

John Carroll, born in Maryland and originally destined to teach theology at the English Jesuit house of studies in Bruges, returned to his native land in 1774. From his mother's home in Rock Creek, Upper Marlboro, he ministered to the surrounding Catholics. At the Treaty of Paris, ending the American Revolution in 1783, the Congregation of Propaganda in Rome approached the new nation in the way in which it had grown accustomed to dealing with Europe. Through the nuncio, the papal ambassador, to Paris, it asked the American minister, Benjamin Franklin, if his government would object to the appointment of a Frenchman as bishop vicar apostolic, were no suitable American candidates to be found. Franklin forwarded this request to the United States Congress, still operating under the Articles of Confederation, and received the reply from the president, James Madison, that the request, being strictly spiritual, lay beyond the competence of Congress to grant or deny.[49] For the first time in modern history, the Holy See had offered a government a say in ecclesiastical matters only to have that government refuse it.

Carroll was furious that the Holy See had excluded the American clergy in its negotiations with the government. He therefore set about to organize the clergy, as a means not only of preserving some semblance of ecclesiastical order but also of preparing for the reestablishment of the Society of Jesus. In the meantime, he had been named superior of the American mission in 1784—a step he resented as a Roman attempt to avoid appointing an "ordinary national bishop" with his own diocese. On March 1, 1785, he submitted his first report to Propaganda on the Catholic Church in the new nation. Virginia's Catholic population was far below that of Maryland, Pennsylvania or New York, which was only then beginning to develop. He reported:

> There are in Maryland about 15,800 Catholics; of these there are about 9,000 freemen, adults or over twelve years of age; children under age, about 3,000; and above that number of slaves of all ages of African origin, called negroes. There are in Pennsylvania about 7,000, very few of whom are negroes, and the Catholics are less scattered and live nearer to each other. There are not more than

200 in Virginia who are visited four or five times a year by a priest. Many other Catholics are said to be scattered in that and other States, who are utterly deprived of all religious ministry. In the State of New York I hear that there are at least 1,500.[50]

Though he did not say it, Carroll was the priest who visited the 200 Catholics in Virginia, where his two sisters had married Robert Brent of Woodstock and William Brent of Richland. The Brents, therefore, continued to be the nucleus of Virginia Catholicism. One of George Brent's great-grandsons, Leonard Neale, would succeed Carroll as archbishop of Baltimore.[51] Of the Catholics Carroll reported to be "scattered" elsewhere in Virginia, little is known. A portion of the Shenandoah Valley in the 1740s was designated as the "Irish tract," but the Irish who settled there were more likely "Scotch-Irish" Presbyterians.[52]

The Catholic population in the nation at the time was roughly 1 percent of the whole. For this mission, Carroll had twenty-four priests, but he was cautious in admitting new ones, for he was "convinced that the Catholic faith will suffer less harm, if for a short time there is no priest at a place, than if living as we do among fellow-citizens of another religion, we admit to the discharge of the sacred ministry, I do not say bad priests, but incautious and imprudent priests." Most of his priests, he continued, "lead a life full of labor, as each one attends congregations far apart, and has to be riding constantly and with great fatigue, especially to sick calls."[53] That situation would change rapidly along the northeastern seaboard of the United States, but it was a fair description of Virginia for more than the next century.

In the decade following the Revolution, meanwhile, Virginia Catholics at last gained freedom to exercise their religion openly. In January 1786, the Virginia assembly passed the Statute of Religious Liberty that disestablished the Anglican Church and provided "that all men shall be free to profess, and by argument to maintain, their opinion in matters of religion, and that the same shall in no wise diminish, enlarge or affect their civil capacities."[54] It was the embodiment of the Enlightenment ideas of its author, Thomas Jefferson. For the Anglican Church, it meant considerable adjustment to voluntary support from the laity. For the tiny Catholic population, it meant there were no longer any civil restrictions on their full participation in public life.

CHAPTER 2

Post-Revolutionary Virginia Catholicism

In 1786, the former Jesuits voted to establish an academy, Georgetown, which would provide a future supply of candidates for the priesthood. They also petitioned Pope Pius VI for permission to elect one of their number as bishop of Baltimore. On May 18, 1788, they elected John Carroll the first bishop in the United States. With the pope's confirmation, on November 6, 1789, the country had its first bishop.[1] Carroll's diocese covered the entire United States, including Virginia. In 1808, he was elevated to the rank of archbishop with the four new suffragan sees of Boston, New York, Philadelphia, and Bardstown, Kentucky.

But Virginia Catholicism was only slowly developing. In a plantation economy, there was no principal center for either church or state. In the east, Richmond was the capital; Norfolk was the principal seaport; and Alexandria was the main port on the Potomac. To the west, Martinsburg, now in West Virginia, and Winchester were market towns. Each of these towns had small Catholic communities, but their only affinity was that they were in the same state. Virginia's economic and cultural centers would be more closely linked only with the advent of the railroad, still decades in the future. Each of these Catholic communities had its own history, but lay trusteeism in Norfolk would ultimately lead to the establishment of Richmond as a diocese. They came into being, moreover, when Virginia was at the height of its national influence and when the older Anglican hegemony was declining.

VIRGINIA CULTURE IN THE EARLY REPUBLIC.

Between 1789 and 1825, a Virginian was president for all but four years: George Washington (1789–1897), and then the Virginia Dynasty of Thomas Jefferson (1801–09), James Madison (1809–1817), and James Monroe (1817–25). Many of Virginia's leaders, moreover, were so enamored with the Enlightenment that they reduced religion to a rational basis at the cost of revelation and doctrine. In the meantime, Virginia was becoming religiously pluralistic. Scotch-Irish Presbyterians and some German Lutherans and Mennonites had settled in the Shenandoah Valley. Episcopalians, as American Anglicans were now called, remained dominant in Richmond and Tidewater. Methodists, who began in Baltimore in 1783, and Baptists, who would ultimately constitute the single largest denomination, moved into small farming communities throughout the state. Catholic newcomers would have to carve out their own niche in the aristocratic state.

The nation and the infant American Church were also subject to European influences. When Carroll became the first bishop in 1789, the French Revolution had broken out. This had a direct effect on Carroll's developing church. Consecrated in England, he immediately began recruiting priests for his diocese. Among them were French Sulpicians who had fled to England rather than take the oath of the Civil Constitution, abjuring loyalty to Rome and accepting the jurisdiction of the French state over the Church. In 1791, the first group of Sulpicians, led by François Charles Nagot, arrived in Baltimore to open St. Mary's Seminary.[2] As Carroll told an English friend, "if in many instances the French revolution has been fatal to religion, this country promised to derive advantage from it. Besides the Seminary, which will be the source of many blessings, I expect some other valuable & useful priests." As one example, he noted that "one, well known to Mr. Nagot, is arrived in Virginia with a number of French Emigrants, who propose forming a settlement there."[3] The identity of these French émigrés is unfortunately unknown, but the priest, whom Carroll described as more "fervent" than others who had come, was Jean Dubois.

JEAN DUBOIS IN RICHMOND

Jean Dubois was twenty-seven years old, when, like the Sulpicians, he fled his native France in June 1791 rather than take the new oath. He made his escape because of his continuing friendship with a school-mate, Maximilien de Robespierre. He first landed in Norfolk, but almost immediately set out for Richmond. He was armed with a letter of introduction from the Marquis de Lafayette, whose own dallying with the anticlerical revolution was countered by his devout Catholic wife's intervention on Dubois' behalf. In Richmond, Dubois presented himself and Lafayette's letter to James Monroe, who had just left the Senate to practice law in Virginia's capital. Like many American patriots, Monroe was an ardent supporter of the French Revolution, for, in his mind, "whoever owns the principles of one Revolution must cherish those of the other." Although many of these cherished revolutionary principles were decidedly anti-Catholic, Monroe graciously received Dubois, and so did Richmond. After all, the young priest had a letter from Lafayette.[4]

Richmond then and later never witnessed the vast numbers of immigrants who poured into the cities of the northeast and mid-west. One foreigner was a curiosity, especially if he was cultured and educated. At the time, the General Assembly had the Episcopalian and Presbyterian ministers alternate in holding religious services in the Capitol. The assembly invited Dubois to celebrate Mass in the courtroom of the new building. But apparently he did not want to press his luck, for Virginia's newspapers were expressing shock that nonjuring priests back in France were still functioning, contrary to the law. After his one appearance in the Capitol, he celebrated Mass in rented rooms or the homes of Richmond's few Catholics. Despite the city's abiding anti-Catholicism, he befriended some leading Protestants, including two clergymen, John Buchanan and John Blair.[5]

Soon, Dubois began to receive invitations to go to other Catholic communities. In November 1791 he informed Colonel John Fitzgerald in Alexandria that, if Carroll approved, he would be willing to make occasional trips to exercise the ministry in the port city. He would

> not ask any contribution for this; I wish but the consolation of being of use. Only, if it will be necessary for me to go there frequently I will ask that a horse be furnished me upon which I may make the trip.[6]

There is, however, no evidence that Dubois actually visited Alexandria. The former Jesuits at Georgetown would soon expand their ministry to include the city across the Potomac River which at that time was part of the District of Columbia.

For over two years, Dubois remained in Richmond, from which he may have ridden a circuit to other Catholic communities. Renting a small wooden house on the James River, he supported himself by opening a "school for the French language," but he also offered to teach English and the classics as well as arithmetic. As he advertised in *The Virginia Gazette* on December 28, 1791: "Such as desire to employ him are requested to leave a line for him at his house next the bridge on the right hand from the capital."[7] Although he advertised that he would teach English, he was himself still learning the language. He later told students that he received "many friendly lessons in our language" from Patrick Henry, who had retired from public office in 1791 to return to his law practice.[8]

In the meantime, the French Revolution was becoming more violent. In September 1792, 191 nonjuring priests were executed. King Louis XVI and his queen, Marie Antoinette, were beheaded. Robespierre, Dubois' friend and protector, was among the victims. In the United States, people were divided. When Citizen Gênet arrived as a representative of revolutionary France, George Washington refused to receive him. After John Marshall led a public demonstration in Richmond to support Washington, James Madison and James Monroe protested that the French people were merely establishing their liberties against the repressions of "priests and nobles."[9] Dubois, as an individual priest, was accepted in Richmond society, but the upper echelons of Virginia society continued to be anticlerical in the name of liberty.

Early in 1794, Dubois moved at Carroll's request to Frederick, Maryland. As he prepared to quit the city, Richmond's leading citizens held a banquet in his honor. Present were his Protestant clergy friends, Buchanan and Blair.[10] Dubois' sojourn in Virginia was short, but his later career was distinguished. He was a founder of Mount Saint Mary's College and Seminary in Emmitsburg, Maryland, from which many of Virginia's priests would come. For a while, he was also the spiritual director of Elizabeth Ann Seton's Sisters of Charity, so many of whom would later play a large role in Virginia's Catholic history. In 1826, he was named third bishop of New York. From Frederick and Emmitsburg, he may also have visited the area around Martinsburg.

The Origins of Martinsburg and Alexandria

Martinsburg was a market town whose original Catholic population had either come across the Potomac River from Maryland or, as with Richard McSherry, emigrated from Jamaica. By early 1795, Father Denis Cahill attended the community from his residence in Hagerstown and traveled as far as Shepherdstown and Winchester.[11] Though remarkable as the pioneer priest in western Maryland and Virginia, he was also one of the Irish-born priests with whom John Carroll had difficulties. He accused the bishop of having purchased his miter from his fellow ex-Jesuits and of having fathered children in Virginia. Three hundred dollars, he said, would buy his silence, an offer Carroll rebuffed with a scorching rebuke.[12]

The Martinsburg area had one distinctive feature—a verified series of ghostly appearances. Sometime in the early 1790s, Adam Livingston, a Lutheran of German ancestry who had settled near Smithfield in Berkeley County, began to experience strange occurrences in his home. He was beset with chickens being beheaded, fireballs rolling across his living room from the fireplace, the sounds of horse hoofs in the house, and, what gave the name of Wizard's Clip to the phenomena, clothing and other material being cut into crescents or thin strips. After unsuccessfully seeking the aid of a Lutheran pastor in Winchester and other ministers, Livingston had a dream of a "minister dressed in robes" who would help him. Seeking out this minister, he went to Shepherdstown, where he was told he was probably looking for the Catholic priest, who occasionally said Mass at the home of Richard McSherry at Leetown. The next Sunday, Cahill said Mass in a Catholic home in Shepherdstown. Livingston attended in the company of the McSherrys. When he saw Cahill in his vestments, he exclaimed that this was the man he had seen in his dream. Despite Cahill's skepticism, the McSherrys and Joseph Menghini prevailed on him to visit Livingston's home and sprinkle it with Holy Water.[13]

For a while, Cahill's ministrations were successful, but then the events reoccurred. Carroll then authorized "Mr. Smith," the pseudonym of Dmitri Augustine Gallitzin, a Russian prince and the first priest ordained in the United States, to go from his residence in Conewago, Pennsylvania, to Martinsburg. For three months in the fall of 1797, Gallitzin remained either at the McSherrys' residence or at Livingston's. He found himself unable to perform an exorcism and called on Cahill, who performed the rite and said Mass in Livingston's house. The bizarre occurrences then ceased. Livingston, up to that time strongly anti-Catholic, converted to the Church, but his wife remained hostile. Among new occurrences, he and some family members began to hear "a voice" that both instructed them in the faith and predicted that his land would become a "place of prayer and fasting and praise." In 1802, he left his land, "Wizard's Clip," to the Church, with Dr. Richard McSherry and Joseph Menghini as trustees. Although there was later litigation over what became known as the "Priest Field," in 1978, it became a retreat center.[14]

In 1802, McSherry had become one of the founding trustees of the Catholic church in Martinsburg, when he, Michael McKewan, John O'Ferrell, and Ignatius O'Ferrell, purchased a lot from the town to build a church.[15] He and his descendants would remain trustees of the church but never sought to intrude into the proper sphere of episcopal authority. But for many years, the area depended on occasional visits from priests at Mount Saint Mary's in Emmitsburg or Jesuits from Frederick, where Father John McElroy, S.J., became pastor in 1822 and where the order later established its novitiate.[16] Jesuits also played a major role in the development of two other Virginia congregations, in Alexandria and Richmond.

Alexandria would vie with Norfolk for the honor of being Virginia's oldest Catholic community. In 1781, a chaplain in Rochambeau's army said Mass, but the community got its real start on St. Patrick's Day in 1788, when Colonel John Fitzgerald, George Washington's Irish-born aide-de-camp, invited prominent Maryland and Virginia citizens, including Washington himself, to his home to discuss, among other things, the building of a Catholic church.[17] In 1791, as was seen, Fitzgerald had attempted to get Dubois to serve the community. But, from 1794 to 1818, Alexandria became a mission of Holy Trinity Church, founded by the priests of Georgetown College. In 1794, Father John Thayer was given charge. A former Congregational minister, chaplain in the Continental Army, and convert to Catholicism, Thayer remained too much of a New England Puritan to deal with Virginia's Catholics. In 1795, he was replaced by Francis Neale, a Maryland native, former Jesuit, and brother of Leonard Neale, who became the second archbishop of Baltimore. But, even as he oversaw the completion of the first St. Mary's Church, he was looking for another site. He followed in Alexandria the unusual mode of Jesuits owning property in their own names and signing wills to two or three other Jesuits. This would create a problem for Archbishop Ambrose Marechal, who succeeded Leonard Neale in 1817.

The Jesuits, who were restored as an order in the United States in 1805, retained ownership and administration of St. Mary's until 1892. But the parish's earliest congregation was drawn from old Maryland or Virginia families, such as the Brents, or Irish newcomers of the professional or merchant classes.[18] Although Marechal had his difficulties with the Jesuits, for the most part he and his successors were quite content to leave the area to the care of the Jesuits, a practice followed by the bishops of Richmond, when Alexandria was annexed to the diocese of Richmond in 1858. But Jesuits from Georgetown ministered in other regions of Virginia.

RICHMOND ON THE EVE OF
BECOMING A DIOCESE: 1811–1820

When Dubois left Richmond in 1794, the Catholic community was largely French, who remained the wealthiest members of the congregation. Its Catholic population was far surpassed by the Norfolk area. It depended, for the most part, on priests who visited from time to time. Father Xavier Miguel, a Frenchman and former student of Nagot in Baltimore, was there from 1811 until 1813 when he left, eventually to enter the Jesuits in his native France, where the order was restored in 1814.[19] In 1818, James Redmond, a former Jesuit, worked briefly in Richmond before going to Martinsburg. After him, Father Roger Baxter, S.J., an Englishman and confidant of Archbishop Marechal, came down for extended periods of time from Georgetown, where he had taught rhetoric. By that time, the Catholic community had the use of "the Rocketts Church," originally built by the Presbyterians and located in part of Hargrave's tobacco factory.[20] Though a minor figure, Baxter was full of self-importance and left the first account of Catholicism in the state capital and of the danger of the trustee problem in Norfolk spreading to other parishes.

In June 1818, Baxter sent Marechal a detailed, if overly optimistic, report. He had arranged with some "of the most respectable members of the congregation" to receive a regular salary, rather than rely on weekly collections. On Marechal's advice, he had provided for four trustees of the congregation but made sure the pastor was president. He thought "the people will be now satisfied, with as little power as you chuse to give them, & besides every thing will wear the appearance of an act of grace & a spirit of conciliation." This system would avoid the havoc then being wreaked in Norfolk. But Baxter found it strange that "the people of Richmond are peculiarly fond of preaching," for he could not "help thinking, that Catholics are in general too fond of it, for the effect is generally, with me at least, very little."[21]

Baxter soon ingratiated himself with Richmond society. He befriended Joseph Gallego, founder of the Gallego Flour Mills, who had left the congregation $4,000 in his will and a lot estimated to be worth $10,000, for building a church. Self-confidently, Baxter informed Marechal that "it is very fortunate for our cause, that I came to Richd when I did, for Mr. Gallego among the rest could not bear Mr. Redmond." When Gallego died that summer, Baxter proudly announced that he alone officiated at his funeral, although four Protestant ministers were also present. He had also been asked to preach in the Capitol.[22] The Gallego bequest of land, located on Marshall Street between Third and Fourth, would, unfortunately, become a bone of contention.

Among the prominent people Baxter cultivated was Jean Auguste Marie Chevallié, who originally came to Richmond from his native France to press the claims of his father for articles furnished Virginia during the Revolution and then remained as the French consul. In 1790, he married Sarah Magee, Gallego's sister-in-law. In the absence of a Catholic priest, John Buchanan, one of Dubois' later friends, officiated at the ceremony. Chevallié then entered into partnership with Gallego in the Gallego Flour Mills and was one of the executors of Gallego's estate.[23] He would remain as one of the stalwarts of Richmond's infant Catholic community.

In the meantime, the Jesuit superior at Georgetown, Anthony Kohlmann, wished to make a permanent Jesuit establishment in Richmond. But he wanted the arrangements to conform with provisions Archbishop Neale had made for the Jesuits in certain parts of the archdiocese. As Baxter now informed Marechal, Kohlmann wanted "a written assertion, that you will consent that the Supr of the Jesuits shall have the power of putting his own subjects in the Richmond mission, so long as the Supr gives that city a proper pastor."[24] Marechal was not about to agree to such a permanent delegation of part of his territory to the Jesuits, with whom he was at odds on other matters.

Until October 1819, Baxter continued to make prolonged visits to Richmond. Far from the handsome salary he had been promised, he found himself with the bare means of subsistence. For the proposed new church, moreover, he had himself collected much of the money in Washington.[25] The Gallego bequest, then in the Chancery Court, had become more complicated. The money had been left in trust to four men, only one of whom, Chevallié, was a Catholic. Since Virginia law did not allow the incorporation of church property, Catholic or otherwise, the trustees of the estate could not legally determine to whom to pay the money and had left the decision to a court of equity.[26] Baxter now had to appeal to the people to contribute, so he "assembled them, pointed out our situation, and treated them almost as severely [as] an Irish priest does an Irish audience in Ireland. They have done a little more, but indeed very little." With the first influx of Irish immigrants, the congregation was then too poor even to rent a church for its use.[27]

Baxter shared Marechal's own reservations about the Irish. On the one hand, he reported, "the Catholics in Richd are prejudiced against Irish priests, & the Irish part of the congregation have the strongest; the cause of this prejudice, I presume is, their having lately seen some of the worst, perhaps in the U.S." On the other, he acknowledged that the people "were well pleased with Mr. [Nicholas] Kerney," whom Marechal had recently appointed to Norfolk to try to assuage the trustees.[28]

The trustee dispute in Norfolk was always in the background of the situation in Richmond. At the end of May 1819, Baxter hastened back from Georgetown to Richmond to protect it from the influence of the Norfolk trustees, who had now brooked the archbishop's authority and hired their own pastor. As he told Marechal, "Mr. Carbery [sic, Thomas Carbry] of famous memory has left N. York. It is more than probable that he is on his road to Virginia."[29] Once in Virginia, Carbry actually visited Richmond but ignored Baxter and spread a rumor that Rome would dispatch two priests with special authority to separate Virginia from Marechal's jurisdiction. Baxter had dispelled this and reported that Carbry was now "unpopular" with the Richmond congregation for "never owning his character in public." With conviction, he declared: "In fine, Car__y [sic] will never come here; he dare not; he had better not; nor shall he go to Petersburg."[30]

During that summer, Baxter had to confront a problem other than shielding his people from trusteeism. John Egan, a young Irish priest whom Marechal had assigned to Augusta, Georgia, had appeared in Richmond. After calling only once on Baxter, he began attending the Episcopal church and then was married to a wealthy Georgia widow by the Episcopal bishop of Virginia.[31] Egan's defection simply added to Marechal's generally negative estimate of the Irish clergy—an attitude that fanned the flames of the Norfolk trustee dispute.

Baxter, meanwhile, had published a broadside against Egan in Washington and was assisting Marechal in drafting a pastoral letter addressed to the Norfolk trustees. His own view was that trusteeism had arisen because Americans were "latitudinarians in point of civil liberty, & they are too apt to bring this spirit with them into the sanctuary."[32]

Late in September 1819, Baxter received orders from Kohlmann to return to Georgetown. Seeking Marechal's intervention, he forwarded a petition on his own behalf from the Richmond trustees.[33] When Marechal failed to respond to the petition, Baxter begged him at least to explain to Giles Picot, acting president of the trustees, that he was being removed because he was ordered back to Georgetown. The Richmond trustees feared that their petition asking for Baxter's return might be construed as an intrusion into the episcopal office, the issue then creating the Norfolk problem.[34]

Richmond was then bereft of a pastor until April 1820, when Baxter managed to recruit John Mahony, whom he had earlier recommended.[35] Mahony, too, faced problems similar to Baxter's.[36] In October 1820, he listed his complaints to Marechal. First, the trustees had not given him the "genteel support" they had promised. His congregation, moreover, consisted of several French who had little zeal for religion and some Irish who were too poor to contribute. Finally, he had been unaware until his arrival that Petersburg was also part of his pastoral charge. He admitted, however, that he was better off in Richmond than in Norfolk, where he presumed Marechal had heard a "Spanish" priest had arrived to assist Carbry.[37] Mahony would remain in Richmond for two years.

Richmond was a minor issue for Marechal. That he chose to enlist the aid of Baxter, however, illustrates the complexity of his relations with the Jesuits, with whom he was then engaged in a prolonged struggle over property he claimed for the archdiocese. He also disputed Kohlmann's argument that the diocesan statutes could not prohibit a religious superior from removing one of his subjects from a mission. Baxter himself had suggested that Marechal use those statutes to argue for his return to Richmond.[38] Perhaps to establish peace with the Jesuits, in 1819 Marechal had Kohlmann invest him with the pallium, the symbol of metropolitan authority. In the fall of 1820, while trusteeism raged around him, he went ahead with plans to dedicate his cathedral and invited Baxter to preach. As Baxter was preparing that sermon late in November, he informed Marechal: "We have heard of the new Southern Bishops, and were justly astonished at it, at least, in as much as regarded a Bp of Norfolk. What will old Carbery [*sic*] do?"[39]

While Richmond was the sideshow, Norfolk was the feature attraction. For some time Marechal and his predecessor, Neale, had been locked in combat with the trustees. The establishment of the new diocese of Richmond represented an initial defeat of Marechal's efforts to defang what Baxter had once called the "wolf of Norfolk."[40]

RISE OF TRUSTEEISM IN NORFOLK

On December 15, 1794, there was an indenture "between Alexander Moseley of the Borough of Norfolk, and Elenor, his wife, of the one part, and Antonio Wallace and John Spelleman for and in behalf of the trustees of the Roman Catholic society of the Borough of Norfolk of the other part." The indenture was for a parcel of land to be used for religious purposes.[41] A short time later Carroll assigned Father James Bushe as pastor. Bushe apparently began building a church but was soon at odds with the trustees—among other things, they complained that he omitted the consecration in the Mass. But there were other issues. In the spring of 1799, Bishop Carroll sent Leonard Neale, then his coadjutor-elect and vicar general, to try to bring peace between Bushe and the trustees. Thinking all was settled, Neale returned to Baltimore, only to receive a letter from William Plume in the name of the trustees. Neale "read with much disquietude the proceedgs. at yr. late elecn. of Trustees." He realized that "it cannot now be expected, he [Bushe] will ever again enjoy either peace & contentment himself, or the confidence necessary to render his ministry available to others." Another priest was now needed for Norfolk.[42]

Only late in 1802, however, did Carroll appoint Father Michael Lacy (or deLacey) as pastor.[43] A former hospital chaplain in the French army, he had remained to serve as a priest in the new nation.[44] In Philadelphia, he had alienated some of the trustees of St. Mary's Church by refusing to use his salary to repair his residence.[45] In Norfolk, he submitted himself totally to the trustees. At a trustees' meeting in May 1804 he agreed to a series of proposals that paved the way for major disputes in the future. The description of the duties "of the Priest and assistant" was a legitimate demand that he say Mass, administer the sacraments, care for the dying, teach catechism, and "inculcate decent and devout behaviour" in the congregation during divine services. What created controversy was the description of the relationship between the priest and the "Council" of trustees. All communication between them was to be in writing. If the priest chose to attend a meeting of the council, he was to sit at the right of the president. He had no vote in the council and could address it only at the president's request. But the provision that caused the most dissension concerned finances. All church revenue was to be collected and administered "under the direction and by order of the Council of Trustees."[46]

The trustees at the time included James Herron, Thomas Moran, John Donaghey, Eugene Higgins, Jasper Moran, and Villalobos, the Spanish consul. On December 26, 1808, they gained complete control of the congregation's finances. The following year, they made their body self-perpetuating and added to their number John F. Oliveira Fernandez, a Portugese physician. Schooled in canon law and medieval thought, Oliveira Fernandez became the genius of the trustee schism that ensued. In the meantime, Lacy was raising funds in Baltimore and other cities to complete the church, but signed a "solemn declaration" that title to the new brick church was to be vested in the trustees.[47] At the time of Lacy's arrival, the congregation consisted of only forty families. Of the twenty-three pew-holders, all but five were Irish. The battle that subsequently developed had, as one dimension, tension between the Irish and French emigrés. But there were other issues—two conflicting visions of the Church in a democratic society. All that was needed was for the French-Irish tension to come out into the open. That would happen with Lacy's death.

On February 25, 1815, Jasper Moran notified Archbishop Carroll that Lacy had died. Carroll responded that he was sending Father Jean-Marie Tessier, S.S., the superior of St. Mary's Seminary to officiate at Lacy's funeral and "confer with you and learn from you the present state of the Church of Norfolk, and the congregation, which probably has suffered and been considerably diminished during the late calamitous times." In particular, he wanted to be able to assure the next pastor of "what will be the certain amount of his means of subsistence," for, in the past, "I have appointed certain of my reverend brethren to undertake the care of souls, which they were soon compelled to abandon, through absolute failure of the assurances previously given."[48]

On April 18, 1815, Carroll informed the Norfolk congregation that he was appointing Father Matthew O'Brien, O.P., as pastor. O'Brien had had a distinguished career in New York at St. Peter's Church, where he received Elizabeth Ann Seton into the Church in 1805. Since O'Brien was then elderly and in failing health, Carroll assigned to accompany him to Norfolk Samuel Cooper, a Norfolk native and convert, then studying at St. Mary's Seminary. Unfortunately, O'Brien was so frail that, after three months, he and Cooper returned to Baltimore, where he died a year later.[49] By this time, Carroll himself was in failing health and died on December 3, 1815. Leonard Neale now became archbishop.

On December 13, 1815, in one of his first acts as archbishop, Neale appointed Father James Lucas to Norfolk, with instructions that he was to read his letter of appointment to the congregation. Like Dubois, Lucas was a French emigré priest. His own letters revealed him to be a devout, committed priest but one unable to deal with the emerging problems in the new republic. Moreover, he was not fluent in English. From his arrival in Norfolk on December 18, he faced opposition. On December 28, the trustees met, without inviting him. Two days later, the trustees again met to elect trustees for the following year, but this time Lucas forced his way into the meeting. Over a month later, he described the scene to Neale:

> I was not invited to that assembly, but desiring to know how they would proceed, I went to the Doctor's [Oliveira Fernandez'], who has a very proper building for such assemblies. At my first entrance, he told me that I was not requested, and that I ought to go

out; and he spoke in French, in order not to be understood by the Irish who were present. I answered in English with calm: "Doctor, you are not polite in your own house; I come only as a spectator; let me see how you proceed; I am curious to see." And I staid— some moments after, the deliberations began.[50]

The trustees then offered Lucas the chair of the meeting, but he refused because of his ignorance of English. Villalobos, the Spanish consul, also declined, so Oliviera Fernandez was then elected, with James Herron as secretary.

At this juncture, the trustees were divided, and some remained loyal to Lucas. Oliveira Fernandez announced that the purpose of the meeting "was to render accounts and to discuss the allowances to be given to the pastor." Herron then "told him, *with warmness,* that they ought only to elect the trustees." The same trustees were then re-elected. But the broader issue was the proper division of the temporal and spiritual spheres. "The Doctor," according to Lucas, "had the intention to exclude the pastor of every administration of the Church, and to take on himself all the right." Oliveira Fernandez argued "that the Pope had no right in the temporal, therefore nor the priests," and "that the trustees had the right to refuse a priest sent by the Bishop, if they judged him not suitable for their Church." When he then proposed that one of the trustees be chosen president, however, most of the trustees opposed him and elected Lucas. He then submitted his resignation from the board, which Lucas tried to prevent. While it appeared that Lucas had won some major victories, he concluded his report to Neale with an ominous note. The trustees said he could not celebrate Mass or preach elsewhere without their consent. By this time, Lucas had already added to his charge visits to Richmond, Portsmouth, and Fredericksburg, with points in-between.[51]

Norfolk was not the only place reeling under the controversy over trusteeism. Charleston was in similar chaos with a French priest, Joseph Pierre Picot Clorivière, assigned to an Irish congregation loyal to Father Simon Gallagher, who had been suspended from exercise of the priesthood. But Norfolk's trustees were to provide some of the most learned treatises in support of the practice. What complicated matters further was an anomaly in the American Church. There was a regularly established hierarchy of diocesan bishops, but technically speaking, there were no parishes that, according to canon law, were benefices or stable sources of income for the pastor. Instead, there were "missions," whose "rectors" enjoyed no tenure and could be removed at the will of the bishop. In Europe, not only did monarchs have the right of patronage, *ius patronatus,* to nominate bishops, but also some prominent families enjoyed a similar right to nominate pastors. Neale alluded to this in his response to Lucas's report of his reception in Norfolk. Determined to prevent "the impropriety of lay trusteeship which I have always been inimical to," he commented:

> Their pretended right of choosing their Priest or Missionary Pastor is perfectly unfounded; for they are not Patrons of the Church according to the language of the Council of Trent, who alone have a right of choosing their Pastor. . . . Hence the trustees can claim no jurisdiction over their Priest, nor prevent his missionary functions, which, with my full permission, you may extend beyond the limits of Norfolk, as you shall see the good of religion requires.[52]

Unfortunately, Neale's letter did not end the controversy.

In November, Oliveira Fernandez wrote an open letter to Neale—forty-four pages of text and a forty-eight page appendix. Amid the lengthy and tedious style common to the age, he argued for the right of the trustees to patronage, similar to that enjoyed by European monarchs. He bolstered his arguments here and elsewhere with citations from saints like Bernard of Clairvaux; medieval and early modern writers, like Jean Gerson and Cardinal Nicholas of Cusa; and eighteenth-century proponents of royal authority over the church, like Justinus Febronius. If not devout, he was at least a learned man.[53] As the flames of lay trusteeism spread down the east coast, many of the proponents argued that, as the pope signed a concordat with a king in a monarchy enabling him to nominate bishops, so in a democracy the pope should enter a similar arrangement with the people.[54] All these ideas became embodied in the Norfolk dispute.

In December 1816, Lucas announced that he was appointing new trustees. The original trustees then proclaimed that they were the lawful board. By this time, some of the original trustees, such as James and Walter Herron, seem to have come over to Lucas's side, but then Lucas was locked out of the church and was forced to rent a room in which to say Mass. Neale then placed the church building under interdict, prohibiting its use for religious services.[55]

Despite the turmoil in Norfolk, Lucas continued to exercise his priestly ministry elsewhere in Virginia. In June 1817, he was in Williamsburg, where he discovered six French and three Irish families. A month later, he was preparing to go to Richmond and Petersburg.[56] Between these trips, he learned Neale had died on June 18. The appointment of Ambrose Marechal, a French-born Sulpician, to succeed Neale now exacerbated one dimension of the feud. Prior to this time, the trustees had as one of their arguments the fact that Lucas spoke broken English at best and represented the French influence in the American Church. Now they were also contending with a French archbishop. They decided to escalate their campaign.

For some time, the Norfolk trustees had been in contact with those in Charleston, where Neale had suspended Simon Gallagher and Robert Browne, O.S.A., for their opposition to Clorivière. In the summer of 1816, at the request of the Charleston trustees, Browne went to Rome to appeal directly to Propaganda. Misrepresenting the issues, he succeeded in having Cardinal Lorenzo Litta, the prefect of the congregation, demand that Neale reinstate the trustees—a decision the cardinal later reversed.[57] Aware of the victory of the Charleston trustees, those in Norfolk now adopted the same strategy. Their delegation to Rome would result in the untimely establishment of Richmond as a diocese.

Virginia's Catholic population was insufficient to support a bishop. Spread between three disparate regions, the people hardly had funds adequately to provide maintenance for a priest in any one church. Martinsburg depended exclusively on occasional visits from priests in Maryland. Richmond, until Baxter arrived in 1817, likewise had no permanent pastor. The only exception was Norfolk, whose trustees now played on the ignorance of Roman officials to get a new diocese for Virginia.

CHAPTER 3

Richmond Becomes
a Diocese, 1820

With Archbishop Leonard Neale's death, Ambrose Marechal became the administrator of the archdiocese of Baltimore. Once he became archbishop, the Norfolk turmoil only increased. On the one hand, Oliveira Fernandez misrepresented the Norfolk situation in his petition to Rome. On the other, Roman officials misunderstood American problems and, for that matter, American geography. Based on their mistaken information, they established the diocese of Richmond.

THE TRUSTEE LEGATION TO ROME

On May 31, 1817, Oliveira Fernandez prepared a petition for two of the trustees, John Donaghey and Jasper Moran, to take to Rome. His main purpose was to have Virginia made into a diocese. Included in the lengthy list of arguments was that Baltimore was so far from Norfolk that pastoral care was difficult; that no prelate had visited the congregation in twenty-two years; and that since the death of Lacy, "who first co-operated to rally this Congregation," and of O'Brien, the community had "been deprived of a Shepherd, whose language we could understand, and whose manners were congenial and agreeable to our own, and to that of our country which we have adopted, and of which we are now citizens." On this point, the petition was misleading. Did it claim that Norfolk had no "Shepherd" or no priest who spoke good English?

Arguing that the majority of Virginia's Catholics were then Irish, the petition called for an Irish bishop and based its claim on the right of patronage, since the trustees had bought the property and built the church. The trustees pledged to establish a seminary and recommended as the first bishop, Father Thomas Carbry, O.P., then in New York. Oliviera Fernandez also gave specific instructions for the two trustees going to Rome; among them was that the bishop needed the trustees' consent for appointing or removing a pastor.[1]

Oliviera Fernandez also addressed a letter to Cardinal Lorenzo Litta, the prefect of the Congregation of Propaganda, commending Donaghey and Moran and pledging "to engage, the first, regularly ordained, Clergyman, that the Divine Providence may bring to our shores."[2] As it turned out, however, only Donaghey made the trip to Rome, where he favorably impressed Litta and other Roman officials. Shrewdly, he made no effort to dispel the Roman impression that Norfolk had no priest, although the petition elsewhere spoke of Lucas exercising the priesthood illegally.

As Propaganda had earlier responded positively to Browne's mission on behalf of the Charleston trustees, it did so now in regard to Donaghey's representation. On September 20, 1817, Litta wrote to Oliveira Fernandez commending his concern for the Church. In particular, he mentioned three points. First, although the archbishop of Baltimore would have to be consulted before establishing a diocese in Virginia, it was likely he would agree, since "his diocese is so large, and Virginia is so distant that he can scarcely exercise care of it." Second, Litta displayed his misunderstanding of the Norfolk situation. While he awaited Marechal's opinion on a new Virginia diocese, he stated that "to provide that congregation deprived of a proper pastor, who may administer the sacraments and other spiritual helps to it, and since the greatest part of it is of English descent, it is clearly fitting that a pastor be chosen from that nation, who can better know their language and character." He then accepted the trustees' recommendation of Carbry as the ideal candidate.

Finally, Litta seemed to acknowledge, at least in part, the trustees' right to the "jus patronatus." "Although the jus patronatus cannot be denied them because of their building and endowing the churches," he wrote, "nevertheless they cannot arrogate for themselves more than the sacred canons for patrons allow." Many of the trustee claims, he continued, "are contrary to Church laws," such as subjecting pastors to trustees. The difficulty was that Litta was quite vague in specifying what else he saw as contrary to "Church laws."[3] Further to complicate the issue, on August 24 and again on November 30, 1817, Pius VII granted Oliveira Fernandez an indult to have Mass celebrated in a private oratory for his family and Catholics in the area, where he was represented as living "more nobilium."[4] Donaghey had carried out his mission well. Roman officials were unaware that this private oratory was in fact the brick church that had served the Norfolk community and was then under interdict. In the hands of Oliveira Fernandez, Litta's letter, together with the indult, became a charter for a new assault on Archbishop Marechal.

THE MOVEMENT TOWARD MAKING RICHMOND A DIOCESE

September 20, 1817, was a busy day at Propaganda. Litta composed his letter to Oliveira Fernandez and then, without alluding to it, he also notified Marechal that he was now officially the archbishop of Baltimore. In passing, he alluded to trusteeism, but then only in regard to Charleston.[5] On the same day, the secretary of the congregation also wrote Marechal that, in light of the Norfolk petition, the congregation was inclined to establish a new diocese in Virginia, since it was so distant from Baltimore, but first wanted Marechal's opinion. In the meantime, since the Norfolk congregation had no pastor and the majority were "of English descent," the congregation recommended that, unless Marechal had objections, he should appoint Carbry as pastor.[6]

Marechal was indignant. In December, he responded with a strong protest against having a diocese in Virginia. Norfolk, he argued, had only about 250 Catholics, could be reached from Baltimore in thirty hours, and already had a priest who was, however, deprived of income by the trustees. He also pointed out that a diocese in Virginia would, at this juncture, divide the archdiocese into two disparate regions: Maryland and the Carolinas. Roman officials, in the meantime, consulted Father Giovanni Grassi, S.J., former superior of the American Jesuits who was then residing in Rome. He thought a bishop in Virginia would help settle the trustee dispute and even argued that a bishop was more necessary there than in Boston, established as a diocese in 1808![7]

As Rome continued to toy with the idea of appointing a bishop for Virginia, Marechal visited Norfolk on June 11, 1818—the first visit of a bishop to the embroiled port city. As he reported to Litta, the trip took only twenty-four hours on a ship that made daily runs from Baltimore. He administered confirmation and then sought to pacify the trustees by visiting Oliveira Fernandez, Reilly, and Donaghey in their homes. When that failed, he had a meeting with the more prominent Catholics to discuss how they could obtain the use of the church. Oliveira Fernandez responded with an "inflammatory letter" distributed among Catholics and Protestants.[8]

Marechal then informed Litta of how his letter to Oliveira Fernandez was being misused. The "impious Fernandez" claimed the cardinal had granted him the privilege of a private oratory and the *jus patronatus* and had ordered Marechal to appoint Carbry pastor. Oliveira Fernandez had gained that privilege "by falsely claiming that there is no priest in Norfolk while there is a very pius and vigilant one." Granting him the use of a private chapel, Marechal continued, "devastates the vineyard of the Lord" and became "an occasion of scandal even among the Protestants." As for acknowledging that the trustees had the *jus patronatus*, the Norfolk trustees, who were supposed to be elected to office for only one year, had constituted themselves a permanent body. Were they now to enjoy the *jus patronatus*, the practice would spread elsewhere. He concluded by warning the Roman congregation to exercise caution "when unknown men without the commendation of the ordinaries ask for certain favors & privileges."[9]

A few months later Marechal sent Litta a report on the archdiocese and the American Church. Before the American Revolution, he claimed, there were only 10,000 Catholics, a figure lower than Carroll's estimate of 30,000 in 1785, but that number had now grown to at least 100,000 not only through natural growth and conversions but "especially through the stupendous number of Europeans who each year emigrate to our republic." He then had fifty-two priests, including only twelve Americans, with each in charge of one or more churches. He proceeded to describe the characteristics of each of the ethnic groups among his clergy, with a decided preference for the English, Belgians, Italians, and Germans. While he had many fine Irish priests, he found that many were addicted "to the vice of drunkenness," which made it necessary for him to withhold faculties until careful examination. He then linked this to the trustee problem.

The Irish, he said, especially those of the lower classes, had little problem with their priests drinking and defended them even to the point that "they enter into and remain with them in schism." In this vein he argued that

It was not the Americans, nor the English, nor the immigrants who came from other countries in Europe who disturbed or are disturbing the peace at Charleston, Norfolk, Philadelphia, etc., etc.; but it was those priests from Ireland who were given over to drunkenness or ambition, together with their accomplices, whom they win over to their side by means of innumerable artifices. Most recently they tried by means of various writings to persuade these ignorant people that the Bishops of Boston [Jean Cheverus], Bardstown [Benedict Joseph Flaget, S.S.], and myself intended secretly to establish a French hierarchy in these provinces and to expel the Irish priests. They did not hesitate to broadcast this absurd calumny at Rome by means of letters and messengers.

Far from conspiring to establish a French hegemony, Marechal noted, he had given faculties to ten Irish priests and the majority of his seminarians were Irish.

But ethnic tension was only part of the lay trustee dispute. Behind trusteeism, Marechal argued, lay the American custom of electing all public officials and that of Protestants electing their pastors. Since the Catholic people raised money to buy land and build churches, they also now claimed the right to appoint their pastors. Where the bishop held title to the property, there were no schisms and the bishop was free to dismiss unworthy priests. By contrast, in Norfolk, "Dr. Fernandez and two drunken Irishmen destitute of all religion ejected from the church their very pious pastor, Fr. Lucas and all his fellow Catholics."[10]

Norfolk Trustees Call Carbry as Pastor

In the meantime, Marechal's efforts to end the schism in Norfolk were fruitless. The trustees invited Carbry to come to be their pastor. In July 1818, Marechal forbade the Dominican under pain of excommunication from exercising the ministry in the archdiocese of Baltimore, a threat that apparently caused Carbry to delay his arrival for almost a year. At the same time, Bishop John Connolly, O.P., of New York roiled the waters by urging Carbry's appointment as bishop of the proposed Virginia diocese.[11] In December 1818, moreover, Oliveira Fernandez penned a lengthy letter to Thomas Jefferson outlining all the trustees' grievances and showing how incompatible Marechal's actions were with American democracy. He published it and sent it to the United States Congress, the governors of all the states, members of the state legislatures, and judges. The Sage of Monticello, however, decided not to become enmeshed in this Catholic quarrel.[12]

The Charleston trustees, meanwhile, formed a plot that would have affected Virginia. Early in 1819, they approached Richard Hayes, O.F.M., an Irish nationalist priest, who had been forcibly expelled from Rome, to seek consecration as a bishop for South Carolina from the schismatic archbishop of Utrecht. Once in Charleston, he could then consecrate a bishop for Virginia. Hayes, however, imprudent though he may have been in his public criticism of the Holy See's Irish policy, remained a loyal priest. In April 1819 he revealed the plot to Cardinal Litta.[13] By this time, Roman officials must have been fed up with the whole situation in Virginia and South Carolina.

Meanwhile, sometime in late May or early June, 1819, Marechal fulfilled his promise to the Norfolk congregation to send an Irish priest, Nicholas Kerney, to assist Lucas and have charge of Portsmouth. Had he done this earlier, he might have avoided much of the controversy. Soon after Kerney's arrival, however, Carbry accepted the call from the trustees. Marechal immediately placed him under censure and informed Bishop Connolly.[14] He then demanded that Carbry show his authorization for assuming the office of pastor before July 1 or face the charge of sacrilege.[15] On June 14, 1819, basing their claim on Litta's supposed authorization, the trustees informed Marechal that he had no authority since he was not "a lawful Prelate of this state."[16]

On June 16, perhaps in reaction to the trustees' letter, Marechal informed Propaganda about his continuing problems with trusteeism in Charleston and Norfolk. The loyal Catholics of Norfolk, he reported, welcomed Kerney, but Oliveira Fernandez had invited Carbry "and that miserable priest of Christ did not refuse." Carbry had obtained from the Protestant civil magistrates the title of "Pastor of Norfolk" and celebrated Mass in the church that Neale had placed under interdict. When asked if he had authority from the pope or archbishop of Baltimore, Marechal continued, Carbry "responds that

that indeed was necessary in the old Catholic regions of Europe which are subject to tyrants, but not in North America where citizens enjoy freedom and independence."[17] At the end of July, Marechal offered further observations about Charleston and Norfolk. He wanted to put the prefect on guard against the intrigues of those who, imbued with the thought of Febronius and other European writers, argued that papal jurisdiction was inimical to American democracy.[18]

In the meantime, on September 28, Marechal issued a lengthy pastoral letter, drafted in part by Roger Baxter, in response to the Norfolk trustees' proclamation the previous June. Noting the difference between the ways in which Catholic and Protestant clergy were selected and the nature of the Catholic priesthood, he appealed to Virginia's Statute of Religious Liberty to refute the argument that he could not exercise jurisdiction in Virginia.[19]

On September 11, Litta responded to Marechal's letter of June. The congregation had decided to accept the archbishop's advice to establish a new diocese in Charleston to embrace both Carolinas and Georgia. Marechal was now asked if he had any candidates. In regard to Virginia, the congregation, "after everything was maturely considered," had also decided to establish a new diocese. The see city would be Richmond, Norfolk, or possibly Washington. Propaganda hoped this would end the chaos fomented by Carbry who had "raised the banner of schism."[20]

APPOINTMENT OF PATRICK KELLY AS
FIRST BISHOP OF RICHMOND

While on August 2, 1819, the Congregation of Propaganda had actually reached its decision to establish the Virginia diocese, it waited until June 25, 1820, formally to decide that Richmond would be the see city and that Patrick Kelly, president of St. John's College, Birchfield, near Waterford, would be the first bishop. His jurisdiction, however, was not to include Washington, as had originally been proposed.[21] Within a few days, Father William Taylor, in Rome to present a petition from a group of New York Catholics against Bishop Connolly, informed Marechal of the decision. He also described the problems some Roman officials had in understanding many aspects of the American republic:

Of the geography of the United States, they are very ignorant here. Cardinal [Francesco] Fontana [successor to Litta as prefect of Propaganda] whose judgment is much seriously affected by years, told me it was their intention to erect Virginia into a Bishopric and to have the Bishop reside at Hartford. I told his Eminence that Hartford was in Connecticut, that Richmond was considered the Capital of Virginia; and it was only by producing the map of America that I convinced His Eminence of their *geographical heresy.*

Taylor, always ready to please Marechal and perhaps angling for a miter himself, added further information that may have led the Baltimore prelate to jump to some conclusions in his correspondence with Rome. "I could not describe to Your Grace," the priest wrote, "the censurable and unchristian conduct of the Irish Friars here; they have attempted even to protect the unprincipled Carbry, who has been invited to Rome to render an account of his conduct."[22]

On July 22, Kelly received official notification of his appointment in a letter that added more detail about Propaganda's motivations. Fontana gave him instructions on dealing with the schism and acknowledged that the decision had resulted from Donaghey's visit to Rome in 1817. Kelly was to proceed to Virginia as soon as possible and first use charity to try to win back Carbry and the schismatics. But, "should they persist in their contumaciousness," he should use "canonical penalties, as often as it seems expedient to you." In regard to Oliveira Fernandez, "the author of the dissensions and schism," it was "necessary to act most prudently." At all costs, he was to avoid altercation.[23]

For some reason, Kelly failed to inform Propaganda officials that he had received notice of his appointment. On August 24, however, he was consecrated in St. James Chapel, Dublin, by Archbishop John T. Troy, O.P., of Dublin, assisted by Bishop Daniel Murray, coadjutor of Dublin, and Bishop Kieran Moran of Ossory. On September 20, he went to Cork to be a co-consecrator of John England, the first bishop of Charleston.[24] Yet, in November, he had still not acknowledged his appointment, but he did inform a Roman friend that he would need travel expenses. Sending him money for the trip, Fontana instructed him to leave for Norfolk as quickly as possible and enclosed a letter to be included in the pastoral letter to Norfolk that Roman officials desired him to issue. He was also to take several priests with him to his new diocese.[25]

The same day Fontana gave Kelly his instructions, he also informed Marechal of the appointments of Kelly to Richmond, England to Charleston, and Henry Conwell to the vacant diocese of Philadelphia. Repeating some of the arguments used the previous year, he said the congregation had its own reasons for rejecting Marechal's advice against a Virginia diocese. "For repelling such a stream of evils," he wrote, "no remedy seemed more apt . . . than . . . the institution of a bishop," who would squelch the schism. Again admitting the congregation was swayed by Donaghey's legation, he argued that Virginia was "one of the more populous provinces of the American union," in which a diocese would more easily provide for the "care of the Catholics and the propagation of our Holy Faith." Although Marechal now governed a smaller diocese, Fontana was sure he would still have "as many Catholics as in all the other provinces combined," with ample scope for his pastoral ministry. With somewhat convoluted reasoning, the cardinal said the population of the archdiocese was one reason why Propaganda chose to establish the new diocese not in Norfolk but in Richmond, "which is the principal city of Virginia and which is more distant from Baltimore." Fontana concluded by saying that he realized Richmond was not prepared for a bishop, so Kelly was first to go to Norfolk.[26]

Not for the first time did a Roman official inform an American prelate that there were good, though unstated, reasons for rejecting his recommendations. What is difficult to determine is whether Fontana thought that the trustee delegation of 1817 was representative of the Catholic congregation of Norfolk as a whole or that some of the trustees' arguments were valid, especially the request for pastoral care for the growing Catholic community in Norfolk. In the letter Kelly was to read to the Norfolk community, Fontana recalled the origin of the dispute and called for an end to the schism. Propaganda had acceded to the trustees' request for the new diocese, he stated, "because after mature deliberation the situation demanded it," but the Holy See did first have to hear Marechal's views.[27] In other words, Fontana seemed to say that the trustees had gotten one of their demands, a separate diocese, but they were not to get their way in ignoring episcopal authority by naming their own pastors. Whatever may have been Fontana's intention, the establishment of the diocese of Richmond and his justification for it did nothing to assuage Marechal's feelings. Unfortunately, Kelly would become the unwitting victim of Marechal's animus toward Rome.

Late in 1820, Kelly, England, and Conwell boarded a ship in Ireland to take them to their American dioceses—Conwell to fall prey to lay trusteeism in Philadelphia, England to Charleston to become one of the most dynamic leaders in American Catholic history, and Kelly to begin a short and ill-fated career in Virginia. Early in 1821, Kelly arrived in Baltimore to present his credentials to Marechal. It was a chilling encounter. Marechal read him a stinging protest against the new diocese and rather boldly interpreted his rights as the metropolitan:

> Although it would be entirely lawful for us to oppose the erection of the said see, whether we consider the wicked means by which it was obtained, or the scandals and calamities of every kind, which will undoubtedly be the result; yet fearing that the said enemies of the Church of Christ will take occasions even from our most justly founded opposition, to inflict the most serious injury on the Catholic religion, your Lordship may, as you judge best, proceed or not to take possession of the new see and diocese of Virginia according to the tenor of the Bulls transmitted to you. But to assure the tranquility of our conscience we hereby distinctly declare to your Lordship, that we in no wise give or yield our assent positively to this most unfortunate action of the Sacred Congregation de Propaganda Fide. If you carry it out, we are to be held free before God and the Church now and hereafter from all the evils and scandals which the Catholic religion suffers or may suffer from it in these United States.[28]

After this frigid welcome, on January 18, 1821, Kelly left Baltimore and arrived in Norfolk the following day.

KELLY'S SOJOURN IN NORFOLK

Meanwhile, Marechal was still intent on explaining his viewpoint to Rome. On January 22, he fired a letter off to Fontana. It began: "A man absolutely unknown to us by the name of Patrick Kelly, first landing in New York from Ireland and then coming to Baltimore, notified us that he had been named and consecrated Bishop of Richmond in Virginia." Although Marechal had his own sources of information in Rome, he claimed Kelly's arrival was the first inkling he had that Richmond was a diocese, so he demanded to see the apostolic letters. Most likely relying on Taylor's intelligence, he was convinced that "two vagabond friars, Browne and Carbry, concocting their schemes with other Irish friars living in Rome, have prevailed; and the Sacred Congregation, deceived by the absurd calumnies of such men, has made itself the instrument to carry out their impious schemes."[29] It would take Propaganda officials six months to respond to Marechal, by which time Kelly's administration was all but unbearable.

On April 19, Kelly reported his initial encounter with Marechal to Propaganda. From his arrival in Norfolk, however, his actions were ambivalent. Since he unfortunately left no records and none are extant in Waterford, Lucas is the principal source for Kelly's brief sojourn. On January 21, Lucas had met Kelly at his arrival by steamboat from Baltimore. He informed Marechal that Higgins, one of the trustees, was planning to support Kelly, but that Higgins had spoken neither to him nor to Kerney. In the meantime, Kerney was concerned when he learned by chance at the home of Thomas Moran that James Walsh, one of the young priests Kelly had recruited in Ireland, had arrived and was lodging with Higgins. Since Kelly wanted to meet Carbry and some of the trustees, Lucas took him to Reilly's house, but then the bishop said Mass in Lucas's small chapel and read his bulls to the assembled congregation, which included most of the Irish. So far, however, Oliveira Fernandez had not made his submission.[30]

A few weeks later, Lucas sent Marechal a "journal" with more alarming information. On February 6, Kelly said Mass in Lucas's chapel, but then refused to stay for breakfast. The next day, he dedicated Oliviera Fernandez' brick chapel. Kerney and Lucas were not invited, but Walsh and a young unidentified Portuguese priest assisted. Apparently encouraged by this show of support, the trustees then announced that "the vacant pews of St. Patrick's Church will be rented on Friday next at 11 o'clock by order of the Trustees." On February 8, Lucas and Kerney visited Kelly at Higgins' house. While the bishop was annoyed at the trustees' action, he vacillated on what course of action to take. Kerney and Lucas left their meeting with the bishop "on good terms."

But Kelly then seemed to shift over to the trustees. After dining with Reilly, Carbry, and the other trustees, he rebuked them for their announcement on renting pews, but then prohibited Lucas from preaching, holding a holy hour after Mass, and teaching catechism to French children. To fulfill their Sunday obligation, moreover, members of Lucas's congregation were now required to attend the "Pastoral Mass" in the brick chapel. Kelly, furthermore, told Lucas "it was wrong for a Priest to say two Masses, since the last was not said fasting." The following Sunday, Lucas said Mass in his chapel, since his parishioners did not have pews in the brick chapel, while Kelly said one Mass in the brick chapel, and Carbry the other. Lucas, moreover, cognizant that Marechal had protested the establishment of the diocese, suspected that Kelly had also seen his letter and had shown it to the trustees. Kelly had made an inauspicious beginning of his Virginia ministry and had already hinted to Lucas that he "might ask to renounce the dignity of being a bishop and return to his college where he could exercise the ministry as a simple priest if His Holiness judged it proper."[31]

Lucas was not the only priest in a dilemma about the new bishop. In March, John Mahony, whom Marechal had appointed to Richmond, informed the archbishop that he had only heard rumors that Kelly had arrived in Virginia, but had neither seen nor heard from him, so he considered himself still subject to Marechal's jurisdiction.[32] In the meantime, Kelly continued to act erratically. In May, he had a falling-out with Carbry, who left for North Carolina. But then he informed Lucas that he was to cease as pastor on June 1.[33] Eighty members of Lucas's congregation then issued a protest defending his care for them during the trustee schism and arguing for the need of a priest who could preach in French. They asked that Lucas be allowed "to officiate in the brick Church as honorary assistant." Kelly interpreted this protest as an interference "with the freedom and purity of the Episcopal office" and declared that Lucas had no canonical ties to the diocese of Richmond.[34] Lucas remained in Norfolk during the summer, however, since he had committed himself to teaching several students.

In the meantime, despite Kelly's efforts to avoid confrontation, he found that the trustees, who had been so anxious to have a diocese for Virginia, provided him with no income. He had to teach school to support himself. On June 30, Bishop England arrived in Norfolk with his sister Joanna. He preached three times, but made no reference in his diary to either Carbry or Lucas. Early in July, however, Lucas reported that the city abounded with rumors about the presence of two bishops. He also attributed to Joanna England remarks about Marechal shamefully treating her brother and Kelly. Rumors aside, England used his conversations with Kelly to initiate a long correspondence with Marechal about holding a provincial council of the archbishop and the other bishops that would produce "a most desirable effect: the union and cooperation of the Bishops of these disturbed States."[35] England would be unsuccessful in persuading Marechal to convoke a council but would be the founder of the conciliar and collegial tradition in the American hierarchy.

While England was proposing councils as a solution to trustee problems, on July 21 Fontana finally responded to Marechal's objection in January to the establishment of the diocese. Repeating many of the previous arguments in favor of the diocese, he flatly rejected Marechal's contention that Rome had fallen under the sway of Browne or Carbry in creating the diocese. He also stated that Carroll had proposed a diocese for Virginia. Not only was Kelly an able prelate, he argued, but the Holy See was developing the policy of establishing a diocese for each state, as some bishops had already indirectly proposed. "At the beginning," he continued,

> there was only one bishop for all the federated states of America, now they have grown to nine. Should there be any wonder, if a proper prelate be given to all the other states that lack a bishop? The Bishop of Bardstown [Flaget] is strongly urging that three states, whose care had been entrusted to him, be separated from his diocese, while he would be satisfied with Kentucky. I have no doubt that you would want to imitate him, especially because exercising care for Maryland alone, which exceeds all the others in the number of the faithful, would not be too small for your labors.

Relying on Marechal's "reverence for the Holy See and this Sacred Congregation," Fontana was certain that the archbishop would not only accept the decision but also "strengthen the new Bishop of Richmond with your advice and support."[36] He was still trying to defend the congregation's decision but would soon have to change his mind.

On August 4, Fontana replied to Kelly's letter recounting Marechal's reception. Not surprised at the archbishop's conduct, he was, nevertheless, "confident that, when he has received our letters, his animus will be soothed." For the time being, Kelly was to remain in Norfolk and report on anything that would prevent the establishment of his see in Richmond.[37] By the time Kelly received this letter, he was about to leave Virginia for good.

In the meantime, early in August, Lucas was completing his preparations to leave Norfolk. "After so many years of war," he told Marechal, "I hope that you have the goodness of letting me take some repose." He planned on returning to Baltimore to make a retreat at St. Mary's Seminary to determine on his future.[38] He later entered the Jesuits and became pastor of Holy Trinity Church in Georgetown. His archenemy, Oliviera Fernandez, had also abandoned Norfolk and the cause of trusteeism to return to his native Portugal.[39] Even with the principals in Norfolk's trustee dispute now off the scene, however, Virginia was obviously not yet ready for a bishop.

On October 5, Fontana again wrote to Marechal. This time, he all but admitted the congregation had made a mistake. When Propaganda received Marechal's letter of October 16, 1820, Fontana was himself in Naples for reasons of health and had not seen the archbishop's arguments against the new diocese. He now regretted the decision that "affected you not only as inopportune but also as troublesome and disrespectful." As a result of Marechal's protestations, the cardinals of the congregation had met on September 27 and "decided there was no other remedy than to transfer the Bishop of Richmond," as soon as a vacant diocese could be found, at which time Virginia was "to be entrusted to the administration of the Archbishop of Baltimore." As a token of the Holy See's good will and appreciation, Fontana then sent Marechal a chalice,[40] which, incidentally, Pope John Paul II would use when celebrating Mass in Oriole Park at Camden Yards in Baltimore in 1995.

KELLY IS TRANSFERRED TO WATERFORD AND LISMORE

Propaganda now engaged in a flurry of activity to find a suitable diocese, in the United States or elsewhere, to which to transfer Kelly. For some time, it had urged the division of Bishop Louis William DuBourg's diocese of Louisiana and the Two Floridas, with Florida made a separate diocese. DuBourg consented to the division and to Kelly's appointment as the first bishop.[41] On October 3, however, Fontana wrote three letters concerning Kelly's future. First, he informed DuBourg of Propaganda's decision to assign Kelly elsewhere.[42] Next, he wrote Bishop John Connolly of New York to see if he would accept Kelly as his coadjutor.[43] Finally, he notified the vicar general of the diocese of Waterford, where Bishop Robert Walsh had recently died, that Propaganda wished to transfer Kelly there as quickly as possible. The vicar general was to prepare the clergy and laity.[44] With three letters to such far-flung dioceses in one day, Fontana seems to have had an assistant dedicated to finding any vacant diocese to solve his Virginia problem. On January 28, 1822, Propaganda formally petitioned Pius VII to transfer Kelly to the newly joined dioceses of Waterford and Lismore. On March 9, Fontana formally notified Kelly of his new assignment to "alleviate the animus of" Marechal and to "avoid any cause whatsoever of offense among the prelates."[45]

In June 1822, probably as soon as he received word of his new appointment, Kelly left his diocese without ever seeing Richmond. On July 10, 1822, England announced Kelly's departure in the *United States Catholic Miscellany,* the national Catholic newspaper he founded, with Joanna as editor. He praised his colleague for his handling of the "disgraceful and unmeaning schism" fomented by "a gentleman, who was, we are informed, a good physician, unsuccessful merchant, and very bad but arrogant and dictatorial divine" whose "object was to make a republican Roman Catholic Church; of which he was to be monarch." During the yellow fever epidemic of 1821, moreover, "the bishop was constant in his attendance upon the sick, and during months, was every day amongst the infected, solacing, cheering, instructing, and administering sacraments to the diseased." England had obviously been in contact with Kelly, for he also reported on the location of Richmond's five priests. England's statement, however, was attacked in the Norfolk *Herald* by "Old Catholic," whom England later identified as Jaspar Moran, one of the dissident trustees. In September, England reported that Kelly had arrived in Dublin on July 15, after a journey of twenty-five days.[46]

BISHOP KELLY'S FINAL REPORT ON THE DIOCESE OF RICHMOND

Once Kelly was back in Waterford, officials of Propaganda had to ask him twice for a report on Virginia. Only in September 1822 did he finally respond with a detailed description of where he had assigned his five priests and the size of their congregations. He had brought with him from Ireland John Walsh, Thomas Hore, and Christopher Delany. From Baltimore, he had recruited John Fitzpatrick and found John Mahony already assigned by Marechal to Richmond. He had appointed Walsh as his vicar general and assigned him to Richmond, where the congregation numbered about three hundred Catholics. South of Richmond, he assigned Fitzpatrick to Petersburg, where there were fewer than one hundred Catholics. To Martinsburg in the northern part of the state, he transferred Mahony, who tended about three hundred Catholics scattered among five small communities spread over six counties. In Norfolk and Portsmouth, Father Hore and the newly ordained Delany ministered to about five hundred Catholics.

Altogether, Kelly listed only 1,200 Catholics in the vicinities of Norfolk, Richmond, and Martinsburg. He could give no accurate statistics on the number of Catholics elsewhere because many of them were immigrants who had not settled permanently and few of them were actively involved with the Church. Nor was he enamored with some American mores:

> Their domestic education is abominable. The mixing of black servants with whites in the same house is a serious obstacle to morality and religion. The corruption and depravity even in the most tender state is universal among them and can scarcely be conceived. No Americans are converted from there.

While he deplored American ways, he did describe his ministry during the yellow fever epidemic the previous autumn. "All the Protestant ministers fled," he reported, but he, by staying, won the "admiration and veneration of the Americans." He received "into the bosom of the church, many foreigners who were converted: but not even one American was added to our congregation."[47] Ministering to yellow fever victims would be a principal way in which Norfolk's future Catholics gained acceptance.

After filing his report, Kelly severed all relations with the diocese of Richmond and had only one additional contact with the American Church. In 1828, the Holy See sought a solution to the lay trustee problem in Philadelphia, where Bishop Conwell proved to be totally incompetent in handling the trustees. Conwell was supposed to retire

to Ireland, where Kelly offered him hospitality, and to accept a coadjutor, Francis P. Kenrick, who would administer his diocese. He
broke his agreement, however, and returned to Philadelphia, where
he repudiated Kenrick's authority, locked him out of the cathedral,
and sided with the trustees. Richmond was not the only diocese that
aroused concerns among Roman authorities. Kelly, for his part, ill-
suited to the American mission, died in Waterford on October 28, 1829.

Trusteeism had arisen in part because of the different modes of
owning ecclesiastical property. Studies have focused on lay trusteeism,
but there were also conflicts arising from religious orders owning
property independent of the bishop.

A Corollary to Lay Trusteeism:
Clerical Trusteeism in Alexandria

Simultaneously with his battle with the trustees in Norfolk and officials in Rome, Marechal was about to enter into a prolonged dispute
with the Jesuits over property. His principal contention was over land
that had provided the income for his two predecessors, both ex-
Jesuits, and that he now claimed for the archdiocese. But he had another dispute with them over property in Virginia. During the colonial period, the laws of Maryland did not permit religious orders, as
such, to own property. Individual Jesuits had held title to property in
their own names and willed it to other Jesuits. In Alexandria, then
part of the District of Columbia, they continued this practice and held
full title to St. Mary's Church. When the Jesuits were reestablished in
the United States in 1805 and by papal decree throughout the world in
1814, they continued their mode of holding property. This was part of
the agreement that Neale made with the Jesuits in regard to Southern
Maryland and that Kohlmann wished to implement in Richmond.
There was a corollary to this—when they could not spare one of their
own to staff St. Mary's, they would call on a diocesan priest. This is
what happened to Joseph W. Fairclough in the 1820s.

Against Marechal's expressed desires, Fairclough imprudently
formed a lay board of trustees, while the property was actually owned
by Francis Neale, brother of the late Archbishop Leonard Neale, even
though Francis was then a pastor in Southern Maryland. Suspended
by Marechal, Fairclough then demanded financial compensation for

his services. At one point, he had to be evicted by court order from the rectory, and he eventually returned to his native England.[48] As his controversy with Marechal was unfolding, however, his case brought forth another dimension. In 1827, Francis Dzierozynski, S.J., the Jesuit superior, informed him that "your continuance there depends neither on *your will nor on the will of your Supr but on the will of the Supr of the Society, whosoever he may be, and also in some measure on your good will & friendship toward the Society, whose property the church & house of Alex.dria are.*" He then let Fairclough know his precise status: "You, Rev. Sir, have lived several years with Jesuits & you know that they have always treated those persons whom they employ either in their churches or houses or farms with kindness unless they deserved a contrary treatment which I am far from expecting from you, particularly as you have imbibed that noble principle which you mentioned in your letter to me: obedience is my watchword."[49] In other words, Fairclough was hired help. But Marechal's controversy with Rome over trusteeism and the diocese of Richmond had a broader dimension.

MARECHAL'S VIEWS ON THE NOMINATION OF BISHOPS

In addition to the problems with trusteeism and the untimeliness of the establishment of the diocese of Richmond, the appointment of Kelly had also raised a question of more lasting concern to the American Church, namely, the method of nominating bishops. On January 6, 1821, soon after receiving confirmation of the appointment of three new bishops from Ireland, Marechal had informed Archbishop Joseph-Octavian Plessis of Quebec of his reservations about the appointments and of his own opinion that American bishops should be consulted in the nomination of bishops. His Canadian colleague agreed that Propaganda seemed to prefer "strangers as bishops to the experienced missionaries who have worked in the ministry of the country." He likewise agreed that Marechal should "ask for the right to nominate or present for vacant sees and to determine on the establishment of dioceses in the future."[50] He then offered personally to present the matter to Rome.

Through Bishop William Poynter, vicar apostolic of London, Plessis then urged Fontana that the archbishop of Baltimore should have more of a say in the selection of bishops. Marechal hoped Plessis' letter would contribute to "establishing a full confidence between Prop and the bishops of the United States." While he acknowledged that there were some exemplary Irish clergy, he and Plessis believed that many Irish, as Marechal had already told Propaganda, were the cause of the problems afflicting the American Church. He proposed that Propaganda allow American bishops to make presentations for vacant sees; specifically, he recommended that, on the death of a bishop, the metropolitan ask his suffragans for nominations. Such a method of nomination would be preferable to leaving the whole matter to the Holy See, which was so far away and not always well informed.[51]

Fontana's reaction was sharp. He informed Plessis that the congregation was in unanimous accord that Marechal had neither a right nor a privilege to nominate episcopal candidates to Rome for approval. "The election of bishops," he continued, "(unless some special agreement be to the contrary) belongs altogether to the Apostolic See, especially in the missionary countries." The cardinals of the congregation were also unanimous that, were Marechal granted any privilege to nominate bishops, this might set a precedent for other metropolitans and, in time, be considered a right. Propaganda would, however, always seek the recommendations of the archbishop of Baltimore and other bishops.[52] While Marechal had the encouragement of both Plessis in Quebec and Bishop Jean de Cheverus in Boston in seeking more of a voice in selecting bishops—especially to avoid unwanted Irish ones—it would, ironically, be the work of John England over a decade later that would introduce the practice of local nominations of bishops into the American Church.

For the time, however, Marechal had won his point. Richmond, while still a separate diocese, was again under his administration. For almost twenty years, Marechal and his successors would have to provide for the widely spread pockets of Virginia Catholics.

CHAPTER 4

A Diocese without a Bishop, 1821–1841

Bishop Kelly's final report on the diocese of Richmond could hardly have served much purpose in Rome, where officials had earlier had little idea of where the state of Virginia was, much less the location of towns within it. Kelly himself had only gotten as far as Norfolk. Yet his list of towns with resident priests at least served to indicate where there were pockets of Catholics. Contrary to his advice, the diocese of Richmond now reverted to the administration of Baltimore. Its story for the next twenty years is largely that of priests and their people functioning in a frequently hostile environment under an archbishop who was far removed. Some priests were immigrant rogues, seeking their fortunes on the American mission. But many were dedicated men selflessly serving their people. All of them faced financial problems, made more complicated by Virginia's laws prohibiting the incorporation of church property. Lay trusteeism continued to exist, but the excesses of Norfolk had been eradicated.

RICHMOND REVERTS TO THE ARCHBISHOP OF BALTIMORE

With the return of Virginia to Marechal's jurisdiction, some of Kelly's priests did not fare well. Late in 1822, Marechal reprimanded John Walsh in Richmond for exercising the authority of vicar general. Walsh admitted that "it is true, I heard some time ago, that your Grace from the competent Authority has again received jurisdiction over Virginia, but having no authentick information of the fact I did not feel myself called on to write." He reported that all the churches in the diocese had resident priests, except for a place he did not name, probably Winchester, seventy miles from Washington. Since Kelly had failed to keep his promise to send a priest from Ireland every three months, Walsh now asked to be relieved of his duties in Virginia.[1]

Marechal charged Walsh with being rash. Walsh apologized, denied the charge, and informed the archbishop that he would take advantage of Kelly's "exeat," or permission to go to another diocese, as soon as possible, either to go to a healthier climate in a northern American city or return to Ireland.[2] Early in March 1823, he left Richmond, after first notifying the other priests that the diocese was again subject to Marechal and passing on to them the archbishop's Lenten regulations.[3] Richmond, the see city, now had no resident priest.

No sooner had Walsh departed from Richmond, when John Fitzpatrick, whom Kelly had recruited in Maryland, asked to leave Petersburg. He suffered from the "bilious fever" and needed to move to a cooler climate.[4] Marechal reminded him that he had permission from his bishop in Ireland only to choose a diocese, not to pass from one to another. Moreover, he concluded, "I respect you too much to suppose that, like the late Pastor of Richmond, your intention is to decieve [sic] me by a willful misrepresentation of the state of your health."[5] Bristling at this accusation, Fitzpatrick told Marechal in June that his bishop in Ireland had summoned him home and enclosed a letter from his doctor testifying to his poor health.[6] Petersburg, too, now lacked a resident priest.

RICHMOND'S QUEST FOR A PERMANENT PASTOR

After Walsh's departure, the Richmond community depended on occasional visits from Christopher Delany in Norfolk. In the summer of 1824, the trustees of the Richmond congregation, Auguste Marie Chevallié, William Burke, John Cullen, and John Gardiner petitioned Archbishop Marechal "either [to] appoint a minister from your own diocese or permit us to nominate one from another diocese subject to your approbation." They wanted their priest to be "a gentleman of refined manners, respectable talents, and exemplary piety; a man who would be stimulated less by emoluments, than by the desire of promoting religion—a man determined to devote his life to the interests of his flock." If they received the Gallego legacy, still under litigation, furthermore, they would "take immediate measures for erecting a suitable church."

With more civic pride than realism, the trustees complained that "Norfolk should have two ministers, while the congregations of Richmond and Petersburg are left entirely destitute," for "Richmond is the emporium of this opulent state, and from its favorable situation, must in time become a city of the first class while the towns of the lower country must sink to comparative insignificance." As the "Metropolis," Richmond could influence the members of the assembly, who would "have the opportunity of having the benign doctrines of our holy faith expounded by an accomplished Preacher. They will return to their homes divested of the prejudices which they imbibed with their mothers' milk, and they will tell their constituents that Catholicks are not such monsters as they are represented."[7]

Father Delany in Norfolk, however, was not so sanguine about the ability of the Richmond trustees to support a priest. He sympathized with their desires but doubted the "expediency & final success" of their proposal to build a church before having a resident priest. Of the trustees, he noted, only Chevallié was sufficiently wealthy to assure a priest's salary, and he intended to return to France. Moreover, a priest would have to live in a boardinghouse, since no Catholic family could provide a residence.[8] Delany's subsequent visit did nothing to change his opinion. The community was divided on whether to obtain a priest or build a church first. Always in the background was the uncertainty of the Gallego estate.[9] Through the fall, Delany kept Marechal informed of the Richmond community. During one of his trips, he had also visited Smithfield, where he found several Catholics. He baptized four adults, whom he then appointed to instruct five others. With no comment about slavery, he reported that he had "also baptized several children, both white & coloured—with the consent of their Parents & Masters or others concerned."[10]

Despite Delany's reservations about Richmond, Marechal decided to transfer Father Thomas Hore from Norfolk to Richmond in April 1825. This left Delany temporarily alone in Norfolk, until he was joined by J. F. van Horsigh. Hore found his congregation unruly. He rented a room on the east side of 14th Street, and, to support himself, opened a classical school for boys.[11] Despite the litigation over the Gallego estate, however, by May 1826 he had built a small church on the property. Many previously unknown Catholics now began to surface.[12] But, in September 1827, Hore found the people to be so uncooperative that he asked to be relieved.[13] Marechal then considered transferring Van Horsigh from Norfolk to Richmond, but Delany argued that Norfolk needed two priests. "Besides," he stated, "I know and am authorized to say that the Revd. Mr. Vanhorsigh [sic] would much prefer to remain in his present situation than to exchange it for an [sic] *never to be satisfied people,* such as those of Richmond prove themselves to be."[14]

Hore then agreed to remain in Richmond until May 1828. Over the previous three years, he had built a church and raised about $600 to support a priest and had procured two houses that would be conveyed to the parish at the death of an aging widow. He had lost the suit for the Gallego case in the chancery court, but the people were now willing to support a priest. He then returned to his native Ireland.[15]

Hore's successor was Father James Hoerner. Arriving in the spring of 1828, he informed Archbishop James Whitfield, Marechal's successor, "that this congregation consists of two hundred members, french or of french extraction, and Irish and children of Irish; no natives but two or three." Many," he continued, "do not attend church, others profess themselves Protestants, and very few, as I suppose, are practical Catholics." The church was "a little frame building, with too scanty room, and too low an appearance, and too far removed for attracting many proud and, at least in this case, indolent Virginians." The trustees had accepted him, but his sole income of $450 came from pew rents and Sunday collections, from which he had to pay his own living expenses as well as the maintenance of the church. He hoped that perhaps Petersburg might at least defray his expenses, but he preferred to have Mass there on weekdays, rather than be absent from Richmond on a Sunday. Richmond lacked many of the necessities for Catholic worship and had some customs Hoerner found strange. He had no ciborium for reserving the Blessed Sacrament and he questioned Hore's practice of simply accompanying the bodies of the dead from their homes to the "protestant burying ground." He noted, moreover, that children were solemnly baptized at home, since "there is no baptismal water, nor baptismal font to be found in the church."[16]

Hoerner soon gained acceptance from the Richmond congregation, but he queried whether "several places around Richmond, and that at a good distance too, as Linchburg [sic], Charlottesville etc. . . . belong to me."[17] There is, however, no record that Hoerner ever visited those distant towns. But, during his tenure in Richmond, Whitfield administered confirmation in the small church in Richmond—the first visit of a Catholic bishop to the capital of Virginia.[18]

In July 1829, Hoerner submitted his annual report. Twenty-five Richmond Catholics received communion during the Easter season and twenty-seven children were in catechism classes. There were two converts, and his income remained $450. Petersburg, however, was in "wretched condition." The people had frequently been asked to support a clergyman, so that "when I repair thither they think I come for their cash." They had "no common place of worship," and the twenty families "are generally at variance and bickering [with] each other." As a result, he continued, "when I say Mass in a house, the few that are on good terms with the owner attend; the remainder trouble themselves no more about it; and vice versa. Of course I go there rarely and ask them nothing." During his four visits there the previous year, only two parishioners had made their Easter duty. He only hoped that, once a church was built, the division would end.[19]

By 1830, Hoerner left Richmond, ultimately to serve in Wheeling. For some time during the summer of 1830, van Horsigh came to Richmond from Norfolk. He recommended the appointment of Samuel Cooper as the permanent pastor of the congregation he estimated to be about 300 with an additional sixty people in Petersburg.[20] A Norfolk native, Cooper had been ordained in 1819 and is reported to have said Mass in Richmond on two occasions in 1823 and 1827.[21] Despite Cooper's credentials as a native Virginian, Whitfield appointed Francis T. Todrig, who left no record of his activities, but was rumored to be a Freemason.

In the spring of 1832, Todrig changed places with Father Timothy O'Brien, pastor of St. Ignatius Church, Hickory, Maryland. Born in Ballina, County Mayo, Ireland, O'Brien completed his theological studies at St. Mary's Seminary in Baltimore and was ordained in 1819. He briefly entered the Jesuit novitiate in Maryland before undertaking a series of pastoral assignments in the archdiocese of Baltimore.[22] After years of relative neglect, Richmond finally received dynamic and—later—controversial leadership. He arrived at a critical period, for Whitfield was pessimistic about the possibility of any Catholic growth in Virginia in general, much less in Richmond.

Soon after O'Brien's arrival in Richmond, Whitfield described the Virginia situation to Propaganda. Catholics numbered only 4,000 out of 1,211,405. He had himself visited Richmond and, of the four priests he had sent there, three had returned saying they saw little hope for any increase in the small Catholic community, then numbering only twenty-five, far below van Horsigh's estimate of two years earlier. He hoped that O'Brien's appointment might bring it about that "our holy religion will flourish in those arid places." He had promised financial support if O'Brien "would build a decent church of brick, for the Catholics have used up to now a small, humble church built of wood in a city where you will find the Protestant churches, and even private homes, as often as not, outstanding for beauty and ornamentation." Elsewhere in Virginia, however, he was about to dedicate a new church in Portsmouth in July and another in Harpers Ferry in October.[23] Whitfield's report played a role in the preparation for the Second Provincial Council in 1833, which recommended the suppression of the diocese of Richmond. The very existence of the diocese rested on the performance of priests like O'Brien—and the opinion of Roman officials.

In the meantime, O'Brien was taking charge in Richmond. As soon as he arrived, he summoned the trustees. He found the "religious instruction of the children . . . greatly neglected," so he immediately initiated catechism instructions every Sunday afternoon at 4, followed by Vespers at 5. By July, he was delighted to tell Whitfield that "several protestants have been in the habit of attending the evening instructions & I am informed have been much pleased." Several women of the parish, moreover, "associated to join the order of the Scapular & go to their communion once a month." Such lay organizations, he asserted, would make Catholicism more public, for "heretofore the practice was to go [to Communion} as privately as possible." He further hoped within a few months to have "15 or 20 candidates for confirmation." Although he had discovered a "much divided" congregation upon his arrival, it was now "again pretty well united," but he feared for the future, since "there is little or no religion at bottom."

From the outset of his Richmond ministry, O'Brien worked to build a proper church. With the appeal of the Gallego case still pending, he feared the congregation would lose its right to the lot on Marshall Street and would only receive "the value of the little church which will not amount to $600 though it cost nearly $2000." The trustees were too poor to build a new church, so he considered pur-chasing a museum that "would make one of the finest churches in the city." With such poverty among Richmond's Catholics, he reflected that "there is but little sympathy for us & unfortunately we are a degraded caste in one of the most aristocratic dens in the world." Finally, he reported that he had visited Petersburg, but to go there often would give "great dissatisfaction here," so he recommended that a priest be assigned there with "help to support him for the first year."[24] O'Brien's first report to Whitfield virtually outlined his agenda for the church in Richmond for almost the next twenty years.

Whitfield had promised O'Brien financial support for building a proper church in Richmond and, in fact, during his tenure as archbishop built more churches in Virginia than in Maryland.[25] In February 1833, O'Brien reported that he had told the people of Petersburg of the "liberality" the archbishop "wished to extend to this part of your diocese," as an incentive for raising money for churches in both Petersburg and Richmond. His strategy was to have the people of Petersburg contribute to the Richmond church with a promise to refund their money if they built their own church. He ap-pointed Colonel McHenry to canvass the people about building a church, but he remained convinced that "an intelligent priest sta-tioned there . . . would not only succeed in building in a short time, but I believe it to be the only way to establish religion in Petersburg." Petersburg, however, would not have a church for several years.

In Richmond, O'Brien had received $4,000 in subscriptions, of which $1,500 was already paid. He had himself contributed $100, but needed a total of $7,000 "to accomplish the design, namely 75 feet long by 45 in width, including a dwelling in the rear." Then he made the first two of numerous proposals that would change the face of Richmond's Catholic community. "Should such a building be put up in the neigh-borhood of the Capitol," he wrote, "& should I be able to buy the present church and convert it into an asylum under the guidance of the Sisters of Charity, with the impulse given to religion we must I think succeed here." For the site he had in mind, however, "it will be neces-sary to transact that business through the agency of some person who may not be suspected as the idea of building a church would greatly enhance its value." Once the property was purchased, it would be vested in the archbishop, for he was determined to avoid the abuses of the Norfolk trustees a decade before. He explained to Whitfield:

As the trustees are not incorporated they cannot hold property as such & I know they are too suspicious of each other to vest the right in either. Besides I would not submit to it if they did. If the matter should come to a discussion this will be the apple of discord & I am almost sure of gaining my point. We must as you see calculate much on our northern friends. There can hardly be a more interesting case placed before them, nor one in which the interests of religion are more deeply concerned.

O'Brien continued to face financial difficulties in building his church. A convert had pledged $1,000, but only "after the death of the daughter who has no notion of dying shortly." If he could get a priest to replace him for a few weeks, he planned on begging for funds in Alexandria, Washington, and Baltimore. Raising money in Richmond, he reflected, had "called forth the malevolence of a few who are fonder of their money than their God or religion. They however are confined to two french & two Irish who are dwindling into insignificance." On a more positive note, he reported that "much edification is derived from the monthly communicants." He continued his Sunday lecturing "from an hour to 1½ hours before vespers after which there is benediction." If the new church were built and the asylum opened, he was convinced "the foundation of religion will be laid on a permanent basis & unless the rising generation is provided for, years will yet elapse before much can be expected."[26]

By August of 1833, O'Brien had obtained the prominent site he desired for his church, a lot "65 feet on one and 165½ on another St. in the genteelist part of the city & within a few yards of the western gate of the Capitol." He paid $3,000 and engaged "a mechanic to build us a church 75 by 45 with a portico supported by 4 large pillars 2½ feet diameter & 25 feet high with a cupola surmounted by a cross." In the rear would be "the sacristies & over them the priest's appartment. Complete for $7500." In the litigation O'Brien would subsequently have with Bishop John McGill, the dimensions of the church would be important, for he later purchased a lot to the rear of the church on which an elderly man built a residence for him with the provision that the builder be allowed to live there until his death.

O'Brien was confident, as he told Whitfield, that he could construct a grand church "with as much ease as an inferior building." He expected that "many will assist us with a view to ornament the city who under other circumstances would not give us a dollar. Indeed we had no alternative, the lot is too conspicuous to admit of an inferior building." To supplement the $4,000 he had already collected, he would make begging tours in Philadelphia and New York, but he still counted "on large aid from your grace, in proportion to the efforts that are being made."[27]

On July 24, 1833, meanwhile, O'Brien had purchased for $500 the Gallego lot on Fourth and Marshall in his own name from Peter J. Chevallie, Gallego's last surviving executor.[28] This purchase opened the way for him eventually to invite the Sisters of Charity to open an asylum in Richmond, but it was another source of his later conflict with McGill.

The work of O'Brien and other priests scattered around the state was going on just at a time when the diocese faced suppression. In October 1833, the American bishops assembled for the Second Provincial Council. As they were discussing diocesan boundaries, they had before them Whitfield's report to Propaganda and recommended "the suppression of the Diocese of Richmond already held in the perpetual administration of the Archbishop of Baltimore."[29] Propaganda officials, however, rejected "the suppression of the episcopal see of Richmond, which the Archbishop of Baltimore will look after with the title of administrator until the S. Congregation shall decree otherwise."[30] The congregation gave no reasons for its decision.

In the meantime, by the spring of 1834, O'Brien had completed his new church, St. Peter's, modeled on St. Phillippe du Roule in Paris. He invited Whitfield to dedicate it on Sunday, May 25. As he told Samuel Eccleston, then the president of St. Mary's College in Baltimore and recently named coadjutor archbishop of Baltimore, he was also inviting "some of the Nabobs as I intend to have a collection made to help to pay the debts of the church, which will be very considerable." If the professors of St. Mary's Seminary attended, moreover, "a splendid display will produce a beneficial result." He was especially anxious for the presence of Father Nicholas Kerney, Lucas's associate in Norfolk during the stormy days of the trustee schism and then pastor of St. Patrick's Church in Baltimore.[31]

The dedication was a grand occasion. Whitfield consecrated the church assisted by Eccleston and Samuel Mulledy, S.J., president of Georgetown College. Adding to the chorus of priests, according to the *Richmond Enquirer,* were "the rich tones of the organ." After the consecration, Whitfield said Mass and administered confirmation.

Eccleston concluded the ceremony with an "able, judicious and liberal" discourse, in which, noted the newspaper, "his appeal to 'the chivalry of the Old Dominion,' was not altogether unheeded." At vespers in the afternoon, however, Mulledy's sermon drew mixed reviews. All were "struck with the talent and learning displayed on the occasion," said the *Enquirer*'s reporter, "but few were equally satisfied with the spirit that characterized it. The contrast to the temperate sermon of the morning was confessed by all with whom we have conversed." The paper attributed the "small collection" to the negative reaction to Mulledy's sermon.[32] Mulledy had preached on "the splendid triumph of the Roman Catholic Church" and the "wisdom, science & virtue" of the popes.[33] Virginia Catholicism was not to be known for its triumphalism.

By July, O'Brien commented to Whitfield that the "great excitement produced by Mr. Mulledy's Sermon" was "fast subsiding." The music in his new church was attracting "a pretty large congregation both in the fore & afternoon" and "the governor & one or two other respectable protestant gentlemen have taken pews."[34] Although Littleton Waller Tazewell was then governor, O'Brien was probably referring to former Governor John Floyd, whose three daughters, Letitia Preston, Lavalette, and Niketti, were baptized at St. Peter's.[35] Niketti would marry John Warfield Johnston, who later served as United States Senator from Virginia. Lavalette married George Frederick Holmes, a professor at the University of Virginia. Floyd's wife, Letitia, was later received into the Catholic Church by Bishop Richard V. Whelan.[36] Another son, Benjamin Rush, a graduate of Georgetown, became a Catholic in 1851 while serving in the legislature.[37] O'Brien's successful cultivation of Richmond's elite stood in sharp contrast to the experience of the Catholic Church elsewhere. The same summer he completed St. Peter's, nativists burned the Ursuline Convent in Charlestown, Massachusetts.[38]

On November 22, 1834, O'Brien had realized his dream of having the Sisters of Charity from Emmitsburg open St. Joseph's orphan asylum and free school in Hore's newly renovated wooden chapel. Sisters Margaret George, Editha Barry, and Ann Catherine Reilly were the first to come. Five years later, they replaced the frame house with a brick one.[39] In June 1838, O'Brien had also arranged for the sisters to provide nurses for the infirmary attached to the Richmond Medical College. Sister Matilda Coskery, a Baltimore native, was the first to work in the small building at the corner of Main and Nineteenth

Streets. Work in the Richmond infirmary, however, was short-lived. In 1841, the sisters withdrew, because, according to their history, "the position of the Sisters at the Infirmary was not enviable; they were under too many restrictions, and the Doctors made use of them as they would of subordinates, and to further their own interests, the patients were mostly colored people, in which be it said, Richmond doth much abound."[40] In 1860, the sisters, now renamed the Daughters of Charity, would found St. Francis de Sales Infirmary in Richmond, totally under their own control.

Although O'Brien's parishioners were predominantly Irish, not all of them were poor. Sometime in 1836, John Dooley arrived in Richmond with his wife and cousin, Sarah—they had been married that year with a dispensation from close kinship at St. Mary's in Alexandria four years after their arrival from Ireland. In Richmond, John became a leading manufacturer of hats and purveyor of furs. In 1838, he and Sarah had their first child, George, who died young. They then had eight more, several of whom played major roles in the diocese.[41] The Dooley family was the most prominent example of middle-class Irish who formed a nucleus around which Richmond's poorer Irish immigrants could gather.

Meanwhile, the nation was being wracked by the first signs of opposition to the national disgrace that would lead to the Civil War. In 1831, Nat Turner had led a slave revolt in Southampton, Virginia. In August 1835, a series of rallies took place around the country protesting the work of abolitionists in fomenting such rebellions. Catholics in the South, furthermore, were accused of being in favor of abolition, a charge that in Richmond they hastened to dispel. In response to a request of the "Committee of Vigilance," O'Brien assembled his congregation on August 30, with J. A. Chevallié as chairman and James Herron as secretary to declare that neither clergy nor laity supported abolition. The assembly heard an address by James Ryder, S.J., of Georgetown College that should have embarrassed his audience.

Ryder stated at the outset that "the fidelity of Catholics to the laws of the land cannot be misunderstood." As evidence, he noted that when the Charlestown convent was burned the previous year, 25,000 Irishmen, "because they valued more the preservation of order and due submission to the laws, . . . raised not a hand to avenge their wrongs, patiently awaiting the dispensations of justice at the hands of their country." But then he proceeded to show the incompatibility of Catholicism and abolitionism:

The wicked interference of some would-be philanthropists, who are jeoparding [*sic*] the peace of our flourishing country, in order to carry out their visionary schemes of emancipation is too alarming to the liberty and prosperity of our national institutions, to be looked upon with indifference by the friend of his country. The Catholic that could countenance such conduct, would be looked upon by his brethren as a madman or a traitor. *They* never will join in fellowship with the miscreant that would sacrifice his country to his wild speculations, however they may be graced by the names of religion and philanthropy.

Had Ryder contented himself with showing Catholics were law-abiding, his speech might not have been reprehensible. But he chose to make an unfavorable comparison between slaves and freemen that bordered on racism.

If abolitionists hoped to "better the condition of the slave," Ryder asserted,

Let them look to the disgusting state of morals among the colored free in the Northern cities—where they are, for the greater part, a nuisance to the white population in almost every department of life; and then let them look to the peaceful, and contented, and secure condition of the Southern slave, under the gentle sway of an upright master.[42]

If Richmond's elite wondered where Catholics stood on the question, Ryder's speech, published in the newspaper by order of Chevallié and Herron, left no doubt. To put the matter in perspective, however, the same issue of the paper carrried similar statements from the Jewish and Protestant communities. Catholics were accommodating to Richmond mores, but at a cost.

DEVELOPMENT OF NORFOLK AND PORTSMOUTH

Norfolk, originally the principal center of Virginia Catholicism, underwent several changes. In February 1823, Hore painted a bleak picture of the community he and Delany served. "It could not ordinarily be expected," he wrote Marechal, that priests so "young and inexperienced in the mission and . . . with as little knowledge of the world's policy, could be able to guide a discordant and convulsed congregation as Norfolk, but when you . . . consider the peculiar situation in which they have been left at the departure of Bishop Kelly it is still less to be expected." The Norfolk church was almost deserted.[43]

In the fall, Delany, Hore's confrere, reported a slight improvement. The number of communicants had increased, principally among the women. Trusteeism seemed to have expired completely, but the community was still composed of both Irish and French. The Norfolk church even had a new organ and bell, but the Portsmouth one needed repair.[44] Like priests of any generation, Delany faced the difficulty of some prominent people demanding special favors. The Portuguese consul complained to Marechal that Delany refused to officiate at his marriage. Delany explained that the consul was married to an Anglican and had joined the Freemasons, but was no longer active in the organization only because of his government's prohibition. The man never attended church and seemed more intent on having his government recognize the legitimacy of his child than on practicing his faith.[45]

During much of 1824, Delany cared for the Richmond community from time to time. In the spring, Marechal came to Norfolk for confirmations.[46] A year later, Marechal transferred Hore from Norfolk to Richmond. Delany then begged the archbishop for "another associate in the Holy ministry as soon as you find it convenient." The number of Catholics in Portsmouth and Point Comfort had decreased, as the economic depression forced the discharge of many mechanics who worked in the Navy yard and on the fortifications. Those who remained agreed to attend Mass in Norfolk, but he would still "attend regularly once a week to the children [in Portsmouth] & to others who may want instructions in Catechism or other duties." In Norfolk too, the membership of the congregation had declined because of the economic slump, but those receiving communion had increased.[47]

In June, Delany submitted his annual report. "In Norfolk," he said, "the number of whites of both sexes is 88 only, and of the colored persons, 12 individuals." He estimated that Old Point Comfort, previously attended by Hore, had an additional twenty-five people, but in Portsmouth, there were only fourteen. Of the grand total of 139, only "40 or 50 attend frequently, the females constituting those numbers being nearly as 3 to 1 male." As elsewhere, women were the dominant church-goers. The total, moreover, was far below what Kelly had reported in 1822.

Delany expressed "humiliation" at "the smallness of the lists" and blamed himself for not being "a fit instrument in the hands of my Savior." He had received no converts into the Church, other than the four he mentioned in Smithfield and a Baptist family of six in Portsmouth. Some of his people were lukewarm at best. If he refused to marry a couple who came to him on short notice, they might go to a Protestant minister.[48] Virginia's Catholics were slow in adapting to ordinary Catholic practices.

In June 1825, Marechal decided to appoint a second priest to Norfolk. At one point, he seems actually to have proposed sending Lucas back. Delany agreed that one priest in Norfolk should have "a thorough knowledge of the French language," but, if Lucas returned, "the old partialities on one side and antipathies on the other, I have too much reason to believe, still exist, and merely want an exciting cause which should it come, it needs not too much penetration to foresee what may be the probable result." Still, he thought "a French Gentleman would be the best selection."[49] A few months later, however, he was so anxious to have a companion that he said he would gladly welcome any priest Marechal sent.[50] But the archbishop had few priests to spare. In January 1826, Delany was still alone. He informed Marechal at the time that Bishop John England had preached in Norfolk—an event that would have hardly pleased the archbishop.[51]

In the fall of 1826, Delany ministered to the victims of yellow fever, which he said was much more serious than the newspapers reported. He had only 118 parishioners in Norfolk, but the numbers in both Old Point Comfort and Portsmouth continued to decline.[52] In the middle of October, however, he finally received an assistant, Joseph van Horsigh, a Belgian. By that time, there was no congregation to speak of either in Portsmouth or Old Point Comfort, and the church in Portsmouth was completely abandoned.[53] Although van Horsigh initially thought "the climate of this country will never agree with my constitution,"[54] he remained long enough to become the builder of the permanent Portsmouth community.

From his base in Norfolk, van Horsigh visited Richmond on a regular basis during 1830. He also rode a circuit. After one such jaunt in July 1830, he wrote Whitfield that, in addition to agreeing to visit Richmond once a month, he had also discovered one hundred and fifty Catholics in Lynchburg and forty in Columbia.[55] In July 1831, under the joint administration of van Horsigh and Delany, the first St. Patrick's Church was built in Norfolk on the corner of Holt and Chapel Streets.[56] But van Horsigh's principal concentration was Portsmouth, which for a time had dwarfed Norfolk as a Catholic center.

In July 1832, van Horsigh had completed a new church in Portsmouth, a stuccoed brick structure, facing High Street.[57] He was, however, a builder and not a fund-raiser, so he asked to be relieved of his assignment. But he recommended that his replacement reside in Portsmouth.[58] By the summer of 1834, he had departed from Norfolk.

Now left alone again, Delany made it clear that, if Whitfield intended to place one priest in charge of Norfolk and Portsmouth, "you may no longer consider me that one."[59] Receiving no response, he left without further ado for New York. James Herron, a parishioner, assured Whitfield that the people wanted his return,[60] but, after more than a decade's service in Norfolk, Delany had left for good.

Portsmouth then had an unidentified German priest, whose lack of facility in English made him ineffective. In Norfolk, the laity took the initiative in finding a pastor. In January 1835, Walter de Lacy, a Norfolk parishioner, told Father Thomas R. Butler, president of Mount St. Mary's College in Emmitsburg, that "we are sadly in want of a clergyman here, for the worthy pastor of the Portsmouth Congregation cannot, I fear, suffice for all our wants, nor effect near as much good among us as he desires." He suggested either Alexander Hitzelberger, then teaching at Emmitsburg, or "some other Pastor of somewhat similar qualifications."[61] In September, Hitzelberger had agreed to take charge of Norfolk, and Nicholas Kerney, Lucas's former associate, came to install Joseph Stokes in Portsmouth to replace the German priest.[62] Stokes would remain for less than two years and was replaced by Walter Moriarty. But, for almost eighteen years, Hitzelberger remained in Norfolk.

Hitzelberger was a native of Baltimore and an alumnus, former professor, and vice president of Mount St. Mary's Seminary. A distinguished orator, he had preached the year before at the dedication of the cathedral in St. Louis.[63] He later confided, however, that his taking the Norfolk parish was not totally voluntary, for Butler was "the originator of many petty vexations & unjust exactions which drove me from the College."[64] Once in Norfolk, he began organizing the community. In 1837, a bequest from Thomas Moran made it possible for the Sisters of Charity to open a free school, which had to close in January 1840, a victim of the national financial panic.[65] In 1848, the sisters would return to Norfolk on a firmer footing when Miss Ann Behan Plume Herron gave $1,000 per annum for St. Mary's "select" school for girls and an orphan asylum.[66] Hitzelberger's own oratorical skills gained the respect of the city, which invited him to speak at the laying of the cornerstone of the City Hall on August 23, 1847.[67]

THE NORTH AND WEST

While priests in Richmond and Norfolk had to contend with financial needs and fluctuating populations in an urban environment, those in the area around Martinsburg tended a vast territory that would be transformed by the building, first, of the C&O canal and then the B&O Railroad. This was Virginia's frontier, where, as elsewhere in the country, priests lived alone, often in rented rooms, and shared the lives of their subjects. The bishop was a distant figure. Priests were independent, but this came at a price.[68]

The population of Martinsburg and its missions was a mix of Irish workers and some of Virginia's more affluent Catholics of Irish descent. Richard McSherry had migrated from Ireland, first to Jamaica, and then to his plantation of "Retirement" in Berkeley County, where he became a trustee of the Martinsburg church. His son, William, entered the Jesuits, became the first superior of the Jesuits' Maryland Province and later president of Georgetown. Farther to the west, in Romney, two boys, Thomas and Samuel Mulledy, came from humbler means, but both became Jesuits and presidents of Georgetown. Thomas served as the second provincial superior, and Samuel had preached at the dedication of St. Peter's.[69]

The priests who served this mixed population were itinerant missionaries, some of whom left detailed accounts of their austere lifestyles. From them would come Richmond's second bishop, Richard Vincent Whelan, who, incidentally, was the first of five bishops who either served in the area or were natives. Thomas Becker, the pastor of Martinsburg for part of the Civil War, later became bishop of Wilmington and then of Savannah. His former student, John J. Kain, was a native of Martinsburg and became pastor before being named bishop of Wheeling and later archbishop of St. Louis. Augustine van de Vyver was pastor in nearby Harpers Ferry in the 1870s before becoming vicar general of the diocese and then bishop. Almost a century later, another native, Joseph Hodges, was ordained for Richmond, and became auxiliary bishop and then bishop of Wheeling. But the mix in the Martinsburg missions between well-to-do and poor workers made it a difficult assignment in antebellum Virginia.

In the 1820s, John Mahony, originally recruited for Richmond, rented a room in a house outside Martinsburg. In March 1823, he described for Marechal his itinerant ministry. On three Sundays of each month, he alternated saying Mass at Martinsburg, Winchester, and Halltown, which was between Charlestown and Harpers Ferry. On the fourth Sunday, he shifted between Shepherdstown and Bath in Morgan County. The size of his congregations varied from twenty-five families in Martinsburg to three or four in Shepherdstown. He also heard that there were three or four more in Hardy and Hampshire Counties, eighty miles from his principal residence. In his far flung missions, "all the Catholics . . . are miserably poor, six or seven persons only accepted, who are tolerably well off."[70]

One of his more "tolerably well off" parishioners was John Jamison, who had moved to the Martinsburg area from Frederick, Maryland. In the fall of 1824, Jamison made a series of complaints about Mahony, ranging from failure to say Mass twice each month in Martinsburg to creating "public scandal" by playing cards and riding with a young woman. While repudiating all these charges, Mahony was convinced that the real issue was that Jamison "never liked me because I was an Irishman & as he was pleased to say a *Democrat*."[71]

Over a year later, Mahony had a physical altercation with another prominent member of his congregation. He had dined at the home of Dennis McSherry, the brother of Richard McSherry, one of the Martinsburg trustees. After the women had retired, he and his host sang songs, but then got into an argument that developed into a fight, the description of which would have made a good skit for the Keystone Kops as one man chased the other up the stairs, out the second-story window to the ground below, and then back in through the front door. They were eventually broken up, with neither showing permanent signs of damage, but Richard McSherry, Robert Boone, and John Piet fired off a petition to Marechal, accusing Mahony of drinking and demanding his removal. They wanted a priest who would be sensitive to the needs of the poor people and especially children and servants. While they preferred to have a Jesuit, they definitely did not want another Irishman.[72]

Mahony pleaded self-defense in his fight with McSherry,[73] but Marechal sent Piet and Boone a letter divesting Mahony of his authority. But Mahony also had his supporters. Nicholas Fitzsimmons, a leading parishioner in Winchester, had heard no complaints about Mahony's conduct and suspected the petitioners' real motives. Fitzsimmons was alarmed, as he told Marechal, that, because "Catholicks are few and I may add the most persecuted society in this part of the country, . . . the present conduct of some of its leading members has rendered their situation still more disagreeable."[74] Once freed from all censures,[75] however, Mahony went to Boston to work with Irish immigrants. He later founded St. Patrick's Church, Lowell, where Richmond's Father O'Brien later took up residence.[76] In light of earlier trustee problems, it is perplexing that Marechal chose to use the trustees of Martinsburg to tell Mahony he was removed. From the reports of later priests, moreover, whatever Mahony's shortcomings, Martinsburg's wealthier Catholics could be demanding.

The Martinsburg area then depended on Jesuits in Frederick and on priests from Mount St. Mary's, until Father John B. Gildea took up residence in 1829.[77] In September 1830, he was planning new churches for both Martinsburg and Harpers Ferry. "The Protestants," he wrote, "are well disposed and evince a great spirit of liberality. The church will no doubt draw many."[78] The Harpers Ferry site was on a high bluff overlooking the Potomac River and shared by an Episcopal church. Later on, the parish procured the adjacent land from the government to build a school.

Weather was sometimes Gildea's enemy. Early in 1831, snow had prevented him going to Bath, but he managed to get to Winchester, where he reconciled several people to the church after they had been away for as many as twenty years. Bad weather also delayed church construction in Martinsburg. His strategy was to build a church to establish a visible Catholic presence before having a resident priest. "Had we churches & time," he told Whitfield, "there is no doubt the flock would increase much."[79] By June 1831, Martinsburg's church was completed. The Catholic population in the district was growing each year, either through the return of lapsed Catholics to the Church or conversions—over the previous year, Martinsburg's congregation alone had grown from 60 to 120, with 40 more at Bath and at least 60 at Harpers Ferry.

Life as a missionary was lonely, so Gildea asked for a second priest. As he told Whitfield, he went "5 months without seeing the face of a priest." "I would give the world sometimes to see a priest for one hour," he continued, "I will assure him a support if he lives as I live. The same house, the same cook & furniture & [illegible] the same victuals will do us both." He foresaw the Catholic population increasing still more with the construction of the B&O Railroad and C&O canal near Harpers Ferry. A second priest would enable him to meet all these new demands, so that his successors "may see our holy religion flourishing in a state from which it has been almost wholly excluded."[80] Martinsburg's population did increase as Irish immigrants came to work on the railroad and canal. With immigration came poverty and disease.

In October 1832, Gildea informed Whitfield that cholera had "commenced its ravages first upon the canal near Harpersferry." For two weeks, he "could scarcely sit upon my horse or drag my legs after me." He grew "depressed at the scenes I had witnessed" and ultimately caught the disease himself. While still recovering, he returned to his ministry only to be stricken again. This time, he arranged to be temporarily replaced by Father Thomas R. Butler from Emmitsburg, while he himself went to Emmitsburg to recuperate. Back at his post, he discovered another difficulty, not dissimilar to Mahony's.

Before the cholera broke out, some members of Gildea's congregation, presumably at Martinsburg, had written to Whitfield asking for a priest. Gildea was "hurt" and "thought [it] strange" that the archbishop paid heed "to their letter without my approbation." He warned that "there has been too evident a spirit evinced by a few of that congregation to dictate to priest & people," for he perceived "a disposition in one who has written to you to dictate as he has on former occasions to Priest & Bishop & cause strife & contention in the congregation." He was willing to remain as pastor, but demanded that "the people must know their place."[81] For three more years, he continued ministering in the area. By April 1833, he had completed St. Peter's Church in Harpers Ferry.[82] He was still trying, unsuccessfully, to gain an assistant to take up residence in Harpers Ferry.

In the spring of 1834, Gildea did receive assistance. Francis B. Jamison, a native of Frederick, former professor and president of

Mount St. Mary's and brother of the resident who had complained of Mahony's conduct, suggested he remain in Martinsburg to attend his dying mother.[83] In the meantime, Gildea, who had been offered a parish in Baltimore, reported that the people of Martinsburg were virtually unanimous in asking him to stay and that they opposed Jamison's permanent appointment. He himself, moreover, needed a year to settle his own affairs before he could leave.[84]

In the meantime, the B&O Railroad was rapidly making its way on the Maryland side of the Potomac River. In December 1834, it had reached a point across from Harpers Ferry. In January 1837, a bridge spanned the river to connect with the Winchester and Potomac Railroad bringing produce from the Shenandoah Valley to be shipped to Baltimore.[85] The days of canals were nearing an end. But the coming of the railroad shaped the ecclesiastical future of the Martinsburg area.

Despite Gildea's reservations, Whitfield considered appointing Jamison to reside at Harpers Ferry. Jamison, however, informed the archbishop that the advance of the railroad on Harpers Ferry meant the employment of many men for at least another year. During "the sickly season," which had already commenced, he found himself making long trips from Martinsburg to answer numerous sick calls. He, therefore, recommended that, instead of Gildea being removed, he should be given extra assistance for the summer, and a resident priest be assigned to both Martinsburg and Harpers Ferry. The day had passed, he asserted, when an energetic priest could "attend the small numbers in the different stations on week days," for "the catholicks have so increased at the ferry, Winchester & Bath as to require a Sunday each." Riding over forty miles on three Sundays each month through inclement weather, he concluded, "would disable me in a short time for the mission and thus throw me a dependent on the charity of my fellow beings."[86]

In 1835, Gildea was transferred to Baltimore, where he was the founding pastor of St. Vincent de Paul Church. But life on the Virginia mission had taken its its toll. In 1845, Gildea was dead at the age of forty-one.[87] Back in Martinsburg, his successor was Richard Vincent Whelan.

Born in Baltimore in 1809, Whelan was educated at Mount St. Mary's and St. Sulpice in Paris before his ordination in Versailles in 1831. He then taught at Mount St. Mary's. Despite Jamison's recommendations to have a resident priest in Martinsburg and Harpers Ferry,

Whelan continued in the itinerant tradition of his predecessors with Mass at Harpers Ferry on the first and third Sundays, at Winchester on the second, at Martinsburg on the fourth, and at Bath on the fifth. He also made occasional visits to Shepherdstown, Waterford, and Romney.[88]

Whelan, however, left little account of his missionary activities. There is only one extant letter from him to Archbishop Samuel Eccleston, Whitfield's successor. On the day after Christmas, 1836, he reported "that the efforts of individuals to excite dissention [*sic*] at the Ferry have been thus far defeated; & altho' they manifest still regret for their privation [of having a resident priest] (which I rather commend than disapprove) I anticipate the final acquiescence of all in the change that has been made." The failure to have a resident priest, however, had prevented raising funds to purchase a priest's house. Whelan also feared losing the lot on which the church was built, since the original donor, Bate Wager, had previously used the land as security for debts he now could not pay. In addition, he complained about "Mr. Gildea's plea for indemnification."[89] Although this "indemnification" was not specified, Gildea may very well have followed the practice of Whelan himself and other priests of purchasing property with his own funds and then seeking reimbursement.

Despite burdens, in January 1838, Whelan was initially successful in obtaining three Sisters of Charity from Emmitsburg to open St. Vincent's Female Benevolent School in the "former pastoral residence" in Martinsburg. Such schools were part of a general strategy to counter Protestant institutions, where young Catholic women might lose their faith, and to dispel anti-Catholic prejudice.[90] The sisters also ran a Sunday school for "colored women." In November 1841, however, they "withdrew as school seemed to serve rich rather than poor."[91] Ministering to the rich may have been a practical necessity in the days of financially strapped mission churches and as a means to enhance the Church's reputation, but it was not in keeping with the sisters' vision. The sisters would not return until 1883. By the time of their departure in 1841, however, Whelan was no longer pastor.

Adaptation was essential for missionary life in Virginia. Whelan and his successors frequently had Mass on weekdays at some of their more distant communities. Moreover, the region was one of the first in Virginia to experience growth in population due to the industrial revolution, as immigrants, particularly from Ireland, arrived to work on the canals and railroads. Whelan remained a circuit-riding missionary until December 1840, when he was named Richmond's second bishop. His immediate successor in the area was, for a short time, Father John O'Brien, whom his brother, Timothy, recruited for Virginia.

During the eighteen years the diocese remained without a bishop, the Catholic urban presence had shifted from Norfolk to Richmond. Whelan's model, however, was his own experience of being an itinerant. Cities could well be left to men like Timothy O'Brien.

CHAPTER 5

Richard Vincent Whelan, Second Bishop of Richmond: 1841–1850

At the Second Provincial Council in 1833, the bishops had recommended the suppression of the diocese of Richmond, but Roman officials rejected the proposal. At the Fourth Provincial Council in 1840, however, Archbishop Samuel Eccleston of Baltimore informed his suffragans that he no longer wanted the administration of Virginia. They therefore proposed the appointment of a bishop for Richmond. In order of preference they named Richard Vincent Whelan, pastor in Martinsburg, Peter Richard Kenrick, coadjutor bishop of St. Louis, and Joseph Chanche, then the president of St. Mary's College in Baltimore and a candidate for the diocese of Natchez. In Rome, the Congregation of Propaganda discussed the proposal and recalled Marechal's anger at Kelly's appointment and the return of Virginia to his administration. On November 16, 1840, the congregation recommended to Pope Gregory XVI that Whelan be named the second bishop of Richmond.[1]

On March 21, 1841, Whelan was consecrated in Baltimore by Archbishop Samuel Eccleston, assisted by Bishop Benedict Joseph Fenwick, S.J., of Boston, and Bishop John Hughes, coadjutor of New York. Hughes's presence was symbolic. A contemporary of Whelan's at Mount St. Mary's, he had been ordained by Bishop Henry Conwell in 1826 in Philadelphia, where he witnessed the turmoil of trusteeism. Within twenty years, however, Whelan and Hughes, two close friends, would be on different sides in the Civil War.

The day after his consecration, Whelan issued his first pastoral letter, published in the *New York Freeman's Journal*. Addressing his

80

people in Virginia, he contrasted the more populated areas of the Midwest with his diocese:

> Why is the solemn chant of the ancient liturgy heard far beyond the Alleghanies [*sic*]? Why are the prairies of the distant West dotted with Catholic temples, while in Virginia the very name is scarcely known, or known but to be abused? It may be that we have not sufficiently appreciated the value of religious truth; that we have neither availed ourselves of such means as were within our reach, nor lifted our voices in humble supplication to Him who has promised to grant what is sought in sincerity and with perseverance.[2]

Whelan had stated his agenda—to recruit priests and more Catholic people for his southern diocese.

Whelan began his episcopate by trying to provide an adequate clergy, first through his own seminary or from recruitment from New York and then from All Hallows College in Ireland. His brief tenure also witnessed the development of the towns of Wytheville and Lynchburg. But he was more a missionary and than an organizer. He soon abandoned Richmond for Wheeling.

PLANS FOR A SEMINARY IN RICHMOND

Whelan initiated his ministry in Richmond with energy, though not with much foresight. In June 1841, he told Hughes he was raising funds for a seminary in Richmond. He also asked his northern colleague's advice on a plan to place in the bishop's hands surplus money from wealthier churches to support poorer missions. He wanted to prevent some priests from accumulating money while others received little reward.[3] He might here have been making an allusion to Timothy O'Brien of Richmond, with whom Bishop John McGill would later be in conflict. Whelan was involved in a missionary venture, and this may have made him autocratic. He once thanked Hughes for sending him a copy of the acts of the New York synod, but noted: "I would prefer a Synod, but we are too few & too scattered." He, therefore, issued his "own diocesan statutes."[4]

By July, Whelan had collected $2,000 to purchase a site for his seminary, about a mile and a half northeast of the city. There he chose to reside rather than at St. Peter's, nominally his cathedral. With assistance from the Society for the Propagation of the Faith, he planned to start with eight to ten seminarians. Asking Hughes for candidates, he listed the qualities for which he was looking. He loathed "avarice & pride, & would be grateful if you would give all who shape their course to Virginia to understand that the priesthood is not to be made a trade for the support of dependents." Until he opened his seminary, however, he would send students to St. Mary's Seminary in Baltimore. At this point, he also seems to have contemplated having the Vincentians staff his seminary.[5] In the meantime, Hughes expressed his fears that trusteeism in Virginia could again lead to schism. Whelan assured him that "the people of Norfolk loathe the thought of former times of schism, & the efforts of an undeserving priest could alone impel them to resistance. That I do not expect. The sense of propriety & religious feeling of the present incumbent [Alexander Hitzelberger] would not permit it."[6] That summer, in fact, Whelan dedicated the new St. Patrick's Church in Norfolk, a symbol of the end of trusteeism.[7]

On January 6, 1842, Whelan ordained the first priest in Richmond, James Hewitt, an alumnus of his seminary, who unfortunately died within a year.[8] He then informed Hughes of the progress of his seminary and of the performance of the priests Hughes had sent him. By April, he had twelve seminarians, of whom two would be ordained in a year. But he was being selective and had rejected many applicants, such as a "schoolmaster" who was a "consummate rascal." He had also dismissed a priest he recruited from Hughes for "his fondness for the bottle," but feared he had "now gone towards N. York and publicly may attempt fraud by asking funds for the Church in Petersburg, for which he has no authority." But Daniel Downey, he reported, was "doing well at Lynchburg where he has established a temperance society," but he was watching him carefully.[9] Whelan was not a man with whom to trifle.

Whelan frequently had to borrow money, especially when his allotment from the Propagation of the Faith failed to arrive. He then usually appealed to Hughes. But his ambitions for education exceeded his means. In November 1843, he opened St. Vincent's College, attached to the seminary. He advertised that its purpose was "to impart to the Southern Student, upon the most modest terms, the advantages of a *complete* literary and moral education." While "the Catholic religion alone" was "professed in the College, there is no violence offered to conscience." The spacious grounds provided a healthy environment where the students could recreate "under the eyes of the professors." Application was to be made to Whelan or O'Brien.[10] Whelan continued to be the rector of the seminary and taught most of the courses, while his brother David was the vice-rector. During the seminary's brief history, it had produced Joseph Plunkett, James Hewitt, Edward Fox, and Francis Devlin.[11] All of them were from Ireland. Some of them, like Fox, seem to have had earlier seminary education before coming to Richmond.[12]

By early 1843, Whelan had ordained Fox and assigned him to Wytheville, which he had himself founded the year before. It was a "destitute mission," he told Hughes as he interceded with him to allow Fox to raise funds in New York.[13] This seems to have been the first introduction of Hughes to the area that occasioned one of the rare times when he offered to support Catholic immigrants moving to rural colonies.[14]

RECRUITMENT OF SEMINARIANS FROM ALL HALLOWS

As Whelan was ambitiously trying to start his own seminary, he received an offer of priests for missionary dioceses like his own. In 1842, Father John Hand, C.M., had founded All Hallows Missionary College at Drumcondra, just outside Dublin. Hand's initial overtures to American bishops, however, were rejected.[15] For two years, Whelan turned down Hand's offer in preference of his own seminary.[16] By October 1845, however, the seminary was floundering. Whelan closed it and St. Vincent's College. He immediately turned to Hand, asking him to select six seminarians to study for Richmond, but, lest there be any doubt, he painted a stark picture of missionary life in Virginia, derived from his own experience.

The state of Virginia, Whelan informed his Irish benefactor, was "one of those known as 'Slave States,'" in which "the Catholics are very few & generally very scattered, requiring a priest sometimes to attend a circuit of 100 miles in diameter." The western part of the diocese he described as "quite unimproved, less so perhaps than many portions of the remote west, exceedingly mountainous, with bad roads, and a very uncultivated population." Any priest who volunteered for this mission, he warned, must expect a life of great labour & fatigue, much exposure to cold, heat & rain, bad roads, very indifferent diet & lodging, but little respect for his dignity, few Catholics, little of society, a compensation barely adequate to support him in the plainest & most economical manner. I wish no one to be taken by surprise. Many of our missions are just such as this; & I want *no* priest who does not come fully prepared to enter upon such a charge, certain that his recompense is not to be expected here, but hereafter. Make the young men whom you may think of selecting fully aware of this; inform them that there are places much more desirable elsewhere, where they may labour advantageously, & that if they select my diocese I shall regard their character & honor compromised if afterwards they flinch, & I shall even refuse an exeat where there is no other good & controlling motive.

Whelan recommended that Hand's candidates for Virginia first read this letter and then write him acknowledging they fully understood what ministry in Virginia meant.

Whelan added several more qualifications for prospective candidates for Virginia. As he had earlier indicated to Hughes, he repudiated the "making the ministry in any manner subservient to the support of parents or relatives." He wanted priests who had "zeal & energy, with a mixture of *devotion* & *piety*," qualities that were essential when priests lived far from one another. "Talent" was "desirable, but good sound sense, a correct judgment is far preferable to brilliant parts without it." Contrary to Baxter's reservations of a generation earlier, he looked for "an aptitude for preaching" and wanted no man who was "rough & without manners," since in American society "the people the most rude themselves are accustomed to see & hear men of fine parts & polished manners asking for their suffrages." It was hardly an attractive picture of priestly life in the Old Dominion, but Whelan assured Hand he would be willing to pay the entire cost of education for any man who met his specifications.[17]

Within a year, Hand had made his first selections for Richmond. But Whelan was still concerned that the candidates be morally prepared for the Virginia mission, where "with the eye of the Lynx do our foes watch the conduct of the priesthood." He had no compunction in advising Hand to adopt Sulpician discipline for Drumcondra, because that tender piety—that tenderness of conscience which scruples the *slightest* fault is almost the only security against the dangers to which we are here exposed, oftentimes far removed from the counsel & the censure or admonition of our brethren, lured on to fault by the deceitful voice of the archenemy & even of dissenting Christians or it may be of Catholics themselves, but pursued with dreadful fury by the public imagination, when its watchful eye has surprised us in crime.[18]

Whelan had almost an apocalyptic view of the Virginia mission, but he also had a practical vision of preparation for the priesthood that would be widely embraced well over a century later. By the end of 1847, he had seven students at All Hallows, but he instructed the acting president, Bartholomew Woodlock, that he did not want them ordained priests before coming to Virginia. "A few months passed here before entering upon the duties of the mission," he wrote, "are almost essential to every foreigner & prevent many sad mistakes."[19] Over the years, Richmond would receive more priests from All Hallows than any American diocese outside of California. But his plan to have candidates get some experience on the Virginia mission before ordination was more of an ideal than a reality.

WHELAN'S HOPES FOR THE WEST: THE FLOYDS OF TAZEWELL

Whelan seems to have been ambivalent about where he thought the future of his diocese lay. While he had personally experienced the first onslaught of Irish workers on the canals and railroads in Martinsburg and Harpers Ferry, he seemed to prefer agricultural settlements for these Irish newcomers. In August 1842, he had made his first visit to Wytheville, where he baptized several converts and began a mission. He was accompanied by James Ryder, S.J., who had spoken in favor of slavery in Richmond in 1835 and managed, while being president of Georgetown and provincial of the Maryland province, to travel extensively in Virginia, without preserving his correspondence or sermons to inform historians of whatever it was that caused his audiences to listen. On this occasion, Ryder gave a series of lectures, after which Captain John P. Matthews, the sheriff of the county, donated an acre of land and a sum of money for a chapel. Subsequently, he, his wife, and seven of their children entered the Church.[20]

But the major Catholic family in the region—though sixty miles away could hardly be considered close proximity—were the Floyds in Burke's Garden, Tazewell County. As was noted above, three of the Floyd daughters, Niketti, Letitia, and Lavalette, had entered the Church in Richmond, and they were the first of a series of conversions in the family. Their mother, Letitia Preston Floyd, delayed entering the Church for several years but had become close to Whelan. His correspondence with her, a rare example of his relations with the laity, reveals a side of his character a bit less austere than that he showed to his clergy. In November 1842, she proposed to him that Catholic colonists be sent to Burke's Garden. Two months later, he promised to "make every exertion" to begin a colony. To her invitation to pay a visit, he replied that "my sure attachments to the West will plead strongly" to be in Tazewell that summer.[21]

In May 1843, Whelan was on the point of leaving Richmond for the Fifth Provincial Council of Baltimore but took time to write Mrs. Floyd in regard to her relations with the Church. He congratulated her on "the very kind dispositions you have manifested & the zeal with which you are forwarding the religious views of your daughters." He had appointed Fox to Wytheville. Whelan saw in him the ideal priest about whom he had written to Hand in Drumcondra and Hughes in New York. "He is quite a zealous & active & pious young man," he wrote, "& I expect much good from his assiduous labor. There is about him a simplicity & devotion that will abundantly compensate for more brilliant qualifications, & which fit him in a peculiar manner, I think, for his mission."[22]

But Mrs. Floyd still hesitated to enter the Church. In August 1844, Fox wrote her from a begging trip in Norfolk. He hoped Lavalette would contribute to the Wytheville mission, but then addressed Mrs. Floyd's spiritual life—"Certainly, Mrs. Floyd, you are very dear to me—would that you would take my advice—in time & eternity it would inconceivably serve you—do." In a postscript, he made an overture to hasten her conversion. "Your term of existence is coming fast to a close," he concluded, "and shall it be that you will leave us without receiving the Sacraments of God your Saviour which He mercifully puts in your way?"[23] Fox was shortly later transferred to Lynchburg, from which he continued to serve Wytheville and Tazewell.

In the meantime, Mrs. Floyd had not given up her efforts to found a Catholic colony and began corresponding with Hughes in New York about procuring a dairyman. Although Hughes had opposed other Catholic colonization schemes because of the lack of priests outside the urban centers, in this case he offered to advertise in the New York *Freeman's Journal* for the dairyman she had requested. He also expressed his "regret that emigrants who arrive in this country with a view of settling on the soil as farmers should not be as convinced as I am of the advantages which they might enjoy in selecting your beautiful valley as the place of their residence." He was far from sanguine about finding recruits, however, since he feared they would reject his advice.[24] For another year, Mrs. Floyd sought her dairyman. She also asked O'Brien in Richmond for assistance.[25] This ended Mrs. Floyd's attempt to woo immigrants to Burke's Garden, but it did not end her interest in the Church.

Whelan continued to pressure Mrs. Floyd to enter the Catholic Church. Her daughter, Lavalette, had married George Frederick Holmes, an Englishman, later a professor at the University of Virginia, and the first president of the University of Mississippi, from which he resigned after one year. On a lighthearted note, Whelan remarked that "with you I regret that" she "did not select a Virginian for her partner. We cannot spare any of our small Catholic population, but particularly such as your daughter, such an ornament to the little Church by her personal qualifications no less than by her position in society." Now that Lavalette might be leaving Virginia, he continued,

> I see no other plan than to prepare yourself for admission. Do, my good friend, do prepare for this desirable event. Subdue the rebellious feelings of proud nature. I feel sure that your intelligent & well informed mind will scarce allow you to admit any resting place between Catholicity & infidelity; I feel equally sure that Christianity carries with it too many evidences of truth to allow you to stake your everlasting hopes upon its rejection. Adopt then the part of prudence, take the *safer* course, subdue proud nature, & make an humble & candid acknowledgement of fault, & I will almost guarantee that all difficulties will vanish. Consider the influence of your example for good or ill; how many may already have attempted before God to excuse or [illegible] this over neglect by your example; how many may still be led astray by it. It is now, my

dear friend, the 11th hour for you, and you still have it in your power to repair much of the past, to do a vast deal of good, by acknowledging before men that Saviour whom you wish to acknowledge you before his Father in Heaven. What a consolation will it be to me if in my approaching visit I shall be allowed to extend the graces of our Holy Religion to yourself, Mr. [John Warfield] Johnston & his mother. Apprise them of my hopes & for me ask them both to pray in the interval most earnestly to God that he may be pleased to enlighten their minds & exercise his gentle influence over their hearts.[26]

It was a hard sell, but Mrs. Floyd held out for several more years. Only in 1852, after the diocese was split and Whelan was permanently in Wheeling, did he pay a visit to Burke's Garden and receive her into the Church.

CANALS AND RAILROADS:
THE BEGINNINGS OF LYNCHBURG AND STAUNTON

While Wytheville and Tazewell had both been the scenes of promising conversions of prominent families and represented an older style of rural Catholic life that Whelan may have preferred, two other towns in central Virginia grew up as the result of the encroaching industrial revolution that he had seen transforming Martinsburg. In 1835, Irish laborers flocked to Lynchburg to work on the 146-mile segment of the James River and Kanawha Canal, linking the town with Richmond. O'Brien had visited the community in 1834 to raise money for St. Peter's in Richmond. He apparently paid another visit in May 1836, for he recorded in the baptismal records of St. Peter's the baptisms of twelve children on one day, including two children of William and Mary Dornin.[27] It was in Mrs. Dornin's home that he said Mass and where he also established under her direction a Sunday school in 1838. Of French parentage, Marie Rosalie Boudar—she later Anglicized her name to Mary—was born in the United States, lived briefly in Cuba, and then with her family moved successively to Philadelphia, Norfolk, and Richmond before settling in Lynch's Ferry, later Lynchburg, sometime around 1812. On a trip to Richmond, she met and married William Dornin, a native of County Antrim, Ireland.[28] Even before

O'Brien's arrival, she had gathered the children in her house for cate-chetical instruction. She was virtually the founder of the Catholic com-munity. In 1841, Father John O'Brien, Timothy's younger brother, vis-ited the town and presided at the marriage of her daughter, Constance, to Patrick Quinn.[29] O'Brien then briefly replaced Whelan as pastor in Martinsburg. In Lynchburg, Daniel Downey became the first resident pastor and the following year built a church, St. Francis Xavier, and founded a temperance society.[30] In 1845, he left Lynchburg to found a new parish in Staunton, St. Francis of Assisi.

Lynchburg then had a succession of pastors: Francis O'Donohoe, who died after a few months in December 1845, and Charles Farrell, who stayed only a few days before returning to his vast mission west of Charleston all the way to the Ohio River. He died in Sommersville, Nicholas County, in 1847. He was from New York, and years later, his brother, Father Thomas Farrell, who played a major role in the history of the church in New York and later flashed across the pages of Richmond's history, moved Charles's body back to the family vault in New York.[31] Early in 1846, Edward Fox was transferred to Lynchburg, where he began a pastorate that lasted a little more than four years. His baptismal records reveal the growing stability of the community and the importance of having a resident priest. On May 19, 1846, for example, he baptized a daughter, aged three, and a son, aged a year and a half, of James and Elizabeth Cahill.[32] The family were clearly newcomers to Lynchburg. James Cahill was a laborer, born in Ireland; his wife was a native Virginian. That they had their children baptized at all could have been due to Fox's effective ministry. More likely, however, they simply had not had access to a church. There-after, they had several more children baptized and frequently stood as sponsors for others. It was not so much that they had come home to the Church, as that the Church had found them.

Fox, for his part, rode a circuit. He was one of Whelan's model priests. He baptized along the canal line, and the *Catholic Almanac for 1847* indicates his itinerary. Under Lynchburg, it states: "Rev. Edw. Fox spends here two months in each quarter, during which time there is mass every Sunday. The 3d month of each quarter he is else-where engaged." Further down the list came St. Mary's in Wytheville, where it noted: "Rev. E. Fox spends here the third month of every quarter. Mr. Fox also attends Burke's Garden, Tazewell County, (where preparations are making for building a church,) and likewise visits several of the surrounding counties."[33] The church in Tazewell was largely the work of Niketti and John Warfield Johnston and Lavalette Floyd Holmes. They also paid Fox's travel expenses.[34] But such travel took its toll. On August 3, 1850, he died of a fever. On the same day, a classmate, Father J. Enraght, arrived for a visit. He remained three weeks to fill in for his deceased friend.[35]

Lynchburg's next pastor was one of the first recruits from All Hallows, Thomas Mulvey. By that time, Lynchburg's parish, composed principally of Irish immigrants, was well established; from 1841 to 1850, its baptisms had grown from 18 to 33. Like Fox before him and his contemporaries in the northern part of the state, Mulvey baptized the children of his Irish workers along the canal line, sometimes using a private home.[36] When Downey had first arrived in 1841, he had also taken care of Lexington, Staunton, Charlottesville, and Union. But in 1845, as was noted, Downey started a new parish in Staunton, to which those missions were now assigned.

While Lynchburg owed its initial Catholic growth to work on the canal, Staunton became increasingly important due to the Louisa Railroad that connected Richmond with the Shenandoah Valley. As in Lynchburg, so in Staunton, the church owed its foundation to the initiative of a lay person, Michael Quinlan, whose home served for Downey's first Masses in the town and who donated land for the original Church of St. Francis of Assisi, completed in 1851. It was, however, a slow beginning. Downey baptized only ten people in 1844, apparently just before taking up permanent residence. Staunton was initially also more ethnically mixed than Lynchburg. Schmidts and Scherers mingled with Collinses and McAleers, but as the numbers of baptisms increased, so did the dominance of the Irish. From a meager beginning of ten or fewer baptisms between 1844 and 1849, the number climbed to over thirty by 1851.[37]

The construction of the railroad sometimes led to confrontation between Irish laborers and local people. It also contributed to the economic development of some areas of Virginia and the decline of others. Downey, under Whelan's successor, John McGill, became a champion of his Irish parishioners, but his weakness for alcohol or at least the reputation for it led the bishop to be his chief adversary. Towns like Portsmouth also experienced the dramatic growth of its Irish population during this period, due not to railroads, but to the development of the navy yard. That story, however, belongs to a later chapter.

WHELAN'S MISSION TO WHEELING

By 1846, Whelan had abandoned not only his own seminary but the city of Richmond. He himself lived and would live the missionary life he described for his Irish recruits. He actually walked from his seminary to say Mass on Sundays in Petersburg, where his brother David was officially in charge until he departed for Cincinnati to work with Bishop John B. Purcell, a fellow alumnus of Mount St. Mary's.

Whelan had expressed to Mrs. Floyd his own "sure attractions to the West," but, in light of later developments, Richmond may have been too small for both a bishop and Father O'Brien. Whelan had remarked to Hughes about an unnamed priest's financial arrangements. He may have meant O'Brien, who owned the property and the house attached to St. Peter's. Perhaps for that reason, Whelan chose to live at the seminary. In 1846, he closed his seminary. Shortly later, accompanied by Father James Ryder, S.J., he moved to Wheeling in the mountainous western portion of his diocese that he had described to Hand. It was on the national pike linking the east coast with the interior, a stopping off place for anyone traveling between the east coast and the Midwest. In the fall of 1833, Father James Hoerner, Richmond's former pastor, informed Archbishop Whitfield that he was taking advantage of Wheeling's being a stagecoach stop to have one of the "western" bishops administer confirmation on his way back from the Second Provincial Council.[38] Whelan now had great hopes that western Virginia could be the locus for Catholic colonies, and one Catholic owned a large estate in that region to which he wanted to draw Catholics. Whelan, therefore, attempted to enlist the aid of Bishop Francis P. Kenrick of Philadelphia in another colonizing enterprise.[39]

In Wheeling, Whelan exhibited the same initial enthusiasm that had marked his arrival in Richmond. He immediately began plans for a Jesuit college and for a Visitation monastery and academy. In August 1846, he wrote Peter Verhaegen, S.J., superior of the Maryland province of the Jesuits. The Jesuits then had a surplus of manpower because the European revolutions of 1848 had driven many of them into American exile from Italy, Austria, and other German-speaking countries. Whelan now asked them to take on new commitments. Wheeling had a population of 10,000, and many of the Catholics were German. While he hoped eventually to open a school for boys, he would in the meantime offer the church and residence to the Jesuits.[40]

Verhaegen expressed some interest in starting a school but initially took little action.

Whelan was more successful in recruiting Visitandine sisters. On a visit to Baltimore in March 1848, he persuaded both Archbishop Eccleston and the sisters' superior to send at least seven sisters to open an academy in Wheeling. To support them, he appealed to the Society for the Propagation of the Faith. He explained that he wanted the sisters' institution on a firm foundation from the beginning in order to leave Protestants with no "doubt of their perseverance and stability in the enterprise." Protestants would be attracted by "the superiority of our schools and even wish them well—when they are well established."[41]

Wearing secular dress, the sisters left Baltimore, took the railroad as far as Harpers Ferry, and boarded a stagecoach for a rough journey of two days to Wheeling. On April 4, they arrived and, a week later, opened their school, later named Mount de Chantal. Whelan had paved the way with newspaper advertisements. The school opened with thirty students; within a month there were forty-nine; and a year later ninety-six.[42] Incorporated in 1852, the school soon attracted girls, Catholic and Protestant, from much of the western part of Virginia.

Whelan now turned back to the Jesuits. With the sisters established, he wrote the new Jesuit provincial, Ignatius Brocard, reminding him of Verhaegen's earlier interest in a school. His greatest need was for a German priest who also had experience in the spiritual direction of women religious.[43] Brocard dispatched Father Roger Dietz, whose coming Whelan thought would "prepare the way for the establishment of a fine school among us. Mr. Dietz will find here many excellent Germans, & nothing can be more opportune than his arrival at the present moment." At the same time, he thanked the provincial for sending German-speaking Jesuits to Richmond, where O'Brien had requested them.[44] But he still wanted the Jesuits to open a school. Early in 1849, he proposed that they could start by taking over the grammar school, then meeting in the church basement, and gradually expand it.[45] By November, however, Brocard proposed that the Jesuits start a second church, instead of founding a school. Whelan approved this, but still urged that the Jesuits open a classical school, which the people would prefer. He even offered to have them live with him, with Dietz as superior.[46]

By late November 1849, however, Brocard had rejected all of Whelan's overtures for a school. The bishop was disappointed and, in view of Dietz's lack of interest in teaching, he had "slackened in the exertions I was making to open a school for boys." "In this, I was confirmed by the (to me) unexpected division of the diocese of Virginia, by which Wheeling is to be constituted an Episcopal See." Here he was less than candid, since he himself had initiated the division of the diocese. He decided to use his recruits from All Hallows to teach and realized the town could not sustain two schools. Repeating his efforts in Richmond, moreover, he was planning a seminary in Wheeling. He did hope, however, that Dietz would remain.[47] In the summer of 1850, however, Dietz departed, but Whelan still begged the Jesuits to send another priest, especially for his German-speaking people.[48] But the Jesuits would not return to Wheeling until 1955, when they opened Wheeling College at the request of Bishop John J. Swint, who realized Whelan's dream of over a century before.

In the meantime, as Whelan had indicated to Brocard, he had received the first of his recruits from All Hallows. In the fall of 1849, Bartholomew Stack and Thomas Mulvey arrived in Wheeling and were ordained on Christmas Day. Mulvey then taught in Whelan's seminary. The next year, three more arrived, Dennis Brennan, John Teeling, and Andrew Talty. But Whelan's ambitious dream to have these men serve on the mission before ordination lacked any practical implementation, at least the way Talty told it. He and Teeling had landed in New York after a frightening thirty-seven-day passage from Liverpool. On September 20, they finally arrived in Wheeling, where they then lingered "until the 30 of December in fact doing nothing[.] We daily expected our ordinations but the confusion that existed relative to the consecration of Mr. McGill, the division of the former diocese of Richmond, and the distribution of the late *imports* broke up all Bishop Whelan's arrangements and detained us as if it were in a *menagerie*."[49] Partly because of Whelan's personality, three of the All Hallows men chose to go with McGill. But as Whelan was seeking a German-speaking Jesuit for his people in Wheeling, the city of Richmond was facing its first influx of non-English-speaking immigrants.

Richmond: The Founding of St. Mary's Parish for Germans

Once in Wheeling, Whelan never returned to the eastern part of his diocese. Back in Richmond, O'Brien remained in charge, but his congregation was starting to undergo the ethnic pluralism that was so

characteristic of the more industrial north. Names like Pizzini, Gian-
nini, and Bonavita joined Purcells, Foleys, and Donovans by the
1830s. More numerous were German Catholics, whose names and
language challenged O'Brien's linguistic ability—in February, 1838,
he simply recorded that he had baptized "two Dutch children,"
whose names he did not give, since he "could not comprehend any
particulars there being no interpreter."[50] These newcomers began settling in the city in greater numbers by 1842 to work on the James
River and Kanawha Canal. At O'Brien's urging, they petitioned for
German Redemptorists in Baltimore to come to Richmond. Among
these early visitors, if later recollections can be trusted, was John
Nepomucene Neumann, who gave a mission at St. Peter's in 1842. He
later became bishop of Philadelphia and was canonized in 1977.[51]
Subsequently, German-speaking Jesuits came from Georgetown
every two weeks. Finally, in the fall of 1848, Father Francis Braun
came to minister to the Germans of Richmond.

Initially Braun used the basement of St. Peter's Church, but, since
he perceived O'Brien wished the Germans to form a separate congregation, he rented a former synagogue on Sixth Street near Marshall.[52]
While the building had no organ, he reported, the Germans made up for
this with their singing, and their congregation was growing. He thought
it imperative to have a resident German priest, since there was already a
"German Protestant minister who attracts Catholics of that nation."
The congregation was paying him $400 a year, and he lived alongside
his rented church in two small rooms he built. Braun was apparently
from Alsace, for he said he was happy to have left revolutionary France,
where he feared too many priests were duped into sympathy with the
short-lived republic by the false expectations that they would have influence on the nation. For him all the talk about republicanism and liberty was "nothing else than impiety." Still, he preached to the few
Frenchmen he found in Richmond.[53] Braun's attitude toward republicanism and liberty hardly made him an apt candidate for ministry in
Richmond. But yet more controversy surrounded him.

Curiously, in light of Braun's controversial stay in Richmond,
O'Brien made no allusion to him in February 1849, when he wrote
Brocard. The ubiquitous James Ryder had just passed through, and
his preaching, related O'Brien,

> has not only arrested the shameless calumnies & misrepresenta-
> tions of the notorious Leahy [a renegade priest], but he has excited

a general spirit of enquiry. I have already heard of more than one who have resolved on becoming Catholic. The strong prejudices against us are now turned in our favor & it is hard to calculate the beneficial results. Would to God his stay could have been longer or even permanent.

While O'Brien was thus optimistic about the good achieved by Ryder's visit, he had yet broader ambitions for a permanent Jesuit presence in Richmond.

O'Brien made several allusions to the Jesuits founding a college. What is unclear is whether he envisioned linking this to a Jesuit parish for Germans, such as Whelan was attempting in Wheeling. He told Brocard that he was "anxious that the establishment of what I spoke to you, could be realized & speedily. I think (of course with great deference) that the consent of the Bishop should be immediately asked, that, if granted, the lot I showed you should be purchased & the building forthwith commenced." What makes O'Brien's remarks all the more intriguing is that he also noted "the condition of poor Petersburg in her widowhood." He had attempted, unsuccessfully, to get Whelan to appoint his brother, John, to the parish and had discussed it with Ryder. While he recognized the "many difficulties to be overcome, the beneficial results will I am sure far outstrip them. Here you will be in the heart of the State—your influence will be felt through all its members. Our youth will be educated—they are now entirely neglected—prejudice will be finally arrested or compelled to hide itself & a better state of things be the result." But he also hinted that his relations with Whelan were not altogether cordial. He suggested that if Brocard should "think of consulting with the bishop on the subject you would do well to say nothing of my anxiety. I believe if he knew it, he would *not* the more readily consent. I believe I have seen this disposition on more than one occasion."[54] While O'Brien's remarks about the German congregation are ambiguous, it is clear that, like Whelan in Wheeling, he was attempting to get a Jesuit college in Richmond or the vicinity.

In the meantime, Braun continued to serve the German congregation until the spring of 1850, when he suddenly departed under mysterious circumstances. In response to a request for information from Brocard, O'Brien said Braun had received over $700 in addition to expenses for the church. The German congregation then numbered between 650 and 700 and, on O'Brien's advice, had "secured the little

Church, which however they only rent from year to year." He would himself be happy to accommodate a priest who came from George-town once or twice a month, but this "would be neither satisfactory to him nor to his congregation & would devolve on me an arduous & often an impossible duty" of adding to his own congregation "700 more, to whose habits & language I am a stranger." While he sup-posed "that Bishop Whelan would expect to be consulted on any per-manent arrangement," he urged that "nothing short of a permanent priest would satisfy them & a pious & zealous one would effect much good." This was all the more necessary, he added, because:

> Mr. Braun certainly has not realized my hopes in anything, altho I never dreamed he would terminate as he has done. Who would give Downey credit for a great show of penetration, yet a year ago he pronounced him an infidel. I suppose they conversed more freely together than either felt disposed to do with me.

He suspected that Braun was then trying "to gain popularity & per-haps to secure him a place as a French Teacher in some of our institu-tions which is what I now understand he aims at."[55]

Brocard complied with O'Brien's immediate request and tempo-rarily assigned Father John Pallhuber, an Austrian Jesuit, to Richmond. Early in July, Pallhuber reported that Braun had apparently stolen $800 from the congregation.[56] On July 18, twenty-two members of the congregation directly petitioned Brocard to assign a permanent priest, to whom they promised an income of $600.[57] Included among the signatories were Joseph Hierholzer, Joseph Mittendorf, Henis Plasmeyer, Joseph Strodmeyer, H. Wienhold, Heinrich Lindemann, and David Kinker. These same men earlier constituted a committee to audit the church books in 1849, during Braun's time, but reported nothing amiss.[58] The petitioners also wrote Whelan, who responded that he was disposed to have the Jesuits "take charge of your Congre-gation," but hesitated to make any "*permanent* arrangement," since the diocese was about to be divided. "Such arrangement might not be pleasing to my successor," he continued, and "he might be displeased that I did not wait his arrival to take such steps as to him might seem best." He concluded by explaining the difference between assigning a diocesan priest and engaging a religious order for a parish. "A secular priest," he noted:

could be removed without difficulty. But probably the Jesuits would expect some permanent arrangement. If *they are willing to attend the Congregation from Georgetown, or to send a priest to Richmond with the understanding that all is to be left subject to the approval of my successor in Richmond, I shall not only be willing, but gratified & thankful.* Of this you can inform them without delay."[59]

The German congregation forwarded Whelan's letter, together with a petition signed by almost fifty parishioners, to Brocard asking that Pallhuber be allowed to remain in Richmond.[60] Brocard complied, but he would have to wait for the arrival of the new bishop before making any formal arrangement with the diocese.

In December 1850, McGill took up residence as Richmond's third bishop and immediately became embroiled in a dispute with O'Brien.[61] In the midst of this, McGill expressed to Brocard his concern for the German Catholics "and the scandal that was given by the uncatholic and strange conduct of their former rector, Mr. Braun. You know how difficult it is for a Bishop, *in the midst of Protestants,* and with very small Catholic congregations, to find worthy, zealous, and disinterested priests." From his brief acquaintance, he was impressed with Pallhuber and asked "to have the congregation of Germans organized and served by some of your fathers."[62] Brocard acquiesced immediately, but only a year later, on the eve of the dedication of the new St. Mary's Church, did he enter into a formal agreement with McGill.[63]

Paulhuber, who had gained the assistance of Michael Tuffer, S.J., sometime in 1851, resigned as pastor in 1852.[64] He left Richmond to go to Australia where he was one of the founders of the Jesuits there. At St. Mary's, he was replaced by Joseph Polk, S.J., who remained until 1860, when Benedictines from St. Vincent's Abbey in Latrobe, Pennsylvania, began their ministry in Richmond, and he joined Pallhuber in Australia, where he became superior in 1862. The Jesuits' decade of service in Richmond produced one vocation, Brother Theodore Vorbrink, S.J.

Whelan had been bishop of Richmond for only ten years, four of them spent in Wheeling. He had succeeded in recruiting clergy for his far-flung diocese and had seen the establishment of several new parishes. In Richmond, O'Brien remained the only church authority and, as was hinted, he may have had some tension with Whelan. This would come out into the open with the appointment of a new bishop, John McGill, for Whelan was convinced of the necessity of splitting his diocese, not because of the size of its Catholic population, but because of the extent of its territory.

CHAPTER 6

Division of Richmond and Wheeling, 1850: John McGill, Richmond's Third Bishop

Between 1846 and 1849, the nation had spanned the continent. Texas, the New Mexico Territory, and California were now part of the United States. The American Church was growing apace at the same time that the European Church was in turmoil. The revolutions of 1848 not only led more emigrants to stream to the United States but also drove Pius IX from Rome into exile in Gaeta, outside of Naples. National expansion, immigration, the Roman situation all shaped the context within which the American bishops voted to split the diocese of Richmond. Their decision led to the appointment of John McGill as Richmond's third bishop. McGill inherited three priests Whelan had recruited from All Hallows, but soon alienated Timothy O'Brien, Richmond's pioneer builder. Like O'Brien, however, the new bishop was intent on winning a place for the Church in the aristocratic state of Virginia.

DIVISION OF WHEELING AND RICHMOND

In May 1849, the bishops of the United States assembled for the Seventh Provincial Council of Baltimore under the presidency of Archbishop Samuel Eccleston. It was the last of the provincial councils, initiated by John England, that was also national. The United States already had two new archdioceses or metropolitan sees, St. Louis and Oregon City. St. Louis had been made an archdiocese in

1847, but the Holy See left it to the council to determine on its suffragan sees. Archbishop Peter R. Kenrick of St. Louis attended the Baltimore council, but Archbishop Charles Seghers of Oregon could not make the lengthy journey across the continent. Altogether, two archbishops and twenty-three bishops assembled in Baltimore. They recommended the establishment of the archdioceses of New York, Cincinnati, and New Orleans; of the new dioceses of Savannah and St. Paul; and two vicariates apostolic for New Mexico and the Rocky Mountains. At the request of Propaganda, they also discussed the vacant diocese of Monterey in California and suggested the appointment of Joseph Sadoc Alemany, O.P., then attending the council as provincial of the American Dominicans.

In the midst of these deliberations about the expanding American Church, the bishops then approved Whelan's proposal to divide the diocese of Richmond and establish a new diocese in Virginia, west of the Allegheny Mountains, with Wheeling as a see. They also supported his request to be transferred to Wheeling from Richmond. Providing that the Holy See approved that proposal, the bishops then listed their candidates for Richmond: John McGill of Louisville, American-born and forty years old; Edward Purcell, Irish-born, forty-one years old, whose brother, John Baptist, was bishop of Cincinnati; and Francis X. Gartland, a priest of Philadelphia.[1]

Propaganda officials were probably mystified at the bishops in Baltimore making recommendations for dioceses thousands of miles apart. They would first postpone and then reject one American proposal: that the archdiocese of Baltimore be named the primatial see. The Americans were simply requesting for the United States what European churches already had as a means of preserving the national unity of the episcopate. From Rome's point of view, however, the proposal illustrated an alarming tendency for the American Church to become too independent, for, were the archbishop of Baltimore to be named primate, he would preside *ex officio* over the plenary council that the bishops had also requested to meet in 1850.[2] The young church across the ocean, growing so rapidly in the midst of political liberty, despite cultural and social prejudice, stood in stark contrast to Europe, where the Church was besieged. It was from his exile in Gaeta that Pope Pius IX approved the council's actions.

In March 1850, Whelan formally tendered to Pius IX his resignation from Richmond. Among the reasons he gave for dividing the diocese and for being appointed to Wheeling was that he had not earlier found priests with whom he could live with "that union of mind and heart that is necessary for promoting the work of God." He did not specify the priests with whom he could not live in harmony, but, as the story unfolded, Timothy O'Brien may have been among them. He further argued that the existing diocese of Richmond had so few Catholics spread over such a vast territory with so little means of sustaining either the bishop or priests, that he could no longer administer it. Finally, rather than have a coadjutor, he preferred a division of the diocese.[3]

On June 10, 1850, the Congregation of Propaganda recommended for the pope's approval that Whelan become the first bishop of Wheeling and McGill the third bishop of Richmond.[4] Richmond finally had a bishop who would take up permanent residence in his see city.

John McGill, Richmond's Third Bishop

McGill had been born in Philadelphia in 1809 but moved with his family to Bardstown, Kentucky. After practicing law, he entered the seminary in Bardstown and was ordained in 1835. Early in 1841, the diocese of Bardstown, established in 1808, was transferred to Louisville. There, McGill served as an assistant at St. Louis Cathedral and editor of the *Catholic Advocate* from 1840 to 1848. He was a disputatious, humorless preacher, whose sermons lasted over an hour and a quarter each Sunday—short by the standards of the day. He also relished religious controversy. When several prominent Protestant clergymen formed an anti-popery "League" in 1844, McGill joined Father Martin John Spalding and a leading layman, Benedict Webb, in combating them.[5] He was emerging as an apt candidate for the episcopacy. In 1848, Purcell and Eccleston had both recommended him to be bishop of either Chicago or Vincennes.[6] That same year, he had also been a candidate for coadjutor of Louisville.[7] With his appointment to Richmond, McGill joined a long line of prelates who began their priesthood in the Kentucky diocese. Francis P. Kenrick had taught in the Bardstown seminary, before being named coadjutor bishop of Philadelphia in 1830, bishop in 1842, and archbishop of Baltimore in 1851. In 1843, Ignatius Reynolds, a native of Bardstown and member of the seminary faculty, had succeeded John England as bishop of Charleston. In 1850, Spalding, another Kentucky native and McGill's partner in defense of the Church, had already become bishop of Louisville.

But McGill had other friends among the newly chosen bishops in 1850. Richmond and Santa Fe would seem to have had little in common at the end of the twentieth century, much less in the middle of the nineteenth. But the new vicar apostolic of New Mexico, Jean Baptiste Lamy, had worked in Ohio and Kentucky. He suggested to McGill that they both receive consecration from Archbishop Purcell in Cincinnati, in order "to unite my humble prayers with yours so that we may be able with the assistance of the divine pastor to fulfill the high duties which are to be confided to our care."[8] McGill, however, was consecrated in Bardstown on November 10, 1850, by Archbishop Peter R. Kenrick of St. Louis, assisted by Bishops Richard Pius Miles, O.P., of Nashville, and James Mary Maurice Landes D'Aussac de Saint-Palais of Vincennes, Indiana. He then set out on his journey to take possession of his see.

DISTRIBUTION OF THE ALL HALLOWS PRIESTS

On his way to Richmond, McGill stopped off in Wheeling, where Whelan offered him his choice of the All Hallows recruits. He immediately chose Andrew Talty and John Teeling, who were then ordained by Whelan on December 29. Thomas Mulvey then opted to go with McGill, who assigned him to Lynchburg. Informing McGill of his actions and offering advice on O'Brien, Whelan noted that he had obliged Talty, "as a condition of promotion to the priesthood, to take an *oath* (from which his Bp. alone can dispense him) to abstain from all intoxicating drink."[9] Both Whelan and McGill were unbending on priests' use of alcohol. Teeling was assigned to Richmond, where he became vicar general. Talty went to Martinsburg as assistant to Joseph Plunkett. Shortly later, he sent Bartholomew Woodlock, rector of All Hallows, an account of how he and Teeling had fared in their early months on the Virginia mission and their opinion of Whelan.

Talty was convinced McGill chose him "simply because I speak Irish and had a good constitution." Teeling, he went on, was "highly pleased at his leaving Wheeling" for he had earlier hoped he might become "vicar general and administrator of Wheeling and that his purse could not contain all the money he would receive for intentions." Granted the rigorous qualifications Whelan had demanded for his Irish recruits, it was no wonder that Teeling and he did not get along. But Teeling was also contentious. As Talty put it, even a question "regarding his health" caused him to shift to "an argument on the slave question or some moral point of Theology unless it was that you began to abuse the Bishop or something belonging to the establishment."

Speaking for himself, Talty was happy to be assigned to the diocese of Richmond, for "all of us hate Bishop Whelan on account of his snapping manner though in my opinion he is a good hearted man." His description of Whelan may also help explain the bishop's relations with O'Brien.

Talty had little time to adjust to being ordained. The day after his ordination, he took up his assignment in Martinsburg, where he immediately befriended Joseph Plunkett. But the "mission is indeed pretty much laborious," as he wrote Woodlock. He recounted the usual priestly routine of saying Mass, hearing confessions, and administering the other sacraments. But he also had "to attend a sick call at a distance of 43 miles from Martinsburg—two Irish struck each other with hammers and gave me the pleasure of riding 86 miles." "The people" in the Martinsburg area, he continued,

> are Irish or descended of Irish Parents. Very few natives. The Irish are very fond of me and would do anything for me. I prefer to speak Irish than to be the second *St. Thomas.* Oh prevail on every person coming to this country to learn some Irish if they can and to retain carefully all of it they possess. I assure you the Irish won't think anything of them unless they know Irish.

He also noted that McGill "is an Irishman both by father and mother" and "all our Priests are Irish but one as also the Wheeling priests."[10]

Talty probably provided a more realistic picture of what All Hallows men could expect on the Virginia mission than the more abstract and apocalyptic portrait Whelan had earlier given. Irish recruits would find their own countrymen in Virginia, where the only non-Irish priest was Alexander Hitzelberger, then in Norfolk, but Talty's allusion to speaking Irish indicates that the Irish coming to work on the railroads around Martinsburg were poor and probably illiterate refugees from the Great Famine that had hit Ireland in 1847. But Talty had also closed his letter to Woodlock with the ominous statement that "Timothy O'Brien after quarelling with the Bishop has left Richmond."

McGill Comes to Richmond and O'Brien Leaves

McGill had arrived in Richmond late in November or early in December 1850. O'Brien had immediately informed him that, far from there being an income to support a bishop, he was himself owed a total of $26,000 for St. Peter's, the house behind the church, and St. Joseph's orphanage. The alternative he offered was unacceptable, as McGill told Ignatius Brocard, S.J., the Jesuit provincial, "I could not consent to remain in my cathedral church and congregation as a salaried assistant of one of my priests." Early in December, O'Brien departed to join his brother John in Lowell, Massachusetts. McGill now begged the Jesuits for help, at least for Christmas.[11]

McGill's narration to Brocard is the only detailed description of the dispute. His letters to Whelan are, unfortunately, no longer extant, but he had apparently accused him of choosing to remain in Wheeling in order to avoid conflict with O'Brien. Whelan was shocked at O'Brien's "open attempt to plunder the Church" and declared his claims to be such "base & groundless fraud" that, if he had even hinted at them, he "would long since have removed from his position one who now manifests himself so unworthy of the confidence reposed in him." He further argued that the property for St. Peter's had earlier been deeded to the archbishop of Baltimore in such a way that "zeal & activity & prudent management of the revenues" would pay off any remaining debt. Since "the law gives Mr. O'Brien no right whatever even to the dwelling," he recommended that McGill "simply . . . eject him from the premises by legal force, if necessary," and "withdraw his faculties instantly, for his claim places him in my eyes in the attitude of a sacrilegious robber, & renders him undeserving of all consideration."

As for McGill's charge that he chose Wheeling over Richmond because of O'Brien, Whelan unequivocally stated that

> I am truly mortified that my successor should have been placed in so unpleasant a situation. Once more I assure you that I had not

the slightest anticipation of any such difficulty; & that my *sole* motive for selecting Wheeling was that here the church was unencumbered with debt, & there was none comparatively. So I declared at the Council.

Whelan's vituperative language in describing O'Brien, however, hints that tension had existed between the two before Whelan moved to Wheeling.

But then Whelan became a bit more cautious as to how McGill should proceed against O'Brien. If O'Brien was "disposed to compromise . . . at a fair rate, say about $5000," for what he claimed to be owed for the orphanage, then Whelan said, "I would do it." He further suggested "$5000 as a fair annuity during his natural life, by way of compromise for all claims & for ceding without him (unless there are bona fide debts) all the property which stands in Mr. O'Brien's name in Richmond. . . ."[12]

McGill also sought the advice of Bishop Francis Kenrick of Philadelphia, who recommended he submit O'Brien's claims to Archbishop Eccleston, but, in the meantime, not pay any rent for the house, for "the presumption naturally is that it was built from public funds for the residence of the clergy," a point, of course, that O'Brien contested. Kenrick encouraged his younger colleague that "the difficulties with which you have to contend are not insurmountable, and great consolations will, I trust, follow."[13]

Even as McGill was corresponding with Kenrick, however, the male members of St. Peter's Church met in the basement on December 21. The meeting was chaired by John Purcell with R. H. Gallagher as secretary. To draft their resolutions, C. W. Purcell proposed the formation of a committee consisting of, among others, Edward McAdams, John Dooley, and Dr. Picot. O'Brien thus had the support of the leading figures in Richmond's Catholic community. For nineteen years, they wrote, he had lifted the church "up with the help of God from a feeble and languishing existence to its present condition," which "caused him to be esteemed not only in his own Church but by the community in which he lived without religious distinction." His building of St. Peter's and St. Joseph's orphanage "were great works in a community where Catholics were few, and where the prejudices against the Catholic Church were a serious obstacle in his path." He had "brought the Church as it were 'through the Valley of the shadow of Death' to its present state of comparitive [*sic*] prosperity." During several epidemics, he had "remained in the city always faithful to his duty under the most trying circumstances of exposure and fatigue." Now, the petitioners continued, "to sever the connection between such a spiritual Father and the congregation which has been so long guided by him in the path of religious duty—many of them from childhood—is to afflict us with a grief which words are too feeble to describe."

The committee concluded its petition with a series of resolutions to McGill and forwarded a copy to O'Brien. Among other requests, the committee asked McGill to join the parishioners in asking O'Brien to return.[14]

Whelan had his own sources of information about the Richmond situation. He was convinced that "O'Brien himself is at the bottom of this project to bring him back to Richmond," so he urged McGill to "be firm & keep him away, or at least avail yourself of the opportunity to prescribe the conditions such as may keep him in his place." The petition was no cause for alarm, he continued, for "if Mr. O['Brien] has some devoted friends, he has many more foes who would rejoice at his removal." Even the friends, he thought, "are not the men to give trouble; they are too conscientious." Whelan was convinced that the deed for St. Peter's he possessed included the land on which the house stood, so he urged McGill to occupy the house, regardless of O'Brien's threats.[15]

Whelan may have been certain that his deed included the disputed property, but O'Brien possessed a different deed. McGill offered him $4,000 for the property and house. Instead, O'Brien sold both to a merchant for $5,000 and forced McGill to repurchase them.[16] Perhaps to protect his investment, the bishop later decided to enlarge St. Peter's Church to cover the land on which the small house had stood.

The final act in the O'Brien case occurred in May 1852, at the First Plenary Council, which, in an extraordinary action, appointed a special committee of bishops to investigate the dispute.[17] McGill submitted his charges against O'Brien, who was now claiming a total of $33,903.30 in repayment for what he had spent on the house and property at St. Peter's, debts on the church itself, the property for the school and orphan asylum, and a lot for a church in Petersburg.

Included in McGill's lengthy list of charges was that it was "a fact notorious that Mr. O'Brien came to Richmond poor, without estate or means. If he has acquired any thing, he obtained it as priest and neither as merchant, trader nor speculator." O'Brien, therefore, had no claim that the church owed him anything he may have expended from his personal income. McGill noted he had already paid $5,000 to regain the house and ground at St. Peter's and an additional $2,000 for the land in Petersburg, when he heard O'Brien might sell that.[18]

The bishops investigating the case were in a quandary. On the one hand, they could be expected to support one of their number, especially one so recently named to the episcopacy. They, therefore, agreed with McGill that whatever money O'Brien had expended had in fact been given him for the purposes of the church in Richmond and Petersburg. On the other, they concluded, "in view of the honest impression of Rev. T. O'Brien to the contrary, and of his long, laborious, zealous and efficient ministry . . . that the Bishop of Richmond should meet his obligations given for the purpose of securing said property, and that Rev. T. O'Brien may without molestation be allowed to enjoy and use for himself" what he had obtained for selling the property, "*Provided* that he shall forthwith make to the Bishop of Richmond a legal deed to all the property now held by him (said T. O'Brien) in the Diocese of Richmond, and relinquish all other his said claims." The bishops of the Plenary Council then unanimously approved this committee report.[19]

On May 17, O'Brien responded that "I must I suppose bow in submission to the decision of the Prelates in my case." He would donate the asylum to the diocese, since that was his original intention, never "thinking that I would have occasion to fall back on it." He likewise relinquished any claim against the church, while "protesting . . . before my God that it is a just claim, & that the money claimed by me was my own and applied by me to the best of my judgement for the good of Religion." His concluding words were sad:

> I am now in my old age. I am a cripple creeping along to my grave after having spent thirty-three years at the altar of Religion & it is hard, after so many years to be obliged to proceed to take an active part in the duties of the mission for my support. God's will be done. I have at all times confided in Him, & in Him I have put my trust. When I stand in his presence I hope & pray I will be judged with mercy."[20]

It was a poignant valediction from one of the most dynamic and dedicated pastors in Virginia's history.

But O'Brien fired one last parting shot. Although he had agreed to donate the asylum to the diocese,[21] he signed the deed to the "Trustees of St. Joseph's Female Academy & Orphan Asylum of the City of Richmond." To McGill's protest, O'Brien replied that the institution was built with the donations "of the poor workmen on the canal," whose orphans he had sworn to protect. He pointed out that the bylaws of the trustees could be amended to provide for the bishop or pastor of St. Peter's to be chairman, but, while he would surrender his own rights, he would not "sacrifice" those "of the good Srs. of Charity & the orphans."[22]

Whether it was a case of a priest making poor financial judgments or of a bishop whose personality could not allow competition for authority, the O'Brien-McGill dispute cast a pall over the early years of McGill's administration. In Lowell, O'Brien took charge of the school his brother founded and, in 1854, led the resistance to the local Know-Nothings who demanded to inspect the convent living quarters. Three years later, he died. His brother, John, who had briefly labored in Virginia and, incidentally, patented "Father John's Medicine," a popular cold remedy, died almost twenty years later. Both are prominently interred together in front of the entrance of St. Patrick's Church. They founded what became known among Lowell Catholics as the "O'Brien Dynasty" that lasted from 1848 to 1922, for John, the pastor, was succeeded by his nephew and he, in turn, by his cousin.[23] To provide three generations of priests to the American mission the O'Brien family had to have had its own wealth, as Timothy had argued in his defense.

Meanwhile, even before the O'Brien case was settled, McGill was taking up other functions of his episcopal office. One of the earliest tasks he had as suffragan bishop of Baltimore was to participate in naming a successor to Archbishop Eccleston, who died on April 22, 1851.

McGill's Role in the Appointment of Kenrick as Archbishop of Baltimore

In 1833, the Second Provincial Council had legislated that each bishop should draw up a list of three names of possible successors and place it in an envelope to be opened at his death, when it would then be forwarded to Rome.[24] In 1845, Eccleston had drawn up such a list. He nominated in order: 1) Bishop John J. Chanche of Natchez; (2) both Whelan and H. B. Coskery, rector of the Baltimore cathedral; (3) and Gilbert Raymond, S.S., president of St. Mary's College.[25] As senior suffragan, Kenrick of Philadelphia opened the envelope after Eccleston's death and discussed it with McGill and Bishop Michael O'Connor of Pittsburgh, who attended the funeral. On April 26, the three bishops forwarded the list to Rome, but commented that they did not think either Coskery or Raymond was qualified to be archbishop and suggested that Bishop John Timon, C.M., of Buffalo be transferred. Timon, they wrote, had been born in 1797 in Pennsylvania, then part of the diocese of Baltimore.[26]

The next day, however, McGill and O'Connor sent a second letter to Propaganda. They now supported Kenrick as the new archbishop. Assured that the cardinal prefect knew Kenrick's numerous qualities, they urged that "it is highly fitting to transfer so great a man to a see of this kind, especially if the Sovereign Pontiff proposes to honor for himself some bishop in this region with a higher dignity."[27] In other words, even at this early date, McGill and O'Connor were hoping to see the archbishop of Baltimore made a cardinal or at least be named primate.

McGill now became the principal spokesman for Kenrick's promotion to Baltimore. Archbishop Anthony Blanc of New Orleans agreed with the original list but recommended to Propaganda that Timon be placed second and Whelan third. This left Chanche in first place.[28] Blanc may well have preferred the one candidate who was French, at least in ancestry. In the meantime, McGill was circularizing the other suffragans about the recommendation he and O'Connor made about Kenrick. On May 16, Whelan wrote that he acknowledged the "worthiness of Bp. Kenrick" but had already declared his "preference for Bp. Timon as American & Baltimorean, & more acceptable, I thought to the clergy & people of the diocese." He agreed that Eccleston's list necessitated "new correspondence with Rome," but he wanted to call McGill's

> attention to the singular fact that *all* our Archbishops are now foreigners. Is it not a disadvantage to the American Church to appear so alien in her government? National prejudice may easily be carried too far, but it should not be without its just influence on our recommendations. When we may safely select a native is it not better to do so?

Using this criterion, Whelan supported Chanche, who was "also a Baltimorean dignified in his manners, & should be well acquainted with a diocese in which he resided so many years."

Whelan further argued that "our province is now decidedly American in the complexion of its hierarchy; more than any other is it American in its Catholic population. Should we not endeavour to maintain for it this character?" He had already discussed his views with O'Connor, who was Irish-born, and Kenrick.[29] Whelan, who was second on Eccleston's list, may have seen himself as a possible native-born candidate, but, in any event, the native-born bishops were divided. Whelan wanted an American-born candidate to present the image, especially in the South, that the Church was governed by Americans, but the Kentucky group of both native and Irish-born bishops saw no importance in this distinction.

Reynolds of Charleston now gave his views to McGill. He began by commiserating with McGill's "mishap" of being "thrown from your buggy" by telling about all of his own ailments, ranging from a "chill" to the "bilious cholic." Since his poor health prevented him from attending a meeting McGill had proposed in Richmond, he dictated to an amanuensis that Eccleston's list "will, and should have no weight at all, here, at Rome or anywhere or with anyone." "I will vote for *no one* save Bishop K. himself," he averred. "And as I cannot write to Rome, I beg you to state in your letter, that I have thus written to you."[30]

On May 28, McGill again wrote to Propaganda. Recalling that he and O'Connor had joined Kenrick in signing the original letter supporting Eccleston's list, he again promoted Kenrick's candidacy and offered his views on the other names on the list. Ranking Kenrick far above Timon and making no mention of Whelan's wanting an American-born archbishop, he also included Reynolds' strong endorsement of Kenrick.[31] A few weeks later, Reynolds himself addressed a letter to Propaganda—he was apparently still so ill that he dictated his letter to James Corcoran, an alumnus of the Propaganda College in Rome and well known to Roman officials. Eccleston's list, he said, resulted from the archbishop's falling from his carriage onto his head, because of which he was "so seriously affected that his brain was injured, and he was somewhat disturbed in his mental health." Perhaps aware of Whelan's views, he acknowledged that each candidate on the list had been born in the United States, which gave them an advantage, but Chanche was born of French parents and the other two of Irish parents, which still made them Irish in the minds of many Americans. Although Kenrick was Irish-born, he concluded, he had been in the United States for thirty years and excelled the other candidates in doctrine and demeanor.[32]

McGill's campaign was successful. On August 3, 1851, Kenrick was named archbishop of Baltimore. All the American archbishops were now foreign-born. Four years earlier, Kenrick's own brother, Peter, had preceded him to the metropolitan see of St. Louis.

Despite Whelan's preference for at least one American-born archbishop, he and McGill took opposite views on the nationality issue when a successor was being named to Kenrick in Philadelphia. Originally Kenrick named in first place John Nepomucene Neumann, C.Ss.R, followed in order by Edward Purcell and Henry Elder, a professor at Mount St. Mary's Seminary. With O'Connor's support, McGill persuaded Kenrick to place Purcell first, but Whelan strongly supported Neumann, though he acknowledged the German-born Redemptorist was not well versed in dealing with Protestants. McGill's principal objection was that Neumann did not speak English well, so that his appointment, "though favorable to the German-speaking populace, would find very little favor with the American people."[33] In this case, Propaganda officials ignored the pleas of McGill and O'Connor and appointed Neumann bishop of Philadelphia. Neumann's life as a missionary before becoming a bishop and his travail in Philadelphia led him to become the only member of the American hierarchy to be canonized.

There were, of course, obvious differences between Kenrick and Neumann, not the least of which was that Kenrick spoke fluent English. But that McGill supported Kenrick's appointment, contrary to Whelan's preference to have at least one American-born archbishop, may have been influenced by his desire to have his Kentucky friend as the archbishop of Baltimore to whom O'Brien was appealing.

McGill Outlines His Plans
for European Benefactors, 1852

In the fall of 1852, McGill made plans to go to Europe. He intended to discuss with Propaganda officials the decrees of the First Plenary Council and Richmond affairs. In Paris, he would present his financial needs to the Society for the Propagation of the Faith.[34] To his French benefactors, McGill outlined his plans for his diocese. Recounting the debts he incurred in settling O'Brien's claims, he announced his plans immediately to expand St. Peter's on the ground that he was compelled to purchase. This, he thought, was necessary in order to accommodate the increased number of Catholics he expected from immigration and conversions. Making no mention of the Jesuit at St. Mary's, he said that Teeling was the only priest with him in Richmond, but he wanted to build a residence sufficient to house himself, at least two other priests, and perhaps two or three seminarians, for, like Whelan, he planned on starting his own seminary. He also hoped to engage the Brothers of the Christian Schools to open a school for poor boys in Richmond. Above all, however, he needed priests, and too many of those who came from Europe with proper recommendations were "disposed to find placement elsewhere" or had bishops who "wished to free themselves of them." From McGill's description, little had changed in the six years since Whelan began recruiting priests from All Hallows.

Much in the vein of Whelan, McGill described the nature of his diocese to the French society. Virginia, he wrote,

> is in one of the oldest and most aristocratic States of our Confederation, known as *Old Virginia,* and colonized by a race of English *Cavaliers* who, with their pride and prejudices, went to the newly discovered continent to increase their fortune. Nothing can attract the attention of their discussions that does not present some external pomp. And to lead them to examine Catholicism and embrace our holy saving faith, it is not necessary that we remain of all the churches the poorest and least important. We ought to act and present ourselves in a respectable manner before the public. I have the hope of finally seeing Virginians turning their attention to the titles and proofs of our Religion . . . . They are disposed to come and to listen, as long as it is possible to offer them a place in our churches.

To attract the curious and aristocratic Virginians, he desired that the church and its ministers present an appearance of success. In this regard, he followed in O'Brien's tradition. Up to this time, he continued, the churches were small in number and size and were laden with debt. The one exception was Norfolk, almost abandoned only twenty years earlier, but now with a debt of only $500. New churches to replace old ones were nearing completion in Portsmouth and Martinsburg, and he hoped to begin a small church in Warrenton.[35]

By December, McGill was in Rome, but there is no record of his discussions with Propaganda officials.[36] While in Rome, however, he played a minor role in a major event. On December 22, 1852, Levy Silliman Ives, bishop of the Episcopal diocese of North Carolina, entered the Catholic Church and transmitted, through McGill, his resignation as a bishop. With Ives's permission, McGill made a copy of the document before forwarding it to authorities of the Episcopal Church. Among the reasons for joining the Catholic Church, Ives listed his long-standing doubts about the validity of his ordination as an Episcopalian bishop.[37]

While McGill had presented his financial needs to the Society for the Propagation of the Faith, he had also mentioned his pressing need for committed priests. He continued to rely on priests from All Hallows and other dioceses.

MATTHEW O'KEEFE TAKES CHARGE IN NORFOLK

In August 1852, as he was preparing to leave for Europe, McGill received from Kenrick the offer of two good Irish priests for Richmond.[38] McGill chose one, Matthew O'Keefe.[39] Born in 1828, O'Keefe had taught Latin, Greek, and geometry for three years at St. John's College in Waterford, where Bishop Kelly had been president, until he reached the canonical age for ordination. In 1852, he was ordained for Baltimore.[40]

Kenrick's offer of O'Keefe to Richmond came at an ideal time, for the people of Petersburg were demanding a permanent pastor. To Petersburg McGill sent Hitzelberger and now introduced to St. Patrick's in Norfolk the priest who would dominate Catholic life in the port city for over thirty years. Although he would serve under three bishops in Virginia, he remained a priest of the archdiocese of Baltimore on loan to Richmond.[41] Much in the way O'Brien had earlier done in Richmond, O'Keefe established a Catholic presence in Norfolk. At his own expense, he paid for the preliminary education of young men he thought had vocations to the priesthood and later opened his own seminary. In May 1854, he recommended his brother, Edmund, then in Ireland, and Michael Farren, one of his Irish-born parishioners, to Tobias Kirby, rector of the Irish College in Rome, to study at the Urban College of Propaganda. He then reflected on the difference in priestly life between Virginia and Ireland. "The laborers are very few, but the harvest most abundant," he commented, for "there are but ten Priests in this immense diocese, which embraces half Virginia." Under McGill's "fostering care," he hoped to see an increase in the number of priests, but he mused that, "if but five or six of the thirty-two Priests in my native city would come out here what an immensity could be done for God's glory." The city of Norfolk alone, he argued, could easily provide enough work for all those potential Irish recruits.

While Whelan and Talty had given descriptions of missionary life in rural Virginia, O'Keefe described his urban setting, where Catholics numbered only 1,100 out of 18,000, and "the only priest within 150 miles" was in Portsmouth. Norfolk, he continued, was "full of Episcopal, Methodist, Baptist & various other conventicles, so that with these & numberless other inconveniences, a young Priest has his hands full."[42] Norfolk was clearly no more of an easy mission than Martinsburg for an Irish priest accustomed to being surrounded by Catholics and enjoying the companionship of fellow priests.

But O'Keefe and McGill had acted too hastily in sending students to Rome for study. The bishop had mistakenly thought Richmond had two scholarships at the Urban College of Propaganda, where student-residents of the Irish College took their courses. As a result, he received "a sharp letter" from Cardinal Giacomo Filippo Fransoni, prefect of Propaganda, reprimanding him for "my infraction of a rule of the Propaganda, of which I was ignorant." He therefore asked Kirby if his two students could reside at the Irish College "at the lowest your charity can make it." McGill had already written an apology to Fransoni, but asked Kirby and Abbot Bernard Smith, who acted as an unofficial agent for the American hierarchy, to intervene with the cardinal to gain the two students admission to Propaganda.[43] As it turned out, O'Keefe apparently paid the bills at the Irish College out of his own income but was frequently late in paying because of his other expenses, especially when he was raising funds for building a new church.[44] As he later told Kirby, "I hope for much from these two young men in this heretical State."[45] O'Keefe would later have more to say about the quality of clergy coming to "heretical" Virginia. At some point before 1860, however, Edmund O'Keefe left the seminary, and Farren was later forced to withdraw for reasons of health,[46] but was ordained in 1862.[47]

The vacancy in Norfolk that O'Keefe had filled in 1852, however, had resulted from the need for a permanent priest in Petersburg. Kenrick's offer of one of his Irish priests to Richmond may in fact have been a response to McGill's frustration of what to do in reply to an angry and articulate letter he received in July from Anthony J. Keiley.

Getting a Priest for Petersburg

Keiley had been born in New Jersey but as a child was brought by his family to Petersburg. At some point, his father abandoned both the Catholic Church and his family. In 1842, Anthony had served the Mass for the dedication of St. Joseph's Church, where there was no regular pastor. First O'Brien and then McGill had sought to have the Jesuits take it over.[48] By 1852, Keiley was a lawyer, editor of the *Southside Democrat,* and, at the age of twenty, the patriarch of his family. He was angry at the neglect of the community of which he was somewhat of a spiritual leader.

Keiley headed his list of complaints with a priest he thought was named "Murdock" (his name was actually Murdagh), who "had left Petersburg *never to return*" after announcing only five weeks earlier that he was "the last chance they would ever have for a priest." After demanding to know if Murdagh spoke for McGill, he recounted a decade of neglect of the community. His list was varied. When the community raised $1,000 to pay the existing debt on the church, Whelan used it "to erect that useless pile near Richmond—the college." He did "not mean to charge the good Bishop with *larceny,* [but] . . . his unfortunate *cacoethes aedificandi* [itch for building] at that particular juncture . . . led him to be less scrupulously exact than he would have been under other circumstances."

Keiley then listed the priests who served Petersburg during the previous decade. One was removed for "a flagrant breach of the 6th commandment." Two had difficulties with alcohol. One of them "once traversed our streets armed with a loaded pistol and in a state of intoxication vowing that he would shoot any one who said he drank."

The only exception to this litany of sinners was David Whelan, the bishop's brother, "a pious devoted, zealous clergy man," after whose departure Petersburg "had no regular service and our irregular visitation were most irregularly irregular—five or six a year." Although Whelan had promised them a resident pastor for years, he had sent them "with one exception drunkards and debauchers," while he dispatched Francis Devlin, Joseph Plunkett, and Edward Fox "out through the back country." Although Richmond was twenty-two miles away, Keiley declared, "unless *business* drew Bishop Whelan or Father O'Brien to Petersburg we had no service."

Murdagh, Keiley went on, was the first permanent priest assigned to Petersburg since David Whelan's departure. During his five weeks of residence, his appearance in church was desultory at best. Murdagh left Petersburg, Keiley concluded, because he thought "he was not regarded enough," a trait common to "the new Irish priesthood in this country, if they *are located immediately after arriving.*" While Talty may have been relishing the opportunity to speak Irish in Martinsburg, Keiley in Petersburg had few kind words to say about Irish priests, because:

> Accustomed to the most abject reverence at home, treated with a deference which seems to me unmanly, they come to this country and find themselves *men*, and they are treated as they deserve and no better; perhaps not as well. They bring with them those feelings which always accompany men accustomed to such exaggerative respect and, unless they fall among a congregation entirely Irish and rather recent arrivals also, they soon give offence and receive it.

Keiley, as an Irish-American, may have been well aware that he was still considered "Irish," but he had adopted the American principle that people had to earn respect.

Keiley acknowledged that the people of Petersburg were not "the most pious people in Christendom," but the bad priests sent them had contributed to many leaving the Church. Whelan, he felt, "was never an episkopos—a looker over, to us, but rather an *overlooker.*" Lack of a resident priest in Petersburg, he concluded, had already led several families to leave. He himself thought "that the Catholic who is a father should, if possible, leave Petersburg as a matter of duty to his children; for those in authority will surely have to render an account of their stewardship and we are taught that children are given by God that they be trained up in the 'nurture and admonition of the Lord.'"[49]

Keiley was a well-educated young man, with broad knowledge of Church history—he cited several errant popes to draw the distinction between personal sins and official functions of ministers. He would have no hesitation writing McGill in the future about the mistakes and limitations of Petersburg pastors. His strong indictment of Irish priests, moreover, probably induced McGill to assign as resident pastor to Petersburg the only non-Irish priest in the diocese, Alexander Hitzelberger, who thus left open his position in Norfolk to O'Keefe.

But McGill's problems with Petersburg were not over. In September 1855, he received a complaint from the son of a parishioner that Hitzelberger visited his parents' home too frequently—the boy's father blamed the complaint on "the persecuting spirit of Know Nothingism, which unfortunately infects all my sons."[50] Whatever the reason, early in 1856 Hitzelberger left the diocese ultimately to enter the Jesuits.[51] Keiley's *South-Side Democrat* enthusiastically reported that Plunkett might be assigned to Petersburg and "would be sure to please."[52] Instead, Thomas Mulvey, then forty-six years old, was transferred from Lynchburg.

For several years, all seemed to go well, but Mulvey was frequently blunt. On one occasion, he wrote McGill for a dispensation for a Catholic man "from the wilds of Rock Bride [sic] Co." to marry an unbaptized woman. Were no dispensation granted, Mulvey feared some "rascally saddle-bag preacher will have to do it."[53] But Mulvey soon ran afoul of the preserver of Petersburg's Catholicism. In April 1860, Keiley complained about the "temper and character of Father Mulvey's preaching." On Easter Sunday, Mulvey delivered "the most vulgar, indecent, intemperate and abusive tirade that ever disgraced a Christian pulpit in this city or elsewhere." William Hinton and his wife, Margaret, both converts, vowed never again to attend the "late Mass," when Mulvey preached. Many people were leaving Mass before the sermon, and Keiley had instructed his younger siblings, who included Benjamin, a future bishop, and Nora, a future superior of the Visitation Monastery, to leave the church during the sermon, if Mulvey again acted in this way. He warned McGill that "unless the 'amending hand' is applied the worst consequences to religion and constitutional accord must ensue."[54] Precisely what Mulvey said is unknown, but McGill must have told him to mend his ways, for, within a short time, Mulvey and the Hintons seemed to be friends.

When McGill assumed office, Talty had remarked that all priests but one were Irish. With Hitzelberger's departure, all the priests were Irish. In Petersburg, Keiley and Mulvey, a layman and a priest, an assimilated Irish-American and an Irish immigrant, symbolized the new composition of the diocese of Richmond. This was the diocese McGill would have to lead through the crises of the Know-Nothings and the yellow fever epidemic on the eve of the Civil War.

CHAPTER 7

The Diocese on the
Eve of the Civil War

In the decade before the Civil War, Virginia's Catholics faced one of the state's rare public displays of anti-Catholicism, as the Know-Nothing campaign drew support from some leading citizens. In the midst of this turmoil, Norfolk was afflicted with an outbreak of yellow fever, during which Matthew O'Keefe and the Daughters of Charity, as Mother Seton's congregation was now known,[1] distinguished themselves with their heroism. Paradoxically, the period also witnessed several extraordinary conversions to Catholicism. In the meantime, Bishop John McGill attempted to put his diocese on a proper footing by holding its first synod, just as he was about to have Alexandria annexed to his diocese. For a brief time, however, he faced the possibility of being transferred to a new diocese in Washington.

PLANS TO MAKE WASHINGTON A DIOCESE

At the First Plenary Council of Baltimore in 1852, Bishop James Oliver Van de Velde, S.J., of Chicago had suggested that Washington become a diocese or that he himself be assigned there as some type of titular bishop. Not the most mentally stable of men, he thought that by resigning Chicago and taking some ecclesiastical post in the capital he would live at Georgetown and "remain more a Jesuit." Noting the bishop's limitations, Archbishop Francis P. Kenrick recommended to Propaganda that, if a bishop were to be assigned to Washington, he should be an American, and Kenrick thought no one more qualified than McGill. There is, however, no evidence that he had discussed the matter with McGill. For the time being, the Roman congregation rejected this proposal.[2] But the question resurfaced in another context.

In the midst of the Know-Nothing campaign in Virginia in May 1855, McGill attended the Eighth Provincial Council of Baltimore. The bishops formally recommended that Washington be made a diocese and that McGill be transferred there. They further stated that McGill was willing to go. Kenrick, however, was now lukewarm on having Washington made a diocese, because he feared a bishop in the capital might become a government tool. If the Holy See approved the transfer of McGill, the bishops recommended as the first of their candidates for Richmond Bernard Maguire, S.J., the president of Georgetown.[3] They may have thought that Maguire could draw on Jesuit manpower to staff the diocese, as both Whelan and McGill had tried to do.

The Jesuits, for their part, seemed eager to have McGill in Washington. On August 2, 1856, Charles Stonestreet, the provincial, asked McGill to ordain three Jesuits in the newly dedicated St. Ignatius Church in Baltimore, in order to relieve Kenrick of his hectic schedule. He added that, "as Providence may soon make more intimate our relations, I wish to take time by the fore lock & show you my preference."[4] McGill agreed to ordain the Jesuits, since, he commented, "I am seldom able to do so for the benefit of my own poor diocess." But, he added, "I am aware that the probabilities of 'more intimate relations' are very remote. I am told that no see is at present to be established in Washington, and that I am to remain in Richmond, with which arrangement I am perfectly content."[5] By October, Propaganda again rejected the proposal to make Washington a diocese.[6]

But Washington was not the only diocese for which McGill may have been under consideration. At the time of the Baltimore council in 1855, O'Keefe in Norfolk picked up the rumor that Norfolk might also become a diocese and McGill would be transferred "south."[7] Since the dioceses of both Charleston and Savannah were at that time vacant, O'Keefe, of course, could just have been reporting diocesan gossip that McGill might be transferred to one of them. But why McGill was willing to go to Washington remains a mystery, unless, somehow, the Know-Nothing campaign led him to think the nation's capital would be more hospitable than Virginia.

KNOW-NOTHINGS IN VIRGINIA

Anti-Catholicism had long been part of the nation's heritage, but it was on the rise in the 1850s, partly in reaction to immigration. When Archbishop Gaetano Bedini, on his way to become nuncio to Brazil, made an official visitation of the United States from June 1853 to January 1854, he left riots and protests in his wake. One of his antagonists was a former Italian priest who charged in inflammatory speeches that, when Bedini was papal governor of Bologna, he committed atrocities against the revolutionaries in 1848.[8] Bedini's visit, unexpected and unwanted by the American hierarchy, simply fanned the flames of the Know-Nothings. They combined reaction against immigrants with anti-Catholicism, but vowed to preserve the union of the United States and thus distracted the nation from the divisive issue of slavery. The Know-Nothings had been founded in New York, and Virginia sent a delegation to the first national convention in May 1854. During the summer, Richmond and Charlottesville established local "councils" of the party.[9]

What gave the party some cohesion in Virginia was frustration at the lack of progress of public works, such as the railroads, on which many immigrants labored. As early as November 1852, J. M. Mason of Selma, Virginia, wrote William C. Rives of Castle Hill, outside Charlottesville, lamenting "the irresistible hordes of Germans & *goths* who are annually poured out on our shores, near making up a majority in the Atlantic cities." Moreover, he continued, "the rude & licentious dogmas & doctrines brought by this class of emigration, are manifesting themselves prominently in political [illegible], and tainting and debauching the political morals of those amidst whom they are thrown."[10] Rives, a former senator from Virginia, would be temporarily off the political scene, as he then became the United States minister to France, but he would later manifest his sympathies for the movement.

As the Know-Nothings grew in Virginia, Catholics did have their defenders and prominent ones at that. In July 1854, former President John Tyler of Virginia wrote his son, Robert, of his reservations about the Know-Nothings then threatening to defeat the Democrats. He was particularly disturbed that the new party

> is said to embrace an element which I am sorry to see gaining wider expansion,—hostility to immigrants. . . . The Catholics seem

especially obnoxious to them, whereas that sect seems to me to have been particularly faithful to the Constitution . . . while their priests have set an example of non-interference in politics which furnishes an example most worthy of imitation on the part of the clergy of the other sects at the North.[11]

James Ryder, of course, had given an example in Richmond of the clergy's "non-interference in politics" almost two decades earlier, when he defended slavery.

In October, the Know-Nothings swept the elections in Massachusetts and Delaware, and contributed to the defeat of the Democrats in Pennsylvania, Ohio, and Indiana. Fearful of a Know-Nothing victory in Virginia, the Democrats moved their gubernatorial convention up to November. After a heated polling, they nominated Henry A. Wise, a former Whig, who had already condemned the Know-Nothings for their attacks on immigrants and Catholics, neither of which, he noted, were much of a threat in Virginia.[12]

Just before the Virginia Democratic convention, McGill was in New York, from where he apparently planned to sail for Rome to be present for the definition of the Immaculate Conception, but then changed his plans. Writing to Tobias Kirby at the Irish College in Rome, he described the Know-Nothing campaign in New York. "We are living in the midst of obloquy and persecution," he wrote:

> Lately there were riots from "the Know nothing faction" in Williamsburg, Long Island, and 3 or 4 persons killed. A church was attacked, but protected by the town authorities. In New York all was excitement last week, processions and meetings, 10,000 in number. This week things are more quiet. But we are in constant apprehension that new troubles will occur. The lava rumbles and roars in the heart of the mountain, and no one can say when there will be an eruption.

Curiously, McGill made no mention of any apprehension he may have had about Virginia.[13]

In the meantime, Rives had returned from France. Although he had not joined the Know-Nothing Party, he let it be known that he was willing to accept a draft as its gubernatorial candidate.[14] Lack of party membership precluded his nomination, but he did support the

Know-Nothing candidate, hoping that the party might "check the extravagances of *modern democracy*" and "install itself as the American *Republican* party, faithful to the tradition of a *Republican* ancestry & consulting the genius, usages, & habits of a *Republican* people."[15] Ironically, one of Rives's descendants, Anthony Rives, would become a Catholic and leave money for building the Church of the Incarnation in Charlottesville.

While Rives saw in the Know-Nothings a means for resurrecting a true "Republican" spirit, other Virginia politicians saw in them something characteristic of Americans then and a century later—the quest to be free from any type of external authority not of their personal making, and that meant Catholicism. Benjamin Johnson Barbour explained that "it is against foreign *politicks* [*sic*] and not foreign *religions* I would have my countrymen combine." The Know-Nothings, or American Party, as they were becoming known, "were quite content that the Roman Catholicks should remain undisturbed in their profession and practices of their peculiar worship," but he believed "that the temporal power conceded to the Pope by his church and the unlimited sway over minds and souls wielded by the priesthood are utterly destructive of individual freedom, and or private judgment."[16]

At their convention in Winchester on March 13, 1855, the Virginia Know-Nothings nominated Thomas Stanhope Flournoy, a former congressman, for governor. Without specifically mentioning Catholics, their platform did condemn any group "which believes and maintains that any foreign power, religious or political, has the right to control the conscience or direct the conduct of a freeman." The platform also restricted election to office to native-born citizens and called for immigrants to get the right to vote only after a "sufficient" residence in the United States.[17] If people doubted where Virginia's Know-Nothings stood in regard to Catholicism, they had only to read Flournoy's acceptance letter, which declared that "intimately connected with this question of foreign immigration is the growth of the Roman Catholic Church in our country. Despotic, proscriptive, and intolerant, its ascendancy, as all history teaches, has ever been destructive of freedom and of opinion."[18]

The campaign was heated. In local elections, Know-Nothings won in urban areas that had experienced immigration. They elected the mayor in Alexandria and the mayor and city council in Norfolk.

They were also successful in Portsmouth, Lynchburg, Fredericksburg, Wheeling, and Richmond.[19] Norfolk even had its own version of what had been popular literature in the North two decades earlier, the disclosures of an ex-nun. Josephine Bunkley had left the novitiate of the Daughters of Charity and moved with her father to Norfolk, where she wrote of her escape from debauchery and of the pope's plot to take over the nation.[20] Her recantation and apology to the Church in 1859 came too late to dampen the flames of the Know-Nothings.[21]

In March, Senator Stephen A. Douglas of Illinois campaigned in Richmond for Wise. Throughout the contest, Anthony Keiley editorialized against the Know-Nothings in the pages of the *Southside Democrat*. On the eve of the election, he quoted extensively from the pastoral letter of the Eighth Provincial Council of Baltimore, firmly stating that the pope's possession of temporal power in Italy in no way gave him temporal authority over Catholics in the United States.[22] On May 24, 1855, Wise received 83,424 votes to Flournoy's 73,244. In the state Senate, the Know-Nothings won six out of twenty-five seats; in the House of Delegates, they elected fifty-three of 149. One Know-Nothing was elected to Congress, although three of the twelve Democrats elected had avowed Know-Nothing leanings. Writing after the Civil War, Governor Wise interpreted the Virginia defeat of Know-Nothings as preventing their growth in the South and paving the way for the election of James Buchanan in 1856.[23]

While Virginia's Know-Nothings may have pretended not to focus as much on anti-Catholicism as their northern counterparts, the immigrants they opposed were mainly Catholics. One Washington Know-Nothing stated succinctly that the Virginia party was defeated by "the increased foreign vote; by the Irish laborers upon the public works."[24]

After Wise's victory, a satirical anti-Know-Nothing novel appeared, *The Life and Death of Sam*, the nickname given the party in Virginia. Sometimes attributed to Wise himself, it might have come from the pen of Keiley, who proved himself quite adept at satire in his later Civil War accounts. A bit heavy-handed, it held the Know-Nothings up to ridicule and portrayed Catholics as truly American.[25]

Wise's outspoken condemnation of Know-Nothing anti-Catholicism, however, may have an explanation that goes beyond his liberal-mindedness. A newcomer to the Democratic Party from Accomack County on the eastern shore of the Chesapeake, he would have to gain acceptance from the Democratic power structure. This included John B. Floyd, Jr., son of a governor and former governor himself and then secretary of war, whose mother, three sisters, and one brother, Benjamin Rush Floyd, had become Catholics.

The summer of 1855 saw a temporary respite from the Know-Nothings but brought yellow fever to the Norfolk area. As the epidemic waned in the fall, the Know-Nothings waxed anew, but this time met a formidable opponent.

McGill as Apologist against the Know-Nothings

In June 1855, delegates of the American Party met in Philadelphia to draw up a series of resolutions. They voted formally to exclude Catholics from membership, after a Catholic delegation of Louisiana Creoles, themselves anxious to curtail Irish immigration, had sought admission. The national party now pledged "resistance to the aggressive policy and corrupting tendencies of the Roman Catholic Church."[26] In October, the Virginia Know-Nothings met in Lynchburg and passed a resolution they thought would downplay the anti-Catholicism of the national party. It stated that the national platform was "not intended . . . to exclude any citizen from public station, on account of his religious faith, but only such as may have reserved a paramount allegiance to a foreign potentate."[27]

McGill fueled the flames of the Know-Nothings in a Thanksgiving sermon in September toward the end of the yellow fever epidemic in Norfolk and Portsmouth. With more rhetoric than prudence, he remarked that such calamities resulted from sin that had "provoked Almighty God to anger." He did not claim that the fever victims were personally guilty of sin, but he did say: "if I were allowed to divine what sin it is which, in our day particularly, has provoked God's displeasure, I should be *inclined* to designate *the sin of Know-Nothingism*: because, holding as I do the Catholic Church to be divine, and the true church of Christ, I consider a secret conspiracy organized for its destruction is *a sin*, which sooner or later, will be visited with God's displeasure and be punished by him."[28]

McGill was not alone in linking yellow fever and the Know-Nothings. William Lamb, later the mayor of Norfolk, wrote: "Poor unfortunate Norfolk. The reign of Know-Nothingism has been visited by a curse."[29] But the bishop was a more available target for Richmond's hostile press. On September 11, 1855, the *Richmond Whig and Public Advertiser* ascribed to McGill the opinion that "the visitation of the yellow fever [was due] to the monstrous sin of Known Nothingism!"[30] The editor of the *Whig* also managed to discern sinister papal motives behind the visit, "immediately after our last Presidential election," of Archbishop Bedini, "a wretch reeking with the blood of martyrs tortured in the dungeons of Italy."[31] For two weeks, McGill kept up an exchange of letters in the *Daily Richmond Enquirer,* a Democratic paper, and sometimes also in the *Whig,* whose editor published them with his own comments. Typical of the nineteenth-century style, the *Whig* editor at one point referred the "reader to an intensely Jesuitical, impertinent, and abusive communication, in another column from 'John McGill, Bishop of Richmond,'" who "clearly demonstrates the truth of the proposition . . . that blackguardism is not inconsistent with professions of superior sanctity, and that the pulpit is sometimes the best school in which to learn the refinements of the Fish Market."[32] McGill was back in the metier of his earlier journalistic jousting in Louisville. From Lynchburg, Mulvey praised him for being such "a knotty opponent," but could not help but remark "what a bitter, jaundiced crew the Church has to battle against."[33] Such published repartee may have entertained readers in the days before television, but it satisfied no one except perhaps the writers and the typesetters.

While McGill was battling the local Know-Nothings, the national party nominated as its presidential candidate Millard Fillmore, who then received the support of many former Virginia Whigs. In the 1856 election, however, Virginia went overwhelmingly for the Democratic candidate, James Buchanan.[34] As a political force, the Know-Nothings were a sideshow distracting the nation from the more pressing issue of slavery, but, for a while at least, Catholics and immigrants were the principal targets of prejudice.

In Norfolk, O'Keefe encountered treachery that he believed was inspired by the Know-Nothings. Sometime between October and December 1855, when he also had charge of Portsmouth, he answered a knock on his door from two men requesting that he come to a dying man in Portsmouth. Dutifully, he responded, but with some caution. When his escorts reached the other side of the Elizabeth River, they said the dying man lay further outside of town. O'Keefe then took a pair of revolvers from his coat, placed the men under citizen's arrest, and marched them into Portsmouth, where he turned them over to the sheriff. They subsequently confessed they had been hired to assassinate him.[35] O'Keefe had drawn attention to himself by his heroic service during the yellow fever epidemic and had not heard the last of prejudice.

THE YELLOW FEVER EPIDEMIC IN NORFOLK, 1855

For Virginia Catholics, the spring and summer of 1855 saw a movement from prejudice to pestilence, especially in the Norfolk and Portsmouth area. Barely recovering from the gubernatorial political campaign, they now faced the worst yellow fever epidemic to sweep through the two port cities.

Until the late 1890s, when Walter Reed discovered that yellow fever was spread by mosquitoes, the disease was largely thought to result from contagion and bad summer air. On July 26, it had spread throughout Norfolk and Portsmouth, carried there, according to a contemporary report, "by a workman on the steamer *Benjamin Franklin*."[36] In August, 80 died each day. For the first ten days of September, the number of burials in Norfolk alone reached as high as seventy-six, and never fell below forty-five. On September 12, a correspondent for *The Richmond Dispatch* reported:

> We hear scarce a sound but that of the hammers and saws, and wagons of the undertaker, and the rattle of the physicians' vehicles. Business has ceased, and the voice of mirth and revelry is not heard. More than 500 have been buried in the two principal cemeteries in eleven days. Many more have been buried in the Catholic burial ground and elsewhere. There have been about 1,500 deaths in the City.

A week later, the city adopted "the plan for burying in pits," with coffins placed eight abreast and sometimes four deep. When it was over, 2,000 had died, including thirty-six physicians, half the number before the epidemic.[37]

Occurring in the midst of the Know-Nothing campaign, the epidemic was the occasion for Catholic heroism. In Portsmouth, Father Francis Devlin died while ministering to the people, Catholic and

Protestant alike; only in January 1856 was he replaced by Joseph Plunkett from Martinsburg. In Norfolk, O'Keefe was twice afflicted with the disease, and the Daughters of Charity added to their duties of teaching and caring for orphans the new task of nursing the victims.

In September, O'Keefe described to Kirby the devastation of the disease. "Only imagine in a population of 16,000," he wrote,

> there have been over 1200 swept away in 2 months, & taking into consideration that at the outset of the epidemic more than half our people had fled, the mortality is truly awful; my poor congregation has suffered much. I was after six weeks incessant labor night & day struck down, & my case considered hopeless, however, God, in his mercy, has again raised me up, & I am once more in the midst of my labors. It is supposed by medical men, it will not abate for another month. Pray God it may soon cease.[38]

While many Protestant clergymen were among those who fled, O'Keefe had stayed and had entered a pact with the Rev. George Armstrong, a Presbyterian minister, that if either died, the other would conduct the funeral. Neither died of yellow fever, but years later O'Keefe did conduct the funeral of his friend, an amicable gesture long before the days of ecumenism.

After the epidemic, the people of Portsmouth erected a monument to Devlin for his work during the "Plague of 1855" that took his life. This caused Archbishop Kenrick to comment provocatively: "What a pity it is that they make a martyr of Devlin. The memory of weak men ought to be suffered to die away."[39] Devlin may have been weak, but he would be remembered for the way he died. But Catholic heroism during that tragic summer had a more lasting monument.

The Founding of St. Vincent's Hospital

The epidemic in Norfolk took the life of one of the local church's principal benefactresses, but also led to the founding of the first Catholic hospital in Virginia. Miss Ann Behan Plume Herron was the daughter of James Behan of Wexford and the niece of Walter Herron, one of the trustees who had remained loyal to Lucas thirty years before. Walter had married Ann Plume, who died without offspring, so, during a trip to Ireland, he convinced his niece to come to Norfolk, legally adopted her, and made her his residuary heir, with the provision that she take on the rather complicated name by which she demanded to be known. When Herron died, she inherited half of his estate, including his mansion in Norfolk. The other half of the estate went to his two nephews, James H. Behan, Ann's brother, and John E. Doyle, both of whom had also moved to Norfolk. In 1848, she had given the property for St. Mary's orphanage in Norfolk to the Sisters of Charity and, as was seen, provided funds for a girls academy.[40]

Like some wealthy Catholics of her day, however, Herron owned slaves, although she was reputedly far kinder to them than her brother was. In July 1855, just before the yellow fever hit Norfolk, she sought Archbishop Kenrick's advice on selling a married slave who was unruly and had recently been returned after running away. Although the sale would separate the slave from his wife, Kenrick counseled her that, "in the actual state of Society in the South," she was "free from any blame, under the circumstances. I praise, however, your humane and christian feeling."[41] No Catholic leaders would yet speak out against the laws upholding slavery. But in this case, his advice was irrelevant.

By the time Miss Herron received Kenrick's letter, the epidemic had begun. While her brother fled the city, she remained to nurse nineteen of her slaves back to health, but then died herself on September 27. She had, however, already turned her home into a hospital where the Daughters of Charity at St. Mary's Female Academy and Orphan Asylum, Sisters Bernard Boyle, Aloysia Lilly, Celine Blackburn, and Baptista Dowd, began nursing the victims. Subsequently, Sister Bernard, the first sister servant of St. Vincent's Hospital, transcribed an account of their work from an unnamed Protestant newspaper. As the "persecution" of Know-Nothingism broke out against Catholics, one man who lived near St. Mary's Asylum stated that "he hoped to see the day when he could wade knee deep in Catholic blood." Instead, he became "one of the first victims of the Yellow Fever." Her source went on to describe how, regardless of the creed of the afflicted, "by the pestilential bedside of their persecutor they [the sisters] sit through the stifling day and night, smoothing his pillow, fanning his hot brow, and cooling his parched lips."[42] The sisters also later ministered to the sick seamen of the side-wheel steamboats that plied the Chesapeake between Baltimore and Norfolk, an act of charity the Old Bay Line still remembered in the 1950s by granting them free passage.

The death of Miss Herron provided the means for making permanent the service the Daughters of Charity rendered during the epidemic. She left them her house for a "charity hospital." She seems also to have specified that Sister Bernard should be superior. Father Francis Burlando, the Daughters' director in Emmitsburg, however, preferred someone else and apparently questioned if the Daughters could run both a hospital and the orphanage. In October 1855, James Behan defended the choice of Sister Bernard. "All the sisters," he wrote, "have acted their parts nobly in the destroying sickness which has visited us. They have become very popular, our people are grateful, and by their acts have done much to remove the prejudice against our holy religion." But "Sister Bernard as superior" of the orphanage, he continued, "was the most prominent and by her conciliating disposition & good sense has become a great favorite with every citizen in the community." There were, moreover, funds available not only for a new asylum but also for a hospital. To remove her, he added, would add to the "chaos caused by the confusion of the epidemic" and increase the cost of the planned building for the asylum.[43]

At this time, hospitals, in anything approaching the modern connotation, were just beginning, and Behan reflected the mentality that heroic dedication to care of patients provided sufficient credentials for nursing. In retrospect, Sister Bernard was not the best choice to found a hospital. As one sister later stated, "Sister Bernard . . . of course . . . was not adapted for the work;—she was elegant, splendid for schools, but totally without experience of Hospital life."[44]

Regardless of the reservations about Sister Bernard, she joined Sisters Jane Regina Smith, Catharine Euphemia Blenkinsop, and Elizabeth Raphael Smith as the incorporators for the "Hospital of Saint Vincent of Paul," in accordance with an act passed by the Assembly of Virginia on March 3, 1856. The board of trustees resolved that James Behan and Ann Behan Plume Herron were to be acknowledged as "Founders and Benefactors of the Institution." One ward, to be named "Miss Ann," was to be reserved for charity patients under the "protectorship of Mr. Jas. H. Behan."[45] The emergency of the yellow fever epidemic had as a side-effect a Catholic outreach to the community on a humanitarian, rather than strictly religious, level. Yet, there was still some abiding anti-Catholicism in the port city.

O'KEEFE BUILDS HIS NEW CHURCH

In March 1856, O'Keefe invited the Redemptorists to give a mission in Norfolk. The preachers for the occasion were Isaac Hecker and Clarence Walworth. For the first time, Hecker had aimed his preaching principally at non-Catholics. After the mission, he then gave a series of lectures, directed at Protestants, on the Bible, the role of the Church, and tradition.[46] His approach was successful and it set in motion a series of events that led to his founding the Congregation of St. Paul the Apostle (the Paulists), dedicated to explaining the Catholic Church to Protestant Americans. But the mission and Father O'Keefe at St. Patrick's Church may also have aroused hostility to their proselytizing efforts. Late in the night of December 7, 1856, the church was burned after "an incendiary" set fire to a neighboring building. Only the walls remained standing. The church was insured for only $10,000, but had cost $20,000. Two valuable paintings were also destroyed: one of the Crucifixion given by the queen of Spain and the other of the Ascension given by Miss Ann Herron.[47]

Whether the "incendiary" had St. Patrick's as the principal target is uncertain, but O'Keefe took immediate action. Almost every week, he took the steamship to Baltimore and then on to Philadelphia and New York to raise funds for a new church. Each weekend, he was back in Norfolk. On Monday, he paid the laborers for their previous week's work and took off again on his journey.[48] In July 1857, he described his progress for Tobias Kirby:

> never in my life have I been so occupied more than now, for as you must have been informed, my little church, which was my pride & on which I lavished all my energies & taste, was burned to the ground on the morning of the 8th of December last, a circumstance which I cannot fail to view as not without meaning & which I have endeavored to turn to account by raising to Our Blessed Mother of the *"Immaculate Conception"* an edifice worthy of Her, & which is not half finished. It is of Gothic structure, about 150 feet long by 75 wide with clerestory & of course, the clerestory roof supported by [illegible] brown-stone columns. My poor people have been so reduced in numbers & circumstances that I am compelled to solicit the aid of the Catholics of the country; hence you can form an idea of the amount of labor in my hands this year; the building will cost

nearly $40,000 the greater part of which must be procured by begging & of course, the burthen is on my shoulders.[49]

O'Keefe was obviously intent on making a statement to those who had burned his church. The dedication of his new church was designed to make sure Norfolk knew the Catholics were there to stay.

On October 2, 1858, McGill began the ceremonies by consecrating the altars. The next day, he dedicated the church. He sang a pontifical Mass, and, he recorded, "the choir performed Mozart's 12th Mass in a very creditable manner." Bishop Patrick Lynch of Charleston preached the sermon "before a great concourse of people." In the afternoon, Lynch sang Vespers and had Benediction, while McGill preached on the authority of the Church. For the next week, the two bishops alternated preaching in Norfolk and Portsmouth.[50] It was the first recorded time that two bishops were together in the port city since England had visited Kelly in 1821. O'Keefe had made his statement. In 1991, Pope John Paul II would name St. Mary of the Immaculate Conception a minor basilica, the only one in Virginia.

Ironically, within six months of the dedication of the Norfolk church, St. Paul's in Portsmouth was burned down. This time, it was completely accidental. The church was across the street from the city jail, to which an "incendiary" set fire in order to rescue some friends. The flames soon spread to the church. For the time being, Plunkett had to use private homes or rented facilities to say Mass.[51] He would have to wait to complete the fourth church in Portsmouth until after the Civil War.

THE FIRST SYNOD OF RICHMOND

Now that his possible transfer to Washington and the Know-Nothing campaign were behind him, McGill convoked the first diocesan synod of Richmond on October 15, 1856. Preceded by an eight-day retreat given by two Jesuits, Joseph Aschwanden and Leonard Nota, the consultative assembly included all the priests of the diocese: John Teeling, the vicar general, Daniel Downey of Staunton, who was also the "procurator of the clergy," Joseph Plunkett of Portsmouth, Thomas Mulvey of Petersburg, Andrew Talty of Martinsburg, and James McGovern of Lynchburg. Of the diocesan priests, only O'Keefe was absent, with McGill's permission, apparently to raise funds for his new church. In addition, Aschwanden and Nota were named advisers, and Joseph Polk, S.J., pastor of St. Mary's Church was appointed secretary. One other new name appeared. Oscar Sears, a convert and former Jesuit novice then studying for the priesthood, was the master of ceremonies.[52]

The purpose of the synod was to bring the legislation of the diocese into conformity with that of the various councils of Baltimore. It renewed the legislative norms for clerical discipline that Whelan had promulgated in 1843.[53] But one piece of legislation may have reflected McGill's battle with O'Brien. No priest was to hold title to any ecclesiastical property in his own name. If he retained the title for three months after the bishop requested it, he incurred *ipso facto* suspension.[54] By and large, however, the synod's legislation was not innovative and simply articulated the norms for administration of the sacraments and clerical conduct.

PROBLEMS WITH CLERICAL DISCIPLINE

Clerical misconduct was one of McGill's major concerns during the later 1850s but, surprisingly, it did not seem to fuel the Know-Nothing propaganda campaign in Virginia. Sometime later in his career, probably at the urging of Father Francis Janssens, he made a "Record" of important points to be recalled in his episcopacy. He began with a list of the priests he removed from the diocese, including L. E. Leonard, who came to Richmond as a priest in 1855 and served at the cathedral for a few months before going to Martinsburg, apparently to help Talty after Plunkett's transfer to Portsmouth. Within a few months, Dr. Richard McSherry, whose family continued to be among the most prominent in the town, reported that, though Leonard said Mass daily and twice on Sundays, he heard confessions only on Saturday. The priest, furthermore, was impatient and had given one boy a black eye.[55] Leonard was dismissed from the diocese for "intemperance."[56] But the people of Martinsburg were to be subjected to a greater trial.

In May 1856, Father William Kenny, a classmate of Teeling's from All Hallows, had appeared in Richmond. Though ordained for Oregon City, he had served in San Francisco. At Teeling's urging,[57] McGill appointed Kenny to Martinsburg, but, in August, he told Father Bartholomew Woodlock at All Hallows how disappointed he was in Kenny "from that cause that ruins so many, indulgence in drink."[58] In this case, McGill was understating the case.

Kenny was guilty of other, more bizarre behavior. Before Mass, he once placed a pistol on the altar, and threatened to shoot Dr. McSherry if he entered the church.[59] After McGill removed his faculties, Kenny tried to excommunicate the people who complained about him. Finally, he stole a chalice and was charged with "snapping" a pistol at the deputy sheriff who arrested him in Maryland. As Teeling informed Woodlock in September, the congregation of Martinsburg insisted on pressing charges, though the bishop had written them to "let the unfortunate man go," once he had returned the stolen item. Both Talty and McGill were then subpoenaed as witnesses in Kenny's trial. Teeling feared that, if Kenny was tried before a "Know-Nothing Jury," he would "be sent to the penitentiary which is as disgraceful here, as transportation in Ireland." As an explanation for Kenny's actions, he opined that "the first cause of his fall has been exposure too young & without experience to that wicked country California."[60] Kenny was convicted in May 1857 and sentenced to a year in prison, but was pardoned by Governor Wise a month later.[61] He subsequently left the priesthood.[62]

Another case of clerical discipline was more tragic and more complicated. Daniel Downey had served the diocese well both in Lynchburg and in Staunton, where he was the founding pastor. On the evening of December 12, 1857, he shot and killed William Mullen, who had gotten Downey's housekeeper pregnant, promised to marry her, but then refused. Before witnesses, Downey apparently tried to talk to him, but they got into an argument, and Downey shot him. The *Staunton Spectator and General Advertiser* reported that Downey was then found "in profound slumber, the result, in the opinion of the Physicians present, of thorough intoxication."[63] At the inquest, however, one witness testified that Downey was "perfectly sober."[64] Downey was then placed under arrest.

McGill sought the advice of Kenrick, who argued that the evidence at hand did not indicate Downey had been attacked, and, furthermore, "it is forbidden to Clergymen, under penalty of excommunication, to carry arms."[65] This was now the nub of the canonical case against Downey, but it should be remembered that O'Keefe had also carried a brace of pistols without receiving any canonical censure.

In the meantime, both Oscar Sears, now ordained, and Teeling visited the Staunton parish from time to time. Only in April 1858 did Downey, at Sears's suggestion, personally explain his action to McGill, and then he tied it to the labor unrest that he had helped settle. Mullen, he stated, had already seduced the woman and then arranged for her to be the priest's housekeeper. He was part of a group "of ruffainly men & women who boast of their Catholicity, who robbed & ravished & burnt & destroyed property in this county, so that my life was endangered by them and the church was in danger of being demolished by the offended citizens in revenge of their bad deeds."[66]

Downey was alluding to the settlement he had negotiated a short time before with striking Irish workers on the railroad tunnel through the Blue Ridge Mountains, engineered by Colonel Claudius Crozet. Catholic "Corkonians," who were originally hired for $.75 a day, demanded $1.50. They called on a newly arrived crew from northern Ireland, "Far Downers," who were probably Protestants, working near Fishersville, to demand the same. When the newcomers refused, the Corkonians attacked the Fishersville camp at night, beat up several of the men, and burned the houses. Staunton was thrown into a panic with rumors of widespread killing and pillaging. The local militia rounded up the Corkonians, but few perpetrators could be identified. Crozet credited Downey with having worked out a compromise, according to which all would work for $1.25 a day.[67]

Regardless of Downey's defense, McGill was determined to stand fast. In the spring of 1858, he prepared to attend the Ninth Provincial Council of Baltimore. First on his list of proposed topics was "whether the bearing of arms for self-defense was forbidden clerics in the sacred canons."[68] The council did not directly treat McGill's proposal but did apply to the Province of Baltimore restrictive legislation adopted at the First Provincial Council of St. Louis in 1855. A priest who protested his removal or transfer was to be suspended from the sacred ministry while his case was heard by the bishop's consultors.[69]

In a third trial held in Albemarle County, adjacent to Augusta County, where Staunton is located, Downey had been acquitted on the grounds of self-defense. He immediately informed McGill that the prosecuting attorney had declared him to be "a pure & proper man and a most orderly & valuable & conservative peace loving citizen." He, therefore, asked to be returned to the active ministry.[70] But, because Downey had carried a pistol, McGill stood by Kenrick's advice that he "treat" the priest "as one altogether cut off from the ministry, and not receive him under your roof."[71]

Downey later expressed strong views about McGill's support of the Confederacy during the Civil War, and he remained in Staunton until his death in 1875.[72] Aside from occasional visits from Sears and Teeling, the parish remained bereft of a pastor until the colorful Joseph Bixio, S.J., arrived in the spring of 1861. Sears, in the meantime, had taken over Lynchburg, where James McGovern, Mulvey's successor, had left his post in 1859, only four years after his ordination in Richmond.[73]

Ending his first decade as bishop, McGill must have had mixed feelings about his clergy. Countering the loss of Kenny, Downey, and McGovern, however, were several converts who became priests right at the height of anti-Catholicism.

CONVERT PRIESTS AND THE TEELING LAW

On May 22, 1853, Talty baptized Thomas A. Becker, a schoolteacher in Martinsburg. Born in Pittsburgh, he received his early education at Xavier College in Cincinnati before coming to teach school in Martinsburg in 1851. He also claimed to have attended the University of Virginia, but there is no record of him among the registered students. He could, however, have lived with his older brother, Samuel, also a convert who taught at the university from 1853 to 1856.[74] In the fall of 1856, he began his studies for the priesthood at the Urban College of Propaganda in Rome,[75] where, in June 1859, he became the first priest of the Richmond diocese to be ordained there. During the Civil War, he was assigned to Martinsburg, where his Confederate sympathies led to his arrest.[76]

Besides Becker, three other converts became priests. Oscar Aloysius Sears was born in Alexandria in 1830 and attended Gonzaga College in Washington. Converting from the Episcopal Church, he briefly entered the Jesuit novitiate before coming to Richmond where he was ordained in 1857.[77] In February 1856, Robert H. Andrews, a graduate of Princeton, was baptized in Alexandria—his sister, also a convert, was one of his sponsors. He was ordained in 1859.[78] Finally, there were the conversions in the Weed family of Richmond. Mary Otis Weed was the first. On September 12, 1855, while McGill was engaged in his journalistic jousting over the Know-Nothings, he received her into the Church.[79] She then entered the Ursulines and founded their convent in Tuscaloosa, Alabama. In 1858, her brother, Ambler J. Weed, a priest in the Episcopal Church, who had served in Accomack County and then in Philadelphia, entered the Catholic Church on June 29, 1858, and was subsequently ordained.[80] Finally, a younger brother, George, also became a Catholic.[81] Sears, Andrews, and Weed did their theological studies under McGill in Richmond.

In the meantime, Teeling in Richmond established an important historical precedent. In 1859, he heard the confession of a woman fatally wounded by her husband, John Cronin. Cronin's attorneys attempted to coerce him to reveal her confession that they hoped would include infidelity and thus exonerate their client. Teeling adamantly refused to break the seal of the confessional and was backed up by Judge John A. Meredith. "To encroach upon the confessional, which is well understood to be regarded as a fundamental tenet in the Catholic Church," Meredith argued, "would be to ignore the Bill of Rights, so far as it is applicable to that Church." In what became known as "The Teeling Law," the judge ruled "that a priest enjoys a privilege of exemption from revealing what is communicated to him in the confessional."[82]

ALEXANDRIA BECOMES PART OF THE DIOCESE OF RICHMOND

As if McGill did not have enough territory to govern, he now received more. In 1858, the bishops at the Ninth Provincial Council of Baltimore forwarded two major petitions to Rome. First, they made one last effort to have the archdiocese of Baltimore declared the primatial see of the United States. Second, they recommended that Alexandria, ceded by the federal government back to Virginia a decade earlier, be transferred to Richmond from the Archdiocese of Baltimore. Propaganda rejected the former and came up with the noncanonical title of "prerogative of place" for Baltimore. It was more amenable to the second proposal, because, as the bishops had argued, the laws of the District of Columbia and of Maryland differed from those of Virginia.[83] On October 1, 1858, Kenrick notified McGill that his diocese now included Alexandria and its Jesuit parish of St. Mary's.[84]

Even before the canonical transfer of Alexandria to Richmond, the Jesuits of St. Mary's were extending their work beyond the city. Alexandria had slipped in its importance as a port because its leaders had initially opted to support the C&O canal rather than the railroad. In the 1850s, however, the Orange and Alexandria Railroad brought Irish workers flocking to construct the new line. In July 1854, Joseph Bixio, one of the Italian Jesuits who came to the United States in 1848, pled with the provincial that he be included among his countrymen chosen for the new Jesuit mission in California because of "my delicate health." He lamented that "this railroad life obliges me often to sleep under the poor badly roofed Irish shanties exposed to the inclemency of the weather, and therefore exposed to yet again the disease which the winter before the last brought me so near the grave."[85] Bixio would get his wish to go to California, but "his delicate health" recovered enough for him to return to play a colorful role in Virginia's later history.

At the end of 1854, John Blox, the pastor of St. Mary's, pointed out the drain this extended ministry placed on his staff, for "we are liable to be called on any day, from any part of Virginia this side of Richmond. On Saturday we had three sick calls more than a hundred miles apart. All the Irish sick calls are *pressing cases.*" He also complained that L. Vigilante, another of the Italian Jesuits, began collecting money in Fredericksburg and "along the railroad" and, therefore, was committing "us to the obligation of attending these churches."[86]

By the time McGill inherited Alexandria, some of the places Blox had mentioned were already developing. On June 27, 1857, McGill laid the cornerstone of St. Mary of the Immaculate Conception Church in Fredericksburg. Funding came from Behan's bequest in memory of his sister, Ann Behan Plume Herron. The priest who visited monthly from Richmond was to offer Mass for her on Monday.[87] Less than two years later, McGill dedicated the new church; as he had done on so many previous occasions, James Ryder, S.J., preached.[88]

Further to the north, Fairfax was apparently the "place along the railroad," to which Blox had alluded. On September 19, 1858, McGill "blessed and laid the cornerstone of a small frame church at Fairfax Station about 18 miles from Alexandria on the Orange and Alexandria Railroad."[89] The small church, St. Mary of Sorrows, would become the locus for important events in the Civil War. It was also the first church to be erected in northern Virginia outside of Alexandria and would serve the community for more than a century.

On the eve of the Civil War, McGill dedicated three more churches. On July 16, 1860, he laid the cornerstone for St. John's Church in Warrenton. It was made possible by a donation from Rice W. Payne, whose wife was Ann America Semmes, a cousin of Raphael Semmes, later the Confederate admiral. Again a Jesuit preached at the cornerstone ceremony, this time John Early, the president of Georgetown.[90] In October 1861, McGill returned to dedicate the church,[91] from which he would soon be cut off by war. Farther to the south, on September 9, 1860, he laid the cornerstone of St. Mary's at Ft. Monroe. Although the military post had been attended from time to time from Norfolk since the 1820s, the new church was an unusual arrangement. On July 9, 1860, McGill and Colonel Rene E. DeRussy of the Corps of Engineers signed an agreement according to which the church would be on the military base but was to be owned by the diocese. Secretary of War John B. Floyd, Jr., former governor of Virginia, approved the arrangements.[92] Plunkett was to serve the church from Portsmouth.[93] During the Civil War, however, the fort remained in Union hands.

Back in Richmond, St. Peter's Irish congregation had expanded into the eastern part of the city, Church Hill, near the tobacco factories where so many of the poorer Irish worked. On June 12, 1859, McGill laid the cornerstone for St. Patrick's Church on 25th Street between Franklin and Grace. In 1861, the building was completed and Teeling was assigned as the first pastor.[94] The see city now had three parishes. By that time, however, Richmond was preparing for war.

Storm Clouds of War

As the controversy over slavery continued to grow, the American bishops, particularly those in the South, sought to keep their priests out of it. At the Ninth Provincial Council of Baltimore in 1858, they decreed that the clergy should "be prudently on guard not to interpose themselves in the judgments of the faithful; for it is necessary that these be truly free on all questions pertaining to civil and social reason, within the limits of Christian doctrine and law."[95] Although they were understandably leery of raising political questions so soon after the Know-Nothings had charged the Catholic Church with having political designs, they apparently thought slavery lay within "the limits of Christian doctrine and law."

By 1860, however, the Civil War was imminent. One of the first indications of its inevitability came from Michael Costello, an All Hallows priest ordained in 1857 and assigned to replace Andrew Talty at Harpers Ferry.[96] On October 16, 1859, he not only witnessed John Brown's raid on the United States arsenal but also played a minor role in the episode. A few months later, he described the scene for a friend back at All Hallows. One of his parishioners was mortally wounded, but Brown's forces, who were then taking hostages, allowed him to pass through their lines to administer the last rites. During the night he attended other wounded members of his congregation. He reported the arrival of a company of United States troops from Washington but apparently did not think its commander, Colonel Robert E. Lee, important enough to mention. Nor did he note the presence among the troops of the Montgomery Guard, a company raised from the parishioners of St. Peter's in Richmond.[97] After the final attack on the engine house, where Brown and his supporters had taken refuge, two Catholic soldiers were wounded, one mortally. Costello gave him the last rites and buried him in the church cemetery.

Five of the insurrectionists had been executed by the time Costello wrote, and two more awaited death. But he was no abolitionist. Brown's party, Costello explained, had hoped "to arm the Negro population to free their coloured brethren in Virginia. They were, however, sadly mistaken, for they could not get a single slave in Virginia to join them, and the first man shot by them was a free Negro who refused to take arms and join their standard." In his own opinion "the slaves are much better off than the free Negroes, and they know this to be the fact, hence it is that they prefer to remain as they are, and it is better for them, I am sure." Costello had actually visited Brown before his execution, but the two engaged in a sharp exchange of views on whether slavery was biblically based. Despite his own anti-abolitionist views, Costello did not think he needed to be "a prophet to predict that if a dissolution of the union of the States ever takes place, it will be on account of the question of slavery." Still, he hoped that "good and sound men in the north and in the south . . . will rally round the constitution and preserve it inviolate."[98]

While Costello defended slavery, he was, however, concerned for the spiritual well-being of his parishioners' slaves. On the second Sunday of Advent in 1857, for example, he announced that "parents & masters & mistresses are . . . requested to send all the members [sic] of their respective children & servants to the Sunday school" to receive proper instruction for First Communion.[99]

Slavery, however, now became the issue that divided the nation. Few Virginia Catholics were slave owners. In Portsmouth, families like the Murphys, Bilisolys, and Webbs owned slaves and dutifully had them baptized.[100] In Norfolk, Miss Ann Herron and her brother, James Behan, both owned slaves. In Staunton, Michael Quinlan had sixteen slaves.[101] In Richmond, John Dooley owned at least five.[102] In the Civil War, nevertheless, Virginia's Catholics would rally to the Stars and Bars, perhaps to prove the loyalty that had been so severely challenged during the Know-Nothing campaign.

CHAPTER 8

The Civil War:
Virginia's Catholics
Rally to the Cause

As the war approached, Bishop McGill joined the other southern bishops in trying to preserve the unity of the church. When it came, he reflected the Confederate sympathies of most of his people who rallied to the Stars and Bars. The Civil War had perhaps a greater impact on Virginia than on any other state, for not only was Richmond the capital of the Confederacy but the state became a major battlefield. As Union forces occupied more and more of Virginia, McGill was cut off from direct communication with parts of his diocese. But the war also provided the opportunity not only for young Virginia Catholic men to prove their loyalty to the state but also for nursing sisters to display their heroism in numerous hospitals. Their work, considered in the next chapter, contributed to diminishing anti-Catholicism.

THE BISHOPS ON THE EVE OF THE WAR

As the clouds of war began to gather early in 1860, McGill and his fellow bishops conducted business as usual. Their correspondence focused on choosing a bishop for Savannah.[1] As late as October, McGill and his clergy traveled to Baltimore to join the archdiocesan priests in making a retreat under the direction of the Sulpicians.[2]

In November, Abraham Lincoln had been elected president of the United States; yet, McGill still did not seem to think war was imminent. In the middle of November, in accordance with the custom that prevailed before the incorporation of diocesan property, he wrote a will leaving all the property held in his name to Archbishop Francis Kenrick or, if he had died, to Bishop Richard Whelan.[3] In early December, Kenrick, for his part, seemed more preoccupied with the Savannah succession than with impending war. He did, however, comment to McGill that the "times are threatening, but I still hope for the permanency of the Union. It is suicidal to separate. Conservative men should step forward at this crisis, to save the country."[4] But the time for conservative men to step forward had passed. On December 20, South Carolina announced its secession from the Union. On February 4, 1861, Alabama, Florida, Mississippi, Georgia, Texas, and Louisiana followed suit. The same day, the states held an unsuccessful peace conference in Washington, and McGill ordered that the collect for peace be said at every Mass in the diocese until Holy Week.[5]

Right after the fruitless peace conference, McGill wrote the Society for the Propagation of the Faith describing the secession of the first six states. "The question of slavery is the origin of our difficulties," he said and laid the blame on "the fanaticism of abolitionists, who represent slavery as a mortal sin." Civil war was imminent, he thought, unless the leaders of both sides could settle their differences.[6] Some of Virginia's Catholics were slave-owners, but none held large numbers. Those who did own slaves were members of the professional classes or merchants in the towns and cities; none owned large plantations. Regardless of whether they were slave-owners or not, Virginia's Catholics would rally to the Southern cause.

Even after the secession of the first six states, however, the bishops of the province of Baltimore were intent on preserving their unity. On February 14, Kenrick asked McGill if "some of your wealthy converts might give a small donation" for the support of Levy Silliman Ives, the former Episcopal bishop of North Carolina who had converted to Catholicism a decade earlier. He also reported that Bishops Patrick Lynch of Charleston and Augustine Verot, vicar apostolic of Florida, both wanted to hold the Tenth Provincial Council of Baltimore "at the usual time" after Easter. Kenrick preferred not "to call it, as the times are so unsettled," but, if McGill favored it, he should "send a list of questions or matters." Verot had "proposed [for the council] a declaration on the subject of slavery to which Dr. L[ynch] objects, but intimates a wish that some moral points bearing on it may be treated of with advantage." Verot had also sent Kenrick

"for publication a sermon preached on July 4 on slavery and abolition, which I have written to him to suppress."

Verot's sermon defended the rights of slave owners, but called for
a drastic reform of slavery itself, specifying the rights as well as
the duties of slaves. Contrary to Kenrick's desires, he published it in
Baltimore. Despite the division among his suffragans, the archbishop
could still state: "I am full of hopes for the Union. Much is due to Old
Virginia, something to Virginia, and a good deal to the cool determination of our Kentucky master [Lincoln]. Folks need to be kept from
doing themselves and others harm."[7]

But Kenrick's hopes for the Union were soon shattered. On
March 4, Lincoln was inaugurated. At 4:30 in the morning of April 12,
General Pierre G. T. Beauregard in command of the Confederate
forces in Charleston opened fire on Fort Sumter, which surrendered
two days later. The war had begun. On April 15, Lincoln called for a
volunteer army of 75,000 to which Virginia was expected to provide
three regiments of infantry. The next day, Virginia's Governor, John
Letcher, informed Lincoln:

> I have only to say that the militia of Virginia will not be furnished
> to the powers at Washington for any such use or purpose as they
> have in view. Your object is to subjugate the Southern States, and a
> requisition made upon me for such an object—an object, in my
> judgment, not within the purview of the Constitution or the act of
> 1795—will not be complied with. You have chosen to inaugurate
> civil war, and having done so, we will meet it in a spirit as deter-
> mined as the Administration has exhibited toward the South.[8]

On April 17, Virginia seceded from the Union, followed over the next
month by Arkansas, Tennessee, and North Carolina. In June, however, fifty counties in western Virginia seceded from Virginia, and, in
1863, were admitted to the Union as the new state of West Virginia.
For the Church, this meant that for more than a century the boundaries of the dioceses of Wheeling and Richmond would not conform
with state lines. Virginia's secession, moreover, meant that Richmond
would now become the capital of the Confederacy.

St. Peter's became the host to Catholic troops from southern
states with higher Catholic populations. It is also highly probable that
Confederate secretary of the navy Stephen Mallory, the only Catholic

in Jefferson Davis's cabinet, regularly worshiped there. Although correspondence to McGill from Confederate authorities is not extant, the proximity of the cathedral and episcopal residence to the Capitol made oral communication more likely than written. Even in the absence of any communication, however, McGill proved himself a loyal son of the South.

In the meantime, on April 19, 1861, the first blood was shed in what was to be the nation's bloodiest war. The Sixth Massachusetts Regiment, answering Lincoln's call to arms, was marching through Baltimore to transfer from one railroad station to another when it was attacked by a mob of southern sympathizers. Four soldiers and twelve Baltimoreans were killed.[9] Regardless of the bishops' desire to maintain business as usual, the Baltimore attack ended the possibility of their holding a council.

As the Civil War began, the Church in the United States was divided, like the rest of the country. Former friends now became enemies. In 1858, for example, Lynch had originally invited Archbishop Hughes of New York to preach at his installation in Charleston. Only because Hughes could not come did Lynch then turn to McGill.[10] Like their people, the bishops reflected the political views of their regions. Both Whelan and McGill made their positions clear.

Late in April, Whelan complained to Kenrick about the "dastardly act" of northern bishops giving in to demands to fly the flag over their churches. Wheeling itself was divided, but he stated that "I privately shall stand by" Virginia's secession.[11] As will be seen, Whelan apparently did not maintain his position "privately" enough to prevent his threatened arrest for treason. A few days later, he challenged his old friend Hughes on why he encouraged men to enlist. "Are Catholics so numerous that you can spare them?" he asked. He then waxed eloquent in defense of Virginia and her cause. The only people whose interests were served, he stated, were:

> New England fanatics, who have ever shown themselves ready to oppress—and against the very people whose general sense of right & honor prompted them to stand up for Catholic & foreigner, tho' Catholics & foreigners were so few among them. I must acknowledge that the blood boils within me when I think of the Catholics & foreigners & other settlers of Ohio & other western states, that are feeling & fattening upon the soil which Virginia generously

gave for the common weal, & who, when *she* officially tells them that as a member of the Union she feels herself aggrieved & asks redress, such as could not injure them, refuse to hearken to her appeal & as tho' their souls were strangers to every magnanimous & grateful feeling, rush aye *rush*, unbidden to slay the children of those who for the Union gave up an empire.

While defending the actions of the Old Dominion, he begged Hughes not to allow Catholics to sacrifice themselves "for the party that contains their most deadly enemies, abolitionists, infidels & red republicans." He concluded by protesting the flying of the national flag over northern churches.[12]

Flag-waving had become a major issue. Probably in response to Whelan, Hughes explained that

the flag on the cathedral was erected with my permission and approval. It was at the same time an act of expediency going before a necessity likely to be urged upon me by the dictation of enthusiasm in this city. I preferred that no such necessity of dictation should overtake us; because, if it had, the press would have sounded the report that the Catholics were disloyal, and no act of ours afterward could successfully vindicate us from the imputation.

At the same time, Hughes chastised his southern colleagues for newspaper articles that justified "the attitude taken by the South on principles of Catholic theology, which I think was an unnecessary, inexpedient, and, for that matter, a doubtful if not a dangerous position, at the commencement of so unnatural and so lamentable a struggle."[13]

In Pittsburgh, Bishop Michael Domenec was forced by antisecessionists to raise the flag over his cathedral. In Baltimore, Kenrick faced a more complex problem. John Carroll had composed a prayer for civil authorities that included the petition that the nation "be preserved in union." It was recited after every Mass. When the priests refused to say the prayer, Kenrick personally read it in his cathedral and aroused such reaction among his secessionist congregation, the newly ordained James Gibbons later recalled, that "many people got up and publicly left the Cathedral, and those who remained expressed their dissent from the Archbishop's petition by a great rustling of papers and silks."[14] Kenrick then discontinued the prayer, especially after the "popular tumult," as he termed the attack on the Sixth Massachusetts Regiment, so that his clergy would not become enmeshed in the divisive politics of his border city.[15] He too faced the demand of Union supporters to fly the flag from every private residence. As he confided to Bishop Martin J. Spalding of Louisville, "I am averse to the practice [of flying the flag], but necessity might determine me."[16]

Kenrick had to contend not only with a city with divided loyalties but also with a divided metropolitan province that extended to Florida. In May 1862, he heard a rumor that General John C. Fremont, in command of the Union forces in western Virginia, planned to arrest Bishop Whelan for preaching treasonous sermons against the United States government. He immediately warned Whelan of the danger and urged him publicly to deny the charge. In the meantime, he had Father Bernard Maguire, S.J., then pastor of St. Aloysius Church in Washington, intercede with both Lincoln and Secretary of War Edwin Stanton. Both the president and secretary thought the rumor was unfounded, but Stanton, nevertheless, telegraphed Fremont to take no action against Whelan. In the meantime, Whelan had replied to Kenrick's letter denying that he had made any anti-Union statement, except in private conversation. Kenrick forwarded Whelan's reply to Washington, and there the matter ended.[17]

McGill and his clergy could be more open than Whelan in expressing their southern sympathies. On April 21, 1861, Father John Teeling told his congregation at St. Peter's Cathedral "to stand firm in the assertion of their rights." At the same time, McGill ordered that the customary prayer for the United States, which had already caused controversy in Baltimore, be changed to one for the Confederate authorities. That change later led to the imprisonment of Father Thomas Becker in Martinsburg.[18] Surprisingly, however, when McGill wrote to Lynch in Charleston on April 25, the only allusion he made to the impending conflict was to remark: "It would *not* be easy *now* to hold a council in Baltimore." He was sure Lynch had heard of "the recent events there," that is, the attack on the Sixth Massachusetts Regiment. He was more concerned about getting a bishop for Savannah. Even as the nation was becoming divided, he suggested that Lynch "might make some inquiries" about an unnamed New York priest who might make a suitable candidate![19]

Only in the middle of May did McGill directly address the issue of the war with Lynch. Firmly convinced that "justice [was] on the

side of the South," he declared that "the party in power [was] organized on principles *unconstitutional.*" So clear was his conviction that
he asked: "can a person, without sin formal or material, volunteer into
the army called out by Mr. Lincoln?" He even considered making his
own episcopal contribution to the Confederate war effort by refusing
Union Army chaplains faculties to hear confessions in Virginia, since
"they come as officials of an invading army." In other words, under
the canon law of the time, Union chaplains might not be able to ab-
solve their own men once they set foot on Virginia soil. "Virginia,"
McGill continued,

> has waited, hoped, and plead for an arrangement which might se-
> cure the union. Her efforts were derided and condemned. I feel
> that the party in power has shown no disposition to respect the just
> claims of the south. They seek to humble & subjugate her.[20]

McGill left no doubts about his political views.

Virginia's Catholics Go to War

Catholics in Virginia and other states of the South, like their northern
counterparts, answered the call to arms. On April 10, ten of the eleven
members of the philosophy class at Georgetown College solemnly presented Father John Early, the president, with a proclamation. They
were leaving the school, they said, because of "our inability to apply
ourselves to our studies . . . while all we have most dear on earth, our
country (the South), our parents and our brethren call loudly upon
our presence at our respective homes."[21] Within a year, four of these
young men were in the Confederate Army. Altogether, 375 Georgetown graduates would serve in the Confederate Army, of whom
167 were Virginians. Among these were Tazewell Tyler, son of former President John Tyler, four Matthews brothers from Speedwell,
near Wytheville, and two Dooley brothers, James and John, from
Richmond.[22] Other Georgetown alumni from Virginia would also
play major roles in the Confederacy, but perhaps none more than the
Dooleys.

In 1849, Richmond's Irish parishioners had formed the Montgomery Guard, Company C of the "Old First" Virginia Regiment,

under Captain Patrick T. Moore, with John Dooley as lieutenant. Moore was a merchant and was an active parishioner at St. Peter's church, where he was one of the founders of the Young Catholic Friends Society,[23] but drew public attention in 1855 when he was charged with "familiarity with a married lady."[24] In 1861, he was elected colonel of the regiment, at which point one company, the Richmond Light Infantry Blues, withdrew from the regiment, whether because he was a Catholic or a philanderer or the regiment had too many companies is unknown. Subsequently wounded, he declined to be reelected colonel of the regiment. Later promoted to brigadier general of the Home Guard, he performed heroically in the defense of Richmond in 1864.[25] He died in 1883 and was buried from St. James Episcopal Church.[26]

When Moore was elected colonel, John Dooley became captain of the Montgomery Guard. His son, James, who had graduated from Georgetown a year before, enlisted as a private in the company. Later wounded in the arm, he became a captain in the reserves defending the city of Richmond. A second Dooley son, John, remained a student at Georgetown until 1862, when he joined his father's company and rose to the rank of captain before he was wounded and captured at Gettysburg, to spend the rest of the war in a Union prison. At the outbreak of the war, McGill had blessed the pikes of the Montgomery Guard, resplendent in their green uniforms trimmed with gold stars and bars, in the basement of the cathedral.[27] The company chose as its chaplain John Teeling, pastor of St. Patrick's and vicar general of the diocese. Colonel Moore may then have misjudged the sentiments of his regiment by appointing Teeling regimental chaplain.

As the First Virginia encamped at Camp Pickens as part of the Fourth Brigade under James Longstreet, Teeling's appointment became controversial. One correspondent complained that "without detracting in any manner from Dr. Teeling's abilities, I would say that his ministry is chiefly confined to Company C, Montgomery Guard." A member of Company D was more outspoken. He wrote that "I find with much regret and indignation that father Teeling a Roman Catholic Priest has been appointed Chaplain to our regiment which I think exceeds all the acts of injustice to us and we have received many." Teeling was soon assigned only to the Catholic troops.[28]

Company C first saw combat in July 1861, in a skirmish at Bull Run preceding the First Battle of Manassas, when it staved off an attack by the Sixty-Ninth New York Infantry, part of the famed Irish Brigade.[29] United in their nation of birth and in religion, but now divided by regions in their adopted country, Irish-American Catholics illustrated the fratricidal character of the war.

When Virginia seceded, Richmond's Irish formed a second unit, the Emmet Guards, Company F of the Fifteenth Virginia Infantry, under the command of Captain William Lloyd. Since the men had enlisted for only one year, however, the company was disbanded in June 1862. Such short enlistment may have reflected a class distinction. Whereas the Montgomery Guard, consisting of Richmond's more established Irish community, served for the duration of the war, some laboring-class Irish immigrants, perhaps including members of the Emmett Guards, later claimed their British citizenship exempted them from Confederate service.[30] In this sudden discovery of loyalty to the Queen, they were not alone. In Harpers Ferry, Father Michael Costello was reported to have flown the Union Jack over St. Peter's Church to ward off attack from either side. Whatever the truth of the story, all the other churches, including the Episcopal church that shared the bluff with St. Peter's, were destroyed by Federal artillery. Back in Richmond, German Catholics were also well represented in the Confederate Army, although they did not form distinct Catholic units. In 1859, the Virginia Rifles elected Florence Miller of St. Mary's Church as captain. Of the twelve officers in the Virginia and Marion Rifles, St. Mary's provided three.[31] In Columbia, Fluvanna County, the Wakeham brothers, Alfred, William, Jr., and John K., and their two cousins joined the Richmond Howitzers.[32] The Wakehams will figure later in the diocese's story.

In Portsmouth, eight members of the Bilisoly family, including Antonio Leon and Leslie Augustus, both physicians, enlisted in the Ninth Virginia Infantry Regiment on April 20. Two other parishioners of St. Paul's parish enlisted the same day.[33] At least five more served in the Third and Sixth Virginia Infantry Regiments. Across the river in Norfolk, O'Keefe's parishioners did the same. Among them was Michael Glennon, who had attended St. Mary's school for boys, and would later become a prominent journalist and Catholic leader in the city. In Staunton, Thomas Collins lied about his age to enlist in the Fifty-Second Virginia Infantry, only to die within a year of causes unknown at the age of nineteen. In Winchester, Patrick Reardon was prevented by an older brother from joining the army in 1862 at the age of fifteen, only to enlist in Mosby's Rangers two years later.[34] One of Mosby's key lieutenants, Fountain Beattie, early fell under the sway of the colonel's Catholic wife, Pauline, and became a Catholic either during or shortly after the war. He would later have twelve children by his wife, Ann Hathaway, and two of his grandsons, Dixon and Robert Fountain Beattie, became prominent priests in the diocese.[35]

In Petersburg, on April 19, 1861, Anthony Keiley enlisted as a sergeant in the "Petersburg Riflemen," Company E of the Twelfth Virginia Infantry Regiment. In 1860, he had been elected to the state Democratic convention that nominated Stephen A. Douglas for president. He openly opposed secession and published his own pro-Douglas newspaper. Once Virginia seceded, however, he followed his state. Wounded at Malvern Hill in 1862, he continued to serve until Gettysburg, after which he was elected a member of the General Assembly.[36] Later, he was a prisoner of war. His brother John enlisted in the Montgomery Guard on April 20, 1861, and rose to the rank of major on General Longstreet's staff. During the final year of the war, a second brother, Benjamin, also enlisted in the Confederate Army—he was later to become bishop of Savannah.[37] Lynchburg's Catholics likewise rallied to the cause. Mary Dornin worked in the town's hospitals. Her son, Anthony, enlisted in the Beauregard Rifles of Moorman's Battery and died of wounds received at Antietam.[38]

In Alexandria, St. Mary's parishioners rallied to the Confederate cause. Two of them had already taken an active part in the 1860 election. William F. Carne and George William Brent were the local leaders of, respectively, the Breckenridge Democrats and the Douglas Democrats. When the war broke out, the parish provided two companies for the Seventeenth Virginia, Company G, the Emmett Guards, and Company I, the O'Connell Guards. Like their counterparts from Richmond, they wore green uniforms.[39] But Alexandria was an occupied city for the duration of the war, and many of these Irish Catholics abandoned the cause and returned to civilian life.

For whatever reason, the Irish in Virginia and North Carolina enlisted in the Southern cause. Father Jeremiah P. O'Connell wrote Bishop Lynch from Columbia, South Carolina, in June 1861, that on a recent missionary trip to North Carolina he found "the great bulk of the Irish Catholics have volunteered & gone to Virginia. The last time I was in Charlotte 45 of them left for the seat of war."[40] Jeremiah

O'Connell and his two brothers, Joseph and Lawrence, were priests of the diocese of Charleston. Their nephew, Denis J. O'Connell, later became bishop of Richmond. Although it is difficult to obtain accurate statistics, Virginia probably never before had a greater percentage of Catholics, the result of regiments from the more Catholic states of Louisiana and Alabama moving north to the theater of war and of Union troops occupying northern and later western Virginia. These Catholic units, moreover, were accompanied by chaplains.

CHAPLAINS, CONFEDERATE AND UNION

As Southern Catholics answered the call to arms, their bishops had the task of providing for their spiritual care. At the outbreak of hostilities, McGill had already informed Lynch that he might refuse Union chaplains faculties for his diocese. He also seems to have wanted to be sure that Confederate chaplains serving in Virginia received faculties from him. In August 1861, Lynch explained to McGill that he wanted to assure that a sufficient number of chaplains be named to accompany the Confederate forces. Father Joseph Prachensky, S.J., he wrote, had been elected chaplain of a Mobile regiment and would present himself to McGill upon his arrival in Virginia. Lynch had applied for an appointment of Father Lawrence J. O'Connell, without specifying any particular regiment, since he was "best known in our up-country S.C. Regiments, but there are very few Catholics among them." He had proposed his name "simply because I thought a priest might be useful somewhere that you ... might designate." O'Connell was actually to serve as the chaplain to the Sisters of Charity of Our Lady of Mercy at the military hospital at Montgomery White Sulphur Springs.[41] Lynch further suggested that "it would be well to have one or two priests to each large division. Norfolk has one, will have two or three. Has Magruder any? Beauregard has Teeling." As an aside, Lynch queried "did B[eauregard] really go to communion as the papers say?" Returning to his concern about chaplains, he thought General Joseph E. Johnston needed at least one and thought McGill would "have to send one with the army in Western Virginia." But he assured his colleague that these chaplains "will of course have faculties from you for our troops."[42] Unfortunately, although the bishops of the Confederacy may have continued to correspond with each other during the war, most of their letters have now been lost.

Up north in Alexandria, Father Peter Kroes, S.J., pastor of St. Mary's, watched as Union troops occupied the town for the remainder of the war. In February 1862, some Orangemen from an Illinois regiment threatened to burn the church down and arrest any priest who did not say the prayer prescribed for Federal authorities. An Irish regiment got wind of their plan, and, when the Orangemen were about to order Kroes's arrest, a witness recounted, "the measured tramp of soldiers was heard at the door of the church. Soon they were marching up the aisles, and to the relief of the Catholics knelt down and blessed themselves."[43]

Chaplains among the Confederate forces may have been the first priests some Southerners had seen. In December 1861, Z. Lee Gilmer from Charlottesville of Company B of the Nineteenth Virginia Infantry witnessed the execution of two members of the Louisiana Tigers who had assaulted the guards in an attempt to free some friends then under arrest. As he described the execution, he seemed equally fascinated by the strange attire and actions of the priest who accompanied the condemned men, most probably Hippolyte Gache, S.J.:

> One of the men made a slight resistance to his eyes being bound, when the old Preast [sic] went & spoke to him & he was quiet. The Capt of the Tigers then gave the 24 armed Tigers command. Make redy [sic], aim, fire. one fire of the Rifle & they were no more. They met their fate without a sigh, without murmur. They feared neither God, man nor the Devil. . . . Soon as they fell the Preast [sic] ran to them & sprinkled 'Holy Water' &c upon them. A clear & beautiful spring like day witnessed their last hours. . . . The Preast was clad in a Black Gown with a singular hat on his head & with his beads around his neck & with a face representing the Virgin Mary &c. This is the sadest [sic] event I ever witnessed & may God forbid another such. What a strange race we are, how Barbarous, as if their hearts were of stone.[44]

Gache refused to wear the officer's uniform donned by other Confederate and Union chaplains, and wore the black cassock and biretta of a Jesuit.

Born in France, Gache was one of six Jesuits assigned in 1846 by the province of Lyons to its new mission in Louisiana and Alabama, where they took over Spring Hill College. When the war broke out, he received an appointment as chaplain to the Tenth Louisiana

Regiment. In September 1861, he had arrived at Camp Magruder, near Williamsburg, where he described for a Jesuit colleague in Louisiana his first reactions to his labors among Virginia Protestants. His only "consolation" came from "the thought that, probably, never before in this land where we now tread has true worship been offered to the true God, and that I and a few Catholics may be the first people in the Old Dominion who know God truly and who worship Him according to His Holy Will."[45] Gache could hardly be styled an ecumenist.

During his stay on the Peninsula, Gache paid visits to both Richmond and Norfolk. In November, he traveled to Norfolk to see Darius Hubert, S.J., chaplain of the First Louisiana Regiment, commanded by Colonel Albert Blanchard, and Prachensky, whom Lynch had commended to McGill. His plan was to "get their ideas on the apostolate, and . . . enjoy simply the pleasure of talking with them." En route, he met Hubert traveling with Oscar Sears, pastor of Lynchburg, on their way to Manassas. The dour Frenchman hardly recognized his former student. "Imagine," he wrote:

> a young dandy: his hair elegant, his beard splendid; gold-braid festooned upon his blue kepi and embroidered upon the sleeves of his high-collared frock coat; the golden buttons of his waistcoat emblazoned with the Louisiana Pelican; his gold-filleted trousers falling neatly into a pair of comely boots. This dazzling sight was none other than Father Hubert himself!

Once in Norfolk, he stayed with O'Keefe and found Prachensky similarly attired and bearded with the assumed rank of major. He bluntly told his fellow Jesuit "that the bishop of Richmond, as well as all the diocesan priests, found it passing strange that a Catholic chaplain should dress up in an officer's uniform. And I told him also that General Blanchard himself, in my very presence, had asked by what right it was that this Father Prachensky had put on a uniform." Like Hubert, Prachensky rejected such criticism, which made Gache query how "the desire to pose as an officer . . . could find its way into the hearts of Jesuits."[46]

Despite his love for military attire and rank, Prachensky grew tired of the more arduous aspects of the job. In March 1962, he resigned from the army. This paved the way for General Blanchard to request that Matthew O'Keefe be named chaplain of Mahone's brigade. On April 16, 1862, Secretary of War George Wythe Randolph issued O'Keefe his appointment.[47] With the occupation of Norfolk in May 1862, however, O'Keefe's military career came to an end, but not his pastoral ministry or his Southern sympathies. He noted in his records the burial of several Union soldiers, but maintained to his death his pride in being the last surviving brigade chaplain of the Confederate Army.[48]

In the meantime, from his camp on the York River, Gache made several trips to Williamsburg. Initially, he went to minister to a young alumnus of Spring Hill who was dying of typhoid. As he conducted the young man's body to the cemetery, he commented that "this was probably the first time the city of King William of Orange ever witnessed a Catholic priest, fully vested in cassock, surplice and stole, walking in procession down its historic streets."[49] Gache was, in fact, the first priest recorded to have been in Williamsburg since 1817, when Lucas reported finding six French and three Irish families there.

Immediately after the young man's funeral, Gache was introduced to Colonel Benjamin S. Ewell, who commanded the Confederate forces in Williamsburg. A native of Georgetown, Ewell had attended the Jesuit academy there as a young boy. He became president of the College of William and Mary, but resigned to enlist in the Confederate Army.[50] He invited Gache to stay with him whenever he was in town. On a later visit, Gache obtained Ewell's permission to say Mass in "the chapel of the lunatic asylum," "the largest and most beautiful building in Williamsburg." His congregation was "a dozen or so Catholic convalescents [in the military hospital] and some twenty Episcopalian ladies"—Ewell's daughter and her friends. That evening he received a personal "visit from the Episcopalian minister [Thomas Ambler], himself." Their initial encounter involved a bit of theological sparring, but Gache remained impressed particularly with the faith of the Ewell women. "I am very fond of the people of Williamsburg," he told his correspondent, "and it seems unfortunate that there is not a single Catholic home here around which a priest might build a parish." If only there were a few devout Catholics, he opined, "it would not be long before one could have a sizable congregation."[51] It would be more than seventy years, however, before Williamsburg got its first parish and a resident priest.

Williamsburg remained Gache's place of "predeliction." On a subsequent visit, Ambler invited him to remain at his home. "We are almost always arguing with one another—and I don't spare him a bit," he recorded, "but that doesn't spoil our friendship." He had also befriended a Baptist minister, William Martin, who "truly treats me like a brother, but I'm not going to give him any encouragement." Instead, the Jesuit took "every occasion to tell him and others of his ilk that I don't see them under any other aspect than as gentlemen, but that certainly I don't consider them as ministers of the Gospel."[52]

During the summer of 1862, Gache was in Richmond and shortly thereafter left his regiment to spend the remainder of the war working in military hospitals in Virginia. He continued to write detailed descriptions of his life as a chaplain, however, including his meeting in Richmond with a Jesuit chaplain in the Union Army, Peter Tissot, who had been a student of his back in Europe and had been captured during the Peninsular Campaign.[53]

Tissot was chaplain of the 37th Regiment, New York Volunteers, the "Irish Rifles." In July 1861, he had witnessed the defeat of the Union Army at Bull Run and the army's chaotic retreat back to the Potomac. A year later, he was with his unit in the Peninsular Campaign. As the Union Army retreated, Tissot fell ill and was left behind. He was joined by another Jesuit chaplain, Joseph O'Hagan. On June 30, both were taken prisoner. Unable to ride his horse, Tissot gave it to O'Hagan's servant. Transported by cart to Savage Station, on July 2, he took a train to Richmond, where he "stepped off without being molested or questioned by anyone" and found his way to St. Peter's.[54]

At the cathedral, Tissot met McGill and three priests stationed there: "Father [John P.] Hagan, a young man; Father [Augustine L.] McMullen, an ex-Jesuit; and Father [R. H.] Andrews, a young convert from Alexandria, an excellent man." "None of them seemed to care about politics," he remarked, but "it was not the same with Father Teeling of St. Patrick's Church. He and one of the Southern chaplains were rabid Secessionists." Tissot actually met four Confederate chaplains, three of them fellow Jesuits, Gache, Hubert, and Joseph Bixio, S.J.[55] Bixio, as will be seen shortly, was versatile enough to pass himself off as a chaplain in both armies. The fourth was a Redemptorist, James B. Sheeran, who was chaplain of the Fourteenth Louisiana Regiment from the Peninsular Campaign to the end of the war—with an interlude as a prisoner in Fort McHenry, Baltimore, because of Bixio's escapades. He may well have been the "rabid secessionist," about whom Tissot spoke, for he sprinkled his vivid account of being a wartime chaplain with references to General "Pope and his

Abolition Robbers" and other less than favorable comments on the Union cause.[56]

In Richmond, Tissot also met up with O'Hagan and another Union chaplain, Thomas Scully from Boston. But Teeling proved to be Tissot's nemesis. While Tissot was quietly reading a book one day, Teeling attempted to preach him "a homily on the North." Tissot "brought him to a dead stop" by returning to his interrupted reading. Unintimidated by the Irish-born Confederate, however, Tissot "was especially careful to avoid talking politics with the Bishop." McGill was "very kind," he recorded, "but very strong in his Southern convictions." As Tissot was about to leave Richmond, he requested faculties of McGill, who

> readily granted me faculties for the Northern soldiers, but did not seem inclined to give them for civilians (Southerners). This did not satisfy me. I explained how I might be in some place where there might be Catholics living. Why could I not hear their confessions? "Well, you may," he said, "provided you do not talk to them against the South." He did me the honor to make his confession to me.[57]

Not every encounter between the Union chaplains and Richmond Catholics was so friendly.

One Union chaplain created a crisis while visiting a Catholic family by indiscreetly remarking "that the only hope of the South was in entire submission." "This gave great offense," said Tissot, "for the Catholics of Richmond, if we except the Germans and a few Irish, were strongly for the South." Anonymous letters soon went to the military commander, General Charles Winder, complaining that Yankee chaplains were loose in the city and claiming that one was scheduled to preach at Mass the following Sunday. Some Catholics grumbled that, while fulfilling their Sunday Mass obligation, they would be "compelled to attend the ministrations of Yankee chaplains." Winder requested that McGill have the chaplains remain in his house and not be allowed to say Mass. Tissot thought that the general's wish would be McGill's command, but the bishop remarked: "I am master at home." The following Sunday, McGill himself preached a sermon on charity. All restrictions on the chaplains' movements were then removed.[58] As Tissot later narrated for a French journal, "the bishop is strongly pronounced in favor of the South; but he is a bishop before all: the mantle of a prelate cloaks over the clothing of a citizen."[59]

As soon as Tissot was well enough, he began visiting the Union prisoners at Libby Prison, where he found them in "in a very pitiable condition," but thought "the authorities seemed to do what they could for them." O'Hagan, in the meantime, had befriended several government officials who had attended Georgetown. Through them, the chaplains obtained permission to take their horses with them when they were exchanged with the other prisoners. As Tissot and O'Hagan were about to leave Richmond, however, they discovered that provisions were not made for their horses. O'Hagan sold his to McGill, and then Tissot sold his to "Father O'Hagan for $200 in good Northern currency, payable in two years after the war. He gave me his note to that effect; it was the last I ever heard of it."[60] Just what O'Hagan did with this horse, for which there was no provision, Tissot did not record.

Tissot made it clear that "we were not paroled, but simply let go without any condition or promise of any kind." At 4 A.M. on July 19, he left Richmond. During the train's layover in Petersburg, "we were visited by Father Mulvey and several Catholic ladies, who brought us food, pies, cakes, etc." That afternoon, the train continued to the James River, where the prisoners were put on boats to proceed to City Point, where they disembarked at 7 A.M. the next morning.[61] Tissot's account provided a vignette of how a people, divided by war, remained united in faith, of how an ardent Confederate sympathizer like McGill overcame his politics to act the part of a bishop. Tissot subsequently wrote up his experiences in a series of letters published in *Etudes,* the French Jesuit journal; some of them were then reprinted in *Annales de la Propagation de la foi,* the journal of the Society for the Propagation of the Faith.[62]

While Tissot kept a diary and wrote letters about his military service, one of the Confederate "chaplains" he met in Richmond was a more shadowy, if more unforgettable, character. Father Joseph Bixio was born in Genoa. His younger brother, Nino, was one of Garibaldi's generals and one of the most fierce anticlericals in the battle for Italian unification. During the revolution of 1848, Joseph and other Jesuits had to flee Italy. Ordained at Georgetown, he served in Alexandria,[63] and Eastport, Maine, before joining his fellow Italian Jesuits in California. As the war approached, he returned to Alexandria, where he recorded a marriage as late as May 23, 1861.[64] But on June 20, he was recording baptisms in Staunton, which had not had a resident priest since 1858, when Father Downey had shot a parishioner. Oblivious to details of geography or ecclesiastical jurisdiction, Bixio made his entries in Staunton's sacramental records with the designation "in missionibus sub Alexandria."[65]

In January 1862, Gache narrated for his southern colleague this account of Bixio's career:

> When the war broke out Father Bixio had been pastor of a parish that lay on both sides of the Virginia-Maryland border. During the battle of Manassas he happened to be in the Virginia part of his parish, and ever since then he hasn't been able to return to the Maryland side. But this hasn't bothered him a bit; he has simply volunteered as a Confederate chaplain.[66]

Bixio may well have told Gache that story, but in the telling, he altered some facts. A later account of his adventures had him explaining to Union officials that he was assigned to the Jesuit parish in Frederick, Maryland, from which he visited the Shenandoah Valley. This would explain Gache's understanding that the Italian Jesuit found his "parish" in Maryland and Virginia cut off by the hostilities. Bixio, of course, was really assigned to Alexandria and had already begun ministering in Staunton before the First Battle of Manassas in July 1861. In April 1862, Tissot had written a letter for the Society for the Propagation of the Faith, describing the work of chaplains on both sides. Bixio, he said, had initially worked with Union troops, with whom he was "very popular," for "he completely won over the hearts of the officers and soldiers."[67]

Bixio may well have been a volunteer Confederate chaplain, the guise under which Tissot next met him in Richmond in July 1862.[68] Yet, in early September, if the reports are accurate, he was back in Fairfax Station, where he conducted the funeral service for two major generals in the Union Army, Philip Kearny and Isaac Stephens, who were killed during the Second Battle of Manassas.[69]

During one of his stays in Richmond, Bixio apparently also ministered to Italian soldiers in the Union Army held at Libby Prison. Among these was Luigi Palma Cesnola, like Nino Bixio a veteran of Garibaldi's campaigns and later the first director of the Metropolitan Museum of Art in New York.

If nothing else, Bixio had flair. Late in the summer of 1864, he engaged in one of his most dramatic exploits. Father Leo Rizzo da Saracena, O.F.M., chaplain of a Connecticut regiment, had fallen seriously ill with typhoid. Father Sheeran, the Confederate chaplain, was then a captive behind the Union lines. He recorded that Bixio "slipped into the sick priest's tent and stole his chaplaincy credential and uniform." In September, he found him "now playing Yankee chaplain in company with several Yankee officers." But he did not betray his erstwhile Confederate companion. In Winchester, the Jesuit used his stolen commission to purchase supplies which he shipped off to Staunton. Among those he deceived was General Philip Sheridan, who was outraged to learn he was the butt of jokes in Staunton at having been duped by the wily Jesuit. He took out his wrath on Sheeran, throwing him into prison for not revealing Bixio's identity.[70]

In the meantime, General Benjamin Butler, better known to Southerners as "Beast Ben," heard a twisted version of the story, in which Father Leo was made the culprit. Butler, with less than ethnic sensitivity, ordered: "Find him, and shoot the Dago at sight." Father Leo, who later became the president of St. Bonaventure College in New York, came close to being shot for espionage but managed to explain that he was writhing with fever while Bixio was cavorting in his uniform in the company of Sheridan. Meanwhile, Bixio was distributing the Yankee goods back in Staunton, where he received the message, probably from Butler, "that, if ever caught, he should be hanged to the first tree."[71]

In February 1865, a correspondent from Richmond, probably Father McMullen, provided some additional details about Bixio, whom he had recently seen with "his hands always full of business as if he were to remain here for life. If the Yankees ever lay hands on him they will make him suffer. Genl. Sheridan swears vengeance against him & will hang him as a spy if he catches him." It seems that "when he was asked in Winchester or Harpers Ferry where he was from he answered Frederick & that he had for years attended the Valley." Sheeran had warned him "that he was playing a dangerous & imprudent game & had better be cautious." The writer concluded:

> The consequence of all this will be that Bixio will have to fly if ever the Yankees go to Staunton again & his church will be always in danger of being burnt. So much for playing tricks. It is said that Bixio is a perfect Pascal Jesuit.[72]

As it turned out, Bixio remained unmolested in Staunton. With the town as his base, he continued to ride a circuit to Harrisonburg, Gordonsville, Middleburg, Lexington, and Charlottesville. He recorded his last baptism in October 1866, when his superiors recalled him to California.[73]

Even in death, however, Bixio remained a man of mystery. The official obituary sent to the Jesuit general in Rome in 1889 focused principally on Bixio's Civil War ministry but glossed over his exploits and invented some facts. When the war broke out, it stated,

> he hastened to Virginia in order to provide the assistance of religion to the men of both armies. He once fell among a cavalry unit of the federals, who suspected him of being sent by the enemy to spy on them and brought him as a captive before Philip Sheridan, the supreme commander of the cavalry. But, when Father Bixio was discovered to have been assigned only to take care of the conveniences and salvation of souls, he not only permitted him to go free, but also ordered his own men to provide him with everything they collected in order for him more easily to carry out his sacred ministry, and assigned one of the soldiers to him, whom he always employed as a servant.

The obituary is an example of the creative rewriting of history. It also said, contrary to the Staunton records, that Bixio was recalled to California before the end of the war.[74] Another acquaintance said that in the spring of 1865, he showed up at Holy Trinity Church in Georgetown "with a trunkful of Confederate script—hundreds of thousands of dollars, expecting to found a college with his treasure."[75] In the archives of Santa Clara University, there are Confederate bonds that might represent Bixio's purchases in Richmond.[76] Though insignificant in regard to the outcome of the war, he was certainly one of the most colorful characters to pass across the Virginia landscape.

In the meantime, Sheeran had paid the price for not betraying Bixio. After the battle of Winchester in September 1864, he received permission from Union General Horatio G. Wright to cross the lines to administer to the Confederate wounded. On October 31, he was arrested together with several other civilians from Winchester. From there, he wrote a letter to the *Freeman's Journal*, edited by James A. McMaster in New York, complaining of General Sheridan's violation of the permission to minister to wounded Confederates. Subsequently transported to Baltimore, he was imprisoned in Fort McHenry, where he remained until December 5. After a brief stay with the Redemptorists in Baltimore and in Cumberland, Maryland, he returned to

Winchester, where he described the Union army's devastation of the Shenandoah Valley. He also had a personal confrontation with Sheridan, who, though himself a Catholic, admitted he had imprisoned the priest out of pique at being duped by Bixio.[77]

CONFEDERATE OVERTURES TO PIUS IX

Chaplains and soldiers, however, were not the only Catholics in Confederate service. After the Union victories at Gettysburg and Vicksburg in July 1963, draft riots broke out in New York as Irish immigrants protested the conscription laws that enabled the wealthy to buy a substitute for $300. The Irish flocking to the northern cities by the thousands each year were too poor to buy a substitute, and their blood flowed on the battlefields in disproportion to their percentage of the population. Lincoln's Emancipation Proclamation, moreover, changed the war from one to preserve the Union to one to free the slaves. Black freedmen were already an economic threat to Irish workers on the lowest rung of New York's economic ladder and became the objects of assault and lynching. The rioting ended only with the arrival of Federal troops, many of them also Irish, and a plea for submission to the draft laws from the ailing Archbishop John Hughes on July 17.[78] Confederate leaders now sought to capitalize on this situation.

On August 30, 1863, Father John B. Bannon, Irish-born chaplain of the First Missouri Brigade, said Mass at St. Peter's in Richmond. In the congregation was Secretary of the Navy Stephen Mallory, who invited Bannon and McGill to his home that evening. As Bannon was about to leave for his appointment, he received a message from Jefferson Davis to come to his home. Davis asked Bannon to go to Ireland as the Confederacy's secret agent to convince potential immigrants not to be lured to come to the North to work on railroads only to find themselves being slaughtered in the Union Army. Bannon proposed the broader strategy of gaining Pius IX's recognition of the Confederacy. Davis now gave him the dual mission to the pope and to Ireland. With McGill's advice and support, Bannon accepted.[79]

Armed with both a letter from Davis to the pope and instructions for Ireland from Judah B. Benjamin, the secretary of state, Bannon went first to see the pope and present Davis's letter explaining the Confederacy's cause. On December 9, 1863, the pope responded with a letter "to the Illustrious and Honorable Jefferson Davis, President of the Confederate States of America," thanking him for the "warm appreciation" he had expressed toward the Holy See.[80] The pope's letter was widely construed in Europe and the South as official recognition of the Confederacy, which Richmond leaders hoped would be forthcoming from other European powers. The Reconstruction Congress also interpreted it that way and used it to justify legislation in 1867 that prohibited further funding for the United States mission to the papal states—legislation that remained in effect until 1983, when its repeal paved the way for establishing diplomatic relations between the United States and the Holy See.

In the meantime, once in Ireland, Bannon waged a propaganda campaign to dissuade the Irish from emigrating to the North. Using the correspondence between Davis and Pius IX, he also drew a comparison between the Southern and Irish quest for freedom. By the end of May 1864, Bannon took credit for stanching the bleeding of the Irish population to the North. Back in the South, Father Aegidius Smulders gained Jefferson Davis's approval to launch a similar effort to convert captured Irish Union soldiers to the Confederate cause. Although Bannon resigned as an official Confederate commissioner, he did take on one more mission—to assist Bishop Lynch in gaining the pope's recognition of the Confederacy.[81]

In February 1864, Lynch was on his way to visit his sisters at Montgomery White Sulphur Springs. Passing through Richmond, he met Judah B. Benjamin, who asked him to undertake the position as Confederate Commissioner to Pius IX. He agreed, provided the assignment would not last for more than six months. In April, he set out for a stay in Rome that would last almost two years.[82] While in Rome, he published a defense of slavery in Italian, German, and French. Joined by Bannon, he made another fruitless effort to have the pope officially recognize the Confederacy. Bannon never returned to the United States, but entered the Jesuits in Dublin. Lynch was able to return to Charleston only after President Andrew Johnson pardoned him at the intercession of the Northern bishops.[83]

Virginia's Catholics had rallied to the cause. Their young men served in the army. Chaplains in both armies had cared for the people of the diocese. But others had also served who wore neither the blue nor the gray. Church life, moreover, continued for the diocese, even if it was divided by war.

CHAPTER 9

Nursing on the Battlefield and a Diocese Divided by War

While Virginia's youth fought in the bloody conflict, others served in nonmilitary ways, especially nursing sisters. But Bishop McGill had to administer a divided diocese. Alexandria had been occupied by the Union as soon as hostilities broke out. In 1863, it became the seat of the "restored" state under Governor Francis Harrison Pierpont.[1] By the spring of 1862, Norfolk fell to the Union, and Martinsburg shifted back and forth between the warring armies. In Richmond itself, the capital of the Confederacy, McGill and his priests maintained a semblance of order and normalcy, even when the city was under siege.

THE DAUGHTERS OF CHARITY IN MILITARY HOSPITALS

The war created truly heroic figures, but none more so than the Daughters of Charity. Two hundred and twenty of them had served in military hospitals or camps on both sides. The first call for their services came in Richmond on May 16, 1861. The Confederate authorities asked them to admit sick and wounded soldiers to the Infirmary of St. Francis de Sales. Two sisters went daily from St. Joseph's Asylum to tend to the sick. In the meantime, Mother Ann Simeon Norris at Emmitsburg dispatched Sister Juliana Chatard, a Baltimore native, to assist the Richmond sisters. When the infirmary proved to be too small to care for the increased number of patients, the government purchased a series of houses that were placed under the sisters' care. Their corporal work of mercy in military hospitals led to numerous conversions.[2]

Sister Angela Heath, a North Carolina native, later wrote a narrative, "Annals of the War," about the work of the Daughters of Charity during the conflict. Perhaps through an unfortunate sense of humility, however, she omitted most of the names of the sisters and most dates. She was more concerned to narrate edifying stories. She recounted that on one occasion a Protestant minister said he could do nothing for a critically ill man. Looking across to where a "priest was preparing a dying man for death," the man

> called the sister and said to her: "I heard my Minister say he could do nothing for me, while my companion there has every hope in the spiritual helps he has received. Therefore, if my church can do nothing for me when I am dying, I renounce it." He was soon prepared by our holy religion for his happy exit.[3]

Although the sisters were hardly ecumenical, they were successful in mitigating hostility toward the Church. One steward likened himself to "St. Paul, as to zeal, in his hatred of Catholicity." On one occasion, "He said to a sister: 'I admire you Ladies for your great charity, but I despise your religion.' Sister calmly replied: 'Without our Holy Religion, sir, we could have no Charity.'" Much later, the man was dining with a group who began speaking of "Catholic errors, absurdities, etc." He announced that "in my presence I will allow nothing said against the Catholics." He was now "convinced, that the Catholic Religion alone can give such proofs of heroic virtue as I have witnessed in those Sisters, and I intend to embrace their religion."[4]

But the sisters did more than nurse soldiers. As Angela Heath recounted, "*Lady* prisoners were brought to us for safe keeping, who otherwise must have been consigned to a common jail." On another occasion, "a female soldier is brought to us that she might be taught to know her place and character in life."[5]

Richmond was not the only Virginia hospital under the direction of the Daughters of Charity. In June 1861, Confederate authorities in Harpers Ferry telegraphed the sisters at Emmitsburg to send nurses to tend sick soldiers. Three sisters made their way by stagecoach through Frederick across the lines of both armies to Harpers Ferry, where Father Michael Costello gave them quarters. When the Union Army advanced, the Confederates blew up the bridge across the Potomac and withdrew to Winchester. Accompanied by Father Costello carrying the Blessed Sacrament, the sisters followed. The church in Winchester, they said, was "the poorest, poorest old stone building ... in the suburbs." Since the sisters were understaffed, the doctor in charge "said ... only the Sisters of Charity could travel now" to gain assistance. One sister set off "partly by car [railroad], then stage, and a dangerous crossing the Potomac in a flat canoe, then on foot as fast as she could walk, and often running for a mile to reach the next car before it would leave, and here the Cornette gained admission for her." Four more sisters, including Sister Euphemia Blenkinsop, one of the founders of the Norfolk hospital, were dispatched to Winchester. Within a short time, they followed the army to Richmond, where they joined the sisters already working there.[6]

In Portsmouth, the Union forces blew up the Portsmouth navy yard early on the morning of April 21, 1861, as they prepared to abandon all but their stronghold at Fortress Monroe. The sisters then opened the doors of St. Vincent's Hospital to Confederate soldiers. In May 1862, when Federal forces captured Norfolk and Portsmouth, the sisters were given charge of the Portsmouth Marine Hospital.[7]

The work of the Daughters of Charity for both of the warring armies, however, did not go unchallenged. In December 1861, Major General John A. Dix informed Archbishop Francis Kenrick of Baltimore that he had received a letter from the government in Washington "charging that ladies in the costume of Sisters of Charity, furnished by the Convent of Emmitsburg have passed the lines into Virginia, for the purpose of keeping up communication with the Confederate States." Kenrick immediately responded that the sisters already stationed in Norfolk and Richmond had "extended their services to the sick and wounded, and from time to time visited the parent Institution." He also stated "that their journeys were open and with formal passports from the Government at Washington and wholly unconnected with politics and not intended in any way to aid rebellion." The archbishop, nevertheless, recommended that Father Francis Burlando, C.M., the spiritual director of the sisters, their superior, and three members of the council "draw up a statement ... bring it to Baltimore and present it to the General. It is proper that all suspicion should be at once removed. *Instant tempora periculosa* [dangerous times are at hand]."[8]

Burlando consulted Sister Ann Simeon Norris, the superior. They then composed a letter to General Dix, signed by other officials of the order. They wrote:

> The only object for which the sisters were sent to Virginia was to nurse the sick and wounded soldiers. The sisters now in Richmond passed the lines at various times via Harpers Ferry, or by Bay to Norfolk, furnished with passports either by Genl. Banks, Maj. Genl. Scott or the Secretary of State. The first two bands that crossed over at Harpers Ferry had no pass, none being then required; two of the number returned to the Central House at Emmitsburg on account of ill health rendering them unable for duty, and one had a number of family letters, principally from Sisters of Charity to their Superiors, which were handed over while crossing by the same sister to the officer of the boat from the other side, and afterwards sent to Washington, thence mailed to their destination.[9]

The superiors of the Daughters emphatically denied that nursing "the soldiers in the South could be interpreted as a disaffection for the Government, since sisters from the same society" had worked or were still working at the request of Union military officers at Albany, St. Louis, Baltimore, Troy, Milwaukee, and other places, even at the cost of their own institutions. They believed "the odious charge" had "arisen from some ill-disposed source, or . . . [from] some misguided female assuming a costume similar to that of the Sisters." The previous October, two women had in fact posed as sisters in Baltimore. The sisters were "mortified" and "indignant" at this abuse, but concluded that "we take the liberty to remark that the duty of the Sisters of Charity is to strive to save their souls by the exercise of charity towards their fellow creatures, the poor & suffering of every nation independent of creed or politics."[10] The letter placated Washington officials, but the episode indicated that the war had not eradicated all suspicion of Catholics.

In the meantime, in January 1862, five sisters left Richmond for Manassas, where they found "500 patients, sick and wounded of both armies." They lived in a small room, in which they had Mass whenever a chaplain was available, but it was a quarter of a mile away, so that "often it was found more prudent to be satisfied with two meals, than to trudge through the snow for a third, which at best, was not very inviting, for the culinary department was not under our control, but under that of negroes, who had a decided aversion for cleanliness." On the average, ten patients died each day, but Sister Angela thought that "I may safely say, four were baptized, either by Fathers Smoulders [sic, Aegidius Smulders, C.Ss.R., chaplain of a Louisiana regiment] or [John] Teeling, or by our Sisters."[11]

On March 15, 1862, the sisters abandoned Manassas with the retreating Confederate Army. Three of them next took over a hospital in Gordonsville, where there were 200 patients, victims principally of pneumonia and typhoid. On Easter Sunday, they withdrew from Gordonsville to begin a new hospital in Danville, where they had "a nice little house . . . a kind of luxury had it not been the abode of innumerable rats, of whom we stood in the greatest awe, for they seemed to be proprietors of the mansion." Most of the 400 patients were Catholics, "at least in name, for many had almost forgotten their duties as such." In November, the hospital was moved to Lynchburg, where five sisters tended 1,000 patients.[12]

While Angela Heath was silent in giving the names of the sisters and focused more on their spiritual conquests, Father Gache filled in some of the gaps. Having left the Tenth Louisiana, he began working with the sisters in Danville sometime in the fall of 1862, when Father Smulders was transferred. He gathered a congregation of eighty people and befriended Mrs. Elizabeth Letcher Stuart, mother of General J. E. B. Stuart. He then followed the sisters to Lynchburg, where he shared thirty hospitals with the local pastor, Oscar Sears. Though each had between 1,500 and 2,000 patients, so few were Catholic that he did not think "the Catholic hospital chaplains . . . are in . . . danger of being crushed by the burden of overwork."[13]

Gache found his efforts to convert the ailing men frustrated either by indifference or by the opposition of Protestant ministers. But he encountered a different situation "in the hospitals of the Daughters of Charity," where:

> normally it is enough for the sick to see these saintly women at work for a period of three or four days; then they are willing to believe in the "sisters' church." For these men the proof of the Catholic church is the life of the sisters. I have asked some men in the hospitals conducted by the nuns if they would like to be baptized Catholics. "Oh, no," they'd reply, "I don't like that church a

bit! I've never seen a Catholic, but I've heard a lot about them. The sisters' church is the church for me!"[14]

Gache was a man who played by the rules. Just as he had been indignant that two fellow Jesuits wore officers' uniforms, he now balked at having to say prayers at the funerals of non-Catholics. He was sure that his superior in Mobile would share his "scandal" to hear that

> there are Catholic army chaplains here in Virginia, and indeed even a bishop, who have made an agreement with the "Protestant chaplains" to take turns in conducting a daily funeral service for all of the military dead brought to the cemetery, whether they be Catholic, Protestant, Jew or Turk. So as not to violate the laws of the church in this respect they recite not the prayers of the Latin ritual, but other prayers, and in English. They also insist that they do not read these prayers for the dead, but rather for those who are present at the funeral service. The pastor at Lynchburg [Sears] is one of these priests.[15]

The French Jesuit may have been able to form friendships with Protestants as individuals, but he was clearly not at home with what had become Virginia Catholicism's accommodating approach to Protestant neighbors.

In the middle of May 1863, Gache described the Confederate victory at Chancellorsville, which claimed the life of General Stonewall Jackson. Jackson was "a very good Christian," he told a southern confrere, and "the face of this austere Presbyterian expressed all of the characteristics of a devout member of that sect; yet, he was not a bigot—at least so far as I have heard." Robert E. Lee, however, was "very religious, not in an ostentatious and wordy manner, but sincerely and genuinely." The general, he reported, was "very favorable toward Catholics and he has the greatest esteem for them." Gache personally knew the general's brother, Commodore Sidney Smith Lee, then in command of Drewry's Bluff on the James River, who had "the same religious sentiments and sympathies towards Catholics."[16] The commodore had even invited eight sisters and fifty orphans from St. Joseph's Orphanage to inspect the fortifications, where they prayed and chanted the litanies of the Blessed Virgin. Gache then offered his opinion on the religious sentiments of other Confederate leaders. The wife of General Joseph E. Johnston proclaimed that "We're Catholics already in our hearts." Her three sisters had converted to Catholicism, and her husband's nephew, John Warfield Johnston, was married to Niketti Floyd. Jefferson Davis's wife, moreover, requested the Daughters' prayers and asked them to recommend a Catholic governess for her children.[17]

In December 1864, Gache had little to do in Lynchburg, partly because the hospitals had few patients and partly because Sears "is not eager that his parishioners have much to do with me."[18] But Gache did take on the special hospital for smallpox patients that had been entrusted to the sisters in Darrington outside Lynchburg. In his account, the sisters were forces to be reckoned with. Sister Aloysia Kane was the head matron of one of the hospitals in the city. She was "a child of the Emerald Isle—a sweet and timid dove who scarcely dares to open her eyes to speak above a whisper in her day to day dealings with the world, but, a dove who shows the boldness and the courage of a lioness as soon as there is a question of defending the Faith." Contrary to army regulations, a Protestant minister was given permission to preach in the wards. She thought she was sucessful in her demand to the doctor in charge that he revoke that permission, when she and her companions "were suddenly startled by a Protestant hymn booming forth from the ward on the other side of the street." She marched over to the ward, threw open the door, and gestured to the preacher to cease as he began the prayer "to let me know my sinfulness." When he ignored her, she

> walked right through the ward straight up to him, and said: "Sir, this place is a hospital; not a meeting house. Please cease your preaching and praying. Otherwise I shall report you to the chief doctor of the division. He has forbidden the holding of all religious services in this hospital."[19]

But the Daughters of Charity were not the only religious order of women nursing in Virginia hospitals.

The Sisters of Charity of Our Lady of Mercy in Montgomery White Sulphur Springs

In December 1861, McGill had asked Bishop Lynch of Charleston to send members of the Sisters of Charity of Our Lady of Mercy to staff a hospital in Greenbrier White Sulphur Springs in what is now West Virginia. He enclosed a letter from Emily Mason, a convert and great-niece of George Mason, who was already working there and requested the sisters' assistance. Lynch met with the superior of the sisters, Mother Teresa Barry, and her council, which voted to dispatch five sisters to the hospital, Sister Mary De Sales Brennan, Sister Mary Ignatius Clark, Sister Mary Bernard Frank, Sister Mary Helena Marlowe, and Sister Mary Stanislaus Coventry. On December 19, the band set out by train for Virginia, accompanied by Mother Teresa and Father Lawrence P. O'Connell, their chaplain and uncle of the future bishop. On December 21, they had reached Richmond, where they stayed with the Daughters of Charity and inspected their hospital. Sometime after Christmas, they set off for Greenbrier White Sulphur Springs, by train from Richmond to Staunton and then by stagecoach to Greenbrier, where they began to work in the hospital that had previously served as a hotel and remains a prominent resort.[20]

In March 1862, Mother Teresa returned to South Carolina leaving Sister M. De Sales in charge. But the sisters faced early difficulties. Upon their arrival, they found that Miss Mason had assumed charge of nursing, a situation that created tension until she left to start a new hospital in Charlottesville. In May 1862, Lynch was visiting the sisters apparently to recover his health.[21] On May 16, however, the Union Army captured Lewisburg, only ten miles away. As the Confederate forces fell back, the hospital and the sisters moved to Montgomery White Sulphur Springs General Hospital, six miles from Christiansburg, where it remained for the duration of the war. With the Union occupation of Greenbrier, rumors circulated in Charleston that the bishop, O'Connell, and the sisters had fallen into Yankee hands. Only when letters from Lynch and Sister M. De Sales arrived in Charleston, did their friends learn that they were safely in their new location.[22]

In Montgomery, the sisters again faced conflict, this time stemming from an undercurrent of anti-Catholicism. In July 1862, Dr. J. Lewis Woodville, who had been at Greenbrier, was appointed surgeon in charge of the Montgomery hospital. A convert to Catholicism, he had appointed O'Connell as chaplain. This brought a charge against him of undue "Catholic influence." One doctor protested to the inspector general of Hospitals, Doctor T. C. Madison, that Sister M. De Sales and O'Connell had usurped the duties of the Protestant chaplain, whose name was also Madison.

In August, Sister M. De Sales told Lynch that Doctor Madison replied to the complaint that "the Hospital was the best organized and best kept in his circuit and he considered the Rev. Mr. Madison a very fortunate man to have his business so well done for him." With that response, the minister resigned, and Woodville dismissed the doctor who had complained. Before resigning, however, Madison accused Sister M. De Sales of refusing to summon a Methodist minister for a young man whom O'Connell baptized. She explained to Lynch that

> Dr. Woodville denied that such could have been the case for he knew me to ask him at the Greenbrier White [Sulphur Springs] to send him miles for a Minister. . . . I have sent for Madison himself. The fact is that they are frantic at the influence we have over the men and at the number that have been baptized, all of whom have died save one who went of himself to Father O'Connell, became instructed and has received baptism and Holy Communion. There are three others studying the catechism and asked for themselves.[23]

By this juncture, the hospital had over 400 patients, and Woodville told the sisters to prepare for 300 more. To assist the sisters in tasks such as laundering, Lynch had earlier recruited several young women from Lynchburg. The hospital now faced a labor dispute. Four of the young women, apparently led by Lizzie Kelly, without whose assistance, said Sister M. De Sales, "my ward would be altogether neglected," were demanding $12 a month instead of $10, a wage Woodville said the surgeon general would not approve.[24]

With the increased number of patients at the Montgomery hospital, Sister M. De Sales requested more sisters from Charleston. On September 24, 1862, Sister Mary Alphonsa Moore and Sister Mary Agatha MacNamara were appointed. Accompanied by Lynch, they arrived in Montgomery sometime in October. Shortly after Lynch left, however, the hospital experienced its first outbreak of smallpox. The one infected patient was isolated, but the other men eagerly stood in line to be vaccinated. Only two of the sisters had to be vaccinated, since all the others had had smallpox. The arrival of more smallpox patients, especially in January 1863, precipitated a new crisis for Woodville.[25]

Under orders of Doctor John Hunter, medical director for the District of Southwestern Virginia, Woodville had to assign a physician to be quarantined with the smallpox patients. One after another, the four contract physicians, whom Woodville assigned, refused to enter the quarantine. Sister M. De Sales then asked Sister M. Helena, assisted by a servant woman and two male nurses, to quarantine herself, lest any patient die without baptism. She accused the contract physicians of cowardice, but they, in turn, accused Woodville of lack of respect in choosing them instead of a commissioned surgeon for the duty. Moreover, in a protest to Doctor Samuel Moore, the surgeon general, three of the four stated that

> There has been ever since the establishment of the Hospital a dissatisfaction on the part of a majority of the surgeons . . . because of favoritism shown and authority given to a religious party placed in the Hospital who are permitted to have control of everything. . . . Mr. O'Connell, a Catholic Priest, and seven Sisters of Mercy together with all of their order they succeeded in gathering around them consisting of Quarter Master, clerks, and nurses is the party referred to above.[26]

Doctor Moore, however, supported Woodville by abrogating the contracts of the four physicians. Major General Sam Jones, commander of the department of Western Virginia, moreover, ordered that Woodville was to place "no restrictions on the movements of the Chaplain or the Sisters of Mercy, except such as are absolutely required by a due regard to the safety of the patients and attendants." Under this authority, Woodville released Sister M. Helena from quarantine, but she was to avoid contact with patients in the General Hospital.[27]

Just when all seem settled, the hospital received a new post commander, Captain D. P. Graham, who issued stricter quarantine regulations, which Woodville construed as designed to remove the sisters from the hospital. Three of the assistant surgeons wrote a letter agreeing with him. Woodville forwarded this letter and other information to General Jones, who ordered an investigation. As a result, Jones ordered Graham not to require that the sisters nursing smallpox patients sleep in the quarantined hospital. All seemed at peace, but it was only a lull before another storm.[28]

On March 6, 1863, while Woodville was warding off Graham's new restrictions, O'Connell informed Lynch that he thought it was time for him and the sisters to abandon the hospital. "The country around us," he wrote, "has been harangued. . . . The people are almost in arms against us (I mean of course the Sisters & myself)." Furthermore, he reported, the number of patients was declining, hospitals in Richmond and Lynchburg were being closed, and patients from hospitals closer by were not being sent to Montgomery, a move he interpreted as a concerted effort "of breaking up the Hospital" or of "removing Woodville." Regardless of the hospital's future, he asked to transfer as a chaplain to South Carolina. But he ended on a testy note:

> In case you treat my letter with the same indifference as those already sent you it is necessary for me to notify you that I will consider myself free from any further duty in Va., after the lapse of two weeks.
>
> You must not regard this last paragraph as apparently severe, since such a course has become necessary on account of yr remissness towards my letters.[29]

A week later, O'Connell again wrote saying that he had failed to mention that he had been ill with "chill & fever, my old inveterate malady," and had been confined to bed. He had written to Father Hagan, then in Lynchburg, to come to Montgomery for a week, so that he could take a train to Charleston. On the way, he would stop in Columbia, where his family had settled. The bishop could reach him there.[30]

Precisely how Lynch reacted to O'Connell's tone is unknown. On May 22, O'Connell replied to a letter from Lynch, now lost, and stated that he had just been appointed hospital chaplain in Columbia. He further reported that McGill and Father Augustine McMullen had just visited the city and the bishop's sermon made him the "Lion of the Day."[31]

Despite O'Connell's hope to obtain the services of Hagan for the sisters, they had to wait six weeks without a chaplain until the arrival of Father C. J. Croghan of Charleston. On April 18, Lynch had petitioned Colonel Lucius Northrop, the commissary general to grant Croghan a commission. He noted that "the Sisters receive no remuneration whatever, and have asked for none." He had himself supplied them with clothing and food to supplement their rations, but he could not take on the "additional expense of supporting a clergyman."[32] Recommending the commission, Northrop wrote in red:

"The Sisters will not remain without a Chaplain. Economy is advanced by yielding to their wish."[33] Accompanied by Mother Teresa and Sister M. Gertrude Murkhardt, Croghan arrived at Montgomery early in June.

In July 1863, Lee's army was defeated at Gettysburg, and Vicksburg surrendered in July. While the hospitals in Lynchburg cared for the sick and wounded of the Army of Northern Virginia, Montgomery received those "from the West—some very badly wounded; others bad cases of typhoid fever."[34] Sister M. De Sales and her companions kept up a running commentary for Lynch on the horrors of war. The hospital treated 653 men in September, and 873 in December. O'Connell's prediction that the hospital would soon be closed proved to be unfounded.

In February 1864, Lynch paid another visit to Montgomery White Sulphur Springs. On his way through Richmond, he received a request from the Confederate government to gain Pius IX's recognition of the Confederacy.[35] Shortly after his visit, the forces opposed to Woodville preferred charges that led to his court martial. Among the accusations were embezzlement of military stores and failure to enforce quarantine regulations. After a two-week trial, he was acquitted. In his own defense, he blamed the controversy on Captain Graham, who had imposed quarantine "regulations so vexatious" that

> there seemed to be a settled purpose in certain quarters to drive from this Hospital these humane and most useful Sisters of Mercy who have been of such essential importance to its proper management, and whose kind attentions have contributed so much to the comfort of the patients. This purpose, originating I presume, in some narrow-minded sectarian prejudices, was manifested in various efforts to make the situation of these Sisters as uncomfortable as possible.[36]

The sisters continued to work at the Montgomery hospital without pay until May 1865. Six weeks after Lee's surrender, accompanied by their chaplain, they abandoned the place where they had labored for almost four years to begin a circuitous route home to South Carolina. Because they were noncombatants, no provision had been made for them to travel directly to Charleston. They went first to Washington and then to New York, where the parishioners of St. Peter's Church on Barclay Street raised funds to secure passage for them on a ship to Charleston.[37]

In the meantime, on February 13, 1865, the Daughters of Charity had abandoned Lynchburg before the advancing Federal Army and moved with their hospital stores to Richmond, where the surgeon general of the Confederate Army asked them to take charge of Stuart Hospital.[38] Gache moved with them. In Lynchburg, he was replaced at Sears's request by Smulders, who a few months earlier had proposed to Jefferson Davis that captured Irish Catholics be isolated from other prisoners so that he could preach to them to convert them to the Southern cause—his plan was the corollary to that of Father John B. Bannon, who was then in Ireland trying to convince the Irish not to emigrate to the United States and serve in the Union Army to begin with. After getting one Confederate commander to set up a special camp for 700 Catholic prisoners, he preached a mission to them, heard their confessions and gave them Communion, but still they preferred not to exchange the Union blue for the Confederate gray. When the Confederates abandoned Lynchburg, Smulders and Sears persuaded first the retreating army and then the advancing Federal troops not to burn the bridges.[39]

While the Daughters of Charity had charge of several hospitals in Virginia, they also tended the Confederate prisoners at the Union prison camp at Point Lookout, Maryland. Even when all female nurses were ordered to leave the site, they remained until August 1, 1865.[40] Among the more prominent prisoners was Anthony Keiley, who wrote a memoir of his captivity, and John Banister Tabb, who subsequently entered the Church and became a priest of the diocese of Richmond.

The hospital work of the sisters on both sides of the fray did much to change the image of the Church in the United States, particularly in the South. McGill later recounted the significance to the Church of hospital work in his first report to Propaganda after the war. In the meantime, he was trying to maintain some semblance of order in his diocese now divided between the warring armies.

PASTORAL LIFE IN A DIOCESE DIVIDED BY WAR

Shortly after the Second Battle of Manassas in August 1862, McGill shared his thoughts with Lynch. He was delighted at the "wonderful things" Archbishop John Hughes of New York had spoken recently in Dublin under "the nose of her Majesty." But he was dismayed at "the account of his war sermon after his return home," in which the archbishop supported not only the call for more volunteers for the army but the initiation of a draft. "I am sad to read these things," remarked McGill; "I really think that the Archbishop of New York is losing his wits. I trust in Providence, who will I hope render vain all their designs and efforts."[41]

The war rendered communications between McGill and some of his priests impossible. In May 1862, Norfolk fell permanently into Union hands. Cut off from Richmond, Matthew O'Keefe wrote Kenrick during February and March of 1863, asking for marriage dispensations and suggesting that the archbishop exercise extraordinary faculties for the region under Union occupation. He further offered to act as a conduit for communication between Baltimore and the other southern bishops.[42]

In Martinsburg, an important railroad center, Thomas Becker confronted more formidable problems. In 1862, he was assigned there to replace Andrew Talty, who had just died. For much of the war, the town was occupied by the Union Army. Becker himself was definitely a Confederate sympathizer and, according to a popular legend in Martinsburg, actually aided one of Colonel John Singleton Mosby's raids on the Union stores in the town. When the Union troops strung a rope from the church to a house across the road to unseat Mosby's cavalrymen, Becker supposedly cut it at the last minute, allowing the band to enter the town.[43]

On March 12, 1863, Becker informed the Congregation of Propaganda that he had not heard from McGill, except indirectly from people who managed to cross the battle lines from time to time. He found himself "now under one authority and then under another. Nearly all my possessions have been taken away by the military, and it is not easy to say when there will be an end to it." In Bath, Confederate forces had burned his little church. Since he now thought it "impossible for me to continue to live in this place where war is raging," he had asked Archbishop Kenrick to arrange his reassignment.[44] His situation was even more precarious than he admitted. He failed to say that he had been jailed earlier that same week for continuing prayers for Confederate authorities.

As was noted earlier, Kenrick had dropped the prayer composed by Bishop Carroll, after his recitation of it in his cathedral caused people to walk out in April 1861. McGill, however, had ordered that the prayer be continued, with the change from the civil authorities of the United States to those of the Confederacy. If nothing else, Becker was a stickler for Church authority. On March 7, 1863, he and other ministers received an order from the Union Army commander in Martinsburg to offer prayers for United States officials, under pain of imprisonment and the closing of their churches. Becker first sought the advice of Kenrick, whose consultors said Becker needed authorization from his bishop. According to Becker's account to Propaganda, Kenrick further advised him that to comply with the Union order would violate freedom of religion and proper church authority.[45] The result was that Becker was arrested, but then released on bail. The church in Martinsburg, however, remained closed.

Kenrick next intervened with Lincoln to gain Becker's freedom. While Whelan urged Kenrick publicly to protest the case, the archbishop preferred moderation. On April 7, Becker refused to obey a second order to recite prayers for the United States government. This time, he was arrested, taken to Washington, where he was briefly imprisoned in the Old Capitol Prison, and then released to the custody of Kenrick, who assigned him to St. Peter's Church in Baltimore. By that time, Kenrick informed Cardinal Alessandro Barnabò, Prefect of Propaganda, that the war originally fought to preserve the Union had become one to free the slaves, especially after Lincoln's Emancipation Proclamation on January 1, 1863. Although the Baltimore clergy remained aloof from the discussion, the Cincinnati *Catholic Telegraph,* edited by Father Edward Purcell, the archbishop's brother, tried to show the Church's opposition to slavery, but this had alienated Bishop Martin J. Spalding of Louisville. The bishops in the border states remained divided on the issue of slavery. In the meantime, Kenrick asked for "full jurisdiction in every part of Virginia when communication with the Bishop of Richmond is interrupted, and the same with the Bishop of Wheeling."[46]

CHOOSING THE ARCHBISHOP OF BALTIMORE

Kenrick, however, apparently never received the faculties he requested from Propaganda. On July 8, 1863, he died, as Becker immediately informed the Roman congregation.[47] Wartime conditions now affected the way in which a new archbishop would be chosen. It was impossible for the bishops of the province to come together or communicate their views on candidates in accordance with canon law. Kenrick had left a list of three priests, all Maryland-born, but none of the suffragans present for the funeral thought any of them had the requisites to be archbishop. Consulting Archbishops Hughes of New York and John Purcell of Cincinnati, both of whom attended the funeral, the bishops added the names of Whelan and Martin John Spalding. Whelan, as the senior suffragan, then forwarded the list to Rome, to the other suffragans who could not be present for the funeral, and to the archbishops.[48]

Later in July, McGill wrote Cardinal Barnabò that Kenrick's death was an "irreparable loss" to the whole church and particularly to the province of Baltimore. Since all the suffragans of the province could not assemble to submit names of candidates to the pope for approval, he recommended that the archdiocese be placed under an administrator until after the war was over.[49] To Lynch he added a further argument that "it will be difficult to find a successor for Abp. Kenrick, and while the province is so divided between North & South, and an uncertainty existing as to which side will have Maryland, it will be difficult to select the proper person for that important see."[50] McGill's remark about Maryland joining the Confederacy, even after the Union victory at Gettysburg earlier that month, was decidedly unrealistic but indicative of his continued support for the Southern cause.

Baltimore remained vacant for almost a year. Then, in January 1864, Archbishop Hughes of New York died. Spalding recorded in his diary the unfounded newspaper reports that the government was attempting to influence Rome in the selection of the two archbishops for New York and Baltimore. Finally, on May 6, Pius IX appointed Spalding to Baltimore and John McCloskey, bishop of Albany, to New York.[51] Although McGill had played no role in Spalding's appointment, as he had earlier in Kenrick's, the new archbishop was part of McGill's old Louisville circle. But this did not mean that their relations were always cordial.

McGill's Efforts to Visit Rome

In October 1864, McGill wrote Spalding granting him faculties for the parts of his diocese he could not reach—the substitute he devised when special faculties were not forthcoming from Propaganda to the archbishop of Baltimore. He also complained that Union forces would not permit him to go to Baltimore, so that he could go to Rome to make his *ad limina* visit to the pope.[52] On November 23, he wrote again to say that when he had earlier sought permission to go to Rome, Secretary of War Stanton "declined to allow it." He now asked Spalding to get permission for him to go to Norfolk and then to Baltimore and New York. Despite living in a city under siege, he noted in conclusion, he had completed an apologetical work, *Our Faith, The Victory,* and was seeking a publisher.[53]

In January, McGill again wrote Spalding asking him to intercede with Lincoln to allow him to go to Europe. "As I am, and have been entirely passive amid the war troubles, and have no connection with them," he continued, "although I think I see what is just and right, I had a hope they not refuse to me this privilege."[54] He enclosed for the purpose a letter to Lincoln, stating that:

> I desire this in the interests of religion, and for the benefit of my health, and I have not the slightest reason or motive connected with the politics or troubles of the day, for wishing to go. I have had no part and taken no part in these troubles, because from the day I became a priest I gave up on politics, and resolved to attend to my profession.

He did not help his plea by adding: "I do not think it right to withhold from you the avowal, that I consider there is wrong done to the south, and that it is my belief that citizens owe their allegiance to the central government through the states, but I hold it my duty as a Bishop not to be party to any movements which involve an interruption of order, and consequent strife and bloodshed."[55]

Spalding did approach James A. Hardie, inspector general of the Army and a convert to Catholicism, who promised to make inquiries at an opportune time but recommended that the archbishop make no note of this in any letter he sent McGill under a flag of truce.[56] On February 17, McGill sent Spalding a copy of *Our Faith, The Victory,* which he had just had published in Richmond and which he wanted to be distributed in the North and West. He also told Spalding to forget his previous letter, since he had found "a more direct way" of approaching Lincoln, who had given him permission to go to Europe. He, therefore, expected to be in Baltimore after Easter.[57] This prompted Spalding to reply that "I strongly incline to the opinion that you will act more prudently to remain for the present in your Diocese, & to delay your European journey to a more favorable time."[58] By Easter, of course, the war was over, and McGill would delay his trip to Rome for two more years.

PARISH LIFE IN RICHMOND DURING THE CIVIL WAR

For a city at war, Richmond went on with life as usual, judging from the announcement book for St. Peter's Cathedral. The ladies of the Altar and Sanctuary Society continued to hold their monthly meetings, and the parish held vespers and benediction every Sunday afternoon. On June 29, 1862, during the Seven Days Battle, St. Mary's Church had first communion, and later McGill administered confirmation. All seemed so ordinary, but mixed in with the announcements of banns of marriage was increasing mention of those killed in battle. The people were informed that the body of Father Ghislain Joseph Boheme, chaplain of the Eighteenth Mississippi Regiment, who had been killed at Ashland, would be brought to the church.[59] The following week, when the Union chaplains, Tissot and O'Hagan, were guests of McGill, the usual request for contributions to reduce the church debt was followed by the announcement that there would be a Mass for Boheme, who was buried in the tiny churchyard, "and for those who have fallen in the recent battles near the city." "We have cause to return thanks to God for the success of our army in the late battles," continued the announcements, but

> those who have sick or wounded soldiers at their houses are requested to send their names & numbers of regiments to Army Intelligence office Bank of Virginia. This announcement is out of our usual order, but the times are exceptional.[60]

As Christmas 1862 approached, McGill proposed "that on that day, the anniversary of the birth of our redeemer, when 'Glory to God on high and peace on earth to men of good will,' was announced, we should all pray, and offer up the holy communion to propitiate almighty God, and ask for peace, and an end of bloody battles."[61] Such pleas became more frequent, and the announcements began to reflect the increasing difficulty in procuring common items. On June 4, 1863, the feast of Corpus Christi, St. Peter's announced it would hold the Forty Hours devotion beginning the following Sunday and ending on Wednesday morning. Its purpose was

> to pray for our country and armies—for peace without more bloodshed, if it please God, or for peace through victories. It will be necessary that those who are able should send in some candles and flowers for this devotion, as we do not wish in a few days ceremony to exhaust our supply of candles.[62]

The congregation was starting to feel the pinch of wartime shortages.

While Richmond's Catholics were displaying their loyalty to the Southern cause, however, they were still subject to some residual anti-Catholicism. On March 5, 1863, Holy Thursday, a thousand women had protested in Richmond first before the governor and then before Jefferson Davis about the shortage of bread. Then they went on a rampage, sacking, as Gache told his correspondent, "the goldsmiths, the jewelers and the fancy shops," but bypassing food stores. "Protestant spitefulness," he continued, "didn't miss the opportunity to heap all of the blame for this riot on the foreign-born—that is, on the Irish and Germans, all of whom, normally, are Catholics," though, he pointed out, the riot started with meetings in both a Baptist and a Methodist church. A few days before, Petersburg had experienced similar protests, and rumors circulated that the violence would spread to Lynchburg.[63] The day after the Richmond riot, the *Examiner* had commented that the women were "prostitutes, professional, Irish and Yankee hags, gallows birds from all lands but our own."[64] Although, at the request of civil authorities, Bishop McGill sought to quell any Irish or German Catholic looters, contemporary research indicates that Catholics, native or foreign-born, played almost no role in the fracas.[65] Nativism was clearly alive even as Richmond's Catholics were dying in the war.

Although their relatives may have been maligned at home, a few months later, on July 3, some of Richmond's Catholics were marching with the First Virginia, the center of Kemper's Brigade of Pickett's Division, in the famous charge that marked the high-water mark of the Confederacy. John Dooley, promoted to captain only that morning, recorded the scene. As artillery raked the ranks of the young southerners, he found himself giving the order:

Close up! Close up the ranks when a friend falls, while his life blood bespatters your cheek or throws a film over your eyes! Dress to left or right, while the bravest of the brave are sinking to rise no more! Still onward! Capt. Hallinan has fallen and I take his place. So many men have fallen now that I find myself within a few feet of my old Captain (Norton). His men are pressing mine out of place. I ask him to give way a little to the left, and scarcely has he done so than he leaps into the air, falling prostrate. Still we press on—oh, how long it seems before we reach those blazing guns. Our men are falling faster now, for the deadly musket is at work.

Thirty yards from the guns that Pickett's Division were to capture, Dooley fell, "shot through both thighs." Lying next to another wounded officer, he longed "to know the result, the end of this fearful charge!" They heard "a new shout, and cheer after cheer rends the air." But "that huzza never broke from southern lips. Oh God! Virginia's bravest, noblest sons have perished here today and perished all in vain!" The wounded Virginian was to spend the remainder of the war as a prisoner.[66] Off to his left, another Georgetown alumnus, Brigadier General Lewis Armistead, was not so fortunate. A convert to Catholicism, he led the remnants of his brigade to the copse of trees toward which the Confederates were advancing. He no sooner penetrated the Union lines, however, than he was mortally wounded. He died in a Union hospital two days later.[67]

Back in Richmond, the congregation of St. Peter's increasingly prayed for the Confederate soldiers who died in the siege of Richmond that began in the summer of 1864.[68] In the meantime, Anthony Keiley in Petersburg was captured in April 1864 and later published his recollections, *In Vinculis; or, The Prisoner of War.* Taken before General Benjamin F. Butler, he described the former Massachusetts politician in most unflattering terms. From his "face," he wrote, "scarce an element is wanting of absolute repulsiveness."[69] But Keiley enjoyed his intellectual parrying with the general. He gave his name and profession as a lawyer but refused to say how many soldiers were then in Petersburg. Butler retorted that he already knew there were none "by this infallible induction: if there was a soldier in town, no lawyer would get into the trenches!" Keiley "joined in the smile that followed," but responded: "You speak of Northern lawyers, I presume. We have contributed our full share to this fight for freedom."[70]

As a prisoner, Keiley was first taken to Point Lookout and then to Elmira. There he heard two sermons on a Sunday, the one "a Christian discourse" by a Catholic priest, the other "one long insult to the prisoners" by "a Reverend Bainbridge, a freedom shrieker."[71] Keiley may have originally been a Union man, but he was no abolitionist. In October 1864, he was included as a nurse in the exchange of prisoners considered to be too weak to serve in the army for at least sixty days. Once home in Virginia, he witnessed the final days of the Confederacy as a member of the legislature.

Even as General Ulysses S. Grant tightened the ring around Richmond, however, parish life continued as if the war was far away. In September 1864 the Altar and Sanctuary Society and the Young Catholic Friends continued to meet, and Father Andrews opened a school for boys. Parishioners were reminded that, if they married before a Protestant minister, they incurred "excommunication reserved to the bishop."[72] In February 1865 the people received detailed rules for the Lenten fast, but were also told that, at the request of "those who have the difficult task to provide supplies for the army, . . . it is of the greatest importance that each citizen should do what is in his power to contribute to this end. It is believed that many keep back articles of food for obtaining high prices, and that those even, who have no intention to sell, could spare something of what they have on hand."[73] Hoarding, the twin of scarcity in wartime, was making its impact on the Richmond Catholic community.

THE END OF THE CONFEDERACY

Father McMullen reported to a Jesuit friend on the final days of the siege of Richmond. Like so many others, he was still blind to the evil of slavery. He pitied

> the poor country people of St. Mary's [County, Maryland] on the loss of their negroes, but the case is no better here and slavery in Va is already virtually abolished. You can scarce get anything for them on the market. They are running off by dozens almost every night. The likeliest negro man will not bring $50 in gold.[74]

Gache described the actual fall of Richmond. On the night of April 2, Jefferson Davis and his cabinet fled from the city. But the

Jesuit and others were ordered to remain at the hospital "until Federal troops arrived" and then "to carry on as circumstances would permit." For three days fire spread throughout the city, but especially on April 3. Gache described the inferno and the attempts of the people to rescue belongings, gather food, or simply to observe. But what seemed to impress him the most was that "no one spoke; everywhere there was grim silence, drawn faces and a sense of hopelessness and horror. Except for an occasional exclamation from a child or from a Negro who had salvaged something from the flames, no human voice was heard." This silence was "suddenly broken again and again by the detonation of whole arsenals as the fire spread," and "then, like phantoms against the background of the burning city, the sudden appearance of the first Yankee cavalry scouts: they came galloping sword in hand and pistol in belt giving the impression, as they looked neither to the left nor to the right, that they were even more frightened than frightening."[75]

On April 9, Palm Sunday, the announcements at St. Peter's gave little clue that Richmond was an occupied city under martial law, except for a passing reference to the evening services scheduled for Holy Thursday and Good Friday, to be held if "it be permitted for persons to come out to attend service, as we hope will be the case." The ladies of the parish were then asked to help clean the church on Monday, Tuesday, and Wednesday in preparation for the sacred triduum. The only direct allusion to the fall of Richmond was the announcement that "during the fire on Monday several things were brought to the yard of this church out of the burning home of Mrs. Stanard, corner of 8th and Franklin, and afterwards taken elsewhere." Whoever took the furniture was asked to deliver it to Mrs. Stanard's new residence.[76] Just about the time the people were receiving their blessed palms, further to the south, in the tiny hamlet of Appomattox Courthouse, Robert E. Lee was surrendering to Ulysses S. Grant. The long and bloody war, the most costly in human life in the nation's history, had come to an end.

By the middle of Holy Week, General Edward Cresap Ord, commander of the Department of Virginia, arrived in Richmond. In Ord's division was Father Joseph O'Hagan, the Union chaplain Gache had met as a prisoner three years before. Gache was paroled to O'Hagan's custody, and, the next week, the two made their way to Georgetown.[77] The war had also ended for this somber Jesuit who left such a detailed chronicle of life in military hospitals.

In February, young John Dooley had been exchanged and returned to Richmond. He rejoined the army and, even after Appomattox, attempted to link up with Johnston's army in Georgia. In Charlotte, North Carolina, he and his companions gave up and decided to return home. On May 6, he arrived back in Richmond. "I shall not attempt to describe my feelings," he wrote, "the city in ruins and the hated and triumphant army of our malignant foes marching through the ruined city."[78] It was the final entry in his diary.

Dooley had echoed the sentiments of Father Abram Ryan, the poet-priest of the Confederacy. Years later, a marker would be erected in Norfolk near Ryan's boyhood home. On it is inscribed part of his poem, "C.S.A.":

> But their memories 'er shall remain for us,
> And their names, bright names, without stain for us:
> The glory they won shall not wane for us,
> In legend and lay
> Our heroes in Gray
> Shall forever live over again for us.[79]

Virginia Catholics were among those "heroes in Gray," but now they confronted Reconstruction.

McGill's Postwar Report to Rome

Shortly after the war, McGill sent a report to Rome. Writing in English, for which he received a reprimand, he recalled his unsuccessful efforts to gain Lincoln's permission to travel to Rome for his *ad limina* visit until the spring of 1865. The surrender of the Confederacy, however, meant he could visit the churches of the diocese and administer confirmation for the first time since hostilities broke out in April 1861. He now decided to postpone his visit to Rome until after the Second Plenary Council of Baltimore, scheduled for 1866. In the meantime, he gave a description of his diocese as the South entered the period of Reconstruction. Even here, his southern sympathies shone through. Only two of his churches were destroyed: "one burned at Berkeley in Bath, while occupied by Confederate soldiers; it is burned by accident; the other in the town of Winchester by federal troops used as a stable and afterwards destroyed." The church at Winchester had, as was seen, been described by the Daughters of Charity as "the poorest, poorest old stone building." The town itself, so close to the important rail center of Martinsburg, had changed hands seventy-two times during the war. The churches in Martinsburg, Fredericksburg, Warrenton, and Fairfax, McGill continued, had been damaged from being used as quarters for soldiers or as hospitals.[80] Those sections of Virginia that were in the diocese of Wheeling also experienced the results of war. At Wytheville, the Union Army sought to destroy the lead mines nearby. Though the town was severely damaged, the pastor, Joseph Heidenkamp, was credited with having intervened with the Union commander not to burn it.[81]

McGill unfortunately gave no details on the damages done to his churches, but some of them had made history in the process. The tiny church of St. Mary of Sorrow at Fairfax had been the site where Clara Barton, the foundress of the American Red Cross, nursed the wounded at the Second Battle of Manassas in 1862.[82] The church in Martinsburg, where Becker was arrested in 1863, was put to various uses depending on which army occupied the town. Though Becker was back briefly in September 1864,[83] the church itself was used as a hospital, the basement as a stable, and the sacristy as a prison. Henry Kyd Douglas, a member of Stonewall Jackson's staff, was imprisoned there for violating his parole after Appomattox because he donned his Confederate uniform to have a photograph taken. He was then accused of complicity in the assassination of Lincoln.[84]

After McGill had completed his report on the damages done to churches outside Richmond, he gave his own account of the fall of the city:

> At Richmond, during the awful conflagration, all our churches and institutions escaped injury. But most of the more wealthy Catholics here as elsewhere in the diocese, in common with all southern citizens suffered great losses, and are in greatly reduced circumstances.[85]

In this context, he also delivered his extremely negative comments on Reconstruction.[86]

McGill acknowledged that he was not sure if any of his letters got through the blockade to Rome. In one of them he had mentioned the case of Father Daniel Downey, still languishing in Staunton. He recounted for Roman officials how Downey had killed a parishioner, while "intoxicated." Having refused Downey faculties to exercise the ministry, McGill referred him to the pope, but now thought he would appeal to the forthcoming plenary council. While he had himself not seen him on his visits to Staunton, he said Downey had "conversed with the priest who attended that congregation."[87] Precisely what advice Bixio, presumably the priest attending Staunton, may have given is unknown, but Downey had not had his last word.

In the fall of 1865, McGill informed Downey in a letter no longer extant, that he could appeal to the pope for rehabilitation. On October 24, 1865, Downey retorted that, far from his needing rehabilitation,

> you and every one of your unhappy Priests who encouraged, I might add, persuaded and forced Irishmen to join the Confederate army are the gents that are wickedly guilty of murder and need Rehabilitation. The widows and orphans and the blood of too many of my slaughtered countrymen cry to Heaven against you.[88]

With this parting shot, Downey, the pioneer of Lynchburg and Staunton, disappeared from the annals of the diocese. He remained in Staunton, where he listed his occupation as an "ex-clergyman" and a teacher.[89]

McGill now had the task of piloting the diocese through Reconstruction. At least his situation was not as bad as that of Bishop Lynch, who was caught in Europe at the end of the war trying to get Pope Pius IX to recognize the Confederacy. In the final analysis, damage to Catholic churches in the diocese of Richmond was not excessive, and McGill's priests had remained at their posts, even when cut off from communication with him. Nursing sisters had done much to overcome the prejudice of southern soldiers. Of equal importance, just as in the North service in the Union Army proved Catholic, and particularly Irish, patriotism,[90] so in Virginia service in the Confederate Army launched the careers of many Catholics in the postwar years. As McGill faced the prospects of Reconstruction, however, one of his greatest responsibilities was reaching out to the newly emancipated African Americans.

PART II

Post-Reconstruction
Catholicism Takes Root

Service in the Confederate Army provided credentials for Virginia's Catholics to assume political office during Reconstruction. In 1870, Anthony Keiley was mayor of Richmond, James Dooley was in the legislature, and John W. Johnston, married to a Catholic, Niketti Floyd, was in the United States Senate. Keiley and Dooley made no secret of their Catholic faith, but they also joined the Conservative Party that had the dual purpose of enfranchising Virginians who had served in the Confederacy and of excluding the newly emancipated Blacks from office.

But the period of Reconstruction found Bishop John McGill with the task of rebuilding a diocese torn by war. With the secession of West Virginia from Virginia, parts of the diocese of Richmond were now in the new state and parts of the diocese of Wheeling remained in Virginia—a situation that prevailed until 1974. He still had the perennial problem of recruiting priests and turned to the American College at Louvain, from which would come several prominent priests, including Francis Janssens, later bishop of Natchez and archbishop of New Orleans, and Augustine van de Vyver, the first priest of the diocese of Richmond to become its bishop.

For a brief period after Reconstruction, Richmond became a stepping-stone to national prominence for its bishops. In 1872, James Gibbons succeeded McGill, but in 1877 he became archbishop of Baltimore. His successor in Richmond, John J. Keane, became the first rector of the Catholic University of America in 1888. It was probably no accident that Gibbons, the nation's only cardinal between 1886 and 1911, Keane, and Denis J. O'Connell, a priest of the diocese serving in Rome, formed the nucleus of what became known as Americanism, as they joined forces with Archbishop John Ireland of St. Paul to have the Catholic Church take a more active role in American society. They attempted, as it were, to apply the accommodating style of Virginia Catholicism on a national level.

Although Gibbons and Keane would achieve their national prominence only later, while in Richmond they did initiate work with African Americans—work that was continued by their successor, van de Vyver. Virginia was ripe for work with Blacks, so few of whom were Catholic. In 1883, the Josephites began their work in Richmond and soon expanded to Norfolk and other places. A decade later, Mother Katharine Drexel, canonized in 2000, and her sister, Mrs. Louise Morrell, opened St. Francis School for girls and St. Emma's School for boys outside Richmond. The Church in Virginia received other benefactions, notably that of Mr. and Mrs. Thomas Fortune Ryan, who built Richmond's new cathedral in 1905, and that of "Major" James Dooley, who left money to build a new orphanage for girls.

Railroads, however, continued to provide the key to the expansion of Virginia Catholicism in the late nineteenth century. Roanoke, which was a hamlet in 1880, had become the principal town in the southern Shenandoah Valley by 1890. The populations of towns in the northwestern part of the diocese, now in West Virginia, fluctuated according to the vagaries of where railroad officials established key depots. As the Church in the northeast and midwest was now settling into an urban structure, Virginia still maintained elements of a frontier experience with priests riding circuits to tend their far-flung flocks. Virginia's urbanization would have to await a world war.

Richmond's bishops during this period reflected the changing American Church. From the moment of his arrival in Virginia, Gibbons knew he was under consideration for Baltimore and lost no opportunity to prove his capacity, if not worthiness, for the position, even in the face of opposition. Keane was perhaps the most spiritual of Richmond's bishops and sought to develop the spiritual lives of both his priests and people, but he seems to have been somewhat of a micromanager. Yet both joined in the antiforeign crusade of Archbishop Ireland that ultimately divided the hierarchy and attempted to prevent the appointment of van de Vyver to Richmond. Gradually dying out was the sense of collegiality that characterized the earlier hierarchy. Van de Vyver, most likely for personal, rather than theological, reasons presaged the bishop of the future who limited his concerns to his own diocese.

CHAPTER 10

The Diocese Faces Reconstruction

During the last days of the war, Bishop McGill had published an apologetical work, which reached the booksellers probably only after Appomattox. He was, however, more concerned with rebuilding his shattered diocese as it now faced Reconstruction. For this, he would turn to a new source of clergy, the American College in Louvain. He would also be among the first Americans to attend an ecumenical council, the First Vatican Council that defined papal infallibility. During Reconstruction, moreover, Virginia's laity assumed unprecedented roles.

McGill as Apologist

McGill arranged his book, *Our Faith, The Victory,* in twenty-five chapters, beginning with the existence of God and the Trinity and ending with the final judgment and Purgatory. In 336 pages, he systematically treated the creation and fall of humanity, the nature and structure of the Church, and each of the seven sacraments. It was not original, but it reflected some of the theology commonly held at the time that would become controversial before the end of the decade at the First Vatican Council. He spoke, for example, of the "infallibility of the Church," a necessary "prerogative" if she was to fulfill her mission to teach.[1]

The pope, McGill continued, "is the head of the body of pastors, and visible head of the whole church. The Pope has not only the primacy of honour, but also of jurisdiction, or authority and power, over the whole body of bishops, and the whole visible church, . . . by divine right, and by the express institution of Jesus Christ." Papal infallibility, he acknowledged, was "not a settled point, some theologians having maintained that he [the pope] is not, while others have contended that he is infallible." Since "no decision [had] been given by the church," "persons can choose the opinion which appears to have for it the best reasons and arguments."[2]

On some issues, McGill was decidedly irenic, probably reflecting his experience of dealing with Protestants. He interpreted "out of the Church, no Salvation" to apply only to those who consciously broke the unity of the Church. A person who, through no fault of his own, he asserted, "may be really of the church by his dispositions, his good faith, and his endeavours, according to the lights and graces he has received, to do all that he thinks required of him by God. God, in his infinite mercy, will not allow such to perish, but, by means known to himself, will attract them into the way that ends in eternal life."[3] McGill was simply reflecting an American Catholic tradition that went back to John Carroll by distinguishing between membership in and communion with the Church, a distinction that some Catholics almost a century later would fail to make.

McGill seemed intent on portraying Catholic doctrine in the most positive light, without polemics. He treated the Virgin Mary in his chapter on the Incarnation, but, while listing doctrines such as the Immaculate Conception, defined in 1854, and the Assumption, not defined until 1950, he made no effort to link these Marian teachings to the theology of Christ and to the Virgin Mary as personifying the effect on humanity of the Incarnation.[4] Intending his work primarily for Catholics, he also noted "among those not of our church, there appears to be a growing disposition to become acquainted with Catholic doctrines, and to examine for themselves into the nature and grounds of our faith."[5] He sent a copy to Archbishop Spalding immediately upon its publication in besieged Richmond in February 1865, and asked assistance in having the book circulated in the north and west.[6] In September, he published a second edition with a Baltimore publisher.[7] But it was to have nowhere near the vast circulation of *The Faith of Our Fathers,* written by his successor, James Gibbons.

ADJUSTING TO RECONSTRUCTION

The days after the war required major adjustments. In May 1865, McGill agreed to allow Thomas Becker to remain in Baltimore to assist Spalding until August. The Richmond priest therefore joined the archbishop's closely-knit household, which included Gibbons, a Baltimore native ordained in 1861 and assigned to be Spalding's secretary in 1865.[8] By September, Becker had returned to Richmond, where he became pastor of the cathedral. By then, McGill told Spalding, the people of Richmond were "building up amid the ruins, but generally with inferior houses."[9]

By the middle of November, McGill had completed the first visitation of his diocese since 1861. In his report to Propaganda on the state of the diocese, he added his views on Reconstruction. The whole South, he wrote, was being devastated,

> because the radical members of the Congress, being politicians who look chiefly to their selfish interests, are seemingly throwing every obstacle they can in the way of a restoration of the Southern States, that they may retain and profit by their present power. The blacks throughout the south, having obtained their freedom though but little qualified to appreciate or use it properly, are in an unsettled condition, disturbed by the efforts of pretended friends, who, having no regard for their real welfare, desire to use them as means to accomplish their purpose which appears to be the subjection and thralldom of the Southern States. This measure, and other causes, are evidently producing bitterness between the two races here, and it is fearful to think in what terrible events it may result, as already in a few instances there have been collisions with bloodshed.[10]

While McGill remained an unreconstructed Southerner and would continue to exhibit racial prejudice, he accurately described the situation in which many of his people, deprived of the right to hold office, would later demand a voice in government.

But McGill did see some positive effects of the war. "The emancipation of the blacks," he told Propaganda, now left "the church free to exert all the influence she can to give them the knowledge of the true religion." In the past, "the unenlightened prejudices of the owners proved in most cases an insurmountable obstacle to the work of their conversion." While few African Americans in Virginia were Catholic, "now that they are free, an effort can be made to enlighten them, but how this may best [be] accomplished it is not easy to say, especially in our present destitution of priests and money."[11] Working with the freed slaves was an incentive McGill would use to recruit more priests.

McGill went on to say the war had helped "to diminish the prejudices against the church of the southern people generally, and to dispose them to hear and examine its doctrines." Throughout the "whole South," he continued, "there have been numerous conversions from non Catholics and nominal Catholics." As a primary example, he noted, without specifically mentioning the nursing sisters, that "in the many military hospitals, great numbers, who had never been baptized, solicited and received this sacrament before death."[12]

THE SECOND PLENARY COUNCIL

McGill's visitation of the diocese was part of his preparation for the Second Plenary Council, delayed from 1862 to 1866 because of the war. In April 1866, he released Becker to assist Spalding in preparation for the council that met from October 7 to 21 in the Baltimore cathedral.[13] While one purpose of the council was to show the unity of the Church in the United States after the divisive war, Spalding told Archbishop John McCloskey of New York that "it is precisely the most *urgent* duty of all to discuss the future status of the *negro*. Four million of these unfortunates are thrown upon our Charity, & they silently but eloquently appeal to us for help. It is a golden opportunity for reaping a harvest of souls, which neglected may not return."[14] McGill, of course, had expressed virtually the same sentiments in his report to Propaganda.

But McGill disagreed on the means for reaping that harvest. At the council, for example, the bishops discussed a schema, drawn up by Spalding and approved in Rome, to have an "ecclesiastical man residing in Baltimore" with jurisdiction over the newly emancipated African Americans. McGill balked at the proposal and argued that, while the city of Richmond had numerous African Americans, few were Catholic and the Daughters of Charity had ably taken care of them before the war. When Spalding pointed out Propaganda's desires on this issue, McGill responded that "the Sacred Congregation had not well understood the situation in our region, they had been badly advised by someone."[15] McGill further objected that the plan promoted "the salvation of the blacks as if they alone were derelict and neglected."[16] Bishop Augustin Verot of Savannah, who had written so forcefully on the eve of the war about the property rights of slave owners, favored the proposal and now became a staunch advocate of the freedmen.

The council rejected the proposal for a separate ecclesiastical superior for African Americans, but did pass other legislation concerning them. The bishops noted that "since we see everyday heretical men spare no labor [with African Americans], . . . it would be absolutely unfitting that we, who are the ministers and assistants of Christ the good Shepherd, desert them through sloth or lack of care."[17] But then they decided that "what should be done in different places . . . would better be left to be determined by the zeal and prudence of the Ordinaries," who could either establish separate churches for African Americans or invite them to join existing ones.[18]

The council went on to decree that "apostolic men institute missions in the places where blacks were more numerous, to which they invite people of color. . . . We exhort and entreat the ordinaries of the place and pastors of souls, that, without delay they procure the benefits of missions to blacks, who are strongly entrusted to their care."[19] Acknowledging the shortage of priests, the bishops nevertheless urged that both diocesan priests and religious orders devote themselves to this work. They further urged that, if there were any priests in Europe, "who are moved by the spirit of God and wish to be of assistance to us, we call to mind for them that the harvest here is indeed great, but the laborers are few."[20] The council also encouraged the establishment of schools and orphanages for African Americans,[21] but left it to future provincial councils to determine what was best for each region.[22]

The American bishops had not passed any earthshaking legislation for the newly emancipated African Americans. Yet McGill would support the plea to recruit priests in Europe. On other matters, however, the council expressed a theology that would soon be challenged in Rome. In its section on bishops, it stated: "Bishops, . . . agreeing and judging together with its head on earth, the Roman Pontiff, whether they are gathered in general councils, or dispersed throughout the world, are inspired from on high with a gift of inerrancy, so that their body or college can never fail in faith nor define anything against doctrine revealed by God."[23] This theology of collegiality would soon be eclipsed at the First Vatican Council, where McGill played an insignificant role.

DEALING WITH THE PRIEST SHORTAGE AND RECRUITMENT FROM LOUVAIN

Once the Second Plenary Council was over, McGill could at long last make his *ad limina* visit to Rome. More important, he used the trip to recruit priests, for his own manpower had become depleted. He had sent John Teeling away to make a retreat at the Jesuit novitiate in Frederick, Maryland, and now gave "him yet a further trial, by receiving him in my house." As he informed Spalding, "I told him I should not allow him to say Mass till by two or three months of sobriety he had shown himself to be in earnest." But Teeling had other physical problems that caused him to have "fits."[24] His place as pastor of St. Patrick's had already been taken by R. H. Andrews, a convert who had so impressed Tissot in 1862 and who had studied for ordination under Teeling in 1859.[25] His assistant was J. Ambler Weed, a former Episcopalian priest. It was probably not accidental that McGill assigned these two converts to St. Patrick's, which was so close to historic St. John's Episcopal Church. After a short period, Weed was assigned to Staunton, where the continuing presence of Daniel Downey, suspended from the priesthood since 1858, may also have induced McGill to send a native Virginian.

Having more than one priest in the same parish was a luxury in Virginia. In 1870, aside from St. Peter's Cathedral and the parishes staffed by the Jesuits and Benedictines, respectively in Alexandria and Richmond, only Norfolk and Portsmouth parishes had more than one priest.[26] Within a few years, only St. Patrick's in Richmond and the churches in Lynchburg and Staunton would also have two priests, but the latter two also served several other missions.[27] With most of its priests still serving alone on the "frontier," the diocese of Richmond had nothing like the configuration of northern dioceses.[28]

McGill could be demanding on his priests, and their lives remained rigorous. Patrick Donelan arrived from All Hallows only in March

1866, and tended Warrenton and Fredericksburg from Richmond. Within a few months, however, he died of sunstroke on the boat between Washington and Acquia Creek.[29] At the end of 1866, McGill wrote Father Barthomew Woodlock at All Hallows College that Teeling had "been useless to the diocese and to himself for years or nearly for years, and is now absent at St. Vincent's College, Pennsylvania, endeavouring to effect a reformation." Another All Hallows priest, Father John Brady, had "left the diocese in the commencement of the war in the fall of 1860 [sic], being a useless priest from the same cause."[30] Teeling, however, seems to have recovered his usefulness, as far as another bishop was concerned. By the fall of 1868, he was teaching in Whelan's seminary in Wheeling, where he had begun his priestly ministry in Virginia. He died two years later in Dubuque, Iowa.[31] It was a tragic ending for Teeling, one of the first Virginia recruits from All Hallows and founding pastor of St. Patrick's.

Still another priest who exercised the ministry in Richmond during the Civil War came to naught. Augustine McMullen, the ex-Jesuit, received faculties for over four years, until McGill removed them sometime late in 1865, "because," as he told Spalding, "I found him under the effects of drink." McGill now had scruples about whether he had proper authority to have accepted the priest in the first place, much less whether he could "again allow him to officiate, on his pledging himself to abstain from all intoxicating drinks."[32]

It was partly to recruit priests that McGill lingered in Europe after making his *ad limina* visit to Pius IX in June 1867. While he was short of manpower, he at least now had a source of some income. In April 1864, James Behan had died in Liverpool, to which he had fled during the war. In addition to sizable bequests to St. Vincent's Hospital and to the Jesuits, he left stock to fourteen dioceses, including Richmond. The total amount of the bequest was estimated to be $60,000, and McGill decided to devote his portion to seminary education. Behan had, in fact, already been paying for some students at All Hallows.[33]

At Louvain, McGill visited the American College, established in 1857 with the strong support of Martin J. Spalding, then the bishop of Louisville, to recruit and educate Belgian and other European seminarians for the American mission. By 1870, the college had sent 122 priests to the United States.[34] J. J. Pulsers, the vice-rector, later recalled that McGill had "exposed to us the unfortunate state of his

Diocese" by stating that, of his seventeen priests, fourteen were suspended for drinking or other misdemeanors. The bishop appealed to the students that "he could offer no gold or silver but only the necessary means of support." Several students responded favorably, but the rector, John De Nève, argued he could consent only if McGill would become a patron of the college by offering $1,000, the amount other American bishops were already paying for the education of seminarians in the college. Otherwise, Richmond would be taking away seminarians whose tuition was paid by other bishops. McGill agreed, but then paid only one installment. With that, Gerard van der Plas and Francis Janssens both volunteered for Richmond.[35]

Dutch-born Van der Plas was ordained for the diocese of Bois-le-Duc in 1867. In Virginia, he was assigned first to Norfolk and then to Petersburg, where he replaced Thomas Mulvey, who, as vicar general, moved temporarily to Richmond while McGill attended the First Vatican Council. In July 1870, he died of typhoid fever at the age of twenty-seven. Janssens celebrated the funeral Mass.[36]

Janssens was born in Tilburg, Holland, in 1843, and was also ordained in 1867. In Richmond, he was assigned to St. Peter's where he began a distinguished and varied career in Virginia and elsewhere in the United States. As McGill's secretary, he seems to have insisted that the bishop make a "record" of important events in the diocese, which he then copied in chronological order in a neat hand. In 1870, Augustine van de Vyver, a native of Haesdonck, Belgium, was ordained for Richmond and joined Janssens at St. Peter's. After serving in various parts of the diocese, he became Richmond's sixth bishop. These were but the first of a long series of priests from Louvain.

During the European trip, on which McGill made his first recruits at Louvain, he also visited All Hallows College in Dublin. Presenting a draft from the Society for the Propagation of the Faith, he reported that the Behan legacy would also help provide scholarships there as well.[37]

New Religious Orders of Women

McGill was responsible for other changes that would affect the future of the diocese. In September 1866, while the city still bore the scars of war, a group of Sisters of the Visitation arrived in Richmond. Their superior was Mother Mary Baptista (Amelia R. Hitzelberger, sister of Father Alexander Hitzelberger, who had served in Norfolk and Petersburg, before entering the Jesuits). They established their monastery, Monte Maria, and opened a female academy in a home McGill had purchased in 1864 for $15,000, on a piece of property fronting on the south side of Grace Street and extending from Twenty-Second to Twenty-Third Streets. Subsequently, the grounds were enlarged to extend to Franklin Street.[38] The school not only provided the education for many of Richmond's rising elite, but its monastery would also attract some of Virginia's outstanding Catholic women. At the same time, the Daughters of Charity opened a new school for girls at St. Patrick's. Two years later, Benedictine nuns from St. Mary's, Pennsylvania, arrived to teach in St. Mary's parochial school in Richmond, which had been briefly staffed by School Sisters of Notre Dame.[39]

In the meantime, McGill was also laying the groundwork for Richmond's care for the elderly. Shortly after Appomattox, he travelled to New York to baptize William Shakespeare Caldwell, a close friend of Archbishop Spalding's.[40] Caldwell would later donate his Richmond home to Gibbons, making possible the first establishment of the Little Sisters of the Poor.

The New Diocese of Wilmington and the Vicariate Apostolic of North Carolina

As McGill was working to staff his diocese after the Civil War, the bishops at the Second Plenary Council in 1866 made several proposals that would affect Richmond. They recommended a new diocese in Wilmington, Delaware, and a vicariate apostolic for North Carolina. They suggested that the diocese of Wilmington include the eastern shore of Maryland and Virginia and nominated, in order, Patrick O'Reilly, Edward Brennan, and Thomas Becker.[41] For the new vicariate apostolic, they proposed James Gibbons, in first place, followed by Matthew O'Keefe and Jeremiah Joseph O'Connell.[42] Archbishop Spalding strongly supported Becker for Wilmington, because he was an alumnus of Propaganda, and Gibbons for North Carolina. Both of these regions, he wrote, were vast missions and needed active and zealous men.[43] Both Becker and Gibbons received their appointments on March 3, 1868. On August 16, they were consecrated in the

Baltimore cathedral, Becker by Spalding, assisted by McGill and Whelan, and Gibbons by Spalding, assisted by Patrick Lynch of Charleston and Michael Domenec, C.M., of Pittsburgh.[44] Becker and Gibbons had lived together in Spalding's residence, Gibbons as the archbishop's secretary and Becker as a refugee from Virginia during the Civil War and as the archbishop's adviser in preparing for the Second Plenary Council. During the next decade, they also developed a less than friendly rivalry.

RECONSTRUCTION IN VIRGINIA AND
THE RISE OF A CATHOLIC ELITE

In the meantime, the South was still going through Reconstruction. McGill had earlier reported to Roman officials that the war had brought new respect for the Catholic Church in the South. In Virginia, at least, Reconstruction ushered in a "Catholic moment" as laymen assumed positions of leadership in politics and journalism. Anthony M. Keiley was the outstanding example. His career during the war earned him the proper credentials for politics. He had served in the army, was elected to the legislature, and had been a prisoner of war. Upon his return to Petersburg, he joined Major E. B. Branch in founding the Petersburg *News* and became its editor. Although, in general, he praised the occupying Union forces for solving the labor shortage, after he attacked the policies of Secretary of War Edwin Stanton he was imprisoned in Castle Thunder in Richmond on June 24, 1865, and his newspaper was suppressed. Released after three days, he went back to Petersburg to found a new paper, *The Daily Index.* In August, he declared his candidacy for the House of Representatives, but had to withdraw because the Radical Republicans in the United States Congress demanded that all candidates had to take the test oath of 1862. On November 1, 1865, he married Rebecca Davis, daughter of a prominent Petersburg Jewish family that had recently moved to Richmond. Father Thomas Mulvey officiated at the ceremony in his rectory, since Church law at the time did not permit mixed marriages to take place in the church. On November 21, Keiley and Branch founded a second paper, the Norfolk *Virginian,* which Keiley himself edited until April 1866, when William E. Cameron, local editor of the Petersburg *Index* moved to Norfolk to assume the position. In the summer of 1866, he was named to the House of Delegates to fill out the term of William Joynes, who had been appointed to the Virginia Court of Appeals.[45]

Keiley now moved to Richmond. By January 1867, he and Branch had sold the Norfolk *Virginian,* which would enable another Catholic, Michael Glennon, to enter the field of journalism, and the *Petersburg Daily Index.*[46] They now purchased the Richmond *Examiner* of which Keiley became editor, while serving in the legislature. In March 1867, however, Congress passed the Reconstruction Acts denying the legitimacy of the governments of the former Confederate states, which were now to be treated as conquered territories. Virginia became Military District I under General John Schofield, who sought to temper the more extreme measures of the Radical Republicans. This temporarily ended Keiley's political career, so he returned to the practice of law and sold the *Examiner.*

In December 1867, meanwhile, the Conservatives held their founding convention in Richmond. Most were prewar politicians, but they were neither old-line States' Rights Democrats nor Whigs. They were united in launching an appeal to the North to spare them from Negro rule.[47] They formed the nucleus of what emerged over the next decade as the Democratic Party in Virginia, allied with northern Republicans on business interests.

The Conservatives organized themselves into a state party in response to the constitutional convention that had assembled in Richmond a few days earlier and elected as its president Judge John C. Underwood, an antislavery man and member of the provisional government established during the war in Alexandria. Members of the convention consisted of 72 Radical Republicans, including 25 blacks, and only 33 Conservatives. The majority of the white Radicals were "carpet baggers," who had come South with the Union Army. The proposed constitution contained many beneficial clauses, such as the ratification of the Fourteenth and Fifteenth amendments and the establishment of public schools in Virginia. What offended the Conservatives, however, was the Radicals' insistence, as part of the organic law, on limiting officeholding to those who took the test oath, affirming that they had not taken any part in the rebellion, and on disenfranchising all who held civil or military office in the Confederacy. The test oath would exclude 95 percent of the white male voters from holding office, and at least 10,000 would be disenfranchised. On

April 17, 1868, the convention completed its work.[48] Opposition to the "Underwood Constitution" now further melded the Conservatives into a cohesive political party, enlisting many of Richmond's Catholics.

On June 12, 1868, Irish Conservatives met at the Odd Fellows Hall to protest the proposed constitution. On Keiley's motion, General Patrick Moore, founding captain of the Montgomery Guards and commander of the First Virginia, was elected president. The assembly then appointed vice presidents, among whom were John Higgins and James Dooley. Keiley was elected to a committee of five to draft resolutions. Dooley then addressed the meeting on the need for concerted efforts "to defeat the miserable production of twenty-four negroes, scarcely able to read their own printed work, fourteen renegade Virginians, fit associates for them, and twenty-seven scallawags, carpet-baggers, and miserable political adventurers from the North."

Keiley then submitted eight resolutions, culminating in the meeting's endorsement of the Conservative ticket. Unfortunately, Radical Republican policy now forced the Catholic Conservatives into a racist position. The first resolution read:

> That in the national struggle for the re-establishment of the lost authority of the Constitution, and in the local struggle for the maintenance of the political supremacy of the white race as a constituent portion of the people of Virginia, [Richmond citizens of Irish birth or descent] will vindicate their respect for the organic law, and their fealty to their own color by every method left them by the power and malice of their enemies.

But Keiley's fellow Irish seemed still to be on the defensive about their role in Virginia life. In the forthcoming opposition to the constitution, they said, "the good citizens of the Old Dominion may confidently rely on the unfaltering support of their Irish fellow citizens, who have never failed to stand by the side of the native children of the soil whenever her rights or interests were attacked." Calling the constitution "the fit work of a mob of angry adventurers, corrupt vagrants and ignorant negroes," Richmond's Irish called on "the Irish of America to witness the single purpose of Radicalism in the South—to plunder the whites, and use the blacks to aid them in the plundering."[49]

The exclusion of former Confederates from holding office deprived the state of seasoned politicians who could restore it to economic prosperity. But the Catholic Conservatives saw Radical Republican policy as a resurrection of the old nativism. One resolution reflected anger at the Radical Republicans' attitude toward immigrants and especially their nomination of Schuyler Colfax, "an original Know Nothing," as General Grant's vice presidential running mate.[50] Opposition to the constitution and fear of the return of nativism provided Keiley, Dooley, and a host of Richmond's Catholic elite with motivation to enter staunchly into the Conservative camp. Moreover, their strategy of showing that, though Irish, they were Virginians paid off.

In July 1869, Keiley was elected as a Conservative to the House of Delegates, probably because he could appeal to the Irish of Richmond to join the "white vote" the city leaders needed to counter the numerically superior Black population. The following year, he was one of six official representatives of the General Assembly at the funeral of Robert E. Lee. In 1870, Virginia was readmitted to the Union, but the choice of a new city council, which would choose a mayor, was disputed by the old mayor and city council appointed by the military government. When the court ordered a new election, the Conservatives put forth Keiley, who won the first of two three-year terms as mayor of Richmond. His election ended Republican rule.[51] Keiley was thus rising in Richmond society and even became a founding member of the Westmoreland Club. He asserted his Irish heritage as he moved into Conservative leadership positions, but at the same time he and Dooley made no secret of their Catholic faith.

Keiley served for several years as president of the Irish Catholic Benevolent Union and was active in other Irish organizations. In 1865, he and James Dooley were also among the founders of the St. Vincent de Paul Society at St. Peter's Cathedral, the charitable organization out of which grew Catholic Charities in the 1920s. He, Dooley, John Ahern, and John M. Higgins alternated as vice president of the association, the highest elected official.[52] On January 2, 1871, the society called for a mass meeting of Richmond's three parishes to protest the loss of papal temporal power when the forces of the Kingdom of Italy entered Rome the previous September. With McGill's approval, the meeting took place at the cathedral on January 12.[53] Keiley served as chairman of the resolutions committee condemning the Italian action and joined Dooley and Bishop McGill in denouncing the usurpation of Pius IX's authority.[54] Keiley's action cost him the post of minister to Rome in 1885, when the Kingdom of Italy declared him persona non grata. His marriage to a Jewish woman likewise caused his rejection as ambassador to the Austro-Hungarian Empire.[55] He later served on the International Court in Cairo. In 1905 he was killed by a taxi while visiting Paris.

While Anthony Keiley was moving into Richmond politics, his brother John moved to New York, where he became assistant editor of James MacMaster's *Freeman's Journal*.[56] Far from being a shortcoming in a northern city, the younger Keiley's service in the Confederate Army may have added luster to his appeal to MacMaster, who had opposed Lincoln. Another brother, Benjamin, was soon to be ordained in Richmond for the diocese of Wilmington. Nora Keiley later entered the Visitation Monastery.[57]

Anthony Keiley was not the only Virginia Catholic who began his rise to prominence through newspaper work. James A. Cowardin was one of the editors of the *Richmond Daily Dispatch*, which had the largest circulation of Richmond's newspapers—his coeditor was Henry K. Ellyson, a Baptist.[58] Perhaps more prominent was Michael Glennon. He had come to Norfolk from Ireland, had attended O'Keefe's school, and had served in the Confederate Army—he originally tried to enlist in a Virginia outfit at the age of sixteen, but ended up serving in a North Carolina regiment. When Cameron took over the editorship of the *Virginian* from Keiley, he hired Glennon as an assistant. In 1876, Glennon purchased the paper with money he borrowed from O'Keefe and became both editor and publisher of the paper until the end of the century.[59] Like Keiley, Glennon championed the Conservative cause, even though this meant sharing southern prejudices against the free Blacks and antagonizing William Lamb, Norfolk's mayor.[60] Also like Keiley, Glennon was active in the Irish Catholic Benevolent Union. Cameron, who began his career as Keiley's protégé, was, incidentally, elected governor of Virginia in 1882.

Keiley was the first Catholic to hold office in Richmond, but James Dooley held equally prominent positions. After the war, he began practicing law. In 1868, his father, Major John Dooley, died, and James took his place on the board of trustees of St. Joseph's orphanage and, in the process, also inherited his father's military title of "Major." Although he married Sallie May of Staunton, an Episcopalian, in 1869, he remained an active member of St. Peter's. In 1871, he was elected to the Virginia assembly, where he would remain until 1877.

But he soon found a more lucrative career than the practice of law. From 1881 to 1882, he was the director of both the Richmond & Danville Railroad and the Richmond & West Point Terminal Railway and Warehouse Company and later became president of the former. He also speculated in real estate and engaged in banking. In 1889, he became one of the organizers of the Seaboard Air Line Railway Company and was chairman of the company's executive committee 1900 to 1902.[61] He became one of the greatest benefactors in the diocese's history. His brother, John, in the meantime, had died at Georgetown in 1873, before being ordained to the priesthood.

The Dooley women were also active in Richmond life. Sarah, wife of John, Sr., was an officer of the Ladies' Benevolent Society of St. Peter's between 1875 and 1885. While her daughter Sarah entered the Visitation monastery, where she took the name Sister Mary Magdalen, Alice, Florence, and Josephine were involved in a wide range of charitable and civic activities, including the movement for women's suffrage.[62]

Within Richmond politics, Keiley and Dooley were not the only Catholics to emerge into positions of prominence. John M. Higgins, a liquor dealer and active member of the St. Vincent de Paul Society at St. Peter's, had tried unsuccessfully during the war to gain a seat on the city's common council. In 1870, however, he ran from Jefferson Ward as a conservative Democrat and held the seat for the next eighteen years.[63] He was later joined on the common council by Andrew Pizzini, scion of one of St. Peter's early Italian families, and later, in 1883, secretary of the committee to investigate building a new cathedral.[64]

But at least one other man with Catholic ties held prominent elected office. The same year Keiley was elected mayor of Richmond, John W. Johnston, the husband of Niketti Floyd, was elected by the assembly to the first of two terms in the United States Senate. Unfortunately, there is no extant correspondence between him and either McGill or Gibbons. While there is no evidence that he himself became a Catholic, his children were raised as Catholics, and he was buried in the cemetery of St. Mary's Church in Wytheville in 1889.[65]

As some Catholics assumed positions of leadership after Reconstruction, the Church was planning for the First Vatican Council, which Pius IX had convoked. McGill addressed both Reconstruction and the council in a letter to Archbishop John McCloskey of New

York in June 1869. He complained strongly of two New York priests, Thomas Farrell, whose brother had earlier served in Virginia, and Sylvester Malone. Both had recently caused "scandal" in Richmond, Petersburg, Norfolk, and Portsmouth. Stressing that his report was based only on what his own clergy had told him, McGill protested that the two priests had spoken:

> not only in the line of Negrophily, which seems a monomania with them, but about the Pope, the bishops and priests, the council, the infalibility [sic] of the Pope, and denounced the sending of contributions to the Pope, saying the Italians were right in their move for nationality; that money had been brought to them to send to the Pope, but they refused to take it &c &c.

For McGill, the two priests had turned the pulpit into a forum for meddling in politics, "but apart from their extravagance about the negro, their views and feelings about the Holy Father and his spiritual and temporal authority, make me fear that they will not prove reliable pastors and spiritual fathers; for if they talk among their people as they talked down here, they will do much harm."[66] By this time, however, the two priests were already well known in New York as members of a group that chancery officials dubbed the "Accademia." Among other things, they tied together sympathy for Radical Reconstruction with opposition to papal infallibility.[67]

The First Vatican Council

McGill had apparently altered his view of papal infallibility since he published *Our Faith, The Victory,* when he considered it to be only an opinion. At the First Vatican Council, which met from December 1869 to July 1870, he played a negligible role and was frequently absent from crucial votes, but he was listed among those in favor of the definition.[68] Despite his earlier love for debate, he was overshadowed by Spalding of Baltimore, who initially favored the definition but thought the time was inopportune. Of several American bishops who opposed the definition, Archbishop Peter R. Kenrick of St. Louis, who had consecrated McGill, was the most prominent and based his arguments on the writings of his brother, Francis, McGill's old friend.

In May, McGill left the council because of hemorrhaging in his eyes, but from Paris he delegated Spalding to cast his vote. He was lingering in Europe, he reported, because the "oculists" dissuaded him from making the ocean crossing until his situation had changed.[69] Bishop Whelan, incidentally, played a far larger role than McGill at the council. As a member of the minority opposed to the definition of papal infallibility, he both feared arousing hatred for the Church and held serious doubts about whether the pope could enjoy infallibility independent of the bishops.[70]

JANSSENS BEFRIENDS COLONEL MOSBY IN WARRENTON

Back in Richmond, although priests in the city now lived in a type of community, they continued to be circuit riders. Priests from the cathedral said Mass once a month in Fredericksburg, which had had a church since 1858. For almost a year, van de Vyver had charge of the mission, until November 1871 when Hugh J. McKeefry became the first resident pastor.[71] Irish-born, McKeefry had served briefly in Harpers Ferry before coming to Fredericksburg. Now he became a circuit rider to missions that included Chesterfield, Tappahannock, and Ashland. He would later recruit his brother, William, who would later also briefly serve as pastor in Fredericksburg.[72] A century later, Fredericksburg began developing into a significant town, part of the extended suburbs of Washington.

Janssens was now paying monthly visits to Warrenton, Culpepper, and Gordonsville. In Warrenton, he alternated staying in the homes of Major Rice Payne, who, with his wife, Ann America Semmes, had originally donated land for St. John's Church, Dr. John Chilton, and the most famous of them all, Colonel John Singleton Mosby, the "Gray Ghost" of Civil War fame. Mosby had been expelled from the University of Virginia and served seven months in jail for the "malicious shooting" of a student bully. Reading law on his own, he was admitted to the Albemarle County bar. In 1857, he married Pauline Clarke, a Catholic, of Franklin, Kentucky. After the war, he sent his children to Catholic schools in Washington and Montreal.[73] In Warrenton, his five sisters also lived with him. On Christmas Day, 1868, Janssens, newly arrived in Virginia, was his house guest. As the younger sisters went to a ball, the oldest, Lucy, remained behind to talk. "Until midnight," Janssens recorded, "I explained our Holy Religion, answering the questions which she put occasionally." The next morning, Lucy and the next oldest, Mary Florentine, expressed their desire to be baptized.[74] On March 28, 1869, Janssens baptized Mary Florentine, then aged nineteen, and subsequently received the remaining sisters into the Church. In December 1871, Florentine or Florence, as she was also known, entered the Daughters of Charity.[75]

Since Mosby worked for reconciliation after the war and joined the Republican Party, he had to move his family closer to Washington, for "the people of Warrenton avoided me and my family as if we were stricken with the plague. You can see then the great wrong I was doing my children to keep them there."[76] He died in Washington, and Father Leo Gill buried him next to his wife, in St. John's churchyard in Warrenton. Though Mosby never became a Catholic, a rumor persisted in the family that his daughter Ada had baptized him on his deathbed while he was unconscious.[77]

Evangelizing the Valley

While Janssens was making conversions among some of Virginia's elite, other priests were establishing a network of missions in the principal towns in the Shenandoah Valley. In Lynchburg, James McGurk also had charge of Lexington. From Staunton, Ambler Weed went to Charlottesville and Harrisonburg each month. In the northwestern part of the diocese, John J. Kain, a native of Martinsburg, had been one of Becker's students and had been ordained in Baltimore in 1866. Like his predecessors, he had charge of Martinsburg and Bath but made Harpers Ferry his headquarters. He had two assistants, Peter J. O'Keefe, brother of the Norfolk pastor, and John McVerry. Twice a month, one of them visited Winchester. In Alexandria, Peter Kroes, S.J., and Bernard Toale, S.J., still had charge of Fairfax Station. In submitting his report for publication in the *Catholic Directory*, however, McGill continued to express his Confederate sympathies. As he had earlier informed Propaganda, the church at Bath "was accidentally destroyed by fire during the war, while used as quarters by Confederate soldiers." But the church at Winchester "was destroyed during the war, chiefly by Federal soldiers, who stabled their horses in it."[78]

McGill's Last Days

McGill had been an austere but able bishop. His twenty-two years in office would be exceeded only by Peter Leo Ireton's combined tenure as coadjutor and ordinary and by Walter F. Sullivan's episcopacy. When he died in 1872, there were seventeen priests to minister to fifteen churches and fifteen mission chapels and stations. The Catholic population was estimated to be 17,000. There were eight parochial schools for boys enrolling a total of 600 and five academies for girls enrolling 800. In Richmond, girls in the schools outnumbered the boys, a situation that may have been true in other dioceses as well. Of Richmond's four parochial schools for girls, St. Peter's Cathedral had 125, St. Joseph's Academy 175, St. Patrick's Academy 200, and the German Female Academy under the Sisters of St. Benedict at St. Mary's 40. St. Mary's had also opened a high school with an enrollment of 30 girls and 30 boys. The Academy of the Visitation had a total of 51 boarders and day students. In contrast, St. Peter's parochial school for boys, which met in the basement of the church, had 80 students, St. Patrick's 75, and St. Mary's 75. In Norfolk, the situation was reversed. St Mary's Academy for girls had 60 students, but the boys' school had 80. St. John's Seminary under the direction of O'Keefe and his assistant, John Doherty, had one student in philosophy and six in theology. In Alexandria, the Sisters of the Holy Cross conducted St. Mary's Academy with 93 students and a parish school with 70.[79]

McGill had won the respect of the people of Virginia with his support of the Confederacy and states' rights. He had weathered the storm of the Civil War and Reconstruction. If he was sometimes harsh in dealing with Irish priests, he still recruited priests from All Hallows, but also turned to the American College, Louvain. In personality, he seems to have been a man without ambition. With his lawyer's mind, he enjoyed verbal sparring in the press with the best of his adversaries. But he left no doubt who was in charge. Whatever happened between him and Timothy O'Brien, the effect was clear—O'Brien had to leave. Yet Matthew O'Keefe seemed to have the same type of personality as O'Brien and was left alone.

From the time of the First Vatican Council, McGill's health was clearly failing. On January 14, 1872, he died at the age of sixty-two. He was buried in St. Peter's, but his body was transferred to Sacred Heart Cathedral in 1961, as will be seen below, in one of the last displays of

Richmond's Confederate sympathies. At his funeral on January 16, Spalding, Frederick Wood of Philadelphia, Lynch, Becker, and Gibbons were in attendance. Gibbons had just gone home to North Carolina, when he received a telegram summoning him back to Richmond. McGill had not appointed an administrator for the diocese. After Gibbons's departure, Spalding, with the approval of the remainder of the bishops present, appointed Gibbons. They thus passed over both Mulvey in Petersburg, who was vicar general of the diocese, and Janssens, McGill's secretary. Shortly after McGill's funeral, Becker wrote Cardinal Barnabò and was careful to note that the deceased bishop had sent him to Rome for study. He now proposed that Gibbons be transferred to Richmond while retaining administration of North Carolina. "Piu degno non v'e [there is no one more worthy]," he commented,[80] a sentiment he was not to utter again. But several months would pass before Rome made its decision. There seemed to be some underlying tensions about the general qualities of the Richmond clergy.

CHAPTER 11

James Gibbons,
Fourth Bishop of Richmond,
1872–1877

James Gibbons was the administrator of the diocese of Richmond from January to July, 1872. After McGill's funeral, Bishop Becker accompanied Archbishop Spalding back to Baltimore, where he remained as Spalding's secretary. On February 6, the archbishop dictated a letter for Becker to send to Cardinal Barnabò, the prefect of Propaganda, supporting Gibbons's nomination for Richmond. Spalding had appointed Gibbons as administrator, he said, because no Richmond priest had both the knowledge and aptitude for the post, no one would be as acceptable to both the people and clergy, and the vicariate of North Carolina was close enough to Richmond that Gibbons could fill both offices.[1] Spalding clearly implied that none of the Irish-born veterans in the diocese, such as Matthew O'Keefe in Norfolk, were suitable to be bishop, and the newcomers from Louvain were too young. Becker enclosed a letter of his own endorsing Gibbons.[2] The next day, Spalding died. The Holy See now had to deal with filling vacancies in two dioceses in the Baltimore province, and the problems with each were intertwined. The death of two bishops within a week of one another, moreover, created a side issue that, in retrospect, pointed out the problems of the Virginia mode of holding church property.

On May 29, 1866, McGill had written his will, leaving everything to Spalding and his heirs. If the archbishop predeceased McGill, then everything was to go to Bishop Whelan of Wheeling.[3] Spalding, therefore, became McGill's heir. With his death, his successors inherited his property. Unfortunately, the archbishops of Baltimore apparently forgot to deed the Richmond property back to the bishop of Richmond until 1924![4]

GIBBONS CHOSEN AS RICHMOND'S FOURTH BISHOP

The Baltimore succession was less complicated than that of Richmond, but it brought to the surface some of the tension that would divide the American hierarchy over the next two decades. In November 1868, Spalding had originally drawn up the required list of his suggested successors. In first place, he named James Roosevelt Bayley, bishop of Newark, a convert and nephew of Elizabeth Seton, followed in order by Gibbons and William Henry Elder, bishop of Natchez. His candidates were all American-born. On August 24, 1869, he added a note that he thought Gibbons would be more acceptable to both the people and clergy and would be zealous in administering the archdiocese. Finally, on January 20, 1872, right after McGill's death, he further added that, if the Holy See appointed Gibbons to Richmond, he would then put Becker in second or third place for Baltimore.[5] As early as 1872, therefore, Becker and Gibbons were both contenders to be archbishop of Baltimore. Becker, of course, was then Spalding's amanuensis. He would also be the secretary of the meeting of the other suffragan bishops after the archbishop's funeral. After all, he was Roman-trained and could communicate in Italian to the prefect of Propaganda.

The suffragans altered Spalding's list. They retained Bayley in first place, but followed him with Patrick Lynch of Charleston and Elder. Conveying this decision to Rome, Becker noted that Bishop Augustine Verot of St. Augustine had not attended the meeting and that Archbishop John McCloskey of New York advised that Verot's opinion be sought. Becker, however, thought this would cause too much delay. In the meantime, he informed Propaganda that the bishops unanimously recommended Gibbons for Richmond.[6]

When the bishops of the province were surveyed about the two vacancies, their opinions varied. Gibbons favored Bayley for Baltimore, because he was Spalding's own choice. If Rome should reject him, however, Gibbons preferred either Elder or Frederick Wood of Philadelphia.[7] Whelan urged the appointment of Elder, who was a

Baltimore native. He also recommended Gibbons for Richmond, commenting that Gibbons had said he wanted to retain the vicariate of North Carolina.[8] All the candidates for Baltimore, except Lynch, were natives of the United States. Perhaps for that reason, Whelan did not take as much interest in this succession as he had in 1850. Other suffragans, however, gave more detailed evaluations.

Ignatius Persico, O.F.M., Cap., bishop of Savannah, submitted separate letters for Baltimore and Richmond. An Italian missionary bishop, who would soon return to Rome to take up various curial and diplomatic posts and be named a cardinal in 1893, he voiced about Baltimore several of the concerns that Roman authorities had about the American Church. He stressed the importance of Baltimore in preventing abuses from creeping into a nation where religion had so rapidly progressed. "There is danger," he wrote, "that Americanism, or rather the spirit of independence peculiar to Americans," will "invade the ecclesiastical sphere," for even the clergy might embrace "this people's mode of seeing and acting shaped as it were by fascination and apparently heterogeneous elements." Baltimore was so important, he continued, that it was, "in a word, the Rome of the United States." His own choice was Bayley, who was in the United States what Henry Edward Manning, the convert archbishop of Westminster, was in England. Gibbons and Becker were both too young to be archbishop of Baltimore, he continued, "and in my opinion they do not have the qualities required for such a position." Returning to the *terna* submitted by the suffragans, he rejected Lynch because of "the part he played in the recent political movement of this country."[9] Persico had virtually outlined the Roman fears of the American Catholic character that would surface when Gibbons later became archbishop of Baltimore.

In regard to Richmond, Persico pointed out that, instead of the three candidates, required by American canon law, the bishops had nominated only Gibbons. Should the Holy See decide not to accept Gibbons's nomination, Persico proposed Matthew O'Keefe and Father Frederick Wayrich, C.Ss.R., then working in Baltimore. He wrote in particularly glowing terms of O'Keefe for having founded a school, a hospital, and seminary and giving life to the Church in Norfolk.[10]

The final suffragan to give his opinion on the successions to Baltimore and Richmond was the unpredictable Verot of St. Augustine. Mentioning his absence from Spalding's funeral, he gave the nod to either Bayley or Elder, but thought Lynch should be excluded. He urged, however, that Gibbons remain as vicar apostolic of North Carolina and not be transferred to Richmond, because "change of persons is harmful to public usefulness. Since the above mentioned Vicar is the founder of the church of North Carolina, it is fitting that he continue to labor in the same place."[11]

In July 1872, the Congregation of Propaganda met to consider the succession to both dioceses. Reporting that North Carolina contained only 1,400 Catholics and quoting from Spalding's letter that no one was more qualified than Gibbons, the *ponenza* or position paper also mentioned that Persico had written positively about O'Keefe. In the meantime, Whelan had also petitioned the congregation to realign the diocesan lines to coincide with the new state lines brought about by the secession of West Virginia from Virginia. The cardinal presenting the material, however, thought it better to wait for the appointment of a new archbishop in Baltimore to get more precise information. The cardinals then submitted the names of Bayley and Gibbons, respectively for Baltimore and Richmond.[12]

Gibbons had had the support of all the suffragans, except Verot. His transfer to Richmond was probably strengthened by the ardent support of Richmond's first Roman alumnus, Bishop Becker, who may have had his own eye on the nation's oldest see. As bishop of Richmond, Gibbons retained the vicariate apostolic of North Carolina. When he was consecrated bishop in 1868, he had just turned thirty-four. At the First Vatican Council, he was the youngest bishop present and would be the last surviving participant. Richmond now received the most prominent bishop in its history, albeit the one with the shortest tenure, aside from Kelly. Hardly had he arrived in Richmond, however, than Archbishop Bayley began suggesting him as his coadjutor, and Gibbons did everything in his power to present himself as an apt candidate.

On October 20, 1872, Archbishop Bayley installed Gibbons as Richmond's fourth bishop, and Becker celebrated the Mass. It was a symbolic ceremony with the two contenders to be Bayley's successor both at this moment displaying public harmony. In attendance were about thirty-five priests. Gibbons then preached in words that he would echo throughout his episcopal career and that may have caused Persico to express his alarm. Many "enemies of the Church," he declared, had stated:

that the submission of the Catholic laity to their pastors was forced and servile, and that their loyalty to their Church would melt away amid the free air of America. The Catholics of the United States have triumphantly repelled, by their acts, the insulting insinuation. As there are none more loyal than they to their country, so there are none more devoted to their Church.[13]

Congratulations came from every level of Virginia society, including one from Sister Mary Charles Weed, a Richmond convert and then the superior of the Ursuline Convent in Tuscaloosa, Alabama. Her brother, Father Ambler Weed, had recently died in Staunton.[14]

Gibbons's Central Administration

Gibbons had a vast territory to administer, a total of 34,808 square miles in his two jurisdictions of the diocese of Richmond and North Carolina. In North Carolina, he had assigned Father Lawrence O'Connell to be vicar general. In Virginia, Catholics numbered only 17,000 out of a total population of 1,225,163. Richmond's population was then 51,038, including 23,110 African Americans. Only two other Virginia cities numbered more than 10,000, Norfolk with 19,229 and Alexandria with 13,570.[15] In addition, O'Keefe and his assistant tended a tiny church in Northampton on Virginia's eastern shore that technically belonged to the diocese of Wilmington.[16] The new bishop would initiate work with African Americans and increase the number of schools. But, like his predecessors, he continued to have problems with priests and, of course, with finances.

Gibbons retained Thomas Mulvey as his vicar general, but the last surviving member of the original group of All Hallows priests died later the same year. Gibbons now appointed Francis Janssens as both his chancellor and vicar general. It was a wise choice. Gibbons was the first bishop of Richmond to keep a detailed diary of his activities in both Virginia and North Carolina. Janssens had earlier put McGill's often rambling reminiscences into order in a diocesan diary. He now transcribed into it the sections of Gibbons's diary pertaining to Richmond. The Dutch priest would become Gibbons's right-hand man; yet the new bishop was decidedly opposed to having his men educated in Europe, with one exception.

Gibbons Americanizes Seminary Education

A little more than a year after coming to Richmond, Gibbons ordained Benjamin J. Keiley, brother of the former mayor, Anthony M. Keiley. For reasons unknown, however, the first Virginia native both to be ordained in Richmond and to receive a Roman education was ordained not for Richmond but for Wilmington, where Becker was bishop.[17] He was one of the younger children Anthony had told to walk out of Mass if Mulvey ever preached a distasteful sermon. After serving in the Confederate Army, he entered the seminary at St. Charles College, Ellicott City, Maryland, and continued his studies at the American College in Rome. But there was one recruit Gibbons sent to Rome.

When Gibbons was transferred to Richmond, he attached to the diocese the most promising seminarian for North Carolina. Denis J. O'Connell had been born in Donoughmore, County Cork, Ireland, but was brought as a young boy to Columbia, South Carolina, where his three priest-uncles, Joseph, Lawrence, and Jeremiah, were already working. At the end of the Civil War, the family migrated to a farm outside Charlotte, North Carolina, and Denis began studying for the priesthood at St. Charles College in 1868, the year Gibbons was named vicar apostolic. The bishop and student became fast friends, solidified by Gibbons's relations especially with Lawrence O'Connell. In the fall of 1872, Gibbons sent Denis to the American College in Rome to study for Richmond.[18] O'Connell would play a major role in Gibbons's life and in the future of the diocese of Richmond.

Just as Gibbons was sending O'Connell off to Rome, he received into the Church a young convert, John Bannister Tabb, a native of the Richmond area and a Confederate veteran. While a prisoner at Point Lookout, he formed a lifelong friendship with the Catholic musician and poet Sydney Lanier. After Tabb's release, he went to Baltimore and fell under the influence of Alfred Curtis, an Episcopal minister, who later entered the Catholic Church and became the bishop of Wilmington. After teaching English at Racine College in Michigan, Tabb returned to Richmond. In November 1872, shortly after entering the Church, he began his studies for the priesthood at St. Charles College. From 1875 to 1877, he was back in Richmond, teaching at St. Peter's school, part of the program Gibbons had designed for at least some of his future priests, who would teach for two years before beginning the study of theology. In 1875, Canon Peter L. Benoit, an English visitor, recorded that Gibbons thought this would make them "more manly, . . . more tried & with a fresh relish for their higher studies." He sympathized with the policy, for Richmond, "like many others, has suffered much from discarded European priests, coming & causing scandal. He is educating youths born here. But he speaks in the highest terms of the Belgian & Dutch Priests." In particular, Benoit praised Janssens, van de Vyver, who was about to go to Harpers Ferry, and John L. Tiernan.[19] Only in 1884, however, was Tabb ordained for Richmond. He spent most of his priestly life teaching at St. Charles College outside Baltimore and developing a reputation as an able if not extraordinary poet.[20]

Gibbons demanded that his seminarians write him regularly about their progress. Failure to do so could bring a strong reprimand, merited even by his favorite, Denis O'Connell.[21] He may have initiated this practice from his first days in Richmond, when he was not really certain where some students for the diocese were studying. In September 1872, he asked Father William Fortune, president of All Hallows College, how many students were studying for Richmond. In the future, he said, he preferred to send over American students rather than accept Irish ones who did not know the country.[22] He even said at one point that he had such an ample supply of priests that he did not need Fortune to choose any more.[23]

One reason for Gibbons's vacillation on recruiting students from the Irish institution was his personal preference for his own Sulpician training at St. Charles College and St. Mary's Seminary in Baltimore. For him, this provided the decidedly American education he thought necessary. O'Keefe, meanwhile, was still operating his seminary in Norfolk, where, on April 25, 1873, Gibbons ordained Patrick J. Hasty and John J. Reilly to the priesthood. Two days earlier, he had also conferred minor orders on John L. Tiernan, whom Benoit would later praise, and two others.[24] In June 1874, Gibbons ordained Tiernan with eleven Jesuits at Woodstock College outside Baltimore.[25] O'Keefe now closed his major seminary but continued to run St. John's preparatory seminary.

In 1877, the final year Gibbons was in Richmond, the official report stated that students for the diocese were at St. Mary's in Baltimore, St. Charles College, and in Rome.[26] There was no mention of either Louvain or All Hallows.

O'KEEFE AND GIBBONS AS APOLOGISTS

In the meantime, both O'Keefe and Gibbons were gaining reputations as apologists. From July to October, 1873, O'Keefe had been engaged in an exchange of public letters with J. D. Blackwell, pastor of the Cumberland Street Methodist Episcopal Church in Norfolk. The debate ensued when Blackwell published a letter in the *Christian Advocate* of Richmond challenging, among other doctrines, the Catholic belief in the real presence of Christ in the Eucharist. In his letter, he specifically mentioned O'Keefe, who then readily took up the cudgels of a frequently sarcastic debate that took place in the pages of the *Norfolk Virginian,* Michael Glennon's newspaper. When it was over, O'Keefe published a book, *The Key to True Christianity.* It contained his own letters, with major selections of Blackwell's, to which he added other letters he had published in the *Norfolk Virginian* a year before, and a refutation of O. S. Barten, pastor of Christ Church, Norfolk, who had charged that Catholics "adored" the Blessed Virgin.[27] With the book's publication early in 1874, Thomas Foley, the coadjutor bishop of Chicago, predicted that O'Keefe would "get a miter in the proximate Baltimore council."[28]

O'Keefe, in the meantime, was continuing to make his presence felt in Norfolk in other ways. Not only had he funded Glennon's purchase of the *Norfolk Virginian* and thus provided a Catholic platform to influence the city, on May 19, 1875, he officiated at the marriage of Mary Pinckney Hardy, daughter of a cotton merchant, and Captain Arthur MacArthur, U.S.A. Supposedly, George Armstrong, pastor of the First Presbyterian Church and O'Keefe's friend from the yellow fever epidemic, refused to have the marriage of a Virginia woman and a Yankee officer. "Pinky's" two brothers, both graduates of the Virginia Military Institute who fought under Lee, likewise refused to attend.[29] Accepted by the Hardy family, O'Keefe had no difficulty in presiding at the marriage of two Protestants, whose son, Douglas, would be one of the most famous generals in American history.

In the meantime, shortly after O'Keefe engaged Blackwell in debate, Gibbons too had to enter into public discussion. In May 1874, Thomas Atkinson, the Episcopal bishop of North Carolina, gave a lecture in Wilmington, N.C., in which he attacked the Catholic doctrine of the sacrament of penance and charged the confessional itself was immoral. He also asserted the moral superiority of Protestant over Catholic countries. Gibbons responded with *The Sacrament of*

Penance and the Moral Influence of Sacramental Confession. Showing the origins of the sacrament from Scripture, he argued for the psychological value of private confessions. He then lined up statistics to refute Atkinson's argument that Catholic countries had more crime and immorality.[30] O'Keefe, who was then under consideration for the miter Foley had predicted, congratulated Gibbons from Montreal, where he was making a retreat.[31] But Gibbons's most famous work was yet to come.

In November 1876, Gibbons published *Faith of Our Fathers.* As he explained in the preface, it was basically a compilation of "the instructions and discourses delivered by him before mixed congregations in Virginia and North Carolina."[32] Aiding him at least in the literary style was Tabb, teaching at the cathedral school for boys. Gibbons then submitted the manuscript for theological scrutiny to Father Camillus Mazzella, S.J., at Woodstock College. By March of 1879, 50,000 copies had been sold, and translations were being made into German and Spanish.[33]

Gibbons's approach to his topics reflected the irenic style of his preaching, often in Protestant churches, in Virginia and North Carolina. He introduced the topic of infallibility, for example, by speaking of the infallibility of the Church, so essential in the postapostolic age to determine the canonical books of Scripture. He then proceeded to analyze "the Primacy of Peter" and "the Supremacy of the Popes," before treating papal infallibility itself. Gibbons's diary is sprinkled with frequent references to the occasions when he preached or lectured on this topic. In *Faith of Our Fathers,* he made it clear infallibility applied only to those instances when the pope acted "in his official capacity, when he judges of faith and morals as Head of the Church."[34] He, therefore, made it clear that papal infallibility did "not in any way trespass on civil authority." The pope, moreover, was "not the maker of the Divine law; he is only its expounder. . . . The Holy Father has no more authority than you or I to break one iota of the Scripture, and he is equally with us the servant of the Divine law."[35]

To illustrate his point, Gibbons drew the analogy between the pope and the Supreme Court in interpreting the "constitution":

> The revealed Word of God is the constitution of the Church. This is the *Magna Charta* of our Christian liberties. The Pope is the official guardian of our religious constitution, as the Chief Justice is the guardian of our civil constitution.[36]

Gibbons had a relatively balanced view of papal prerogatives, but he illustrated how far his ecclesiology deviated from that of his predecessors. He denied that the supreme "tribunal" of the Church could be either a "General Council" or "the Bishops scattered throughout the world," for it was necessary that there be an authority to act quickly to prevent "the poison of error" from spreading in the Church.[37] Gone were the days when American bishops envisioned infallibility enjoyed by the "college of bishops."

GIBBONS AND HIS PROBLEM PRIESTS: VIRGINIA AND NORTH CAROLINA

While Gibbons was defending the Catholic faith and recruiting more priests, particularly from the United States, he experienced some of the same difficulties with priests already in the diocese that had plagued his predecessors. As had frequently happened in the past, one place of tension was Martinsburg. John J. Kain had been assigned there soon after his ordination in 1866, but sometime in 1872 he was released to preach missions around the diocese. Father Peter J. O'Keefe, Matthew's brother, was then assigned to Martinsburg. Initially, he seemed to do well, but unlike his talented brother he seems to have been an incompetent and imprudent administrator. He had grandiose designs for a school but then ran the place into debt, possibly as a result of the panic of 1873.[38] Early in 1874, his difficulties made Gibbons curtail a tour of his North Carolina missions and return to Virginia. He withdrew O'Keefe's "faculties for very urgent reasons," and added the comment: "I think his mind is impaired & that he is hardly responsible for his acts." In an understaffed diocese, the removal of one priest upset the delicate balance of manpower; Gibbons now had temporarily to reshuffle his other priests between Richmond, Martinsburg, and Warrenton.[39]

O'Keefe's situation now became intertwined with the rising tension between Bishop Becker and Gibbons and may have contributed to the developing alienation between Gibbons and Matthew O'Keefe. At Peter O'Keefe's request, Becker wrote Gibbons, who remained adamant that O'Keefe should find another diocese. Then Becker wrote Matthew O'Keefe stating that in Peter's "serious trouble . . . may readily hinge his and your good name." Urging Matthew to intervene with Gibbons, the bishop argued: "You may be the means of preventing much scandal, which you certainly are obliged to hinder, if you can."[40]

O'Keefe was annoyed at the implication that his own reputation depended on that of his brother. Forwarding Becker's letter to Gibbons, he then informed Becker of his long-strained relations with his brother. With a touch of sarcasm, he added: "I cannot forbear expressing . . . my surprise at the unexpected interest manifested by your Lordship in any one so nearly allied to myself than poor Peter, & for him, & his part in the matter, I am deeply grateful." Such an intervention had overcome the "alienation" he had experienced from the bishop, so he now sent him a copy of his published debate with Blackwell.[41]

Becker forwarded O'Keefe's letter to Gibbons with the comment: "I plead guilty to the charge of writing to the Rev. M. O'K certainly not in the spirit of bravado by any means, and yet it has been so paraphrased by him. I refuse to comment on his note, but I enclose it to you for inspection." While Becker had previously urged that Matthew O'Keefe intercede with Gibbons on Peter's behalf, now he said Peter was "always an enormous and thoughtless fabricator of stories [as] I always knew from the time he came to Richd." Still believing Peter had not "committed enormities," he agreed with Gibbons's decision that he should seek another diocese. "That he will crop up again is, I fear, too probable," he said, "so that a very far off land wd be the best for him."[42]

Matthew O'Keefe, at this point, was a candidate to be bishop of Wheeling, the possibility of which may have shaped his attitude toward his disaffected brother. To Gibbons, he wrote: "I have only to say that I have always appreciated your extreme delicacy towards me as regards him & I *assure you I am deeply grateful*." "From my heart," he asserted, "I deplore the day that I ever took steps towards preparing him for the Priesthood."[43]

While Peter O'Keefe's difficulties seemed to have been financial, other priests presented greater problems. In April 1874, Gibbons had removed Father J. V. McNamara as pastor in Raleigh, North Carolina, and replaced him with Father Mark Gross, whose brother William was the bishop of Savannah. But McNamara did not give up easily. He first appealed to James MacMaster, editor of the New York *Freeman's Journal,* who had long campaigned for priests' rights.[44] He then refused to surrender the keys to the church and asked the mayor to arrest the parishioner who gave Gross a duplicate key. The immediate occasion for his difficulties occurred when Gibbons reversed McNamara's decision not to allow his parish to hold a ball on St. Patrick's Day, for fear of the scandal it would cause. But the congregation had a long list of other grievances against him, ranging from his abolishing Sunday school to holding only Sunday Mass during Lent. When Gibbons went to Raleigh to install Gross, McNamara "had the hardihood to sit in the sanctuary . . . during late Mass, & attempted to speak after I had preached, but I forbade him, & had an officer in court to arrest him, if he disturbed the congregation." The next Sunday, Gross reported McNamara had attended Mass from the sacristy, but had made no disturbance. But the priest then telegraphed Gibbons that he was appealing his sentence to the Holy See, so the bishop himself then wrote Cardinal Alessandro Franchi, the new prefect of Propaganda.[45]

Gibbons's friend, Bishop Thomas Foley, coadjutor of Chicago, told him how he handled such appeals to Rome. McNamara, he said, had every right to appeal to Rome, which would await Gibbons's report before hearing the case. He himself had two similar cases—"they appealed to Rome, I received a letter from the cardinal, which I laid in my portfolio, and never answered. Rome never bothered me again."[46] Gibbons was sustained in his case against McNamara, but the priest's appeal to Rome was one of several that drew the Holy See's attention and led to a change in priestly discipline in 1878.

In April 1874, Gibbons reported to Archbishop Bayley that "I have been lately weeding my two big gardens of Virginia and N. Carolina. It is hard work while one is at it, but gives pleasure when it is done." For O'Keefe, he had "warm sympathy, as his head was more at fault than his heart," so he "procured him a subordinate & safe position in another diocese." McNamara, however, a former Vincentian, "has been a constant source of affliction to me during the four years that he was under my charge, as he had been to his former superiors." Gibbons had delayed so long in taking action only because of "the struggle that a suspension would involve."[47]

While McNamara was off the scene, in the fall of 1874, Peter O'Keefe made one last effort to be reinstated, with the support of Bishop Gross of Savannah, where he had found a "safe position." He asked Gibbons the precise charges against him.[48] Gibbons then sought the advice of Archbishop Bayley, who gave his own views on holding priests' trials. There were times when he favored "giving a refractory priest a trial," for

> it shuts his mouth so effectively but I hardly know what to advise in regard to such a fellow as O'Keefe. It is like trying a skunk for smelling bad—everybody knows it, and no one better than the skunk. If ever informata conscientia came in, it would be in such a case as this. If his scandal was public and notorious I would not give him a trial, if otherwise I would."[49]

Gibbons decided O'Keefe's case was sufficiently serious that he would not grant a trial.[50] He found his "weeds" vexatious, but the attitude he and his fellow bishops expressed toward the cases of O'Keefe and McNamara, each of them different, illustrated how bishops exercised their authority over priests.

In the meantime, Kain had returned to Martinsburg, only to be appointed bishop of Wheeling. Gibbons then sent Charles van Queckelberge, a Louvain alumnus on temporary loan from Bishop Elder, to the troubled town, where he remained until late 1877 when he was recalled to Natchez.[51] At the same time he assigned van de Vyver as resident pastor of Harpers Ferry. The Louvain alumni were serving the diocese well, but soon after he came to Richmond Gibbons faced the possible loss of Janssens.[52]

Gibbons, however, did far more than shuffle manpower around his vast diocese. In the city of Richmond, he took the first steps toward evangelization of its Black residents.

Gibbons's First Attempt to Work with African Americans

Soon after taking office, Gibbons attempted to start organized work among African Americans in Richmond, who then numbered approximately 25,000 out of a population of 60,000. To work among these people, he sought the assistance of St. Joseph's Society of the Sacred Heart for Foreign Missions, founded in 1866 by Herbert Vaughan in the London suburb of Mill Hill. In 1872, Vaughan accompanied the first four Mill Hill priests to Baltimore, which they would make their American headquarters. He then set out on a tour of the South, where he was appalled at the treatment of Blacks even by white Catholics.[53]

On February 25, 1872, Vaughan visited Richmond. After he preached in the cathedral, Gibbons showed him a lot "in the midst of Negroes." "Bp anxious to have us," Vaughan wrote, and would give him the lot, if an unidentified donor in New York would consent. During his stay, he had met "an old Negress called & looked upon by Visitation sisters as a saint. Her name is Emily I think (or Sally) has brought many to Church & got one of her relatives into the colored convent [the Oblates of Divine Providence] at Baltimore."[54]

Vaughan found "Richmond . . . one of the nicest towns in the South . . . on 7 hills like Rome it is said," but fewer than 100 Negroes were Catholic. He also learned about what he termed "Methodist politicians." Janssens told him of a recent Black convert who said he came for instructions because, in his former church, "in one meeting I asked to have religion & not politics & they turned me out at last; so I have come to see if you have politics or religion in your church."[55] Unfortunately, Vaughan could do nothing at this time for Richmond. Almost immediately upon his return to England, he was named bishop of Salford—he later became archbishop of Westminster and a cardinal. While he remained in charge of Mill Hill, he delegated much of his authority to Canon Peter L. Benoit of the Salford cathedral. This change in administration may have accounted for the delay in any further action for Richmond's African Americans.

But word of Gibbons's desire to open a school for African Americans had reached as far as Boston. Father Edward Holker Welch, S.J., scion of a wealthy Boston family, Harvard graduate, and a convert, wrote Gibbons from Boston College early in 1874. He had heard of Gibbons's intention to open a school and warmly recommended a young black woman, Jeannette E. Davis, for a position. A Catholic and graduate of a normal school, she was then teaching in Smithfield, where the school term lasted only five months, too short a time for her to earn a sufficient income. She had, moreover, run into prejudice for her religion and missed being able to attend Mass and go to confession.[56] What happened to Jeannette is unknown, but her plight showed another reason for having black Catholic schools in Virginia. Northern Protestants were already very successful in evangelizing Southern Blacks, and the few Catholics who answered the call to serve ran the risk of losing their own faith.

Over three years later, Gibbons again received an overture from Mill Hill. During a tour of the United States in 1875, Benoit visited Richmond. On Sunday, March 7, he said Mass at the Little Sisters of the Poor. But he also learned that some Catholics harbored deep prejudices. "An Irishman came to inquire about the address of the Chaplain of one of the prisons in England, where his son is," he recorded in his diary; "then referring to our Negro mission, he said: yr Rev. don't bother yourself about this bad lot—why?—because they are a thieving crew. Well, they have a soul as we—not a bit, yr. Rev. they have no souls, the blackguards." The plight of Richmond's African Americans was still deplorable, for they were "all Baptist, Methodist or nothingist," with only a few of them Catholics. After again visiting the site Gibbons had shown Vaughan, Benoit outlined a plan. The Franciscan Sisters of Mill Hill could first start schools and attract students through teaching music and showing kindness. Next, the Little Sisters should add a wing for "colored." Then, two priests could begin work. Gibbons approved and offered to defray all initial expenses.[57]

Benoit also recorded his impressions of the rest of Richmond. The Daughters of Charity, he wrote, conducted their schools and orphanage in a manner "wonderfully adapted to the wants of America" and were "ready, well trained & never causing trouble to the Bp." Gibbons he found to be "a very saintly & punctual bp, much respected by all. Full of admiration for America." In regard to American politics, he believed "the elections are peaceful periodical revolutions, Society's safety-valves." Gibbons also discussed his reservations about the Vatican Council with Benoit. He "was unhappy . . . , being afraid of a schism. Being the youngest Bp of all he did not open his mouth in public." He "was annoyed at the hot-headed French & Italians" who cut off debate since they were "unaccustomed to free parliamentary debates." He also thought the principal "deputations [to prepare topics for the council's discussions] sh'd have been composed of Bps of the principal shades, so as to have all disagreements discussed in committee, rather than in public session."[58] When Gibbons was later under consideration to become archbishop of Baltimore, his attitude toward papal infallibility was called into question. His outspoken criticism of the conduct of the council, at least with Benoit, may have been the basis for this.

Benoit left Richmond with the promise to consult the "Abbess" of the Mill Hill Franciscan Sisters about opening a school in Richmond.[59]

Back in London, however, he and the sisters' superior both agreed that the community was too new and inexperienced at this point to take on such a distant mission. Benoit now returned to another part of the plan he proposed to Gibbons—to send two priests for the Richmond work with African Americans. In the meantime, he suggested that Gibbons have two or three Daughters of Charity begin working with "the negro children in order that you may not have to embark at once into heavy expenses."[60] On June 7, Gibbons replied to Benoit's offer of two priests, promising "to pay traveling expenses & one thousand dollars a year for three years."[61] Despite Gibbons's willingness, Mill Hill apparently could not spare any priests for Richmond. The first Josephites, the American successors to Mill Hill, would not arrive in Richmond until the next decade. But Gibbons was more successful in developing other apostolates.

THE LIFE OF A MISSIONARY BISHOP
IN POSTBELLUM VIRGINIA

The extension of railroads within Virginia had made travel easier. Richmond had direct rail connections with Washington by 1867, and within five years both Norfolk and Old Point Comfort had rail connections to the west. Many priests regularly commuted by rail to visit their missions. Gibbons shared in the circuit-riding experience, but his descriptions left no doubt that it was still an ordeal.

On November, 8, 1872, Gibbons took the train from Richmond for Lynchburg at 9:30 in the morning and arrived at 8 in the evening—there was a three-hour delay due to an accident. In Lynchburg, Father J. J. McGurk and his assistant, Father Thomas Murray, not only ran a school for boys and girls, but also had charge of Lexington, which they visited once a month, and of Liberty (now Bedford) and Danville, which they attended less frequently. The trip from Lynchburg to Lexington was still an adventure. After confirming thirty-three people in Lynchburg on November 11, Gibbons and Murray took a packet boat along the canal from Lynchburg, but then had to resort to a carriage "from Thomson's Ld. to Lexington," due to "a break in the canal." On November 12, Murray said Mass in the engine house in Lexington, and Gibbons confirmed ten people. The bishop then officiated at the marriage between John B. Purcell and Olympia

Williamson in her parents' home. Always conscious of the contacts he made with Virginia society, Gibbons was careful to note that in attendance were "Gen. Custis Lee son of R. E. Lee, the officers of the Washington & Lee University & the Military Institute & a large number of the gentry & ladies of the neighborhood." Canals and railroads made travel easier than it had been when McGill first became bishop, but Virginia was still not an accommodating place for travel. At 2:00 A.M. on November 13, Gibbons took a stagecoach from Lexington to Goshen, and then a train that reached Richmond at 6:00 P.M.[62]

Although Lynchburg was still difficult to reach by rail, it was becoming a principal Catholic center. On September 14, 1879, Gibbons, then the archbishop of Baltimore, returned to dedicate a new church, now named Holy Cross. Bishop John Keane, his successor, then confirmed eighty-one people, including fifteen converts. Despite a cost of $30,000, the church was free of debt. The speaker on the occasion was Father Patrick Healy, president of Georgetown University. That Healy's mother was of mixed African ancestry and had, theoretically at least, been his father's slave, was apparently unknown to Lynchburg's Catholics.[63]

Sometimes, however, Gibbons faced dangers other than travel hazards. Early in January 1874, he had gone to Halifax in southern Virginia to preach in the courthouse. Early the next morning, he was awakened by the barking of dogs, enabling him "to hear, at first indistinctly, & soon afterwards with tolerable clearness a noise in my room, which was caused by a thief who was searching for plunder." He jumped from his bed shouting and scared the thief off. "It was fortunate I did not seize him," he recorded, "as he probably would have overpowered me."[64]

New Schools and Other Institutions

Back in Richmond, Gibbons made new educational institutions a priority. From the time of the failure of Whelan's seminary, the only education for boys in the cathedral parish took place in the church basement. While he was still in Richmond, Becker had begun subscriptions for a school. With further collections, a site was purchased at Marshall and Ninth Streets in 1870, while McGill was attending the First Vatican Council. Soon after his installation, Gibbons tried unsuccessfully to have the Christian Brothers in New York open the school in the fall of 1873.[65] He then decided to staff the school with laymen and with seminarians. On September 28, 1873, he dedicated the new school, which enrolled 187 boys within a few days. He entrusted it to the administration of Charles Van Quekelberge, on loan from Elder.[66]

Parochial schools in the United States at that time provided separate instruction for boys and girls, with religious sisters teaching only the latter. In November 1872, after learning that the Christian Brothers could not open a boys school, Gibbons consulted Archbishop John B. Purcell in Cincinnati about his experience in having sisters teach boys. "I write to the oldest & consequently the most experienced Prelate in the U. States," he said, "that he might give the benefit of his advice to the Benjamin of the Episcopate family."[67] Only in April 1875, however, did he succeed in having the Daughters of Charity agree to begin a school for both boys and girls in Petersburg, where there was already a school run by the laity.[68] On January 30, 1876, Gibbons accompanied five sisters to Petersburg, where they opened a school "with 90 children including 35 small boys, whom at my request of Mother Euphemia, they are permitted to teach."[69] At the same time, Gibbons obtained Daughters of Charity to open a school for girls in Portsmouth. In September 1875, he also received an offer from the Visitation Sisters in Abingdon in the diocese of Wheeling to open a school in Lynchburg,[70] but this he refused. During the five years of his episcopate, other parochial schools opened either under the direction of the local priest or, more frequently, of laypeople in Harrisonburg, Keyser, Staunton, Martinsburg, Lynchburg, Old Point Comfort, and Winchester.[71]

Gibbons also started other diocesan apostolates. As he was completing preparations for the Cathedral boys school, he requested that the Little Sisters of the Poor start a home for the aged in Richmond. In the fall of 1873, the assistant mother general and a companion came to inspect a building on Brooke Avenue that Gibbons intended to give them.[72] On March 30, 1874, Gibbons received from William Shakespeare Caldwell of New York the gift of a piece of property with a house at Marshall and Ninth Streets, across the street from the newly dedicated Cathedral boys school. Caldwell had purchased the property the previous year from the estate of his sister, Mrs. Dean, for $20,000. Although Gibbons originally wanted to use it for "a male orphan asylum,"[73] Caldwell preferred that the house be used by the Little Sisters of the Poor. On April 16, the General Assembly incorporated the institution for "poor, aged white persons, to be called 'St. Sophia's Home for Old People.'"[74] On October 13, 1874, the first sisters arrived to take possession of the property. "The Community numbers six members," Gibbons recorded, "of whom the Superior is Sister Virginia—very appropriately called. The other sisters are named: Srs. Angela of S. Peter, Marcian, Blanche, Teresa & Pauline la Pié." Included among the incorporators were two of Richmond's leading Catholics, Mrs. Anna Maria Cowardin and Mrs. Sara Anne Robinson.[75] Shortly before his transfer to Baltimore, Gibbons purchased a new site for the Little Sisters, "Warsaw," forming the square bound by Harvie, Main, Plum, and Floyd Streets.[76]

THE DONATION OF BELMONT ABBEY

Some of the existing parishes in Richmond were undergoing change. In May 1872, while Gibbons was still administrator, Abbot Boniface Wimmer in Latrobe informed him that he was replacing Father Leonard Meyer, the pastor of St. Mary's, with Father Benno Hegele, to ward off a potential schism. Without specifying the nature of the conflict, Wimmer took great pains to describe Hegele's new assistant, Hermann Wolfe, as a convert, the son of a Lutheran bishop, and a medical doctor. He was, moreover, a southerner, who, while residing in Missouri "sided at the time of the war with the Southern [sic]." Perhaps part of the conflict at St. Mary's was some residual pro-Confederate sympathies that Wolfe was expected to placate. Wimmer also hoped to send a brother, an Irishman, to teach in the high school and attract Richmond's Irish, who had been indifferent to the institution.[77] By 1876, the Benedictines had begun a mission at Buckner's Station, St. Boniface (the name was later changed to Immaculate Conception), where Gibbons later commented there was a "very bad spirit of clannish discontent among the Germans."[78] Whether Wolfe was intended to placate Richmond's southern sympathies, however, he was not to remain long, due to another benefaction Gibbons received.

On July 26, 1875, Gibbons had just returned from a four-week visitation of North Carolina. In Gaston County, Father Jeremiah J. O'Connell, another of Denis O'Connell's uncles, had offered him a "farm of 500 acres with stock, for the purpose of establishing in it a community of Regular Priests [members of a religious order] who would cultivate the land & evangelize the missions." O'Connell estimated the value of the property at $65,000, since it included a gold mine. After the Redemptorists refused the offer,[79] Gibbons turned to Abbot Wimmer, who appointed Wolfe as first prior of what developed into Belmont Abbey.[80] The arrival of the Benedictines in Gaston County, outside Charlotte, provided the first stable supply of clergy for Gibbons's far-flung vicariate of North Carolina. Jeremiah O'Connell, incidentally, then entered the Benedictines. His brother, Joseph, had already left North Carolina, with Gibbons's reluctant permission, to serve in Brooklyn.[81]

First Signs of Growth in Falls Church and Fairfax

The northern part of the diocese had now begun its slow development. Again, it was the railroad lines that created new communities. Early in January 1873, Dennis O'Kane, S.J., newly appointed pastor in Alexandria, reported that, while the Jesuits still took care of Fairfax Station, a new mission was developing at Falls Church. In May, Gibbons administered confirmation in Alexandria and then accompanied O'Kane to Falls Church to select a site for a new church. "The Catholics within an area of five miles from Falls Church village," Gibbons recorded, "number probably 250 souls,"[82] an estimate that seemed rather high by O'Kane's later accounts. But choice of a site led to the type of division in the community with which pastors are familiar. Some preferred a site close to the railroad depot for easy access, while others wanted a more distant piece of property available at a better price.[83]

Even while this dispute was going on, Father Charles Stonestreet, S.J., pastor of St. Aloysius in Washington promised to take up a collection in his parish and donated an altar to be used in a large hall in the Taylor family home in Falls Church, where O'Kane said Mass in September for about a hundred people from both factions. O'Kane called for cooperation and raised about $250, but one parishioner from the other faction refused to contribute.[84]

In December, O'Kane seems to have hit upon a compromise between his warring factions when the Reily family donated another lot. Money now became his principal concern. Most of the congregation, which he estimated to be one hundred, was poor, and the money for the church was coming principally from Holy Trinity in Georgetown, St. Aloysius in Washington, and St. Mary's in Alexandria.[85]

On October 18, 1874, Gibbons dedicated the first St. James Church, a simple frame structure, a substitute for the ambitious brick building O'Kane had originally planned. The building had cost $3,000, all paid for, as Gibbons happily recorded. Six hundred people gathered from Alexandria, Georgetown, Washington, and the neighborhood around Falls Church. The railroad ran a special train from Alexandria for the dedication. A Jesuit from St. Mary's would attend the church the third Sunday of each month.[86] This was the first of several buildings that the parish would occupy in West Falls Church. The village was still far removed from the hustle of Washington, which, at its best, was populous for only part of the year. The community of Falls Church, moreover, was still too poor to support itself. It relied on parishes like St. Aloysius, now in the "inner city," for funds. The same was true for Alexandria's other mission, Fairfax.

In May 1873, when Gibbons was looking at a site for St. James, he also accompanied Father Charles Cicaterri, S.J., to Fairfax to administer confirmation to twenty-one people. He estimated that there were two hundred people then in the congregation, but he may again have exaggerated.[87] But all was not well in the small community. In July, the officers of the St. Joseph Society, John R. Taylor, Patrick Cunningham, and John Mawdeley, signed a petition to Gibbons asking for Mass twice a month and complaining that the priest had failed to show up the previous Sunday.[88] Whatever the legitimacy of the complaints of the Fairfax people, they would have to settle for Mass once a month for more than a generation.

LAY ORGANIZATIONS, TEMPERANCE, AND PARISH MISSIONS

The mention of the St. Joseph Society at Fairfax is one of the rarest indications of organized lay activity in the diocese during this period. St. Peter's in Richmond had had a Sanctuary Society and St. Vincent de Paul Society since the 1860s, and places like Harpers Ferry also had sanctuary societies. In the 1840s, Daniel Downey had founded a temperance society in his early days in Lynchburg. Temperance societies continued to be popular. In December 1872, Janssens formed one for fifty members in the basement of St. Peter's Cathedral.[89] Gibbons himself spoke on temperance before non-Catholic groups in North Carolina.[90] It was one of several issues that later led to his close association with Archbishop John Ireland of St. Paul. But it was not always popular with his other episcopal friends. In 1874, Bishop Foley wrote him from Chicago: "The west is all crazy with Temperance. I am sorry in some places clergymen have courted popularity by joining in the hue and cry against liquor." "Intoxication is a sin before God—and it leads men to commit many sins," he agreed, "but it is a sin with Protestants because it is external." Too many Protestants, he thought, ignored "the crimes against the V & VI commandments," such as infanticide and "adulterous marriages . . . , because they don't manifest themselves in the streets."[91]

Gibbons himself had difficulties with other lay societies. In 1874, Father Thomas J. Wilson in Petersburg reported that the Hibernian Society had postponed its celebration of St. Patrick's Day because its members wanted to use the church for a dinner with their wives, followed by a dance. Since the society consisted of both Protestants and Catholics, Wilson approved the dinner, but said only the bishop could approve the dance, which he feared would be a cause of scandal and an occasion of sin.[92]

Gibbons's response to Wilson is not extant, but he elsewhere gave his views on another Irish organization, the Ancient Order of Hibernians, one faction of which, under the name of the "Molly Maguires," had been involved only a few years before in a series of murders in the coal-mining regions of Pennsylvania. In October 1874, Bayley had addressed Catholic societies in his cathedral and had condemned suspect secret societies. Gibbons commented:

> I was very glad you thought of giving a thrust to the secret societies, as we have one here composed largely of Catholics, which is suspected of secrecy, though it tries to wear an honest face. I allude to the ancient Order of Hibernians towards whom I am unwilling to take any *direct* hostile action, till I consult my elders, though I don't hesitate to throw as much cold water on them as I can. I wish I could freeze them quietly.[93]

Gibbons, however, would later play a major role in gaining the Hibernians' exemption from the Church's condemnation of secret societies.

While Gibbons may have been cold toward certain lay organizations, he promoted lay spirituality, especially through parish missions.[94] On April 25, 1874, he was in Winchester, where a parish mission had "been crowned with great results." The preachers of this "Catholic revival" were John J. Kain of Martinsburg and Harpers Ferry and John J. Keane of Washington.[95] Both had been classmates at St. Mary's Seminary, and the mission marked Keane's first recorded entry into Richmond's history. A few weeks later, the two priests began a mission at St. Peter's Cathedral. Starting with the First Communion of the children of the parish, each day for the next week was filled with instructions, concluding in the evening with a sermon, benediction, and confessions. The mission ended with Gibbons conferring confirmation on one hundred and thirty-three people, twenty-one of whom were converts. "Eminently successful," Gibbons commented, and "a large number of Catholics who have for years abandoned their religious duties approached the sacraments."[96]

Gibbons also commissioned religious orders to give missions. In April 1875, four Redemptorists came to Richmond, two to St. Mary's, and two to St. Patrick's. The band then spread out through Virginia and North Carolina, with one group of two going to Petersburg, Lynchburg, Lexington, Staunton, Harrisonburg, Martinsburg, and Warrenton, and the other to Norfolk, Old Point Comfort, Portsmouth in Virginia, and then New Bern, Goldsboro, Samson County, Wilmington, Charlotte, Concord, the Gaston County Mission, and Raleigh in North Carolina.[97] This Redemptorist work in North Carolina may have led Gibbons later that year to offer them the farm in Gaston County donated by Jeremiah O'Connell.

Jesuits, too, conducted a mission in Richmond. In October 1875, only a year after Kain and Keane had been there, three Jesuits began a two-week mission at St. Peter's. At its conclusion, Gibbons recorded there were 2,300 confessions and 2,000 went to communion.[98] To Bayley, he reported that "they carried out my wishes to the letter by avoiding controversy in their sermons. My little experience in this region, has convinced me that polemical discussions don't effect as much good as moral discourses interlarded with some points of doctrine."[99] Here he echoed the approach to Catholic doctrine that would make his *Faith of our Fathers* so popular. That he omitted similar instructions to the Redemptorists might be an indication that he had feared the Jesuits were too apt to engage in controversy.

Gibbons had honed his administrative ability in both North Carolina and Virginia. His episcopate witnessed the humble origins of places like Fairfax Station and Falls Church that would become wealthy centers a century later. In addition, his writing and speaking brought him national fame. But it was his friendship with many American bishops and his aptitude at handling affairs both within the American hierarchy and with Rome that led him to be transferred to Baltimore after only five years in Richmond.

CHAPTER 12

Gibbons Achieves
National Recognition

Gibbons was more involved with broader Church affairs than any other bishop of Richmond in history. His education, like that he preferred for his own seminarians, had taken place exclusively in the United States. What he lacked was experience in dealing with the Holy See. That he gained within a year of coming to Richmond when the Congregation of Propaganda threatened to take Francis Janssens away from him. He learned more about dealing with Propaganda both in participating in the nomination of bishops and in preventing a new division between Richmond and Wheeling. In each of these issues, however, he exhibited the character flaws noted by his biographer, vanity and vacillation.[1] Always on the horizon was the possibility of becoming archbishop of Baltimore, the prospect of which had arisen even before he was appointed to Richmond. In this, he would find Bishop Thomas Becker of Wilmington not always a friendly rival.

Janssens Considered as Rector
of the American College, Louvain

While Gibbons was "weeding" his gardens of undesirable priests, he had to prevent the loss of a valuable one. Francis Janssens had won wide respect since his arrival in Virginia in 1867. Late in 1872, Edmond Dumont, bishop of Tournai and former vice-rector of the

American College in Louvain, recommended to Propaganda that Janssens be named rector of that institution to replace the ailing John de Nève.[2] At the same time, Father James J. Pulsers, the acting rector, wrote to Bishop William Henry Elder of Natchez that Dumont was proposing to all the episcopal "patrons" of the college that Janssens be named rector.[3]

That Pulsers was writing to the patrons of the American College illustrated the problem Gibbons faced. When McGill first recruited seminarians from Louvain, he had agreed to become a patron at the cost of $1,000, but he paid only $250 toward that amount and owed the college money for Janssens, Gerard van der Plas, and Augustine Van de Vyver.[4] Those bishops who had contributed the full $1,000 now had a say in the choice of the new rector. Gibbons, who unknowingly inherited the debt, was excluded from the consultation, although it involved one of his most valuable priests. Bishop Becker of Wilmington, moreover, began to play a key role in attempting to gain Janssens' appointment.

On January 9, 1873, Becker informed Janssens that, at Dumont's request, he was nominating him as rector and would ask the other bishops to do the same. "I suppose," he added: "that Bp. Gibbons may object; but 'in conflictu praeceptorum praevalet fortius'; his needs are as nothing compared with the good you can accomplish yonder."[5] He also claimed to have written both Gibbons and Bayley urging that the rectorship of Louvain take priority over the needs of Richmond.[6]

Janssens had, however, already written Pulsers stating that he was too young and inexperienced for the position.[7] Gibbons also informed Pulsers that he opposed losing Janssens at that time, but would be willing at a later date if he could procure another priest from Louvain.[8] Despite Janssens' demurrer, Pulsers now told Elder that he was "very acceptable" to all the bishops polled, "except to the Bishop of Richmond who is not desirous of losing Father Janssens."[9] Gibbons was clearly in the middle and seemed to hedge his opposition to losing Janssens.

In March, Gibbons informed Elder that "the loss of this good priest will, I fear, be a serious embarrassment to me; he is my factotum." He had, however, "no hesitation in strongly recommending him for the office though I will part with him with a heavy heart."[10] In the meantime, the papal nuncio to Belgium was also urg-

ing Propaganda to appoint Janssens, but the congregation replied
that it would first have to get Archbishop Bayley's opinion.[11] By
the summer, Janssens' appointment appeared certain. Elder had
even softened Gibbons's loss by loaning him Father Charles van
Quekelberge, ordained at Louvain in 1861.[12] But the ailing Bayley
was sending mixed signals. On July 5, he told Janssens that he opposed his removal from Richmond, for a good rector could be found
in Belgium, but "it would be very difficult for Bishop Gibbons to
replace you."[13] But he then informed Propaganda that Gibbons
would agree to Janssens' appointment if another Louvain priest was
sent in his place.[14]

On August 27, the congregation informed Bayley that, though it
understood his objections to Janssens' appointment, he should consider the greater good of the American Church rather than that of
a particular mission. He should therefore forward Janssens' nomination.[15] Without waiting for Bayley's reply, the congregation appointed Janssens as rector. After several weeks, however, Janssens
rejected the offer. "I am still quite young," he wrote, "not yet thirty
years and without experience." Moreover, when he left the American
College, he wished "to devote my whole life to the missions and the
Bishop of Richmond thinks that I shall be able to do more good in
Virginia than in Louvain." Finally, he pointed out that in the previous
year both Bishop McGill and Mulvey, the vicar general, had died,
"and all the diocesan priests are young."[16] On November 18, the congregation accepted his arguments and instructed him to inform
Bayley to submit another candidate.[17]

Bayley had played a major role in preventing Janssens' appointment, sometimes by inactivity. Why Becker took such an interest in
Janssens' promotion remains unknown. If he did it to show his influence in Rome and thwart Gibbons's own chance of further promotion, he made a serious blunder. While Gibbons had not yet learned
the ropes of dealing with the Roman congregation on a major issue, he
did know how to consult his older and more experienced colleagues.
His glowing praise for Janssens, moreover, indicated that at this time
he did not think foreign birth was a detriment for service in the
American Church, a position he would change. But the arguments of
Roman officials used for appointing Janssens illustrated they did not
think the diocese of Richmond was a suitable place for a talented
priest.

GIBBONS'S INVOLVEMENT IN THE SELECTION OF BISHOPS

Gibbons's nominees for vacant dioceses within the province of Baltimore illustrated the qualities he sought in fellow bishops—and also prepared him to assume the reins of the nation's oldest see. The first diocese in which there are detailed records of his choice was Wheeling. In March 1874, Bishop Richard Whelan had paid his first visit to Richmond since he departed for Wheeling almost thirty years earlier. He had preached in St. Peter's, where he had never lived, perhaps because of his friction with Timothy O'Brien. "I hope & believe that many years will pass before you will have to name his successor," Gibbons told Bayley; "the venerable man is reverenced wherever he is known."[18] "The venerable man" was, in fact, only sixty-five years old. Years of being on the mission, however, had taken their toll. On July 7, he died in Baltimore. Three days later, he was buried in Wheeling, and Gibbons was present, together with Archbishop John B. Purcell of Cincinnati and Bishops Frederick Wood of Philadelphia and Elder.[19] Bayley was absent from Baltimore on one of his many stays in New Jersey.

Gibbons now became involved in the succession to Wheeling, only to learn of a further complication. As Bayley asked his opinion on the best way of consulting the suffragans about naming a successor, he informed Gibbons that:

> There is one point connected with this affair which it is necessary for you to know, and that is, that at the same time that I write to the suffragans in regard to Wheeling I intend to ask their consent to my requesting the Holy See to name you Coadjutor of Baltimore cum jure successionis so that you will have to keep in mind, in choosing three names for Wheeling, the probability of having soon to name a successor to the Bishop of Richmond.[20]

Upon receiving Bayley's letter, Gibbons first listed in order his candidates for Wheeling: Matthew O'Keefe, John J. Kain of Harpers Ferry, and Frederick Wayrich, C.Ss.R. of Baltimore.

Gibbons's comments on his candidates, especially O'Keefe, are interesting in light of his later attitude toward the Norfolk pastor:

> Father O'Keefe is a good financier (a desirable qualification for the diocese of Wheeling.) He is a man of extraordinary physical

endurance, & very abstemious in his habits. His moral record is above suspicion. He has also very respectable abilities. His natural sternness of character is calculated to inspire the clergy with more than affection for him. I endorse him the more willingly, as he was recommended by the late Bishop [Whelan]."

O'Keefe, moreover, had already been proposed as a possible candidate for the vicariate apostolic of North Carolina in 1866 and for the diocese of Richmond in 1872. Gibbons had also considered Kain as a candidate for North Carolina, which he had hoped to separate from his dual jurisdiction. He now placed Kain second for Wheeling because he was a "polished speaker, & is calculated to win more affection than Fr. O'K." About Wayrich he only stated that Bayley already knew him.[21]

Then Gibbons turned to the issue of the coadjutorship. "I have a grounded fear that I would not satisfy your Grace's expectations," he wrote Bayley, "& that I would not improve on closer acquaintance." The "one thing [that] would reconcile me to the marriage," he continued, was "the reasonable prospect of your long life." While he prayed that "God's will may be done," he added that "things are now thank God, in such splendid order in this diocese, that I have little trouble directing affairs." Although Gibbons was leaving the coadjutorship to "God's will," he also made it clear that he had been successful in governing his diocese—an essential qualification for a promotion.

To the archbishop whose own health constantly grew weaker, Gibbons added an account of his own strenuous travels and the reputation he was gaining nationally. At Whelan's funeral, he recounted:

> The Patriarch from Cincinnati [Purcell] was there, & was very naturally selected as the speaker. He very kindly invited me to speak, but although primed & loaded, I would not go off. On the following Sunday, I discharged my gun in Martinsburg, one of Bp. W's first missions.

On his way back from Martinsburg, he had also "dedicated a handsome church at Lexington, a Presbyterian hotbed."[22] His was a strenuous regimen indeed, and he did not even bother to tell Bayley that, on his way to Wheeling, on July 2, he had selected a site for a church in New Creek, West Virginia, and on July 5 administered confirmation in Staunton; after the funeral, he went first to Martinsburg and, on July 17, administered confirmation in Charlottesville, before dedicating the new Lexington church on July 19.[23] He obviously was a man with stamina. For the time being, however, the coadjutorship of Baltimore was put in abeyance.

In the meantime, the diocese of Wheeling was still vacant, with two priests of the diocese of Richmond as candidates. On July 30, O'Keefe sent Gibbons the "notations" necessary to fill in his official biographical sketch sent to Rome.[24] What caused the delay in filling Wheeling was the Holy See's desire, which Bayley had earlier mentioned to Gibbons, to establish new metropolitan sees. This would alter the composition of the metropolitan province of Baltimore, of which both Richmond and Wheeling were suffragans.

At last, on February 12, 1875, Propaganda issued a series of decrees on the Church in the United States. Kain was named bishop of Wheeling. Four new metropolitan sees were established: Milwaukee and Santa Fe, separated from the province of St. Louis; Boston, divided from that of New York; and Philadelphia, detached from that of Baltimore. At the same time, the United States received its first cardinal, Archbishop John McCloskey of New York.

Gibbons now illustrated the political acumen that would make him the dominant figure in the American hierarchy. On April 27, McCloskey was to receive the red biretta of a cardinal in New York, so Gibbons asked Bayley whether bishops from outside New York were expected to attend. "If duty, or even courtesy requires it," he wrote, "I shall make it my business to be present."[25] On June 17, Archbishop Wood was scheduled to be invested with the *pallium*, the sign of metropolitan authority, so Gibbons likewise queried Bayley whether it was expected that suffragans of Baltimore be present at the ceremony for their former colleague. "I should like to do him every honor in my power," Gibbons remarked.[26] He was dutifully present for both ceremonies.[27] On May 23, between the Philadelphia and New York ceremonies, he journeyed to Wheeling, where he joined Becker as a coconsecrator, with Bayley, of Kain.[28] A year before, he and Becker had performed the same function at the consecration of William Gross of Savannah.[29] While attendance at so many of these ceremonies may have merely expressed his solidarity with his fellow bishops, he was also gaining greater visibility in the American Church at large. That he and Becker were the coconsecrators on several occasions may also have represented each contending for the prize of being Bayley's successor. But, before Gibbons became archbishop of Baltimore, he had to defend the territorial integrity of Richmond.

Kain's Attempt to Realign Diocesan with State Lines

Within a year of Kain's consecration, Gibbons faced a difficulty with his former subordinate. In November 1875, Kain wrote Cardinal Alessandro Franchi, the prefect of Propaganda, proposing that the boundaries between the dioceses of Richmond and Wheeling be readjusted to coincide with the state lines. Wheeling then had seventeen counties of Virginia and part of another county; Richmond had eight counties in West Virginia. To reach some of these areas, Kain argued, it took three days by train, while they were only a day's journey from Richmond. By the same token, he continued, the West Virginia counties in the Richmond diocese were closer to him than to Gibbons. Finally, he pointed out that the states had such different laws it was difficult to administer church territory that crossed the civil boundaries.[30] Believing Gibbons would have no objection, Franchi accepted Kain's arguments.[31]

But Gibbons did have serious objections. On January 19, 1876, he protested to Bayley that neither of them had been consulted. The action, he said, would "take from Richmond its most flourishing, I might add, its only flourishing part, where I have in two years, constructed two churches, & give in return a *tabula rasa,* where there is but a handful of Catholics with a Visitation Community [in Abingdon] who are trying to escape for want of support." Determined to keep the boundaries of his diocese, he refused "to surrender its most populous Catholic territory." Whether or not he was conscious of the theological implications, he also alluded to the older collegial tradition of the American hierarchy. The boundaries between the two dioceses, he reminded Bayley, had been made at a council in 1849 with concurrence of the archbishop and his suffragans and was "more equitable than the civil division which was consummated during the war, against the wishes of Old Virginia." In regard to the argument that the two dioceses crossed over civil jurisdictions, he pointed out that other dioceses, such as Mobile and Wilmington, did not follow "civil boundaries." In refutation of Kain's argument that he was closer to the West Virginia sections of the diocese of Richmond, Gibbons appealed to geography. "The town of Martinsburg, which is the center of the Catholic population in these counties," he wrote, "is actually nearer to Richmond than to Wheeling, by 96 miles."

Gibbons further stated, erroneously, that Whelan had never asked for a realignment of the diocese, "and he occupied that See from 1850 to '74. The present Bishop is only eight months in Wheeling, being scarcely warm in his seat." This realignment, Gibbons complained, would add seventeen counties to what he already had, to give him "a territory covering 92,000 square miles—the size of all Italy." But then he vacillated. He acknowledged that the railroad gave him easier access to the Virginia counties than Kain, so he would agree to the new division, "as soon as your Grace names a Bishop for N. Carolina, which I hope, will not be long delayed." To suggest that Bayley could name a bishop to North Carolina was probably a slip of the tongue, but it did illustrate part of the mentality that Gibbons would display in regard to who should nominate bishops.

On January 25, Gibbons informed Franchi that he refused "to accede to the wishes of Bp. Kain."[32] The next day, he forwarded to Bayley a copy of Kain's letter to Franchi and of his own response to the cardinal. He also enclosed "a map of the two Dioceses, which I think will eloquently endorse the wisdom of the division made by the Fathers of the Balto. Council in 1849. It is the boundary formed by nature itself, for the boundary runs along the Alleghenies." Bayley had suggested that the bishops of the province could meet to discuss the matter after Easter, but Gibbons retorted that Kain had precluded that by referring the matter to Rome. In the meantime, he accepted Bayley's advice to retain North Carolina, especially because, as was noted, he had just received Jeremiah O'Connell's gift of a farm that became the basis for Belmont Abbey.[33] Behind Gibbons's altercation with Kain, however, was an ecclesiological issue. The bishop of Wheeling had appealed to Rome without consulting his fellow American bishops.

On February 1, Gibbons wrote to Franchi repeating some of the arguments he had used with Bayley and enclosing the map of the two dioceses.[34] On March 25, he received word that he had persuaded the congregation that "it is not expedient to make any change in the existing limits of the dioceses of Richmond & Wheeling." "Exaudivit me Deus justitiae meae! [The God of my justice has heard me]," he commented to Bayley.[35] While Gibbons was writing to Bayley and Cardinal Franchi, there is no extant evidence that he directly approached Kain, who now appeared unabashed at how Gibbons perceived his actions.

Two weeks after Franchi's decision, Kain wrote Gibbons. He provided the additional information that he would "like to renew the proposition which I once made to you, to petition the Holy See to transfer to Richmond that part of Va, which is now in this diocese." Gibbons, of course, had complained that Kain had written to Rome without any previous consultation. Perhaps in an effort to assuage Gibbons, Kain added:

> With your consent & that of the Archbp & other Bishops of the Province, I have no doubt that it [the division] could be effected. I do not care to acquire any additional territory & additional trouble; yet I see good reasons for thinking that the diocesan limits might perhaps be so defined as to correspond with the civil boundaries of the two states.

He had suggested the division, he continued, only in order to "prevent future difficulties, arising from a diversity of laws in regard to the possession & transfer of property."

As though Kain actually had before him Gibbons' arguments to Bayley and Franchi, he asserted that

> The more flourishing condition of religion at one or two points— as at Martinsburg—might form a greater difficulty in the estimation of the next incumbent in Richd than in yours. But to one who knows it, that unfortunate congregation is not an object to be much desired. My allusion to the next incumbent of Rd means no anticipation of your Lordship's early demise, but to the probability of other changes to which none will give a heartier acquiescence than myself."[36]

Kain, of course, was simply repeating the arguments he had used with Franchi, with the added reminder that the "flourishing" section was his hometown, where he had been pastor and which had always been a contentious assignment. His final remark about "other changes," however, may have indicated his desire to be on good terms with his future metropolitan, for Gibbons's appointment as coadjutor to Baltimore was by this time almost certain. When that appointment came, however, Kain did not initially give it the hearty "acquiescence" he promised.

GIBBONS BECOMES ARCHBISHOP OF BALTIMORE

While Gibbons knew he had been Bayley's choice to succeed him, the outcome in the beginning was by no means certain. On April 3, 1876, Bayley formally petitioned Cardinal Franchi for a coadjutor. He specifically recommended Gibbons, who was also favored by John Lancaster Spalding, the nephew of Archbishop Spalding, who had been named bishop of Peoria in 1875. The bishops of the province then drew up their *terna* with Gibbons first, Thomas Foley, the co-adjutor of Chicago, second, and Becker third.

Becker now began a campaign to prevent Gibbons' appointment. In September, he wrote Cardinal Franchi that Gibbons was too young and not learned enough "to occupy the primatial see of North America." Moreover, he claimed Gibbons spoke in an unorthodox manner both at Vatican I and about the Syllabus of Errors. Franchi, who drew up the *ponenza* or position paper for the Baltimore co-adjutorship, reminded the cardinals of Propaganda that Becker had made similar charges against Spalding as a candidate for Peoria. Just in case there was any doubt about Gibbons's orthodoxy, however, Franchi had consulted the Vatican archives about the bishop's role at Vatican I. If silence or theological limitation constituted orthodoxy, then Gibbons passed the test. The "note of the archive" stated that "in 1870, Monsig. Gibbons was irreprehensible. He had not signed the postulate *against* [the definition of papal infallibility]: he was always in favor; he never spoke at all." In fairness to Gibbons's theological acumen, however, it should be recalled that he had mentioned his reservations about the conduct of the council to Canon Benoit.

But Becker had proposed his own candidates for Baltimore: Foley in first place; Lynch of Charleston in second; and James Corcoran, a priest of Charleston, in third. The other suffragans of Baltimore were divided. On the one hand, Gross of Savannah thought Gibbons would be the most acceptable choice to Bayley. On the other, Kain of Wheeling shared Becker's view that Gibbons lacked sufficient knowledge for the post and proposed that, instead of a coadjutor, an auxiliary bishop be appointed for the ailing Bayley.[37] Kain, of course, may simply have been following the lead of Becker, his former schoolmaster in Martinsburg, but he would later tell Gibbons that he had in fact placed his name first.

Six of the ten archbishops also gave their opinions. Cardinal McCloskey of New York supported Gibbons and did not think Foley should be removed from Chicago. Archbishops Joseph Sadoc Alemany, O.P. of San Francisco, Peter Kenrick of St. Louis, Wood of Philadelphia, and John Williams of Boston all favored Gibbons. Purcell recommended that Gibbons be put in third place behind Bishop Sylvester N. Rosecrans of Columbus and Bishop Elder of Natchez. Elder was a Baltimore native, and Rosecrans an Ohio native and convert. Franchi noted that both were alumni of the Urban College of Propaganda in Rome, but Elder was known to be hesitant in action. The cardinal then quoted what Bayley had recently written about Gibbons: "there is no one more worthy than he; the place fits the man and the man the place." On March 7, 1877, the cardinals in a general congregation approved the nomination of Gibbons as coadjutor of Baltimore.[38]

Gibbons had the support of the majority of the archbishops, but the suffragan bishops of the province over which he would preside were clearly divided, with Becker almost hostile. This would shape the discussions for choosing Gibbons's successor as bishop of Richmond. In the meantime, he began receiving congratulations, one from a man whose personal loyalty to Gibbons was sometimes indistinguishable from his own ambition, his favorite seminarian then approaching ordination in Rome, Denis J. O'Connell. Immediately upon receiving word of Gibbons's promotion, O'Connell wrote:

> I never forget my obligations to you, and doing all that remained in my power to satisfy them I went to my Rector [Silas Chatard] the night before taking the oath [binding him to his diocese], and declaring to him my indebtedness, asked him if it were possible to bind myself directly to you instead of to the diocese. He answered no, and to satisfy me said, I could do much good in Virginia, and that you would consider no more my obligations to you, when you learn through himself your impotent debtor's readiness.[39]

O'Connell was to remain a priest of Richmond, but in the years to come he was for all practical purposes personally bound to Gibbons rather than to Richmond.

On May 26, O'Connell was ordained in Rome. The next day, he described the ceremonies for Gibbons and then continued in his usual effusive vein: "God has great designs upon you, and his finger is most strangely apparent in the course of your life. Whatever else awaits you here, the government of many cities certainly awaits you hereafter." On May 27, he and the other newly ordained priests then had an audience with Cardinal Franchi. Also present was Father Edward McGlynn of the archdiocese of New York, who was accompanying a group of American pilgrims and would later play a major part in the careers of both Gibbons and O'Connell. O'Connell described for Gibbons his conversation with Franchi:

> I told him he took away my Bishop. "How so?" he asked. "You have given him to Baltimore." "Oh! si, si," he exclaimed laughing. "Monsig. Gibbons for they all wanted him." "And cum jure successionsis too, Eminenze?" interposed Dr. McGlynn who stood near. "Yes," replied the Cardinal, "all the Bishops were in favor of him, and the people of Baltimore were most eager to obtain him." "And he is very young," added the Dr., "not much above thirty." "Thirty-four [sic; Gibbons was then forty-two]", his Eminence responded. Then Dr. McGlynn continued: "He is most amiable and learned and has written some very valuable works, especially one on the Faith." "Si, si," said the Cardinal, "lo so," (I know it) "è molto bravo."[40]

In the meantime, Janssens was visiting his family in the Netherlands, where he learned of Gibbons' appointment and of his own designation by Bayley to administer Richmond upon Gibbons's departure. He had actually heard that he himself might be named bishop, but begged Gibbons, "if you will add one more act of kindness to the many you have shown me, pray use yr influence to counteract it; the very idea of being a Bishop now frightens me, and I feel entirely incompetent for such a responsibility,—my youth, inability, foreign blood, lack of piety and many other things make me unfit for such a position."[41] These may have been the words of a humble man, but Janssens' allusion to his "foreign blood" would become a factor in later successions to Richmond.

During the spring and summer of 1877, Bayley was in Europe attempting to recover his health. There he received the official documents about Gibbons's appointment. Only on his return in August did he forward them to Gibbons. On October 3, shortly after Gibbons visited him in Newark and anointed him, Bayley died. Gibbons then automatically became the archbishop of Baltimore, before he had even finished his affairs in Richmond and North Carolina.[42]

On September 19, Gibbons had preached at St. Peter's at a Mass for the Irish Catholic Benevolent Union, then meeting in Richmond. Recalling his almost ten years of service in North Carolina and Virginia, he painted a positive picture for the visitors from other states of the relations between Catholics and Protestants in Virginia:

> unless I have very much mistaken the character and disposition of those people, I can say to you with confidence, that you will here seek in vain for social ostracism or religious animosity. Prejudices indeed there may be & are among us, but they are relegated to the private family & to the churches. You will find in the public walks of life, a broad religious toleration & a social fraternal spirit. And the friendly smile you will see before you on Richmond's face, will reflect the warm & generous feelings of Richmond's heart.[43]

The sermon was an apt summary of the relations Virginia Catholics had developed with their Protestant neighbors.

On October 14, Gibbons bade the people of Richmond farewell in a sermon at St. Peter's. Both Catholics and Protestants attended. On October 16, the priests hosted a dinner in his honor, and O'Keefe presented him with a chalice in their name. Gibbons then praised the priests of the diocese and especially of the cathedral.[44] On October 19, he departed for Baltimore. Richmond's Catholics had purchased for him a set of vestments, which unfortunately did not arrive before he left. Anthony Keiley, the former mayor, forwarded them to Gibbons with a letter stating

> Its value, were it a hundred fold greater, would feebly image the reverent respect and affectionate gratefulness with which the name of Bishop Gibbons will ever by borne in the hearts of the faithful of this city and see.

You have filled your diocese with monuments of your enlightened zeal and fervent piety; you leave it tarnished by the memory
of no scandal, and weighted by the burden of no debt; and you
bear to your new home the palm of successful labors and a faithful
duty, and the crown of a good will, genuine and universal.[45]

Keiley, of course, had seen many scandals in the diocese, so such remarks from him were high praise indeed.

There was only one dark cloud hovering over Gibbons' departure.
By this time, his relations with O'Keefe, the most senior priest in
the diocese, were strained. In May, O'Keefe had written to congratulate
Gibbons on being named coadjutor, but regretted to say that, while
he had always considered Gibbons a friend when he was in North
Carolina, he could not say the same once he became bishop of Richmond. The source of their tension arose from a conflict the priest
was having with the superior of the Daughters of Charity over fund-
raising for the orphan asylum. She had written to Gibbons, who
replied that he was ordering O'Keefe to take up a collection for the
asylum. O'Keefe bristled that "you would give a verbal order to one of
your Priests through a woman."[46] It was more than pique at receiving an episcopal order "through a woman," however, for his continuing conflict with the sisters would contribute to his departure from
Norfolk. But that was a matter for Bishop John J. Keane to handle.

Although Gibbons had been only five years in Richmond, he had
built seven new churches, bringing the total to twenty-two; he increased the number of chapels or mission stations from fifteen to
twenty-four. Despite the loss of some priests, Richmond now had
twenty-five, an increase of eight, most of whom were educated in
the United States. It was in the area of education, however, that
Gibbons left his greatest legacy. In 1872, the diocese had five female
academies and eight parochial schools for boys; in 1877, it had six
female academies and fourteen parochial schools for boys and girls.
When he went to North Carolina, he found no parochial schools; now
there were four.[47]

Gibbons had been meticulous in recording in his diary the number of people he confirmed and the percentage of those who were converts. He later estimated that in North Carolina, thirty-five percent
were converts, and in Virginia fourteen. Most of these, he noted, came
from the Episcopal Church.[48]

Before leaving Richmond, Gibbons confirmed Bayley's original appointment of Janssens as administrator of both Richmond and the vicariate apostolic of North Carolina. But he had by no means severed all relations with the priests of his former diocese. Late in the summer, Denis O'Connell had returned from Rome to take up residence in St. Peter's. When Gibbons automatically succeeded Bayley on October 3, he appointed O'Connell his procurator to obtain his *pallium* and faculties to exercise his full authority as metropolitan. O'Connell returned to Rome, from where he sent Gibbons a series of detailed reports on the Roman Curia that presaged his future career in the Eternal City. On January 22, 1878, he arrived in Baltimore, *pallium* in hand. Gibbons had originally planned an elaborate ceremony for its imposition on February 10, but decided to simplify it out of respect for the death of Pius IX on February 7, ending the longest pontificate in the Church's history.

The Church, both universal and American, was in a period of transition. Right after the cardinals in Rome had elected Leo XIII as the new pope, Gibbons had another assignment for O'Connell. Present for the imposition of the *pallium* was Bishop George Conroy of Ardagh in Ireland and temporary apostolic delegate to Canada. While in the United States for his health, he received a commission from Propaganda to tour the country and submit a report. The Americans were leery of such Roman visitors, so Gibbons appointed O'Connell to accompany the bishop around the country as far as California. One purpose of Conroy's visit was to investigate the relations between priests and bishops in light of the many appeals of priests to Rome, such as the one Peter O'Keefe threatened against Gibbons. Conroy's report was a blistering condemnation of the American bishops with few exceptions, Gibbons prominent among them. Even before receiving the report, however, Propaganda issued an instruction on clerical discipline.[49] Despite Conroy's strong criticisms of the American hierarchy, O'Connell had performed well in his task of mentoring his Irish visitor through the American countryside.

In May, O'Connell had returned to Richmond, where Janssens assigned him to St. Patrick's and the Visitation Monastery. He had not only received a Roman education but also had broader exposure to the American Church than most other priests in Richmond or elsewhere. He awaited Gibbons's next assignment, and that would come in five years. Richmond, meanwhile, awaited its new bishop.

CHAPTER 13

John J. Keane:
Richmond's Fifth Bishop,
1878–1888

Gibbons's successor, John Keane, would initially still be encumbered with the administration of North Carolina. Almost immediately, he began to organize a centralized diocesan administration. More than any of his predecessors, he concentrated on developing the spiritual life of both clergy and laity. In the process, however, he adhered to many of the approaches of Gibbons. He had no problem preaching in Protestant churches and he preferred a distinctly American education for his clergy.

CHOOSING GIBBONS'S SUCCESSOR

Before he had even left Richmond, Gibbons had summoned the suffragans of the Baltimore province to draw up a *terna* for the vacant see. They named in order: Silas Chatard, Baltimore-born, rector of the American College in Rome, and also a candidate for Vincennes; John J. Keane, a native of Ireland and at that time rector of St. Patrick's in Washington; and Henry Northrop, born in Charleston and a convert, then on loan from Charleston to North Carolina. Gibbons strongly recommended that Chatard remain in Rome, regardless of the diocese for which he was considered. If Chatard were retained in Rome, the other bishops would move Keane to first place. They also recommended a new vicar apostolic for North Carolina. On February 4, 1878, Propaganda rejected Gibbons's arguments against removing Chatard and named him to Vincennes. It then recommended Keane for Richmond.[1] In short, as far as Propaganda was concerned, Richmond was less important than the Indiana diocese.

The congregation then turned to the matter of a new vicar apostolic of North Carolina, for which Gibbons and other bishops of the province had been asking since 1876. In his final report on the vicariate, Gibbons noted that it took six months to make a visitation, but that, under his administration from 1868 to 1876, there had been an increase in the number of priests from two to eight, of churches from seven to thirteen, of mission stations from eleven to twenty-one, and Catholics from 700 to 1,700. The bishops then submitted a *terna*, consisting of Mark Stanislaus Gross, a priest of the vicariate, whose brother William was the bishop of Savannah, Northrop, and Francis Janssens, vicar general of both Richmond and the vicariate. Despite this second request for the vicariate to be separated from Richmond, Propaganda decided that Keane should first submit a report on North Carolina, to determine its future status.[2] Keane, therefore, like Gibbons before him, became both bishop of Richmond and administrator of the vicariate apostolic of North Carolina.

KEANE'S ADMINISTRATION

On August 25, 1878, John J. Keane was consecrated Richmond's fifth bishop in St. Peter's Cathedral by Archbishop Gibbons, assisted by Thomas Foley, coadjutor of Chicago, and John J. Kain of Wheeling. Born in Ireland in 1839, Keane was taken as a boy by his family first to New Brunswick, Canada, and then to Baltimore. His first official act was to reappoint Janssens as vicar general, but he soon relieved him of his responsibilities for North Carolina by appointing Lawrence O'Connell, Denis O'Connell's uncle, as vicar general for the vicariate.[3] Keane was somewhat of a micromanager. He took over from Janssens the task of maintaining the diocesan "diary." Four years later, he began annual clergy meetings to discuss a wide range of issues. He was, moreover, diligent in making annual visitations of his diocese and the vicariate, which eventually was separated from his jurisdiction.

Like Gibbons, Keane took an active part in civic affairs. In March 1879, he recorded that he was invited to open "the House of Delegates with prayer—said to be the first time in the history of Va. that a Cath.

clergyman has thus officiated."[4] He seems not to have known that John Dubois had done the same thing almost ninety years earlier. A year later, he joined with the Episcopal bishop of Virginia for a rally at Mozart Hall to raise funds for the starving people of Ireland. Anthony Keiley was the president of the meeting, and James Dooley also delivered an address. The money was to be distributed through the Catholic and Protestant archbishops of Dublin.[5] A few months later, he was invited by Protestants in Boydtown, Mecklenburg County, to preach in the courthouse on a Sunday morning and evening and the next evening. "Great impression produced, & prejudice removed," he wrote; "the first time Catholicity was ever preached in the county."[6] In October, 1881, he agreed to a request from the Yorktown Centennial Association to conduct religious services—after first seeking the advice of Gibbons and Cardinal McCloskey.[7] This type of activity, some of it later called "ecumenism," would arouse suspicion in Roman circles over the later movement known as "Americanism," in which Keane, Gibbons, and Denis O'Connell would be leaders.

But Keane came to office in a period of transition in the American Church. Roman authorities were becomng increasingly involved in American affairs. An early indication of this was a new "instruction" from the Holy See in regard to clerical discipline, which Keane received within a few weeks of his consecration.[8]

Denis O'Connell, as was already mentioned, had accompanied Bishop George Conroy on his visitation of the American Church. Although the bishop's report contained several recommendations for improving relations between priests and bishops, it is doubtful if it reached Propaganda in time to influence its decision in regard to clerical discipline. In 1878, it issued an *Instructio* on clerical trials. Rescinding the legislation that had bound the province of Baltimore since 1858 and the whole country since 1866, it decreed that every bishop, preferably in a diocesan synod, was to appoint a commission of five or at least three priests, trained in canon law, to examine the evidence in disciplinary cases, collect testimony, and interrogate witnesses in order to assist the bishop in rendering his decision. If a priest protested his removal from a mission, the bishop had to have the advice of at least three members of this commission. In the event of an appeal, the metropolitan or senior suffragan was to proceed in the same manner and his investigating commission was to have access to the records of the trial in the first instance.[9] This was the first step towards the Holy See's demand that priests be granted greater rights that would lead in 1883 to the convoking of the Third Plenary Council. But this was precisely the type of Roman intervention into the American Church that the bishops had long sought to avoid.

Keane did not convene a diocesan synod, as the instruction recommended, but early in December 1878, appointed as consultors for clerical trials Matthew O'Keefe of Norfolk, Denis O'Kane, S.J., of St. Mary's, Alexandria, Benno Hegele, O.S.B., of St. Mary's in Richmond, John Hagan of Winchester, and Thomas Kelly at St. Patrick's in Richmond. For unexplained reasons, which he would later regret, O'Keefe asked to be excused and was replaced by James McGurk of Lynchburg.[10] Keane thus attempted to have each section of his diocese represented on his commission, but he also had appointed two members of religious orders, who, as such, were not directly involved in the issues the Holy See wished to address about relations between priests and their bishops.

EDUCATION IN THE DIOCESE

One of Keane's principal endeavors was to increase the number of parochial schools, especially as Virginia began to develop public education, a result of the Reconstruction Constitution. Early in 1880, John Hagan, pastor in Winchester, proposed that he have his school, staffed by lay people, be "recognized as a public school," if this met with Keane's approval. The members of the school board were favorably disposed, and Hagan suggested using the basement of the church for the school with the provisions that the pastor would choose teachers subject to the school board's examination, have access during school hours, and choose the textbooks with the board's approval. While the school board would pay the salary of the teacher, he was willing to "give the basement gratis," for "it would be a great relief to our people to be freed from the double taxation which they would be subjected to in case we had to keep the school at our expense."

One of the major controversies in which Keane would be involved in his later career was precisely this type of arrangement between the parish and the public school board, an arrangement that Archbishop John Ireland had worked out in Minnesota. While Keane would be one of Ireland's strongest supporters, at this juncture he peremptorily wrote on Hagan's letter: "Decided agst compromise with the public school system."[11]

Back in Richmond, Keane worked to increase the availability of Catholic education. Within a year of his arrival, he sought first the Christian Brothers and then, through Gibbons, the Xaverian Brothers to open a new school for boys at the cathedral. By June 1879, Brother Alexius, the provincial and president of Mount St. Joseph's High School in Baltimore, promised to open the new school at St. Peter's Cathedral in the fall of 1881.[12]

At the end of the school year, Keane attended commencement exercises at the schools in Richmond, Petersburg, and Lynchburg, a practice that he generally followed during his years as bishop. "Great satisfaction given by condition of all our schools this year," he wrote in his diary; "the Xaverian Bros. have given special satisfaction during this their first year in charge of our boys' school, & especially in the sanctuary of the Cathedral."[13]

While Keane wanted to increase the number of parochial schools, he was equally attentive to their quality. In August 1887, at the last meeting with his clergy, he instituted "examiners of schools and school teachers." These were to assess the qualifications of any lay teacher hired by parishes in the areas of "grammar, arithmetic, and the elementary branches," unless the candidate could present other credentials. But "Religious who have been trained for the schools are exempted from the ordeal." Beginning at the end of the 1887–88 school year, the examiners were also to visit each parish and examine the children.[14] This board of examiners would gradually evolve into the office of superintendent of schools. While Keane was busy founding schools for the diocese of Richmond, however, he continued to administer the vicariate of North Carolina during the early years of his episcopate.

VICARIATE OF NORTH CAROLINA SEPARATED FROM RICHMOND

Immediately after Keane's consecration in August 1878, Gibbons had the suffragans present resubmit the same *terna* for the vicariate that he had sent to Rome the previous year—Gross, Northrop, and Janssens.[15] A few weeks later, Keane informed Cardinal Giovanni Simeoni, prefect of Propaganda, that he "found everything both in the Diocese of Richmond and the Vicariate Apostolic of North Carolina calm and prosperous." He also asked that a new vicar apostolic be appointed as soon as possible. In November, Simeoni responded that, in accordance with its decision in naming him bishop, the congregation first wanted him to submit "a special report on the state of that mission" and to consult the other bishops of the province about possible candidates for North Carolina.[16] The cardinal said nothing about the list of candidates already sent the previous August.

Keane's jurisdiction between Richmond and North Carolina necessitated that priests from elsewhere have faculties for sections of North Carolina outside his reach. In September 1878, for example, he renewed the faculties for Father Joseph Mullen in Wytheville who tended a floating congregation of Irish in Ash County, North Carolina.[17] At the same time, he gave faculties to the Jesuits in Frederick and Southern Maryland, and Jeremiah O'Sullivan in Westernport, Maryland, who frequently served in neighboring sections of the diocese of Richmond.[18]

During the summer of 1878, Mark S. Gross in Wilmington, one of the priests on the list to be vicar, described his missionary journeys in North Carolina. He reported that the aging Lawrence O'Connell, the vicar general, "makes no appearance at all before the people. He is old, feeble and without any address. My visits to Greensboro were altogether gratuitous and I may say unremunerative." He suggested that "in regard to Charlotte, if you could obtain a good English speaking priest of piety for that mission, it would be a great blessing to that languishing mission. Fr. O'Connell is a very good old man, but very inefficient."[19] Several months later, Gross suggested that the priest who visited Danville might also go to Greensboro every third month. This would enable Gross to tend to the missions closer to Wilmington.[20]

Early in 1879, as Keane continued his pleas to be freed from the burden of North Carolina, Cardinal Simeoni's only advice was to be careful in admitting priests to the vicariate who lacked the necessary qualities of a missionary.[21] In September, however, the public press announced that Gross had been named the new vicar apostolic. He had received confirmation from James McMaster, editor of the New York *Freeman's Journal,* who managed to keep his finger on the pulse of Roman affairs. Gross commented to Keane that "this call is a kind of punishment of my secret pride and presumption."[22] In this instance,

McMaster jumped the gun. In September, Propaganda had, in fact, decided that North Carolina should be withdrawn from the administration of the bishop of Richmond, but only in December did it propose Gross to Pope Leo XIII as the new vicar apostolic and then it waited until March 10, 1880, formally to notify Keane of Gross's appointment.[23]

Just when the issue seemed settled, Gross informed Keane that he had gone to Baltimore to see Gibbons, who was on the point of departing for Europe and recommended postponing Gross's consecration. Gross now felt "relieved as the reprieve has come. His Grace will explain to the Cardinal in Rome the reason of the delay. My bulls I read and the Archbishop put them in his safe." In the interim, he intended to "return home quietly next week, and attend to my humble work."[24]

Whether Gibbons had reasons other than his forthcoming trip for postponing Gross's consecration is unknown. When Gross's name had first been proposed, Propaganda received a report that he lacked sufficient theological knowledge, but Gibbons still supported him.[25] Though not yet consecrated, Gross now had the administration of North Carolina. In September 1880, however, he sent his resignation to Rome. Keane explained to Gibbons that "it seems the long delay was such a strain on his nerves that he broke down at last, and sent back his bulls." Although Gross thought he was now automatically free of the administration of the vicariate, Keane informed him "that he must retain his office . . . till Rome's reply to his resignation had been received. And so the matter stands now. I deeply regret his step,—but it is now too late to indulge in regrets, and we must await the decision of the Holy See."[26] When Rome accepted Gross's resignation, Keane again had the administration of North Carolina.

In November 1880, the suffragan bishops again assembled in Baltimore to draw up a list for North Carolina. Keane now suggested that it might be best for him to resign Richmond and take the vicariate. Should the pope accept his resignation, the bishops would then drew up a *terna* for Richmond.[27] In December, Gibbons forwarded these proposals to Propaganda. In the meantime, Janssens was named bishop of Natchez. "In consequence," Keane recorded on February 23, 1881, "I have . . . written to Rome, that it would now be seriously injurious to this See if I too were taken away, either for N.C. as I have offered, or to be coadjutor of San Francisco for which I have been recommended."[28] Rome, therefore, asked for a new list for North

Carolina. In May 1881, Gibbons submitted a second list, from which, on September 16, 1881, Propaganda selected Northrop. In January 1882, Keane and Becker joined Gibbons as Northrop's coconsecrators in Baltimore.[29] After almost a decade, the bishop of Richmond could now concentrate exclusively on his diocese.

JANSSENS APPOINTED BISHOP OF NATCHEZ

Just as Keane was being relieved of the burden of administering North Carolina, Richmond lost one of its most valuable priests, Francis Janssens, the vicar general. Independently wealthy, Janssens sometimes served without salary when the diocese was financially strained.[30] During his years in Richmond, he had drawn the attention of the hierarchy for his dedication and missionary zeal. In addition, he administered the boys school at the cathedral.

Janssens had been on the *terna* for North Carolina, and, in 1873, he was actually named rector of the American College, Louvain, but turned it down. Among his strongest supporters at that time was Bishop William Henry Elder of Natchez. In April 1880, Elder was nominated as coadjutor of both San Francisco and Cincinnati. As he awaited the decision of the Holy See, he informed Keane that he had placed Janssens first on his list of suggested successors, because Janssens' financial independence made him all the more desirous a candidate for a poor diocese.[31] The bishops of the province of New Orleans, of which Natchez was a suffragan, also placed Janssens first, followed by Henry Northrop and Nicholas Gallagher.[32] Keane described Janssens to Elder as "my right arm." He added: "he is a favorite with all the priests who know him, as far as I am aware, and is greatly loved by the people of Richmond, and of other parts of the Diocese where he has done missionary work." Elder forwarded Keane's letter to Propaganda to be included in the congregation's deliberations about Natchez.[33]

On February 15, Keane received the news that Leo XIII had named Janssens bishop of Natchez. To his diary he confided: "That see will have a model Bishop, but this See loses its right arm."[34] On May 1, Janssens was consecrated by Gibbons in St. Peter's in Richmond.[35] The ceremony, less than three years after Keane became the first bishop consecrated in Richmond, attracted the largest crowd for a Catholic event in the history of Virginia up to that time. Keane and Becker were coconsecrators. Archbishop Elder, who had become the coadjutor of Cincinnati, preached. Also in attendance were Bishops John Moore of St. Augustine, Kain of Wheeling, Gross of Savannah, and Lynch of Charleston. In the congregation were Senator John W. Johnston and Anthony Keiley, who was then the Richmond city attorney and chairman of the Virginia Democratic committee.[36] With Janssens the bishop of Natchez, Keane now chose a new vicar general, Janssens' fellow Louvain alumnus, Augustine van de Vyver, then the pastor of Harpers Ferry.[37] While Louvain had provided two successive vicars general to Richmond, Keane, like Gibbons, however, now sought to sever any relations with the American College.

SEMINARY EDUCATION

Early in 1879, James Pulsers, the vice rector, wrote him reminding him that the diocese still had paid nothing for the education of Janssens and very little for van de Vyver, Andrew Habets, Peter Coris, and van de Plas, who died soon after his arrival. The issue was that, even at this date, the bishop of Richmond still had not become a patron of the college, as McGill had promised.[38] In August, Pulsers wrote again, recounting McGill's plea for priests and his promise to become a patron. Although he knew Gibbons's preference for St. Mary's Seminary in Baltimore, he thought Keane could work out a better arrangement with Louvain. He recognized that the Sulpicians were distinguished for their discipline and "scientifical training in Paris," but Louvain was known for moral and dogmatic theology, Scripture, and liturgy. "Rome, of course, is preferable to any other place," he acknowledged, but Louvain was superior in spiritual direction, the principal function of a seminary, for "we have the help and assistance of the Jesuit Fathers."[39] When Keane apparently accused the college of careless bookkeeping, Pulsers retorted that he did not want to disagree with a bishop, but asked "the favor, if favor it be, so for myself as for my predecessors [sic], not to be accused and condemned of carelessness in keeping accounts, before being heard." Though John de Nève, the rector, "had the misfortune of becoming insane; his books however were correct." He then sent a detailed account of what the diocese owed.[40]

In the meantime, de Nève had resumed the rectorship and visited the college alumni in Virginia in April 1880. He again brought up the issue of Richmond's debts. But Keane felt that "as this Diocese has no need of continuing relations with the College & as I have no personal knowledge of the facts, I have taken no part in the matter, & leave it to whose whom it concerns."[41] For the next five years, de Nève tried unsuccessfully to have Keane fulfill McGill's promise to become a patron.

In December 1885, Keane recorded his reactions to de Nève's insistence on paying the diocesan debts. In his mind, he had no obligation, since only van de Vyver remained of the recruits from the college, and he had no intention of applying to the college in future.[42] De Nève now wrote Janssens, who thought the diocese should pay the debt. Keane himself, like Gibbons, thought that a sufficient supply of seminarians could be found in the United States and that the Sulpicians charged less. Although van de Vyver also rejected the validity of de Nève's claims, early in 1886 Keane sent Louvain the money, so that "Henceforth, therefore, the Bishop of Richmond has the privileges of a 'Patron' of the College."[43] There may, however, have been more to Keane's reaction against Louvain than annoyance at having to pay a debt or preference for an American education for his seminarians, namely, an antipathy to foreign clergy.

While Keane himself used his new status as a patron to recruit only two priests from the American College, Andrew Habets and Peter Coris, he had paved the way for his successor to resurrect the relationship with Louvain. He sent most of his seminarians to St. Mary's in Baltimore. He did however, have one burse or scholarship at the American College in Rome and one at All Hallows. During his episcopate, he assigned two seminarians to Rome, Edward M. Tearney, ordained in 1883, and W. Gaston Payne, ordained in 1886, whose parents had been the original benefactors of the church in Warrenton. Once priests were ordained, however, he continued to be concerned about their ongoing spiritual development.

ANNUAL MEETINGS OF THE CLERGY

Even before Keane held the second synod in the diocese's history, he turned the Holy Thursday gatherings of the priests for the blessing of the oils into quasi-synods, to advise him, among other things, on the selections of members for the commission on clerical discipline. Some of his concerns would seem trivial by later standards, but they provide a glimpse into Catholic practices of long ago that may have needed explanation to Catholics even of that time. At the first meeting in 1882, for example, Keane called on his clergy to replace "altar stones" that were "invalidly consecrated" because the "opening of the sepulchre" containing the relics had not been sealed with stone. He would, moreover, not consecrate any church "in which canonical confessionals have not been erected," that is, confessionals that were permanent structures with a screen between the priest and penitent.[44] A year later, Keane was still worried about the invalid altar stones, but added a new concern about having more than one "corporal . . . in each burse," for "it was morally certain that some particles of the sacred species remained in each corporal." While he was at it, he reminded the priests that Church law required "that the key of the tabernacle should be kept under lock & key beyond the reach of laity."[45] But the clergy meetings dealt with far more important issues than church furniture.

Keane was committed to the continuing intellectual and spiritual formation of his clergy. In 1882, he asked his priests to consider instituting during the next year regular clergy theological conferences to be held by regions throughout the diocese. He also recommended the establishment of a diocesan union to support "aged or disabled priests" and for the revitalization of the "Virginia Mission Union" that drew support for poorer missions from wealthier parishes.[46] The union was essential for his work in establishing black missions.

On March 22, 1883, Keane formally instituted the theological conferences which were to be held twice a year, in June and October, in Richmond for the eastern part of the diocese and in Harpers Ferry for the western—the place for the latter was later changed to Alexandria. He would himself try to attend as many of these conferences as possible. He then suggested that all pastors exchange positions during the Easter season to allow the people to have a different confessor. He also "commanded" that every parish with a resident priest and one hundred people hold the Forty Hours devotion every year, for he found this practice "always does good, and sometimes as much or even more than a mission." Far from demeaning the value of missions, however, he and his priests voted to have a diocesan-wide series of missions the next year.[47]

At subsequent meetings, Keane addressed other issues that affected the diocese. He mandated that every parish have a daily recitation of the rosary in the church and called the clergy's attention to the low collections for specific needs of the diocese.[48] But Keane also left his priests free to discuss matters among themselves. In 1885, he left the meeting to allow van de Vyver to preside over the discussion on two issues: a special collection for the orphanages and the place for the annual priests' retreat. In regard to the first, some felt that there were already too many collections, but they ultimately decided to hold a collection, not on Christmas as was originally proposed, but on the First Sunday of Lent.[49] The question of the annual retreat, however, indicated some resentment among the clergy.

For many years, the Richmond priests had usually made their annual retreat in Baltimore, attendance at which was mandatory at least every two years. Now, one priest objected to this practice, "not that he had any dislike for the Baltimore priests or was unwilling to associate with them and to pray with them, but, he thought, our clergy did not occupy the position to which they were entitled and did not feel perfectly at ease there," for he sensed "there was an air about them which seemed to say that they were doing us a compliment to allow us to make our retreat in Baltimore with them." When a vote was taken, twelve out of sixteen priests voted for a separate retreat. The clergy then voted unanimously to hold the annual retreat at Georgetown University. When Keane returned to the meeting, he said he "was sorry the change was made, but since it was such a general wish of the clergy, he would cheerfully acquiesce, and would make the necessary arrangements at Georgetown."[50] From that time the Richmond priests made their annual retreat at Georgetown until the 1960s, when summer school at that institution and the availability of other accommodations led to a change.

On April 10, 1886, in place of the usual priests' meeting, he conferred with them about revising the statutes of the diocese and preparing for the second diocesan synod. On August 18, the three-day synod opened. Its main purpose was to bring the diocesan regulations into line with the legislation of the recent plenary council. But it also addressed issues peculiar to Richmond. Willibald Baumgartner, O.S.B., pastor of St. Mary's Church in Richmond, drafted a decree on the care of Germans, and John R. Slattery, S.S.J, of St. Joseph's Church in Richmond, presented a similar decree on care of the Blacks. In accordance with the Baltimore Council, every priest ordained less than five years was to take an annual examination in theology. The synod also designated the territorial boundaries of all parishes and missions and then legislated for the Mutual Aid Society for priests that Keane had frequently urged.[51]

One piece of the conciliar legislation upon which the synod did not act, however, was the requirement that every diocese designate certain missions whose rectors were irremovable. This omission in 1886 may have been due, however, to a battle that Keane was then waging with Matthew O'Keefe in Norfolk, who, incidentally, was not present at the synod.[52]

In 1887, the priests did not meet on Holy Thursday but on August 26, 1887, at the end of their retreat at Georgetown. It was their fifth—and last—annual meeting. Keane announced that St. Patrick's Church in Richmond, whose pastor was Patrick Donohoe, and Holy Cross Church in Lynchburg, where James McGurk was still pastor, would enjoy irremovability. In the future, he anticipated raising St. Paul's in Portsmouth and St. Mary's in Norfolk to that status.[53] O'Keefe, after thirty-five years, had just been forced to leave Norfolk. If his parish were now declared to enjoy irremovability, he might have the basis to demand a formal trial.

By this time, Keane was preparing to leave Richmond to become the first rector of the Catholic University of America. At this meeting, he was clearly trying to leave the diocese in order for his successor. Each parish was to have "a pew book, a cash book, and a ledger" ready for the bishop's inspection on his visitation. In what may have been an allusion to O'Keefe, he said such bookkeeping was necessary, because "business must be transacted according to sound maxims." He concluded this final meeting with the announcement that he was starting a new parish in Richmond. He had sold property in Richmond to use the income to make improvements on the bishop's residence and to build "a new parish church in the West end of Richmond." He had already purchased a lot and transferred Henry J. Cutler from Norfolk to the new parish of the Sacred Heart of Jesus.[54] This new parish was the first step toward building a new cathedral.

In relation to his priests, Keane was more consultative than most of his contemporaries in the hierarchy. He was still a product of his age in regard to his exercise of episcopal authority. But, perhaps more than most bishops of the time, he was concerned with developing a lay spirituality.

KEANE AND THE DEVELOPMENT OF LAY SPIRITUALITY

Deeply influenced by Isaac Hecker's devotion to the Holy Spirit, Keane had once petitioned Archbishop Bayley for permission to join the Congregation of St. Paul the Apostle, more familiarly known as the Paulists, which Hecker had founded in 1859. Keane, as noted, had conducted missions in the diocese of Richmond before becoming its bishop, but he used other means to encourage lay devotional life. In October 1879, he issued a pastoral letter requesting that every parish establish a Confraternity of the Servants of the Holy Ghost and that every Catholic who "has made his or her First Communion should be enrolled in this beautiful devotion."[55] In 1880, he published *A Sodality Manual for the Use of the Servants of the Holy Ghost*. In it, he included "The Little Office of the Holy Ghost," adapted from the priest's breviary and devoting each of the seven hours to a gift of the Holy Spirit.[56]

Initially the clergy were enthusiastic. From Keyser, Father Peter Fitzsimmons wrote in February 1880 to announce that he already had forty-eight members enrolled in the society.[57] In Winchester, Father John Hagan reported that he was organizing a sodality and that Father Walter Elliott, a Paulist then conducting a mission, promoted the devotion as well as the Mission Union.[58]

Missions remained for Keane a principal means of revitalizing Catholic life. The Paulists had perfected the method, and they were Keane's favorites. The mission to which Hagan alluded in Winchester was part of a series begun in January 1880 and ending in mid April. The Paulists covered the territories around Harpers Ferry, as well as Martinsburg.[59] They returned in the fall to preach in Staunton, Harrisonburg, Lexington, Fredericksburg, Petersburg, and in Richmond at both St. Patrick's and the cathedral, where they concluded on December 12. They then gave "three evenings for the colored people," with whom Keane had begun his own ministry.[60]

In 1884, with the agreement of his clergy, Keane again arranged for the Paulists to conduct missions throughout the diocese. Writing to Keane from Hampton in February 1884, Father E. B. Brady reported

that he was beginning a mission there and would then go to Martinsburg, while Father A. P. Doyle had started one in Harrisonburg. Even
if he had to return to New York before completing his planned missions, he promised "I shall give all the time I can to 'Old Virginny' for
it is a pleasure to me to labor in the missions in this model Diocese."[61]

When Doyle had completed his missions in April, at Isaac Hecker's
insistence he wrote back to Keane in glowing terms of his experience.
After hearing over 4,000 confessions, he altered his view of the Church
in Virginia:

> I went to the diocese rather prejudiced. I had heard a great deal of
> southern torpor and of the proud worldly spirit of the Virginians
> but I have left the diocese with my idea of Va. catholicity entirely
> changed. I think after going through the diocese I am in good con-
> dition to give an accurate statement of the spiritual conditions of
> the people and I frankly say that I have never met with on the
> whole a better lot of Catholics than the Virginia Catholics. Of
> course my experience is not very extended, but in the sixty odd
> missions I have taken part in I do not now remember one where
> the people were on the average better than on some of the missions
> in Va. I found more unostentatious piety more real devotion to
> prayer more practical religion among them for example keeping
> the laws of the church with regard to fasting and various other
> things that necessitate sacrifice for conscience sake than can be
> found anywhere else that I know of.

There is, unfortunately, no documentary evidence for what Virginia
Catholics did when Mass was not available, but Doyle provides a clue
that they maintained their faith through "unostentatious piety" and
adherence to such Church laws as fasting.

But Doyle also praised the material contributions of Virginia
Catholics. "If these facts were put before some N. York pastors," he
declared, "they would appear incredible." He and Brady both concluded that there was no "diocese better equipped to do the work of
the church than the diocese of Richmond."[62]

Keane continued to have his pastors include membership in the
Sodality of the Holy Ghost in their annual reports, many of which are
unfortunately lost. The ones available, however, indicate that, in addition to St. Peter's Cathedral, Alexandria, Harrisonburg, Martinsburg,

Portsmouth, Staunton, and Winchester had sizable enrollments, with Portsmouth soaring to 250 in 1885, the last year for which the reports are available. But the devotion died out when Keane was transferred, and it never had the popular appeal of practices such as Forty Hours.[63] From the available evidence, moreover, it appears that Keane's successors never tried to organize diocesan-wide missions on the scale Keane had done.

Keane had proven himself an able administrator as well as a spiritual leader. For that reason, he had been under consideration in 1881 as coadjutor archbishop of San Francisco. He could be meticulous in regard to the proper care of churches and sacred vessels. But he also had not neglected the directly pastoral side of his office of bishop.

CHAPTER 14

Pastoral Life during Keane's Episcopate

While Keane focused on issues such as education and the spiritual development of his people and clergy, the diocese continued to expand during his episcopacy. The Catholic population continued to grow in the Shenandoah Valley and the northern portion of the diocese in West Virginia. Simultaneously, however, he took personal responsibility for one apostolate in which Gibbons had failed—work with Black Virginians.

Down the Shenandoah Valley and East

Railroads continued to provide the key for the expansion of Catholic presence in the valley, as they extended south down the valley and west from Norfolk to Roanoke and on to Tennessee. When Keane assumed office, there were two principal missionary centers, Harpers Ferry in the north and Staunton for the central valley. Within a decade, that would change. For some years, Winchester, one of the oldest Catholic settlements, had had a parochial school, conducted by laypeople, whose names, unfortunately, are unknown.[1] In June 1879, Augustine van de Vyver, then the pastor in Harpers Ferry, recommended that John P. Hagan be permanently assigned to Winchester, not only to minister to the Catholics already there but also to influence the Protestant community.[2] Once in Winchester, Hagan tried to make some accommodation with the local school board to make his parochial school, in fact, the public school.[3] Unfortunately, in June 1882, Hagan had to be removed, and Winchester then received a series of pastors.

The first was Denis O'Connell, who also had charge of starting a new church in Front Royal, made possible by a gift from Eliza Jenkins of Baltimore as a memorial to her brother, a Confederate soldier who was killed in the Civil War. Although Keane dedicated the church in September 1882,[4] it was still incomplete. Keane blamed O'Connell. Writing Gibbons from Rome in June 1883, he remarked: "I hope I will find the Front Royal church finished on my return—as I have done all in my power to push it on. But Dr. O'Connell is slow, & the people he has to deal with there are still more so."[5] This was, in fact, O'Connell's only stint as a pastor and it would be short-lived. Even as Keane was commenting on O'Connell's slowness, Gibbons had summoned him to Baltimore to help prepare for the Third Plenary Council, summoned by the Holy See for 1884.[6] O'Connell would not return to pastoral work in Richmond until he arrived as its bishop in 1912. After his departure, Winchester received permanent resident pastors, but its parochial school did not survive.

Further south in the valley, Staunton had two priests, John McVerry, the pastor, and Hugh J. McKeefry, the assistant. McKeefry had been in Keyser, but now had charge of riding a circuit of missions, which included Harrisonburg, where Gibbons had dedicated a former Methodist church in 1876, and Charlottesville. Both towns had Mass once a month. In Charlottesville, incidentally, the most prominent parishioner remained Lavalette Floyd Holmes, wife of Professor George Frederick Holmes at the University of Virginia. She and her husband seemed concerned to raise their children Catholic; yet, there is hardly any reference to their activity in the church, other than Gibbons staying with them when he administered confirmation in Charlottesville.[7]

Despite an apparently amicable relationship with McVerry, however, McKeefry asked Keane to be reassigned as an assistant in Norfolk for reasons of health.[8] McVerry was "grieved" and informed Keane that he could not pay James T. O'Farrell, his new assistant, any salary. Instead, he suggested that he give O'Farrell "board, washing & lodging gratis. And he can have Harrisonburg & Charlottesville & attend them two Sundays in each month as in the past & receive all their income. And thus he will have an independent mission of his own." To this Keane tersely commented: "New arrangement not agreed to."[9] In 1881, Charlottesville finally had a church, the Church of the Paraclete (it later changed its name to the Church of the Holy Comforter), but it still depended on Staunton for Mass once a month.

Early in 1884 Keane received an offer that would later contribute to the education of African Americans. Father Richard Wakeham, a priest of the diocese who joined the Sulpicians, was then teaching at St. Charles College in Ellicott City, Maryland. His father lived in Columbia and offered a site for a church. While Wakeham acknowledged that it would be "many a day before we shall be able to assemble a congregation of 100 there," he was concerned about "some Catholics scattered in the neighborhood, on the RR, & in the mines & quarries" and others "who have never acknowledged themselves [to] be Catholics, or have said very little about it, when seeing themselves entirely surrounded by protestants." Many Catholic orphan boys, he continued, were transported there and dispersed among Protestants.

While Wakeham knew it would be impossible to have Sunday Mass even once a month, he proposed the technique adopted by Virginia's missionary priests fifty years before: "possibly a Priest might go there almost once a month, *on a weekday*. Arriving there in the afternoon, he could preach in the evening, & say Mass early next morning, (i.e. at 6 o'clock) & be back in Richmond by 10 A.M."[10] St. Joseph's church in Columbia became a mission station to the cathedral and had Mass once a month until it became an important mission for the Josephites.

The church in Columbia was not the only contribution the Wakeham family made to the Catholic Church. Father Wakeham's sister, Alice, became a Daughter of Charity. His brother, Alfred, a Confederate veteran, had contributed to Richard's seminary education and, in 1895, became the first Josephite brother.[11]

ROANOKE BECOMES THE CENTER OF THE VALLEY

While missions sprang up between Richmond and Staunton, the southern part of the valley grew most rapidly during Keane's administration. Roanoke and Botetourt Counties were originally served from the church Gibbons had dedicated at Lexington. In 1882, the principal town in Roanoke County, Big Lick, adopted the name of the county. It was the crossroad of the Norfolk and Western Railroad and the Shenandoah Railroad and was developing as a Catholic center as laborers came to work on both. In August 1882, H. M. Meade, a rail-road employee, told Keane he had already contacted Father John W. Lynch in Lexington, but the actual proposal for a Catholic church in Roanoke came from W. Welch, master mechanic of the Shenandoah Valley Railroad, "who said it was vitally necessary to the success of the road." The founding of the church was due to a collaborative venture of the people and the railroads. Meade argued:

> R. R. people are better adapted to carrying out such designs, than the people in a settled place. There are so many passing through, who would willingly contribute something, even if they do not belong to the faith, so that we are not dependent on the place alone, but can rely on all who belong to the road, as well.

He also said that "Father O'Connell [then in Winchester] was so good as to come down last Friday & say Mass for us" in the room of one of the mechanics' houses.[12]

In October, S. M. Brophy of the Shenandoah Valley Railroad Company held a meeting to discuss purchasing land for a church building that could later become a school. The Roanoke Land and Improvement Company had already promised to donate a lot. Brophy then chaired a committee to canvass the town for contributions.[13]

According to a newspaper report, Lynch had come down from Lexington late in October and "held services" at Rorer Hall. When he returned on November 19, however, he found the hall unavailable, so Brophy procured for him the use of Shenandoah Valley Railroad Passenger Coach, number 6.[14] Although O'Connell had certainly said Mass near Roanoke the previous summer and Lynch was later said to have "held services," Lynch testified that the Mass in the railroad coach was the first Mass in Roanoke.[15]

On July 2, 1883, the Roanoke Land and Improvement Company sold three lots on the northeast corner of Jefferson and Harrison Streets to Keane for $1.[16] Construction of St. Andrew's first church began that summer and was complete by September.[17] Lynch came down from Lexington at first once, and later twice, a month to say Mass. Though he was later fondly remembered with a monument put up to his memory in Roanoke, he was not universally beloved.

A year after the church opened, a parishioner complained to Keane that Lynch had failed to preach the previous Sunday. Lynch explained that he had purposely not preached, because "the subscription had fallen off & I had to do something to raise it—hence my 'scold' as the gentleman was pleased to call it. However, it had the desired effect, and I have not had to speak of money since." He intended to speak of money only when it was necessary, but, since many of his people were from the Pittsburgh area, they "were raised by Bp [John] Tuigg and are used to it." In further defense, he pointed out that he had made over $10,000 in improvements, that the people knew he was available to serve them, and that, should the complainant take the trouble to investigate, "he wd find the people instructed in their religion."[18]

In the meantime, Lynch purchased adjacent pieces of property on an installment plan with parish funds but registered them in his own name.[19] This would later cause his downfall. But the people of Roanoke had built a rectory, and, late in 1889, Bishop van de Vyver, Keane's successor, appointed Lynch the resident pastor. By that time, Roanoke already had a "Little School" conducted in the school hall. Mrs. Hester White McGeehee taught the boys and her sister, Agnes White, the girls.[20] Lay initiative in beginning schools was already a pattern in the valley with which the people and their pastor would have been familiar. But before Roanoke got a parochial school staffed by religious women, it also had an orphanage.

According to Lynch's later account, McGill had received a legacy for a boys orphanage. When Keane made his last visitation of the diocese in 1888, he chose Roanoke as the site, which van de Vyver later ratified. Lynch himself was not, as he put it, "stuck" on orphanages but preferred schools. He realized, however, that, where there was an orphanage, a school would follow.[21]

Keane's account was somewhat different. Looking for a site for an orphanage in 1886, first in Alexandria[22] and then in Lynchburg, he was persuaded by Lynch and several leaders of the Catholic and Protestant communities to visit a site in Roanoke. Keane and his consultors agreed on Roanoke,[23] but then Lynchburg made another bid and the Daughters of Charity agreed to operate it. When they could not provide personnel for two years, Keane's successor, van de Vyver, then chose Roanoke as the site for the orphanage and invited the Sisters of Charity of Nazareth to staff it.[24]

By the fall of 1892, Lynch had seventy-three children in his "Little School." In February 1893, the orphanage, St. Vincent de Paul, was completed. By the end of the month, six members of the Sisters of

Charity of Nazareth, headed by Sister Mary Vincent, arrived to take over the orphanage and school.[25] This congregation thus made its first entry into the diocese—it would later staff the school at the Cathedral of the Sacred Heart—and would ultimately give the name to Roanoke's second parish, Our Lady of Nazareth.

Within five years, Lynch had built a larger school with funds from a source familiar to Virginia Catholics over the next decade, Mrs. Thomas Fortune Ryan. In 1902, he saw the completion of the present massive St. Andrew's Church on the site of the old one, on one of the dominant hills in the city. But then something happened. Without warning, on November 6, 1910, he announced that he was being transferred to Harpers Ferry, even though the people of the parish and the "colored residents of city" petitioned van de Vyver to allow him to return.[26]

But Lynch was gone from Roanoke, first to Harpers Ferry, then to Danville, and finally as chaplain in St. Leo's Hospital in Greensboro, North Carolina. While none of his correspondence to van de Vyver is extant, his letters to Bishop O'Connell several years later indicate that some of Roanoke's Catholics accused him of becoming a rich man and landowner at their expense.[27] The problem arose from his practice of holding property in his own name. Nevertheless, during his tenure, first as missionary and then as resident pastor, Roanoke was a success story. Within less than three decades, it had moved from being a mission station to one of the most important Catholic centers in the diocese.

MISSIONARY PRIESTS OF THE NORTHWEST

The Shenandoah Valley may have been developing, but the diocese of Richmond still contained extensive missionary territory. In the northwestern part of the diocese within West Virginia, priests frequently had to cross jurisdictional lines to minister to the people. They also faced unpredictable obstacles in the choice of sites for churches. Keyser was a case in point. In that region, the Baltimore and Ohio Railroad determined where churches would be located. When the railroad changed its plans, the people followed along—and so did the church. When Catholic workers first moved into the area, the nearest priest was actually in Maryland, in the archdiocese of Baltimore. Early in 1873, Father Jeremiah O'Sullivan, pastor in Westernport and later Bishop of Mobile, thought he had found a good site for a church in Piedmont.[28] A little over a year later, he learned that Piedmont would be only a second-class agency, since it lacked sufficient space to make up the trains. The first-class agency would be in New Creek, soon to be renamed Keyser City, about six miles away. O'Sullivan, therefore, informed Bishop Gibbons that a new church would soon be needed there, but that the Catholics were too poor to contribute to it. He proposed that a resident priest there could attend the rest of Mineral, Hampshire, and Hardy counties.[29]

In July 1874, Gibbons and O'Sullivan inspected a site in Keyser.[30] While the church was being built, O'Sullivan said Mass in Keyser on the Mondays following the first and third Sundays of each month.[31] On August 22, 1875, Gibbons dedicated the little Church of the Assumption.[32] O'Sullivan continued to minister to the small community until December, when Hugh J. McKeefry became the first pastor. Then the B & O moved the division, where trains were made up, to Piedmont, the site that was originally thought too small. McKeefry's parishioners were reduced to about a dozen when the railroad moved the division back to Keyser.[33] Such stress may have taken a toll on the priest. In September 1878 he was assigned as assistant to McVerry in Staunton, and Peter Fitzsimmons was transferred from there to Keyser.[34]

In November 1878, Fitzsimmons wrote to Keane that he was taking a census of all who claimed to be Catholic. If they all lived up to their promises, he expected to establish a congregation in Paw Paw, further along the railroad. In Keyser, and eventually in Paw Paw, he hoped to establish schools for boys and girls.[35] A short time later, however, he reported that some of his missions were actually in the archdiocese of Baltimore. While all the pastors involved were cooperating, he recommended that Keane and Archbishop Gibbons make some permanent arrangements regarding faculties for missions that crossed state and diocesan lines.[36] Fitzsimmons was a priest in the missionary mode of Richard Whelan and the All Hallows recruits of a generation earlier. He soon fell victim to one of the scourges his predecessors had feared.

In August 1880, Keane cut short his visitation of the diocese to hasten to Fitzsimmons' deathbed. The priest had contracted typhoid fever, and died at the age of only thirty-two. It was a loss the bishop could ill afford. Within a few months, he had lost four priests. One priest had returned to his diocese. Of his Louvain recruits, Andrew Habets was now totally deaf and Peter Coris was dying in a hospital after less than two years on the mission. To supply Keyser, Keane now appealed to Bishop John Loughlin of Brooklyn,[37] but waited several months for a reply.

In April 1881, Keane transferred P. J. Hasty from Harpers Ferry to Keyser, where he remained only a few months. In October, Keane made an extensive visitation of the area, preaching in Martinsburg, Bath, Paw Paw, and Keyser on his way to dedicate a church in Leesburg. All the missions, he assured Gibbons, "are wretchedly poor. Keyser especially causes me a good deal of solicitude."[38] By this time, however, Loughlin had responded to his request and sent Father Eugene P. Mahony, who worked first in Martinsburg and then in Keyser. In six months, Mahony had built a church as well as a school for both Catholic and Protestant children. In February 1882, however, he was recalled to Brooklyn by his bishop. He explained to Keane that the decision was not his own, for he thought Loughlin had agreed to let him remain, especially since the people of Keyser and Paw Paw were "working heart & soul with me." Sadly, he locked up the church he had worked so hard to build.[39] On Easter Monday, he departed.

For the next year, J. H. Cutler was the pastor. He gave "great satisfaction," Keane remarked, but then, in December 1882 requested to go to Norfolk where he had served earlier. Joseph Frioli, newly ordained in Baltimore, then assumed charge of Keyser.[40] West Virginia's outpost was a difficult mission. Few priests would remain more than a few years. But Frioli here began his distinguished career in the diocese.

Despite the frequency with which priests, especially younger ones, were transferred, some finally found more or less permanent homes. In April 1881, at the same time Keane transferred Hasty to Keyser, he sent McKeefry from Norfolk to be pastor in Martinsburg, an appointment that later opened the way for Cutlar to go to Norfolk.[41] McKeefry immediately set about to reopen the school, which had been closed with the departure of the Sisters of Charity in 1841. It was an expensive proposition if the building of a schoolhouse and residence for sisters was included, but, in 1883, he found a more economical solution by purchasing the Berkeley Female Academy, which already had both a school and a residence.[42] He had already contacted the Daughters of Charity and even offered his own residence for them. Sister Euphemia in Emmitsburg now accepted the new charge, but the sisters delayed their arrival because "their appearance might excite Protestant prejudice and create difficulties. After the property is secured, they can go, and suggest any little arrangements necessary to be made."[43] McKeefry quickly raised subscriptions from his congregation and purchased the property, for other parties were also interested in it. "The Lutherans are sadly disappointed," he told Keane, "but my poor people are delighted." On November 25, four Daughters of Charity returned to Martinsburg to open the school after an absence of over forty years.[44] After a succession of assignments across the diocese, McKeefry remained in Martinsburg for eighteen years before becoming pastor of St. Patrick's in Richmond, where he died in 1921. His brother, William, incidentally, would later become pastor in Martinsburg. Both had also both been pastors in Fredericksburg.

Martinsburg and Harpers Ferry were the only settled parishes in Richmond's northwest territory. As if finding a priest for such distant outposts as Keyser were not enough, Keane also inherited a burden that was not of his own making.

The Keileyville Colony

At the opposite end of the diocese, "Southside" became the site of one of the few postbellum efforts to establish a Catholic colony outside the Midwest. The purpose of these colonization projects was to woo immigrants from the overcrowded cities of the northeast to rural farming country. Samuel Barnes owned a plantation of 7,000 acres, "Barnesville," in Charlotte County. In addition to the land, the plantation consisted of forty former slave cabins, a steam sawmill, a grist mill, a tannery, and a distillery. It was an attractive site for immigrant families to make a new beginning. At some point, Barnes began negotiations with the Philadelphia Catholic Colonization Society, formed by the local branch of the Irish Catholic Benevolent Union (ICBU) to sell the property for $11 an acre. It was named Keileyville in honor of the ICBU's national president, Anthony Keiley, former mayor of Richmond.[45]

On July 1, 1878, Janssens, the administrator of the diocese, recorded the beginning of what promised to be a new Catholic enclave in Virginia: "The colonists up to date, to the number of about 120 are a sober and industrious class of people, and the colony bids fair to succeed. The colony is attended once a month by a priest from Richmond."[46] His evaluation was, unfortunately, far too optimistic. Other Catholic colonies at the time had a priest as leader of the colony. Keileyville, instead, had Thomas Hannon, the representative of the Philadelphia ICBU who had first negotiated the agreement with Barnes. Fifty-two families migrated there, not directly from Ireland or other nations, but from other states. At first, a priest, probably Janssens, came from Richmond once a month. People who died between those pastoral visits had no priest in attendance. For that reason, Archbishop Hughes of New York and other bishops had previously opposed movements of immigrants from cities to rural areas.[47] But a visit from a priest once a month was the rule in Virginia outside the more urban areas.

From the beginning, however, the colony suffered from more than lack of a priest. The settlers produced a good crop of potatoes in 1877, but the land had been overworked. On October 1, 1879, Keane finally appointed a priest, Andrew Habets, as resident pastor. One of the Louvain recruits, who suffered from deafness, Habets was also to attend Danville, previously a mission of Lynchburg, and other places along the Richmond and Danville Railroad. Keane himself had preached in Danville on September 27 and accompanied Habets to Keileyville. He found the "colonists greatly cheered by the appointment of Father Habets to reside among them."[48] But Keileyville had other, more serious, problems.

In July 1879, Martin I. J. Griffin, an official of the ICBU and member of the Philadelphia board, visited Keileyville. In a conversation with Keiley, then the city attorney for Richmond, he learned that Samuel Barnes was not the sole owner of the property conveyed to the Philadelphia group. The other owner had, in fact, been involved in a scheme to induce Catholic colonists to settle in North Carolina. Griffin suspected the owner was engaged in land speculation, resigned from the board, and accused Hannon, the board's resident agent, of mismanagement or possible collusion in a fraud. Habets protested that Griffin's resignation jeopardized the future of the colony. "Though somewhat gloomy seems its [the colony's] aspect for the present," he wrote, "yet I hope it will be a success, which I am sure it will be if the people can pay their installments and make a living." He recognized that "this will be hard if not impossible for a couple of years more, but by that time I think they ought to be able to get along better."[49]

Habets continued to serve in Keileyville without salary, but, as his deafness grew worse, he was so frequently absent to see physicians that he was present only for Sunday Mass. In December, Keane temporarily replaced him with James O'Farrell from Harpers Ferry.[50] By February 1880, however, the Philadelphia colonization board had dissolved, and its rights and title to the colony returned to Barnes, who was supposed to pay $2,000.[51]

But Keileyville was to continue only briefly. Habets had returned, but in August 1880 he chastised Griffin for his attacks on the management of the colony. With perhaps a reflection on the type of Irish colonist recruited, he said he still thought the colony would flourish if "real" farmers settled there.[52] By December, however, Habets had grown so deaf that Keane had to remove him permanently. Keileyville would be served from the cathedral, and Danville was reassigned to Lynchburg.[53] For two more years, the colony went on. In January 1883, a group of colonists petitioned Keane for a resident priest. Father Francis X. McCarthy from Lynchburg had come in November 1882, and again in January, but said he could not return until sometime after Easter. Already strapped for priests to man his many mission stations, Keane scribbled across their petition that he could not provide a priest until at least June.[54] Keileyville gradually faded away as a colony, but some Catholic families remained. Visiting priests would say Mass in the small wooden church into the 1930s, when it was dismantled and its timbers later used for the first church of St. Catherine of Siena in Clarksville.[55]

Keane had been an able diocesan administrator in managing his extensive missions, even with a severe shortage of priests. He had also shown his concern for the spiritual development of both his priests and the laity. But one of his abiding legacies was his pioneering work with the Black community.

KEANE'S FIRST WORK AMONG BLACK VIRGINIANS

In January 1879, Keane began holding special services for African Americans in the basement of St. Peter's. He recorded his reasons for this experiment:

Out of 36,000 Negroes in the city, we have only 22 Caths! The project of a separate church for them has been long entertained. But before venturing on it, it seemed prudent to test the experiment by exercises in the Cathedral. The opening proved a grand success. The church was *crowded* by them in every part. They behaved in the most respectful manner & seemed greatly pleased with the singing, prayers, & instructions. I intend to devote my own exertions to it whenever I am in Rd. May God grant fruit to our labors."[56]

A month later, even in the face of opposition from white and Black ministers, Keane began holding biweekly catechetical instructions.[57] By June, he had gained twelve converts.[58] In the process, he seems to have fueled some anti-Catholicism that unsettled Richmond's usual practice of religious tolerance.[59] But he recognized the need for more regular work with the African American community.

In September 1883, Keane wrote Alfred Leeson, American superior of Mill Hill, for a priest. Pointing out the tiny number of Catholics among "over 32,000 negroes in the city," he said that his ministry among them for almost five years had "made some impression and about 25 converts, in the face of bitter prejudice and desperate opposition." He then outlined the strategy that would be followed in future work among Virginia's Black population. He had a school with about fifty students, "the bulk" of whom were "of Protestant parents and through them access might be had into their families."[60] In the fall of 1883, Keane appealed directly to Canon Peter Benoit, the vicar general of Mill Hill, who was again in the United States. This time, Benoit promised a priest, if a church and school could be provided. Keane judged the cost, estimated between $8,000 and $10,000, was "evidently a duty."[61]

Richmond still remained heavily dependent on the Society for the Propagation of the Faith. Unfortunately, the French organization sometimes forgot about its Virginia beneficiary—it sent nothing for Richmond in 1878. But it would be a major contributor to this new endeavor. In June 1883, it had already sent 10,000 francs and would send another 12,000 the next year. The society was contributing so much, said its president, because "of your need among so many thousand non-catholics and because of the negroes who are the object of your paternal solicitude."[62]

In November, John R. Slattery, S.S.J., was assigned to the Richmond mission. For him, it was a form of exile, for he had been defeated in his bid for reelection as provincial by Leeson. At the request of Bishop Herbert Vaughan, Benoit then offered Keane advice in regard to Slattery. They both wanted Slattery to succeed in order to repay Keane "for the Sacrifices which you are making for the poor coloured race." Since Slattery was a "tried man," Vaughan thought Keane could simply tell him:

> Here is a large field, set to work as you think best, under my sanction. Look out for some eligible plot of building; buy when you can; here is so much that I have gathered from the contemplated coloured missions. Let it be the first payment for the land or building. As soon as you see your way call the English sisters to open a school at it.

Slattery himself had said that he was "not afraid of working in means for his own support, in thus being launched," although Benoit and Vaughan were sure Keane would not leave him in want. They wanted Slattery to be as independent as possible, because Vaughan in particular was "altogether unwilling to let F. Slattery occupy himself with white people. And yet this is scarcely avoidable if he lives at the cathedral & sees pressing white work before him." Finally, Benoit suggested that, if Keane had not already bought a chapel or land, he should tell Slattery on his arrival "that you wish him to set to work to the best of his judgment, in securing land etc. & that you will help him by your influence & means whenever you can."[63]

By January 6, 1885, Slattery had arrived in Richmond. His "mission" was a congregation of about forty who met in the basement of the cathedral. The school of which Keane spoke actually consisted of one teacher holding classes in the basement of the bishop's residence. But Keane had already purchased a lot on First Street between Jackson and Duval for a church.[64] He now set about to raise funds to build it. From January 25 to February 8, he preached in several New York churches, including the newly dedicated St. Paul the Apostle, the headquarters of the Paulists, and St. Patrick's Cathedral. Altogether, he raised $2,700.[65] He was to make other such fund-raising journeys.

Slattery tried a different approach to raise funds. In an appeal to parochial school students throughout the country, he received 800,000 pennies. From his base in Richmond, furthermore, he opened mission churches in Petersburg, Columbia, Keswick, and Union Mills and founded schools in Petersburg and Keswick.[66]

Keane had used his annual Holy Thursday conference in 1884 to urge his priests "not to be content with the general services of the church but to have special services for them [African Americans], something after the manner of those in the cathedral." He reminded them that "God will demand an account from them for those souls and judgment will befall them unless they can say: 'If I have failed, I still did my duty.'"[67] The following year, he told them it was a "duty incumbent upon all of helping this unhappy race" and announced his "desire to have a missionary in the diocese to travel around and work among the negroes." His priests were to "receive such missionaries kindly and . . . lend them all the assistance in their power."[68]

On April 12, 1885, Keane laid the cornerstone of St. Joseph's before a crowd in the streets he estimated to be 10,000. Within a month, he had begun a school funded by an anonymous woman donor from the North.[69] He hastened to have it ready in time for the arrival of Franciscan sisters from St. Mary's Abbey, London, who had turned down Gibbons's request in 1876. Upon their arrival in the fall of 1885, they already had a hundred students. Keane then purchased additional property adjacent to the church to expand the school. On November 22, he dedicated the new church, and he preached a mission during the following week. Most of the $24,000 for the church and school, he recorded, came from outside the diocese.[70]

To increase funding within the diocese, in 1879, Keane had established the Virginia Mission Union, the bulk of whose funds would now be directed to work with Blacks.[71] In the meantime, the bishops were preparing to meet for the Third Plenary Council of Baltimore in 1884. To prepare for this, Vaughan wanted to make some recommendations to Gibbons, who had been delegated to preside. But first, he sought Slattery's advice. Slattery knew from Keane's visit to Rome in 1883 that Propaganda would insist that the bishops call for an annual collection for Indian and Negro missions. He now suggested that the money collected be sent to the Society for the Propagation of the Faith that had "greater experience—would be more careful than the Bishops." He then proposed that the bishops establish American branches of the society, the management of which would be given to the Josephites. In regard to evangelization of the Blacks, he recommended that more churches be established in cities than in rural areas, the churches to serve as centers from which missionaries could go out to the rural areas.[72]

When the council met, it did legislate that there be an annual collection throughout the country for Indian and Negro missions. To administer this fund, however, it rejected Slattery's suggestion and established a Commission for Catholic Missions among the Colored People and Indians." At the council, Keane echoed another of Slattery's proposals and recommended a separate American seminary for training missionaries for Indians and African Americans.[73]

In the summer of 1886, the second synod of Richmond convened to review diocesan legislation in light of the recent council. Included in its legislation was a decree, drafted by Slattery, on the necessity of working with Blacks.[74] In October, Slattery sent Gibbons, chairman of the newly established Commission on Indian and Colored Missions, a detailed description of the progress of the Virginia missions. St. Joseph's then had eighty-nine parishioners, and five sisters were teaching in the school. Petersburg had a school with forty-four children taught by the Daughters of Charity, whom Keane had procured. Alexandria had a school with fifty-five children under the Sisters of the Holy Cross. The school in Norfolk, with twenty children, was taught by laypeople. But, aside from Richmond, all these places needed new school buildings. Slattery also recommended a second priest for Richmond and the assignment of a priest to Petersburg to work exclusively with the Black people.

Slattery then contrasted Catholic with Protestant philanthropy. "For two and one half centuries," he wrote,

> heresy has held the unfortunate people in that slavery of ignorance and sin, which surpasses beyond all conception the yoke which galled their necks. And Protestantism has been lavishly generous. Massive buildings, higher schools, numerous professors, educational paraphernalia are all at the disposal of the Blacks, to educate whom the Protestants of the country annually give millions of dollars. Add to these efforts, the public school system of the States, which is a new enemy sprung up since the war. To do anything, the Catholic missionaries must meet these efforts on something like a fair footing. They must be well equipped; notably so in schools and also in churches. Exterior show is a power, as Your Eminence's personal experience in North Carolina and Virginia may well testify.[75]

Slattery had well outlined how far Catholics had to go in serving the Black community.

Slattery had also touched upon the contrast between Catholic and Protestant philanthropy in regard to work with Black Americans. Although there was to be an annual collection on the first Sunday of Lent for the Commission for Catholic Missions Among the Colored People and Indians, it was a failure. The first one in 1887 yielded only $82,000, a figure that dropped to $66,000 in 1892. Congregationalists, by contrast, were far more generous and raised the equivalent of $1.50 per person for their home missions in 1893. A similar levy on Catholics would have garnered $12 million, instead of the contribution of $80,000 in 1893, or an average of a penny a person. Admittedly, Catholics were less affluent than Congregationalists, but their numbers would have dictated a far greater contribution.[76] Failure of American Catholics to raise money for work with African Americans placed a greater burden on a poor diocese like Richmond.

Late in 1887, Slattery left Richmond for Baltimore, where he founded St. Joseph's Seminary. P. J. Fahey now replaced him at St. Joseph's, which soon received a second priest, J. Oud, S.S.J.[77] Keane had succeeded in starting diocesan work among Black Virginians. To do so, however, he had to expend much of his own energy in preaching in northern cities to raise funds. Moreover, he devoted much of the funds from the Society for the Propagation of the Faith and his own Virginia Mission Union to his Black missions and churches.[78]

To judge from Keane's journal entry, his principal concern about the Third Plenary Council was its decree on Indian and Negro missions, for he noted only that "We hope for some assistance in work among negroes."[79] But the council was to have far-reaching effects on him and the diocese of Richmond.

CHAPTER 15

Richmond:
A Diocese in Transition,
1883–1888

For John Keane, like James Gibbons before him, Richmond was a stepping-stone to other positions. The American Church was going through a period of transition, and Keane was to play a large role in it. There were a number of tensions between the Vatican and the American Church, including the continued appeal of priests to Rome against their bishops. For some time also, the bishops of the Midwest had been calling for a council, but Gibbons and others had resisted it. The Holy See now stepped in to convoke the Third Plenary Council of Baltimore, the last national council and the only one not summoned at American initiative. The council would have several direct effects on the diocese of Richmond. First, it would provide for increased priests' rights and would change the manner of selecting bishops. Second, it legislated to establish the Catholic University of America, of which Keane became the first rector. Preparations for this new office would mean Keane would be frequently absent from his diocese. Finally, the council set into motion a series of events that would cause Denis O'Connell to leave the diocese until he returned as bishop.

PREPARATIONS FOR THE COUNCIL

In the summer of 1883, Keane was in Rome making his *ad limina* visit, or official report to the pope, on his diocese, when Propaganda summoned a meeting in Rome of all the American archbishops to prepare the agenda for the council. He assured Gibbons that the call was "issued in a spirit of the most entire friendship towards the American hierarchy, and through the desire to have all their relations with their priests and with the Holy See placed on the footing that will be the most advantageous & agreeable to our Hierarchy." He also reported Roman overtures about appointing a legate to the United States. Other bishops had informed Gibbons of this in the preceding months and had recommended, as an alternative, the appointment of an American agent in Rome. Keane too had discussed such an agent with Propaganda officials, but offered the opinion that "they never will recognize it when it is advanced as a substitute for the appointment of a Papal Delegate."[1]

O'Connell, then serving in Winchester, now received Gibbons's summons to come to Baltimore to help him prepare for the council and accompany him to Rome for the meeting of the archbishops in November 1883. The cardinals of Propaganda had previously drawn up an agenda for presentation to the archbishops, partially based on Bishop George Conroy's report of 1878. The Americans were confronted with a series of proposals that reflected Roman concerns, but they succeeded in recasting some of them in an American mode. Roman authorities did not present one item, however, that Propaganda had already discussed with Keane—the establishment of a permanent apostolic delegation. Such a permanent Roman official must be distinguished from the appointment of a delegate to preside over the council, an issue on which the archbishops and Propaganda officials had divergent views. At the previous plenary councils in 1852 and 1866, Archbishops Francis P. Kenrick and Martin J. Spalding, respectively, had been appointed as delegates. Toward the end of the 1883 meetings, however, the Americans learned that Propaganda proposed to elevate Bishop Luigi Sepiacci, a consultor to the congregation, to the rank of archbishop and appoint him to preside over the council. Only after the Americans protested Sepiacci's appointment did Pope Leo XIII rescind it and name Gibbons as the delegate.[2]

Gibbons's appointment brought out into the open some of the tension already developing within the American hierarchy. Michael A. Corrigan, coadjutor archbishop of New York, had represented the ailing Cardinal McCloskey at the Roman meetings but had departed before the discussion about Sepiacci. Ella Edes, an American convert and journalist, who had acted as an unofficial Roman agent for the archbishops of New York since the 1860s, now informed Corrigan of her own reactions. She accused Gibbons of waiting for Corrigan's departure before representing to Propaganda that McCloskey's ill health prevented him from being named delegate. Next, she described how she had met "His Grace and Denis marching along the Piazza di Spagna," outside the headquarters of Propaganda, and then went herself to the congregation, where she learned that Gibbons was not named "Apostolic Delegate," as he claimed, but was merely delegated to preside over the council. Later on, she recounted, "Denis arrived on one of his exploring expeditions," and she confronted him with a report in an Italian newspaper about Sepiacci's rejection and Gibbons's appointment. To O'Connell's expression of surprise that the story was public, she replied "that the Sulpitians [sic] . . . had the name in Rome of being tremendous gossips." She then lectured O'Connell on how she had discovered Gibbons's plot to capture the appointment after Corrigan's departure. "I then told Denis," she concluded, "that it was very silly of his Archbishop to go around talking in that style the more so that it was not true he knew very well he had not discovered it [Sepiacci's appointment] and that he had not checked it."[3] Her disclosure at this early date revealed that tension was already developing between Gibbons and Corrigan, a tension that would soon embrace both Keane and O'Connell. It was also the first of many colorful comments she would make about Gibbons and O'Connell in the coming years.

The Third Plenary Council

Gibbons and O'Connell now returned to Baltimore to prepare from the Roman draft the documents to be discussed at the council itself. On November 8, 1884, fourteen archbishops or coadjutor archbishops, fifty-seven bishops, seven abbots, and thirty-one superiors of religious orders processed into the Baltimore cathedral. They would remain in session until December 7. As secretaries of the council, Gibbons appointed O'Connell, Sebastian Messmer, and Henry Gabriels.

At the council, the bishops passed far-reaching legislation that would continue to govern the American Church to the present, except as modified by the codes of canon law of 1917 and 1983. They tried to strengthen their own authority over the proposed Roman drafts and introduced legislation of their own. Sometimes, however, they acted only from Roman pressure. At the Roman meetings, Propaganda officials and the archbishops had drafted a proposal for "irremovable rectors," priests in certain parishes who would enjoy tenure and could not be removed without a formal trial. When the topic was discussed at the council, Bishop John Ireland of St. Paul asked for the opinion of Gibbons, who replied that Rome was so insistent on having them that, if the bishops failed to legislate for them, the Holy See would intervene to the embarrassment of the hierarchy. The council further legislated that every diocese was to have consultors to advise the bishop on financial matters. In future episcopal nominations, moreover, the consultors and irremovable rectors were to draw up a *terna* for a vacant diocese or a coadjutor. The bishops of the province were then to meet, examine the priests' list, and then submit one of their own, giving their reasons if they rejected any name on the first list. The council also decreed that every parish was to have a parochial school within two years of the end of the council.[4]

Among the Roman proposals the bishops modified was one concerning secret societies. The bishops wished to provide for uniform discipline and prevent the confusion arising from one bishop condemning a society while another tolerated it. They decreed that each case of a suspect secret society was to be submitted to the full body of the archbishops. If they failed to reach unanimity, the case was to be referred to Rome. Finally, the council legislated for the establishment of a Catholic University of America. Both these decrees would have direct impact on the diocese, for Keane became a defender of the Knights of Labor and would be chosen as the university's first rector.[5]

Once the council was over, Keane returned to Richmond. His only comment on it was: "Not much legislation that can affect small and poorly organized Dioceses." But while Keane was back in Richmond, O'Connell was again going to Rome, this time as one of the procurators to gain papal approval of the conciliar legislation. He had "been in the service of the Abp. & the Council since Nov. 1883," Keane recorded; "it is a great embarrassment at the Cathedral here, leaving us short-handed. But he was considered indispensable, and he will still be needed for several months to put the decrees in order, be one of the committee to take them to Rome, & then prepare the final publication."[6] In June 1885, however, Keane received news that O'Connell would not be returning. He had just been named rector of the American College in Rome. "It is a great loss to us," Keane noted, "but as it is expressed that he will have a quasi-representative character in Rome, his appointment will be a great blessing to the Church in this country."[7] Gibbons intended that O'Connell would act in Rome as the agent for the American hierarchy that Keane and others had suggested as the substitution for the Roman intent of appointing a delegate in the United States. But O'Connell was already under consideration for two dioceses. William Gross of Savannah had just been transferred to Oregon City. Thomas Becker in Wilmington, Gibbons's former rival for Baltimore, asked to be transferred to Savannah. The bishops of the province of Baltimore, therefore drew up two lists. If the Holy See approved Becker's transfer, O'Connell was placed second on the list for Wilmington; if Becker was not transferred, O'Connell was placed first for Savannah.[8] Becker was named to Savannah and, incidentally, took Benjamin Keiley with him; Alfred A. Curtis, John Bannister Tabb's former mentor, was named to Wilmington. For the moment, O'Connell remained in Rome.

KEANE NAMED RECTOR OF THE CATHOLIC UNIVERSITY OF AMERICA

In May 1885, just before O'Connell's appointment, Keane became a member of the committee appointed by the council to initiate work on the Catholic University. In November, he was named to the fundraising committee for the institution. While collecting funds in New York early in 1886, however, he learned of Corrigan's opposition to the university. In May 1886 the university's newly formed board of trustees named Keane its first rector. As he told O'Connell, "I pleaded that it was simply absurd for a man to undertake to organize and run a university who had never been in a university in his life."[9] Until the Holy See approved the plans for the university, however, his appointment was to be kept secret.

But there were more changes coming for the American Church. In October 1885 Cardinal McCloskey had died. Seven months later, Gibbons learned he was to be the nation's second cardinal. On June 30, 1886, the twenty-fifth anniversary of his ordination to the priesthood, he received the red biretta in the Cathedral of the Assumption before a large crowd, including Keane and a delegation from Richmond.[10] Early in 1887, he then went to Rome to receive his red hat from Leo XIII. Richmond's former bishop now became the acknowledged leader of the hierarchy, while Keane, the diocese's incumbent, would play a supporting role.

With his nomination as rector, Keane began a two-year period of increasing involvement in the national church. But he had by no means abandoned Richmond. During this period, he arranged for the Daughters of Charity to staff a school for African Americans in Petersburg, looked for a site for a new orphanage, and entered a dispute with O'Keefe. In June 1886, moreover, he implemented one of the council's decrees. For the first time, the diocese had a chancellor, Edward M. Tearney.[11] Elsewhere in the world, the chancellor was merely the keeper of the records or archivist, but the American bishops transformed the office, so that the chancellor became the bishop's real delegate and, therefore, more important than the vicar general.[12] Tearney was new in a new office. Two years later he was still trying to find out what the job entailed. Fortunately, he had Roman classmates, like Thomas Shahan of Hartford, whom he could consult.[13] In the meantime, Keane confronted some of the issues dividing the American hierarchy right in his see city of Richmond.

KEANE AND TERENCE POWDERLY OF THE KNIGHTS OF LABOR

In 1884, just before the plenary council, Archbishop Eleazar Taschereau had gained a Roman condemnation of the Knights of Labor, a pioneer labor union. Bishop James A. Healy of Portland, Maine, then promulgated the condemnation in his diocese. The Canadian condemnation now led to an application of the conciliar legislation regarding secret societies. In this case, many Knights were Catholic, including the Grand Master Workman, Terence V. Powderly. But the Knights also claimed a membership of fifty thousand in the South, where they had struck twenty-two times for better wages. They included dock workers in Newport News and miners and foundry workers elsewhere in Virginia.[14] The Church in Virginia now had to confront the rights of workers. On October 4–20, 1886, the Knights held their annual convention in Richmond, the largest assembly of working men up to that time. Keane met Powderly on at least two occasions to discuss the organization's relations with the Church and urged him to present his case before the university committee of bishops meeting in Baltimore at the end of the month. He had even drafted a speech for the convention, but Powderly did not ask him to deliver it.[15]

Gibbons, too, was anxious to avoid a condemnation of the Knights of Labor. He had already written Cardinal Giovanni Simeoni, prefect of Propaganda, deprecating such an action, and had obtained a copy of the Knights' constitution, which Powderly was already revising to make it conform with Church teaching. On October 27, the bishops of the university committee met in Baltimore. Since Keane and John Ireland were to go to Rome to gain approval for the university, Gibbons also assigned them the task of defending the Knights. The next day, Gibbons presided over the first meeting of archbishops to investigate secret societies. They were originally to examine only the Grand Army of the Republic, a benevolent association of Union Army veterans, but Gibbons added the Knights of Labor and the Ancient Order of Hibernians to the agenda. Nine metropolitans were present. Of the three who were absent, all voted either against any condemnations or to follow Gibbons's views. Those present unanimously voted against a condemnation of the Grand Army or the Hibernians but failed to reach unanimity about the Knights of Labor. The case now had to be referred to Rome.[16]

KEANE'S STAY IN ROME:
ISSUES DIVIDING THE AMERICAN HIERARCHY

Soon after the university board meeting in October 1886, Keane and Ireland set out to Rome where they lodged at the American College. Keane's reunion with O'Connell at the college marked the formation of the liberal party in the hierarchy, as the triumvirate took a united stand on several controversial subjects. Not only were they working to gain approval of the Catholic University and prevent a condemnation of the Knights of Labor, they now confronted the question of ethnic tension.

Father Peter Abbelen of Milwaukee had come to Rome to complain of the treatment of German-Americans and demand that German-speaking parishes be declared to enjoy irremovability as the English-speaking ones did, that the pastor of a national parish would have to give his formal consent for the children of immigrants to join a territorial one, and that dioceses with large German-speaking populations have a German-speaking vicar general. Tragically, in light of what ensued, Propaganda had already consulted the American bishops, who agreed that national parishes should have irremovable rectors, just as territorial ones did, but that adult children of immigrants should be free to choose to join a territorial parish. The congregation was merely awaiting Gibbons's presence before issuing its response when Abbelen arrived in Rome. Keane, in the meantime, joined Ireland in distributing Abbelen's memorial to the American hierarchy and alerted Gibbons to the danger.[17]

In February 1887, Gibbons arrived in Rome. In April, at a meeting that Gibbons attended as a cardinal member of the congregation, Propaganda rejected Abbelen's proposals, except for what it had already decided before he arrived.[18] What lay behind the reaction of Keane and his friends was what it meant to be American. German-Americans saw the necessity of preserving their culture and language in order to preserve their faith. For men like Gibbons, Keane, Ireland, and O'Connell, this suggested that the American Church was still "foreign" to American society, that it was to be permanently divided among ethnic groups. Keane and O'Connell had had little experience of ethnic division in Richmond, where St. Mary's was the only German parish, whose pastors, the Benedictines, were not eligible to be irremovable rectors. This new experience, however, and their growing friendship with Ireland may also have shaped their attitudes toward those who were not native English-speakers in Richmond, especially van de Vyver.

Gibbons's defense of the Knights of Labor was more complicated. In New York, Powderly and the Knights had supported the mayoralty campaign of Henry George, whose social theories skated close to socialism. So had Father Edward McGlynn. After McGlynn had given a speech in George's behalf, against Corrigan's orders, he was suspended and threatened with excommunication unless he went to Rome for a hearing. Amid public outcry at his treatment, he refused to go unless he knew the specific charges against him. Although Keane thought McGlynn was a "disobedient and cranky priest," as he told Cardinal Edward Manning of Westminster, still he and Ireland, at Simeoni's request, cabled McGlynn to come to Rome, where he would receive a "fatherly" hearing. Keane then personally wrote Father Richard Burtsell, a canon lawyer and one of McGlynn's closest supporters, urging him to use his influence to have the priest come to Rome. The New York newspapers were soon reporting that Gibbons and Keane were in Rome working for McGlynn's restoration.[19]

As this controversy raged, Gibbons, with the assistance of Keane and Ireland, now submitted a memorial to Propaganda against the condemnation of the Knights of Labor. Unfortunately, the full text leaked to the press. It contained a reference to the reaction against Archbishop Corrigan's suspension of McGlynn. While this seemed criticism enough of Corrigan, Gibbons further widened the gap between his New York colleague and himself by submitting a second memorial deprecating the condemnation of George, for which Corrigan was then working. Instead of a condemnation of a social thinker, the American cardinal called for the pope to issue an encyclical on the social question, a suggestion that led to *Rerum Novarum* in 1891. Gibbons then met with officials of the Holy Office, the body charged with safeguarding orthodoxy. Keane was convinced, as he told Cardinal Manning, that the mood in Rome had been for condemnation, but "to-day the keynote was that the convictions of the Bishops of America are the safest guide to the Holy Office in its action on American affairs, and that they will let well enough alone."[20]

After Gibbons left Rome, Keane was still awaiting approval of the university. In the meantime, he presented both Propaganda and the Holy Office with French translations of all the endorsements of Gibbons's memorial in favor of the Knights of Labor. After consulting O'Connell, he had also presented the Holy Office with the constitutions of the Knights, with the amendments made at the Richmond convention. As he informed Gibbons, "they will be apt to see that this mass of English print is an elephant on their hands and they will be very slow to touch the matter again."[21] The Holy Office must have found the "elephant" difficult to digest. Only in the summer of 1888 did Simeoni forward to Gibbons the Holy Office's decision that the Knights of Labor could continue, provided they amended their constitutions to omit any expressions of socialism or communism.[22]

While Keane, O'Connell, and Ireland were busy dealing with Abbelen's memorial, the Knights of Labor, and Edward McGlynn, they were still working for the approval for the university. One reason for the delay was Corrigan's opposition. Finally, on April 10, 1887, Leo formally approved the university. In a subsequent audience with the pope, Keane asked to be relieved of being rector. Instead, the pope confirmed his selection but told him not to resign from Richmond until the future of the university was "solidly & practically under way."[23]

On May 15, 1887, Keane left Rome. He spent some time touring European universities and arrived back in Richmond on June 17, after an absence of over seven months. Among those welcoming him home was Governor Fitzhugh Lee.[24] He soon took off on his last visitation of his diocese, where he found "religion is in a healthy condition everywhere, allowance being made for the great disadvantages of the poor little missions which can have the visit of a priest so seldom."[25] His extensive Roman experience seems to have left him with a certain sense of ambiguity. On the one hand, his defense of McGlynn would seem to render him hesitant to risk an ecclesiastical trial of one of his own priests. He nevertheless chose to take on Matthew O'Keefe of Norfolk. On the other, his coalition with Ireland on the Abbelen memorial seems to have induced him totally to endorse the St. Paul bishop's Americanizing program. He worked strenuously to prevent the appointment of van de Vyver as his successor.

O'KEEFE FORCED TO LEAVE NORFOLK

While Keane was an exemplary bishop in caring for his diocese, he ended his episcopate on a sour note in regard to one of the veteran pastors of Virginia, Matthew O'Keefe. O'Keefe's problems had begun under Gibbons for supposedly deflecting his parish's collection from the orphanage to pay off the church debt.[26] Now another issue surfaced. James Behan had left property in Norfolk for the Jesuits eventually to build a college. The Jesuits, in turn, delegated O'Keefe to administer the property. One parishioner complained that, because O'Keefe failed to pay taxes on it, the city would soon take possession.[27] The Jesuit superior in Baltimore, however, assured Keane that the province procurator paid any bills O'Keefe sent and "that all his dealings with Fr O'Keefe have been satisfactory."[28] O'Keefe's accuser was R. Devereux Doyle, a cousin of James Behan. Though the Doyle family had been beneficiaries of Behan's will, O'Keefe later claimed they had "squandered" the money and now relied on "the well-known hostility of the people of Virginia to the Jesuits" to appropriate the property for themselves by filing "suit in our Norfolk Courts."[29]

In January 1879, Keane went to Norfolk personally to investigate the matter.[30] At this point, he seems to have supported O'Keefe, for in March 1879 Sister Euphemia in Emmitsburg informed him she was replacing Sister Mary Alice as superior of the orphanage with Sister Mary Augustine Wilson.[31] At the end of May, the transfer took place, at which point Sister Mary Alice, as Keane recorded, "astonished the community by putting off her habit."[32]

But the controversy was far from over and focused increasingly on O'Keefe's business practices. Much of this was due to the manner of holding property in Virginia. As had happened with O'Brien a generation earlier, O'Keefe purchased property with his own income and held it in his own name until the debt was paid off. A man of simple personal tastes, at one point he rented a room for himself and leased the rectory to two nieces of Archbishop Spalding to pay the debt on his church. When they fell into arrears in their rent, he evicted them. This contributed to his feud with the Doyle family.[33] Further to complicate the story, one of the Doyle women was married to the brother of Sister Isidore, director of St. Vincent's Hospital, which O'Keefe later asserted was the center of a conspiracy against him.[34] Keane now sided with the Doyles and ordered O'Keefe to cease his business ventures by 1882, a date that had to be extended.[35] In March 1885, Keane received new accusations that O'Keefe continued to be engaged in "business" and was the "real owner" of *The Virginian*. Again, the priest defended himself and explained that he had helped Michael Glennon financially in purchasing the newspaper.[36]

Keane's next action raised the controversy to a new level. On January 3, 1886, he ordered O'Keefe to change places with Father John Doherty at St. Patrick's in Richmond by the beginning of February.[37] O'Keefe acquiesced in Doherty's taking over Norfolk, but, in regard to going to Richmond, he begged "leave to say that my future happiness must be consulted on that point, and I now feel convinced that my future peace of mind can be attained only by seeking occupation elsewhere." He planned on applying to Gibbons for readmission to Baltimore, for which he had been ordained, or, if refused, to apply elsewhere. He had, in the meantime, ordered the tenants out of his rectory.[38]

O'Keefe then asked for several more postponements of his departure, so that he could conclude his personal business "without occasioning scandalous accusations."[39] Keane explained to Gibbons that O'Keefe wished there to be silence about his departure "to represent his return to his own diocese as an act solely depending on his own volition and the kind good will of his Archbishop as well as of the Bishop of the Diocese in which he had been working."[40]

For more than thirty-four years, O'Keefe had been an admirable pastor. In his annual report for 1885—which he did not send until May of 1886—he listed 1,200 people in the parish with 6,000 to 7,000 communions. His parish societies included the Living Rosary, St. Patrick's Benevolent Society, St. Augustine's, the Emerald Beneficent Society, and the Children of Mary.[41] He did not, however, list Keane's favorite, the Sodality of the Holy Ghost.

O'Keefe's departure had become public and his correspondence with Keane more heated. He had received letters of support from priests around the country and from newspaper editors promising they "will make it hotter for you than during the Plenary Council." He was now appealing to Gibbons as the metropolitan for "redress from an unjustifiable aggression on these rights, beginning years ago, and culminating January of this year. This course is now forced on me."[42] He also demanded a formal trial in accordance with Propaganda's instruction of 1878 and threatened to appeal to Rome. Keane flatly rejected his argument for a trial, "after careful consultation with the best authorities in Rome, that I have acted all along in entire accordance with law, I am quite content to await his Eminence's decision on your appeal."[43]

As the tension between Keane and O'Keefe was increasing, Gibbons's cooler counsel prevailed. While refusing to hear O'Keefe's appeal, Gibbons did recommend that Keane allow him another year, until July 22, 1887, to wind up his affairs,[44] an arrangement Keane thought was "not too much to pay for peace."[45]

The painful episode ending O'Keefe's service to Norfolk occurred, ironically, just as Keane held the Second Synod of Richmond, which promulgated the decrees of the Third Plenary Council but did not yet establish which parishes would have irremovable rectors. Had St. Mary's in Norfolk enjoyed the right of irremovability, O'Keefe could not have been removed or transferred without a formal trial. But Keane was still worried that O'Keefe might appeal to Rome.

Here, he relied on Denis O'Connell, whose own pastoral experience had been limited to the cathedral and a short stay in Winchester. O'Connell inquired if Propaganda had received an appeal from O'Keefe. Archbishop Domenico Jacobini, the secretary of the congregation, he informed Keane,

> said "he will have to go to the Archbishop of Balto. first." Then he asked me about the particulars of the case and I informed him. "Oh pshaw!" he replied, "it is only about a transfer, he can do nothing." I hope Father O'Keefe for his own sake will not make the mistake, for I wish him well. It only shows how delusive were all hopes of his being able to alter his course in Norfolk.[46]

In a few years, O'Connell would play an active role in the restoration of Edward McGlynn to the Church, but O'Connell's attitude then was not so much to support priests' rights as further to embarrass Corrigan.

On July 12, 1887, a month after his return from his lengthy stay in Rome, Keane formally released O'Keefe from service in Norfolk to go to Baltimore.[47] O'Keefe was then fifty-nine years old, having begun work in Norfolk at the age of twenty-four. Although ten years later he again attempted to have himself restored to Norfolk so that he could voluntarily resign, he was to pass the remaining years of his life in Baltimore, where he became editor of *The Catholic Mirror* and later founded a parish on a hill in Towson, Maryland, a suburb of Baltimore. The church he built there was named the Immaculate Conception and was built in a French Gothic revival style, reminiscent of his beloved St. Mary's of the Immaculate Conception in Norfolk. He died in January 1906, the last surviving brigade chaplain of the Confederate Army. The newspapers recalled his being awarded the Legion of Honor by Emperor Louis Napoleon of France for his care of men stricken with yellow fever on a French frigate in 1869.[48] They also reported his frugal life—to the end he ate only one meal a day, at noon. He was buried in his Towson church with the Confederate battle flag and the flags of Maryland and Virginia.[49]

Like the case of Timothy O'Brien in Richmond thirty-five years earlier, that of O'Keefe is ambiguous. Had he been so long in Norfolk that he regarded himself as autonomous? Had he made bad financial arrangements? Or was he the victim of false accusations about his business successes? Unlike O'Brien, he did not get support from Norfolk's most prominent Catholics. Nor did other priests express any concern about his removal. Whatever the truth, O'Keefe's departure marked the end of an era in Norfolk and cast a dark shadow over the end of Keane's episcopate.

KEANE'S RESIGNATION AS BISHOP OF RICHMOND

For the first six months of 1888, Keane was principally occupied with preparing for the opening of the university in the face of growing opposition. The choice of Washington as the site for the institution had, among other things, aroused the hostility of the Jesuits, who already had their own Georgetown University in the city, and led to Corrigan's temporary resignation from the board of trustees. Keane's new job was no sinecure. Nevertheless, in June, he formally submitted his resignation as bishop of Richmond. It was accepted on August 28.[50] When he received word, he was visiting the University of Notre Dame, from which he wrote to Gibbons: "While I cannot but feel the separation from the dear old Diocese, where I was truly the happiest bishop in America, I rejoice that the suspense is over, and that the Diocese can now soon have a bishop who can stay home and attend to it." He appointed van de Vyver, who had administered the diocese so often in his absence, as the apostolic administrator.[51]

True to his meticulous nature, Keane left a series of detailed recommendations for his successor. He began by listing the twenty-six priests of the diocese, excluding O'Connell, with their ordination dates—T. J. Brady, ordained in 1867, was then the senior.[52] Among his "General Observations," he wrote that "the work of giving schools, chapels, teachers, & pastors to the colored people throughout the Diocese, is of paramount importance. The Josephites & the local pastors should cooperate in it. The funds may be hoped for from the annual general collection, & from the Drexels."[53] He then proposed ways to free up the priests in the valley. He thought "it would be desirable that there were a priest at Charlottesville, although Catholics are so few & resources scant." Roanoke needed either an assistant or to be divided. The priest in Charlottesville could take care of Gordonsville and Culpeper, allowing the priests in Staunton to assume the missions on the C & O Railroad then extending up the valley from

Roanoke. Once the pastor of Manassas was freed of Gordonsville and Culpeper, he could then "take Fairfax from the Jesuits of Alexandria, who would be glad to give it up." Keane was still playing the game of movable priests.

He encouraged his successor to continue his practice of making annual visitations of the diocese, for "it gives good opportunity to lecture to the Protestants of Virginia & break down ignorant prejudice." Though he had shown himself to be almost picky about how churches and their liturgical furniture were maintained, he had "never insisted on the technicalities of visitation prescribed in the ceremonial,—things being in too primitive a condition for such formalities." Finally, he knew that Bishop Kain in Wheeling had again petitioned for a realignment of the diocesan boundaries. Although this would be to the "material disadvantage of the Diocese Rd.," he thought "it would be only fair to the Bp. of Wheeling," since the bishop of Richmond could "easily" reach the southwestern part of Virginia by the Norfolk and Western Railroad."[54]

Keane, like Gibbons, had been a circuit-riding prelate, as his entries in the diocesan diary illustrate. Unfortunately, unlike his predecessor, he recorded little detail of his journeys, other than the bare facts of where he was and what he did. What he did was not insignificant, despite his long absences. The diocese now had thirty-nine priests, in addition to two Jesuits in Alexandria and two Benedictines in Richmond. It had thirty-nine churches and twenty chapels, where Mass was said at least occasionally. But Keane could particularly claim credit for progress in two particular areas, work with Black Virginians and education. St. Joseph's in Richmond now had a school with eighty-nine students, of whom fifty-three were girls; and St. Francis orphanage, which developed from a foundling home, had ninety-seven. St. Mary's in Norfolk also had a nascent school for Black children, who now numbered fifty. The school for African American children at St. Mary's in Alexandria then enrolled sixty. For white students, Keane had introduced the Xaverian brothers to Richmond where they operated the Cathedral Male Academy and the parish school for boys. Altogether, the diocese now had five academies, two for boys and three for girls; and thirty-two parochial schools, evenly divided between boys and girls.[55] Keane had also laid the groundwork for a new boys orphanage eventually established in Roanoke.

Keane's successor would have a good foundation on which to build. But the choice of that successor was not to be without controversy. The process brought to the surface many of the problems latent in the broader American Church.

CHAPTER 16

Augustine van de Vyver: Pastoral Life in the Diocese of Richmond, 1889–1911

Augustine van de Vyver began his episcopate knowing that he was not the choice of either of his predecessors, Cardinal James Gibbons or Bishop John J. Keane. Whether because of his reaction to this antagonism or his own disposition, he remained uninvolved in the turmoil that divided the principal members of the hierarchy, with Gibbons and Keane strongly in the camp of the progressives. He chose, instead, to focus on his own diocesan administration. But here he seems more to have reacted to developments than to have had a concrete vision. Yet he also won the respect of his clergy. In one area, however, as will be seen in the next chapter, he did have a more articulated set of goals—work with African Americans.

OPPOSITION OF GIBBONS AND KEANE TO VAN DE VYVER AS BISHOP

Choosing Keane's successor was the first time that Richmond would use the new method legislated by the recent plenary council. As soon as Keane submitted his resignation, he appointed van de Vyver administrator. Theoretically, this created an irregularity, since Keane retained jurisdiction until his resignation was accepted. In June 1888, nevertheless, van de Vyver asked Gibbons to set a date for the eligible priests of the diocese to meet to draw up a *terna*. He added that all the priests were sad "at their separating of one who has been a model and a true father to all."[1] Before the ordeal was over, he might have had other sentiments.

On July 1, the Richmond priests chose, in order, Daniel Riordan of Chicago; Francis Janssens, then the bishop of Natchez; and van de Vyver. The most influential clergy, therefore, favored two of the diocese's priests recruited from Louvain, both of whom had served as vicars general. But the bishops of the province submitted a different list: van de Vyver, O'Connell, and James Cleary of Milwaukee. Their list differed from that of the priests, they explained, because Riordan had ill health and Janssens had, in the meantime, become archbishop of New Orleans. Although van de Vyver was in first place on the bishops' list and third place on the priests', Keane and Gibbons now began urging the appointment of O'Connell, who was only on the bishops' list. Immediately after the bishops' meeting, Keane told Gibbons that he regretted "that the notion of Dr. O'Connell's leaving Rome should have to be entertained at all, yet, since it evidently *is* entertained, I rejoice that his name is on our list. I hope that its being in the second place will make little or no difference and I pray that he may be the man."[2]

Further to complicate matters, this correspondence with Rome went through O'Connell, who pointed out to Gibbons that Keane's resignation had not been officially accepted.[3] More to the point of what unfolded, however, was Keane's attitude toward van de Vyver. He seems to have been so influenced by the controversy over the Abbelen memorial and John Ireland's Americanizing program that he now sought to prevent van de Vyver's appointment.

Although van de Vyver had ably served as a missionary priest in Harpers Ferry under Gibbons and as vicar general under Keane, the cardinal informed Propaganda that he lacked the necessary eloquence in English to appeal to both Catholics and Protestants. He further argued that O'Connell would have been the bishops' first choice, had they not thought he should remain in Rome. Cleary, he noted, had spent all his life in the Midwest and would perhaps find it difficult to live in Richmond. O'Connell, he made sure to mention, also had Keane's backing. Propaganda assigned the *ponenza* or position paper to the one cardinal with some experience of the United States, Camillo Mazzella, S.J., former dean of Woodstock College in Maryland, to whom Gibbons had submitted *Faith of Our Fathers* for theological review.

Named a cardinal in the same consistory as Gibbons, Mazzella would frequently oppose Gibbons and his friends. At this point, however, he displayed none of his later reservations about Gibbons. He did include in his position paper what was now a familiar issue—Kain in Wheeling had again proposed the realignment of the dioceses of Richmond and Wheeling. When the cardinals of the congregation met on December 10, 1888, Gibbons' influence from afar prevailed. They approved O'Connell's appointment to Richmond but deferred dealing with Kain's request until the new bishop of Richmond was installed. On December 16, however, Leo XIII rejected the nomination, "in order that the Rev. D. O'Connell might remain here some time as rector of the American College." Instead of asking the congregation to propose another name from the *ternae,* however, the pope called for new lists for Richmond.⁴ Ella Edes wondered from the beginning why O'Connell would want to give up his Roman position for a "one horse diocese."⁵

On February 5, 1889, the eligible priests of Richmond nominated, in order: van de Vyver, Daniel Riordan, and George Devine, a priest of Baltimore. On February 12, the bishops then submitted their own list. They were unanimous in placing van de Vyver first; this meant he had Gibbons's vote at this point. By a vote of four to three, they placed Devine second and unanimously named Ignatius Horstmann, a native of Philadelphia, third.⁶ Now van de Vyver was first on both lists, but, again, Gibbons attempted to thwart his nomination. He wrote strongly in favor of Horstmann as preferable to van de Vyver in preaching and to Devine in aptitude for governing a diocese. Keane, in the meantime, was in Rome recruiting faculty for the Catholic University. He disagreed with Gibbons in regard to Horstmann and urged Devine as his choice. As he told Gibbons, Devine was "not a strong man, but seems the best available."⁷ "Poor old Richmond," Keane wrote to O'Connell, knowing Gibbons would be hurt at his failure to support Horstmann.⁸

In the meantime, the leading priests of the diocese had all signed a petition to Rome, asking for van de Vyver's appointment. Bishop Kain of Wheeling personally presented it to Propaganda.⁹ In short, some of the tensions earlier manifested between Kain and Gibbons again surfaced. Within six years, however, Kain must have regained the cardinal's confidence, for he was named archbishop of St. Louis. The petition effectively countered Gibbons's and Keane's efforts. On June 3, 1889, Propaganda, for whom Mazzella had again presented the *po-*

nenza, choose van de Vyver. As they had done the year before, however, they still postponed any decision about the boundaries between Wheeling and Richmond until the new bishop took office.[10] Van de Vyver's appointment evoked a comment from O'Connell to Gibbons that "I am afraid you will find your province rather heterogeneous."[11]

Van de Vyver had to have known that Gibbons did not want him. On June 6, he wrote to Gibbons that he had learned of his appointment by a telegram from *The Catholic News* of New York. He had also received Gibbons's congratulations, but, in what may not have been a display of modesty, he said he hoped the news was false.[12] At the end of the month, he thanked Gibbons for his congratulations, but added that

> I must see you & consult with you about this matter. I am convinced that my accepting this high office would dishonor the American Hierarchy & ruin what the saintly Bishop McGill, your Eminence and dear Bishop Keane have built up. A very great mistake has been made & it is not too late to remedy it.[13]

Finally, on July 8, he informed Gibbons that he wished to reject the appointment and would come to consult him once the letters of appointment reached Baltimore.[14]

Van de Vyver had also written Monsignor de Nève, rector of the American College, for advice. On August 3, de Nève replied in a letter that the bishop must have later entrusted to his nephew, Louis Smet:

> In reply to your very interesting letter, I sent immediately a cable: *rien demander, rien refuser.* That is the golden rule of St. Francis of Sales. *Tuto progreditur qui illam sequitur.* . . . An application to daily duties makes a man soon acquainted with things that he must know. And the grace of God! *Si Deus vocat, Deus dat. Ergo esto robustus, et noli timere. Esto pater et frater cum omnibus, semper in gravitate. Vriend met iedereen, maar met niemand gemeen.* I will pray much for you.[15]

Regardless of his hesitation, van de Vyver became Richmond's sixth bishop. On October 20, 1889, he was consecrated in St. Peter's by Cardinal Gibbons assisted by Keane and Leo Haid, O.S.B., who had succeeded Northrop as vicar apostolic of North Carolina. Among the attending priests was O'Connell, who had returned to the United

States to help Gibbons prepare for the centennial of the hierarchy and the opening of the Catholic University in November.[16] Richmond was now but a memory for the young priest who was a rising star in the Roman galaxy.

Van de Vyver's Diocesan Administration

Van de Vyver seemed to be intent on being as different from his two predecessors as possible. Unlike them, he concentrated exclusively on his diocese, but he kept no diary of his activities. Initially, he made no major changes in Keane's structure. He retained Edward Tearney as his chancellor and secretary, before assigning him to Falls Church, after which he seems frequently to have done without a chancellor. From the pattern of some of his appointments, he also seemed to develop an informal method for testing young priests. In 1889, for example, he summoned Joseph Frioli from his first assignment in Keyser to serve in the cathedral until 1900, when he assigned him as pastor in Staunton. He then tried Charles Donohoe out in Keyser before giving him the new parish of St. Vincent's in Newport News. Although Keane had left a series of "observations" or recommendations for his successor, van de Vyver largely ignored them. The Holy Thursday meetings were abolished, as were the semiannual theological conferences.

Some of Keane's recommendations were initially difficult to follow, such as the appointment of a resident priest in Charlottesville to free the priests in Staunton for ministry in the valley. McVerry from Staunton or one of his assistants still crossed the mountain twice a month to Charlottesville until 1896, when John Massey became the first resident pastor. Van de Vyver then did follow part of Keane's directives and assigned to Charlottesville the missions in Culpepper, Gordonsville, and Orange County, along the railroad line going north to Alexandria. The next parish north of Orange was Warrenton, which was then under the care of the Benedictines.

Van de Vyver and Gibbons

Van de Vyver remained aloof from the controversies that began to divide the hierarchy in 1886 over the Abbelen memorial, the Knights of

Labor, and the Catholic University. In fact, there are only three extant letters from him to Gibbons during his episcopate. In light of Richmond's chronic shortage of priests, one of these was ironic, as he may have intended. In 1889, he informed Gibbons that he had two students from Lynchburg at St. Charles Seminary, one of whom was F. Joseph Magri, who later played a prominent role as a priest in the diocese. Since he already had nine seminarians, he suggested that Gibbons adopt the two for Baltimore.[17] His relationship with his metropolitan seemed cordial enough, but certainly not warm. During his episcopate, one of the few recorded times that the cardinal visited Richmond was on June 3, 1900, to consecrate Benjamin Keiley as bishop of Savannah to succeed Becker, who had died the previous year. While van de Vyver's correspondence with Gibbons was sparse, there are also few extant letters between him and Janssens, his fellow Louvain alumnus. He was bishop during a tumultuous period in the American Church, but he chose the part of a distant spectator as his predecessors played out their roles on the national, and ultimately international, scene.

RICHMOND'S CONNECTION WITH AMERICANISM

Richmond's former bishops, Gibbons and Keane, and one of its priests, O'Connell, were in the forefront of the controversies that divided the American Church. In the process, they would alter the face of the Church and bring it under the suspicion of heresy.

In 1892, the hierarchy was publicly divided on the issue of parochial schools and the religious education of children attending public schools. In 1890, Archbishop Ireland of St. Paul had initiated the argument by supporting the right of the state to educate during a period when the European Church was trying to preserve that right against state intrusion. He went further by arranging for two local school boards to rent his parochial schools during class hours, supervise the secular instruction, and determine the qualifications of the teachers. This was the type of plan John Hagan had proposed to Keane for Winchester in 1880. The arrangement, moreover, was not unique for it had existed in Poughkeepsie in the archdiocese of New York since 1875. For Ireland and his friends, however, it was part of his general program of Americanization. In an era when German-American

Catholics clung to their language as a means of preserving the faith of their children, he exacerbated the issue by supporting a law proposed in Wisconsin that would require English as the language of instruction in all schools, public and private. His plan aroused the hostility of German-American Catholics and several bishops, including Michael A. Corrigan of New York. But he had the ardent support of Gibbons, Keane, and O'Connell.[18]

Van de Vyver's only extant contribution to this debate was to tell Gibbons that pastors should arrange for children in public schools to receive religious instruction outside school hours.[19] His letter was dated October 15, 1892, only three days after the arrival in the United States of Archbishop Francesco Satolli, who came ostensibly as the Vatican representative to the Columbian Exposition in Chicago and to discuss the "school question," as it was known, with the archbishops at their November meeting. O'Connell and Ireland had orchestrated his arrival to keep Corrigan ignorant of the time and place of the ship's docking and thus make his absence from the reception committee appear to be disrespect to the papal emissary. Both, moreover, knew Satolli was to remain as the first permanent apostolic delegate to the American hierarchy, but they even kept Gibbons ignorant of that plan.[20] O'Connell would later make a point of recalling his role in establishing the delegation when giving his qualifications to be bishop of Richmond. Satolli, moreover, under the influence of Gibbons, Keane, Ireland, and O'Connell reconciled Edward McGlynn to the Church in December, without consulting Corrigan, his archbishop.[21]

In February 1893, van de Vyver wrote Gibbons in regard to Matthew O'Keefe's request that he again be appointed pastor in Norfolk with the understanding that he would voluntarily resign after one month. O'Keefe's purpose was "self-vindication," but van de Vyver thought it was "an attack" on both Gibbons and Keane. With perhaps a note of sarcasm for the role he knew the cardinal played in having McGlynn reconciled, the bishop voiced his fear that, if he did not reply, O'Keefe would take his case to Satolli, who, by that time, had been appointed apostolic delegate.[22] Gibbons's response, if there was one, is unfortunately lost.

As the divisions between the American bishops increased, Satolli shifted to support of Corrigan and his camp. Part of the delegate's criticism of his former friends stemmed from the prominent role Gibbons, Keane, and Ireland had played in the World Parliament of

Religions, held in October 1893 in conjunction with the Columbian Exposition in Chicago. Gibbons himself had reported to the Vatican secretary of state that the opportunity to explain Catholic doctrine far outweighed the danger of religious indifferentism. He and Keane both had had years of experience of relating to non-Catholics, joining with them in common projects and even preaching in their churches. As Satolli told his Roman superiors, however, he could not help but view Catholics participating with Protestants in prayer as undermining the integrity of Catholicism as the one true Church of Christ.[23] Satolli now increasingly joined forces with the conservatives.

O'Connell was the first victim of the conservative reprisals. As rector of the American College, he was supposed to act as agent for the entire hierarchy, but, for him, this meant Gibbons, Keane, and Ireland. In May 1895, Leo XIII, who had originally thought O'Connell so valuable as rector, now demanded his resignation. Instead of returning to the diocese, however, he became vicar of Gibbons's titular church in Rome, Santa Maria in Trastevere. A year later, Satolli, who had recently been named a cardinal but temporarily remained in Washington, recommended that the pope remove Keane from the Catholic University of America, for the sake of the discipline, intellectual life, and economic welfare of the university. Keane now joined O'Connell in Rome where he became a consultor to the Congregations of Propaganda and of Seminaries and Universities.[24] The stage was now set for what became known as Americanism.

Americanism grew out of a number of factors. First, in France, Archbishop Ireland became the darling of those seeking to show the compatibility of Catholicism with republican government at a time when most French Catholics sought the return of monarchy. His speeches were translated into French, and, in 1892, he himself toured the nation in a self-appointed mission to have Catholics support the new papal policy of rallying to the French Republic. The Italians, too, adapted his speeches to call for Catholic support of the constitutional monarchy. Second, *The Life of Father Hecker*, by Walter Elliott, was translated into French. Hecker, the founder of the Paulists, had, among other things, said that if Catholic doctrine were presented in a positive way, American Protestants would embrace it. In Europe, he was accused of watering down doctrine. Underlying this view was the American separation of Church and State. O'Connell entered the fray by delivering an address at the Fourth International Catholic Scientific

Congress at Fribourg, Switzerland, in August 1897. Considered to be the definitive theological description of authentic Americanism, his paper, "A New Idea in the Life of Father Hecker," praised the notion of "unalienable rights" in the Declaration of Independence. It further argued that the American separation of Church and State worked better to grant freedom to the Church than a union between Church and State that appeared to many theologians actually to be authentic Catholic doctrine. Many of these problems would, in fact, not be solved until the Second Vatican Council. Early in 1899, however, Leo XIII addressed an apostolic letter to the American Church, *Testem Benevolentiae,* condemning what he saw as heretical elements in Americanism.[25] Van de Vyver's papers reveal nothing of these controversies in which so many people with ties to him and his diocese were involved. He remained content to govern his diocese.

VAN DE VYVER AGAIN RECRUITS FROM LOUVAIN

Although Keane had finally fulfilled McGill's pledge to make the bishop of Richmond a "patron" of the American College in Louvain, van de Vyver was slow in renewing the association. In the alumni bulletin for 1903, only two Louvain priests were listed as functioning in the diocese, Cyril de Muynck, ordained in 1895, and Felix Kaup, ordained in 1902. Born in Prussia, Kaup was first assigned to Portsmouth, where he started a night school to teach boys typing and machinery.[26] In 1904, he was the pastor of Sacred Heart in Manchester, from which he was collecting funds for the new cathedral residence.[27] Then, he was back in Portsmouth, from which, in 1907, he was appointed vice rector of the American College. After only a year, however, he was recalled to Richmond and served as chancellor. But van de Vyver soon gained other Louvain recruits.

In 1905, van de Vyver travelled to Louvain to ordain his nephew, Louis Smet, for the diocese. Smet would hold a series of appointments in the diocese before becoming pastor of St. Mary's in Alexandria, from which he returned to Louvain as vice-rector of the college. In 1905, the bishop also recruited John Konicek, an Austrian subject, to work with a Bohemian settlement near Petersburg. Three years later, Joseph De Gryse of Belgium began work in the diocese. But just before he died, van de Vyver had also recruited his great-nephew, Joseph

Govaert, who was, however, ordained under O'Connell.[28] While van de Vyver was recruiting young priests from his alma mater, he gained a windfall—another Belgian, not an alumnus of the American College.

AMADEUS JOSEPH VAN INGELGEM

Amadeus Joseph van Ingelgem was born in Lippeloo, Belgium, in 1852. He studied at the Grand Séminaire in Mechlin (Malines) where he formed a lifelong friendship with Désiré-Joseph Mercier, then a seminarian and later archbishop of Malines, a cardinal, and a hero during World War I. Each had made a promise to offer his second Mass on Christmas Day for the other. Ordained in 1875, van Engelgem then pursued a degree in canon law at the University of Louvain. Assigned to pastoral work in Brussels, he was active in work among the poor and in supporting a nascent newspaper, *Le Patriote,* which was later renamed *La Libre Belgique.* He became the director-general of the Society of the Priests of St. Francis de Sales but resigned early in 1900 to go to the United States. Although Van de Vyver had heard of his arrival and begged him to come to Virginia, he initially refused and, instead, associated himself with the Josephites to work among African Americans in Oklahoma. But van de Vyver was not to be put off. Assisted by Julia Ward of Norfolk, who had been under van Ingelgem's spiritual direction in Paris, the bishop persuaded him to come to Virginia. He first assigned him to Lynchburg, where he replaced the controversial Joseph Anciaux in 1902. But then van Ingelgem took up residence in Staunton. From here, he began a whole new apostolate—not to African Americans but to the illiterate and unchurched people of the mountains.[29]

With Father Joseph Frioli as his nominal superior in Staunton, van Ingelgem, then over fifty years old, began missionary treks through Augusta, Rockingham, Rockbridge, Bath, and Highland Counties. He soon set up his headquarters at Vanderpool, about five miles south of Monterey, in Highland County. On October 28, 1904, he induced Van de Vyver to come for confirmations. The fifty-four-mile trip from Staunton took a day and a half, according to an account in *The American College Bulletin,* probably written by van Ingelgem himself. They traveled along "one of the finest mountain-roads to be seen in America . . . laid out and graded by Mr. Le Long, a French engineer of acknowledged ability." People by the hundreds turned out, for "our non-Catholic brethren are ready to listen to the preaching of Catholic doctrine and, once they see the truth, are willing and eager to accept it." But, van Ingelgem continued, these people were "Protestant in the strictest sense of the word . . . [and] to make the change from any form of non-Catholic Christianity to that of submission to the Roman Catholic Church, means to acknowledge that they have, up to the time of their conversion, been in the wrong all the while." Without the support of a Catholic community, in a situation where Catholicism was "almost entirely unknown," "singularly misunderstood and studiously misrepresented, . . . to become a convert and submit to the true Church, generally means the exercise of a vast unflinching courage and dauntless determination." Once in Vanderpool, van de Vyver gave a lecture on Saturday evening on the marks of the Church. The next morning, after saying Mass and administering confirmation, he addressed a crowd of 400, some of whom were gathered outside the church doors.[30]

For six years, "Father Van," as he became affectionately known, criss-crossed the mountains on his black stallion "Dixie." He had a series of places where he stayed overnight, often with Protestants who constituted his congregation for his daily celebration of Mass.[31]

The Belgian missionary captured the imagination of Joseph Hergesheimer, a popular early-twentieth-century novelist, whose character "Father Merlier" is a minor but significant protagonist in *Mountain Blood,* transformed by literary license into a Jesuit.[32] Unfortunately, van Ingelgem's community at Vanderpool, which he numbered at the time to be forty, did not long survive. In the 1990s, there was no Catholic presence in Highland County.

But van Ingelgem's service to Virginia had not ended. In August 1906, van de Vyver assigned him to the diocese's first "mission band," together with Thomas F. Waters, ordained in Rome in 1896, and W. Gaston Payne. They were to visit all the churches in the diocese and the small congregations without churches, to conduct temporary missions. Initially making their headquarters at Barnesville, the site of the ill-fated Keileyville colony, the three started a monthly magazine to publicize their efforts, *The Catholic Virginian,* with van Ingelgem as editor. The paper continued only until the middle of 1909, when van Ingelgem received the double appointment of secretary to the bishop and chaplain at "Oak Ridge," Thomas Fortune Ryan's estate. He soon alienated the cathedral's benefactor by using the estate as the base of operations for missionary tours. This experience probably colored his reaction to Ryan later on, when he referred to the "Siegneur of Oak Ridge."[33] Early in January 1910, van Ingelgem was appointed pastor of St. James Church in "West End," Falls Church. There was a certain irony in his new assignment. Although he had chafed under Thomas F. Ryan's imperious demands on a chaplain at Oak Ridge, he now came to a stone church built by Mrs. Ryan in 1902 to replace the frame structure of 1872.[34]

FALLS CHURCH AND BEYOND:
THE FIRST DEVELOPMENT OF NORTHERN VIRGINIA

In 1892, the Jesuits had transferred their parish of St. Mary's in Alexandria, with its missions in Falls Church and Fairfax, to the diocese. Falls Church received a resident pastor, Edward Tearney, native of Harpers Ferry, who had been Richmond's first chancellor. He now became the only priest between the parish of his birth and Alexandria and had two missions, in Fairfax Station and Leesburg. With the exception of two years, 1897–99, when he was rector of the cathedral in Richmond, he remained at St. James until 1910. He presided over the building of the new church and, in 1905, opened a school, for which he invited the Sisters of Perpetual Adoration.[35] Tearney left Falls Church to become pastor of Lynchburg, where he died in 1935. But Falls Church in 1892 was still a sleepy little town.

What slowed down development in northern Virginia was the lack of a bridge across the Potomac from what was then Alexandria County to Washington. A canal bridge crossed at the site of the future Key Bridge and a streetcar line ran to Falls Church. In October 1908, Tearney wrote van de Vyver that his parish included Balston and Clarendon along the river. He estimated that there were 200 Catholics in the territory, mainly Irish laborers, few of whom came to Mass. They could afford neither the twenty-cent trolley for the five-mile trip to Falls Church nor the pew rents at Trinity Church, the Jesuit parish in Georgetown. The Jesuits, moreover, had been saying Mass at Fort Myer, but had to discontinue the practice and felt no responsibility for Catholics in the neighboring diocese. In addition, Tearney reported thirty-two Catholics in the hamlet of Ingleside, so he proposed a new parish to include Balston, Clarendon, Fort Myer, and Ingleside. The priest assigned to the parish could temporarily live with him in Falls Church until the new parish was self-sufficient.[36] From this proposal came St. Charles Borromeo, the first daughter parish of Falls Church. It would still be some years, however, before the area experienced great growth. When it came after World War I, van Ingelgem and his fellow Louvain alumnus, Louis Smet, would see the first, slow growth of northern Virginia. Other areas of Virginia were also in need of a catalyst to aid development.

Newport News and Norfolk

In Newport News, the story began in 1881 when Charles W. and Margaret E. Hogan Lohmann of Richmond moved to the hamlet that was starting to develop as a result of the extension of the Chesapeake and Ohio Railroad to Old Point Comfort. They gathered a Catholic community in their home, which became a mission of St. Mary's, Fort Monroe. On Sundays when Mass was not available in Newport News, they rode in their carriage to Fort Monroe. Early in 1890, the congregation petitioned van de Vyver for a resident priest. For a time, Father Richard A. Drake came down from Richmond twice a month to say Mass either in a hall or a Baptist chapel, but, in November, Charles E. Donohoe was transferred from Danville to become the first resident pastor. In April 1891, a church, named after the patron of the diocese, St. Vincent de Paul, was completed for a congregation of only 175 people, with twelve more in its two missions in Williamsburg and Smithfield.

The catalyst for the growth of the Newport News region came with the opening of the Newport News Shipbuilding and Dry Dock Company, which launched its first two ships for the Navy in 1895. By 1900, the parish had 1,000 members, but the population of its missions had increased only to twenty-five. By 1902, it had a new pastor, Thomas J. Wilson, and a school for boys run by the Xaverian Brothers. On October 5, 1903, the Sisters of Charity of Nazareth opened a school for girls, made possible by a gift to the parish from Mr. and Mrs. Thomas Fortune Ryan.[37]

Across Hampton Roads in 1894, after a century of Catholic presence, Norfolk still had only two parishes, St. Mary's and St. Joseph's.

A third parish, Sacred Heart, was now carved out from the territory of St. Mary's, along the Elizabeth River near the Norfolk and Western Railroad, and placed under the care of Father Francis X. McCarthy.[38] Thirty years would pass before the parish even had a permanent building and almost that long before more parishes would be established in the area. The cradle of Virginia Catholicism had ceased to be its nursery. Norfolk would receive a catalyst for growth only when the United States government chose it as a Naval Operating Station, but that would have to await a world war.

Sisters in Norfolk and at the Medical College of Virginia

Norfolk's Catholic presence, of course, continued to find expression through St. Vincent's Hospital. In 1892, a clinic for poor patients was opened. A proposed reorganization of the hospital in 1896, however, threatened this new outreach and increased tension between the physicians working in the clinic and those in the hospital, with Sister Isidore Kenny strongly defending the clinic physicians.[39] Part of the friction may have stemmed from the growing professionalization of nursing and the changing role of hospitals.

In 1893 the Medical College of Virginia in Richmond contracted for the Sisters of Mercy from Newberne, North Carolina, to take over the nursing care of its new hospital, founded as a teaching institution by Doctor George Ben Johnston, son of Senator Johnston and Niketti Floyd and a pillar of the Catholic community.[40] The sisters' "use and occupancy" of the building were to be continued until ended by mutual consent. They were to have the use of the upper floor, and the faculty "will at all times give their professional services to the hospital."[41] In December 1894, however, the faculty passed a resolution to notify the sisters that their contract would be terminated on May 1, 1895. No reason was officially given, but the sisters were not trained in nursing.[42] It was to remedy this deficiency, in 1893, that St. Vincent's Hospital had opened a nursing school, one of the first such Catholic institutions. Six years later, however, fire completely destroyed the hospital, which was rebuilt in 1901.[43]

Neither the Norfolk area nor northern Virginia would ever grow because of immigration. For that matter, as van de Vyver pointed out in his speech at the dedication of the new cathedral, Virginia and the Church within it had not been the destination of large numbers of European immigrants. But some did find their way to the Old Dominion.

VIRGINIA'S IMMIGRANTS FROM EASTERN AND CENTRAL EUROPE

In the late nineteenth century, small numbers of immigrants, usually recruited as laborers or farmers from eastern and central Europe, settled in Virginia's countryside. In 1905, van de Vyver had engaged John Konicek from Louvain to work with "Bohemians" who had come to the area around Petersburg. In November, Konicek reported that few of the people spoke English and most had settled in two regions, one group in Prince George County and the other in Dinwiddie, with a few scattered families in between. Since the community in Prince George had been there for fifteen years and had twenty-seven immigrant families and three others, he recommended a church be built there. Moreover, he continued, these people had to travel an average of ten miles to Petersburg, along roads that were impassable during flooding or in the winter. He further pointed to the danger of defection because of the presence of a Protestant church with a Bohemian minister. Konicek had already begun subscriptions for a church.

In regard to the Dinwiddie community, Konicek revealed how loosely the term "Bohemian" was applied. This was a new settlement, and he found there eighteen Bohemian families and one German. But these all came from Russia and Hungary, where there were few Catholic churches. They were between four and eleven miles from Petersburg and twelve miles from Prince George. He counted sixty children among them, but, up to this point, the people had shown little religious zeal. He now recommended building a chapel where a priest could say Mass twice a month. In regard to the families dispersed between Prince George and Petersburg, he thought they could go to either church. Finally, he proposed that he reside at the main church in Prince George, say Mass and conduct Sunday school for two weeks and then go to Dinwiddie every third Sunday.[44] Curiously, Konicek specifically asked van de Vyver to respond in English, so he could read it to the people. His own use of English was still poor, but he seemed to be making a point that the language should not be an obstacle. As a result, Sacred Heart Church, New Bohemia, opened in 1906. Konicek, unfortunately, was forced by ill health to retire in 1911 and died the following year. But most of Virginia's immigrants continued to be Irish.

MINES AND RAILROADS IN THE ALLEGHENY HIGHLANDS

West of Lexington, a few scattered families had lived in Allegheny County before the Civil War. With the expansion of the Virginia Central Railroad (later the Chesapeake and Ohio) that connected Staunton and Clifton Forge by 1857, and the development of the Low Moor mines in the 1870s, more Catholics, mainly Irish, moved into the area. In 1882, John Lynch, while already building St. Andrew's in Roanoke, built Mt. Carmel Church in Low Moor. With Lynch's permanent transfer to Roanoke, Lawrence Kelly became pastor of Lexington with missions at Low Moor, Covington, and Clifton Forge. The railroads made it less difficult, but still not easy, for a priest to answer sick calls. The family of a dying man in Clifton Forge, for example, once telegraphed the priests both in Lexington and Staunton. McVerry from Staunton got there first to administer the last rites.[45]

The further expansion of the railroad, however, made Clifton Forge into a more important center than Covington, so Kelly transferred his residence there from Lexington in 1892. Two years later, van de Vyver dedicated the first Sacred Heart Church in Covington and appointed a new pastor, William A. Fallon, who also had charge of Lexington, Clifton Forge, and a chapel, the Shrine of the Sacred Heart, at Hot Springs in Bath County. Lexington was now being bypassed by its own missions. In 1901, Gaston Payne was assigned to Clifton Forge, but Lexington was made a mission of Staunton, the status it would have until well into the twentieth century.[46] His Virginia birth and relation to a Confederate admiral may well have helped him mediate between the predominantly Irish settlers and the Protestant establishment. He was also a member of the original diocesan mission band.

The Irish were not the only immigrants to go to Allegheny County. Between 1900 and 1914, young Italian men came to work in the mines; at least fourteen of them died in accidents. From the available evidence, they were for the most part single, and, unlike the Irish, had not come to take up permanent residence but to make money to return to Italy. When the mines and furnaces began to decline during World War I, they departed.[47]

BENEDICTINES IN NORTON, BRISTOL, AND POCAHONTAS

Mining also attracted immigrants to Norton and the surrounding area of southwest Virginia in what was then part of the diocese of Wheeling. They came from Hungary, Slovakia, Ireland, Germany, Lebanon, and Poland. In 1896, the Stonega Coal and Coke Company had built St. Anthony's Church for the Catholic miners in Norton, which was tended from time to time by Emil Olivier, the pastor in Bluefield, West Virginia. But the nearest priests were the Benedictines of St. Bernard's Abbey in Cullman, Alabama, then in charge of a series of missions in the diocese of Covington, Kentucky. They initially became involved in Virginia through pastoral necessity. In 1902, Thomas Roach of Stonega lost both his legs in a railroad accident. He sent for Ambrose Reger, O.S.B., the pastor in Middlesboro, Kentucky, who may also have made subsequent calls to Stonega. Bishop Kain of Wheeling then formally petitioned the abbot for the Benedictines to take over the missions in southwest Virginia.[48] Father Vincent Haegle, O.S.B., took up residence in Stonega, while Father P. Theodore, O.S.B., became the first resident pastor of Bristol.

Bristol, or Goodson as it was originally called, had had a church, St. Anne's, since 1871, visited once a month by the priest from Abington or Wytheville, Virginia. In 1873, the pastor of Wytheville reported he received no regular income from the mission but depended on what the people gave him. He took a train to Goodson, but covered the rest of his missions on horseback.[49] In January 1903, Father Theodore arrived in Bristol to find that he had for his living quarters only a small room at the back of the church. Apparently not suited for such a rugged life, he was replaced in a year by Fridolin Meyer, O.S.B., who was to remain for twenty-four years.[50]

From Norton and Bristol, the Benedictines established a string of missions, the churches for which were built with contributions from miners and the company. They remained until the Depression forced the closing of the mines and the departure of many Catholic miners to northern cities.[51]

Further to the east was Pocahontas, where Hungarians had settled. By 1896, they had a church, St. Elizabeth's, and were served by Olivier from Bluefield. In 1909, Olivier retired, and the Benedictines added this mission to their charge. They remained until 1942, when Oblates from Princeton, West Virginia, took over. The Oblates, in turn, were replaced by the Pallotine Fathers–Irish Province. Pocahontas became a center for missions in McComas, West Virginia, and Tazewell, Richlands, and Grundy, Virginia.[52] These sections of Virginia would be assigned to the diocese of Richmond in 1974.

Van de Vyver had been an able administrator, though he seems to have kept most diocesan affairs in his own hands. Like many bishops, he had simply responded to the demands of the pastoral needs of his diocese, and so far these were not great. The period of his episcopacy was not one of growth in population. While he steered a course independent of his two predecessors, he did develop one of their key projects and place on it his own character—work among African Americans. In addition, he was the beneficiary of an outpouring of financial bequests, the most notable of which was that of Thomas Fortune Ryan to build the cathedral Keane had originally planned.

CHAPTER 17

Benefactors of the Diocese and the Drexels' Work with African Americans

Although van de Vyver's episcopate was largely uneventful in terms of diocesan initiatives, it witnessed an increase in benefactions not only to the diocese but for work specifically with Black Virginians. The Josephites not only expanded their activity beyond Richmond, but the Drexel sisters opened their schools in Rock Castle. Another benefactor made possible the institutions of the Benedictine sisters and priests in Bristow, of which only Linton Hall, under the sisters, would remain. By far, the largest gift to the diocese up to that time, however, was Thomas Fortune Ryan's donation of money for a new cathedral, perhaps the crowning achievement of van de Vyver's tenure in Richmond.

African Americans and the Josephites

While Gibbons, Keane, and O'Connell were embroiled in national and international controversy, van de Vyver made major advances on the work Keane had begun with African Americans. In 1888, the Josephites reported that of the 750,000 Black Virginians outside of Norfolk, very few were Catholic. Two years later, Richmond had not only St. Joseph's Church, but also an industrial school and several mission schools. The Josephites had, moreover, opened a mission in Norfolk and schools in Petersburg, Lynchburg, Alexandria, and Keswick, outside of Charlottesville. The Black Catholic population had grown to 600.[1] The following year, van de Vyver appealed for "liberal appropriations" from the Catholic Bureau of Indian and Negro Missions. Norfolk then had a convent and two schools, but the accommodations were so small that applicants had to be turned away. But the congregation also needed a church, the bishop continued, for "hundreds of old Maryland colored Catholics who went to Norfolk after the war are now fallen away. If we had a special church for them, many of them could be reclaimed."[2] In 1894, the Josephites opened St. Joseph's Church in Norfolk.

The work among Black Americans proceeded slowly. In 1896, Father L. J. Welbers, pastor of St. Joseph's in Richmond, reported that both the Richmond and Norfolk parishes had schools with twelve Sisters of St. Francis, while Lynchburg had a school run by two lay teachers. He himself served three mission stations and had opened a home for infants, St. Francis Foundling Home, the only institution of its kind in Virginia, where "a considerable number of children have been baptized, who, but for this institution, would perhaps never have received that grace." While baptisms were steadily increasing, he also warned that Protestants were everywhere active.[3] When Welbers left Richmond in 1897, there were still only 700 Catholics out of a total Black population in Virginia of 650,000.[4] Despite the slow progress in terms of numbers, the Josephites followed the pattern of evangelization established by Keane—schools would precede churches in many places.

A prime example was the school in Lynchburg for African Americans, founded in the 1890s. The small Catholic community received occasional visits from a Josephite priest in Richmond. In 1900, when Joseph Anciaux became the first pastor of St. Francis de Sales, the school had an enrollment of one hundred and forty, only four or five of whom were Catholic. A Belgian, Anciaux was then an oblate of the Josephites and was not admitted to full membership until 1904.[5]

Unfortunately, Anciaux shortly became involved in the public controversy over Father John R. Slattery's decision to leave the priesthood and the Church. In a sermon at the first Mass of John Henry Dorsey, the first African American Josephite in 1902, Slattery accused the American Church of complicity with the racism then rampant in the nation. On August 27, Anciaux issued a broadside to the American hierarchy, "Plain Facts for Fair Minds," in which he charged that "the Protestant idea of a radical and unchristian separation of the races" had found its way into the Church. As an example, he cited the pittance American Catholics contributed to the annual collection for missions among the Black people. Slattery, he said, was "almost the only one who always courageously raises his voice against the wrong done the unfortunate Negro," while Gibbons and van de Vyver were too cautious in the face of "negro-haters." The opposition to the ordination of Black priests, he claimed, derived "from . . . unchristian negro-phobia; from the horror of thinking that a colored seminarian will sit beside a white seminarian . . . and . . . being a priest . . . will consecrate and bless as any other priest." For Anciaux, "that hurts the feelings of Southerners, [who] . . . cry 'Down with colored priests.'"[6]

In 1903, Anciaux followed up with a pamphlet, "The Miserable Condition of Black Catholics in America," and sent a copy to his cousin, Cardinal William van Rossum, prefect of Propaganda. Though there were ample "decrees of the Council of Baltimore and synodal rules" for charitable work among African Americans, he asserted that "prejudice" left them "without force. . . . Excepting the noble-hearted Archbishop [John] Ireland and Bishop [Anthony] Durier (Natchitoches) and the very saintly deceased prelate, Archbishop [Francis] Janssens, I know of no one who had the audacity to protect and to defend the rights of the Negroes openly."[7] As evidence for white prejudice against Blacks, he had only to cite a speech by Bishop Benjamin Keiley of Savannah criticizing President Theodore Roosevelt for inviting Booker T. Washington to a dinner at the White House.[8] Thus, two bishops with strong Richmond connections took opposite views on the race question: Janssens, recruited for the diocese from Holland, and Keiley, a native of Petersburg.

Anciaux received the support of Archbishop Ireland, as might be expected, but van de Vyver withdrew Anciaux's faculties necessitating his departure from the Richmond diocese.[9] The bishop then temporarily appointed Amadeus van Ingelgem to the parish.

In its early years, 1901–5, St. Francis de Sales Church experienced a dramatic number of baptisms. In the first quinquennial report, there were 113 baptisms and 78 converts, but then the numbers began to drop, with no more than 20 baptisms and 8 converts in any year until 1917. The enrollment in the school also began to decline from a high of 155 in 1901 to only 35 in 1907.[10] Yet the school provided a model for evangelization of African Americans in Virginia. One of its earliest students, Rebecca Clifford, was a graduate. Baptized by

Thomas B. Donovan, who succeeded Slattery as superior general of the Josephites, she was the first member of her family to become a Catholic. She then attended St. Francis de Sales Institute in Rock Castle. In 1908, she entered the Oblates of Divine Providence in Baltimore and, as Mother Consuela, served as superior for eleven years. In 1937, she died at the age of only fifty-two, but her life bore testimony to the value of the schools both in Lynchburg and in Rock Castle.[11]

Back in Richmond, St. Joseph's Church had become such a familiar part of the Catholic scene that white Catholics had begun going there, "occupying," as a newspaper story reported, "seats apart from the colored people." In 1902, van de Vyver ordered "that no confessions are to be heard at St. Joseph's to [sic] white people."[12] Parishes, however, were not the only apostolates among African Americans.

KESWICK AND KATHARINE DREXEL

While the Josephites were almost exclusively responsible for the overall pastoral care of Black Catholics in Virginia, Rock Castle with its dual institutions for male and female students was the product of Katharine Drexel and her sister, Louise Morrell, daughters of a wealthy Philadelphia family. Katharine founded the Sisters of the Blessed Sacrament for the explicit purpose of working with Indians and African Americans, and Louise married Colonel Edward Morrell, a graduate of the University of Pennsylvania law school and officer in the Pennsylvania National Guard. The Morrells devoted their wealth to service of Black Americans. For both sisters, Virginia became an early focus for their philanthropy. Katharine had approached van de Vyver in August 1891 about funding an existing school at Keswick in Albemarle County in order to turn it into a boarding school to train Black catechists for rural Virginia.

The school in Keswick had its beginning in 1886 with Wales R. Tyrrell, an African-American native of Virginia and a schoolteacher. Hired to teach in the public school, he conducted a Sunday school on the side. In January 1886, he asked Slattery to come from Richmond and say Mass. As a result, he was brought before the public school board in Charlottesville in February 1887. In Tyrrell's account, the chairman of the board informed the members:

you have before you the teacher of school No. 5 who is charged with being a Catholic, teaching a Sunday school composed of day pupils in general, and has led many astray. He is further accused of making many people believe a man can forgive sin. A third accusation is that he allows a Catholic priest to preach in his school room.

In the exchange that followed, Tyrrell stated he had not declared he was a Catholic when he was hired because he was not asked "about my religion." His accuser responded that "religion is something omitted sir, but Catholicism is a different thing. In general that is not regarded as religion." When Tyrrell was challenged on his authorization "to have services in a public school room," he produced a letter from the clerk of the board granting his permission. The clerk responded that he recalled granting permission, but "thought it was a minister of the Gospel. Had he said a Catholic Priest, he would have received a different reply." The board then instructed Tyrrell "in the future [to] let Catholicism alone; keep your much loved faith to yourself and no doubt you will succeed as well as when you were a Protestant."[13] Catholicism still had not found a welcome in some parts of Virginia, and being Black only exacerbated the situation. But Tyrrell was not the only Black Catholic who faced prejudice because of his religion.

In 1887, Tyrrell and another Black Virginia student, Joseph Griffin, entered the seminary for the Mill Hill Fathers at St. Peter's College, near Liverpool, England. Poor health, however, forced Tyrrell to withdraw from the seminary and return to Virginia. Griffin later left the seminary before ordination.[14] Tyrrell returned to Keswick, where he concentrated on a catechetical school, supported by Slattery's personal funds, that prepared at least some students to enter Epiphany Apostolic College, the Josephite preparatory seminary in Walbrook, near Baltimore, Maryland.[15]

It was Tyrrell's school that Mother Katharine now proposed to develop into a boarding school. But van de Vyver had reservations, some of them about Tyrrell. Her offer, he said, was "sufficient to put up a good building & furnish it in a plane [sic] style. But there is no one to look after the daily expenses except the teacher himself who cannot be trusted with any money." The potential students could not be expected to contribute much, and the diocese was already too strapped to "cover the expenses of the various schools throughout the diocese." He acknowledged that a good boarding school "would no doubt be the means of great good and it could be made successful if we had some good prudent and economical manager to take matters in hand." Finding such a manager presented a problem, but the bishop explained that "a white person will hardly undertake it and a colored person such as is needed is very rarely found." He, therefore, proposed that he use her funds to "put up in Norfolk a wooden structure for our little ones in Norfolk," where the building in use had never been "fit for the purpose" and "fell down." Father Albert Lightheart, the Josephite pastor in Richmond, seconded the view that "the needs in Norfolk are much greater than those in Keswick."[16]

At issue were two different approaches to evangelization. Katharine Drexel looked to the rural south where most African Americans then lived. Van de Vyver and Lightheart took into account the cities to which many Blacks were then beginning to move. They differed not so much in concern for African Americans as in where to reach them. But the bishop had by no means abandoned the rural approach.

On September 2, 1891, van de Vyver again wrote Mother Katharine. This time he articulated more of his views on a rural apostolate:

> I have the interests of our colored people at heart as much as that of the whites; I acknowledge that I am inclined to favor them even a little more, their needs and wants are indeed much greater. It is probable that we may educate in such a school some good teachers who will be of incalculable benefit to country missions. Were we able to start little schools in country districts we would be able to spread the light of faith. Father Lightheart tells me now that he feels able to secure a proper person to take charge with the present teacher of our school in Keswick.
>
> I have always held that if we can establish schools in rural districts we will be as successful as we are in Keswick. We can do but little in the cities where the colored people are banded together wonderfully well but it is difficult in the country districts where in a measure they are left to themselves.

In short, his principal reservation about Keswick seemed to focus on Tyrrell's ability to run a boarding school. In this, he seems to have been influenced by Lightheart. In closing, he thanked Mother Katharine for her donation to the school in Norfolk and promised to make it "go as far as possible."[17] But Mother Katharine was not so easily persuaded to abandon Keswick. In addition to a donation of $1,900 for a school in Norfolk, she sent an additional $1,000 for the one in Keswick.[18]

Several months later, van de Vyver sent Drexel an account of how he had used her donation. Lightheart was trying to purchase additional land adjacent to the Keswick school but discovered Tyrrell "had deceived" him "as to the number of scholars who were attending the school & those who according to his statement had promised to come." The bishop and Lightheart had, therefore, temporarily abandoned plans for building in Keswick and had appointed a new teacher. In Norfolk, building the new school was delayed because Father Alfred B. Leeson, the provincial of the Josephites, had not approved the building plans on property that the Josephites owned. Van de Vyver now asked for a further donation to be devoted exclusively to Norfolk. Mother Katharine referred the matter to Archbishop Patrick Ryan of Philadelphia, her ecclesiastical superior, who "heard from a very reliable source that the Josephites were breaking up." She and Ryan agreed that van de Vyver should "apply both sums to the Colored Missions according to what your conscience deems best."[19] What Ryan reported to Mother Katharine, however, was not a "breaking up" of the Josephites but the separation of the American province from Mill Hill that was finalized in 1892.[20]

St. Emma's and St. Francis in Rock Castle

While Katharine Drexel was subsidizing work among Virginia's Black people, her sister took a more direct approach. In 1894, Louise and her husband, Edward Morrell, purchased "Belmead," a 1,600-acre estate formerly belonging to General Philip St. George Cocke at Rock Castle on the James River in Powhatan County, about forty miles west of Richmond. The Morrells proposed to open an industrial school, a type of "Catholic Tuskegee," modelled on what the Drexel sisters had already seen in Europe and on what Elizabeth Drexel Smith, their deceased sister, had already established in Eddington, Pennsylvania. The school was to be an industrial and agricultural school for "colored boys" from the South and was to be named St. Emma's, after Mrs. Morrell's mother.[21]

In the meantime, even as she was dispatching the first sisters of her young community to begin their work with the Pueblo Indians, Katharine Drexel joined her sister's educational endeavor in Virginia. She purchased the 600–acre estate, adjacent to Belmead, "Mount Pleasant," which was also owned by General Cocke. In June, she received van de Vyver's permission for her sisters to open a school for girls, St. Francis, named after her father.[22] The bishop promised to make his first visit to Belmead in August but, in the meantime, thought from her description of the property that a "⅛ of a mile separation between the buildings intended for the boys and girls is amply sufficient."[23]

On January 3, 1895, van de Vyver dedicated St. Emma's Industrial and Agricultural College. The next day, the Brothers of the Christian Schools took over the administration under the supervision of Brother Anatole. At their installation, Colonel Morrell gave an address as which he stated the "object" of the school "is to give many colored boys of the South a good, practical education, it is to teach them to use their brains and hands properly." He envisioned it as a school where they would learn to be "American citizens, . . . ruled by the standards of justice and honesty." The boys would "learn, besides reading writing, ciphering, U.S. History etc., lucrative trades, and all kinds of useful works."[24]

For the next thirty years the Christian Brothers and their successors, first lay teachers and later Benedictines, stressed the trade aspect of the school. Only in 1947, when the Holy Ghost Fathers took over the administration, did the institution respond to pressure from students and alumni to introduce a more academic curriculum to enable their graduates to undertake higher education. In the beginning, however, the school also faced a combination of racism and anti-Catholicism. Some locals set fire to the buildings of both St. Emma's and St. Francis.[25] Yet another problem arose when the Drexel sisters arranged for chaplains of their schools without consulting van de Vyver.

At its inception, St. Emma's chaplains were Holy Ghost Fathers, the first of whom was William Healy, C.S.Sp. Early in 1898, as Mother Katharine was completing arrangements for opening St. Francis, she proposed that she draw on the same congregation for chaplains for her convent and school. Having objected to Archbishop Ryan about the appointment of the Holy Ghost Fathers to Belmead, van de Vyver now wrote to Mother Katharine that "Still they came. I still object to them but I grant them faculties of the Diocese. Since they are on the place it is better that they should have charge of your house as well." He left it to her to determine where the chaplains would live.[26] During the summer, however, he advised her to accept their "terms . . . at least for one year. During that time we will confer together about future plans."[27] As the story unfolded, van de Vyver objected to more than the fact that the priests had arrived without his approval.

Although the building for St. Francis was virtually complete by the spring of 1898, changes in personnel and illness among the Sisters of the Blessed Sacrament delayed the school's opening for over a year. In the meantime, van de Vyver was intent on removing Father Healy as chaplain. In February 1899, he informed Mother Katharine: "I will replace at any cost the present chaplain at Belmead, but considering my position you might possibly allow two of the Josephite Fathers, under Father Slattery to take possession. I shall remove them any time they do not give satisfaction." If she did not agree to this, he would "borrow priests from outside & supply your home with priests of the diocese as I am anxious to give your religious & inmates the very best attention."[28]

Van de Vyver's problem with the Holy Ghost Fathers seems to have been specifically with Healy, but he generalized about the quality of the priests of the religious orders who came to work in the diocese. He told Mother Katharine that, from his own experience, "religious communities have many calls and they generally confide outside work to members less usefull for the work mapped out for their intended work." In his opinion, moreover, "the Holy Ghost Fathers have been far from successful in their work among the Negroes." Since he preferred "to take up the work with my own priests as I had hoped to do from the beginning," Mother Katharine was now to inform the superior of the Holy Ghost Fathers that the diocese would "take charge of Belmead and St. Elizabeth's Convent on the first day of June 1899."[29] He then appointed Cyril DeMuynck, ordained in Louvain in 1895, and William O'Hara as chaplains to both schools.[30]

On October 1, 1899, the school opened with Mother Mercedes, a veteran of work at St. Catherine's Indian School in Santa Fe, as superior. The first student, in fact, was Mary Boyd, a Native American from Wyoming, who, after graduating from St. Francis in 1903, entered the Sisters of St. Francis and worked with the Indians in Oklahoma.

As the year got underway, thirty-one girls had enrolled. Initially, the school used a system of indenture, according to which a girl would remain at the school, winter and summer, until her twenty-first birthday, but it then modified this to accept the daughters of the "best families" of Richmond.[31] Until St. Francis closed in 1970, seventeen young women entered religious life, of whom sixteen became Oblate Sisters of Divine Providence, including Mother Consuela, mentioned above, and Mother Teresa Shokley.[32]

From their inception, both schools were to be boarding schools, but they were also to provide an outreach to the surrounding areas. The sisters from St. Francis taught in the Sunday school held at St. Emma's. One of the more enduring of the sisters' endeavors in the neighborhood began, however, early in 1900. Mother Katharine had paid a visit to Rock Castle to inspect the final stages of construction of the chapel in honor of her father. While there, she was asked to look into the possibility of a school for African Americans in Lynchburg. On her way, the train stopped in Columbia, and she saw a cross shining through the trees. She asked her traveling companion, Mother Mercedes, if it was perhaps a Catholic church. Mother Mercedes replied that she did not think there was any Catholic church between Richmond and Lynchburg, but upon her return to Rock Castle she learned from a student from Columbia, Rebecca Kimbro, that it was, in fact, a Catholic church tended by her father, "Uncle Zach Kimbro," the only Catholic among the African Americans who had settled in the vicinity. It was the church Richard Wakeham had built for his father in 1884 and had, at least until 1890, been tended from the cathedral. A week later, Mother Mercedes returned with Sister Mary of the Sacred Heart to initiate a Sunday school for twenty-five children and seventy-five adults. She read the Epistle and Gospel and explained their meaning. Scrupulous about "preaching" in the church, she received van de Vyver's assurance that this "was God's way of bringing souls to Him." The bishop further recommended that Josephites from Lynchburg send a priest for a monthly Mass at Columbia.[33] During the first year, thirty adults and several children were baptized. Within two years, a school opened under the direction of Mrs. Lydia E. Nicholas, who remained for forty-seven years and would be the first woman in the diocese to receive the *Pro Ecclesia et Pontifice* medal. The Columbia mission continued to grow under both the Josephites and later under the diocesan mission band.[34]

Whatever may have been van de Vyver's initial reservations about the Holy Ghost Fathers, on May 3, 1903, they returned to establish Holy Cross Mission on the grounds of St. Francis de Sales High School. Fathers William Stadelman, Joseph Cronenberger, and David Fitzgibbons were assigned to be chaplains and religious instructors at the two schools as well as to evangelize Powhatan and Goochland counties. In 1907, Stadelman undertook a five-week tour of the South to recruit students for St. Emma's, where Colonel Morrell had offered fifty scholarships to young men interested in agriculture. At the same time, he recruited students for St. Francis.[35] The sisters from St. Francis also began weekly visits to State Farm Prison, in Maidens, Virginia, about twenty miles east of Rock Castle. In the summer of 1908, Stadelman began saying Mass in the prison once a month.[36]

St. Francis at Rock Castle was not the only focus for Katharine Drexel's philanthropy in the diocese of Richmond. In 1910 van de Vyver and Dr. George Ben Johnston, son of Senator Johnston and Niketti Floyd, apparently proposed building a hospital for Black patients. When they submitted their preliminary plans to her, she remarked that it was easier to raise money for a building than to endow free beds in an existing hospital. With Archbishop Ryan's approval, she pledged to give $50,000, if they could raise other funds.[37] Van de Vyver and Johnston, unfortunately, abandoned their plans, presumably for lack of funds.

The Christian Brothers remained in charge of the administration of St. Emma's until 1924, when they were replaced by lay teachers. In 1929, Benedictines from St. Vincent's Archabbey in Latrobe, Pennsylvania, took over the administration of the school and of Holy Cross Mission, but they focused almost exclusively on running the school rather than on outreach to the surrounding area. They remained until 1947, when the Holy Ghost Fathers returned to Rock Castle and assumed administration of the school.

While the two institutions at Rock Castle were getting underway, sixty miles south of Richmond at Jarratt, where Keane had dedicated a mission church in 1880, Black lay catechists, graduates of the Josephites' Epiphany Apostolic College in Baltimore, opened a school in October 1899. Initially, they enrolled over ninety students with sixty in regular attendance. Their day school taught elementary subjects, and their night school, conducted twice a week, principally attracted adults. None of the students were Catholic. Every Sunday, the catechists conducted a prayer service with hymns in the church attached to the schoolhouse. But they faced opposition from local ministers. In one Baptist church, the preacher said two young girls in his congregation were going to hell because they attended the Catholic school. In another, a white preacher worked up the Black congregation with a variety of charges including that "the unjust judges who accused the chaste Susannah . . . were Catholic priests." Still another preacher attacked the Catholic Church and then challenged any one to disprove his charges. One of the catechists was in the congregation and took him on, with results that are not recorded.[38]

Overcoming the anti-Catholicism of Virginians, Black or white, took courage for the catechists and others who opened schools. But education was a principal means of winning converts. The school at Jarratts and the institutions at Rock Castle were but a few examples of this outreach to the non-Catholic community. For years to come, the majority of the African-American students in the elementary schools throughout Virginia were non-Catholic—a preponderance that was reversed when high schools were opened.

BENEDICTINE SCHOOLS AT BRISTOW

The Benedictine Fathers from Belmont Abbey and the Benedictine Sisters from Richmond were offered a site in trust for homes for "poor friendless white boys" and "poor friendless white girls" on the Linton estate in Bristow, near Manassas. The Linton family bequest may have been intended to provide for white children what the Morrells and Katharine Drexel were beginning in Rock Castle for poor Black students. In 1894, Father Julius Pohl, O.S.B., a native of Richmond, became the prior of St. Maur in Bristow, which initially had only eight other monks, and opened St. Joseph's Institute. Although the institute was intended to be an industrial school, it never advanced beyond its initial agricultural work. A man of more energy than vision, Pohl failed to develop sufficient financial support for the school. Complaints against the condition of the school and his administration forced his removal in 1922 and the eventual closing of the school.[39]

But, meanwhile, Pohl established St. Joseph's parish for Prince William County, subject to the priory, while Patrick Donlon, O.S.B., became pastor of St. John the Evangelist Church in Warrenton with a mission in Manassas—he later made All Saints in Manassas his head-quarters with Warrenton as a mission.[40] When the Benedictines later claimed to have permanent pastoral charge of the area, van de Vyver's successor, O'Connell, would have to demand their removal.

The Benedictine Sisters were more provident. In May 1894, five Benedictine sisters from Richmond arrived in Bristow. Their superior was Sister M. Alphonse Bliley, O.S.B., a Richmond native. Among the other four was Sister M. Agnes Johnston, O.S.B., an alumna of St. Mary's Academy. They then purchased a separate piece of prop-erty and opened St. Edith's Academy in September.[41] Unlike the Benedictine priests, they were convinced that they would need an aca-demic school to support the school for poor girls. In 1897, they opened St. Ann's Industrial School for "poor, friendless white girls" who would receive their academic education at St. Edith's. When St. Mary's School in Richmond closed in 1901, the Benedictine Sisters then transferred their priory to Bristow. St. Edith's Academy now drew many of the girls from Richmond families. When it closed in 1922, it was replaced by the Linton Hall School for boys, and the sis-ters then opened St. Gertrude's High School for girls in Richmond.[42] But Bristow remains the priory for the Benedictine Sisters of Virginia.

Cathedral of the Sacred Heart and Thomas Fortune Ryan

Perhaps the highlight of van de Vyver's episcopate was the dedication of the new Cathedral of the Sacred Heart, the result of a remarkable gift from Mr. and Mrs. Thomas Fortune Ryan. On November 17, 1882, Keane had gathered several prominent Catholics in the base-ment of St. Peter's to discuss building a new cathedral. They rejected the possibility of tearing down the old cathedral to build a new one because the property was not large enough. In addition, Keane real-ized the need for a parish in the city's expanding western section. McGill had already purchased property across from Monroe Park after the Civil War. Keane then procured the adjacent property. But still, there were insufficient funds to build a new cathedral. As a tem-porary measure to meet the growing need of the western part of Richmond, Keane bought a lot at Short Street and Floyd Avenue in the summer of 1887 and built Sacred Heart Church.[43] The plan for a new cathedral, however, was realized by the personal donation of $500,000 from the Ryans in New York.

Thomas F. Ryan was a native of Nelson County, where he later maintained his estate, "Oak Ridge." A self-made man, he started amassing his fortune by forming a syndicate to build part of the New York subway system. He later founded the American Tobacco Company and took over the Equitable Life Assurance Society. Although he had his offices in New York, he and his wife did not forget his native Virginia, where both were generous benefactors of a number of enterprises. Simultaneously with their bequest for the cathedral, Mrs. Ryan also gave money for building Sacred Heart Church in Manchester (South Richmond) and Blessed Sacrament Church in Harrisonburg.[44]

For the cathedral, van de Vyver chose Joseph H. McGuire of New York as architect. Built in Italian Renaissance style, the basement was of Virginia granite and the superstructure of Indiana limestone. At its extremes, it measured 206 ft. x 114 ft. It was unique for its age. Until the Cathedral of Mary Our Queen was built in Baltimore from money given by Thomas J. O'Neill, Sacred Heart was the first cathedral built from the generosity of one family. On June 4, 1903, Archbishop Diomede Falconio, the apostolic delegate, laid the cornerstone. He arrived the night before, accompanied from Washington by Denis O'Connell, who was now the rector of the Catholic University. They were met at Ashland by Bishop Benjamin Keiley of Savannah and Father J. J. Bowler, the vicar general, to be conveyed to the bishop's residence at St. Peter's. The entire party then proceeded to St. Peter's for the official exchange of greetings between the delegate and representatives of the Church in Richmond. In his remarks, van de Vyver traced the history and development of the diocese. He said in part:

A little more than fifty years ago, when the Diocese of Virginia formed what are now two distinct States, it contained but six priests, seven churches and three schools. Only three cities were so fortunate as to have the Holy Sacrifice celebrated each Sunday.

Notwithstanding the fact that in 1850 West Virginia was formed into a new diocese, now, in the See of Richmond, proper, there are ten times as many priests as then, and, instead of seven churches, there are more than fifty. In place of three educational institutions in the State, now every parish of the diocese is blessed with its own parochial school. Then there are in addition a college, several high schools and academies, industrial schools, infant and orphan asylums and other charitable institutions.

Fifty years ago there was but a handful of Catholics. Now there are more than thirty thousand. In every portion of the State where there are gathered even but a few faithful souls, zealous priests have been sent to establish churches and schools, and thus propagate the Kingdom of Christ in this portion of the Lord's vineyard.

That the increase in Catholic population was not even greater, the bishop continued, is due to "the almost entire absence of Catholic immigration into the South. Unlike the more flourishing North, where thousands of faithful annually arrive from Europe, to swell the Catholic population, here the growth in numbers results almost exclusively from the natural increase and conversions to the true faith, of which, thanks be to God, we have annually large numbers."[45]

John C. Hagan, representing the laity, then struck a patriotic chord by noting the role of Virginians in founding the country. He added:

> And as our old State has given so freely of her brain and brawn to the cause of liberty, so has this dear old church, within whose walls we now stand, sent forth from its hallowed precincts those who have become famous in the hierarchy of Mother Church: a prince whose fame is world wide, His Eminence, the Cardinal Archbishop of Baltimore; that distinguished linguist and scholar, the late Right Reverend Bishop of Savannah [Becker], and his brilliant successor, the present right Reverend Bishop of that diocese [Keiley]; His Grace, the eloquent Archbishop of Dubuque [Keane]; and, last, but not least, the present Rector of the Catholic University of Washington [O'Connell], who has filled with such distinguished ability every position to which he has been called.[46]

After the cathedral exercises, the clergy repaired to a reception at the home of Dr. George Ben Johnston, where Governor Andrew J. Montague, the lieutenant governor, and several prominent Protestant ministers were also present.[47]

The next afternoon, the delegate and other prelates vested in the residence of Judge S. B. Witt, a prominent Protestant, while from four blocks away at Sacred Heart Church, a procession of the clergy and laity began moving to the cathedral site. Again among the guests was the governor, in addition to Mayor Richard M. Taylor. Joseph Geisinger recorded the scene for the *Times-Dispatch*. Throughout the ceremonies, he wrote, "there was present the thought of the patriotic Catholic, the existence of which some men choose to deny." The ceremonies had, in fact, expressed Catholicism, Virginia style. Flag and cross were intertwined for Virginia's small Catholic population, which endeavored to show by the presence of the government leaders and ministers of other denominations that Catholicism was an integral part of Virginia life. Geisinger strove to illustrate the theme:

> On Wednesday evening the Stars and Stripes and the Papal flag were draped over the episcopal throne [in St. Peter's], caught with the American eagle; yesterday the trowel used in the ceremony was decorated with ribbons of red, white, and blue, and a parchment scroll placed in the stone was tied in the same manner. English hymns were sung; the Governor of the State was present and the Mayor of Richmond.

Father William Pardow, S.J., superior of the Maryland-New York province of the Jesuits, gave the opening sermon in which he "spoke of the American flag, showing wherein Catholics were ready to die for their country's good and wherein they stood for all those things that made to the betterment of this great land."[48]

On November 29, 1906, Thanksgiving Day, Falconio returned to consecrate formally the new building. Present with him were Cardinal Gibbons, Archbishops Ireland, Keane, John Glennon of St. Louis, and John Farley of New York, Bishop Keiley, and Monsignor O'Connell. This time, Keane was the principal speaker at the morning's ceremony. It was the end of one era and the beginning of another. It may have been the only time that van de Vyver was in the presence of John Ireland, the leader of the Americanist party, from which he had so studiously remained aloof. Gibbons and Keane also represented the party and its tenets which had been nurtured in Virginia. Glennon and Farley represented a new order, but they were moderates. Both would become cardinals, Farley in 1911 and Glennon in 1946, only a few weeks before his death. But O'Connell's presence was a look into Richmond's future. He had been the theologian of Americanism but was the only principal member of the group who was not a bishop. He was then more than half-way through his single term as rector of the Catholic University, to which his past successes in Rome did not flow over. For the moment, at the cathedral of the Sacred Heart, the hierarchy was in harmony.

Even as the cathedral was being built, Archbishop Farley had requested that Pope Pius X give a papal honor to Mr. and Mrs. Ryan. On April 13, 1904, Falconio notified van de Vyver that the pope had named them to the papal nobility and that he had further given Mrs. Ryan the cross *Pro Ecclesia et Pontifice* for her work for the diocese of Richmond.[49] In the years to come, the Ryans would contribute yet more to the diocese.

Van de Vyver's Last Years

Van de Vyver had reason to be proud of the growth of the diocese. In 1903, as he reported in his speech as he prepared to lay the cornerstone of his new cathedral, the diocese had forty-five diocesan and ten religious priests. Thirty-two churches had a resident priest, with an additional thirty-seven mission churches. Twenty-one parishes had parochial schools, educating over 5,600 students. In 1898, moreover, the Xaverian Brothers had opened Old Point College at Fort Monroe.[50] But the work seems to have been taking its toll on van de Vyver.

On June 16, 1897, van de Vyver had preached the funeral eulogy for his old friend Archbishop Janssens, who died during a sea voyage.[51] Three times, he attempted to resign. In 1903, Archbishop Falconio refused to forward his request to Rome. In 1905, van de Vyver personally submitted his resignation during an audience with Pius X, who rejected it. As might be expected, he did not on either occasion consult Gibbons, who simply offered his opinion in 1905, when asked by the apostolic delegate, that the bishop must have had good reason for resigning.[52]

Finally, in April 1908, van de Vyver again submitted his resignation to the prefect of Propaganda, Cardinal Gotti. On May 5, Pius X accepted it.[53] In the meantime, word of his resignation had leaked to his clergy and the people of Richmond. The priests sent him a petition asking him to remain. Then, on May 17, 1908, a mass rally was held at the Bijou Theater, at which the speakers were Governor Montague,

Dr. Johnston, and L. Z. Morris, representing, respectively, the Protestant, Catholic, and Jewish communities. The meeting then adopted a formal resolution "to request and urge our good Bishop to withdraw his resignation." Smet later described this meeting in *The American College Bulletin* after his uncle's death.[54]

Forwarding these petitions to Falconio, van de Vyver now withdrew his resignation. Unfortunately, the delegate had just received Gotti's notification that the pope had accepted it.[55] He now forwarded this new request to Rome, where, on June 16, Pius X "was pleased to take into consideration your petition of remaining at your post as Bishop of Richmond notwithstanding your former resignation and the Holy Father has graciously granted the favor that you remain in the government of your diocese." Transmitting this information, Falconio added his own comment: "I am highly pleased that the Holy Father has been pleased to listen to the petition of your clergy and people and I earnestly hope that the attachment which on this solemn occasion has been shown to you will be a tie which will keep you united to your flock during all your life even if it should cost you any amount of sacrifice."[56] Falconio may, however, have had a more practical reason for his pleasure that the pope had accepted the petitions that van de Vyver remain as bishop.

Other than their devotion to their bishop, the priests of the diocese may have had other motives in initiating the petition to retain van de Vyver. On May 3, 1908, two weeks before the mass rally in Richmond, O'Connell, then finishing his term as rector of the Catholic University, was consecrated a bishop in Baltimore. He would have been a likely candidate to succeed van de Vyver. Moreover, on June 11, while waiting to see if the pope would allow him to withdraw his resignation, the bishop wrote the rector of the American College, Louvain, recalling Felix Kaup to the diocese after only one year as vice rector.[57] Without documentary evidence, it is difficult to determine precisely why van de Vyver decided to continue as bishop, but, immediately upon Kaup's return, he made him both chancellor and vicar general. The bishop might have intended to groom him as his successor and prevent or at least delay the succession of his old rival, O'Connell. Whatever O'Connell desired at this point, he was named auxiliary bishop of San Francisco, where he was virtually forced on Archbishop Patrick W. Riordan, who at the time wanted, not an auxiliary, but a younger coadjutor who would succeed him. O'Connell, for his part, languished unhappily at the Golden Gate yearning for an opportunity to return east.[58] He had only a short time to wait.

On October 16, 1911, van de Vyver died. Gibbons was present for his funeral, and Keiley preached the eulogy, which, the rector of the American College recorded, "did not, from all accounts, meet with everybody's expectations."[59]

Van de Vyver was not necessarily a great bishop, but he was a good one. He represented the best of the missionary zeal that led European priests to volunteer for American dioceses. He also seems to have passed that zeal down to two more generations of his family back in Flanders, for both his nephew and his great-nephew came to serve in Virginia. His support of work among African Americans by the Josephites, Blessed Sacrament Sisters, and Holy Ghost Fathers was etched in the memory of the Black Catholics of the diocese. In 1910, they renamed St. John the Baptist Institute at St. Joseph's Church the van de Vyver College and Parochial School for boys and girls.

Richmond remained a missionary diocese, dependent on clergy from outside. But it also benefited from the philanthropic commitment of families like the Ryans and Morrells and individuals like Katharine Drexel. Its next bishop could well build upon the work that van de Vyver and these benefactors had initiated.

Coat of Arms of the Diocese of Richmond

Rev. Patrick Kelly (1779–1829), first bishop of Richmond (1820–1822)

Rev. Richard V. Whelan (1809–1874), second bishop of Richmond (1840–1850)

Rev. John McGill (1809–1872), third bishop of Richmond (1850–1872)

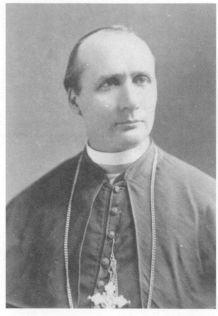

James Cardinal Gibbons (1834–1921), fourth bishop of Richmond (1872–1877)

Rev. John J. Keane (1839–1918), fifth bishop of Richmond (1877–1888)

Rev. Augustine van de Vyver (1844–1911), sixth bishop of Richmond (1889–1911)

Rev. Denis J. O'Connell (1849–1927), seventh bishop of Richmond (1912–1924)

Bishops of the Diocese of Richmond

Rev. Andrew J. Brennan (1877–1956), eighth bishop of Richmond (1926–1945)

Rev. Peter Leo Ireton (1882–1958), ninth bishop of Richmond (1945–1958)

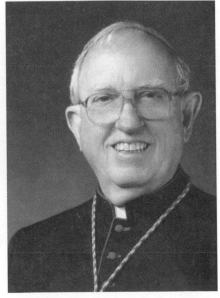

Rev. John J. Russell (1897–1993), tenth bishop of Richmond (1958–1973)

Rev. Walter F. Sullivan (1928–), eleventh bishop of Richmond (1974–)

Rev. Thomas A. Becker (1832–1899), bishop of Wilmington (1868–1886) and bishop of Savannah (1886–1899)

Rev. Francis Janssens (1843–1897), bishop of Natchez (1881–1888), archbishop of New Orleans (1888–1897)

Rev. John J. Kain (1841–1903), bishop of Wheeling (1875–1893), archbishop of St. Louis (1893–1903). (Courtesy of Diocese of Wheeling)

Rev. Benjamin Keiley (1847–1925), bishop of Savannah (1900–1922) (Courtesy of Diocese of Savannah)

Rev. Vincent Waters (1904–1974), bishop of Raleigh (1945–1974)

Rev. Joseph Hodges (1911–1985), auxiliary bishop of Richmond (1952–1962), bishop of Wheeling (1962–1985)

Rev. Ernest Unterkoefler (1917–1993), auxiliary bishop of Richmond (1962–1964)

Rev. Carroll Dozier (1911–1985), bishop of Memphis (1970–1982)

Rev. Timothy O'Brien

Rev. Matthew O'Keefe

Rev. John R. Slattery, S.S.J.

Rev. Felix Kaup

Rev. F. Joseph Magri

Rev. Louis Smet

Rev. Amadeus Joseph van Ingelgem

Mrs. Lydia Elizabeth Nicholas, first woman in diocese to receive *pro ecclesia et pontifice* medal. (Courtesy of Josephite Fathers Archives)

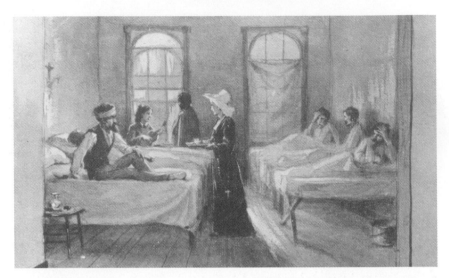

Pen sketch by Union prisoner of Daughters of Charity nursing in Richmond. (Courtesy of St. Joseph's Mother House, Emmitsburg)

Catholic suffragettes in Richmond. Standing on far left, Adele Clark. In car, far left, Josephine Dooley Houston, third from left, Nora Houston, fifth from left, Alice Dooley. (Courtesy of Virginia Historical Society)

Mr. Thomas F. Ryan

Mrs. Thomas F. Ryan

Major James H. Dooley

The Drexel sisters, Mrs. Louise Morrell and St. Katharine Drexel. (Courtesy of the Archives of the Sisters of the Blessed Sacrament)

Cathedral of the Sacred Heart,
Richmond

Cathedral of St. Thomas More,
Arlington

St. Peter's, Richmond

Basilica of St. Mary's, Norfolk

Some Places of Worship

St. Peter's, Harpers Ferry (Courtesy of St. Peter's, Harpers Ferry, W. Va.)

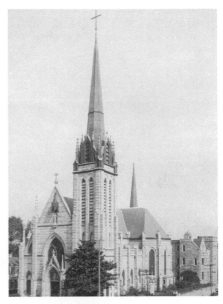

St. Paul's, Portsmouth

St. Mary of Sorrows, Fairfax. (Courtesy of St. Mary's Parish)

St. Mary's, Alexandria

St. Mary's, Richmond

St. Andrew's, Roanoke

St. Joseph's, Richmond

St. Mary Star of the Sea, Fort Monroe

St. Vincent's Hospital, Norfolk, circa 1892, founded by Anne Behan Plume Herron. (Courtesy of The Carroll Walker Collection, Kirn Memorial Library, Norfolk)

St. Emma's Industrial and Agricultural College, Rock Castle

Dedication of the Cathedral of the Sacred Heart.

Corpus Christi Procession at St. Joseph's Villa, 1960. (Courtesy of *Catholic Virginian*)

Annual outdoor Mass at Brent Cemetery, Aquia, 1930s

Fr. Chester Michael on Motor Chapel at Camp Pickett, 1943

Bishop Brennan at confirmation at St. Vincent de Paul Church, Berkley Springs, W. Va., 1932

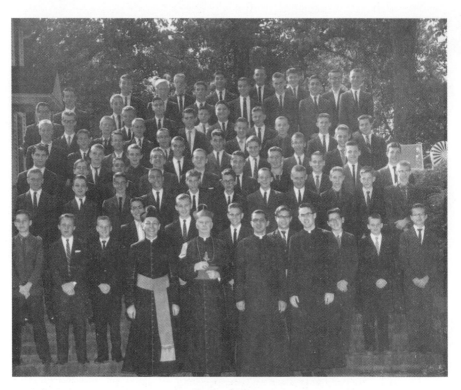

St. John Vianney Seminary student body, May 1961

PART III

Keeping the Faith in a Changing Environment

The first real urbanization of Virginia occurred through somewhat ironic circumstances. Although Virginia's Catholics had been in the forefront of wanting to rid their state of the hated Union occupation, World War I introduced the military as a significant factor in reshaping Virginia. In 1917, the United States Navy opened its first Naval Operations Station at Norfolk. The oldest part of the diocese, after a century, now began a rapid expansion that slowed down as the nation retreated into isolationism. The bishop who oversaw this first development was Denis J. O'Connell, close friend of Gibbons and the second priest of the diocese to become its bishop.

While Virginia Catholicism continued its style of accommodation to culture, Virginia experienced one of its rare outbreaks of public anti-Catholicism, part of the nationwide movement that occurred after the war. In the 1920s, the Ku Klux Klan held anti-Catholic rallies in the Shenandoah Valley and distributed the "Bogus Oath" of the Knights of Columbus. Klan members even protested that a proposed statue of Columbus in Richmond was a Catholic symbol. These protests were but a dry run for the anti-Catholicism that surfaced in the Al Smith campaign in 1928, when Virginia's Democratic vote held firm, but many others turned out to vote for Herbert Hoover. For the first time, Virginia's Catholics organized to defend their rights, but then reverted to their policy of accommodation by taking active parts in civic and patriotic affairs.

But Virginia was slowly undergoing urbanization, especially in Richmond, northern Virginia, and the Norfolk area, as streetcars made more pleasant living areas accessible to urban workers. Yet even in northern Virginia in the 1920s, railroad schedules continued to determine the allocation of missions to principal parishes and the schedule for Masses. As Virginia's Catholics were beginning to move away from downtown areas, African Americans left the rural countryside to move in. The Church responded by focusing on schools to educate these newcomers, most of whom were not Catholic. During and after World War II, moreover, Bishop Peter L. Ireton focused on creating new Black parishes, a trend that would be reversed in the name of integration in the 1960s.

Ecclesiastically, Richmond was a diocese in transition. In 1926, O'Connell, given the honorary title of archbishop, had resigned to be replaced by Bishop Andrew J. Brennan from Scranton. Hardly had Brennan assumed office than the nation faced the Great Depression. In 1931, nevertheless, he presided over the silver jubilee of the cathedral, the dedication of St. Joseph's Villa, made possible by James Dooley's benefaction, and a special celebration at the two schools opened by the Drexel sisters in Rock Castle for African Americans. While urging participation in patriotic displays, he was also intent on showing the strength of Catholic presence in Virginia. But the depression took its toll on him. In 1934, he suffered a stroke from which he never recovered. A year later, Ireton, a Baltimore pastor, was named coadjutor bishop of Richmond.

Ireton's episcopacy saw Virginia begin its change from the Old Confederacy to the New South. When he first took office, he lamented that many more Virginians had moved from the state than had come from other states. Within a decade, that trend was completely reversed. World War II had definitively changed the face of Virginia. As in other wars, Catholics had proven their patriotism through their military service, a fact Ireton was careful to record. The United States, moreover, did not retreat into isolationism but remained involved in world affairs, with an increased military presence in Virginia. The strong presence of the military, which had been integrated by President Harry S. Truman, provided a catalyst for Ireton's decision to integrate Catholic schools in 1954, before the Brown decision. Yet Virginia's Catholics, so many of whom were now newcomers, introduced the more "muscular Catholicism" with which they were familiar in their hometowns. New schools and churches strained the economic resources of the diocese. When Ireton died in 1958, his diocese bore little resemblance to what it had been in 1935.

CHAPTER 18

Denis O'Connell as Bishop: The Diocese and Virginia Culture, 1911–1926

Richmond's next bishop, Denis J. O'Connell, would preside over the diocese as it went through its first substantial growth, due to World War I, and the first outburst of anti-Catholicism in the state since the Know-Nothing campaign in the 1850s. He would also develop a systematic approach for evangelizing rural Virginia, while not neglecting its urban regions. He distanced himself from van de Vyver, at least in regard to recruitment of seminarians. But by the time he assumed office, he was already sixty-three. He no longer had the energy and panache that characterized his earlier career.

CHOOSING A SUCCESSOR TO VAN DE VYVER

Since van de Vyver failed to name an administrator, Gibbons had immediately named J. J. Bowler, pastor of St. Peter's.[1] On October 23, 1911, Archbishop Diomede Falconio, the apostolic delegate, asked Gibbons to call a meeting of the clergy and bishops and gave detailed instructions on presenting the "notulae" or brief biographies and qualifications of the candidates.[2] The procedure looked normal, but only on the surface.

By coincidence, on the day van de Vyver died, Denis O'Connell was in Washington representing Archbishop Riordan at the Golden Jubilee of Gibbons's ordination.[3] On October 19, even before writing Gibbons, Falconio summoned O'Connell to the delegation. In pencil,

O'Connell filled out his "notulae," recounting his early service in the diocese of Richmond, his rectorship of the American College in Rome, and his role in establishing the apostolic delegation, "incurring thereby great ill will in America." But then he erroneously gave 1902 as the date of the delegation. His appointment to Richmond, he wrote, "would be only closing the long and trying parenthesis in my life and restoring me to my own diocese where I was before." He followed up his pencil-written "notulae" with one in ink. In neither did he mention his role in Americanism.[4] The official lists, of course, had yet to be composed.

Before the priests of Richmond and the bishops of the province of Baltimore met, Riordan urged Gibbons to place O'Connell on the *terna*. He reminded him that O'Connell had been originally nominated for the diocese in 1888.[5] Only on November 15, did Gibbons preside at the meeting of the eligible priests of Richmond to nominate van de Vyver's successor. They put O'Connell in first place, followed by James T. O'Farrell, pastor of St. Joseph's in Petersburg, and Charles E. Donohoe, pastor of St. Paul's in Portsmouth. On November 22, the bishops of the province assembled and drew up their list, with O'Connell in first place, Joseph D. Budds, chancellor of the diocese of Charleston, in second, and Donohoe in third.[6]

In the meantime, Falconio had become a cardinal and returned to Rome. During the interim before the arrival of the new delegate, Archbishop Giovanni Bonzano, Monsignor Bonaventura Cerretti was the chargé d'affaires of the delegation. On November 30, Cerretti forwarded the *ternae* to Cardinal Gaetano de Lai, secretary of the Consistorial Congregation, but pointed out that the bishops' list had several canonical irregularities. Among other things, they had failed to give their reasons for rejecting O'Farrell's name and substituting Budds.[7] In addition, Cerretti consulted religious priests: Edward Meyer, O.S.B., pastor of St. Mary's Church in Richmond; A.P. Doyle, C.S.P., of the Apostolic Mission House in Washington; and Rev. William F. Stadelman, C.S.Sp., of Rock Castle.[8] For the candidates other than O'Connell, the extant letters in the Vatican archives all pertain to Donohoe's qualifications.[9] While no one spoke directly against Donohoe, some thought he lacked the ability to bring leadership to Richmond. Doyle, for example, who had earlier conducted a mission in Virginia, said nothing negative about Donohoe, but thought that Richmond had stagnated and needed strong leadership. He was convinced that there were thousands of potential converts, if only there were a real missionary crusade. He remarked that there were only 41,000 Catholics out of 2,000,000 people within the boundaries of the diocese. He said nothing, however, about either O'Connell or Budds.[10]

The lack of archival information available on O'Connell is somewhat surprising, considering his earlier role in Americanism. His performance as rector of the Catholic University, however, may have proven his orthodoxy in Rome. During his tenure, both he and Gibbons played disgraceful roles in forcing the resignation of Professor Henry Poels, a leading Dutch Old Testament scholar.[11] On January 19, 1912, Cardinal Rafaele Merry del Val, the secretary of state, cabled Cerretti that Pius X had chosen O'Connell as bishop of Richmond. Cerretti immediately notified Gibbons and O'Connell.[12] From San Francisco, O'Connell telegraphed: "Thanks, dear Friend, for the news and for the things."[13] Gibbons also immediately thanked Cerretti. He had already received "a telegram from Mgr. O'Connell early in the week announcing his appointment, but did not wish to announce it till it was officially confirmed."[14] O'Connell obviously still had his Roman sources of information.

O'Connell's appointment, of course, was a foregone conclusion before the lists were even drawn up. He had never liked San Francisco and, in 1910, had to be encouraged by Gibbons to remain there with the expectation that he would succeed Riordan as archbishop.[15] O'Connell, for his part, probably thought that, once in Richmond, he would be a likely successor to Gibbons, but by this time he was sixty-three, and Gibbons would live for almost another decade.

As soon as he received official word of his appointment, O'Connell headed east, stopping on the way to visit his old friend, Archbishop Ireland, in St. Paul. On March 19, the feast of St. Joseph, he was installed as Richmond's seventh bishop. Cardinal Gibbons preached for the occasion. With rhetorical flare he stated that, if the clergy were offered a choice, "like the people assembled in the Church of Milan who suddenly cried out: 'Let Ambrose be our Bishop,' you would have exclaimed: 'Let Denis J. O'Connell be placed over us.'"[16] Gibbons probably intended no irony, but by this date the clergy and people of Richmond had most likely forgotten O'Connell, after an absence of twenty-nine years.

In many ways, O'Connell was a tragic figure. Few bishops in American Catholic history were his intellectual superiors. He had loyally served Gibbons as rector of the American College in Rome, and that had been his undoing. Forced by Leo XIII to resign in 1895, he was replaced as rector by William Henry O'Connell, whose ideals and vision of the American Church were diametrically opposed to those of Denis O'Connell and Gibbons. William O'Connell then began a rapid rise in the hierarchy: first, in 1901, bishop of Portland, Maine, and, then, in 1906, coadjutor archbishop of Boston, though he was never nominated for either position. In 1911, he became a cardinal, as Denis O'Connell finally became bishop of Richmond. Among the few extant letters between them is a poignant one of November 1922. Bishop O'Connell had sent the minutes of the annual meeting of bishops at which he had been secretary. With a shaky hand, he suggested to the cardinal that, once printed, the minutes be sent "out direct from Boston without returning them to Richmond. You have fine equipment and I have neither secretary nor stenographer."[17] A year before, moreover, he had lost his patron, Cardinal Gibbons. The new Archbishop of Baltimore, Michael J. Curley, once remarked that he found that among the changes he had to make was to tell O'Connell he was not welcome in Baltimore.[18]

As bishop of Richmond, however, O'Connell proved to be a capable administrator. He retained Felix Kaup as his chancellor but appointed James T. O'Farrell of Petersburg as his vicar general. Initially, he also held regular meetings of his consultors, but then either ceased the practice or left no records. Furthermore, he found a body of distinguished clergy recruited by his predecessor. He used one of these, Louis Smet, van de Vyver's nephew, as a troubleshooter with the Benedictines in Bristow.

Benedictines Cease Pastoral Work in Bristow and Warrenton

In July, 1913, Julius Pohl, O.S.B., prior of St. Maur and director of the boys home in Bristow, asked O'Connell to urge Abbot Leo Haid to appoint a second priest to assist in Warrenton and Manassas.[19] O'Connell interpreted this request as an effort of the Benedictines to establish jurisdiction over the territory surrounding their monastery similar to that exercised by Belmont Abbey. To regain control over Warrenton, he immediately assigned Smet, who strongly opposed the

Benedictines having jurisdiction.[20] In March 1914, Abbot Leo Haid explained that van de Vyver gave Pohl permission to build a church in Bristow and for another Benedictine to serve other places from his residence in either Warrenton or Manassas.[21] On April 9, O'Connell brought the matter before his consultors, who decided that the Benedictines had jurisdiction only on the grounds of their monastery and that the arrangements for them to staff parishes in Bristow and Warrenton were only temporary.[22] This ended the Benedictines' parochial ministry in the area.

Smet, meanwhile, had redrawn the lines of the missions in Prince William County. He had wanted to avoid any quarrel with Pohl "as I had reasons to believe that the Catholics around Bristow would be the sufferers, if any trouble arose between Father Julius and myself." Catholics, who remained part of his Warrenton-Manassas mission, should be free to attend Mass at Bristow, but Pohl should have no right to compel them. Yet it also seemed appropriate that the Benedictines tend to the sisters at St. Edith's Academy. In the meantime, Smet had procured the deed to the Benedictine land at Bristow from the Manassas courthouse.[23] But he remained in Warrenton only until 1915, when he was appointed pastor at St. Mary's in Alexandria. He and van Ingelgem in Falls Church then became the key figures in the initial expansion of northern Virginia. Pohl, in the meantime, remained in charge of the Benedictines' school for boys in Bristow, St. Joseph's Institute, until he was replaced in 1922 after numerous complaints about his administration and the care of the students. Shortly later, the school closed.[24] But, aside from the strained relations with Pohl, the diocese benefited from other Benedictine establishments.

Benedictine College and St. Gertrude's High School

When O'Connell arrived in Richmond, Benedictine College, the city's first Catholic high school, had just opened. It had grown out of van de Vyver's desire for a new parish in the West End, which he assigned to the Benedictines, whose German parish of St. Mary's was then declining. For the time being, the school building served as the church for what now became known as St. Benedict's parish. The Benedictines had founded it as a military school, perhaps reflecting the desire of

Richmond Catholics to prove their patriotism. Since it was not a diocesan institution, however, friction soon developed with the parochial schools, whose students were not being admitted. In April 1916, Abbot Haid admitted to O'Connell that "I am certainly tried severely with the Benedictine College in Richmond & wish you could tell me what to do!"[25] In 1917, the Knights of Columbus throughout the state had, furthermore, contributed to a scholarship fund.[26] In July 1918, Benedictine College addressed a circular letter to the Catholics of Richmond pledging to raise funds so that no deserving boy would be refused admission. Now it asked all Catholics to give "moral and material support and influence to the Benedictine College" and parents to consider the school for their sons.[27]

But this was not enough for O'Connell. Although he had been somewhat lukewarm toward Catholic education during his Roman days, he now wished to provide high school education for all boys graduating from parochial schools. He therefore instructed Kaup to consult Mark Cassidy, O.S.B., pastor of the parish and rector of the school, about providing funds for tuition. Kaup was then to convene all the pastors of the city to establish "harmonious" relations between the parochial schools and Benedictine College.[28] Apparently Kaup's negotiations were successful. For years to come, Benedictine was the only high school for boys in Richmond.

Early in 1913, the Benedictine Sisters from Bristow had opened St. Gertrude's school for young girls, a short distance from Benedictine College. The sisters from St. Mary's parochial school commuted by cab until their new convent was ready. Then they responded to a proposal from Father Thomas Verner Moore, professor of psychology at the Catholic University, to open a school for "feeble minded" girls. From their experience in Bristow, however, the sisters knew they would have to operate a regular high school in order to support the special institution. By 1918, they opened this new institution, devoted now exclusively to mentally retarded girls.[29] They could not, however, realize their intention of running a regular high school in tandem, and, from the outset, their special school faced opposition.

Cassidy, the pastor of St. Benedict's, wanted the sisters to open a parochial school and postpone "opening the school for feeble minded at St. Gertrude's Convent or open it at another place," but the sisters refused. He had, moreover, purchased a house closer to his new church, where he thought the sisters should live for fear that "should the Sisters live at St. Gertrude's Convent the feeble minded children would have a depressing effect on them to the detriment of their school work."[30]

The sisters' work with the mentally retarded lasted only a few years, but Moore himself came at least twice to examine the children.[31] But from the begining the project was impractical. None of the sisters were trained in either nursing or psychology. With the closing of St. Edith's Academy in Bristow in 1922, the high school moved to Richmond. The school for the retarded was closed, and St. Gertrude's now became a regular high school for girls.[32] In 1924, St. Gertrude's enrolled thirty-one students. Benedictine College then had one hundred and thirty-seven.[33] The city of Richmond at last had the beginning of secondary education for its young Catholics, but neither institution had been founded by the diocese. In this regard, the diocese continued to be hampered by the perennial problem of lack of priests.

SEMINARIES AND RECRUITMENT OF PRIESTS

While O'Connell accepted Joseph Govaert, van de Vyver's great-nephew, from the American College in Louvain, and tried to recruit one or two others to work with Polish and Bohemian immigrants, in general he followed the lead of Gibbons and Keane and ended his association with the Belgian institution. He sent his students to St. Mary's in Baltimore, Mount St. Mary's in Emmitsburg, Belmont Abbey, and the North American College in Rome. He again recruited from All Hallows College, which van de Vyver abandoned, and from several other European seminaries: St. John's, Waterford, of which Bishop Kelly had been president, St. Peter's College, Wexford, and, especially, the Albertinum in Fribourg, which he had visited personally in 1913 to begin recruiting students. Several of these European recruits never arrived in Virginia because of their obligation to serve in the military during the First World War.[34] After the war, O'Connell did recruit both Nicholas Habets and Joseph Jürgens. Recruitment of eastern and central European priests was necessary to care for the small but growing number of immigrants from eastern Europe to Virginia.

The diocese also received the assistance of other American bishops in educating priests. When Sacred Heart Cathedral was dedicated, Bishop Bernard McQuaid offered the diocese a scholarship in St.

Bernard's Seminary in Rochester. Only O'Connell, however, availed himself of this burse from his erstwhile foe, McQuaid, and sent two Richmond students to Rochester, William Meredith, who later transferred to St. Mary's, and Anthony Tohill. Cardinal John Farley of New York likewise offered a burse for a Richmond student at Dunwoodie,[35] where William Winston received his theological education. At the same time, O'Connell continued to recruit priests from other dioceses. In 1913, he wrote Bishop Michael J. Hoban of Scranton for the loan of a "few nice young priests for a few years." Hoban made the noncommittal response: "Will do what I can."[36] While he apparently could do nothing at that time, Scranton would soon make its contribution to Richmond.

As a seminarian in Rome, O'Connell had once been sharply reprimanded by Gibbons for failing to write. As bishop, he imposed the same requirement on those seminarians he sent to Europe. Some of these letters reveal the changing theological climate in Rome. As a leader of the Americanist movement, O'Connell had befriended many of the outstanding European scholars, some of whom would later be held suspect of Modernism. In 1921, Francis Byrne, a student in Rome, reported that he was then studying Church history under Monsignor Umberto Benigni.[37] Benigni had been the Roman coordinator of a secret organization ferreting out suspected Modernists, many of them O'Connell's former friends, until Benedict XV stopped the investigations.[38]

One of Richmond's students in Rome, however, never had the chance to write the bishop. Francis Parater had arrived at the North American College in November 1919. On December 5, he wrote out his will in which, among other things, he declared that he wished to offer "my all for the conversion of the non-Catholics in Virginia." Not moved by either "melancholia or morbid sentimentality," he wished for nothing but "the spread and success of the Catholic Church in Virginia." He then expressed his desire to die on Good Friday, 1920.[39]

On February 7, 1920, Parater died of influenza. Two days later, Monsignor Charles O'Hern, the rector of the North American College, informed O'Connell that, after Parater's death, Byrne found the will among his personal effects. O'Hern was considering showing it to the pope and commented that several people had recommended its publication. Parater had also left a letter for the Boy Scouts and had explicitly requested to be buried at Campo Santo in Rome.[40] The

Osservatore Romano subsequently published an Italian translation of his will. Back in Richmond, Benedictine College, Parater's alma mater, unveiled a tablet in his memory.[41] Later on, the diocese established a summer camp in his honor. Publicity about Parater's death, moreover, may have spurred Virginians to establish burses for the education of seminarians, for the diocese soon received numerous bequests.

For the first five years of his episcopate, O'Connell was engaged primarily in recruiting priests to fill his existing parishes and missions. Virginia's Catholic population remained small and increased only through natural growth and conversions. The state still continued to receive only a trickle of immigrants. All that began to change with World War I.

WORLD WAR I AND THE DEVELOPMENT OF NORFOLK

The entry of the United States into the First World War brought dramatic changes in Virginia, particularly in the Hampton Roads area. In 1907, the state of Virginia had sponsored the Jamestown Exposition on Sewalls Point in Norfolk. Each state had built a replica of one of its most distinguished buildings. After the exposition was over, the state tried unsuccessfully to find a buyer for the site and then surrendered it to the Fidelity Land and Investment Corporation. The Navy had been urging its purchase as a base, but, as late as January 1917, Secretary of the Navy Josephus Daniels rejected an offer to purchase it. On April 6, however, the United States declared war on the Central Powers. The next day, Daniels made an offer to the corporation to purchase the property. On July 4, Admiral Walter McLean formally took possession of the land to inaugurate the Naval Operating Base, which was commissioned on October 12. The exposition buildings now became the officers' quarters. Within the first month of the Navy's ownership, housing and other facilities were built for 7,500 men.[42] Hampton Roads would never be the same again.

The war meant a general mobilization of church efforts to meet the needs of Catholic service personnel. As part of the Catholic participation in President Woodrow Wilson's preparedness campaign in 1916, the archbishops had appointed Father Lewis J. O'Hern, C.S.P. to act as liaison with the government in procuring Catholic chaplains, at that time severely restricted by the War Department to a proportion far below that of Catholic enlistment. With American entry into the war, O'Hern was also given charge of providing for entertainment and recreational facilities for Catholic servicemen.[43] At the end of May 1917, he informed O'Connell that, because of the more moderate climate, many training camps would be located in the South. Many priests were applying to the War Department to serve as Army chaplains and, in addition, Secretary of the Navy Daniels was already appointing Navy chaplains.[44] A few days later, Daniels assigned one of three new Catholic chaplains to Portsmouth, which O'Hern had seen as a priority.[45] During the war, however, only thirty-five Catholic priests served as commissioned Navy chaplains.[46]

In the Army, too, the number of Catholic chaplains was far below the percentage of Catholics. To pick up the slack, the Knights of Columbus mobilized to provide for priests and recreation centers in the rapidly expanding camps.[47] Each Knight was assessed two dollars to raise a total of $1 million to support the war work, which included subsidizing Catholic chaplains the government would not provide.[48] The funds for chaplains serving in the diocese were distributed through O'Connell, who likewise gave them diocesan faculties.[49] In November 1917, however, the Holy See named Bishop Patrick J. Hayes, then the auxiliary bishop of New York, as the military bishop with jurisdiction over the armed services. From this would later emerge first the Military Ordinariate and then the Military Archdiocese.

The military buildup had the greatest effect on the Norfolk-Hampton Roads area. In July 1918, Walter A. Hoker of the National Catholic War Council in Washington informed O'Connell that, after a recent inspection tour of the region, he was appropriating $5,500 for Father Thomas Wilson of Fort Monroe to erect a building for Catholic servicemen and another $500 for him to buy a car, $10,000 to Father David Coleman in Newport News to build a service club and other facilities, and $25,000 for Father William T. Whearty in Portsmouth to build a facility for Navy personnel. In addition, he had appropriated $20,000 for a "visitor's house" at Camp Stuart similar to the Hostess Houses already established by the YWCA.[50] In Norfolk, furthermore, the Women's Auxiliary of the National Catholic War Council sold Liberty Bonds.[51]

The Virginia war effort was not limited to the Hampton Roads area. In February 1918, O'Connell dedicated a new building at the Quantico Marine base. The chaplain, Joseph Pastorelli, O.P., assigned there by his provincial, told of the cooperation he received "from the officers, men & the Y.M.C.A. which is indeed quite consoling & an incentive to greater activity."[52] In Richmond, O'Connell actively participated in the United War Work Campaign, a national endeavor requested by the president. His speech to the Virginia convention, in November 1918, drew praise from G.K. Roper, director of the Virginia Division of the Campaign.[53] As in earlier wars, Catholics and their leaders used this one to prove their patriotism. Bishop Peter J. Muldoon of Rockford, Illinois, chairman of the administrative board of the National Catholic War Council, informed O'Connell that "Catholic cooperation in every activity of the campaign has been most marked and generous and we believe that the Catholics of the country have done their full share."[54]

A year after the United States entered the war, Norfolk was a changed city. John A. Baecher, the diocesan attorney, reported that the city was then overcrowded and rents and real estate prices had soared. Fortunately, the diocese had purchased property for new parishes in Ocean View and Virginia Beach just before the war. As Baecher now searched for other property, he thought it better to wait until the end of the war to see how far prices would fall.[55] With the armistice in November 1918, the nation returned to normalcy. Shipbuilding ceased. The number of workers at the Norfolk Navy Yard declined from 11,000 to 2,538 by the end of 1923.[56] Yet across Hampton Roads at Fort Monroe, the population remained high enough for William A. Gill to realize the long-time desire of his predecessor, Thomas Wilson. In 1923, he invited the Dominican Sisters of Nashville to staff his new school.[57] Normalcy in the Norfolk area would never be what it had been prior to 1917. Although Virginia's Catholics had proven they were American during the war, they now had to defend their position.

THE KU KLUX KLAN AND ANTI-CATHOLICISM

In 1915, the second Ku Klux Klan was organized in Atlanta. It combined racism with anti-Catholicism and anti-Semitism. In Georgia, it influenced the passage of a Convent Inspection Bill allowing authorities periodically to enter Catholic institutions for religious women to make sure none were being held against their will. But the Klan was

not limited to the South. In Oregon, it was responsible for electing a
governor and for passing legislation outlawing private schools. The bishops of the state appealed the law. With the assistance of the National
Catholic Welfare Conference, the umbrella group of the American hierarchy, and the Knights of Columbus, the Sisters of the Holy Names
formally filed suit. In 1924, the Supreme Court in *Pierce v. Society of
Sisters* declared the Oregon law unconstitutional on the grounds of
parents' right to choose the means of their children's education.[58]

As late as 1920, Virginia's lay leaders did not see any cause for
alarm. In June 1920, John J. Blake, the diocesan attorney and state
deputy of the Knights of Columbus, met with J. H. Farrell of Augusta,
Georgia, who came to discuss founding in Virginia an organization,
similar to the Laymen's Association in Georgia, to defend Catholic
rights. His Georgia group had been successful in making the Convent
Inspection Bill "virtually a dead letter no longer enforced." In Michigan, he had also organized "the opposition to those who were attack-
ing Catholic Schools." But Blake did not think such a group in
Virginia was necessary at that time. As he told Bishop O'Connell,
when the Virginia legislature tried to pass a Convent Inspection Bill a
few years before, "the quiet work done by our own men was most effective and resulted in keeping the bill from even being considered in
Committee and that this piece of work confirmed our position, that
local men would always know best the means of defense to be employed." If the need arose in the future, however, he pledged that
"every Knight in Virginia . . . [would] respond to our Bishop's call."[59]
For the time, Virginia's Catholics were maintaining their *modus
vivendi* with the cultural majority. Within a few years Blake would
have to fulfill his promise to O'Connell, but for the moment he and
the Knights were concentrating on the familiar theme of proving how
patriotic Catholics had been from the time of the Revolution.

VIRGINIA CATHOLICS AND PATRIOTISM

In May, 1921, the State Council of the Knights of Columbus met in
Portsmouth and passed a resolution to have a chapel or memorial
placed at Yorktown to commemorate the French who died to win
American independence. At a later meeting in San Francisco, the
Supreme Council of the Knights empowered the national board of di-

rectors to take charge of the memorial. In January 1922, Blake sent O'Connell a copy of the resolution with the comment that the memorial, "if erected upon this field shortly to be set apart as a National Park, . . . would be a perpetual reminder that Catholics have from the beginning ever been in the forefront for liberty, and but for the assistance of Catholic France, our liberties would never have been won at Yorktown." The attached resolutions recounted the roles of General Rochambeau and Admiral De Grasse and concluded that "without the assistance of Catholic France there had been no Yorktown."[60] The Knights of Columbus placed a bronze plaque at Yorktown inscribed with all the names of French military men who lay in unmarked graves in the vicinity. Sixty years later, President Ronald Reagan and President François Mitterand of France dedicated a larger monument on the bicentennial of the surrender of the British at Yorktown.

THE KU KLUX KLAN AND THE BOGUS OATH OF THE KNIGHTS OF COLUMBUS

But Catholic displays of patriotism did little to assuage the growing anti-Catholicism, which, however, remained restricted principally to Virginia's rural areas. In May 1922, Father F. Joseph Magri in Portsmouth told O'Connell that arsonists attempted to burn his mission church in Cradock. This followed shortly after two other incidents. Bricks had been thrown through the windows of the girls school in Portsmouth, and some of the sisters riding a streetcar, which stopped in front of the public high school, experienced verbal abuse. "Many of the pupils jeered and hissed the sisters," he reported, and "some boarded the car and insulted the sisters." But he "took the matter up with the principal who gave the pupils an awful call down."[61]

Two years later, Magri was forced to move his Cradock church to a new site, in the "face of opposition of some bigots who got 81 names to a petition." Now he "thought the time to fight had arrived," so

> The Sunday before church was moved I told the congregation that I had tried gentleness long enough and that those who were looking for a fight would get all they wanted. Said that in a fight the Catholic Church does not usually come out second best. Told them we bought new site with express stipulation of later moving

church to it; that we had the permission to move from Norfolk County Engineer and from Cradock head of Housing Corporation and that we would not allow any body [to] stop us from moving. The bigots did not want us to have best site in the place. Last Sunday we had Mass at new site with increased attendance.[62]

Magri was obviously not a man with whom to tangle. But what he was experiencing in the Portsmouth area was part of a more widespread explosion of anti-Catholicism in Virginia that year.

Harrisonburg became the scene of conflict, fortunately limited to verbal assaults. On April 14, 1924, the Ku Klux Klan began a week-long rally in the city. On the opening day, "Dr. Bulgin" entertained the crowd with a long rambling speech, reminiscent of the Know-Nothing attacks seventy years earlier. He declared that the Catholic Church was "not a church, but a most dangerous and non-American political organization, acting behind stone walls, wearing its black gowns and receiving orders across the water, most of whom are opposed to Americanism." All true churches, he asserted, "are American and are ruled by officers selected in this country by and from the membership, which makes them American and democratic." In contrast, "papal Rome is ruled by a foreigner who calls himself the Pope, occupies a throne, the Vatican, wears a triple crown and represents sovereignty over all people and all princes."[63]

He went on to condemn the Church "because wherever she has spread her black devastating wings she has kept the people in ignorance and poverty, fleecing and robbing all the uninformed and ignorant." As examples, he chose Mexico, where a bloody revolution and slaughter of priests was then going on; the Philippines; and California before the arrival of Protestant missionaries. The rest of Bulgin's speech brought up the accusations that Catholics rejected the Bible and opposed public schools; repressed religious liberty and sought a union of Church and State; and, though they comprised only fifteen percent of the population, made up fifty percent of prison inmates. Finally, he remarked: "when I am asked by some good, old honest Protestant if I believe the fourth degree oath of the Knights of Columbus, which is a part of the Congressional Record," he replied that, even "if the men never took the oath," "anyone who reads history knows all that oath contains and what they have been guilty of."[64]

The so-called "bogus-oath" had come into circulation in 1912. Besides swearing total blind obedience to the pope and other Church officials, the Fourth-Degree Knight was supposed to "promise and declare" to "make and wage relentless war, secretly and openly, against all heretics, Protestants, and Masons . . . to extirpate them from the face of the whole earth." He was to "spare neither age nor sex or condition" and would "hang, burn, waste, boil, flay, strangle, and bury alive these infamous heretics, rip up the stomachs and wombs of their women, and crush their infants' heads against the walls in order to annihilate their execrable race." Failing in such overt warfare, he was to resort to "the poisonous cup" or any other means of assassination. The bogus oath had, as Bulgin said, been published in the *Congressional Record,* but it was part of evidence submitted to Congress in 1913 as proof of fraud in the contested Philadelphia congressional election of an opponent to a Fourth-Degree Knight.[65]

Bulgin's speech was published in the *Bridgewater Times* four days later, as Father William Meredith, pastor in Harrisonburg, informed William J. McGinley, supreme secretary of the Knights of Columbus in New Haven. While the Harrisonburg paper had not published the speech, he said, it was "rather favorable toward the whole idea." Apparently Bulgin had not actually delivered the speech in its entirety but had given its text to the paper in Bridgewater, where "there is not a Catholic." While "the better class of citizens are thoroughly disgusted with the man and his preaching," the priest continued, "he has sewn seeds of dissension and bitterness in many of the ignorant, gullible people." He himself had "not considered it wise to publish any statement as yet," but would follow the advice of the Knights about "mailing literature to residents of the town and country."[66]

Even as Meredith was writing for advice, however, the Klan rally was coming to an end in Harrisonburg, but not before Bulgin had again addressed the assembly. On April 29, he praised the "principles of Klandom" for thwarting "a dangerous black gown organization which every Protestant should fight." He had himself investigated the charges leveled against the Klan and found "that those crimes are committed by men masquerading as the Klan." He was present at one well-publicized investigation of Klan atrocities and assured his audience "that of the 103 newspaper men present 97 of them were Knights of Columbus, and three of them were owners of Catholic newspapers."

To combat this, he wanted "to see every minister a member of the Klan and every Klansman a member of the church."[67]

McGinley told Meredith that he had referred the matter to the association's "supreme advocate," Luke E. Hart in St. Louis, who was monitoring the distribution of the bogus oath. He also sent Meredith pamphlets for distribution to repudiate the "bogus oath."[68] That summer, the oath was further circulated in Clarksville in Halifax County, near the North Carolina border, and in Norfolk.[69]

A year later, the bogus oath received wider circulation during John M. Purcell's campaign for election as state treasurer. A leading member of the Richmond Catholic community, Purcell had been appointed acting treasurer in 1924. In July 1925, the oath appeared in Wytheville, just before the Democratic primary that nominated Purcell to a full term. Ordinarily in Virginia politics at the time, winning the Democratic nomination assured election—the newspapers already treated Harry Byrd as governor-elect. But the Republicans now made a bid for the treasurer's office and nominated John David Bassett, who had the support of the Klan, which distributed a pamphlet purportedly sent from the "Grand Order of Knights of Columbus" to the "Faithful of Mother Church." As the *New York Times* reported, the pamphlet called upon every Catholic "to prepare yourself to cast your ballot on Nov 3 for a strong supporter of the mother of all churches and an officer of the Grand Order of the K. of C. to fill the important office of State Treasurer of Virginia." With an allusion to Alfred E. Smith's attempt to gain the Democratic presidential nomination in 1924, it went on to describe a wider conspiracy "to place at the head of the Government of the U.S.A. a most faithful servant and obedient to the Holy Father at Rome, whose infinite power cannot be questioned." Catholics who ignored this call to action would face excommunication. Attached to the pamphlet was a message addressed "to the Protestants of Virginia," asking "Will any red-blooded American stand for this—Roman Catholic control of this State?"[70]

From the pulpit of Sacred Heart Cathedral, Kaup denounced the proclamation and denied that the Church discriminated against any candidate for political office simply because of his religious affiliation. He also announced that the Knights of Columbus was preparing to take legal action against "the perpetrators of this bogus proclamation." As it reported Kaup's speech, the *New York Times* added that the Klan had "not been much of a force in Virginia" but drew its "greatest strength around Norfolk, in Roanoke City, in the southwest and in Danville and Pittsylvania Counties to the south." Altogether, the Klan claimed to have 25,000 members in Virginia.[71] But lacking a centralized structure in Virginia, it failed to develop the political power it had in other states.

Despite the anti-Catholic crusade, on November 3, 1925, Purcell was elected state treasurer, the first Catholic to win statewide office in Virginia. But, as Kaup had announced, the Knights of Columbus still considered taking legal action against the distributors of the inflammatory literature. Walter J. Conaty, Grand Knight of Richmond Council no. 395, the largest in the state, and supervisor of valuation for the Chesapeake and Ohio Railway Company, led the fight. The policy of the Supreme Council of the Knights in New Haven, however, was to prosecute printers of the bogus oath but leave to the local branches bringing legal action against the distributors of the propaganda. In this case, the bogus oath was distributed in Harrisonburg, and the pamphlet addressed "To the Faithful of Mother Church" was disseminated in Richmond, Newport News, Norfolk, Portsmouth, Petersburg, and Roanoke. The national office of the Knights was hesitant to become involved in a case where there was not assurance of victory. Conaty's strategy, however, was to focus on Wytheville, the residence of former Governor Elbert Lee Trinkle, where he thought he could obtain a successful prosecution. Ultimately, however, the Knights decided to drop their proposed libel suit. On the one hand, it was difficult to prosecute the distributor in Wytheville, where he might have sympathy. On the other, Hart, the Supreme Advocate, feared that, if they hired a non-Catholic attorney, as Conaty proposed, he might charge a "Standard Oil fee."[72]

But even before Purcell's nomination, another event occurred in Richmond that may have contributed to the national coverage of his campaign. On May 28, 1925, a Richmond city council committee overwhelmingly rejected the gift of a monument to Christopher Columbus from the Italian-American community. First proposed by Frank Realmuto, a Richmond barber, the statue was sculpted by Ferrucio Legnaioli who, with his business partner, Frank Ferrandini, employed thirty men in manufacturing stone and plaster artwork. The base was provided by Alphonso Grappone's family stone-cutting company. All these Italian immigrants had been part of Richmond's business community for some years. Some opposed the monument because the original site chosen was too close to the statues of Confederate heroes on Monument Avenue. But E. F. Miner, a metalworker, presented a "protest," in the name of 200 subscribers, "against the city donating any part of our streets . . . to any . . . sectarian body or organization for the purpose of erecting any statue, monument or other building to the memory of any man, be he native, naturalized or foreign born."[73] The opponents of the monument were for the most part, like Miner, from the laboring class and the Klan. As the Knights of Columbus entered their campaign against the bogus oath, their patron, Columbus, now became a hated Catholic icon.

On June 8, 1925, the city council's Committee on Streets approved the monument but moved its site to the southern end of the Boulevard near Byrd Park. "Richmond got back to normalcy," commented one reporter.[74] The original vote rejecting the monument had occurred when Richmond was hosting the annual convention of the National Editorial Association, which then publicized it in newspapers across the country as part of its reportage on the Klan in Virginia. Richmond's Italian-American community then numbered less than one percent of the city's population. Its leaders primarily intended to celebrate their Italian, not their Catholic, heritage—an intention that became clear in the ceremonies at the monument's dedication, originally scheduled for Columbus Day, 1927, but changed to December 9 in order for the Italian ambassador to participate. Governor Harry Byrd attended and may have later regretted his efforts to gain support from his Italian-American constituents by pronouncing that Benito Mussolini was "one of the few great supreme leaders that the world has produced."[75] The episode of the Columbus statue illustrated that immigrants still did not receive a warm welcome in Virginia's capital. The anti-Catholicism the statue evoked flowed into the Purcell campaign, but that was simply a dress rehearsal for the campaign against Alfred E. Smith three years later.

By the time of the Purcell campaign and the bogus oath controversy, O'Connell was nearing the end of his episcopate. He was ill and virtually retired. But, while the diocese, particularly its southern part, was going through the outbreak of anti-Catholicism, it was also expanding in the Norfolk and northern Virginia areas during and after World War I.

CHAPTER 19

Virginia's
First Suburban Growth,
1915–1924

In the years following World War I, Virginia experienced the first major development of "inner suburbs" connected with the downtown areas by the streetcar lines radiating out from the core of the cities to nearby regions. Richmond, in fact, was the first city to employ the new means of transportation and gave to Frank Julian Sprague's invention of the "troller," the little wheeled carriage that connected the car to an overhead electrical cable, the nickname by which the streetcar became known, the "trolley."[1] Between 1915 and 1924, the diocese of Richmond had to adjust to this new phenomenon, particularly in the city of Richmond, sections of northern Virginia, and the Norfolk area. In the more affluent regions, moreover, laypeople took the initiative in establishing parishes.

RICHMOND'S FIRST SUBURBS

The city of Richmond lagged behind the postwar development of northern Virginia and Norfolk. During his episcopate, Bishop O'Connell established only two new parishes in his see city, St. Paul's and St. Elizabeth's, both in the northern "suburbs."[2] In 1910, the Catholic families in the Barton Heights and Ginter Park areas belonged to St. Peter's, St. Mary's, or the Cathedral. Father Louis Smet, van de Vyver's nephew, was the first of several assistants at St. Peter's assigned to direct the "Barton Heights Catholic Club" that these families had formed with a view to developing a future parish. Prominent among these early lay leaders were Mr. and Mrs. Frank H. Nott, who would play a major role in founding Catholic Charities. Their older son, Walter, was then a seminarian at the North American College in Rome. The Catholic Club's feting of his ordination in 1919 became the occasion for it formally to petition the bishop to begin a new parish. On July 4, 1920, Father Edwin P. Shaughnessy, the assistant at St. Peter's, was named the first pastor and moved to the club's Fendall Avenue residence. In a little over a year, he had an assistant, Joseph V. Brennan. Though rapidly growing, the parish still had no name. It originally intended to build a school on the existing property and use the auditorium as a church, but the diocese then purchased the former Barton Heights Methodist Church on North Avenue. On August 6, 1922, O'Connell dedicated the church but recommended that the Barton Heights Catholic Club take the new name of St. Paul's.[3]

Shaughnessy soon began a school in the rear of his church, staffed by five Benedictine sisters, led by Sister Cecilia Bahen, O.S.B., a native Richmonder, as superior. The early membership of the parish indicated that Richmond's suburbs, like those of larger cities, were becoming an ethnic melting pot, with families like the Notts and Morrisseys joining the Biagis and Hoffmans. Within two years, however, Shaughnessy died from complications of appendicitis at the age of thirty-one. The second pastor was Thomas E. O'Connell, who had briefly been pastor of St. Mary's in Fairfax and would remain until 1960. The parish became one of the most active in the Richmond area. Among its earliest altar boys were two who would play a major role in the diocese, Harold Nott, who followed his brother into the priesthood, and Paul Williams, who became a pioneer for racial justice. Father O'Connell became one of the earliest spokesmen for integration.[4]

Like St. Paul's, St. Elizabeth's in the Highland Park area owed its origin to the commitment of several lay leaders, Lawrence H. Wittkamp and his wife and two brothers, Louis and Bernard, and especially their uncle, Fritz Sitterding. Like the women in Alexandria, as will be seen, the women in Highland Park formed a "St. Rita's Society," to place their endeavor under the patronage of the saint of the impossible. Sitterding then donated both land and money for building a church named for St. Elizabeth in honor of both his mother and his deceased daughter. On July 3, 1923, Father Louis Rowen said Mass on the porch of the Sitterding residence, the first floor of which served as a chapel until the community had its church completed in time for Christmas, 1925.[5]

NORTHERN VIRGINIA'S FIRST GROWTH AFTER WORLD WAR I: CLARENDON AND CHERRYDALE

In 1913 Father Frederick P. Lackey, pastor of St. Charles in Clarendon, had started saying Mass in Cherrydale, first in a grocery store and then in Pioneer Hall, a movie theater.[6] In June 1918, he received from Admiral A.W. Weaver an offer of $1,300 to purchase property for a new church.[7] By February, he had formed a building committee for the "Cherrydale Mission," now named St. Agnes after the admiral's sister, a Daughter of Charity, and had raised $3,200. For the time being, the congregation still had Mass in the "moving picture hall," which was about to be torn down. Wartime construction had increased the cost of labor, but the government's surplus of material could be purchased cheaply. St. Agnes's congregation numbered only about 100 people, but Lackey reported "the real estate men of Washington say this section will grow rapidly as soon as the new bridge is completed, and the Virginia cars run across the bridge into Washington."[8] The Key Bridge would link Washington with northern Virginia and definitively change the northern Virginia landscape.

Since St. Charles then had no debt, Lackey was concerned that "the people have no outlet for their energy, and they will be tempted to take it easy financially." He was also convinced that "a parish without a school is only half finished," so he urged O'Connell to write a letter urging his parishioners to raise funds for a school.[9]

On January 18, 1920, O'Connell dedicated the new church of St. Agnes with a seating capacity of 250.[10] Initially, Lackey said an early Mass at St. Agnes and a later one at St. Charles. By 1923, some parishioners at St. Charles petitioned O'Connell to appoint a resident pastor to St. Agnes, because the present arrangement necessitated that some parents with young children had to attend different Masses in separate churches.[11] Instead, O'Connell decided to assign Lackey an assistant, and St. Agnes would have to wait until 1936 before it got a resident pastor. By the middle of 1922, moreover, Lackey was already proceeding with his school for St. Charles, which he predicted would "be a credit to the Catholics in this growing community."[12]

MISSIONARY JOURNEYS FROM FALLS CHURCH

While the northern Virginia suburbs of Washington around Clarendon and Alexandria were being linked by trolley cars, west of Clarendon railroads or unpaved roads still provided the links between towns. Van Ingelgem's village parish in Falls Church had begun its expansion. He had missions at Fairfax Station, Pleasant Valley, El Nido, Herndon, Leesburg, and Purcellville. For much of his time as pastor, he covered this territory on "Doc," the horse he purchased from Father Edward Tearney, and later on "Louis." He especially disliked the muddy track he had to ply to Annandale. "I sing three High Masses every time I go over it," he remarked, "and Louis answers me."[13] Writing to his old friend Cardinal Désiré-Joseph Mercier, Archbishop of Malines, late in 1912, he said O'Connell was "a very charming man and devoted bishop," but "he has just charged me with building a fifth church in my very vast parish. Think of that! At my age!"[14]

In September 1919, van Ingelgem hosted Mercier in Falls Church.[15] The cardinal was making a triumphal tour of the United States, receiving accolades and honorary degrees from numerous prestigious secular universities in recognition of his patriotic defense of Belgium during the war. To convey him around the country, Thomas Fortune Ryan had provided him with the use of his own railroad car. Since van Ingelgem's own dealings with Ryan had not always been amicable, he may have looked askance at the cardinal's association with the millionaire. For that matter, one Belgian residing in New York attempted to dissuade Mercier from accepting Ryan's hospitality because of the scandal of the millionaire's unseemly haste in remarrying only two weeks after his first wife's death.[16] Nevertheless, after leaving Falls Church, Mercier journeyed south to the Ryan estate of "Oak Ridge," in Nelson County, where he and O'Connell remained for a day.[17]

Mercier's was the first recorded visit of a cardinal to van Ingelgem's village parish—Gibbons, of course, had visited it when he was the bishop—but Falls Church was starting to become a Washington suburb. Van Ingelgem already had one assistant, Valentino D. Cuevas, a priest of the archdiocese of Anteguera o Oajaca in Mexico, who, like many other Mexicans, had to flee his country during the bloody revolution that had begun in 1917. He had charge of the mission of El Nido, now part of McLean.

FAIRFAX GETS A RESIDENT PASTOR

In April 1919, Cuevas asked O'Connell to be assigned as the resident pastor of Fairfax Station, in whose little church Clara Barton had nursed after the Second Battle of Manassas.[18] Van Ingelgem approved of the arrangement for in El Nido there was little income, but in Fairfax Cuevas was "'persona gratissima' with the people. . . . 'Moto proprio' they asked him to come, promising to take care of him." Relieved of the Fairfax and Pleasant Valley missions and "those long trips," van Ingelgem could concentrate "more my work on a still extended territory."[19]

By the end of June 1919, Cuevas had taken up residence in Fairfax.[20] Enthusiastically, he asked O'Connell to pay a visit immediately after the priests' retreat at Georgetown. "The people of St. Mary's Fairfax, are most worthy of a reward from their Bishop," he wrote; "their Pastor begs of you to give them the one of your presence at our 3rd meeting on Sunday the 13th inst." It was a simple enough jaunt in Cuevas's mind, for the bishop could stay overnight in Alexandria, take the 7:37 Sunday morning train and arrive in Fairfax at 8:17 in time for Mass. At 2:30, he could then take the train back to Alexandria on his way to Richmond.[21] If the trains ran on time, the Alexandria-Fairfax trip in 1919 would be the envy of commuters in the 1990s.

Cuevas applied to the Church Extension Society for funds for his struggling mission. He was also negotiating to purchase a house and land from Dr. Swetnam, but he still needed the bishop's support, since he could not ask his "poor people" for more.[22] By December, Cuevas had procured the Swetnam property.[23] For years to come, the postal address of the parish would be "Swetnam" to distinguish it from Fairfax City, only then developing, and the house he purchased remained the rectory.

MISSIONS FROM FAIRFAX TO CHARLOTTESVILLE ALONG THE RAILROAD

Having a resident priest in Fairfax led to the reallocating of missions attached to parishes. While automobiles were becoming the standard means of transportation, train connections still dictated the assignment of missions to parishes that superficially had nothing in common.

Fairfax was the northernmost parish on the rail line stretching through Warrenton to Charlottesville. Late in November 1921, William Winston, the new pastor in Warrenton, urged that Manassas be assigned to Fairfax and Culpeper to him. Manassas had fifty Catholics with Mass every Sunday. But Winston also said Mass on weekdays every month or so for one hundred and twenty-five Catholics in the towns of Haymarket, Gainesville, The Plains, Marshall, and Delaplane. By train, these towns were closer to Manassas than to Warrenton. If they were detached from him, he would have only 100 Catholics in Warrenton but could then add Culpeper, which he could reach by train every Sunday without omitting a Mass at Warrenton.[24] Not only would Manassas give Cuevas increased income, Winston argued, but he feared that "if the masses were reduced to two a month, I believe that a considerable falling off in attendance would follow." Although Warrenton's congregation was small, it was "really the [financial] source of support for the whole mission." All that was now needed was for Father Joseph J. De Gryse in Charlottesville to give up Culpeper.[25]

In Falls Church, van Ingelgem liked the proposed changes. "Swetnam with Manassas," he told O'Connell, would make "a good little parish."[26] Down in Charlottesville, De Gryse likewise agreed to the new arrangements. He claimed he already had too many missions but hoped to make his parish self-supporting. Culpeper had only fifty people, but they were generous. He suggested, moreover, that Orange, Madison, and Greene Counties be included with Culpeper. Greene County had no Catholics, and those in Madison and Orange already attended Mass in Culpeper.[27] O'Connell added Rappahannock County to Winston's charge in Culpeper and gave the Keswick mission, formerly served by the Josephites in Richmond, to Charlottesville.[28]

Assigning missions to a priest resident in a sometimes distant town according to such practical issues as train schedules was not a negligible matter. According to the discipline of the Catholic Church at that time, the priest who said Mass in one town and then took a train to another was obliged to fast from all food and drink from midnight. He might not eat breakfast until noon.

Van Ingelgem congratulated O'Connell on the new arrangements, for "Charlottesville with a mass every Sunday could be worked up— and get out of a kind of lethargy: it would not take long before the sacrifice of Culpeper would be entirely forgotten." With a touch of sarcasm, he added: "If the Pastor would paint a nice 'Christus,' whose type is familiar to his Church, and offer it to the 'Seigneur of Oak Ridge,' he would become at once 'persona gratissima'—and this may go a long way."[29]

THE HIGH COST OF A BENEFACTOR: CONFLICT WITH RYAN

Van Ingelgem's remark about Ryan arose from his own personal experience when he used Oak Ridge to evangelize the area. But other priests had had unpleasant encounters with Richmond's benefactor. While pastor in Lynchburg, Thomas A. Rankin also had charge of Ryan's private chapel at Oak Ridge. In June of 1913, he complained that he was treated like a servant in Ryan's employ, with no meals provided for him when he arrived to say Mass. In reply to his complaint, Ryan's attorney in New York stated that, before leaving for Europe, Ryan had ordered the mansion closed to everyone, but had instructed the keeper of the local boarding house to provide the priest with meals when he came to say Mass.[30] Rankin remonstrated with O'Connell that he had to bring his own lunch with him to Oak Ridge and that, when he had eaten in the boardinghouse, he was simply seated with the regular boarders.[31]

In December 1914, O'Connell assigned William Gill to Oak Ridge, where he hoped through his "zeal to give a new impulse to that mission and to extend the confines of religion."[32] Gill lasted only a short time before being transferred to Warrenton. Ryan did, in fact, place great burdens on the clergy. In April 1917, for example, he requested that, beginning the next Sunday, O'Connell have the pastor in Lynchburg say Mass at Oak Ridge until the middle of June and during September and October. In the fall, he intended to visit Richmond to make permanent arrangements for his estate.[33] In a diocese that was always short of priests, Ryan was making a great demand. Van Ingelgem was not alone in his evaluation of the "Seigneur of Oak Ridge."

In the meantime, Rankin had been transferred to Charlottesville, where he again ran afoul of Ryan. The two locked horns over a gift of $30,000 Ryan and his wife had agreed to give through a parishioner either to build a new church on a different site or to replace the original one built in 1881. As Ryan told the story to O'Connell, the situation by February 1919 had "drifted into a very unfortunate position. When Mrs Ryan and I agreed to help the Parish, it was at the earnest solicitation of our friend Mrs. Randolph, and the credit whatever it amounts to belongs to her and no one else." He found it "distasteful" that the pastor and Mrs. Randolph were then publicly airing their differences as to how the money was to be used. Under these circumstances, he offered the bishop his opinion on the proper running of a parish:

> I think it must have a very bad effect on the Parish, and tend to the destruction of the harmony which should exist between the Pastor and his prominent Parishioners. This I think is especially emphasized as Charlottesville contains the University, where Dr. [Edwin A.] Alderman [president of the university] tells me he has 25 to 40 Catholic boys each year from all parts of the country.

While not wanting to burden O'Connell, he was going to suggest that Mrs. Randolph go to see him.[34]

A year later, the tension had not abated, so Rankin decided to humble himself and take the train to New York to see Ryan personally. Writing ahead of time, Rankin tried to put a bold face on his action: "It is said that Fortune favors the brave and I hope he will in this case for it requires all my courage to make this trip in spite of my reluctance."[35] But millionaires are seldom intimidated by village pastors, even brave ones. Forwarding Rankin's letter to O'Connell, Ryan said "our little Charlottesville friend is after me as you will see from the enclosed which I did not answer. He called at the house this morning and I told him that the Charlottesville Church matter was entirely in your hands and that he must see you."[36]

The controversy continued for several more years, even after De Gryse replaced Rankin in 1921. Late in 1923, O'Connell became personally involved and succeeded in having Ryan take a more active role. The bishop now had "some hope for peace and for reasonableness [sic] dealing." On a visit to Charlottesville, he found three opinions on how to improve Holy Comforter. Rankin had proposed a church built in Roman style; De Gryse suggested a Gothic church; and others wanted to build on a new site closer to the university. Laying these issues out in a sermon, O'Connell invited the congregation's comments. He now found himself at odds with "Mrs. Randolph [who] insists the money was donated to her by Mrs. Ryan and that it must be applied as she, Mrs. Randolph, wanted." This he refused to do, but would agree to

Ryan's personal allocation of his gift. He further reminded Ryan that "you wrote me you could not support the plans made by Mrs. Ryan and Mrs. Randolph for a new church and a new rectory on grounds near the University but that, as a compromise you would give me $30,000 for the improvement of the present church, if agreeable to me." As bishop, O'Connell was demanding the right to make the final decision, whereas Mrs. Randolph wanted De Gryse and him

> to work under her orders. I certainly cannot allow her to destroy or to dismantle the present church unless I have a guarantee for another one nor can I risk to assume responsibility for all her orders. If the responsibility rests with me I shall claim the authority and act as ably and as conscientiously as I can with the gift you made me.[37]

Charlottesville's new church was built on the site of the old one. It was a brick structure along classical lines, perhaps the design Rankin had favored. Despite Ryan's generosity in building the cathedral and other buildings, only the correspondence on this episode remains extant in the archives. He was generous, but he expected priests and the bishop to bow to his authority.

FALLS CHURCH AND BEYOND IN NORTHERN VIRGINIA

In August 1922, Cuevas left Fairfax to return to Mexico. For a time, Carmelites from Washington said Mass at St. Mary's and in Manassas.[38] Then, Fairfax again fell under Falls Church. Almost a year passed before Thomas E. O'Connell came for eighteen months before becoming pastor of St. Paul's in Richmond. In 1924, Nicholas Habets, one of Bishop O'Connell's recruits from Fribourg and a native of Belgium, came for five years. He was remembered in Fairfax for his successful campaign to have the roads paved after horses had to pull his car out of a muddy ditch,[39] but he has a place in the story of the diocese of Richmond for founding Our Lady of Victory in Portsmouth for African Americans and for later being pastor of Star of the Sea in Virginia Beach, from which he founded a mission that now bears his name. Aside from Alexandria and Falls Church, northern Virginia was still a series of scattered settlements of small farmers and railroad workers. But Habets's Belgian neighbor was still making his mark.

When van Ingelgem arrived in Falls Church, he found that Tearney had engaged the Sisters of Perpetual Adoration to run the parochial school. Based in New Orleans, the congregation's rule had not been approved by either the Holy See or the archbishop of New Orleans.[40] To support their teaching in the parochial school, the sisters opened a boarding academy that in 1920 had forty students. By August of 1922, they had decided to leave, but charged that van Ingelgem had given them so little support that they were in debt to the mother house. Van Ingelgem countered that they incurred their debt by trying to raise $100,000 for a new building for the academy and, now that they were leaving, "they complain of our poor little Parish. How cryingly unjust it is!" Although their superior continued to demand compensation, he urged O'Connell first to gain title to the property before offering them any recompense.[41]

In 1923, van Ingelgem had already arranged for the Sisters, Servants of the Immaculate Heart of Mary, from Philadelphia, to staff his school and begin their extensive work in Virginia. In their convent, they opened Villa Maria Academy as a high school for boarders. In 1936, Mother Mary Clotildis, the superior in Virginia, decided to close the high school, due to low enrollments, but to continue the academy as an elementary school. In 1952, the academy relocated to "Oak Lawn," near Lynchburg, where it remained a resident and day school for girls through grade 8 and a day school for boys through grade 4, until it closed in 1983. Falls Church, however, remained their major center. Mother Mary Claudia, who began more than thirty years of service to Virginia in 1937, recalled traveling from St. James to Leesburg on Sundays to teach catechism, as the Daughters of Charity had done in Virginia Beach in 1915.[42]

ALEXANDRIA AND ST. RITA'S

While Falls Church was becoming the principal Catholic center between Washington to the north and Charlottesville to the south and Harpers Ferry to the west, Alexandria, the oldest city in northern Virginia, underwent its first major growth as trolley lines made the area accessible to workers in Washington. In November 1912, a group of women who called themselves the Ladies Seminarian Society began holding Sunday school in a cobbler's shop in Del Ray. Intent on starting a new parish, they had already chosen a name, St. Rita, the same patroness of impossible causes the people of Richmond later chose for building St. Elizabeth's. Within a month, three of these women, Mrs. M. R. Sullivan, Mrs. Frank Hill, and Miss Virginia R. Burke, notified Bishop O'Connell that a non-Catholic had donated two lots for a church midway between the trolley stations of Del Ray and Mt. Ida.[43] A few months later, Sally Teagan took a census of the Catholics in the area and outlined plans for a church.[44] All this occurred before St. Rita's had even had its first Mass, which van Ingelgem celebrated on July 16, 1913.[45]

Within a few months, St. Rita's had a building committee, chaired by Patrick J. Conlon, which coordinated efforts with Henry Cutler, the pastor of St. Mary's. In May 1914, the cornerstone for the building was laid. Because O'Connell had to be in Rome for his *ad limina* to the pope, Conlon arranged for Archbishop Giovanni Bonzano, the apostolic delegate, to preside over the ceremonies and for Father William Kirby, professor at the Catholic University, and James Regan, national president of the Ancient Order of Hibernians, to speak. As president of the Union of Holy Name Societies of the archdiocese of Baltimore, he also invited their members in Washington as well as the Hibernians to make sure to swell the attendance.[46] They were to wear their identifying pins, "as we are isolated in a locality where a Holy Name button is regarded as a curiosity of Magnetic Charm. We hope by your presence on this occasion you will demonstrate to our separated Brethren that there is some real substantial backing to our little Band located in the woods."[47]

But then the plans hit a snag. James S. Groves, a parishioner of St. Mary's, was president of the Mt. Ida Realty Company; at the same time, he was president of a realty company in Virginia Beach, where he was also selling the diocese property. He had originally donated a lot for St. Rita's, but O'Connell exchanged it for one in a better location. Groves then promised to contribute the cost of the original lot. For three years, his role in the building of St. Rita's became a major bone of contention with which Cutler's successor, Louis Smet, would have to deal.

Groves had never contributed either the amount he had originally pledged to the building fund for St. Rita's or the cost of the lot that O'Connell had exchanged. Smet grew suspicious of Groves's generosity. "I learned too late," he told O'Connell, "that lots much better situated sell less than $300. It is plain enough that the Groves' are getting out of St. Rita's church all they can." He urged that the bishop come personally to Alexandria to complete the financial transactions for Groves's lots.[48] Only in October 1916, did Groves fulfill his commitment to O'Connell.[49]

Smet continued to have charge of St. Rita's until 1924. In May, he urged O'Connell to appoint a pastor for the new parish, for "the missions interfere with the main church and Father [Lawrence] Kelly [his assistant] is doing the best he can, but he is really very feeble."[50] Shortly later, Leonard J. Koster became resident pastor of St. Rita's. In June 1924, Smet, in the meantime, had witnessed one fruit of his ministry, when John Samuel Igoe, a parishioner, was ordained in St. Mary's. Two years later, his brother, Michael Francis, was also ordained in the new Shrine of the Immaculate Conception in Washington. Like the McKeefry brothers a generation earlier, they sometimes followed one another in their assignments.[51] St. Mary's was beginning to produce native vocations. A generation after the Igoes were ordained, Julius and John Cilinski were ordained, and their sister, Amelia, entered the Sisters of the Holy Cross.[52]

But St. Mary's during the period of World War I was by no means an easy mission. On the eve of the war, the region continued to be mission territory, including not only Mount Ida but also the "country," with Lorton and Occotineck. Like his predecessors a century earlier, Smet still encountered "numerous Irish families who went to live in Virginia, far from any church, and are lost to the Faith."[53] The war brought renewed growth to Alexandria itself as shipyards attracted more workers. Smet now turned to his long-standing dream of building a parochial school. Alexandria already had St. Mary's Academy, run by the Sisters of the Holy Cross. In 1919, Smet opened a school for boys under the Xaverian Brothers.[54] Simultaneously, however, he entered into conflict with the Sisters of the Holy Cross.

Smet objected to the children of the parish attending the sisters' academy as day students, "for the obvious reason that the distinction between the select 'and the not select' children is the main evil which we wish to remedy." He, therefore, sought assurance "that the parochial school can freely develop in every way, unhampered by the presence of Saint Mary's Academy." Smet's problems were similar to those van Ingelgem faced in Falls Church. He feared that if his parochial school was "simply . . . a feeder to the Academy . . . , the sisters in the parochial school will probably not be heart and soul in *their* own work, and we will have the same trouble recurring that exists now." Should the sisters not be committed to the parochial school, he foresaw that the "position of the pastor might yet be made uncomfortable."[55] Smet's problems with the sisters at the academy were, in fact, making his position "uncomfortable."

In October 1919, without consulting either Smet or O'Connell, the sisters obtained the services of a chaplain, R. D. McGowan, then working for the National Catholic War Council.[56] Although Smet had no objection to McGowan, he saw the sisters' move to have their own chaplain as one more step toward a future declaration "that they are not supposed to have anything to do with Saint Mary's church or Saint Mary's parish," including even teaching in the Sunday school. He, therefore, recommended that O'Connell approve the sisters' chaplain, but he also wanted to preserve his school and his authority as pastor. With a play on the words of the *Aeneid,* he concluded: "Timeo sorores et dona ferentes [I fear the sisters, even when bearing gifts]. As I said, dear Bishop, judging from their methods and from past history I do not know what to expect, and being powerless myself I should like to have some ground under my feet."[57]

Smet's conflicts with the sisters were not unusual. He wanted a comprehensive school for all his children. The sisters, for their part, also had a point inasmuch as they had originally provided teachers free of charge to the parish. In the end, they remained at St. Mary's Academy and also staffed the parochial school.

A Gift from the Episcopal Diocese and Smet's Return to Belgium

In the postwar years, Smet continued to be a missionary priest. Even with Father Koster at St. Rita's, St. Mary's had two missions, St. Anthony's near Baileys Crossroads and Sacred Heart in Groveton. At the height of the Ku Klux Klan crusade against the Church in Virginia, St. Anthony's received an unexpected gift. In June 1924, Bishop William Caleb Brown of the Episcopal diocese of Virginia donated to the diocese of Richmond an acre of land belonging to the Virginia Theological Seminary.[58] As he registered the deed in Fairfax County, Smet commented to O'Connell: "This transaction is certainly unusual and remarkable: may the good relations so continue."[59] The deed stipulated, however, that the property would revert to the seminary, "should it not be used for purposes of maintaining a house of worship thereon." St. Anthony's used the site until late in 1949, when the widening of the road nearby made the site unusable for a church.[60]

In 1927, Smet returned to his native Belgium, where he became vice-rector of his alma mater, the American College in Louvain. His place was taken in Alexandria by Father William A. McKeefry, who, like his brother before him, was pastor in Martinsburg. Four years later, van Ingelgem retired from Falls Church to become chaplain at Monte Maria in Richmond. A short time later, Nicholas Habets left Fairfax to found Our Lady of Victory Church in Portsmouth, the first parish for African Americans staffed by diocesan priests. The last of the pioneer Belgians who watched the first developments of northern Virginia had departed, but their legacy remains. When Smet died in 1940, Sacred Heart Church at Groveton, one of his missions, was renamed St. Louis in his honor.

Expansion in Hampton Roads

Within Virginia, the Hampton Roads area experienced its greatest surge in population after the First World War. In 1920, Norfolk had only two parishes, in addition to St. Joseph's, which will be treated separately. St. Mary's, the original parish served missions in Virginia Beach and Berkeley and a summer station at Ocean View. Sacred Heart had a mission at Lambert's Point. Within four years, each of these missions became a parish with a resident pastor, and Sacred Heart had a new church. There was also a type of mentorship for pastors being developed. The pastors of each of the new parishes had been assistants at the mother parishes. For the most part, they would spend their priestly lives in the area.

Birth of a Parish in Virginia Beach

While Cutler and, later, Smet had their problems with James Groves in Mt. Ida, farther to the south in Virginia Beach, the realtor was also offering lots to the diocese at a discounted rate, but here he met an opponent. As early as 1909, a visiting priest took care of the resort's summer community.[61] On February 2, 1914, however, the people concerned with founding a parish had a meeting at St. Vincent's Hospital in Norfolk. Present were Bishop O'Connell and Father John Doherty, still the pastor of St. Mary's Church since O'Keefe's departure in 1887. Among the laypeople was Mrs. Emma Post. Sister Pauline Strabel, D.C., later described Virginia Beach as "an Aristocratic Southern watering place with many hotels and private dwellings." An hour's ride on the trolley line from Norfolk, it had a summer population of approximately a thousand. The Daughters of Charity agreed to start a Sunday school, beginning in March in Mrs. James E. Allen's parlor.[62]

But this was where Mrs. Post took the reins. Soon after that initial meeting, she told O'Connell of her vision of a church near a new luxury hotel in plain sight of the Norfolk and Southern Railway station, so that it would be the first thing travelers would see. She was already gathering contributions and hoped the bishop would soon reach an agreement with Groves for a site. She was a woman with a mission and threw down the gauntlet with the remark: "Well—to the future now, and Bishop O'Connell's 'Star of the Sea'—to the Point? [sic] and to our donor, the Honorable James Groves."[63] This was but the beginning of a long correspondence in which Groves, Doherty, and O'Connell proved to be no match for her determination.

The first problem was the site. Mrs. Post had already indicated her decided preference for one on the "point," but Doherty told O'Connell that the majority of the Beach Catholics would be satisfied with a more modest site that "will answer every purpose."[64] At one juncture, O'Connell and Doherty passed her letters back and forth to one another, as each sought to avoid a confrontation.[65] With such vacillation between a bishop and a pastor, a person like Mrs. Post was sure to become the victor.

In April, Groves had met with Mrs. Post and Mr. Esby Smith, representing the Catholic residents. He then described to O'Connell a lot on the "lake front" and pointed out that his Virginia Beach lots were larger than the ones he offered at Mt. Ida. At a discount of $275, he would sell the diocese a lot for $500.[66] Mrs. Post now took on both Groves and O'Connell about the size and precise location of the lot. She attended a meeting at Groves' Norfolk office with Doherty, his assistant, "young Leo Judson," and Mrs. James E. Allen. When Grove's representative said the proposed lot was 135 feet deep, she "asked Leo to write that down, which he did." In her mind, "a gift is a gift, but Mr. Groves is unprincipled," for the lot he was selling was in the middle of the block with the corner lot reserved for a cottage to be built by a "Mr. St. Clair," who she heard was a "real estate chum of Mr. Groves." She did not want some next-door neighbor, like those near Riverside Church in New York, complaining about church bells. The corner lot was essential, not necessarily for building a church, "but, for exclusiveness and a neutral ground to plant with trees—where the Cardinals? (for I hear we are to have a few more) can walk in the shade and enjoy the grounds."[67]

In the meantime, Mrs. Post confronted Groves. As she reported their conversation to O'Connell, she had said:

> no one knows better than you what a disadvantage such a location would be for a church and why should you expect us to build a church for Mrs. St. Clair to build a Bungalow on one corner, and Mrs. Some one else to build on the other corner and hem us in like that—We must have the St. Clair Corner on the South Side.

She had further learned that the lots in question were actually 150 feet deep, whereas Groves's agent had said they were 135 feet. When Doherty had conceded that he needed only 100 feet, she "pulled his coat."

Money was no object, Mrs. Post told O'Connell, for

> Our Star of the Sea is not got to be a "little cheap affair." Taste can take the place of money at times, and far surpass that old lucre. But St. Vincent said, in his writings, "be sure to pick the stones of the foundations right at first"—and that is what I'm standing out for.

In the meantime, she was busy planning to plant her trees on the corner lot. "No need to hurry up the building," she concluded, "for you know Father D. is not so well and the Phillistines take advantage and if you were here—we could be preparing during your absence, a good builder don't need to destroy trees when constructing an edifice besides we expect to 'box them.'"[68]

Mrs. Post had won. On April 23, Groves accepted her terms. Enclosing a copy of the letter he had written to her, Groves told O'Connell he hoped to have the matter settled before the bishop left for his *ad limina* visit to Rome, for "this Church is very much needed at the Beach."[69] He told Mrs. Post that he would exchange the lot he originally offered for the corner one, for which he would ask $500, $325 less than he was getting for similar ones, and the church would still retain the neighboring lot that he had donated. His only condition was that building begin by June 1.[70]

But Mrs. Post was still not finished. The new lot ran only 100 feet deep, so she queried that, if the bishop was going to pay $500 for it, "why not get generous? Mr. Groves to give us the full value—at least 135 ft. deep." After all, she observed, "all that talk of his about how the lots run is [']nonsense'—he owns the land and can make them run as he chooses."[71]

Mrs. Post was the type of person who would have tried the patience of the most virtuous of pastors or real estate brokers or, for that matter, bishops. Her foresight that Star of the Sea needed a site larger than Doherty originally thought sufficient was probably due more to sentimental piety than demographic sagacity. The little chapel originally built on the lot she chose eventually outgrew the congregation, still limited principally to summer residents. Before long, other lots were added to the original property, but Mrs. Post and her church at the beach would have to wait until after World War I to get a resident pastor. In the meantime, it remained a mission of St. Mary's, where Monsignor James T. O'Farrell, the vicar general, replaced Doherty as pastor in 1918.

During the summer of 1917, John A. Baecher, the Norfolk attorney for the diocese, commented to O'Connell "that your purchases made at Virginia Beach and Ocean View, were far-sighted and wisely made, and were made just in time to escape higher prices which are now resulting from the great developments at Jamestown and vicinity."[72] World War I was dramatically changing the area, but, on its eve, the diocese had managed to begin another parish in Ocean View.

OCEAN VIEW

Ocean View, a few miles north of Norfolk on the Chesapeake Bay was the site where Union Forces landed to take the city of Norfolk in May 1862. It had begun as a private resort in 1854 but became more accessible when the Ocean View Railroad Company began to run eight trains a day from its station in downtown Norfolk and was even

more so when a trolley line replaced the railroad. From a favorite resort area for wealthy residents of Norfolk, army and navy officers,
and people heading south to Florida who stopped off and sometimes
stayed, it was becoming an integral part of the city of Norfolk to
which it was annexed in 1923.[73]

In November 1916, the diocese began looking at property in Ocean
View. As Baecher was completing arrangements for purchasing the
property at Virginia Beach, he also recommended that O'Connell
purchase lots in Ocean View on Government Avenue, a site that was
only a fifteen-minute walk to the railroad station.[74] Ocean View, unlike Virginia Beach, however, did not have a Mrs. Post to drive a hard
bargain. Baecher had to pay full price.[75] The diocese had completed its
real estate transactions right on the eve of Norfolk's wartime boom.
Once the war was over, Ocean View remained a mission station of
St. Mary's, with Sunday Mass each week only during the summer. But
that situation rapidly changed.

As the summer of 1919 came to an end, Father Robert Kealey, recently ordained and assigned to St. Mary's, had alternated with Father
George Dunn in caring for Ocean View. When Dunn was transferred,
O'Farrell assigned Kealey alone to Ocean View. Kealey now asked
O'Connell for instructions. Dunn had vacated his old quarters at the
resort, and the casino where he held Mass had no heat for the winter.
He had, however, built a small chapel for the permanent congregation. In the summer, there were over seven hundred at each Mass, but
the winter attendance dropped to below three hundred. While Kealey
claimed he was not asking to be made the pastor, he did recommend
that the bishop make permanent arrangements.[76] O'Connell appointed
Kealey, who now had to build a church. While using Dunn's small
chapel, he moved into a cottage provided by one of the summer residents with his mother as housekeeper.[77]

Ocean View's permanent residents were for the most part laborers, with little money for building a church. Most of the financial support came from the summer residents. Kealey and the other Norfolk
pastors approached the people in Norfolk who had summer homes
there but who could see no point in building an "elegant" church at
the seashore.[78] Despite this opposition, Kealey argued that "brick will
greatly add to the beauty and permanence of the structure." He also
asserted the need of an innovation—electric lighting for the sanctuary![79] Kealey won his point and, by May 1920, he was ready to move
into his new brick church of Holy Trinity.[80]

BLESSED SACRAMENT

Simultaneously with the founding of Holy Trinity, the first parish split off from Sacred Heart—Blessed Sacrament. For some time, Sacred Heart under Father Thomas Waters and Father Leo Ryan had had a mission at Lambert's Point, St. Francis de Sales. By 1919, it had grown large enough to become a parish. But here Waters ran into a problem arising from the mode of owning church property in Virginia, this one dating back to the 1870s. Gibbons had apparently purchased several lots in Lambert's Point, but the title was not clear. In Gibbons's will to his successor, as Waters described it, his use of a phrase "excluding such property as he may have aliened [sic] is fatal." Someone now claimed Gibbons had in fact alienated the property. To avoid this in the future, Baecher recommended that O'Connell make sure his own will specify the parcels of diocesan property.[81] The attorney had already had several history lessons as he had tried to trace some deeds in the Norfolk area back as far as 1819, sometimes discovering that the incumbent bishop of Richmond was in fact not the legal owner of some property.[82]

With the title to the Lambert's Point property in dispute, Waters and Ryan sought a new location on Colley Avenue, where Ryan, the first pastor, began to build Blessed Sacrament Church.[83] At the same time, Waters began construction of the new Sacred Heart Church, completed in 1925.[84]

The expansion in Norfolk brought the diocese its first real urban experience long familiar to the American church elsewhere. It was a new experience for a bishop of Richmond to contend with such issues as urban parish boundaries and jurisdiction. In this case, the pastors disagreed on who had charge of the Army hospital, where a patient had died without a priest, and the Public Service hospital. Finally, Waters, Ryan, O'Farrell, and Kealey amicably agreed on parish boundaries and assigned both hospitals to Blessed Sacrament.[85] But the Norfolk priests were already making plans that presaged the city's future growth.

In the fall of 1923, O'Farrell was recovering from a heart attack. "My working days are over," he told O'Connell, but, as vicar general, he summoned Waters and Ryan to his hospital room to discuss plans for yet another parish, planned for Cottage Toll Road and Lafayette Boulevard.[86] During the next few months, even as Waters was building his own church, he and Baecher were purchasing more property in the Winona neighborhood as the future site of Christ the King, which would not have even a chapel for another decade.[87]

In the meantime, O'Farrell's health continued to decline. In December 1923, he had Kealey write for him to O'Connell. "He has to give up," Kealey wrote, but O'Farrell wanted Father William O'Hara transferred from Sacred Heart in South Richmond to Norfolk, since O'Hara had supposedly agreed that O'Farrell could remain as "pastor emeritus."[88] Such arrangements are always perilous, for the "pastor emeritus" might not give up the reins of power. O'Connell rejected O'Farrell's resignation.

By May 1924, as O'Farrell continued to weaken, he received a delegation from Berkley asking for a resident pastor. He told them to consult Father Philip Brennan, one of his assistants.[89] In September, O'Connell finally accepted his resignation as pastor, but retained him as vicar general, a post he held until his death early in 1926.[90] Brennan now became administrator of St. Mary's until late in the year, when Edward Brosnan was appointed pastor, and Michael Hartigan became the first pastor of St. Matthew's in Berkley. The shape of the Norfolk area was now virtually set for the next generation, except for Virginia Beach.

For more than four years, Philip Brennan had been angling to be assigned to Virginia Beach. Born in Ireland and educated at the North American College, he was originally assigned as an assistant at St. Mary's to work with Italian immigrants. While he complained to O'Connell about having to take on the work of a host of other assistants who enjoyed being ill, he also chafed at serving under O'Farrell. As he put it to the bishop in one of his early entreaties for a transfer: "Monsignor is not really a lovable person. He is a little mite in soul when I put him near you who have always had such a broad vision and such a power to encourage! My exalted idea of him as a dear, sweet, lovable old dear has met with disillusionment." With a touch of that persuasive ability characteristic of his native land, he concluded: "Here I am knocking . . . [sic] but feelings are pained simply because I can never mention the child of my heart: Virginia Beach."[91] Late in January 1924, he finally got his wish.

Within a few years, all the new parishes in Norfolk proper had parochial schools, with the Daughters of Charity at Blessed Sacrament and St. Matthew's, and the Sisters of the Holy Cross at Holy Trinity. Of the new parishes, only Star of the Sea in Virginia Beach lacked a school, though Brennan did expand his church in 1929 enough to increase the number of pews from twenty to fifty.[92] The growth of the "Beach" had to wait for another world war. When it came, Brennan had to weigh the "child of my heart" against the burden of building a school. He chose to go to Berkeley Springs, West Virginia. To his successor, Nicholas Habets, fell the task of building a school, but that belongs to a later part of Richmond's history.

For the most part, O'Connell left the development of these new urban centers to the priests who were in place, van Ingelgem and Smet in the north and Doherty, O'Farrell, and Waters in Norfolk. He was more of a reactor than an initiator. In other pastoral aspects of his diocese, however, he was more active, particularly in developing a strategy for rural evangelization, continuing the work of his predecessors with African Americans, and initiating work with immigrants, still few in number, who came from Italy, eastern and central Europe, and Lebanon.

CHAPTER 20

Evangelization in the Country and City

While sections of the diocese of Richmond were becoming urbanized, many Catholics remained scattered in isolated railroad towns. Bishop O'Connell began focusing on rural parishes from which priests would evangelize the surrounding areas. But his episcopate also witnessed the arrival of small groups of non-English-speaking immigrants who soon gave Virginia Catholicism a bit of the ethnic mix so characteristic of the North. At the same time, he did not abandon van de Vyver's policy of evangelizing African Americans in cities rather than rural areas, but that topic will be treated later. By this point, however, O'Connell, increasingly ill after 1922, was nearing the end of his episcopate.

Small Parishes Replace Roving Missionaries

Shortly after assuming office in 1912, O'Connell approached A.P. Doyle, the Paulist director of the Mission House at the Catholic University, to inquire about four scholarships established for Richmond priests. Doyle replied that he had "been personally interested in the Mission work in Virginia, since the days when thrity [*sic*] years ago, I went through the entire state and gave missions in every parish." Since its inception, the Mission House had provided a burse for van de Vyver and had trained Thomas E. Waters, A.J. van

Ingelgem, Thomas A. Rankin, and James A. Brennan. Doyle especially mentioned Waters' "excellent service" and remained convinced there would be a "thoroughly organized mission band," were
it not for van de Vyver's lack of enthusiasm. In giving his views
about van de Vyver's successor, it will be recalled, Doyle had already
noted the lack of efforts in evangelization. Now, he guaranteed that
he would accept the four young priests O'Connell might send, for
even if they became parish priests, "they can give missions in out-of-
the-way places where there are no churches or even any scattered
Catholics."[1]

O'Connell turned for advice to the priest Doyle had praised so
highly, Thomas Waters, then in Newport News. Waters was the last
priest on the old mission band until the shortage of priests, as he put
it, "made my removal also necessary." While the Paulist concept of
"the diocesan mission work" was then "suspended," he argued that
"all the priests of the Diocese are more or less doing that kind of work
all the time." Although he praised the Mission House program as "of
great value even in parochial work," he admitted that "I have never
been able to view this missionary movement with the whole-souled
enthusiasm of its promoters."

In regard to parish missions, Waters had practical objections to
maintaining a mission band in a small diocese. Within a year, the band
would give missions in most of the parishes "and then one of the chief
charms about the band has vanished." Once the missionaries had
visited a parish, "the pastors as well as people prefer other priests for
another mission." As far as "the broad field of the non-Catholic
world" was concerned, he believed few priests could make friends
with Protestants, "nor present the Catholic Truth in a manner that the
Protestant mind can grasp it. . . . When a missionary leaves town after
a well attended mission his influence goes with him and his labor is
apparently lost."

As an alternative to an itinerant missionary, Waters recommended the parish system be adapted by placing a priest in a small
town and offering him permanent support. With a series of such
small-town centers, the priest could be transferred from one to another from time to time.[2] O'Connell followed Waters's advice. Over
thirty years would pass before the diocese again fielded a mission
band, ironically with Waters's nephew, Vincent, as one of its principal members.

CREWE: A RURAL MISSION CENTER

While rural parishes usually received funds from the Church Extension Society, founded for this purpose in 1905, individual benefactors were also responsible for such parishes. Late in 1917, O'Connell received an offer from Hugh A. McMullen of Cumberland, Maryland, the comptroller of the state and a personal friend, to give up to $1,500 for a church named after St. John and another $500 a year for five years to support a priest doing "a sort of special work."[3] Soon, McMullen proposed Crewe as the site, a station on the Norfolk and Western Railroad.[4]

Before entering into a final agreement, O'Connell sought the advice of Father Martin J. Haier of Petersburg, within whose territory Crewe then fell. Haier was enthusiastic. Although some parts of Virginia were becoming urbanized, he suggested that one "take a map of Virginia & draw a line from Portsmouth to Petersburg thence to Lynchburg & Danville & within that territory there is not a single priest." A priest stationed either in Farmville or in Crewe "could do a wonderful work, & build up a Catholic Community especially among the farmers, as many Catholics would move from the severe climate of the North Western States if they had a priest in either one of those towns." Although few Catholic farmers would choose to move from the north, Haier was prescient in proposing a type of twinning between settled urban parishes and undeveloped rural ones. He suggested that St. Joseph's in Petersburg could raise $500 a year until the new parish was self-sustaining, for "Protestant Churches do this & I think our City Churches ought to help some poor Country Mission." "Mr. McMullen," he continued, "is setting a grand example for our Catholics & I only hope there will be many others follow [sic] in his steps."[5]

In accordance with Haier's suggestion, McMullen now added Farmville to his benefaction.[6] In April 1918, O'Connell dispatched Father Edward A. Brosnan from the cathedral to look over the situation in Crewe. Brosnan said Mass for forty-three people and informed them they would have Mass the first Sunday of each month. Altogether, he found twenty-four adults and forty children, in addition to another man who had not been to Mass for fifteen years but promised to bring his two children for baptism. He had described a situation similar to that of Lynchburg or other towns almost a century before. People had not attended Mass or had their children baptized simply because there were no priests. He concluded that "Crewe is a railroad town, on the boom, and the sooner a church is built there and the oftener Mass is said there on the Sundays the greater good for souls will ensue. It should develop into an active missionary centre for a section long neglected because of lack of priests."[7] The "boom," of course, never occurred, but the strategy of placing churches in railroad towns characterized the rural apostolate of the diocese.

In 1922, Crewe became a mission of Petersburg with Mass on the first and third Sundays, and Farmville became a station with Mass once a month.[8] Both Crewe and Farmville remained subject to Petersburg until 1940, when the Precious Blood Fathers took over Crewe as a parish with Farmville as a mission.

THE SHENANDOAH VALLEY FROM ROANOKE TO HARRISONBURG

Railroads continued to determine the development of the Catholic population. Crewe was but one example, but there were others out in the Valley at Roanoke and Harrisonburg. By 1916, Roanoke's Catholic population had expanded to the point that O'Connell established a second parish, Our Lady of Nazareth, named after the Sisters of Charity of Nazareth who staffed St. Andrew's school. The first pastor, James Gilsenan, had been an assistant at St. Andrew's and initially continued to live there with the pastor, Joseph Frioli. He remained pastor of Nazareth for almost forty years. He immediately opened a school, staffed by the Sisters of Charity of Nazareth, in a small house on property purchased on West Campbell Avenue. In 1925, he laid the cornerstone of what was intended to be a school but served as the parish church until 1978. As he began his parish, however, he faced a problem new to Virginia. Lebanese of the Maronite rite had also founded a parish in Roanoke in 1916. When they too wanted to send their children to the Nazareth school, Gilsenan argued he could not accommodate both them and the children of his own parishioners, until O'Connell intervened to have the Lebanese children admitted.[9] Roanoke would continue to grow and eventually have five parishes in the area. Further to the north, Harrisonburg was also expanding.

Blessed Sacrament Church in Harrisonburg was built in Gothic style with Celtic crosses indicating the heritage of the majority of its parishioners, originally railroad workers. A product of Mrs. Thomas F. Ryan's generosity, it was completed in the fall of 1907. But it remained a mission of Staunton from which priests initially came twice a month, and then weekly, to celebrate Mass. In September 1916, Joseph De Gryse, the pastor in Staunton, urged O'Connell to have the Blessed Sacrament reserved, or kept in a tabernacle, in the Harrisonburg church. Without a resident priest, however, the Holy See's permission would be necessary. His arguments revealed how at least one Louvain alumnus saw the relationship between the presence of the Eucharist in the church and proper Catholic piety:

> Those people, as long as they will not have the presence of the Blessed Sacrament[,] will always be more like Protestants than like Catholics. Their church, to them, is not the House of God, but a mere place of meeting. They are good enough people but they have not imbibed the whole spirit of the Faith and I believe that it is mostly due to the absence of the Blessed Sacrament from their midst.[10]

What was needed was not merely the reservation of the Blessed Sacrament, however, but a resident priest.

In 1920, De Gryse was transferred to Harrisonburg, then so poor that he could only "hope things will not be as bad as they look just now."[11] After only a year, he was transferred to Charlottesville, where he had to contend with demanding and wealthy parishioners.[12]

Probably in view of the growing anti-Catholicism in Harrisonburg, O'Connell next assigned to it William Meredith, a native of Staunton. Meredith's previous pastor in Winchester, Thomas A. Rankin, strongly supported his appointment because he "preaches well" and "is very popular with all classes and even the non-Catholics would regret his departure owing to his interest in the Boy Scout movement."[13] But then Rankin indicated the peripatetic life of a priest in the upper valley, now made more so by the automobile. Up to then, the town of Shenandoah had been a mission of Winchester. Rankin recommended it be attached to Harrisonburg. Like Crewe, it was a railroad terminal for the Norfolk and Western Railroad, and had a population of 2,000. The dozen or so Catholics, however, sought transfer to Roanoke because they had no church. De Gryse, moreover, had already attended Elkton, six miles south of Shenandoah, to which the trip from Winchester was seventy-eight miles by rail or sixty-eight by car on a road that went through Harrisonburg.[14]

Meredith accepted his appointment to Harrisonburg, with missions in Shenandoah and Elkton. He remarked, however, that he had earlier found the people in Harrisonburg "were always not pleasant."[15] He had the task of countering the attacks on the Church when Harrisonburg hosted a meeting of the Ku Klux Klan.[16]

Over the next fifty years, the Catholic population in the Valley only gradually increased. Roanoke alone was an exception as it developed into more of an urban center similar to Norfolk or Northern Virginia. But, in addition to providing priests for these rural missions, the diocese had to care for the small groups of immigrants who came to Virginia between 1900 and 1940.

IMMIGRANTS IN VIRGINIA AFTER WORLD WAR I

During the 1920s, the Ku Klux Klan had made immigration a major focus for its attack on the Church. One reason for its relative weakness in Virginia may have been that few Virginians actually encountered either Catholics or immigrants. In 1913, O'Connell responded to a request from Cardinal Gaetano de Lai, secretary of the Consistorial Congregation in Rome, for a report on immigrants in the diocese. Most, he said, were Bohemians, Poles, and Ruthenians. After the death of John Konicek, who had served in New Bohemia, however, he was unable to find a Czech-speaking priest, so he arranged for a priest from the Polish college in Washington to visit the settlement. The Poles and Ruthenians, however, presented a different problem, for, unlike the Bohemians, they were scattered in a number of places.

The Italians fell into two classes, those who had come after the revolutions in 1848 and 1860 and a smaller number who had arrived later. For the most part, they had concentrated in Richmond, where O'Connell had assigned an Italian-American priest, who had studied in Rome, to work with them. In Norfolk, he appointed Father Philip Brennan, another Roman alumnus, to take charge of the small Italian colony there. At Fort Monroe and nearby Phoebus, there were about five hundred Italians, of whom three hundred were American-born, and the pastor was trying to obtain an Italian-speaking priest for them. Far to the west at Harpers Ferry, there were approximately five hundred Italian railroad workers, whom the pastor tried, unsuccessfully, to have come to Mass, although they did have their children baptized. In general, O'Connell concluded, the Italians were doing well and were not in poverty.[17]

O'CONNELL'S RECRUITMENT FOR IMMIGRANTS

Despite his preference for other seminaries, O'Connell now turned to the American College in Louvain for priests to work with immigrants. In particular, he asked for another Belgian and a priest to work among the Poles. In May 1913, J. de Becker, the rector, responded that he was making the final arrangements for Joseph Govaert, van de Vyver's great-nephew, to come to Richmond and that he also had one Belgian and several possible Polish candidates. Sending Govaert's letters of incardination into the diocese, O'Connell instructed de Becker to choose the better of the Polish students, and obtain a Bohemian one.[18] Unfortunately, none of these priests ever came to Virginia.

Unlike the major dioceses in the northeast and midwest, where national parishes for particular European ethnic groups abounded, Richmond was to have only six: St. Mary's and St. Anthony's in Richmond for Germans and Lebanese, respectively, St. Elias in Roanoke for Lebanese, St. Mary's in Bowers Hill for Poles, St. Mary of the Annunciation, founded in 1914 for Slovaks in Woodford, and Sacred Heart of Jesus for Czechs in New Bohemia, for which O'Connell obtained the services of Father Leopold Stefl sometime after writing to de Lai. In addition, St. Theresa's in West Point was in fact, though not in official designation, a Polish parish.

MARONITES

In his report to de Lai, O'Connell made no reference to the Lebanese who had begun trickling into Virginia in the 1890s. Since they belonged to the Maronite rite, which retained a distinctive liturgy and a married clergy, providing clergy for them presented a new problem. Like Ruthenian and Ukrainian members of the Byzantine rite, the Maronites frequently faced outright hostility from the Latin-rite hierarchy in the United States. Archbishop John Ireland of St. Paul, known for wanting to accommodate the Church to American culture, bitterly opposed these newcomers and even sought to gain the Holy See's approval to require that all these immigrants conform to the Latin rite. Instead, the Congregation of Propaganda issued a decree requiring that any priest of an Oriental rite who immigrated had to have the permission of his own bishop, his patriarch, and the congregation. In addition, the Holy See legislated that Ruthenian priests were to be celibate in those countries where their rite was not dominant.[19]

Richmond's Lebanese community initially attended Mass at St. Patrick's or, when a Maronite priest was visiting, in a private home. By 1902, its leaders formed the Star of the East Syrian Society. But van de Vyver, known for his work among Virginia's African Americans, was not as open to the Lebanese. In 1903, they approached him to purchase plots in Mt. Calvary Cemetery, but he refused, "because they were not white people." He did, however, sell them a section at the far end of the cemetery. Under O'Connell, they fared better. He allowed them to have their visiting priest use St. Patrick's between the regularly scheduled Masses on Sundays.[20]

By 1914, Richmond's Lebanese community was large enough that it needed a permanent priest. Father James T. O'Farrell, the vicar general, had found a Maronite, Father Gabriel El Zehenni, but he wrote to Edward Dyer, then president of St. Mary's Seminary, for additional information. Dyer's response was laced with humor but showed the confusion in the American Church about how to treat these priests from other rites. Zehenni was of good character, he reported, and received good testimonials from several priests and Archbishop Henry Moeller of Cincinnati, but "the poor fellow is however afflicted with a Mrs. and three little Zehennis. The Archbishop of Cincinnati was under the impression that married Maronite Priests were not allowed in this country, so he got another for his work."

Although Zehenni did not have the requisite letter from Propaganda, Dyer had Cardinal Gibbons write to Zehenni's patriarch stating that Syrians in the United States could benefit from his services. In the meantime, he sought canonical advice from the apostolic delegation about Zehenni's being married. He reported that "Monsignor [Bonaventura] Cerretti says without hesitation that, as the legislation on this ground refers explicitly to the Ruthenians it is not to be considered as affecting any others." He, therefore, thought "there would be no difficulty whatever" in "employing him temporarily to attend to the actual religious needs of these people."[21] Although Zehenni never came to Richmond, the canonical issue regarding his being married cleared the way for later having a married Maronite priest.

The first Maronite priest to take up permanent residence in Richmond was Father Dimitry Abdallah Terbay, who originally came to the United States in 1909 and had worked in several dioceses, including St. Paul and, most recently, Scranton, before coming to Richmond.[22] On August 14, 1915, O'Farrell informed the Syrian Catholics of Richmond that Terbay was now the pastor of all the Syrian people in the diocese and that no other Syrian priest could say Mass without his recommendation.[23] Terbay had a letter from Father Andrew J. Brennan, the chancellor of the diocese of Scranton, stating that he was leaving the diocese in good standing.[24] Over ten years later, when Brennan was bishop of Richmond, he no longer listed St. Anthony's among his parishes and reported that most of the Lebanese were attending local parishes.[25]

Early in 1916, Roanoke also had a Lebanese community of two hundred and fifty. In January, Elias Peter Hoyek, the Maronite patriarch, had given letters of testimony to Father Peter Rabil.[26] By the summer of 1917, Rabil had made arrangements to purchase a former Baptist church for his community. O'Connell approved the purchase and appointed Rabil as temporary pastor. Because he was either unaware of or refused to accept Cerretti's interpretation in regard to Zehenni, he originally gave Rabil permission to remain only for the duration of the First World War, provided that his wife did not join him.[27] Rabil was in fact married and had three children, one of whom, Fred, was a cardiologist, who later treated President Dwight Eisenhower. Despite O'Connell's original restrictions on his exercise of the ministry, he was later named a monsignor and remained pastor of St. Elias until his death in 1964.[28] Both St. Elias in Roanoke and St. Anthony's in Richmond continued to be under the jurisdiction of the bishop of Richmond until the diocese of St. Maron was established in 1966 for all Catholics in the United States of the Maronite Rite.

RUTHENIANS

O'Connell had reported to de Lai that the few Ruthenians in Virginia, like the Poles, were scattered. At O'Connell's request early in 1913,

Bishop Soter Ortynsky, the quasi-vicar general for Byzantine-rite Catholics, appointed Father Zachary Orun of Curtis Bay in Baltimore to conduct a visitation of Ruthenian Catholics in Virginia.[29] In the middle of February, Orun told O'Connell that "the Ruthenians in your diocese are going to procure a priest for themselves behind your shoulders, because they wish to gather themselves maybe without knowledge of local priest. Will you kindly inform me, what I have to do, write to them and appoint certain time to hear their confession, or you will notify them ex officio, that you have a priest for them."[30] Although Ortynsky became ordinary of the Byzantine rite in August 1913, O'Connell apparently attempted to recruit a Ruthenian priest himself from Fribourg to meet the needs Orun mentioned.[31]

Virginia was not, however, to get a Byzantine parish for several more generations. In 1931, however, some Ruthenian priests began agitating against the imposition of celibacy on them in the United States. Asked his opinion of this by the apostolic delegate, Bishop Brennan stated that there were only twenty Ruthenian families in his diocese and no clergy. From his earlier experience with Ruthenian married clergy in Scranton, however, he found them "good men and had the respect of the people and clergy." They caused "little scandal," but "most of our Latin [C]atholics did not consider the Greeks real Catholics." Reflecting the opinion of most of his contemporary bishops, he concluded that maintaining the requirement of celibacy would lower this barrier between the people of the two rites.[32]

POLES

O'Connell initially had difficulty procuring a priest for the increasing Polish population. Having failed to get a priest from Louvain, he attempted to recruit a Polish priest through Saints Cyril and Methodius Seminary in Orchard Lake, Michigan. After several tries, he obtained Lawrence Budny, who was ordained in 1916 and worked in Bowers Hill outside of Portsmouth. He also tried to recruit Polish priests already working in other dioceses.

Beginning in May 1909, meanwhile, Polish Franciscans in Baltimore cared for Virginia's Polish Catholics. In April 1913, Father Francis Pyznar, O.M.C., rector of St. Stanislaus in Baltimore, asked O'Connell to renew his faculties. Many Poles in Virginia had no permanent priest, he said, and he had also received a request to visit the Yorktown area. He wished to discuss a proposal for a permanent missionary outreach to the Poles.[33] Granting him a renewal of faculties for himself or any priest he designated, Felix Kaup, the chancellor, asked him to report on his visits and include statistics.[34]

What Pyznar was proposing was a type of Polish Catholic colony. While the government was attempting to have immigrants move to farming areas, he argued that many feared being isolated from the spiritual resources of the large cities, as he had discovered in Virginia, Maryland, and North Carolina. His reflections echoed the problems that beset Keileyville and other nineteenth-century efforts at colonization. His solution echoed the rural strategy O'Connell had already developed. The "only way to induce" immigrants "to settle on farms," he said, would be to form "one central residential place for a greater number of priests conversant with the languages of the various nationalities settling in certain States, who would be ready to go whenever and where necessary and render spiritual aid or service to the people there located." He further thought Virginia was especially in need "of spiritual aid and assistance," for "there are more Slavish and Polish people in that State than in any other Southern State in the Union," but they were so "scattered throughout the State . . . that it is impossible for them to establish a parish and maintain [a] priest permanently."

Pyznar reported, moreover, that Gibbons had spoken to Thomas Fortune Ryan, who said he wanted Poles on his estate, "because they are good Catholics, thrifty persons, industrious and desirable element." In the meantime, he requested O'Connell's permission to begin a mission at Bowers Hill, outside Portsmouth.[35] O'Connell rejected Pyznar's offer,[36] and, instead, designated St. Mary's Chapel at Bowers Hill as a Polish mission of Portsmouth.

Jakubowski at West Point

A number of Poles had moved to the area around West Point in King William County, as Pyznar had reported. By late 1917, O'Connell had recruited Father Ceslaus Jakubowski from Saints Cyril and Methodius Seminary and assigned him to this new Polish settlement. But Jakubowski initially had to learn something about Virginia's ways. The issue arose over the selection of the site for a cemetery. G. W. Fitzgerald complained to O'Connell early in 1918 that Jakubowski, or "Father Jack," as he was known, rejected an offer of free land from a Polish real estate agent for a cemetery near West Point in favor of a site four miles away where he wanted to build a church. In Fitzgerald's opinion, the priest

> has made a mistake in opposing from the beginning those who, Catholic and Protestant, have been engaged in the work of draw-ing Catholic Polish immigrants here. The situation is that a goodly number of Polish families are "out of touch" with the Church practically.

Fitzgerald predicted a "further cleavage" in the community because Jakubowski had recently refused to enter the Protestant cemetery, the only one available, for "the burial of a dead Pole" and had made of-fensive remarks about those already buried there because they were not Catholic. Fitzgerald hoped that Jakubowski would "put aside his disposition" but thought "his temperament is not amenable to secular suggestions."[37]

Although O'Connell overruled Jakubowski and accepted the land for the cemetery closer to West Point, the two remained on good terms.[38] By 1920, Jakubowski had made West Point his headquarters, while he had missions in New Kent, King and Queen, and York Counties—he later added Gloucester County, where Mass had been said during the summers of 1898 and 1899 in the home of Colonel C. O'B. Cowardin by his brother, William Cowardin, S.J.[39] Jaku-bowski's mission churches were built largely with funds from the Church Extension Society in Chicago. The postwar retrenchment, however, was having its effect on his people. His twelve families in New Kent were too poor to support themselves, and the closing of the shipyards in West Point left many of his people unemployed.[40]

Jakubowski's missionary excursions and grand plans for the fu-ture again met Fitzgerald's opposition. In April 1920, Fitzgerald complained to O'Connell that Jakubowski was overextending him-self by planning to start a school and erect other buildings. The cost, he said, would be too great for the small community that depended on a "few acres of miserable soil in a climate that has caused a par-tial failure of the crops every one of my thirteen summers here."

The people would have either to seek factory work or leave, and industry in West Point was limited to a pulp mill and the Southern Railroad. Since Jakubowski himself was dependent on a reasonably well-to-do parishioner, Fitzgerald doubted whether the twelve loyal families could raise money to support a schoolteacher. He was also skeptical about the people relying on the largess of outside benefactors, and here he seemed to have meant the Church Extension Society, for

> If I am not presumptuous I look across the river and see a great big church [in New Kent] just finished for a half dozen or so, without any sacrifice on their part, possibly spoiling them, instead of having had the heart and centre in West Point for all. It is none of my business to look down toward Yorktown, with a still more "unprofitable" settlement of Slavs, except for the relation our priest may have to similar cares there.

He added in a postscript that he had sent a copy of his letter to Jakubowski.[41]

Despite Fitzgerald's reservations, Jakubowski continued to expand his missionary endeavors. In 1924, he purchased property in Port Richmond, now annexed to West Point, where he built Our Lady of the Blessed Sacrament, which became his new missionary headquarters.[42]

THE SAGA OF BOWERS HILL

In the meantime, Bowers Hill continued as a Polish mission under Portsmouth, but the people wanted a Polish-speaking priest. For several years, Father Lawrence Budny served the community, while residing at St. Paul's. In June 1925, however, he applied to be accepted by the diocese of Cleveland, on the grounds that Bowers Hill was declining.[43] In July he left Portsmouth and imparted the news to Father F. Joseph Magri at St. Paul's by handing him the keys to Bowers Hill. Judging from Magri's remarks to O'Connell, the congregation was not just growing smaller but was also contentious. He thought one of the priests of St. Paul could say Mass at Bowers Hill the following Sunday, but reasoned that it would do the people good out there to have them worry for [a] Sunday or two without Mass. Am afraid if we make it too easy for them, they will do nothing for the Church.[44]

Later on, Budny wrote to both O'Connell and Magri in a "cringing and plaintive tone"—among his complaints was that he was accused of stealing strawberries he himself had planted. He owed the diocese for his seminary education and proposed paying the debt in yearly installments, but Magri suggested he borrow money, pay half of what he owed, and then O'Connell could formally release him from Richmond to be accepted in Cleveland.[45]

In November 1923 the parishioners thanked O'Connell for finding them a Polish-speaking priest and promised their cooperation with a new priest, Father H. Olszewski, who offered to come from New Cumberland, West Virginia.[46] Olszewski had written to Magri to tell O'Connell "that I am not bad priest."[47] The priests of St. Paul's and the Poles of Bowers Hill thought Olszewski acceptable. Among his other qualifications in Magri's mind was that he cooked for himself.[48] Olszewski, however, lasted only a short time.

Bowers Hill remained a fractious community. Some may have been influenced by the socialism and opposition to the hierarchy that divided Poles elsewhere as they sought a greater voice in American urban politics and in the Church.[49] Joseph Janusz, representing the Farmer's Political and Industrial Association, for example, asked O'Connell in April 1924 to receive a delegate to discuss "the welfare and further development of our Colony."[50] Magri learned, however, that Janusz was actually a Mason who opposed having a resident priest in Bowers Hill.[51] Finally, O'Connell appointed Father John Kociela, his second recruit from Saints Cyril and Methodius, to reside in Portsmouth and serve Bowers Hill.

Late in 1931, however, Philip Blackburn, newly appointed pastor of Suffolk, recommended that Bishop Brennan join the troublesome Polish mission of Bowers Hill to Blackburn's parish.[52] Under that new arrangement, Blackburn notified the bishop of his plans to hold a celebration at Bowers Hill of the Liberty Group of the Polish National Alliance and to observe Polish feasts.[53] By August 1932, however, the Bowers Hill parishioners complained that they had not had a Polish priest for several years and could not understand Blackburn.[54] A year later, they again petitioned for a resident priest.[55] Magri then proposed transferring Blackburn to Holy Angels in Cradock, which had begun as a mission in 1919, and assign Kociela full time to Bowers Hill and Suffolk.[56] Brennan agreed to transfer Blackburn to Cradock, but left Kociela in Portsmouth to continue serving St. Mary's at Bowers Hill. But Poles were not the only eastern European immigrants who found their way to the Portsmouth area, as Joseph Brennan, the first resident pastor in Suffolk had discovered in 1927.

HUNGARIANS NEAR SUFFOLK

St. Mary of the Presentation in Suffolk owed its origins to Felix Kaup, who founded it from Portsmouth in 1909, tended it for five years, and purchased the land on which its church was later built.[57] When Brennan became pastor in Suffolk in 1927, he found some fifty Hungarians within his parish, about twenty-five miles away in Courtland. The presence of immigrant farmers in such a non-Catholic area prompted *The Virginia Knight* to urge that "we, the Catholics of Virginia, will have to stretch in order to provide the apostle of Nansemond [Brennan] with means to prevent the story of the 'lost Irish' being repeated in this day."[58] Brennan's discovery of this colony later led to the establishment of missions, served from Suffolk, in Franklin and Courtland and the ultimate establishment of St. Jude's in Franklin, where some of the descendants of these original Hungarian settlers still reside. In 1929, Blackburn replaced Brennan in Suffolk, from where he made his brief attempt to serve the Poles in Bowers Hill.

The immigrant communities in the diocese of Richmond were always relatively small. Some of the people rapidly blended in with the rest of the Catholic population. The Poles who settled in Virginia, moreover, seem to have been skilled farmers. O'Connell, for his part, would depend on occasional visits from religious priests, but definitely preferred his own diocesan clergy to take permanent pastoral charge. Care of immigrants was an important, yet minor, part of O'Connell's episcopate. Care for such a vast diocese had taken its toll on the aging O'Connell—as it would on his successor, Andrew Brennan.

The 1920s were a period of transition for the Catholic community in Richmond and the diocese. The city of Richmond had not been as much affected by World War I as either northern Virginia or Hampton Roads. But the living links to the Civil War were fading, as the last Confederate veterans died. For the diocese, the link to the days of Gibbons and Keane was also growing more tenuous, as O'Connell's health grew worse.

A City in Transition: Death of "Major" Dooley

In November 1922, Bishop O'Connell said a requiem Mass for "Major" James Dooley in the cathedral at the request of Dooley's sisters. It was actually the second funeral for the eighty-one-year old pillar of the Catholic community in Richmond, who had died on November 16. Over a year before, he had suffered a serious stroke, and his wife, Sallie May Dooley, an Episcopalian, carefully guarded him from any visitors, including priests. During one of her brief absences, however, his doctor summoned Father Edward A. Brosnan from the cathedral to hear the Major's confession and anoint him. But, when Brosnan returned the next day with communion, Mrs. Dooley blocked his way. She then invited her minister, Walter Russell Bowie, rector of St. Paul's Church, to visit and pray with her husband. Bowie then conducted Dooley's funeral at Maymont. Among the honorary pallbearers were Bishop O'Connell and several surviving Confederate veterans.[59] It was the end of an era for Richmond Catholics, the death of one of the steadfast defenders of the Confederacy and the diocese's greatest benefactor. In his will, Dooley instructed that a monument be erected just east of his Maymont estate, which he willed to the city of Richmond, with the coat of arms of the diocese on one face, and on the others his own coat of arms and the seals of the Commonwealth of Virginia and the City of Richmond.

But Dooley had left a greater bequest in his will, $3 million to St. Joseph's Orphanage for a hospital for crippled children and two orphanages for girls to be built on land adjacent to Maymont. The bequest, however, was to take effect only after the his wife's death. When she died in September 1925, the board of trustees of St. Joseph's passed a resolution "that through the death of Mrs. Sallie Dooley, the orphans have lost a life-long and sympathetic friend, whose name we shall hold in benediction and whose memory we cherish as a constant inspiration in the cause of Christian charity."[60] It was a generous enough remark, considering that she had prevented a priest from bringing communion to her dying husband only three years before.

The site Dooley had chosen for the new St. Joseph's complex, adjacent to Maymont, was later changed and the buildings would not be erected until 1931, as a display of Catholic presence in Virginia in the aftermath of another outbreak of anti-Catholicism.[61] Dooley had represented an older style of accommodation to the predominant culture. He had no children, so the question of their Catholicism never arose. But, from his wife's actions toward the end, she was not sympathetic to his Church. While Dooley's death marked the end of an era for Richmond Catholicism, the end of another era in the history of the diocese was rapidly approaching.

Retirement of Archbishop Denis O'Connell

For some time O'Connell's health had been failing. In the spring of 1924, Alice Dooley, the Major's sister, expressed her concern, for "We can't afford to lose men like you especially as you can't be replaced by any *woman* at present. There is no telling how you men are going to be superseded after a while."[62] In a day long before women were taking such an active role in political and civic life, Alice had been a founder of the Catholic Women's Club, an ardent supporter of women's suffrage, an issue on which she was opposed by her brother and sister-in-law, and a member of the Richmond Women's Club until she resigned when it disseminated birth control information.[63]

O'Connell's health continued to decline and so did his administration of the diocese. In September 1924, he had accepted O'Farrell's resignation as pastor of St. Mary's in Norfolk, but retained him as vicar general. He was also losing interest in ecclesiastical affairs. Asked by Archbishop Curley in 1925 for the names of any priests he thought worthy of being bishops, O'Connell seemed confused and responded "while I hope you will find in the diocese some priest suited to take up the succession . . . at present I do not think I have any clergymen whose names I would like to send you for a list of candidates. Our need of priests is very great in the diocese at present and we would not like to lose any of them especially the best among them."[64] He seemed to think Curley was asking for candidates for a specific see. By failing to submit any names, he provided the Holy See with no Richmond priests who might succeed him. Growing increasingly feeble in mind, late in 1925 he tendered his resignation to Pius XI but informed no one but Felix Kaup, his chancellor. On January 26, 1926, he was named archbishop of Mariamne, an abandoned diocese in Syria, and administrator of Richmond.

Before O'Connell received notification of these Roman actions, he grew so ill from uremia that Kaup anointed him. With O'Farrell's death in January, Kaup reported to Rome that he was now the only member of the episcopal curia and that only he knew O'Connell had submitted his resignation.[65] When the news of O'Connell's appointment as an archbishop became public, Abbot Vincent Taylor of Belmont remarked to Kaup: "It is a travesty that these honors should be showered upon the good Bishop when he can scarcely appreciate them, certainly not enjoy them. May the fullness of his reward be everlasting."[66] It was, indeed, a travesty. If ambition for personal preferment had driven him in his younger days, loyalty to the Church sustained him in the end. All his friends, Gibbons, Keane, and Ireland, had long since died. His fourteen years in Richmond witnessed the unprecedented growth of the Norfolk and northern Virginia areas, as the nation was making its first hesitant steps onto the world stage during World War I.

Sometime in late March or early April, Archbishop Pietro Fumasoni-Biondi, the apostolic delegate, came to see O'Connell. He subsequently wrote simply that he had enjoyed the visit and was now relieving him of the office of administrator of the diocese and appointing Kaup.[67] For the first time, Kaup now held that office in the diocese. Rumors persisted among the Richmond clergy that, so certain was he of ultimately being named bishop, that he actually purchased his episcopal regalia. On May 13, the delegate conveyed to Kaup instructions for the administration of the diocese and reported that the Consistorial Congregation had approved an annual pension of $1,500 for O'Connell.[68] By that date, however, Rome had already named a new bishop.

CHAPTER 21

Bishop Andrew Brennan and Civic Life in Virginia: 1926–1934

APPOINTMENT OF ANDREW J. BRENNAN

On May 22, 1926, the apostolic delegate notified Bishop Michael J. Hoban of Scranton that Pius XI had named his auxiliary, Andrew Brennan, the new bishop of Richmond.[1] Born on December 14, 1877, in Towanda, Pennsylvania, Brennan graduated from the College of the Holy Cross in Worcester, Massachusetts, and then attended St. Bernard's Seminary, Rochester, New York, before going to the North American College in Rome, where he was ordained in 1904. He was the first bishop appointed to Richmond since the procedures for nominating bishops were changed in 1916. The new system was one of the elements in the erosion of the earlier collegial tradition of the American hierarchy and allowed one or more prominent prelates to gain the appointment of their candidates. In Brennan's case, it seemed obvious that the source of his appointment was his close association with Michael J. Curley, archbishop of Baltimore, a contemporary in Rome who had preached at Brennan's episcopal consecration in Scranton.[2]

For reasons unexplained, Brennan did not receive the official bulls of his appointment for another six months. With the Holy See's approval, moreover, he delayed going to Richmond for several months to tend to his own affairs. He then effectively became the administrator of the diocese of Scranton during the final illness of Bishop Hoban. After Hoban's death on November 13, Brennan then seems to have needed another four weeks to recuperate.[3] During that period, he continued to reside at St. Mary's, Dunmore, Pennsylvania, where he had been pastor since 1924. In the summer, however, he learned about some of the problems in Richmond. Despite many bequests for seminary education that O'Connell had received, the diocese owed bills to several seminaries, among them, the North American College.[4] Brennan also discovered that O'Connell had failed to complete the process for the incardination of at least one student at Mt. St. Mary's Seminary.[5] Richmond was not going to be a sinecure.

On December 15, Brennan finally bade farewell to the people of Dunmore and boarded a train for Richmond. The next day, though he still had not received the official bulls, he was installed as Richmond's eighth bishop by Archbishop Curley.[6] Curley's presence in Richmond was symbolic, for it was no secret that he had little love for the retired bishop. The installation was a grand affair with the pageantry of the cathedral ceremony followed by a banquet in the afternoon at Murphy's Hotel and a reception in the Cathedral Hall in the evening. But it was overshadowed in only two weeks by the death on January 1, 1927, of Archbishop O'Connell. Perhaps at Brennan's own gracious suggestion, O'Connell's death and funeral took up the bulk of the January issue of *The Virginia Knight*, the monthly newspaper of the Knights of Columbus that served the diocese. The report of Brennan's installation appeared a month later.[7]

Brennan soon learned that O'Connell had neglected a number of diocesan affairs other than paying seminary bills. Early in 1928, for example, he discovered that the diocese had not sent the Congregation of the Sacraments in Rome any statistics for marriage dispensations from 1923 to 1927.[8] Sending those statistics, Brennan announced that he was initiating a diocesan policy of charging a fee for dispensations.[9]

DIOCESAN ADMINISTRATION

Brennan set about to reorganize the administrative structure of the diocese. Here he relied on Archbishop Curley's advice. In December 1926 he had written Curley for the norms pertaining to diocesan consultors. Always at his desk, Curley responded on Christmas Eve that

Brennan should appoint at least four consultors for three-year terms within six months of taking possession of his see. Any vacancy that occurred should be filled with the advice, but not the consent, of the other consultors. The vicar general, furthermore, should not be a consultor, as he had been under O'Connell, since he was the bishop's agent. Curley then turned to a problem that had plagued the Church in Richmond from its inception—the incorporation of Church property. Since diocesan property was held in the name of the bishop, Brennan should write a will as soon as possible, leaving the property to the metropolitan in Baltimore. With characteristic humor, Curley remarked: "On the death of the Testator, or on his being promoted to the Archdiocese of Timbuctoo, the Metropolitan of Baltimore blanket deeds the property back to the Successor in Richmond."[10] O'Connell's will left all his property, unless otherwise specified, to Curley, and Kaup had obtained the opinion of the attorney general of Virginia that diocesan property actually held in O'Connell's name automatically passed to Brennan as O'Connell's successor. Curley advised him, however, to file the opinion in order to avoid any future dispute.[11] This rather tenuous arrangement for property ownership would continue well into the 1930s.

Brennan retained Kaup as vicar general, but appointed Leo Gill as his chancellor. He also reinstituted the annual clergy conferences, apparently abandoned since Keane's administration. During the clergy's annual retreat at Georgetown in June 1928, he further informed the consultors that canon law required the appointment of deans. Initiating this policy in the diocese, he named Edward M. Tearney in Lynchburg, William McKeefry in Alexandria, Thomas E. Waters in Norfolk, and Francis P. Lackey in Martinsburg.[12] All but Lackey were also consultors. In 1929, he broke from another of O'Connell's policies. On December 27, 1929, as he was celebrating the silver jubilee of his ordination to the priesthood, he announced the first monsignors in several years: Tearney, Waters, and Kaup.[13] A few months later, he requested the same honors for Louis Smet, then vice rector of the American College in Louvain.[14] By 1930, Richmond's listing in the *Official Catholic Directory* looked like that of other dioceses. It now had directors of the Holy Name Society, Catholic Charities, League of the Sacred Heart, Laymen's Retreat League, and Priests' Eucharistic League. Brennan was also apparently the first bishop of Richmond formally to institute a Vigilance

Committee, mandated in 1907 by the Holy See to safeguard against Modernism. More importantly, the diocese for the first time had priests appointed full-time to diocesan apostolates: Francis J. Byrne, superintendent of Schools, Thomas A. Mitchell, director of Catholic Charities, and Walter J. Nott, diocesan director of the Pontifical Society for the Propagation of the Faith. The designation of a full-time director for the Propagation of the Faith was significant. Richmond, while still a poor diocese, now began to be a contributor to the charitable agency of which it had so long been a beneficiary. Moreover, the director, relieved of other pastoral duties, devoted his time to preaching in all the parishes of the diocese to raise funds for the missions.

Brennan was determined to make Richmond into a model diocese. In 1927, he proposed to hold a diocesan synod, only the third in Richmond's history and the first since 1886. The synod, however, was postponed until February 16, 1933. Its principal purpose was to bring diocesan legislation into conformity with the Code of Canon Law of 1917. The decrees presented little that was original, but one appendix indicated that the Richmond diocese was still leery of modern inventions. "Business with the Chancery should be transacted by mail or by personal call," it stated; "Telegraph or telephone should not be used except in cases of necessity."[15] The work of Brennan's chancery office was not to be interrupted by electronic contraptions. To staff this newly structured diocese, Brennan, of course, needed priests.

RECRUITING SEMINARIANS AND PRIESTS

Like other bishops of Richmond before and after him, Brennan continued to have the problem of recruiting priests. But he and seminary officials sometimes exercised caution that would evoke amusement from later generations. In 1927, a young man had been strongly recommended by a Richmond priest for adoption, but he had earlier been dismissed from the seminary at Dunwoodie, New York, for writing a letter to a young woman. While "there was nothing wrong in the letter," Dunwoodie's rector, James T. McEntyre, informed Brennan, "it indicated a strong inclination for the opposite sex."[16] Father John Fenlon, rector of St. Mary's Seminary in Baltimore, acknowledged that the young man seemed to be of admirable character, but, because "of the very large number of students we have, we feel that it is necessary for us to be even more careful than the average seminary about admission of students." He therefore felt "hardly justified, in the circumstances, in admitting him. Men with a past are apt to remain doubtful characters in a large institution like this."[17] With a plentiful supply of candidates for the priesthood, Richmond and other dioceses could afford to be choosy in accepting candidates. The Great Depression created another problem. By 1933, some dioceses had too many seminarians and could not afford to ordain them. Brennan was asked if he could take any of them.[18]

ROMAN CONCERN FOR NATIVE VOCATIONS IN VIRGINIA

The failure of the diocese after so many years to provide its own clergy drew Roman attention. In June 1928, after making a visitation of the diocese, Archbishop Fumasoni-Biondi, the apostolic delegate, reported that the Congregation of Seminaries and Universities praised Brennan's work but wanted to "call to your attention the need of supplying *Native Priests* for the work of your diocese." Brennan was to urge his priests and people to promote vocations.[19] Almost a year later, he wrote Rome of his hopes to increase native vocations.[20] He then addressed a circular letter to his clergy, stating:

> The Diocese of Richmond is, at the present time, singularly blessed with native vocations to the priesthood. Heretofore, we have been, to a great extent, dependent on the outside for priests to carry on the work of the Church in Virginia. Now, however, I feel that we have sufficient native vocations to supply our needs. In the past two years twelve young men, natives of the diocese, have answered the call of God and are preparing to carry on the work of the Church amongst you. God has singularly blessed us with vocations, and we are perhaps, the only diocese in the South which can make this boast.[21]

Brennan seems to have wanted to replicate his own educational experience among as many of his recruits as possible. Among the native Virginians who entered the seminary, two, Carroll Dozier and Louis Flaherty, first went to Holy Cross and then to the North

American College. Flaherty had already decided to enter the seminary before going to the Jesuit institution in Worcester, Massachusetts, but his family was hard pressed to pay the tuition. A college official assured both him and Brennan that, if the diocese could not pay the tuition, he would make other arrangements. As he remarked to Brennan:

> We know only too well that the depression is very severe. In fact we are almost overwhelmed with requests for reductions and opportunities for work. But our first help, we feel, should be given to those who are striving to reach God's Altar and become His representatives to the poor and afflicted.[22]

Flaherty also became instrumental in obtaining another student for the diocese. During a summer vacation, he invited a Holy Cross classmate, Thomas Scannell from Brooklyn, to his home in Norfolk. Scannell was then recruited by Edward L. Stephens, assistant at Blessed Sacrament, Flaherty's parish, to study for the diocese. Like Flaherty, he too was sent to Rome.

Altogether, Brennan sent at least nine students to Rome. In 1933 alone, Richmond had a total of eight students at the North American College. Besides Dozier, Flaherty, and Scannell, there were Vincent Waters, the nephew of Thomas E. Waters, himself an alumnus, Joseph Hodges, a native of Martinsburg, Francis Bradican, who had been recruited from Scranton, Robert O'Kane, a native of Wheeling, Bernard Moore, and Andrew Simonpietri, who left the college before ordination.

Late in 1933, Moore wrote Brennan that Dozier, then in his second year of theology, had been dubbed "the aristocrat" by the rector.[23] Dozier held informal seminars in his room that included, among others, John Wright, a student for Boston, who became the first bishop of Worcester in 1950, bishop of Pittsburgh in 1959, and a cardinal in 1969, when he was appointed prefect of the Congregation of the Clergy in Rome.[24]

By 1929, the diocese had thirty-eight men studying for the priesthood, but at a cost of $450 per seminarian and only $4,500 in burses, the diocese had a deficit of $12,000.[25] Brennan continued the policy of having an annual collection for seminaries on Easter Sunday, but it fell far short of the actual need for that year, and he considered making parish assessments.[26] The Depression may have induced many young men to enter seminaries, but it also made their financial support more difficult. Brennan refused, however, to accept William L. Lane, a Black seminarian, for the diocese and, likewise, rejected a proposal of Vincent Waters to adopt a Roman-trained Black priest.[27]

Brennan's decided preference for Rome meant a decline in students at Louvain. Bradican had studied philosophy there before going to the North American College, but Brennan sent only two seminarians to Louvain for theology, Edward Jones and Dixon Beattie. Both of these men, however, were from St. James Church in West Falls Church, where Amadeus J. van Ingelgem, a loyal Louvain alumnus, continued to be pastor. At van Ingelgem's request, Brennan had already ordained Dixon Beattie's brother, Robert, to the priesthood in Falls Church, a first for the village, in 1931. The Beattie brothers, it will be recalled, were grandsons of Fountain Beattie, Colonel Mosby's lieutenant. Robert Beattie's ordination prompted Louis Smet to remark from Louvain:

> It does our hearts good, so far from "home" to read of all the splendid work that is going on in the diocese. How happy old Father Van [Ingelgem] must be since you ordained Father Bob Beattie in his dearly beloved little church! He has had the happiness of seeing several vocations to the Priesthood flourish in his mission. I do hope and pray that he may live long enough to see *our* two boys ordained.[28]

It was not a bad record for what was still a village parish. Unfortunately, Jones had to leave Louvain for reasons of health early in 1932.

Priests Recruit Seminarians

Even before Brennan received the Holy See's request for more native clergy in Virginia, however, several pastors were recruiting seminarians locally. In August 1926, William Gill, the pastor of Fort Monroe, told Kaup, then the administrator of the diocese, that his predecessor, James F. McConnell, had recruited three boys to enter St. Charles College in Catonsville: Vernon Bowers, Edward Ritchie, and another student who later left the seminary. A generous parishioner in the soldiers' home offered to pay Bowers's tuition, but Gill requested diocesan support for the other two.[29] Transferred to Berkeley Springs, West Virginia, McConnell used his summer camp to recruit seminarians. He also asked if the diocese could assume the support of one seminarian at St. Charles, whose tuition he himself had been paying. He was already paying the tuition of two other students, George Bliley and Chester Michael.[30] Several other priests had established burses or scholarships at various seminaries, but McConnell both targeted students and paid their tuition.

Among the seminarians recruited under Brennan was Joseph Harris Findlay, a convert, who became a Catholic while studying at St. Paul's Episcopal School in Baltimore. He studied Latin at an Episcopal school in Lynchburg before going to St. Charles College in Catonsville, Maryland, and later St. Mary's Seminary, where he was ordained.[31]

Brennan was clearly intent on following Fumasoni-Biondi's request to develop a native clergy. He did, however, accept those students already recruited by O'Connell at Fribourg. But here he ran into a series of problems. Richmond had five students ordained at the Swiss institution under Brennan. Three, however, never made it to Richmond, partly because they could not obtain visas under the immigration quota bill. In November 1931, the other two finally obtained visas and arrived in Virginia, Peter Schouten and Peter A. van Ganzenwinkel. Van den Wildenberg, the rector, informed Brennan of the difficulty in recruiting for the diocese. Aside from the difficulty in obtaining visas, he noted: "Formerly, newly ordained priests were most anxious to leave for work in the U.S.A.; at present there seems to be prevailing reports that their services are no longer needed."[32] These "prevailing reports" could have meant either that American seminaries were filled or that, during Depression times, European recruits might find themselves across the ocean without a salary.

BRENNAN ATTEMPTS TO RECONCILE A "FALLEN CHRIST"

While Brennan was busy with administration, he displayed a more pastoral side to his personality by working for the reconciliation of a former priest. Augustus J. Halbleib had been pastor in Danville, where he wrote articles and gave speeches elsewhere to raise money for his parish—on one occasion in 1924, he informed O'Connell he had raised $41,000.[33] He then left the priesthood, married his housekeeper, and began writing against the Church. He moved to Richmond, where he initiated contact with Philip Blackburn, his former associate in Danville and then the pastor in Suffolk. Early in June 1932, at Blackburn's suggestion, Halbleib wrote directly to Brennan. In the first of several long rambling letters, Halbleib recounted that he had suffered a breakdown but had now regained his faith.[34]

Brennan responded that he would do all he could, but would have to refer the matter to Archbishop Fumasoni-Biondi.[35] The delegate advised Brennan that Halbleib's case would have to go to the Holy Office in Rome because of his "attempted marriage" and that he should submit copies of all his writings, since he would probably be required publicly to retract them. In any case, he continued, it was doubtful if Halbleib would be allowed to return to the active priesthood.[36] Brennan transmitted this information, but graciously used the salutation "Dear Father Halbleib."[37] The bishop followed this with an invitation to pay a personal visit.[38]

For several weeks during the summer of 1932, Brennan was in Ireland on vacation. On his return in August, Halbleib wrote to say he could not find the copies of all he had written, but he did send a copy of his book, *The Fallen Christ*. He then noted that he still had his former housekeeper with him. She had prevented him from committing suicide on several occasions and had offered to follow him wherever he went. He had therefore insisted that they enter a civil marriage to protect her. In a veiled reference to O'Connell, he contrasted Brennan's kindness with the actions of another bishop. Stating his desire to say Mass again, he then asked for a personal interview.[39]

On September 12, he had his interview. He was "nervous," he stated, as he sent the first in a series of disjointed letters. In one, he asserted that he might have to advertise his book again in order to pay for an operation he needed. Brennan advised him to go to any Catholic hospital for treatment but warned that advertising his book would be contrary to the conditions laid down for Rome to hear his case.[40] Halbleib was clearly a disturbed man. He wrote to Blackburn threatening suicide, and then tragically took his own life before the letter could even reach his former associate.[41] Before and after leaving the priesthood, Halbleib had shown the power in those days of the written word in disseminating information about or against the Church.

The Diocese Begins *The Catholic Virginian*

For many years, Richmond did not have its own diocesan newspaper but depended on the Baltimore *Catholic Mirror,* published for the entire metropolitan province. In 1924, the Knights of Columbus began publishing the *Virginia Knight,* which in fact served the diocese. In February 1928 the diocesan consultors discussed giving official recognition to the *Virginia Knight.*[42] Over a year later, they recommended that the diocese take over its management.[43] Only in April 1931, however, was the diocese able to complete the arrangements and formally begin publication of *The Catholic Virginian.* William Winston was named editor, and Walter J. Nott, director of the Propagation of the Faith, was also named to the staff. Receiving the first issue in Louvain, Smet commended both the contents of the new paper and the composition of the staff. He was delighted, he told Brennan, "to see how the diocese is making wonderful strides in every respect under your administration."[44] The new paper, like its predecessor, was a monthly publication—it became a weekly in 1946, when its editorship passed to a layman, John Daly, who had previously worked for a radio station, WBRY, owned by the *Waterbury Republican,* in Connecticut.

What precipitated the decision of the diocese to begin its own newspaper was the presidential campaign of 1928 that had severely challenged the usual rapprochement between Catholics and the Commonwealth. The diocese needed an authoritative publication setting forth the Catholic position in Virginia.

The Presidential Campaign of 1928

In 1928, Governor Alfred E. Smith of New York received the Democratic nomination for president. As the first Catholic to be nominated to the nation's highest office, he immediately aroused opposition. In July, Brennan warned his clergy that the pulpit was to be used only for preaching the gospel. He added that "I am fully aware that, under ordinary circumstances, there would be no necessity for calling your attention to the sacredness of this duty, but I feel that, during the next few months, we should all be extremely careful and say nothing in the pulpit which might be construed, even remotely, to refer to the present political situation."[45]

Other religious leaders did not feel the same constraint in remaining aloof from politics. Soon after Smith's nomination, Methodist Bishop James Cannon, the "Dry Messiah" who had long supported prohibition, opened his headquarters in Richmond to work against the Democrat's election. While he claimed that he opposed Smith because he was a "wet" and that only Smith's campaign manager, John Jacob Raskob, had introduced the religious issue, his speeches in favor of the anti-Catholic Mexican revolution and on other issues before the nomination made it clear that he did not regard the Catholic Church as Christian.[46]

Virginia, usually so tolerant, hearkened to the call to bigotry. In August, Senator Thomas Heflin of Alabama, who had won a reputation for conjuring up imaginative dangers of popery on the floor of the Senate, spoke in Norfolk as the guest of the Ku Klux Klan. He regaled his audience of two thousand with the story of how he had prevented the president from intervening in Mexico where the Church was being persecuted. Neither the mayor nor city manager of Norfolk, however, had accepted an invitation to the meeting.[47]

As the election grew closer, *The Virginia Knight* editorialized on "the duty of every Catholic to so inform himself on the doctrines of his Church that he can answer his traducers and explain the many things that have proven such stumbling blocks."[48] In the same issue, the paper announced the continuation of a series of articles on "Catholic Confederate Heroes" by Joseph D. Hebert of Roanoke. They displayed, said the editor, "just what the Catholic people have done for their country, and just how far they have gone in the Confederacy."[49] Patriotism would continue to be a means by which Virginia Catholics proved they belonged. But in this case, it was not persuasive. Virginia, usually so solidly in the Democratic camp, voted for Herbert Hoover.

After the election, *The Virginia Knight* remarked on the campaign's "most rabid bitterness." Smith's opponents had distributed "the terrible and notorious bogus oath of the Knights of Columbus . . . knowing at the same time that it was a tissue of lies." The editor saw far-reaching implications for the defeat of the Catholic candidate:

> Catholics have been accused of a divided allegiance, and, therefore, they must be excluded from public office; it cannot be understood how we can have a spiritual head without secular powers. It

has even been said that Catholics have no right to send their children to the school of their choice. Organizations are setting themselves up as being superior to the parent, and they wish to take from our hands the children we reared. It is plainly evident that those advocating these changes wish to destroy the Church, and they think that by destroying the parochial school they will ultimately destroy the Church.

But the editor remained optimistic for the future. In the face of "this terrible calumny," "Many prominent men of the various Protestant faiths have defended us," and "the leading daily newspapers loyally defended our right to worship as we would." The outbreak of bigotry had also led "large numbers" to convert to the Church and unmasked the "preacher politicians." "The defeat of the Catholic candidate," concluded the editor, "was therefore not without its good results."[50]

FORMATION OF THE LAYMEN'S LEAGUE

In February 1929, however, Father William Winston addressed the question further in *The Virginia Knight*. He argued that an analysis of the election would "make us better aware of the obstacles which the Church in Virginia has to overcome and may, perhaps, even suggest some of the means calculated to overcome them." For the "average Virginian Democrat" to overcome "his hereditary dislike for and distrust of the Republican party, coupled, as it was, with his fear of new Force bills and of negro domination," there had to be a "prejudice even older and deeper-rooted than themselves, and this prejudice was found in the fear of and hatred for the Church of Rome, which many Virginians have inherited from their English ancestors and which generations of evangelical parsons have spared no effort to nurture and make grow." A Catholic candidate, Winston declared, was sufficient to bring to the polls people who had never voted before. Statistics showed that Smith actually "received in Virginia about the normal Democratic vote; but his adversary received the bulk of the new vote, garnered from all sorts of odd nooks and corners out of which votes had seldom come before."[51]

Winston proposed a twofold course of action: first, education on Catholic belief and practice for both poorly instructed Catholics and non-Catholics; and, second, the encouragement of "our people, particularly the women, to an intelligent, honest and open interest in political affairs."[52] What Winston advocated had, in fact, already begun. On January 20, 1929, the Holy Name Society met in McGill Hall in Richmond, under the sponsorship of Father Edward A. Brosnan, then at the cathedral, to form the Laymen's League, modeled on those established in "other progressive sections of the country." This was the type of organization that the Knights of Columbus had advised O'Connell to reject in 1920, but the prejudice brought forth in the Smith campaign now made it necessary. The league's purpose was to create a cadre of "lay Catholic missionaries," who could go where priests could not, "among the people," in order to "let them know the teachings of our faith." Its strategy was to have a body of literature prepared, so that a Catholic could "then hand to his Protestant neighbor some authoritative printed matter bearing on the question under discussion, and this will dispel the untruth held by his Protestant friend and the bigotry in this instance will be broken down." Brennan appointed Brosnan to institute branches of the league in Portsmouth, Alexandria, Lynchburg, Roanoke, and Staunton.[53]

The league used the existing structure of the Holy Name Society, organized in every parish. Women of the diocese were initially invited to associate with the league through the Sodalities of the Blessed Virgin Mary or other associations that were likewise parish-based.[54] Late in 1931, they were admitted to full membership.[55]

From its beginning, however, some leaders of the league broadened their areas of concern. In March 1929, John E. Milan, president of the Tidewater Catholic Laymen's League, saw the league addressing "the serious conditions with which we are surrounded." "Wherever one turns today," he continued, "he cannot help but observe evidence of the gradual decadence of the moral standard." The evils he saw ranged from public advocacy of birth control to laws in favor of eugenics, sterilization, and divorce, which, in turn, separated children from the normal family environment and increased juvenile delinquency. For him, "the Laymen's League, therefore, can be of greatest good in promoting true Christianity and giving full explanations of Catholic doctrine on these important subjects."[56]

But Milan then moved beyond the moral evils of American society. "There is the higher criticism of the Bible in the halls of the seminaries of so-called religious and Christian organizations," he stated; and "we are always hearing of the Fundamentalist, the Modernist and the Evolutionist." To this catalogue of doctrinal errors, he added the story of "a so-called professor in one of the New England colleges" who declared at a scientific congress that "God was a myth." But then Milan returned to the real purpose of his essay: "the spread of religious prejudice, the utterance of vile calumnies against our Holy Mother Church," which "was greatly intensified during the recent political campaign." Trying to broaden the appeal beyond Catholics, he argued that, "if my rights can be abridged on account of my religion, then no man is secure in his religious rights."[57] Milan was convinced that much of the "bigotry emanates from ignorance," to counter which he proposed not only the dissemination of Catholic literature, but also advertisements in the secular press and radio addresses by qualified lecturers.[58]

Milan was soon applying his principles. By this time, the diocese was entering final negotiations to take over *The Virginia Knight* as its newspaper, but Milan now turned to the use of radio. Beginning in March 1930, his Tidewater Laymen's League arranged for WTAR to broadcast nine programs explaining Catholic doctrine on a wide range of topics. Later in the year, the Richmond league succeeded in having WRVA carry "The Catholic Hour."[59]

But Milan had addressed a wide range of topics in his essay. In speaking of religious liberty, he fell within the mainstream of the American Catholic tradition, of which such Virginia churchmen as Gibbons, Keane, and O'Connell had been strong exponents and which would be vindicated at Vatican II. In linking the evils of his age to "higher criticism" of Scripture, however, he would not have been at home with the council's teaching, but he did reflect the ethos of his contemporary Catholic world, still in the throes of reaction against Modernism. Early in 1931, for example, Archbishop Fumasoni-Biondi informed Brennan that Vittorio Macchioro from the University of Naples, who had a "reputation as a modernist," was to lecture on archaeology and history of religion at the University of Virginia. The delegate wanted to know "in what way he treats the subjects of his lectures and what impression he is making at the University."[60] Whether Brennan reported on Macchioro's address is unknown, but Fumasoni-Biondi's letter illustrated Roman concerns for American propensities for freedom, whether of religion or of discussion. American Catholics were isolated both intellectually and socially from the rest of society.

In the aftermath of Modernism, condemned in 1907, Catholics consciously established their own academic and intellectual subculture. If the Catholic Laymen's League was to be successful in its educational mission, it had to be aware of how Protestants, even well-intentioned ones, regarded the Church. Mary McGill, associate editor of *The Catholic Girl* in Indianapolis, explained the problem well to Father Wilfred Parsons, S.J., editor of *America,* in 1927. Only a "well instructed Catholic" could appreciate "Catholicism," she wrote, for "no matter how *broad* our friends on the outside say they are, I find them quickly sensitive. We are so *SURE.* I think I would hate people who are so certain and set apart."[61] Virginia's Catholics had previously kept their certainty to themselves and tried not to be "set apart." Smith's defeat now put them in the same category with Catholics elsewhere. But there was another way of looking at it. Editorializing on the 1928 election, James Gillis, C.S.P., editor of the Paulists' *Catholic World,* prophesied: "We shall not wither up and blow away."[62] Far from withering up and blowing away, Virginia Catholics reverted to their previous accommodation to the prevailing culture through displays of patriotism and cooperation with other religious bodies in civic matters, including nascent ecumenism.

Virginia Catholics Show Their Patriotism

One way for Virginia Catholics to show they were Americans was to look back to the role Catholics played in earlier periods. In 1925, Bishop O'Connell had purchased the old Brent family graveyard on Aquia creek in Stafford County, north of Fredericksburg. On October 6, 1929, eleven months after Smith's defeat, it was the site of the first annual field Mass, with the American flag prominently displayed and music provided by the Marine Band from Quantico.[63] Less than a year later, Brennan purchased more property along U.S. Route 1 on which to erect a large crucifix with a plaque commemorating the early work of the Brents. This became the personal project of Walter J. Nott, director of the Propagation of the Faith. In October 1931, the diocese celebrated the twenty-fifth anniversary of the cathedral, renovated for the occasion, and the opening of St. Joseph's Villa. In conjunction with it, a field Mass was said at Aquia.[64] As time went on, however, the desire to show an early Catholic presence in Virginia conflated the location of the Brent estate with the site of the early Spanish Jesuit mission.[65]

While there were some informal contacts between the Church and other denominations, the Church was far more prominent in participation in patriotic observances. During Brennan's administration, the largest such observance was the one hundred and fiftieth anniversary of the victory at Yorktown. Brennan was invited to give the invocation at the official celebration on October 17, 1931, and to offer a pontifical Mass. Extending the invitation in the name of the Yorktown Sesquicentennial Commission, William A. R. Goodwin added: "We sincerely trust that your Church, which rendered such distinguished service during the struggle for our national independence, will be graciously pleased to cooperate in this great national endeavor."[66] The invitation to Brennan, incidentally, conflicted with a report Father John Burke, C.S.P., general secretary of the National Catholic Welfare Conference in Washington, had heard. Jules Baisnee, a church historian, Burke told Brennan, had looked over the program and found the religious observance was strictly Protestant.[67] Whether Baisnee was misinformed, or whether someone lobbied with the commission to get the invitation, it was significant that Goodwin had alluded to the Catholic role in the Revolution only a decade after the Knights of Columbus had erected a memorial to the French who had died at Yorktown.

As time for the celebration approached, there were a few indications that Brennan would have to tread cautiously in his interfaith endeavors. He declined an invitation to participate in a "union service," on Sunday, October 18, but announced that there would be Mass that day.[68] To show that Catholics were truly American, he designated Richard B. Washington to say the Mass.[69] Over the coming year, first for the sesquicentennial celebration of Yorktown and then for the bicentennial of George Washington's birthday, Father Washington, the first president's collateral descendant, would be in great demand around the country.

After the ceremonies, Burke commented to Brennan: "I wish to say how pleased I was to know that you had offered pontifical Mass at the Yorktown celebration. I think that was as it should be."[70] Subsequently, S. O. Bland, congressman from Virginia and secretary of the commission, asked Brennan for copies of his invocation and his sermon at the Grandstand.[71] The celebration at Yorktown, moreover, occurred only a month before the diocese's own celebration of the silver jubilee of the cathedral and opening of St. Joseph's Villa. Virginia's Catholics were determined to have both patriotic and religious visibility.

The next year, the nation observed the bicentennial of Washington's birth. Governor John Garland Pollard extended an invitation to both Brennan and Archbishop Fumasoni-Biondi, as well as to other religious leaders to take part in a "civic service" at Fredericksburg on October 16, 1932.[72] The delegate was a bit confused as to the meaning of a "civic service" and asked Brennan "will it really be civic without religious character?"[73] Unfortunately, Brennan did not keep a copy of his response, but Fumasoni-Biondi declined the invitation.[74] Reading between the lines, the delegate seemed willing to tolerate the unusual American custom of bishops taking part in quasi-religious ceremonies without wanting to compromise his own position by participating himself. Roman officials had difficulty understanding such Catholic participation in "services" with Protestants from the time that Gibbons, Keane, and Ireland participated in the World Parliament of Religions in 1893.[75]

At the same time, Father Washington was lecturing throughout the country. He gave addresses in Ogdensburg, Mobile, Springfield, Washington, and Albany, where, incidentally, he was the guest of Governor Franklin D. Roosevelt.[76] Early in February, he had received one of the more interesting invitations. Mayor James Michael Curley of Boston offered to fly him in a private plane to Boston to speak on February 21, but he refused, since "I am not very brave about flying." He agreed, however, to be the guest of the Friendly Sons of St. Patrick in Boston on March 17.[77] Worn out after ten years in Hot Springs and from making so many appearances to commemorate his famous ancestor, he now gained a transfer to Fort Monroe to replace William Gill.[78] There, he would encounter the itinerant Catholic lay missionary, David Goldstein, who did not think Washington had made enough of his relationship to the "Father of His Country."

EARLY ECUMENICAL CONTACTS

Despite the tension engendered by the Al Smith campaign, Virginia still engaged in what would later be called ecumenism. On February 1,

1931, Walter Nott preached, at Brennan's suggestion, at Toano Charge Methodist Church.[79] In Roanoke, the Knights of Columbus planted a tree in honor of Columbus in Elmwood Park and received the "assurance of the Masonic lodges that they will attend."[80] Yet there were still strains. The *Southern Churchman,* the official organ of the Episcopal Church in Virginia, published an editorial strongly criticizing a radio broadcast of Pius XI, the first ever made by a pope, for insulting non-Catholics. The address was translated into English over the radio by a young curial monsignor, Francis J. Spellman, later archbishop of New York.[81] Father Washington, still pastor in Hot Springs, was designated to write to the journal pointing out that the translation of the papal address did not contain the offending passages.[82]

Virginia's Protestants seemed to show surprising sensitivity to their Catholic neighbors, despite their differences with them. On February 9, 1933, for instance, Brennan accepted an invitation to deliver an address under the auspices of the YMCA at Randolph-Macon College in Lynchburg, after he was assured that, although the addresses were usually given in the auditorium of the Methodist Church, he could speak in the college auditorium.[83] At the same time, he appointed John A. Kelliher to give the closing prayer and benediction at a meeting at Ginter Park Presbyterian Church.[84]

Long before ecumenism was a word used in Catholic circles, Bishop Peter Leo Ireton, then the coadjutor of Richmond, established a structure for contact with other denominations. On December 16, 1935, Edward Stephens, William Winston, the editor of *The Catholic Virginian,* and Louis A. Rowen, pastor of St. Elizabeth's Church in Richmond, met for lunch with three Protestant and three Jewish clergymen to discuss the ways in which they could initiate in Virginia the work of the National Conference of Jews and Christians—its name was later changed to the National Conference of Christians and Jews.[85] The next day, Ireton announced to his consultors that he was appointing the three priests to an "Interdenominational Committee."[86] His action was ahead of its time in putting in place diocesan machinery for contact with other faiths in promoting understanding and diminishing prejudice.

Only a few weeks after Ireton established the committee, Leo Frierson, O.S.B., of Belmont Abbey, wrote Brennan, who was still officially the bishop, that he had been invited by the National Conference of Jews and Christians to accompany Dr. Everett Clinchy of

New York University, the executive director of the conference, and Rabbi Morris Lazaron of Baltimore to make a "brotherhood tour" in Norfolk, Williamsburg, and Richmond.[87] Leo Gill, the diocesan chancellor, responded that Ireton had already appointed a "diocesan committee of priests for the National Conference of Jews and Christians" which was "prepared to take care of the other meetings in the diocese."[88] The committee had, in fact, already met on December 30 with the other six clergymen and interested laymen to prepare for a series of round-table discussions, sponsored by the National Conference at the John Marshall Hotel on January 14, 1936.[89] The diocese had made a good beginning in what was then only a nascent ecumenical movement. Catholics were free to participate in such an organization, since it involved only social concerns and not any effort to work for reunion.

The outbreak of anti-Catholicism in 1928 had placed Virginia Catholics on the defensive. They became not only militant but also more overt in their displays of patriotism. By 1931, they settled back to their former easy relationship with most of their Protestant neighbors. Nineteen thirty-one was a milestone. Not only was it the bicentennial of Washington's birth, it also marked the high point of the diocese's social outreach, the dedication of St. Joseph's Villa, the gift of James Dooley.

CHAPTER 22

Social Outreach
and the Depression

The diocese of Richmond had long been engaged in social outreach. From the 1830s, it had had orphanages, and, from 1856, one hospital, St. Vincent's in Norfolk. In 1921, Bishop O'Connell had Louis Smet in Alexandria investigate the possibility of the Sisters of Mercy at Georgetown University Hospital opening a hospital in Richmond, but they did not have sufficient personnel at the time. Richmond would have to wait another forty years before it got a Catholic hospital.[1] A hospital may not then have been in the immediate future, but the 1920s marked a systematic development of the diocese's social programs, as it established one of the earliest Bureaus of Catholic Charities in the country. Aiding this social outreach were both the Dooley grant for St. Joseph's Villa and the Robinson bequest for a boys orphanage in Norfolk, both of which were completed during the Depression. During the early years of the Depression, the diocese was actually able to undertake an extensive building campaign that came to a halt in 1933. During the New Deal, the diocese also had to provide priests for Civilian Conservation Corps camps.

FOUNDING OF CATHOLIC CHARITIES

Since 1865, Richmond's Catholics had had branches of the St. Vincent de Paul Society in various parishes tending to the needs of poor parishioners. In addition, the St. Vincent de Paul Auxiliary, composed mainly of women, worked to provide food baskets for the poor of the various parishes. Just before Christmas in 1919, Felix Kaup, rector of Sacred Heart Cathedral, called a special meeting of the auxiliary in his parish. The society's work had decreased during the war, since the Red Cross had drained away many of its volunteer workers. Kaup now called for a reorganization. At the meeting, Walter J. Nott, who had been ordained in Rome the previous March and whose parents, Mr. and Mrs. Frank Nott, were active in the parish, was appointed chaplain. Marie Leahy was named to chair the reorganized group that initially took the name St. Vincent de Paul's Guild for the Poor.

Nott and Leahy, however, soon recognized that the economic conditions of postwar Richmond required more than the traditional type of charity work, for the city now included children in need of institutional care and men and women in need of housing and legal assistance. They, therefore, approached Bishop O'Connell, who gave his approval for the establishment of a Bureau of Catholic Charities, as other dioceses were already doing.[2] With the advice of Monsignor William J. Kerby, national director of Catholic Charities and a professor at the Catholic University of America, Nott and Leahy gathered a small group of men and women and formally inaugurated the bureau on October 22, 1922. Father John Bowler of St. Peter's offered the use of the basement of the church for offices. The meeting also elected as officers Frank H. Nott, president, Joseph Dart, vice president, Mrs. Walter Mahoney, second vice president, Leahy, recording secretary, William Powers, treasurer, and Walter Nott, chaplain. The board of trustees included each pastor and the president for the society of the poor in his parish. Mrs. Frank Nott, president of the Catholic Women's Club, and Marie Leahy, president of the St. Vincent de Paul's Guild at the cathedral, then visited each pastor to explain that the new bureau was not to take the place of the parish charitable organizations, but was to act as a central clearing house for the local groups and to care for major needs, such as family aid, children requiring institutionalization, court cases, and other requests for assistance outside of parishes. On December 8, 1922, the bureau launched a fund-raising campaign with a goal of $10,000. Each local society was to receive a quota from the general fund, according to its need, through application of its president to the bureau.

The money came in very slowly, but the bureau opened in St. Peter's under the direction of Catherine Harahan, the executive secretary. Subsequently, Mrs. Mary O'Neil volunteered her services to assist her in the office, which relieved the strained budget. These two women, as Marie Leahy later reported, were probably the ones most responsible for the survival of the bureau in its beginnings. The problem of funding was partially settled when the bureau became part of the Richmond Community Chest a year later.[3]

The founding of Catholic Charities in Richmond, as elsewhere, represented a new role for women, married and single, who were professionally trained as social workers. This new corps of women professionals differed from both religious women who had operated schools and orphanages and earlier generations of female volunteers.[4] Harahan was representative. A graduate of Trinity College in Washington, she had taken courses at both the Richmond School of Social Work and the New York School of Social Work. Her father was president of the Chesapeake and Ohio Railroad, one of the principal employers of Richmond's Catholics. In 1926, the Community Fund commissioned a member of the staff of the Child Welfare League of America to make a survey of the bureau. The surveyor found Harahan to be "a person having intellectual ability, and one who is acquainted with the principles of modern social work." The survey also recommended that her "time should be largely reserved for educational and administrative duties," and that two full-time caseworkers and a full-time stenographer be added to the staff.

The bureau was divided into two departments, family work and children, with the former handling 265 cases in 1925 and the latter 156. But budget continued to be a problem. The Community Fund had granted only $13,015 of the $22,272.38 requested for 1926. The difference was made up from private donations and parents who could pay for their children's board.

By that date, the bureau, whose services were limited to "needy Catholics," was discharging four functions: (1) General family relief and rehabilitation; (2) a limited amount of casework on children applying for admission or already admitted to St. Joseph's Academy and Orphan Asylum and to St. Vincent's Institution for boys at Roanoke; (3) Care of children in foster homes; and (4) casework with Catholic wards of the Juvenile Court or State Board of Public Welfare. Although the surveyor recommended discontinuing the fourth function,[5] the bureau continued its case work for Catholic children.[6] He also raised the question of the use of the funds Major Dooley had left for St. Joseph's Orphanage. The Dooley bequest was soon to make possible the building of St. Joseph's Villa and provided funds for girls who would be admitted through the Bureau of Catholic Charities.

By the time the survey of the Bureau of Catholic Charities was made in 1926, however, O'Connell had retired, and Kaup, who was administrator, could make no permanent appointment of a director of the bureau until the arrival of the new bishop, Andrew Brennan. Writing to John W. Moore, the president of the bureau, Kaup explained that he was temporarily appointing Walter Nott as director. He did this "in view of the present shortage of competent workers acceptable to the Budget Committee of the Richmond Community Fund." As diocesan director, Nott was to act as liaison with the local bureau and be one of its officers.[7] Nott was confirmed by Brennan and would remain as director until the late 1920s when he was replaced by Thomas A. Mitchell. Under his administration, however, the bureau also handled applications for admission to St. Vincent's Orphanage for boys in Roanoke, but not to St. Joseph's Orphanage for girls.[8]

THE DEDICATION OF ST. JOSEPH'S VILLA

The site Dooley had chosen for the new St. Joseph's complex was adjacent to Maymont. The trustees, however, preferred another site, Hollybrook, three miles north of Richmond, and succeeded in having the court change the decree in the will. With the change of site, the Daughters of Charity were obliged by the court to erect on the grounds a monument similar to the one at the original Maymont site, with the inscription: "These buildings were dedicated to charity by James H. Dooley in memory of his father, Major John Dooley; his mother, Sarah Dooley; of his wife, S. M. Dooley and of himself."[9]

Before the new buildings were completed, however, the Bureau of Catholic Charities was placing girls eligible under the Dooley bequest in boarding homes at a total cost of $5,000 a year. With the completion of St. Joseph's Villa, girls over school age were transferred to the new facility, where the bureau had charge of admissions and withdrawals. When it subsequently became necessary for the bureau to add a caseworker for girls at the Villa, the Dooley fund paid the salary.[10]

But there were restrictions on the Dooley request. It was open only to white girls. This may have been why Bishop Brennan arranged a combination of elaborate ceremonies for the dedication of the new St. Joseph's Villa in November 1931. The opening of the new facility, the building of which cost an estimated $1 million during the early part of the Depression, coincided with the celebration of the twenty-fifth anniversary of the dedication of the cathedral. The ceremony at the cathedral was on November 8, followed the next day by the dedication of the Villa. Brennan scheduled the events to occur immediately before the annual meeting of the hierarchy in Washington, and then extended an invitation to all the bishops to attend. At some point in October, shortly before the ceremonies, Brennan then arranged a trip to Rock Castle the day after the dedication of the Villa.

The decision to add Rock Castle to the list of sights for visiting bishops to see may have occurred after Brennan accompanied Mrs. Morrell on a tour of the Villa.[11] He invited her to participate in the events and sent her a copy of the letter he was sending to all the bishops. Expressing her appreciation for the invitation and for the letter, which she had sent to Katherine Drexel, then in South Dakota, she commented: "Your desire to further the great work among the nation's tenth men, is a truly God-sent one."[12]

Brennan received widespread response to the invitations he had sent to the bishops. Bishop Vincent Wehrle of Bismarck was unable to attend but stated: "I am glad that you intend to celebrate the Silver Jubilee of the Consecration of your Cathedral in a solemn way. It will help to strengthen the Catholics and to set the Non-Catholics thinking."[13] And Brennan, a Scrantonian, probably had just such an effect in mind, but he also wanted to impress the bishops of other dioceses that Richmond was not so out-of-date. As Bishop James A. Griffin of Springfield, Illinois, remarked: "Your forthcoming celebration is getting very favorable and generous publicity. You are certainly putting the Church on the map in the Southland."[14] The Villa was a model for institutional care of female orphans. Each of eight cottages could accommodate twenty-four girls. In addition, there was a school, swimming pool and gymnasium, chapel, and administration building, all designed by the architects, Carneal and Johnson. When the day for the dedication arrived, Archbishop Michael J. Curley of Baltimore blessed the school and Bishop Richard O. Gerow of Natchez blessed the buildings.[15]

On November 10, Brennan took a group of bishops on a tour of Rock Castle. Some had to turn down his invitation because of board meetings of the National Catholic Welfare Conference, the organization of the hierarchy, or of the Catholic University, both of which met prior to the general meeting of the bishops. Of those who were so impeded, Archbishop John T. McNicholas, O.P., of Cincinnati commented: "it is a matter of sincere regret to me that I cannot express my appreciation of the work that Mother Katherine Drexel is doing. We are deeply indebted to her here in Cincinnati for the extraordinary work she is doing for our Negro children in both the grade and high schools."[16] Among those who altered other plans to attend was Bishop Edmund J. Fitzmaurice of Wilmington, who declared: "I feel, like yourself, that the Bishops should do anything within reason to show their appreciation of the noble work of Mother Catharine [sic] & Mrs. Morrell."[17]

Just prior to the dedication, Brennan had received over ten positive responses from bishops who wanted to visit Rock Castle as well. Mrs. Morrell admitted she was "surprised at the number of Bishops who have accepted your invitation to Rock Castle. Both of the institutions will feel very much honored to entertain such distinguished guests."[18] When it was over, she and Mother Katherine were even more enthusiastic. Both felt

> so grateful to you for having arranged the coming of the Bishops to Rock Castle. We feel a distinct boost has been given the work for the Negroes by having put the Bishops in closer touch with what is being done for them. The ones who were formerly uninstructed, from now on will have an entirely different view in their contacts with the "darkee brothers."

While congratulating him on the successful conclusion of the three-day event, she was especially thankful for "what you have done for Rock Castle and the Negro Work."[19]

Brennan passed on Mrs. Morrell's letter to Archbishop Pietro Fumasoni-Biondi, the apostolic delegate, who "read with pleasure in your letter of the interest stirred up in the work for the colored as a result of the trip to Rock Castle. I am also happy to learn that Mother Catherine [sic] and Mrs. Morrell were delighted at the results."[20] From Bishop John J. Cantwell of Los Angeles-San Diego came the type of observation Brennan was trying to gain. Cantwell could not "hope to emulate" St. Joseph's Villa, he wrote, but added:

> Our days at "Rock Castle" were a joy ride and a picnic. May God be good to the ladies who for so many years have had compassion on his colored children.
>
> There is a great future for Richmond and in your celebration you did much for the standing of the Church in your state.[21]

Bishop Christopher E. Byrne of Galveston had been unable to attend the ceremonies but added a comment in regard to the anti-Catholic Methodist bishop, that "Our poor brother James Cannon Jr. [the Methodist bishop] must have been grieved at such a display of Romanism in the Old Dominion."[22] Several months later, Katherine Drexel invited Brennan to the laying of the cornerstone of Xavier College in New Orleans, for she wrote, "Your Excellency has shown such wonderful interest in the Colored work in your diocese that I am emboldened to ask the privilege of your presence on this occasion."[23] The triple events of the anniversary of the cathedral, the dedication of St. Joseph's Villa, and the trip to Rock Castle made a forceful display of Catholic influence in Virginia and of work with the poor and African Americans, all of it due to lay benefactors: the Ryans, Dooley, and the Drexel sisters.

But the Villa played another role in Virginia's expression of public Catholicism. It became the site for the annual Corpus Christi procession in the diocese. Such outward display of a more militant Catholicism, though common in more Catholic areas of the country, led Smet in Louvain to comment to Brennan: "What a consolation to yourself! And what a grand thing too, to dear old Father Van [Ingelgem], that he could witness it! Such events show the progress of the Faith in Virginia."[24]

In the meantime, once the festivities were over, Brennan returned to reality. Two weeks after the ceremonies at the Villa, he dedicated a new building at St. Vincent's Orphanage for boys in Roanoke. In a letter to the diocese, he noted that the Villa was a "monument to the generosity and benevolence of Major James Dooley." It provided for female orphans "without any burden to the Diocese," but boys were not as fortunate. The diocese would have to support them through an annual Christmas collection for orphans.[25] Admission to the Villa and

St. Vincent's fell under the Bureau of Catholic Charities, which in 1932 absorbed existing diocesan charity organizations, ceased to be an independent corporation, and became an official part of the diocesan structure with the bishop as honorary president and the diocesan director of Catholic Charities as the executive secretary. Father Thomas E. Mitchell was in charge of this new organization until 1938, when he became dean of the School of Social Work at the Catholic University of America.[26] Further care for needy boys, however, was in the offing.

THE BARRY-ROBINSON HOME FOR BOYS, NORFOLK

In December 1918, John Baecher, the diocesan attorney in Norfolk, wrote to O'Connell for information on the charter and regulations for a boys school or orphanage, for he had a client who wished to found such a school. In Baecher's proposal, "the final object is the creation & running of such a school for Boys, to educate them well, & to give those who lack aptitude for intellectual pursuits, trades, &c. If I succeed in this matter, it will be a magnificent creation, as the estate is ample." He asked the bishop for a prompt response since his unnamed client was not well.[27] This was the first notice of what was to be the Barry-Robinson School for Boys.

Frederick J. Robinson, a Norfolk realtor, had made his bequest in honor of himself and his grandfather, James Barry. Philip Brennan in Virginia Beach later recalled Robinson's style and character. When Robinson was asked why he had not consulted James O'Farrell, the pastor of St. Mary's and vicar general, about his bequest, Brennan wrote that he replied:

> "No! this is my work and my gift." . . . and he added; "In days gone by if a bequest was made to a pastor for a stain-glass window, he chose a door . . . and vice versa." He died as he lived . . . adamant in his resolution. So, Bishop felt a bit slighted when in addition to his endorsement, other security was required, but it is a sequel to Fred Robinson's bolshevism. He was an awfully eccentric old gent.[28]

In October 1927, Bishop Brennan approached the Xaverian Brothers, who then operated a similar school, St. Mary's Industrial School, in

Baltimore, to which needy boys from Virginia were sent. But their superior replied that he had no men to spare.[29] Finally, during the summer of 1933, Archabbot Alfred Koch of St. Vincent's Archabbey in Latrobe, Pennsylvania, paid a visit to the Benedictines staffing St. Emma's at Rock Castle. Brennan requested that the Benedictines also take over the administration of the new school. On September 7, Koch informed him that the chapter had agreed to the proposal.[30] The new school would now allow Catholic Charities to care for boys within the state and hence obtain state funds for their maintenance.[31] Up until this time, if they sent a boy to St. Mary's Industrial School in Baltimore or a similar institution outside the state, no funding was available.

Even before the Benedictines had agreed to staff the Barry-Robinson School, however, Father Mitchell, director of Catholic Charities, was making plans for the actual operation of the institution. He requested through Baecher, chairman of the board of trustees of the school, that the institution accept applications through Catholic Charities, as was the case with St. Joseph's Villa.[32] The Barry-Robinson School, however, would never be as financially secure as the Villa.

The first Benedictines to staff the new school came from Rock Castle. Exchange of personnel between the two institutions continued over the years until the Benedictines were replaced at Rock Castle by the Holy Ghost Fathers. But almost immediately after the Barry-Robinson school opened in January 1934, its primary purpose was changed. The number of Catholic orphans in Virginia was declining, but not the need for a school for boys from broken and needy homes. In the beginning the home also operated its own farm, while offering a junior high school curriculum. It continued as an industrial school until 1961, when it became an academic high school. Ironically, Bishop Peter Ireton had proposed a similar arrangement in 1944. The declining neighborhood around St. Mary's necessitated the closing of the parish high school to the chagrin of one of its leading alumni, John Baecher. Ireton suggested using part of the Barry-Robinson bequest to fund a regular high school for boys.[33] In 1967, the Third Order Regular Franciscans took over administration from the Benedictines.[34] But, in the 1970s, the school closed, and the Barry-Robinson Center became a home for emotionally disturbed boys and girls or children with learning disabilities. From the Benedictine community at Barry-Robinson, incidentally, arose the parish of St. Gregory the Great, which began worshiping in the school chapel in 1957.

As the needs of the Virginia Catholic community changed, St. Joseph's Villa, too, would cease to be a girls orphanage. With the withdrawal of the Daughters of Charity by the 1970s, it closed as an orphanage, but took on a new life as a multipurpose institution addressing a wide range of needs of young people, from victims of child abuse to children with learning disabilities. Long since forgotten, perhaps, was the way the diocese showcased the opening of the Villa to display the influence of the Catholic Church in Virginia. In 1931, in the midst of the Depression, it was a sumptuous affair. While it was the diocese's most ambitious project, it was representative of a widespread building program during the first years of the Depression.

Expansion and New Parishes

From the inception of his episcopacy, Brennan had wide-ranging plans for developing parishes. At a consultors' meeting in September 1927, less than a year after taking office, he proposed appointing resident pastors in Lexington, Emporia, Suffolk, Fair Oaks (Highland Springs), Waynesboro, Cradock, Bristow or Manassas, and Berkeley Springs.[35] Within a few years he had successfully appointed priests in all those missions, except Lexington, a mission of Staunton, and Emporia, which was served from Petersburg until the Franciscans made it their missionary headquarters in 1940.

By the fall of 1930, Brennan had a new set of priorities. Despite the Depression, he published a "Five-Year Plan" for the diocese. He proposed parochial schools for Keyser, Ridgeley, Winchester, Danville, and Hopewell, and new churches for Waynesboro, then undergoing an "industrial boom," and Williamsburg, where "the number of Catholic students at William and Mary College is constantly increasing and the need for a permanent church is sadly felt."[36] The new churches were made possible by a bequest from Margaret Burns of Staunton, who left money for a "Burns Memorial Church of St. John the Evangelist." This was the name given to the new church in Waynesboro, which remained a mission of Staunton, but the bishop was also able to draw on the funds to build a church in Williamsburg. The town, moreover, would be the only one that would increase because of a Catholic student population.

Williamsburg's Parish Begins
as Cardinal Gibbons Center

Williamsburg had received only occasional visits from priests since the Civil War, when Louis-Hippolyte Gache, the Confederate chaplain, had left such a vivid description of the town. In 1908, Father van Ingelgem, then on the original diocesan mission band and temporarily in residence in Newport News, seems to have been the first priest to return to the town on a regular basis. In September, with his encouragement, the tiny Catholic community held a two-day fair to raise funds for a church. One of the principals in the movement to start a church was Mrs. Isaac Wright, who delighted the readers of *The Virginia Gazette* with her human interest articles, signed "Plain Country Woman," and who wrote for journals elsewhere under her full name, Lydia Wingfield Wright.[37] For the time being, however, the Catholics could not build a church, and the money raised in the fair was invested.[38] After the fair and until his departure for Roanoke in 1912, Father Joseph Frioli from Newport News paid occasional visits to Williamsburg. Other priests then came from time to time.

The reason for the failure to get a church in Williamsburg in 1908 was, unfortunately, not merely lack of funds. In the summer of 1912, a land agent, F. H. Ball, recalled that he had earlier tried to recruit Catholic families to settle on the farms nearby, but they were hesitant to live where there was no Catholic church. Ball offered to donate two lots for a church and school, and one of the prospective families agreed to give $900 for the buildings. But then he "learned that four of these prospective buyers were driven away from town because of the anti-Catholicism of people who call themselves 'citizens.'"[39] Williamsburg would have to wait for a more auspicious time before it got a parish.

In 1923, Carlos Eduardo Castañeda had accepted a faculty post at the College of William and Mary. Though a trained historian, he was hired to teach Spanish. A Texas native, he had graduated from the University of Texas, where he was active in the Newman Club, of which Father John Elliott Ross, then a Paulist, was the chaplain. In Williamsburg, he was alarmed to find very few practicing Catholics in the student body and decided to found a Catholic club. Modeling the organization on what he had experienced in Texas, he opted to build upon Virginia's Catholic tradition and named it the Gibbons Club. In

December, it held its first meeting. Its purpose was to obtain a priest for Mass each Sunday and to provide a forum for Catholic students to socialize and discuss religious and other questions.[40] The original membership numbered twenty-seven, of whom one third were women, for, unlike other Virginia institutions, William and Mary began accepting women as well as men in 1918. A charter member was J. L. Muscarelle, who later endowed the college art museum. Initially, Castañeda and the student leaders arranged for only a monthly Mass celebrated by a priest from Newport News. During the club's second year, however, they increased the Masses to two a month. In 1926, Castañeda invited Ross to celebrate the third annual "Field Mass," the first ever celebrated on the college campus.[41] In January 1927, however, Castañeda left William and Mary to take charge of the Latin American collection at the University of Texas, where he completed his multivolume *Our Catholic Heritage in Texas.* But he had left behind in Williamsburg the nucleus of a permanent Catholic community. By that time, John D. Rockefeller, Jr., had begun the Williamsburg Restoration that would definitively change the town.

For several years, the Benedictines from Richmond sent a priest to Williamsburg to offer a weekly Mass. The Gibbons Club, under the direction of Father Gregory Eichenlaub, O.S.B., now reopened the campaign to build a chapel, the funding of which was made possible through the Burns bequest. On October 30, 1932, Brennan dedicated the chapel, which, as *The Virginia Gazette* noted, was "of Georgian style of architecture and follows closely, the colonial design that is revealing itself in all of the restoration work in Williamsburg."[42] It was dedicated to St. Bede, which, as *The Flat Hat,* the college newspaper commented, was "very appropriate for a chapel in a college town as St. Bede was a great scholar himself," who had written an "early history of England in the 6th century while in a Benedictine Monastery, in England."[43] Put in other terms, as Virginia Catholics throughout the state were endeavoring to show that they were American, in Williamsburg they were illustrating that the Catholic intellectual heritage even within England was far more ancient than either William and Mary or "Colonial Williamsburg."

Benedictines from Richmond continued to serve the Williamsburg chapel once a week until 1939. Bishop Brennan seems to have been content to leave it that way. In 1936, however, Ireton, who was then the coadjutor, proposed that there be a resident pastor. He had an apt candidate. Father Speer Strahan had been ordained for the diocese of Grand Rapids, but then taught English at the Catholic University of America. Since his own bishop did not like his men doing nondiocesan work, he was incardinated into Richmond. Ireton proposed that he become the resident pastor in Williamsburg and teach at William and Mary. Strahan pointed out, however, that there was already a professor in his field at the college. He recommended, moreover, that any priest sent to Williamsburg either be qualified to be a full professor or be classified as a part-time lecturer, to avoid academic tensions.[44] Although Ireton was ignorant of the requirements of the American academic scene, his proposal was provocative for what it revealed about his recognition of the need for Williamsburg's pastor to relate to the academic community.

For the time being, Ireton left Williamsburg under the weekly care of the Benedictines. In the spring of 1938, however, the diocesan consultors discussed, without taking a vote, the possibility of inviting the Dominicans to take over the parish.[45] Over a year later, they urged that Williamsburg have a resident pastor.[46] The first pastor was Thomas J. Walsh. He fit the profile Ireton has sought in Strahan. An alumnus of the North American College in Rome, he had a doctorate in theology.

CHARLOTTESVILLE AND THE UNIVERSITY OF VIRGINIA

But Williamsburg was not the only town whose Catholic population was increasing as more Catholic students attended state educational institutions. Charlottesville had had a parish church, Holy Comforter, since 1881 and had been the scene of a bitter dispute between Thomas Rankin, the pastor, and Thomas Fortune Ryan in the 1920s. Although the church was downtown, by the 1930s it was beginning to influence the University of Virginia. H. R. Pratt, professor of music at the university, was also the music director of the parish. Early in April 1931, he invited Bishop Brennan to attend the Virginia State Musical Festival at the university. He was going to put on Shubert's Mass in E flat and a composition of his own. "The program of this festival," he commented, "proves again that you can *talk* Protestantism, but you cannot *sing* it."[47] Pratt and John J. Brochtrup, the pastor, were intent on making Holy Comforter a showplace for music. Early in 1932, Brochtrup proposed to Brennan the installation of a new pipe organ.[48] Despite the Depression, he thought the cost of the organ was more than justified, because "this is predominantly a University community and parish." His permanent congregation then numbered 253, of whom 119 were children, but he pointed out there were between fifty and seventy-five Catholic students, numerous tourists, and seven Catholic professors, of whom five were converts. Good music, he argued, would provide the parish with a "cultural" outreach to the university. The choir was already composed of university people, and a pipe organ would encourage congregational singing.[49]

By April 1932, Holy Comforter had its new pipe organ. Pratt, who had composed a special piece for its dedication, filled the bishop in on the religious situation at the university. Included among the Catholic faculty were Garrod Glenn of the law school and Scott Buchanan in the philosophy department, but he added that the attitude of Stringfellow Barr, professor of history and editor of *The Virginia Quarterly Review,* was "militantly pro-Catholic in all his lectures and writings." Pratt and a "fairly large group" were

> convinced that this place is ripe for a big Catholic Revival. Many Episcopalians, sick of the way their church is becoming protestantized, are ready to come over to us. These folks who are either Catholic or Pro Catholic are amongst the most influential people here and their influence is not confined to this university. Can't we have a brief talk about all this some day?[50]

Pratt may have been too optimistic about the Church's future role at the university at this juncture, but he did have insight into the opportunities presented. While Williamsburg and Blacksburg had active Catholic student centers, Charlottesville did not have one until 1947.

In the meantime, Brochtrup had to abandon some of his ambitious plans. While he was arguing to buy an organ, he also told Bishop Brennan he was trying to purchase property for a parochial school. By May of 1932, however, he reported that Mother Alphonse (Bliley), superior of the Benedictine Sisters in Bristow, who had supplied sisters for a summer vacation school for the previous six years, probably would not send sisters the following summer, because they would be attending summer school at the Catholic University of America.[51]

Charlottesville would have to wait a generation before it had a school, but Brochtrup's problem that summer was significant. Religious women were now beginning to fulfill academic requirements before being sent out to teach.

While Brochtrup and Pratt appear to be the principal movers in relating Charlottesville's Catholic community to the university, they did have temporary, though significant, assistance. For the summer of 1931, Brochtrup had been replaced in Charlottesville by J. Elliott Ross, who had had such an influence on Castañeda at the University of Texas and had said the first Mass on the campus of William and Mary. Ross had left the Paulists and had then taught at the Newman Center at the University of Illinois in Champaign. In September 1931, he asked Brennan's permission to move to Charlottesville, where he would be self-supporting.[52] At the time, because of his departure from the Paulists, he was caught up in a canonical nightmare. Because the Paulists were technically not a religious order but a congregation, their members were theoretically diocesan priests. At Ross's ordination, however, it was not made clear for what diocese he was ordained. None of the bishops for whom he may have been ordained acknowledged ecclesiastical jurisdiction over him. In October, Brennan simply decided to authorize him to move to Charlottesville, where he resided off and on between lecture tours until 1942, when he returned to the Paulists.[53]

BLACKSBURG: THE VIRGINIA POLYTECHNIC INSTITUTE

The needs within the diocese were sufficient to keep the clergy busy, especially during the Depression. But calls for priests also came from those sections of Virginia in the diocese of Wheeling. Since 1900, Blacksburg, the site of the Virginia Agricultural and Mechanical College and Polytechnic Institute, had been a mission of Wytheville, with a priest visiting on weekdays every month or so. The community gathered in the homes of Mary Kammitt Linkous or Marie Giffendal Keister. During World War I, the increased student enrollment at VPI occasioned the building of a small chapel, but in the postwar years the college administration learned that Catholic parents hesitated to send their sons to a school where there was no provision for weekly Mass and encouraged the diocese of Wheeling to build a regular church.

With funds from the Church Extension Society, St. Mary's Church was constructed and dedicated in June 1924. Simultaneously, a Newman Club was founded, one year after the Gibbons Club at William and Mary. But the priest from Wytheville could no longer take care of the Blacksburg mission. Bishop John J. Swint of Wheeling, therefore, arranged with Bishop Brennan to have the mission served from Roanoke. Father John A. Kelliher, pastor of St. Andrew's, began saying a monthly Sunday Mass in Blacksburg, until he was transferred to St. Peter's in Richmond.[54]

Late in December 1931, Swint requested that Brennan allow Father James Gilsenan of Our Lady of Nazareth in Roanoke to serve the growing Catholic community in Blacksburg.[55] Gilsenan readily complied and announced to the people of Blacksburg that he or his assistant would begin having Mass in Blacksburg every Sunday, beginning on January 3, 1932.[56] He soon discovered, however, that the people of Blacksburg had concerns other than the care of the students. There were two factions in the mission, and one of them was headed by Mrs. Keister. Immediately after his second visit, he informed Swint that "today, all the rival factions were present, though not formally reconciled. (A thing not to be expected, and not so necessary, but which I believe will come with time and God's grace.)" Mrs. Keister expressed her delight at his appointment, but had written him not to come on the first Sunday of January, since the "boys are home." Gilsenan decided "then and there . . . no one could tell me when to come or not to come." On his first visit, he saw representatives of both factions and reported that "before leaving, everyone was happy, and they declared they were right with me and would be at Mass today. They were, and a crowd of students and others that filled the little Church; twenty received Holy Communion. I could sense a feeling of willingness to cooperate in that congregation, which was at least encouraging." He hoped to have sisters from his school begin to go on Saturdays to teach catechism.[57]

Swint sympathized with Gilsenan's experience. Mrs. Keister once phoned him not to come on the appointed day for Confirmation, since "many of the students and some of the people were going to a football game. They asked that I come at some other time—four hundred miles to confirm a handful of children. Of course I went anyway, just as you did, and we had a very nice Confirmation." Swint suggested that Gilsenan keep Brennan informed of the progress of his

Blacksburg adventure, since, as he carefully pointed out, most of the students were residents of the diocese of Richmond.[58] Gilsenan or his assistant continued their weekly visits to Blacksburg for two years, when it again reverted to Wytheville. In 1938, it received a resident pastor, and in 1974 it was incorporated into the diocese of Richmond.

THE DEPRESSION: PHASE I, A BUILDING SPREE

Until 1932, the Depression did not fully affect the diocese. Initially, in fact, there was a building spurt, some of it made possible, as was the case in Waynesboro and Williamsburg, by a large bequest. At St. Andrew's in Roanoke, Brennan had transferred his Roman classmate John Kelliher to St. Peter's in Richmond in 1930 and replaced him with Thomas B. Martin, who immediately began to build a new or-phanage and a high school to serve both his parish and Our Lady of Nazareth. He was going to use bricks from a hotel that had burned down and pointed out that contractors were then anxious to keep their laborers employed.[59]

Martin's building projects did not win him the support of all his parishioners. A flurry of complaints went to Brennan, each signed with a different name and typed, but with similar grammatical errors that leads one to believe they emanated from the same source. They accused Martin of allowing children to skate in the vestibule and of arming the ushers with pistols at the Christmas Masses. More to the point, one letter argued that the people had no money for building and were tired of hearing about purchasing a school bus to bring the children to the new school. Since many Protestant children also at-tended the school already, the writer ended on a less than ecumenical note: "Let the protestant children go to their own school's, if the sis-ter's teach our own catholic children as they should-be taught they wont have no time to-be teaching protestant ones." In the writer's opinion, the Protestants were interested in the school only because the school bus made it easier and cheaper to get to.[60]

Behind many of these complaints was a mentality familiar to every bishop, as parishioners compared their new pastor unfavorably with his predecessors. One writer noted that neither Lynch nor Kelliher would have allowed children to play ball around the church on Sundays. The complainant's solution to the problem was simple;

he wanted Kelliher back, "for the people of Richmond can do without Father Kelliher, better than the people of St. Andrew's, for St. Andrew's certainly needs Father Kelliher back to run the hill in a proper manner as it should-be."[61] If Brennan responded to any of these complaints, he left no record. Regardless of the opposition, the high school was completed in November and the orphanage in December 1931.[62]

Martin was not alone in taking advantage of the early stages of the Depression to undertake building campaigns. In Newport News, David Coleman dedicated a new school in January 1931.[63] Late in 1931, Magri in Portsmouth suggested that the diocese take advantage of deflated prices to purchase the property next to the school.[64] But the end of such undertakings was near. One indication of the effect the Depression had on the diocese was that of the five places where Brennan hoped to build schools in his five-year plan in 1930, he was successful only in Hopewell, where Father James Gacquin opened a school in 1931, staffed by Sisters of Mercy from Scranton.[65] Within a year, the diocese reflected what was happening elsewhere. Three years of depression had reduced the national income by more than half. After a temporary rally in the summer of 1932, the economy had again collapsed. It got worse during the winter of 1932–33.[66]

THE DEPRESSION: PHASE II, ECONOMIC CRISIS

The financial crisis for the diocese covered a wide spectrum of problems. Holy Trinity in Ocean View had earlier issued bonds to pay off its debt. In 1932, an English priest working in Arizona had purchased some of them and wanted to cash them in to return to England. Leo Gill, the chancellor, patiently explained that the notes could not be paid until they had matured, but that they could be sold like other securities.[67] The priest was not persuaded. The brokerage firm in Chicago that had sold him the bonds had said they could be cashed at any time, but admitted it could not sell them for him. Threatening to appeal to the apostolic delegate, he caustically commented that "Apparently in some dioceses Catholic credit would be placed with the devil himself if he supplied the money."[68] Two years later, Bishop Brennan received another complaint about the bonds, this time from a lawyer.[69]

By 1933, the Depression was having a direct impact on parish life. In Alexandria, Rankin reported in the summer that he had to sell the parish car, reimpose tuition in the school that up to that time had benefited from a large bequest from Michael Ahern, and lay off his servant. He also asked to be relieved of his assistant, whom he could no longer afford.[70] Alexandria's black population suffered yet more. Joseph Kelly at St. Joseph's reported that, even in good times, there was "lack of employment to be had here for colored people." The Depression only made this worse.[71]

If the poor suffered the most and the diocese was in general hard-pressed, the Depression also exacerbated the weaknesses of some priests. Rankin had to recommend the removal of one pastor in his northern Virginia deanery whose heavy debts may have contributed to so severe a drinking problem that he could not read the Gospel at Mass.[72] Rankin himself had to fill in. At the same time, John A. Curran, the pastor of St. Charles in Clarendon, advised Brennan that, despite the petition of the parishioners of his Cherrydale mission, the appointment of a resident pastor for St. Agnes be deferred.[73]

To the south, in Virginia Beach, Philip Brennan wrote that the Catholic population was the lowest in years and so few were preparing for confirmation that he did not think the bishop should bother making a special trip.[74] To the west, in Staunton, Emmett Gallagher informed the bishop of a strange phenomenon. Collections were down in Staunton but not in Lexington and Waynesboro, which, incidentally, then had more children than Staunton.[75] But the Depression added yet more burdens to the diocese.

THE CIVILIAN CONSERVATION CORPS IN VIRGINIA

In addition to the financial crisis the Depression created for the diocese, as for other institutions, Virginia also was the site of numerous Civilian Conservation Corps (CCC) camps established as one of several emergency measures by President Franklin D. Roosevelt. In September 1933, John A. Burke, general secretary of the National Catholic Welfare Conference, the national association of the hierarchy, wrote to Bishop Brennan of the desire of Archbishop Amleto Cicognani, the new apostolic delegate, for all the bishops to be informed of the need of chaplains for the CCC camps. He noted further that of the 102 reserve army chaplains called to active duty to serve in the camps, only twenty-three were priests, and only three were assigned to the region that included Virginia.[76] Brennan then sought the opinion of Edward Stephens, director of the Society for the Propagation of the Faith, who reported that most of the camps were in the Shenandoah Valley and recommended that a priest be assigned to the parish nearest each camp to say Mass on a weekday.[77]

On September 26, 1933, Brennan met with his consultors to determine how to respond to the influx of Catholics from other states into these camps.[78] He then circularized his pastors about the camps within their parishes. Writing from Lynchburg on October 31, 1933, Edward Tearney reported two camps within his parish, one near Bedford and the other at Spout Spring, each with 200 men, about half of whom were Catholic. He was arranging to say Mass every Sunday at Spout Spring and have the men from Bedford driven in to Lynchburg.[79] Six weeks later, Edmund C. Kiefer in Danville said there were two camps about fifty-five miles away, at Bassett and Scottsberg. The one had 450 Catholics out of 600 and the other 101 out of 175, but he could not visit the camps on Sundays. A Vincentian priest, however, had agreed to live in the camps, if his provincial approved.[80] Martin in Roanoke was also concerned about the Bassett and Scottsberg camps and thought he could say Mass in them on Saturdays, which seemed to be agreeable to the men.[81] Altogether, Brennan reported to the consultors in December, there were sixty-one CCC camps in the diocese with 1,400 Catholics.[82] On February 20, 1934, Brennan met with his consultors to discuss a proposal from the regional director of the CCC that he appoint a reserve chaplain for the camps. The consultors at the time, however, made no suggestions.[83] This was Brennan's last act as bishop.

Soon after Peter Leo Ireton became coadjutor bishop of Richmond, he appointed as chaplain to the camps Father Eugene P. Walsh, who served until 1939, when he was replaced by Julius Schmidhauser.[84] The chaplain's main task was to coordinate the efforts of the pastors within whose territories the camps were located. Through the late 1930s, reports continued to flow in to the bishop on the pastoral care of these workers. When gathering statistics on African American Catholics in white parishes, in 1937, for instance, Philip Brennan in Virginia Beach reported there were eight, "all CCC boys."[85] But it was difficult to keep up with the new demands on the priests. In

November 1938, Joseph Brennan in Danville informed Ireton that there was a CCC camp "on the outskirts of our parish, 76 miles distant" with forty Catholics. Since it was only thirty miles from Blacksburg, he suggested that the priest there take charge.[86] The difficulty was that Blacksburg was itself a mission of Wytheville.[87]

The Depression had strained the limited resources of the diocese. The decade of the 1930s had begun with Brennan's optimistic program for increasing the number of parishes and schools. As the decade progressed, he had to curtail many of his projects. What, of course, ended the Depression for the nation and especially Virginia was the coming of World War II. But the stress of those years had a more immediate effect on the diocese, for it was while dealing with the new burden of providing for the CCC camps that Bishop Brennan suffered a stroke from which he would never recover.

CHAPTER 23

Peter L. Ireton as Coadjutor, 1935–1940

When Andrew Brennan arrived in Richmond as bishop, he was just short of his forty-ninth birthday. He celebrated the silver jubilee of his ordination to the priesthood as the bishop of Richmond. A little more than seven years later, he was an invalid incapable of governing the diocese. Peter Leo Ireton's coadjutorship, on the one hand, built upon some of Brennan's administrational reforms, but, on the other, marked a return to rural evangelization through a roving mission band, abandoned since van de Vyver's administration.

BRENNAN SUFFERS A STROKE
AND IRETON BECOMES COADJUTOR

On February 20, 1934, immediately after the consultors' meeting to discuss the appointment of chaplains to the CCC camps, Brennan departed for Norfolk, where he was admitted to St. Vincent's Hospital for a bad cold the next day. On February 26, just before noon, he had what was described as a "bad spell." The sisters immediately notified Leo Gill, the chancellor in Richmond, who arrived late in the afternoon and described Brennan as "very weak but able to talk." The bishop's condition deteriorated and, during the evening, he had a "worse spell" that led to his "loss of speech." Gill immediately administered "Extreme Unction, Holy Viaticum & Last Blessing." This began Brennan's protracted illness that would last twenty-two years.

He remained at St. Vincent's until May 5, 1935, when he went to Mercy Hospital in Scranton, from which he returned to St. Vincent's on September 8. This became a pattern. A report in 1941 put it succinctly and tragically: "Bishop Brennan's condition has remained substantially the same. Does not read; cannot write; spends nine months at St. Vincent's Hospital Norfolk and three months—summer—in Mercy Hospital Scranton. Each hospital paid two hundred per month out of the cathedraticum. Bishop Brennan feels he is subject to the canonical laws of residence."[1] In other words, Brennan still regarded himself as the bishop.

As he had been after Bishop O'Connell's retirement, Felix Kaup, the vicar general, was again appointed administrator in August 1934. But again he was passed over as bishop of Richmond. On July 27, 1935, Archbishop Amleto Cicognani, the apostolic delegate, notified Father Peter Leo Ireton, the pastor of St. Ann's Church in Baltimore that he was coadjutor bishop of Richmond. Asking that secrecy be preserved until the official announcement, he stated: "You will have full episcopal jurisdiction in the Diocese of Richmond as long as the Bishop is incapacitated. I may add that Bishop Brennan has been informed of the aforementioned intention of the Holy Father and seemed to be very much pleased with the arrangement."[2] Ireton's appointment, as Brennan's, was obviously due to Archbishop Michael J. Curley's influence, to the chagrin of Brennan's Roman classmate, John J. Kelliher of St. Peter's Church, who publicly proclaimed he should have been coadjutor.[3]

On September 23, the Consistorial Congregation issued a decree officially naming Ireton coadjutor.[4] On October 23, he was consecrated in Baltimore by Archbishop Curley, assisted by Thomas C. O'Reilly of Scranton and James Hugh Ryan, bishop-elect of Omaha. Born in Baltimore in 1882, Ireton received his seminary education at St. Charles College, Ellicott City, Maryland, and at St. Mary's Seminary. Ordained in 1906, he then attended the Apostolic Mission House run by the Paulists at the Catholic University of America. He had been in the Baltimore entourage that attended the silver jubilee of Sacred Heart Cathedral in Richmond and the opening of St. Joseph's Villa in 1931. St. Ann's, his parish in Baltimore, was, incidentally, the parish where both Cardinal Lawrence Shehan, later archbishop of Baltimore, and Bishop John J. Russell, Ireton's successor in Richmond, grew up.

IRETON'S DIOCESAN ADMINISTRATION

On November 6, Ireton was met at the Richmond railroad station by an honor guard of the Knights of Columbus and escorted to the cathedral. That evening, he attended a banquet held in his honor by Kaup, after which he summoned the consultors to a meeting in his hotel room. There he presented them with a rescript, as the secretary recorded, "adding to his coadjutorship the rights of Resident Bishop and apostolic administrator. This meant the cessation of Msgr. Kaup's vicar-generalship. The Bishop requested that no more publicity be given these matters than the law requires."[5]

Although Brennan had supposedly been informed of all these arrangements, he did not take his retirement from power gracefully, as an entry in the diocesan *acta* indicates:

> apparently . . . the Bishop did not appreciate the apostolic administration character of the Coadjutor Peter L. Ireton on his coming to the Diocese Nov. 6, 1935. Bishop Brennan sought to make important changes prior to the coadjutor's coming, e.g. to send Msgr. Kaup, V.G. from the cathedral after 30 years to pastorate at Lynchburg [where Edward Tearney had died in October]; to make Bishop Ireton rector of the cathedral; to make Monsignor Waters of Norfolk V.G. etc. etc. All these Bishop Ireton prevented.[6]

Stories abound that, whenever Ireton visited Brennan, the bishop would point two fingers at him and one at himself to indicate he was still in charge.[7] Soon after arriving in Richmond, Ireton sought Curley's advice. As he had done earlier with Brennan, the archbishop instructed Ireton to write a will to the archbishop of Baltimore. He then told him to pick as pastor for Lynchburg whomever he wanted, and use his consultors and other priests he could trust. Finally, he also recommended that he consult Kaup.[8] Ireton named William Meredith to Lynchburg and retained Kaup as both his vicar general and rector of the cathedral, positions Kaup held until his death in 1940, in spite of Ireton having many reservations about his services.

Almost as soon as Ireton took office, he found difficulties with Kaup's financial administration. While Brennan had handled some accounts, Kaup had overseen diocesan investments, for which "there was apparently no *record.*" While Ireton made a point that he had no "complaint or criticism of anyone," in February and March, 1936, he personally "took over the handling of the deposit and check books, from the hands of Msgr. Kaup." Almost a year later, he and Kaup went into deposit boxes in two separate banks, where he found that the records had been kept, not in "book record of investments," but "each fund was in an envelope, with captions written on the outside of each." Only in April 1937 was Ireton able to get further financial files from Kaup's office.[9] Although Ireton had received from Brennan full power of attorney late in February 1936,[10] he was obviously displeased with the financial administration of the diocese. Paradoxically, though he was so critical of the freedom Brennan had given Kaup, in later years he himself developed the habit of leaving signed, blank checks behind during his many trips either to Florida or to the Poconos.[11]

DIOCESAN STRUCTURE AND INTELLECTUAL OUTREACH

Ireton built upon the diocesan structure Brennan had initiated. He accepted, if he did not actually promote, some projects, but in other areas he took more of a lead, especially in the religious education of his people. In October 1936, he announced the establishment in the diocese of the Confraternity of Christian Doctrine (CCD), organized nationally in 1933 with an episcopal committee named in 1934.[12] He had arranged for Miriam Marks, the national director of the CCD, to visit each of the five deaneries of the diocese to assist in establishing religious discussion clubs in each parish.[13] He appointed Edward Kilgalen of St. Joseph's Church in Petersburg as diocesan director. Each pastor was to appoint a leader of the discussion club who, in turn, was to invite eight to ten adults to join. On November 9, Ireton himself attended the Richmond meeting, at which Marks spoke of the work of the CCD throughout the country.[14]

On a wider, more cultural level, Ireton invited Fulton J. Sheen, professor of philosophy at the Catholic University, to lecture in Richmond. Announcing the lecture at the auditorium then known as the Mosque, on January 27, 1937, Ireton urged his priests to have their people come and to invite non-Catholics.[15] Sponsored by Ireton and the Catholic Business and Professional Men's Club of Richmond, Sheen drew a crowd of 4,000. Introduced by F. W. Boatwright, president of the University of Richmond, he denounced Marxism, a constant theme in his writings and speeches.[16] He returned again to the Mosque in April to speak on "The Divine Sense of Humor." His speeches, usually on the themes of the dangers of communism and the value of democracy, became annual events in the Mosque until 1940.[17] Sheen's oratory in Virginia was not limited to Richmond. In May 1941, Thomas B. Martin, pastor of St. Andrew's in Roanoke, informed Ireton that the manager of the American Theater had offered the facility to Sheen on any Wednesday. The mayor would be on the stage, and Martin hoped the bishop could attend.[18] Later named a bishop, Sheen had a popular television show, "Life Is Worth Living," that sometimes upstaged the popular comedian, Milton Berle. Though diminutive in stature, his glittering eyes, humor, and articulate explanation of Catholic teaching and the dangers of communism perhaps did more than anything else in the 1950s to make Americans realize Catholics might not be so bad after all.

Sheen's lectures were only part of the program to show Richmond's people how compatible the Church was with American culture. On November 17, 1939, the Catholic Business and Professional Men's Club that had cosponsored the lectures also joined Ireton in having an open forum at the John Marshall Hotel on "the Catholic Church and Dictatorship." The speakers were Elizabeth Morrissy, professor at the College of Notre Dame of Maryland, John Cronin, S.S., professor of moral theology at St. Mary's Seminary in Baltimore, Raymond A. McGowan, assistant director of the Social Action Department of the NCWC, and Wilfrid Parsons, S.J., editor of *America*.[19] Ireton also invited Bernard Hubbard, S.J., the Alaskan missionary known as the "glacier priest," to lecture in Richmond in April 1940.[20] Although Hubbard's lecture may have been considered "secular," it fit in with the diocese's efforts to show the contribution of Catholicism to the nation.

But Ireton's promotion of speakers was not limited to those with a religious message. In the spring of 1938, he wrote to his clergy urging them to make a pulpit announcement to get a good turnout to hear Postmaster General James Farley, a Catholic, speak in the Mosque.[21] What preaching had been earlier, now the lecture in the theater attracted large audiences of Catholics and Protestants, especially if accompanied, as Hubbard's had been, by a motion picture. Radio was already making its inroads into this medium of communication.

Television would all but destroy it. In 1939, Ireton himself had a program on radio, "From the Bishop's Study," the first in the diocese's Lenten series.

IRETON'S STATE OF THE DIOCESE ADDRESS IN 1936

When Ireton assumed the coadjutorship in 1935, he found ninety-seven diocesan and twenty-three religious order priests spread out over fifty-eight parishes and fifty-four missions. He also had fourteen seminarians. By 1953, he would have established thirty-one more parishes, some of which had already been missions. These eighty-nine parishes would be served by one hundred and eight diocesan and one hundred and forty-two religious priests, and he would have seventy-six men in the seminary. The number of Catholic schools would increase from thirty-five to sixty-three. More significantly, the Catholic population would grow from 37,366 to 103,407. Most of this new growth was in northern Virginia and most occurred after World War II.[22] Such development would, of course, have occurred regardless of who was bishop, but Ireton would preside over the greatest increase in Virginia's Catholic population up to that time. But in 1935, he could not have foreseen that.

In a brief article for the American Catholic Mission Board in July 1936, Ireton painted a bleak picture of his diocese. What was needed was "money and priests," for if the money was there to maintain parishes and support priests, "the vocations are here." He estimated that the population was "at a standstill," due to "migration and lessened birth-rate." The Chamber of Commerce recently reported "that there are more than five hundred thousand more native Virginians residing in other States than there are natives of other States residing in Virginia." Some urban parishes had "dwindled to dependency in the industrial upset, with its cessation of opportunity for work." Some rural parishes had such a small population "that the revenue must be insufficient to afford the priest anything but a precarious support." As an example, he noted that "within forty miles of the National Capital, there are three resident priests, each with two Missions; these have been established many years; in all this territory of nine centers, there are but six hundred souls. The distances between these nine places defeats any suggestion of combination." He judged that approximately ten towns with populations over 5,000 were served once or twice a month by a priest who lived between twenty-five and seventy miles away. He was particularly worried about those towns with colleges and teachers schools, for "in practically every one of the many Virginia Colleges, an ever increasing number of young men and women, Catholics from the North, are being enrolled." Turning to the "negro population of Virginia," he noted there were only four parishes, in Richmond, Norfolk, Alexandria, and Portsmouth. Altogether, he estimated that less than 3,000 of Virginia's African Americans were Catholic.[23] Ireton's list of concerns provided the agenda he followed for the first half of his tenure in office. He would again field a diocesan mission band to reach rural Virginia. But the groundwork for such a freewheeling group of Catholic evangelists had a precedent in Virginia.

Evangelizing Rural Virginia: David Goldstein's Campaign

One of the most interesting efforts at evangelization of Virginia came from David Goldstein, who toured the state in July of 1933. A convert from Judaism and a former socialist, Goldstein and Martha Moore Avery, like himself a convert and former socialist, won the support of Cardinal William O'Connell of Boston in 1917 to form the Catholic Truth Guild and engage in lay preaching. They had a car custom-built, originally with a sounding board to amplify their voices, and painted the papal colors of white and gold. By the time Goldstein asked Brennan for permission to come to the diocese, Avery had died, and Goldstein's car was now an open Buick with loudspeakers.[24] Brennan readily welcomed Goldstein, who had already conducted successful campaigns in Florida, Alabama, and North Carolina and had the warm endorsement of Bishop Thomas J. Toolen of Mobile.[25] Goldstein carefully targeted the cities he would visit and would depend on the local Catholic pastors to look for suitable outdoor sites for his preaching. By the middle of April, he sent Brennan a list of Virginia priests to whom he would appeal and said he hoped to begin late in June after completing forty-three "meetings" in North Carolina.[26]

By early May, Goldstein had received favorable responses from most of the pastors, but F. Joseph Magri, promising to advertise the meetings in Norfolk, feared arousing anti-Catholicism in Portsmouth. Goldstein noted that "there is no reason to fear trouble anywhere for our work is a positive setting forth of what Catholics believe and not an attack upon the belief of others." He had encountered trouble only once and that was in Sacramento, California, from communists.[27]

By the time Goldstein came to Virginia as part of a four-year tour of thirty-one states, he had developed a program of six lectures to be delivered over six consecutive evenings:

(1) The Credentials of the Catholic Church
(2) The Catholic Church and the Toiling Masses
(3) Christ: Who Is He?
(4) The Iconoclasts and Mary
(5) The Catholic Church and the Family
(6) The Catholic Church and Birth Control.[28]

After his lectures, he would remain to answer questions and to find people interested in becoming Catholics. These he would refer to the local priest. He and his assistant, Theodore H. Dorsey, began the Virginia tour with two meetings in Danville, then three in Lynchburg, and three in Elmwood Park in Roanoke. Goldstein himself described the setting in characteristically immodest terms: "An audience of a thousand persons greeted the speakers at the first meeting who came to witness the novelty of laymen commissioned by the Bishop and priest to meet all inquirers for information regarding the Catholic Church and who had been advertised as ready to meet all objections to her teachings and practices." By the third meeting in Roanoke, he had a crowd of 1,500.[29]

From Roanoke, Goldstein drove to Fort Monroe, whose pastor, Richard B. Washington, arranged for a meeting in Phoebus. Washington was so impressed that he asked Goldstein to return, and the two became "very much attached to each other." Goldstein found his host "young, not well, very priestly but pessimistic." Apparently unaware of Washington's treks around the country just a year before, Goldstein remarked: "I hit him hard for his disregard of his Washingtonian inheritance after outlining how it could be coined into advantage for the Catholic cause. He knows not as much about Washington as one would expect him to know. Nice fellow, needs stabilization."[30] At Norfolk, he held three meetings, followed by two in Hopewell, an address in Fredericksburg, and two meetings in Alexandria. He completed his tour in Winchester.[31] In August, he wrote an account of his mission in *The Pilot*, the newspaper of the archdiocese of Boston, and sent a copy to Brennan. By that time he was in Lincoln, Nebraska, but he was to be in Washington in October, when he suggested the possibility of holding three meetings in Richmond.[32] Goldstein was a showman and virtually indefatigable. At the age of sixty-three, he did all his travel in his "lecture car" long before the days of air conditioning. In 1938, he wanted to return to Virginia, but found no interest.[33] One reason was that the diocese had itself organized its own mission band the previous year that virtually duplicated his approach, but with priests giving the lectures and waiting around to answer questions.

THE DIOCESAN MISSION BAND

Ireton himself was a product of the Paulists' Mission House in Washington, and, contrary to what O'Connell had decided, on March 18, 1937, he announced the formation of the mission band the following fall.[34] Then a problem arose. He had also said that St. Mary's Church would be closed so that the mission band could use it as its headquarters but had failed to inform Father Ignatius Remke, O.S.B., the pastor. Remke first learned from visitors to the church during Holy Week that the parish was to be closed. He was understandably upset.[35]

Only on April 20 did Ireton directly address Remke and the St. Mary's parishioners. After tracing the history of the parish from its founding in 1848, he notified them officially that the parish would close to make way for the mission band. Since he would publish the letter in the *Catholic Virginian*, he instructed Remke to read it at all the Masses, but not to "go outside the text of the letter, or attempt any comment on it."[36] The situation then became more rancorous. Remke planned a formal closing of the parish with a sermon in German on the Fourth of July, the day before he formally left office. In his invitation to Ireton, he pointed out that neither "you nor Bishop Brennan has ever appeared publicly in this church nor has either of you ever spoke of this little congregation. Since you have never attended a service here while the church was alive, would you wish to attend what a secular priest recently called, 'The funeral service of St. Mary's?'"[37]

Ireton bristled at the remark. First of all, he wanted the celebration shifted to the previous Sunday, June 27, and demanded that the sermon be only in English, since "there is no German or Irish, Black or white—to me they are Catholics." As to the remark of the priest about "funeral services," he could only comment that "for the sake of religion and of St. Mary's and the Mission Band appeal and work, such priests are not aiding." In response to the charge that he had never "appeared publicly at St. Mary's," he bluntly stated: "I do not recall that in the year and a half I have been in Richmond, that you ever so invited me."[38] Remke accepted the change in schedule, but added that "I never invited you, Bishop, because I did not think it was customary, much less necessary. Had I invited you, I really think that you would have laughed at me,—the idea of a priest inviting the Bishop to visit a church in his own diocese."[39] On June 27, Ireton spoke after the Mass, thus ending almost ninety years of the only German national parish in the diocese.

On September 1, 1937, Ireton formally announced the beginning of the mission band, with Edward Stephens, Conrad Hoffner, and Patrick Tierney, as the first members.[40] Only a few days before he was to preach at the formal inauguration of the band, he was absent on one of many trips to Scranton—and recovering from poison ivy that he got while playing golf.[41] He nevertheless made it back in time on September 12 to preach at St. Mary's. Recalling the history of the earlier band under van Ingelgem and Thomas Waters, he noted that the present one would have as its task the evangelization of the unchurched, black and white, in rural Virginia.[42] Traveling in a motor chapel, at this point a specially outfitted trailer with loudspeakers, the missioners would crisscross the state to many areas that had never seen a priest.

Stephens informed Vincent Waters, the chancellor, of one of the more moving experiences of the band during the 1939 season. Near South Boston, he had discovered a family of converts who had fallen away from the Church. The son in the family, however, had agreed to drive his mother eighteen miles to attend Mass at South Boston in the mayor's courtroom over the firehouse. This, wrote Stephens, would be the first Mass in the area since "your Uncle Tom" had been there.[43]

The mission band was not the only Virginia Catholic agency concerned with evangelization. In March 1938, Richmond hosted the annual convention of the Rural Life Conference. Addressing the convention, Arthur Taylor, the diocesan director of rural life, noted that in the diocese 93 percent of Catholics resided in urban areas. Such an imbalance provided a challenge for the diocese to reach out to the rural areas. He suggested holding evening services in mission chapels, for, he stated, "In the country the people are inclined to be more gregarious on Sundays, they love to go to meeting or to church and we would probably find that they care little for the sophisticated humor of Charlie McCarthy, Jack Benny and the other Sunday radio comedians who are depleting our city churches on Sunday nights." A good service on Sunday night, he concluded, might induce the people to attend Mass on Monday morning.[44]

The following summer, Ireton gave a lecture on the history of the diocese. He began with a history of the Brent family at Aquia and the placing of the large bronze crucifix there, but, like others, he then conflated the site with that of the earlier Jesuit mission. He wanted to show how deep Catholicism's roots were in Virginia, but how small the Catholic population was. Out of a total population of 2,100,000, Catholics accounted, by his reckoning, for "only one to five-hundred," most of whom lived in urban areas. He queried what would have happened had the earlier mission band continued. The new missioners, he said, would have as its field "the whole diocese . . . from the smallest village where there is not even a mission or a station to the Cathedral itself," where they would conduct a two-week mission, one for Catholics and the other "a series of lectures or mission to non-churchgoers." He envisioned that their work would "react upon the priests of the Diocese generally to make one and all of us more mission-minded, more conscious of the need of bringing those outside the fold into membership of the Church."

Perhaps alluding to complaints from men like Nicholas Habets in Portsmouth who worked with African Americans, he added that "the fact that these secular priests [on the mission band] have shown and will continue to show an interest in members of the colored race will likewise react favorably in the minds of many of our secular priests who in the generations gone by at least felt that the work among the white[s] was exacting enough without branching out in the tremendous field of more than a half million colored people."

The band had begun its work the previous September in Danville, Ireton continued, and along the North Carolina border. From Danville, he noted, east to Suffolk, north to Lynchburg, northwest to

Roanoke, and northeast to Petersburg, there was not "a single resident priest." In the fourteen counties of south central Virginia, there was a population of 300,000, of whom only 500 were Catholic. In addition to this, there were 600,000 African Americans within the diocese, only one third of whom lived in cities, and of these only 2,500 were Catholics. He attributed the slow growth of the Church among both white and Black to the high emigration from the state, as he had already written to the American Catholic Mission Board a year before. He was determined to make rural Virginia the field of work for the diocesan mission band.

For seventeen years, the mission band used "St. Mary of the Highway," its motor chapel, which, upon its retirement, was designated "Number One." Funds for it had been raised by popular subscription, including a generous donation from St. Ann's Church in Baltimore.[45] In 1953, Ireton again employed a popular subscription to purchase a new trailer. The missioners asked for no stipends for either missions or retreats but only for special occasions like Forty Hours.[46] From March to September, they crisscrossed the diocese and, during the winter months, resided at St. Mary's, from which they were available for parish missions or other needs. Their support came from annual collections in all the parishes during September.

Over the years, the composition of the band changed. John C. Donovan had replaced Tierney by 1940. In June 1943, Vincent Waters joined the band, to be replaced as chancellor by Robert Hickman.[47] By that point, Vernon Bowers and Chester Michael had taken over from Donovan and Hoffner.[48] Before the mission season in 1945, when Waters was named bishop of Raleigh, Ireton named Joseph Hodges as the director.[49] Future members would include John Cilinski, Walter Malloy, and Carl Naro. On one occasion, the mission band had an unusual encounter, this time not with Protestants who had never seen a priest, but with members of a quasi-religious order whom the priests had never seen.

In August 1942, Fathers Michael and Bowers were conducting a mission in Chase City, south of Farmville, when two women dressed as sisters came into town in a pickup truck and bought cold drinks in several drugstores. The older of the two had "mannish, weatherbeaten features." Witnesses became suspicious, wrote down the truck's license number, and the state and local police unsuccessfully set out to find them. Bowers then informed Vincent Waters, still the chancellor.

Waters, in turn, asked Father Thomas Albert, O.F.M., in Emporia to investigate. As it turned out, the two women were well known to Father Joseph Brennan and his associate, Joseph Wingler, in Danville, as the "Sisters of Christ the King."[50] The "sisters" were in fact not a religious order but a group of women living in community under the leadership of Sister Teresa, who had originally been a Carmelite nun in the Oak Lane Monastery in the archdiocese of Philadelphia but had never bothered to ask for dismissal from the order. Ireton had, nevertheless, accepted them for work in Danville, where they taught Sunday school and supported themselves by farming.[51] Always desperate for personnel, he seems to have tolerated their unusual lifestyle until 1951, when *Time* published a picture of a new outfit Sister Teresa had Hattie Carnegie design for them to replace the Carmelite habit they had been wearing. Ireton was furious and refused to allow them to have a chaplain.[52] This colorful group came to an end in 1974, when, reduced to Sister Teresa and one other member, it was disbanded. Its Danville property was sold to the Goodyear Rubber Company.

IRETON AND PREWAR URBAN CATHOLICISM

Ireton's intention was to have the roving mission band evangelize rural Virginia, after which he would establish rural parishes, much in the manner O'Connell had attempted. In 1938, the Precious Blood Fathers obtained permission to purchase a house in Charlottesville as a retreat for their own men.[53] By June 1939, with headquarters at St. Richard's in Crewe (later renamed St. John's), in Nottaway County, they had missions at Meherrin and Farmville in Prince Edward County and in Charlotte County.[54] At the end of World War II, they would extend their work yet further, even into urbanized northern Virginia.

Ireton's concentration on rural Virginia, however, may also have led him to neglect the cities, with the notable exception of parishes for Black Catholics. His correspondence for the period indicates little concern for the growing urbanization of the diocese. In the absence of episcopal guidance, Thomas Rankin of Alexandria, dean for northern Virginia, took the initiative. With single-minded determination, according to Edward Stephens, his successor in Alexandria, he insisted on purchasing a tract of land at U.S. Route 50 and Thomas Street as the site for St. Thomas More Church, which opened in 1938, with Edwin Lee as the first pastor.[55] Late in 1937, Rankin attended a consultors meeting and "called attention to the rapid development along the Lee Highway in Arlington." Ireton "stated that Fr. Rankin is the best acquainted with conditions in that section, therefore he should continue to get information, and keep the bishop acquainted with developments and prospects." At the same meeting, the consultors rejected Ireton's proposal that the clergy conferences should be split, with one meeting in Richmond and the other in northern Virginia.[56]

Regardless of Ireton's interest or lack thereof in urban development, by 1940 northern Virginia had a total of eight churches with resident pastors: St. Mary's, with the mission of Sacred Heart in Groveton, St. Joseph's and St. Rita's in Alexandria; St. Charles, St. Thomas More, and St. Agnes in Arlington; St. James in Falls Church, with a mission in El Nido; and St. Mary's in Fairfax Station, with missions at St. Timothy's in Centreville and St. Anthony's in Baileys Crossroads.

On the eve of World War II, the Norfolk area remained virtually unchanged from 1924. In the late 1930s, pastors were principally concerned with having to tend to the Navy base in the absence of chaplains. The parishes, moreover, were in a state of flux. When Thomas Scannell arrived at Sacred Heart in the summer of 1937 for his first assignment after ordination in Rome, the pastor, Thomas Waters, had just died, and the pastor of St. Mary's, Edward Brosnan, would die in 1940. The city was in the throes of the Depression, with the only employment in the area at either the navy yard or the Newport News Shipbuilding and Drydock Company. With little guidance that first summer, Scannell decided to take up a census of the parish. He started a boys basketball team for which he begged used uniforms from Holy Cross, his alma mater, and Fordham—only Fordham responded. By then, St. Mary's was rapidly declining in membership.[57]

The two parishes in Roanoke, in the meantime, were in an uproar because the central governing body of the Knights of Columbus had dismissed the officers of the local council for insubordination. This, in turn, became intertwined with the dedication of a monument to John Lynch, the founding pastor of St. Andrew's. In January 1937, James Gilsenan, pastor of Our Lady of Nazareth, had protested to Ireton about the Knights' action. Both he and Thomas Martin, pastor of St. Andrew's, attested that the dismissed officers were good Catholics and "respected citizens." After a visit to Roanoke, Ireton intervened with the Supreme Grand Knight, Martin H. Carmody. "For the welfare of the Church, not only in Roanoke but in all Virginia and for the well being and advance of the Knights in this jurisdiction," he wrote, "I ask the Supreme Council to lift the suspension now in force nearly a year and in addition, the reinstatement of the group expelled."[58] Carmody, however, remained adamant.[59]

That fall, the dispute worsened as those Knights who remained in good standing began distributing invitations to the dedication of a monument for Lynch. Gilsenan was particularly incensed, for, though he had served as Lynch's assistant, he had received no invitation and saw it as a scheme to win general approval for the expulsion of the other Knights.[60] Aside from illustrating internal tension within the Knights, the case depicts how passage of time can alter a parish's memory of a previous pastor. Lynch, it will be recalled, was removed from Roanoke for mishandling parish finances. Despite his strained relations with some Knights of Columbus, however, Ireton would make use of them in the Church's campaign against communism.

The Threat of Communism, Mexico, and the Spanish Civil War

In the spring of 1937, Ireton had distributed Pius XI's encyclical, *Divini Redemptoris,* condemning communism. In June, he announced the formation of a committee of priests under the chairmanship of John A. Kelliher to instruct the people on the dangers of communism. He was acting in accordance with a letter from Bishop Karl J. Alter of Toledo, then subchairman of the Social Action Department of the National Catholic Welfare Conference. Each deanery was to develop a cadre of a few informed laymen to disseminate information. He had already asked the Knights of Columbus to have the Grand Knight in each of the ten cities where there were councils to work closely with the pastors to distribute questionnaires and information on communist tactics, particularly in the labor movement.[61]

While Catholics were united with other Americans in seeing the danger of communism, however, two other issues were more divisive, the persecution of the Church in Mexico and the Spanish Civil War.

Although the Mexican government had ceased its persecution of the Church and toned down its anticlericalism since 1935 in an effort to assuage President Roosevelt,[62] it still imposed severe restrictions on the Church—the number of priests was limited, no foreign priest could serve in Mexico, and the bishops were forbidden to operate seminaries. Throughout the revolution, the Mexican government had, moreover, waged a propaganda campaign in the United States to show that it was merely trying to liberate the people from the tyrannical hold of the Church. In Virginia, Methodist Bishop James Cannon readily defended Mexican actions.[63]

In November 1935, at their annual meeting, the Catholic bishops appointed a Committee for Mexican Relief. Chaired by Archbishop Curley of Baltimore and consisting of two other bishops, the committee then appointed Ireton and two more bishops to form "The Catholic Bishops' Commission, Incorporated, for Mexican Relief." Although the new commission gained papal approval, it had been formed without the knowledge of the apostolic delegate, Archbishop Amleto Cicognani, or the administrative board of the NCWC, which accused Curley of exceeding the bishops' mandate. As a result, Curley resigned from the NCWC.[64] Ireton left no recorded reaction to the disbanding of his commission, but he usually preferred a more low-key approach to such a situation than his irascible metropolitan did. By the late 1930s, moreover, another issue on the international scene occupied the attention of Americans, Catholic and non-Catholic alike. And, on this issue, Ireton would be more vocal.

In 1936, General Francisco Franco launched his campaign against the Loyalists, or supporters of the Spanish Republic, which had the backing of the Soviet Union. There were atrocities on both sides. The Republicans massacred numerous Catholic clergy and religious, and Franco's forces slaughtered Loyalists. The American people were divided. Supporters of the Republic organized the Abraham Lincoln Brigade to fight against Franco, while many Catholic bishops and their people identified the cause of Franco with that of the Church.

At their annual meeting in November 1937, the American bishops issued a statement in support of the Spanish hierarchy, in which they declared:

Tragic are the true facts of the religious persecution in Spain by men who before the world sought to appear in the role of vindicators of human rights. You tell us that ten bishops, thousands of priests and religious, and tens of thousands of laymen have been put to death, often with unspeakable cruelty, because they were active in teaching the world to promote the works of the Gospel. Your words horrify us who are wont to accept liberty of conscience and freedom of speech as an axiom.[65]

Quoting this passage, Ireton announced a diocesan collection in January 1938.[66] Acknowledging Richmond's contribution, John J. O'Shea, the director of the America Spanish Relief Fund told Arthur Taylor, the diocesan director of the Society for the Propagation of the Faith, that "it would seem that the populous city of Barcelona would soon be in the hands of *General Franco and his Christian forces*" [emphasis added].[67] During that year, Ireton sent $1,300 to the Relief Fund, followed by $700 a year later.[68] This was hardly a princely sum, but it was generous for a small diocese like Richmond's.

The Mexican persecution of the Church and the Spanish Civil War had caused domestic strains between the American Church and large segments of the American population. The two issues also became intertwined with Richmond's nascent ecumenical movement. Early in 1939, Edward Stephens was preparing to address the Conference of Jews and Christians in Jacksonville, Florida. A Jacksonville man complained to Ireton, however, that a rabbi on the same program had supported the Loyalists in Spain and praised the work of the government in Mexico without ever expressing any sympathy for the state of the Church in either country. He urged that Stephens point out what communists in Spain and officials in Mexico had done to Catholics. He added the ominous note that "lack of sympathy for Catholics or aiding the cause of their persecutors calls for condonation of the persecution of Jews. If this is done *vigorously* good may come out of the conference; if not, Jewry will be using a Catholic priest."[69]

Vincent Waters, the chancellor, replied that he appreciated the writer's concern, but noted that not only was Stephens a good speaker but was also an attorney licensed to practice before the Supreme Court.[70] Stephens, for his part, seems to have been unaware of any reservations about his ecumenical work. In fact, on his way to Florida, he stopped off in Atlanta to address Methodist seminarians at Emory University.[71]

The Spanish Civil War, which ended in 1939 with Franco's victory, was not a major issue in the life of Virginia Catholics, but the significant support for the Republic by Americans seemed to indicate that the Church was still associated in the American mind with repression and Fascism. In a short time, they would have to rally to the flag again—this time to fight against Fascism and Nazism.

CHAPTER 24

Virginia Catholics in War and Peace

World War II would change Virginia and Virginia Catholicism as no other event in history up to that time. As they had done so many times in the past, Catholics rallied to the flag. Virginia became the site of expanding military bases and of government projects. Its prisoner-of-war camps placed a further strain on Richmond's clergy. When the war was over, Virginia was a far different state than the one Bishop Ireton described in 1936. Its population soared during the war and did not subside, for unlike the years after World War I, the United States did not retreat into isolationism, but remained involved in international affairs as the world entered the Cold War. Before the war there was, however, the first threat that northern Virginia might be severed from Richmond, as Washington was made an archdiocese.

ADJUSTMENTS IN THE DIOCESE ON THE EVE OF THE WAR

The Church in Richmond had long enjoyed good relations with the Protestant and Jewish communities. When Pope Pius XI died in February 1939, Edward N. Calish, the rabbi of Beth Ahabah, and Irving May, the president of the synagogue telegraphed Ireton that the congregation "mourns with you the passing of your revered and beloved leader Pope Pius the Eleventh. The world has lost a Prince of Peace and Humanity an earnest friend."[1] T. Rupert Coleman, secretary of the Richmond Ministerial Union, together with several Jewish rabbis as guests, likewise passed a resolution expressing their condolences.[2] Ireton's ecumenical overtures, albeit somewhat hesitant, were paying off in terms of good community relations. Soon the Church had a new pope, Eugenio Pacelli, who took the name Pius XII. He would shepherd his flock through the horrors of the war.

Before hostilities had broken out, Richmond already was experiencing the distant rumblings of war. In 1937, the American College in Louvain was forced to close, so Louis Smet asked Ireton if he should return to parish work in the diocese. Ireton, however, thought he would be better placed at the Catholic University teaching moral theology.[3] Smet was making plans to return to the United States when he died in August 1940—he was fifty-seven years old.[4]

Closer to home, Richmond lost another Louvain alumnus and three-time administrator of the diocese, Felix Kaup, who died in March 1940. Ireton now summoned Leo Ryan from Blessed Sacrament in Norfolk, where he had been pastor since 1919, to become vicar general and rector of the cathedral. But the northern part of the diocese would continue to be affected by the growing importance of Washington.

In 1940, the Holy See established Washington as an archdiocese, but left Archbishop Michael J. Curley of Baltimore as ordinary of both sees. This may well have been the Vatican's reaction to President Roosevelt's failure to establish diplomatic relations with the Holy See. After years of negotiation, he had compromised by naming Myron Taylor as his personal representative to Pius XII, an appointment that did not need Senate approval. But then he proposed that the pope name as the first archbishop of Washington Bishop Bernard Shiel, who had been the auxiliary to the late Cardinal George Mundelein of Chicago, a strong Roosevelt supporter. Leaving Curley, an opponent of the president, in charge of both archdioceses may have been a subtle way of letting Roosevelt know that, if he compromised on establishing diplomatic relations, he could expect to have no voice in suggesting a candidate for the nation's capital.[5]

Ireton had his own reaction to the new archdiocese. Commenting to Curley that Archbishop John Carroll might well grieve to see the daughter outgrowing the mother, he provided a rare glimpse of his attitude toward the New Deal. "There has been enough red over the Capitol," he wrote; "I seem to see a new shade of Red over the Capital. May it come quickly."[6] Curley would never receive the cardinal's red hat, and Ireton was probably being simply flattering in suggesting it, but the growth of Washington and its establishment as an archdiocese would have an effect on northern Virginia.

VIRGINIA CATHOLICS PREPARE FOR WAR

As World War II approached, Virginia's Catholics began to prepare. Sometime in the fall of 1939, Monsignor George T. Waring, chancellor of the military ordinariate in New York, sent Ireton a memorandum about the need for army chaplains. There was at the time only one chaplain for every 1,200 men, and, by policy, not law, the War Department appointed only one Catholic to three Protestant chaplains. He noted the need to recruit more Catholic chaplains before January 1, 1940, and pointed out that of the 1,075 in the Reserve Corps, only 225 were Catholic, of whom only a third was likely to pass the physical examination. As evidence of the situation, he mentioned that in recent field maneuvers involving 26,000 men at Manassas, there were twenty-four chaplains, of whom only one was a Catholic priest.[7]

Ireton had already begun his own preparations. In July 1940 he wrote Virginia's senators and representatives urging them to enact legislation exempting priests, religious, and seminarians from the draft. He encouraged the five diocesan deans to write their representatives.[8] In October, he instructed the pastors in the Richmond area to have all men eligible for the draft register with the Knights of Columbus. His purpose was twofold: "that contact may be kept with our Catholic men through their term of service. And for future reference, the record of Catholic service to our Country, can be more readily identified."[9] This proposal resulted in the postwar publication of a list of all Virginia Catholics who served in the military. Virginia's Catholics would soon have another chance to prove their patriotism.

Even before the United States entered the war, however, Virginia Catholics were already displaying their faith and patriotism. In May 1939, the Knights of Columbus of the Washington area and the Catholic societies of the District of Columbia, Maryland, and Virginia held their first annual field Mass at Arlington National Cemetery. Ireton, the honorary chairman, preached. Two years later, he celebrated the first Solemn Pontifical Mass offered in the cemetery.[10] By the summer of 1941, war preparations were brought closer to home.

The Precious Blood Fathers on Lewis Mountain in Charlottesville were officially appointed to be observers to watch for enemy planes flying at night.[11] No one bothered to ask why any such planes would be flying over Charlottesville.

PEARL HARBOR AND RICHMOND'S CHAPLAINS

When the Japanese bombed Pearl Harbor on December 7, 1941, one of Richmond's priests, Speer Strahan, a former professor at the Catholic University, was an eyewitness. He had "just begun mass when the Japs passed directly over us, and began their deadly work." He was on his way to say a second Mass, when he "passed directly through a second attack, and didn't miss anything except being hit." For days after the bombing, he was busy

> going out into the field, confessing our boys, and giving them communion on the spot, fasting or not. The Japs have been good to us, no mission was ever like it. Imagine me coming up on a group, hearing their confessions, then twenty or thirty men kneeling in a circle, uniting themselves with each other and God by the three acts and Our Father, then receiving Holy Communion. I have given over 400 communions in the field since December 7th, and have done it, because every man is in periculo.[12]

Ireton had the letter published in the *Catholic Virginian*, but in a slightly edited version, for Strahan was prone to make ethnic slurs.

A few weeks later, Strahan added some further details of the bombing for Thomas Rankin in Alexandria, where he had been in residence. "On the fateful Sunday," he wrote, "we enjoyed the unenviable distinction of being shelled not only by the Japs but also by our own navy. . . . Anyone who was here Dec. 7th will never blame the French for being surprised by 'blitz' warfare; it happens so quickly everything is over before you realize it." He had "expected the interest in religion to die down," he continued, "but no! it holds up, and even seems to be rising above what it was."[13]

Strahan was not the only Richmond priest to serve as a chaplain during the war. He was joined by Thomas Scannell, Eugene Walsh, Louis Flaherty, Edward Johnston, James H. McConnell, and William

Byrne.[14] Religious priests who had served in the diocese and who became chaplains included Vincent Campbell, O.S.B., Michael G. Downing, C.SS.R., Cletus Henry Foltz, C.Pp.S., John Stanton, C.Pp.S., and Alexis St. Onge, S.S.J.[15] Flaherty would win the Silver Star for bravery under fire during the Italian campaign in October 1944.[16] At home, the diocesan mission band temporarily abandoned its work among Protestants to focus exclusively on the Catholic soldiers at Camp Pickett.

THE EFFECTS OF GOVERNMENT EXPANSION ON VIRGINIA

On the domestic front, the wartime build-up permanently altered the face of Virginia. Norfolk's expansion, arrested after World War I, would continue during the war and the postwar years. Northern Virginia experienced its first real growth since the 1920s, as the Federal government expanded first its activities during the New Deal and then its war preparations, stemming from the Pentagon, completed in January 1943. So much had the Federal bureaucracy expanded into Virginia that, on March 25, 1942, Senator Patrick A. McCarran of Nevada proposed that the government reannex the region to the District of Columbia.[17] Ireton wrote to the senator strongly opposing the proposal, which, he presumed, would make the area part of the archdiocese of Washington. Reannexation, he argued, would have dire consequences for what he hoped would be the area's growing Catholic influence on the state. Arlington County and Alexandria, he estimated, already accounted for one-sixth of all the Catholics in the state.[18] Ireton also enlisted the aid of Senator Harry Byrd, who spoke with McCarran against the proposal.[19] There the matter ended, but northern Virginia's Catholic population during the next thirty years would dwarf that of the rest of the state, and, when Patrick O'Boyle became the first archbishop of Washington in 1947, Ireton again became alarmed that the region would be separated from Richmond.

As the nation mobilized for war, Ireton had a special admonition for his priests. In May 1942, he received word from the National Catholic Welfare Conference that priests would be granted special rationing cards for purchasing gasoline "for essential use." The bishop added his own codicil to "this auto, rubber and gas question." The law imposed a forty-mile-an-hour speed limit. "Just because we are priests," he said, who had been given a "preferred rating," "our observance or non-observance will be subject to observation and criticism both of our own people and outsiders." He, therefore, recommended that "Mass schedules [be arranged] between the Home church and the Mission churches on a wider spacing, since to observe the forty-mile limit will require more time." He concluded with a practical note for those who might be tempted to drive faster: "it will not be edifying to have any of our priests picked up for speeding."[20]

On an issue affecting the future of the diocese, Ireton had to withdraw Harold Nott from graduate studies at the Catholic University to become director of Catholic Charities, of which his brother, Walter, had been founder. The shortage of priests made it necessary for everyone, even those who were not chaplains, to sacrifice.[21]

Parish Life in Wartime Virginia

During the war, parish life maintained a semblance of normalcy. In Richmond the Catholic Theater Guild, founded in 1940 under the direction of Father Robert O'Kane, assistant at St. Paul's, continued its productions, particularly its popular Passion Plays at The Mosque. The guild was a major outreach to Richmond's young Catholics and was closely linked to the Legion of Mary.[22] When Father John Hannon later succeeded O'Kane as director, he added a fifteen-minute Saturday evening program on WRNL.[23] But there were also signs that the urban population of Richmond and elsewhere was in flux.

To gain a more accurate assessment of his population and to provide for the religious education of Catholic children not in parochial schools, Ireton initiated the new apostolate of home missionaries. He began in Richmond, where the Xaverian Brothers had just ceased teaching in the cathedral boys school in 1942 and vacated their residence. First, he tried, unsuccessfully, to have the Mission Helpers of the Sacred Heart from Towson, outside Baltimore, take over the residence, to engage in parish visitations and other work in the neighborhood.[24] He then recruited the Missionary Servants of the Most Blessed Trinity from Philadelphia, the Trinitarians, to be distinguished from the men's order of the same name that would also work in the diocese.[25] One of the Trinitarians' chief tasks in Richmond was taking a census of the cathedral and other parishes as an aid to pastoral care and future development. By July 1944, they had concluded 11,438 home visits and found 1,398 Catholics in the area; they had also discovered 1,289 Catholics in the neighboring regions of Westhampton and Lakeside-Hermitage, data that would lead to Richmond's postwar western development.[26] Reacting to the new phenomenon of two working parents in a family, they also opened a day nursery and could be seen driving children to and from school or other activities—a rare sight when few religious women drove cars.[27] In 1949, they began similar work in Norfolk, where they resided at Blessed Sacrament.[28] Later still, they opened a residence in Winchester.

Wartime growth in northern Virginia led to other stopgap measures. Early in 1943, Ireton again turned to the Mission Helpers. The population of Alexandria had almost doubled during the war, Ireton told their superior, and Arlington County was among the fastest-growing areas in the country. Some 1,500 Catholic children had no access to parochial schools, so he begged the sisters to organize catechetical work, take a census of the area, and perhaps open a nursery, as the Trinitarians did in Richmond. In October 1943, the Mission Helpers agreed to send three sisters to Alexandria, but they did not begin a nursery.[29] In 1950, they would also open the Sacred Heart Mission Center in the former rectory of St. John's Church in Crewe, the mission headquarters for the Precious Blood Fathers.[30] While the Trinitarian sisters and Mission Helpers were lessening the burden on the diocese's priests, particularly in urban areas, Norfolk was a harbinger of a developing urban crisis.

During the war, the diocese of Richmond had one of its first experiences of exodus to the suburbs—an urban blight that had already beset larger dioceses. In May 1944, Ireton announced the closing of St. Mary's High School in Norfolk. John Baecher, the diocesan attorney and a member of the first graduating class of 1914, protested the decision.[31] While Ireton, too, lamented the decision, he pointed out that the area around the church was becoming a red-light district and was no longer safe for the sisters. The enrollment in the high school had dropped to only sixty-two students, but he proposed retaining the grammar school and having the sisters reside near Blessed Sacrament. The decision to close the school was part of a larger problem, he explained, "and if that area cannot be salvaged by public spirited citizens of Norfolk, I fear for the future of the church itself. It is the sad story of thousands of beautiful churches in cities everywhere."[32] Ireton had already had a similar experience in Richmond, where St. Peter's closed its school as Catholics moved away from downtown. In the postwar years, the diocese would still face this problem, but, for the time, its attention was focused more on problems directly related to the war.

PRISONERS OF WAR IN VIRGINIA

During the war, Virginia also became the site for another pastoral activity—prisoner-of-war camps. In this instance, the Vatican seemed to be particularly interested in the plight of Italian prisoners. On June 12, 1942, Archbishop Amleto Cicognani, the apostolic delegate, personally visited 108 Italian sailors detained in the Federal reformatory near Petersburg after they attempted to scuttle their ships in American waters. He confirmed nine of them, said Mass, and the next morning ate breakfast with them and distributed gifts.[33] In September 1943, he asked Ireton to report on and possibly visit the 700 Italian prisoners he had heard were housed at Camp Lee, outside of Richmond.[34] Robert Hickman, the chancellor, responded, however, that no Italian prisoners had yet arrived at Camp Lee but that Italian diplomats, formerly housed in the Hotel Ingleside, near Staunton, had been transferred to the Shenvalee Hotel in New Market.[35] Cicognani asked for the number of diplomats and expressed the wish to make a confidential visit to them.[36] His overture may have been related to the negotiations then going on between the Vatican and the United States about a separate Italian peace and declaring Rome an open city.[37]

By late November, Ireton informed Cicognani that Italian prisoners had been transferred to Camp Hill and Camp Patrick Henry, near Newport News. Together with one chaplain and two of his own priests, he had himself spent three hours in the camps, where he found great need for Italian books, missals, and other literature. In this Mr. Obici, "the peanut king of Suffolk," had offered to help. The bishop also reported another alarming development. "It seems," he wrote, "that the International YMCA is the only agency that can operate as liaison between the prisoners and their relatives back home or with relatives here in America." As a result, many prisoners had not received mail for months. In the meantime, Ireton recommended that

Cicognani request assistance from one of the Italian Trinitarians in Hyattsville, Maryland.[38]

Cicognani consulted the Trinitarians but recommended that Ireton write to their provincial directly, requesting a priest. But the delegate had picked up on Ireton's comment about the men receiving mail. "It is not true," he stated, "that the International YMCA is the only agency for communications between the prisoners and their families. The Vatican Information Service is approved for this work among prisoners in this country." Under separate cover, he sent Ireton several thousand message forms to be distributed to the prisoners.[39]

By March 1944, Father Paul Paolucci, a Redemptorist Army chaplain, was visiting the 1,000 prisoners at Camp Hill and Camp Patrick Henry. But as the only chaplain for the port of embarkation, he had heard 1,200 confessions of departing servicemen in the previous ten days. Since the Italian prisoners had already modified existing buildings into chapels, Ireton, therefore, proposed that Cicognani visit the camps to bless the chapels and to say Mass for the internees.[40] With the permission of the provost marshal,[41] on Saturday, April 15, Cicognani visited Camp Patrick Henry. The next day, he said Mass at Camp Hill and then returned to Camp Patrick Henry to bless the new chapel and to give benediction.[42]

While the extant correspondence with Cicognani indicates more of a concern for Italian than German prisoners, there may well have been reasons for this other than his ethnocentrism. Several priests working with German prisoners of war submitted mixed reports. In 1943, Strahan, then in Aliceville, Alabama, said many German prisoners at a local camp were still pro-Hitler.[43] Early in 1945, Ireton requested more information on this from other priests working with German prisoners. From Roanoke, Father J. Harris Findlay replied that, while a few prisoners went to Mass in the nearby camps, they seemed to be under pressure from the other prisoners to remain away.[44] From Rock Castle, Father Denis Strittmatter, O.S.B., complained that Nazis still dominated the prison camps and prevented Catholics from coming to Mass.[45] Yet, in the previous fall, John Brochtrup in Petersburg had informed Ireton that the German prisoners were "generally very agreeable & peaceful." They were working on farms, and more could be employed but for the regulation that at least ten must work together at a time.[46]

CATHOLIC EFFORTS ON THE DOMESTIC FRONT

Not only did Virginia's Catholics march off to war, but those who stayed at home played a major role in the war effort. The National Catholic Community Service (NCCS) became a member of the United Service Organizations (USO). Before Pearl Harbor, St. Mary's in Alexandria had already organized an NCCS unit. In addition to providing entertainment and meals for service personnel, the parish Boys Club, the Golden Gloves champions of the Washington area, staged boxing matches for the servicemen.[47] In an age when the parish was still very much the focus of social life, young Catholic men had to prove their masculinity. On September 21, 1941, Ireton dedicated the Catholic Service Club in Norfolk. Within a few months, clubs were functioning in Newport News and Petersburg, where nearby Camp Lee had 20,000 men.[48] In Richmond, the parishes took turns providing meals for servicemen in the basement of St. Peter's, and many young women joined forces with the Knights of Columbus to provide dances and other entertainments.[49] Hampton Roads Naval Operations Base received a new chapel, dedicated on February 15, 1942, by Bishop John F. O'Hara, C.S.C., then auxiliary for the Military Ordinariate and later archbishop of Philadelphia. Camp Pickett, near Blackstone, had four Catholic chaplains and substantially increased the Catholic population of Nottoway County. Through the influence of the USO and at the request of the Army, Mass was said at Blackstone's Memorial Armory and also in the auditorium of Farmville State Teachers College.[50] As would be noted after the war, these service clubs not only cared for Catholic military personnel but also provided many Virginians with their first association with Catholics.

On the home front, Americans were made to feel the pinch of the war with scrap drives. In 1942, Lynchburg led the nation with the scrap metal collected, and Holy Cross Academy's students, 150 strong, led all the city's other schools by collecting 60,621 pounds of scrap, an average of 440 pounds per student.[51] Virginia's Catholics, whether in the military service or at home, were proving their willingness to sacrifice for the war effort.

Even in the emergency of the war, however, the problems of racism did not go away. In June of 1943, Nicholas Habets of Our Lady of Victory in Portsmouth wrote Ireton with a special request.

The Norfolk Naval Yard had just put in new shifts. As a result, he proposed a new Mass schedule that

> would give a number of the colored workers a chance to go to Mass if there would be a Mass. They do not want to go to St. Paul's because they do not want to be pushed into a restricted area. Moreover, they do not want to go into a white church in the late afternoon when so many whites are on High St.

He, therefore, asked to say three Masses, at 5:45 A.M., 7:30 A.M., and 11:30 A.M.[52]

The war also had an effect on one of the diocese's more revered institutions. Early in 1940, The *Norfolk News Index* reported that St. Vincent's Hospital, the oldest in Norfolk, might have to close for lack of paying patients.[53] The Federal government had earlier recommended enlarging the hospital with government funding, but that proved impossible on the original site. The trustees procured land composed of a former airfield and soybean field on Kingsley Lane and Granby Street. In May 1944, the new building, renamed De Paul Hospital, admitted its first patients.[54]

De Paul was one of several Catholic hospitals that proved beneficial to, and that benefited from, the victims of the Nazi persecution of the Jews. Because of a dramatic decline in qualified medical school graduates, many residencies and internships in Catholic hospitals were not filled. De Paul took in at least one Jewish physician fleeing from Hitler's Europe.[55]

In the meantime, the city of Rome had fallen to the Allies on June 4, 1944, two days before D-Day. This set in motion a series of events that would plague the American Church in the postwar years—a new outbreak of anti-Catholicism. During the war, Harold Tittmann, Myron Taylor's assistant, was named chargé d'affaires, an official diplomatic title, and lived in the Vatican. Within a few months of the Allied occupation of Rome, however, Taylor attempted to resign. By May 1945, the State Department recommended that the office of personal representative be terminated as soon as hostilities ceased.[56] Probably sensitive to this growing sentiment, Monsignor Giovanni Battista Montini, the substitute secretary of state, in February sent a form letter to all the American bishops, detailing the work the Vatican had done during the war in providing for refugees, arranging for the sending of messages from prisoners and giving asylum to escaped British and American prisoners in the Vatican.[57]

By this time, the war was drawing to a close. On May 7, 1945, Germany surrendered to the Allies. On August 11, after the United States dropped atomic bombs on Hiroshima and Nagasaki, Japan sued for terms of surrender. As the victorious American forces entered Tokyo and raised the flag over the United States Embassy on September 8, Father Eugene Walsh, a priest of the diocese and at that time a lieutenant colonel, was present and offered the prayer:

> On this historical day, as peace comes to all mankind, we humbly entreat the abundant blessings of Almighty God on all nations throughout the entire world. Long and valiantly have men fought and died to see this day of peace; and now may the Lord God order our days and deeds in His peace forever and ever. Amen.[58]

BRENNAN RESIGNS AS BISHOP AND VIRGINIA RETURNS TO PEACETIME ACTIVITIES

As Virginia Catholics returned to peacetime activities, however, they underwent another transition. On April 14, 1945, Bishop Brennan, unable to read or speak for a decade, finally resigned the see of Richmond. He was assigned the titular see of Telmissus and named an "Assistant at the Pontifical Throne." He would live on until May 23, 1956, but Ireton now automatically became bishop of Richmond.[59] On May 15, 1945, moreover, Ireton consecrated Vincent Waters, then on the diocesan mission band, as bishop of Raleigh. Ireton was now completely in charge, but he lost one of his most stalwart aides. To replace Waters as head of the mission band, he named Joseph Hodges, former assistant at St. Andrew's in Roanoke.

As Virginia's men and women came home from war, the diocese issued *For God and Country,* a pamphlet listing by parish the Catholic men and women who had served in the armed forces, the result of Ireton's foresight in having all those eligible for the draft register with the Knights of Columbus. Altogether, 6,996 men and 241 women had served in the military. Included was a separate roster of the 215 who gave their lives in the conflict.[60] Virginia's Catholics had again proven they were Americans by shedding their blood in one of the nation's wars.

POSTWAR GROWTH

Virginia's Catholic population grew dramatically after the war. Whereas Ireton had reported in 1936 that far more Virginians had emigrated from the state than people from other states had immigrated into it, in the postwar years the trend was reversed. He now faced the danger of an ecclesiastical annexation of northern Virginia to Washington. In 1947, Archbishop Curley of Baltimore had died. In June, Ireton told Archbishop Cicognani that "gossip is rife that the limits of the Archdiocese of Washington will be extended somewhat into Maryland and even into Virginia. It is this last that concerns me." He explained to the delegate his earlier interventions with both Senator McCarran and Representative John McCormick of Massachusetts, the House majority leader, to prevent the reannexation of Arlington and Fairfax counties to the District of Columbia in 1942. Now, he argued,

> if the limits of the Archdiocese of Washington should in our time be extended into Northern Virginia, the act might well be considered civilly and politically in Virginia, as an entering wedge, *occasioned by the Church's action,* for the re-annexation of the old Virginia-District area politically. And such an interpretation would mar the work for the Church, my predecessors and I have sought to do to advance the Faith in the Diocese of Richmond.

About six weeks earlier Ireton had informed Cicognani at a meeting in Wheeling that the diocese "had grown from 40,000 souls in 1936 to 70,000 in 1947. Not all, but most of this increase has been in Alexandria, Arlington and Fairfax Counties. There are at least 23,000, perhaps 25,000 in those three places."

Ireton then outlined the specific development of the parishes in Arlington and its ramifications for the financial and political stability of the diocese. In 1936, Arlington had one parish, St. Charles, with two resident priests and one mission, St. Agnes. But, he continued, "in 1947, in Arlington, there are St. Charles—three priests, St. Agnes—two priests, St. Thomas More—three priests, Our Lady of Lourdes—two priests, Blessed Sacrament—two priests, and Our Lady Queen of Peace (for the Negro) one priest. Except for the last named, each of these churches has additional relief from Washington from one or

other Religious house." St. Ann's was already in the planning stages between these Arlington parishes, and the diocese had already purchased
"two additional locations for future development." In both Alexandria
and Falls Church, the population had more than doubled.

In terms of education, in 1936, St. Charles had the only parochial
school; now both St. Thomas More and St. Agnes had schools, with
Thomas More already constructing a new wing. But Ireton had another argument—the role of the diocese of Richmond in the South.
Ireton asserted:

> The added strength of the Church in Northern Virginia means
> a stronger diocese, numerically, financially, influentially. (In the
> Virginia Assembly of 40 Senators and 100 Assemblymen, there is
> but one Catholic [John A. K. Donavan]. He is from Arlington.)
>
> The stronger the Church is in Richmond, the stronger will she
> be in the South. If Arlington County were to be subtracted from
> the Diocese of Richmond in favor of Washington, this diocese
> would be set back 20 years, and I think, the cause of the Church
> likewise in the Southland.

While Ireton realized the Vatican may not have had any intention of
placing Arlington County under the jurisdiction of the archdiocese
of Washington, he deemed "it better to enter these reflections before
the contingency, rather than after an accomplished fact." He enclosed
for the delegate's perusal his earlier letter to Senator McCarran and
Senator Byrd's response.[61]

Whether the Vatican actually intended this new division is unknown. On November 27, 1947, it named Patrick J. O'Boyle as the
second archbishop of Washington. Two days later, Francis P. Keough
succeeded Curley in Baltimore. For the time being, northern Virginia
remained part of the diocese of Richmond.

In the meantime, Ireton confronted a problem related to this new
growth—the need to establish diocesan credit in order to purchase
new property. To meet this need, he sequestered funds, such as those
at St. Peter's from the sale of the school property, on which the diocese could borrow for future land purchase.[62] He also restructured his
diocesan administration to reflect the new, growing population centers. While he retained Harold Nott as the diocesan director of Catholic
Charities, by 1950 he created regional directors, with Norfolk under

Richard H. Rivard, Portsmouth under L. Joseph Baran, Newport News under John T. Cilinski, and northern Virginia under Thomas P. Scannell. He appointed Louis Flaherty as superintendent of schools and Carroll T. Dozier, then at St. Peter's, as director of both the Propagation of the Faith and the Catholic Students Mission Crusade and of the new office of vocations.

Ireton also increased the number of deaneries to six. Frederick Lackey in Martinsburg, James Gilsenan in Roanoke, and Joseph Govaert in Portsmouth remained "vicars forane," and Edward Stephens had replaced the deceased Thomas Rankin in Alexandria. William Gill of Newport News was now appointed vicar forane of the new Peninsula Deanery and James P. Gacquin of Staunton to the new Valley Deanery. In 1946, Ireton had also appointed John Daly as the first lay editor of *The Catholic Virginian,* which was still a weekly publication. As he organized his central diocesan structure, moreover, he took other steps to promote lay initiative.

In February 1946, Ireton informed the women of the diocese that he was establishing in every parish a branch of the diocesan Council of Women, an affiliate of the National Council of Catholic Women, founded in 1920. The new diocesan council was not to supersede existing parish organizations but to coordinate their activities.[63] Over the next two decades the organization, linked regionally to each deanery, formed a series of standing committees dealing with topics such as decency in motion pictures, social action, child labor, and juvenile problems. Its Committee on Legislation addressed issues such as segregation, sterilization, right-to-work laws, child welfare, and Sunday commercialism. As Ernest Unterkoefler, the chancellor, informed a correspondent in 1961, the diocesan Council of Catholic Women performed in Virginia much of the same functions as the Pennsylvania Catholic Welfare Committee.[64] In the meantime, Virginia's Catholics continued to increase well beyond what Ireton had reported to Cicognani in 1947.

In July 1952, Justin McClunn, the vice-chancellor, provided a researcher with statistics on the growth of the Catholic population. From 1946 to 1952, the diocese had grown from 69,660 Catholics to 97,256.[65] A month later, McClunn provided additional information, with the observation that "You will probably note that the number of children under 13 of age is high in proportion to our total population; this is due to the large number of young families in Alexandria,

Arlington, and Fairfax."⁶⁶ Northern Virginia continued to be the region most influenced by this population explosion. Four years later, McClunn indicated this as he tried to recruit seminarians from All Hallows College in Dublin. By 1956, he said, the Catholic population had soared to 130,000.⁶⁷ The diocese, of course, continued to include eight counties in West Virginia, but the increased population in northern Virginia in such a short time would soon be mirrored in the Norfolk-Virginia Beach area.

POSTWAR PASTORAL ISSUES: REFUGEE RESETTLEMENT

One of the most pressing issues confronting the postwar American Church was the care and resettlement of people displaced by the war. In October 1947, Ireton appointed Chester P. Michael, a member of the mission band, to chair a committee to relocate displaced persons within the diocese, particularly in rural areas. On Michael's recommendation, Ireton then asked each pastor to name a man and woman as cochairs on the parish level to help the central committee process applications.⁶⁸ By March 1949, 233 members of the diocese had applied to sponsor 486 adults and their 342 children.⁶⁹ But the work of Virginia's Catholics was not limited to sponsoring refugee families. On the parish level, the Holy Name Societies visited the newcomers, helped them adjust to their unfamiliar surroundings, and assisted them in getting to Sunday Mass.⁷⁰

By 1950, 1,200 Catholic refugees had resettled in the diocese.⁷¹ Among these was Father Alexander Goldikovskis from the diocese of Riga, Latvia, who joined Father Isadore McCarthy, C.Pp.S., in Crewe to take care of five counties where refugees had settled. Goldikovskis' knowledge of Latvian, Lithuanian, Polish, Russian, and German also made him in demand to go to other parts of the state where European displaced persons had relocated.⁷²

VIRGINIA, A FIELD RIPE FOR CONVERSIONS

The resettlement of refugees was but one of the issues confronting the diocese as it returned to peacetime. In 1946, Ireton found himself dealing with the cases of women who married servicemen who never returned after their discharge. Despite some of these pressing problems, some priests found the postwar years a providential time for gaining converts. World War II had created a situation like that at the time of the Civil War. In Alexandria, one priest, probably Edward L. Stephens, the pastor of St. Mary's, asserted before a clergy conference that "there was never a time in the history of the United States when our country was more ripe for conversion." The war had transported northern Catholics into small southern Protestant towns that had seen few Catholics. Southern Protestant men were stationed in Catholic centers of the North. As a result, much of the prejudice against the Church had broken down. Stephens then outlined how his fellow clergy could capitalize on this by-product of the war. For one thing, he suggested greater sensitivity to the non-Catholic party in a mixed marriage, for in such marriages there was hope of a conversion.[73]

How successful the convert campaign was is difficult to determine, but the number of adult baptisms steadily increased from 568 in 1940 to 1,144 in 1955, with a slight decrease only in one year. Virginia was also in the midst of a "baby boom," with infant baptisms rising from 1,233 in 1940 to 5,826 in 1955. There were more mixed marriages than those between Catholics. In 1944, the first year mixed marriages were listed separately, they accounted for 962 out of 1,571; in 1955, they numbered 876 out of 1,366.[74] While Stephens encouraged outreach to the non-Catholic party, this did not diminish the early ecumenical contacts that Stephens had made.

IRETON'S STYLE OF LEADERSHIP IN INTERFAITH MATTERS

During and after the war, Ireton personally enhanced the Church's presence in Virginia life. In 1943, he accepted the invitation of the superintendent of the Virginia Military Institute to give the baccalaureate address.[75] In 1949, he was invited to give the baccalaureate address at the University of Virginia. Although Father Edmund Walsh, S.J., founder of Georgetown University's School of Foreign Service, had addressed the graduates a few years earlier, Ireton learned that, in the 1890s, Cardinal Gibbons had been invited, but it "raised such a furor that the committee had to withdraw its invitation."[76] Conscious of the historic significance of the invitation, Ireton gave the address in full episcopal regalia and then informed William Weedon, then professor of philosophy, that he had endorsed the check for his honorarium to the newly founded Newman Club.[77]

By and large, however, Ireton was a bishop who let things happen. In regard to the diocese's nascent ecumenical work, he simply filed away a clipping from *The Brooklyn Tablet* for February 1945, reporting that Archbishop John T. McNicholas of Cincinnati had prohibited priests from taking part in interfaith conferences.[78] Early in March, he received an invitation from Rabbi Edward Calish of Beth Ahabah Synagogue, one of the original organizers of Richmond's Conference of Christians and Jews, for a priest to take part in the annual Institute of Religion.[79] He replied immediately that his policy was to leave it to individual priests to attend such functions, but pointed out that the proposed date, Easter Monday, was a difficult day for most priests.[80] At this time, a disagreement was arising among the bishops about Catholic participation in the Conference of Christians and Jews.[81] On the one hand, Ireton seemed to opt for a policy of allowing his priests to engage in such activities as long as he was not asked to give official approval. On the other, he agreed to be on the honorary board of governors for the annual Brotherhood Week, sponsored by the Conference of Christians and Jews, in February 1946.[82]

CONTINUATION OF THE
CATHOLIC COMMUNITY SERVICE CLUBS

While Virginia seemed ripe for a harvest of converts, the diocese continued to share responsibility with military chaplains for the pastoral care of military personnel. Some agencies created during the war remained in place. Ireton enlisted the assistance primarily of women in the diocese to participate in the operation of the National Catholic Community Service Clubs (NCCS), which had been part of the United Service Organization (USO). The USO had been disbanded after the war, but late in 1948 the Department of Defense authorized its reactivation, and the board of trustees of the NCCS had approved the reestablishment of the wartime relationship with it. At that time, the Virginia NCCS clubs were located in Alexandria and Norfolk.[83] Early in 1950, however, the government again disbanded the USO, but the hierarchy voted to continue the NCCS clubs. Norfolk was to receive the highest priority, but there were by then two USO clubs in Petersburg in danger of closing.[84]

The NCCS clubs in Petersburg had by 1951 taken on an ecumenical dimension. They had established a Hospitality House, on the board of which sat Father John Brochtrup, the pastor of St. Joseph's, a rabbi, and the president of the ministerial association. This arrangement grew out of earlier collaboration with the YMCA and Jewish organizations. The Hospitality House began providing similar services at Fort Lee, where the presence of many members of the Women's Army Corps drew servicemen from elsewhere.[85]

When the Korean War broke out in 1950, however, Ireton found he could not be as generous in having his priests serve as chaplains as he had been in World War II. Answering a request from Cardinal Francis Spellman, archbishop of New York and military ordinary, the bishop pointed out that five Richmond priests had served as chaplains during the war but that he was so shorthanded that he could spare only those who were in National Guard units that might be activated.[86] The Diocese would need all the priests it could find simply to staff the growing number of parishes.

Although the diocese could spare no priests for the Korean War, it had continued to staff many projects that began in World War II, such as the NCCS clubs. Military personnel now constituted a large segment of the diocese's Catholic population and would contribute to the movement toward desegregation in the diocese. But, most of all the bishop had to accommodate the booming Catholic population in northern Virginia.

CHAPTER 25

Postwar Population Explosion Hits Virginia

As Washington expanded in response to the nation's newfound status as a super power, government workers and military personnel poured into northern Virginia. To the south, Norfolk's navy base and other military installations in the area continued to grow. The nation enjoyed prosperity it had not seen since before the Depression. Virtually every family had an automobile, which gave people new mobility and added "car pooling" to the American vocabulary. What the railroad had been for the development of Virginia in the nineteenth century, the interstate system would be for the latter half of the twentieth. The advent of air-conditioning, moreover, made Washington and the southern states more habitable all year long. The diocese now faced a new Catholic population that was both mobile and affluent.

Coping with this new population required more parishes and schools and, of course, more priests, a need that Ireton partially met by inviting more religious orders of men to the diocese. To meet the educational demands of the newcomers, the diocese made a greater commitment to secondary education than in any other period. This necessitated the introduction of more religious orders of women. In view of this dramatic growth, Ireton needed assistance. In 1952, for the first time in the diocese's history, Ireton obtained an auxiliary bishop, Joseph Hodges, who had headed up the mission band. The diocese, however, continued to be plagued by lack of vocations.

SEMINARY RECRUITMENT

From 1935, the year Ireton became coadjutor, to 1953 the diocesan clergy had risen from 97 to 142,[1] but Ireton's letters to the diocese still noted the pressing need for vocations. In April 1946, he wrote that, of the eighteen men then in the seminary, only six were from the diocese.[2] By 1951, he reported most of his forty-eight seminarians were from the diocese.[3] In May 1953, he ordained three priests, Walter F. Sullivan,the future bishop, Anthony Malabad, and Floyd Keeler, a former Episcopal priest and grandfather, who had earlier entered the Catholic Church.[4] The following year, he ordained eight priests, the largest single class in the history of the diocese up to that date, but of them only two, R. Roy Cosby and Frank J. Hendrick, were from the diocese.[5] In 1955, he had sixty-five young men in various stages of seminary preparation but said he needed a hundred.[6] In view of the rapid development, particularly in northern Virginia, he had to find priests elsewhere.

RECRUITMENT OF RELIGIOUS ORDERS

Ireton now requested religious orders already in Virginia to expand their work and invited others to come. In 1940, the Franciscans had begun working in Emporia. In 1946, Ireton requested funds from the Church Extension Society to enable the Franciscans to found new missions in Clarksville and Tappahannock, later taken over by the Trinitarians.[7] In 1946, the Precious Blood Fathers, already working in Crewe and Farmville, sent Aloys G. Selhorst to St. Patrick's in Lexington as resident pastor. Only in 1953 did a new church replace the one dedicated by Gibbons in 1874.[8] In 1953, the Precious Blood Fathers also took over St. Anthony's in Falls Church. The Holy Ghost Fathers, who already staffed St. Emma's in Rock Castle, expanded their activities to run parishes in northern Virginia. In addition, Ireton recruited other religious orders to supplement his own clergy in parishes, the Stigmatines in Prince William County and the Carmelites on the Peninsula above Newport News. But, like his predecessors, he still had to look to Europe for priests.

In 1946, Father Ernest Dieltiens had been living at the Maryknoll Central House in Ossining, New York, for two years trying to start a permanent American mission and house of studies for the Congregation of the Immaculate Heart of Mary (C.I.C.M.), more familiarly known as the Missionhurst Fathers or, in Belgium where they were founded, "The Scheut Fathers." He and Ireton signed an agreement for Missionhurst to establish its American headquarters in Arlington in exchange for taking charge of several parishes. In October, Dieltiens informed Ireton that new priests would be arriving from Belgium, one of whom, Maurice du Castillon, would become resident pastor in Culpeper with missions in Orange and Gordonsville. Since Dieltiens's Belgian superiors had originally denied permission for their men to take up parish work, he explained that Culpepper was, strictly speaking, a mission.[9] On November 11, 1946, Ireton dedicated Missionhurst's new central house in Arlington. Joining him was Bishop James E. Walsh, pioneer China missionary and superior of Maryknoll, who would return to China, where he would be imprisoned. Originally intended as a place for the Belgian priests to learn English, the central house later became a novitiate.[10]

During the postwar period, some religious orders came to Virginia for the first time, primarily to establish seminaries for their own students. In 1945, the Capuchin Custody of the Stigmata of St. Francis established a house of studies, the Monastery of Our Lady of the Angels, outside Staunton.[11] Gradually, however, they took over several parishes. In 1954, the Missionary Servants of the Most Holy Trinity, the Trinitarians, also opened a major seminary, the Holy Trinity Mission Seminary, outside Winchester.[12] A year later, they staffed the new parish of St. Pius X in Norfolk and would later take over St. Elizabeth's in Colonial Beach. In 1960, they opened the Father Judge preparatory seminary, at Monroe, Amherst County.[13]

Virginia also received the first foundation of the Church's contemplative tradition. In November 1950, thirty-two members of the Order of Cistercians of the Strict Observance, the Trappists, under Owen Hoey, O.C.S.O., opened the Monastery of the Holy Cross in Berryville, near Winchester. Originally dependent on the abbey in Spencer, Massachusetts, Berryville became an independent abbey in 1958.[14] By the nature of their vocation, the Trappists would play no role in the development of parishes, but they provided a spiritual focus for the state's developing Catholic population.

Postwar Growth of Northern Virginia

In 1940, Alexandria, Arlington, and Fairfax had only eight parishes. Between 1946 and 1957, eleven new parishes were either founded or received resident pastors. By 1949, five new parishes had been established in Arlington and Alexandria alone. One of the first resulted from a request of several Black Catholics for a new parish. Ireton established Our Lady Queen of Peace with Joseph Hackett, C.S.Sp., as the first pastor. In September 1946, Ireton personally led the community in procession from the Dunbar Center, where they had temporarily worshiped, to the site of the new church at 19th and Edgewood Streets, where he broke ground for a new building, dedicated the next year.[15]

In 1946, Ireton also established Our Lady of Lourdes in Arlington, with Robert Beattie as the first pastor, not far from National Airport, and Blessed Sacrament in Alexandria, which took over St. Anthony's at Bailey's Crossroads as a mission. That same year, a group of parishioners met with Ireton to draw up the preliminary plans for St. Ann's Church in Arlington, which opened its doors in October 1948, with Dixon Beattie as the first pastor.[16] The two Beattie brothers, Robert and Dixon, it will be recalled, were natives of Falls Church. In 1949, St. Louis in Groveton, previously called Sacred Heart, received its first resident pastor and was separated from St. Mary's. These new parishes represented the first postwar growth out of Washington to Arlington and Alexandria, the nearest Virginia suburbs. What came next was the development of Fairfax County.

In 1950, St. Joseph's in Herndon, formerly a mission of St. James in Falls Church—and for a time of St. John's in Leesburg—was placed under the Holy Ghost Fathers, with Joseph Hackett, C.S.Sp., as the first resident pastor. Only in 1964, however, did the community build a new church to replace the small stone chapel erected in 1926.[17] A year later, St. James's other mission, St. John's, became a parish, and its location, El Nido, was soon swallowed up in the new, up-scale housing development that took the name McLean. By this time, the Missionhurst superiors had apparently overcome their reservations about staffing regular parishes and agreed to assign Paul R. Cauwe, C.I.C.M., as the first pastor.

Such rapid development caused changes in existing missions. In 1949, Martin T. Quinn, pastor of Blessed Sacrament, had St. Anthony's at Bailey's Crossroads as a mission. He now needed a larger church and wanted to use the existing land as a parking lot. By this time, Quinn had merely "heard" that the land had been donated by the seminary of the Episcopal diocese of Virginia, as long as it was used for a church; if it was not, it was to revert to the seminary. In 1954, the land was deeded back to the seminary. In transferring the property, Justin D. McClunn, the chancellor, wrote the seminary's treasurer that "this Diocese sincerely appreciates the courtesy of the Seminary's Board of Trustees through the years during which we have had the use of this property."[18] The old frame church on the land was sold to the Romanian Orthodox Church, and the new St. Anthony's Church, actually part of a new school, was completed in 1953 and assigned to the Precious Blood Fathers.[19]

The population was growing so swiftly that, in the summer of 1953, the deanery of northern Virginia had to be split. The first division covered Alexandria and Fairfax Counties south of U.S. Route 50 to Fredericksburg and Colonial Beach. The second division comprised Arlington County, Falls Church, and the territory north of Route 50 to the next deanery, headed by Lackey in Martinsburg.[20]

The automobile provided the key to northern Virginia's development, especially in Fairfax County. Thomas Scannell, fresh from a chaplaincy in the army, took advantage of the GI Bill to attend the Catholic University for one year and then became the founder and director of Catholic Charities of Northern Virginia. Like Rankin and others before him, he engaged in land speculation to purchase property for the diocese before its increase in value would make its cost prohibitive. In 1953, he founded St. Michael's in Annandale. But he was also concerned for education. He not only had a parochial school, staffed by the Sister Servants of the Immaculate Heart of Mary (I.H.M.), but had also purchased a parcel for a high school. In the meantime, he operated a fleet of school buses—at one time seventeen—to bring children to the school and convey others to the Catholic high schools in Washington.[21]

Other parishes in Fairfax County followed in rapid succession: Our Lady of Good Counsel in Vienna (1955), served by the Oblates of St. Francis de Sales, St. Leo The Great in Fairfax (1957), St. Bernadette in Springfield (1959). But the automobile and the newly constructed roads, especially the Capital Beltway and Interstate 95, enabled people to live yet further from Washington. Prince William County became the next site for development. St. Francis of Assisi opened in Triangle, near Quantico, in 1957. Next came Our Lady of Angels in Woodbridge in 1959 under the Stigmatine Fathers who already staffed All Saints in Manassas.[22]

Each of these new parishes had a parochial school, except Our Lady of Lourdes and Our Lady Queen of Peace. Of the previously existing parishes, only St. Mary of Sorrows in Fairfax Station lacked a school. On the eve of Vatican II, the population of the diocese had clearly shifted to the north.

POSTWAR DEVELOPMENT OF THE PENINSULA

The Norfolk-Hampton area lagged behind northern Virginia in the years immediately after the war. That would change with the completion of the bridge tunnel crossing Hampton Roads and as more relatively young military retirees moved into the region. Hampton, however, was one of the first areas to experience an increase in population, as the various establishments of the federal government and the Newport News Shipbuilding and Dry Dock Company continued to draw employees to the area. The diocese had already purchased property in the Wythe area and had leased it to the government to house female workers during the war. In June 1948, this became the site of St. Rose of Lima to which William P. Byrnes was assigned as pastor. The parish territory was carved out of St. Vincent's in downtown Newport News and St. Mary Star of the Sea at Old Point Comfort. Until a church was built in 1952, the congregation used the buildings left by the government. In 1949, however, the Benedictine Sisters from Bristow opened the parish school.[23] A year later, Julius O. Schmidhauser, pastor of St. Mary Star of the Sea, began to say Mass during the summer months in Buckroe Beach. By 1955, the community had built a chapel, dedicated to St. Joseph, and it became a year-round mission of St. Mary's until it became an independent parish in 1968, first under Father Edward Tobin and then the Redemptorists, who staffed the nearby Holy Family Retreat House.[24]

Further up the Peninsula in Warwick came the next development, due to the pioneering efforts of the Carmelites. Early in 1953, Norbert Piper, O.Carm., and his assistant, Frederic Manion, O.Carm., arrived to found Our Lady of Mount Carmel. From there, Piper took over St. Joan of Arc in Yorktown, originally founded by Father Chester Michael from Williamsburg. Except for the years 1963 to 1967, he remained at Our Lady of Mount Carmel in one capacity or another until the Carmelites left the diocese in 1990. In the fall of

1954, the Dominican Sisters of Nashville opened a parochial school. In 1956, Ireton gave land, originally intended as the site of the church, to the Poor Clares to open a monastery. In the meantime, the parish congregation worshiped in the Warwick High School auditorium and later in a theater until an "activities building" was erected in 1958 to serve as a temporary church. Later on, the Carmelites also established a mission in what became St. Jerome's in Newport News.[25]

POSTWAR DEVELOPMENT IN TIDEWATER AND RICHMOND

Across Hampton Roads, Norfolk and Portsmouth were experiencing their first major growth since World War I. In 1949, Ireton established the new parish of Christ the King in Norfolk, property for which had been purchased in 1924. A mission of St. Mary's since 1937, it was the first parish founded in the city since St. Matthew's in 1926. Conrad Hoffner was the first pastor, but he was succeeded in 1954 by Carroll T. Dozier, who also became dean of the Tidewater area. Dozier would virtually preside over the development of the Norfolk-Virginia Beach area until he became bishop of Memphis in 1971. In 1955, a second new parish began in the Little Creek area, St. Pius X, and was placed under the administration of the Trinitarians. The first pastor, Michael Giblin, temporarily resided at Christ the King.[26] In 1957, Ireton asked the Benedictines staffing the Barry-Robinson Home also to begin a parish, St. Gregory the Great. Father Urban Lux, O.S.B., director of the home since 1944, became the first pastor, and the community used the chapel of the home as their first church. In 1958, Lux was reassigned to the home and was replaced as pastor by Damian Abbaticchio, O.S.B., who had served at the home since 1945, except for two years. When land for the new church was purchased, however, it was over the border in Virginia Beach.[27] The next two decades, however, would far overshadow this initial growth.

SLOW DEVELOPMENT IN THE CITY OF RICHMOND

Despite the dramatic growth in the north and the beginning of expansion in the Norfolk area, Richmond itself had not yet developed. Aside from Holy Rosary and St. Gerard's (to be treated elsewhere),[28] Ireton founded only two parishes in the see city, Our Lady of Lourdes and St. Bridget's. Our Lady of Lourdes grew out of a praesidium of the Legion of Mary that met at the home of Mr. and Mrs. J. A. Lyons. In August 1943, the group was having weekly Mass at the Lakeside Community Center for what became a mission of the cathedral. Ireton, however, resisted creating another parish until the community numbered eighty. By "borrowing" people from other parishes, the community reached that quota, and Ireton appointed Thomas J. Healy as the first pastor. On October 29, 1944, the people gathered for the first time in a renovated farmhouse that served as their chapel, until the new church was finished in 1955 on a fifty-acre tract.[29]

Seven men paid Ireton a visit early in 1948 about establishing a parish in the "West End" on property the diocese already owned on Three Chopt Road. Again the bishop expressed reservations about the number of parishioners in the new area, but agreed to have the Trinitarian Sisters, stationed at the cathedral, take up a census. They discovered 150 Catholics in the area. The deciding factor for a new parish, however, was a bequest from Annie Irvin for $200,000 for a church named after her mother, Bridget Murphy Irvin. In May 1949, Ireton appointed Francis Byrne, the diocese's first superintendent of schools, as pastor of St. Bridget's, and the congregation began to attend Mass at Westhampton Theater in September until the new church was ready by May 1950. A parish school, staffed by Religious of the Sacred Heart of Mary, the Marymount Sisters, opened in 1951.[30] The sisters, moreover, would begin Marymount High School in 1953, as the diocese grew increasingly concerned for secondary education.

New Educational Institutions

The population spurt in both northern Virginia and the Norfolk area required new schools. In Arlington, the Religious of the Sacred Heart of Mary had already opened Marymount College in 1952. Later elevated to university status, it enrolled over 3,800 students by 1998. Most of the new parishes, moreover, had started parochial schools. But more secondary schools were needed. In the spring of 1947, Joseph Govaert, the pastor of St. Paul in Portsmouth, formed a committee consisting of Francis J. Byrne, the diocesan superintendent of schools, and Edward W. Johnston, pastor of Sacred Heart, to discuss a new central high school for Norfolk. Govaert had already purchased a tract near De Paul Hospital. Each of the parishes in the vicinity was assessed for the building: Sacred Heart, Holy Trinity, Blessed Sacrament, St. Matthew's, St. Mary's, and Star of the Sea in Virginia Beach. On September 17, 1950, Norfolk Catholic High School was formally dedicated. It was staffed by two priests, four Daughters of Wisdom, three Holy Cross Sisters, two Franciscan Sisters, and two Daughters of Charity.[31] This arrangement with several religious orders was necessitated by what would become a growing problem—insufficient personnel to meet growing demands.

In northern Virginia, five parishes, St. Ann, St. Agnes, St. Charles, St. Thomas More, and St. James, initiated plans for a new high school in the spring of 1952. Although new parishes had formed in the meantime, these were not involved in the building. The new school, named after Bishop Denis J. O'Connell, was to accommodate 1,500 students with the Sister Servants of the Immaculate Heart of Mary teaching the girls and the Brothers of the Christian Schools the boys.[32] In May 1955, 2,000 volunteers raised over $1 million within a month in a door-to-door solicitation.[33] In September 1958, the new school opened with 400 students. Gradually, the parishes, such as St. Michael's, Annandale, founded after the building began, also sent their students to O'Connell High School, when it became apparent that a second high school would not soon be built further out in Fairfax.[34]

CATHOLIC HOSPITALS

While the Catholic population was now principally concentrated in the northern part of the state, the diocese made no efforts to establish a hospital there. As early as 1941, Ireton was planning a hospital for Richmond, but that would have to wait until Russell's episcopacy. De Paul Hospital, after almost being closed in 1940, survived the war and broke ground for the Smith-Nash Memorial Wing to commemorate its centennial in 1956.[35] But the diocese also opened or took over hospitals elsewhere in the southern region.

In 1945, Harold Nott, then the assistant pastor of St. Paul in Portsmouth, negotiated with the Daughters of Wisdom to open Maryview Hospital, a structure originally built with federal funds.[36] In

1952, moreover, the diocese entered an agreement for twenty Bernardine Sisters to operate the 150–bed Elizabeth Buxton Hospital in Newport News, with its nursing school, under the new name of Mary Immaculate Hospital.[37]

The diocese's efforts to extend health care elsewhere, however, did not go as smoothly. In 1950, the board of trustees of Kings Daughters Hospital in Martinsburg, founded in 1895, invited the diocese to take over the institution. In February 1951, the Sisters of the Holy Ghost assumed operation of the hospital. Late in 1950, however, a public meeting of about fifty people voted overwhelmingly against the arrangement. Although the sisters took over administration of the hospital, the West Virginia Board of Health refused to give approval for its application for federal funds to complete a new building. As a result, it received no federal funds until the fiscal year 1952–53. On March 24, 1954, the new building was dedicated.[38] While the diocese was expanding its hospital apostolate during the 1950s, it had to abandon one other institution. In 1937, the Felician Sisters had assumed responsibility for the Potomac Valley Hospital in Keyser, West Virginia, but had to withdraw in 1945.[39]

In the postwar years, the diocese had increased its work in secondary education and health care. But these years also marked a change in Virginia Catholicism's public expression of its faith.

"Muscular Catholicism" Comes to Virginia

Virginia Catholics had adopted an accommodating style with their Protestant neighbors. They generally had not gone in for public manifestations of their faith, except on rare occasions. The dedication of St. Joseph's Villa, coinciding with the silver jubilee of the cathedral, was one such occasion in the aftermath of the Al Smith campaign. The annual Corpus Christi processions at the Villa were others, but these were limited to the Richmond area and to diocesan property. Catholics had, of course, taken part in civic and patriotic events, but these were used to show that they were truly American. In the postwar years, however, they joined other American Catholics in more militant displays of their faith and strength. Whether these emanated from inmigration from the north, where such demonstrations were more common, or from Ireton, who now felt he had sufficient numbers to make such displays effective, they represented a shift in Virginia Catholic identity.

The postwar years were an era of "muscular Catholicism," lost on a later generation used to the unostentatious religious life of the suburbs. But it was also an era of renewed hostility to the Church. Protestants and Other Americans United for the Separation of Church and State argued that the increase in Catholic population threatened the First Amendment, for, in popular perception, if Catholics ever constituted a majority, they would seek a union between their Church and the State.[40] In May 1954, Archbishop Karl J. Alter of Cincinnati, chairman of the administrative board of the NCWC, repudiated this charge in a sermon for Archbishop John J. Swint's golden jubilee in Wheeling. As *The Catholic Virginian* reported: "'It can be stated categorically,' Archbishop Alter declared, 'that there is no doctrine of the Catholic Church which places upon its members the obligation to work either individually or collectively for a change in respect to that religious freedom which is guaranteed to all of us by the Constitution of the United States.'"[41] Alter fell well within the tradition of three of Richmond's previous bishops, Gibbons, Keane, and O'Connell, but he was a bit optimistic in regard to Catholic agreement on the Church's teaching about Church and State. A little over a year after his sermon, John Courtney Murray, S.J., the American theologian who had reopened the question of religious liberty that had been virtually dormant since the condemnation of Americanism, fell under a cloud and ceased writing.[42] The question would arise again in John F. Kennedy's campaign for president in 1960, but would be definitively settled only at Vatican II.

Independent of the Church-State debate, the pre-Vatican II Church had, as one characteristic, devotion to the Virgin Mary. On May 1, 1946, Pius XII sought the counsel of the world's bishops about defining the Assumption of Mary. For the United States, this provided little difficulty—the cathedral in Baltimore, the first one in the nation, had been dedicated to the Assumption. When Ireton polled his pastors for their opinions, all recommended the definition.[43] On November 11, 1950, the pope solemnly defined that the Virgin Mary was assumed into heaven. It was only the first time since Vatican I had defined papal infallibility that a pope had exercised this prerogative. In fact, a pope had defined a doctrine on his own authority only once before, in 1854, when Pius IX defined the Immaculate Conception.

Although the definition of the Assumption drew little American Catholic attention,[44] this did not mean a diminution of popular devotion to Mary.

Simultaneously with the national discussion over the Catholic teaching on Church and State and, incidentally, with Ireton's decision to integrate the schools,[45] Virginia's Catholics joined their coreligionists in the nation to celebrate the Marian Year of 1954, commemorating the centennial of the definition of the Immaculate Conception. They used it as an occasion to show they had arrived not only as Americans but also as Catholics. Ireton initiated the year by obtaining papal honors for seven priests and twenty-one lay people. Louis Flaherty, superintendent of schools, Harold Nott, pastor of Holy Cross in Lynchburg and director of hospitals, Justin McClunn, the chancellor, and Carroll Dozier, pastor of Christ the King in Norfolk, were named papal chamberlains; Francis Byrne, pastor of St. Bridget's, and Anthony Korkemaz, pastor of St. Anthony's Maronite Church in Richmond, were named domestic prelates; and Leo Ryan, rector of the cathedral, was named a protonotary apostolic, which entitled him to wear episcopal regalia on certain occasions.

Knighthoods of St. Sylvester were conferred on Rupert Bliley, John A. K. Donovan, and Thomas Dyson; of St. Gregory on John Daly, editor of the *Catholic Virginian*, Frank Fannon of Alexandria, Lawrence Monahan of Wakefield, Alphonse Pennartz of Richmond, the cathedral organist. Although Ireton had in 1951 already obtained the *Pro ecclesia et pontifice* medal for Mrs. Lydia Elizabeth Nicholas, an African American teacher,[46] the following now joined her as recipients of the honor: Mrs. Emma E. Holmes of Norfolk, Mrs. Mary Lovell O'Neill of Richmond, founder of Catholic Charities in 1922; the *benemerenti* medal went to Lily Albert of Covington, Margaret A. Cragin of Portsmouth, Mary Dowd of Richmond, Mary T. Gill of Richmond, Marie A. Greene of Alexandria, Henrietta Knightly of Richmond, Mrs. Lucille Lancaster of Charlottesville, Emily Lonergan of Harrisonburg, Claire McCarthy of Richmond, Mrs. Helen K. Nolte of Richmond, Mrs. Teresa Sullivan of Richmond, Mrs. Elizabeth L. White of Falls Church. Other honors were conferred on women who were active in the Catholic Alumnae, Catholic Charities, and the Diocesan Council of Catholic Women.[47]

In anticipation of the year, McClunn issued a series of regulations. Each parish was to observe the opening of the Marian Year with a novena in honor of the Blessed Virgin ending on December 8, 1953, and its closing with a similar novena ending on December 8, 1954. After the feast of the Immaculate Conception in 1953, the Memorare was to be recited before the "Leonine Prayers" at the end of every Mass. Each parish that had not had a recent mission or retreat was urged to hold one during the year. Each parish, moreover, was to have three additional novenas, one in March for vocations, a second before Pentecost, and a third in June in honor of the Sacred Heart. Approximately twenty parishes in the diocese were named after the Blessed Virgin, and these were encouraged to hold an additional novena.[48]

The highlight of Richmond's observance of the Marian Year, however, occurred on Sunday, October 10, 1954. Each of the seven deaneries celebrated an outdoor Mass in the evening, taking advantage of the new laws regarding the Eucharistic fast. Norfolk attracted 16,000 to Foreman Field, Richmond had 9,000, northern Virginia 8,000 in the George Washington High School Stadium, the Peninsula 4,000 at the Xaverian Brothers' Novitiate at Old Point Comfort, Roanoke 2,500, Staunton 1,000, and Winchester 500. Marines from Quantico took part in the Richmond celebration, and Navy personnel formed a human cross in Norfolk. Three of the Masses were pontifical, with Ireton presiding in Richmond, Hodges, the auxiliary bishop, in Alexandria, and Ryan in Norfolk. The theme struck in each of the sermons was the relationship between Catholic devotion to the Blessed Virgin and the Incarnation.[49] In his report, Ireton noted that 40,000 people had attended the observances, roughly one third of the 121,000 Catholics in the diocese. He had, in addition, dedicated three new churches to the Blessed Virgin, in Blackstone, Romney, and Luray.[50] While Catholics thus displayed their faith and devotion in public, their militancy may have contributed to fears of what would happen if Catholics became too numerous.

IRETON'S JUBILEE AND THE
JUBILEE OF THE CATHEDRAL, 1956

A second major event toward the end of Ireton's episcopate likewise provided the occasion for a Catholic display. In June 1956, Ireton was celebrating the golden jubilee of his ordination to the priesthood, but moved the observance to November 29 to coincide with the fiftieth anniversary of the dedication of the cathedral, renovated for the event. The joint celebrations brought the largest number of bishops to Richmond since the celebration of the twenty-fifth anniversary of the cathedral and the dedication of St. Joseph's Villa in 1931. Archbishop Amleto Cicognani, the apostolic delegate, presided at the Pontifical Mass, surrounded by over thirty members of the hierarchy, priests from Richmond and other dioceses, and laymen who had received papal honors. The Mass itself was televised. Francis Cardinal Spellman of New York was originally scheduled to preach, but his appointment as papal legate to the Eucharistic Congress in the Philippines left his sermon to be delivered by his auxiliary bishop, Joseph F. Flannely.[51]

Spellman, who had the highest visibility among the American bishops, had done some homework on the history of the diocese. Noting that the first Mass in Richmond had been celebrated by Jean Dubois, who was one of Spellman's predecessors as the ordinary of New York, he recalled that Gibbons went on from Richmond to Baltimore and that Keane became the first rector of the Catholic University. "And one could go on with name after name of men who crossed through Richmond to other fields," he continued, "and did their work there the better because they had been here." In somewhat of a stretch of historical fact, he added that "perhaps your first Bishop, Patrick Kelly, started a tradition, who came from Kilkenny and finished his days as Bishop of Waterford and Lismore in Ireland. Your second Bishop became Bishop of Wheeling."[52] Spellman seemed to imply that Richmond was a stepping-stone to other assignments.

Spellman then turned to the significance of a cathedral as "a symbol of the apostolicity and unity of the Church," whether it was the "old Cathedral of St. Peter" or the more splendid new one, because "the Cathedral houses the Cathedra, the chair of the bishop." Drawing on Ignatius of Antioch, he gave his views of apostolic succession, in which he declared that "the fullness of the Sacrament of orders given to every Bishop is carried back to one of the apostles, from Richmond to Palestine it stretches. Perhaps John, perhaps James, perhaps Peter of Galilee holds the first link and Peter of Richmond the latest link, binding Richmond to our Christian origins."[53] Spellman was simply and simplistically reflecting the theology of the episcopacy that would be challenged within a few years at Vatican II. He concluded with a catechesis on the priest as "ambassador of Christ" and minister of the sacraments with a particular application to Ireton.[54] Spellman's sermon was not noteworthy, but it was somewhat of a coup for Ireton that the cardinal agreed to write it and have his auxiliary deliver it.

Spellman, incidentally, had already paid at least one visit to Virginia. In April 1952, he dedicated St. John the Evangelist Church in Marion, where he gave a ringing speech on one of his favorite themes—the necessity of all Americans to unite against the threat of communism. He then drove to Bristol to speak to the parishioners of St. Anne's.[55] Such a public link between Catholicism and anticommunism paved the way for Catholic acceptance in the nation.

While the joint jubilees of 1956 provided a grand occasion to show where the diocese of Richmond stood within American Catholic life, they also served to display where Catholics and Ireton in particular stood within Virginia's civic life. On December 2, 651 laity attended a dinner in Ireton's honor and presented him with a check for $60,600, part of which he gave to Catholic Charities in lieu of the annual Christmas collection that he had canceled that year. The leaders of Virginia's political life were all in attendance. Governor Thomas B. Stanley delivered greetings in the name of the Commonwealth. Senator Harry F. Byrd read a telegram from President Dwight Eisenhower. Senator A. Willis Robertson, Representative J. Vaughan Gary, and Mayor Henry Garber of Richmond were also present.[56] Ireton seemed to have arrived on Virginia's civic and religious scene. But, in fact, he had already departed from a major aspect of Virginia tradition. By 1956, his schools had been integrated for two years.

BEGINNING OF LITURGICAL RENEWAL

Such public displays of religion as the celebration of the Marian Year and the jubilees of Ireton and the cathedral were characteristic of Catholic devotion and liturgical practices before Vatican II, which would make major changes in the liturgy. In anticipation of some of those changes, several of Richmond's priests were more progressive than their bishop. By 1957, Thomas Scannell, pastor of St. Michael's Church in Annandale, had initiated a "dialogue Mass" at all his parish Masses. On December 6, however, Ireton issued a letter to all the priests of the diocese warning of the dangers of this innovation.

Quoting a document from the Congregation of Rites that "things that are in themselves licit are not always expedient," he argued that the practice of the dialogue Mass might, therefore, "be praiseworthy," but it might "actually cause distraction to both priests and people rather than further devotion." The Holy See had therefore left it to each ordinary to determine when the Dialogue Mass would be appropriate. Ireton then issued the following norms:

1) In no church or chapel of this Diocese may the Dialogue Mass be had without the previous permission of the Ordinary.
2) When permission is granted, there may be only one such Mass in any church having four or less Sunday Masses; if a church has more than four Sunday Masses there may, with special permission, be a second Dialogue Mass.
3) The Dialogue Mass does not dispense with the use of a server.
4) The celebrant is NOT to slow down his recitation of the Mass prayers; it is for the people to keep up with the celebrant.
5) For the Dialogue Mass Latin is obligatory. The people may recite in Latin the parts sung by the choir during High Mass (Gloria, Creed, Sanctus and Agnus Dei) and the responses made by the altar boys, with the exception of the Psalm "Iudica me" at the start of the Mass. I do not approve of the recitation of this Psalm in the Dialogue Mass because it is difficult for the people to recite it in unison. The people may recite the Confiteor at the start of Mass and before their Communion.
6) The Dialogue Mass is never to replace the parish High Mass on Sunday. If the people can recite the Gloria, Creed etc., they can, with a little more training, be induced to sing in unison some simple Mass.[57]

If nothing else, Ireton gave proof that he was not in favor of too much liturgical innovation in his diocese.

Not every parishioner in Annandale agreed with these norms. In January 1958, Mrs. Kenneth M. Sullivan praised Scannell and complained to Ireton about the new restrictions.[58] Replying for Ireton, McClunn commented that "moderation must temper our zeal for the Dialogue Mass. The Holy Father has allowed it as an *occasional* practice but has never consented to having a Dialogue Mass at all the Sunday Masses in a large parish. In fact, the Holy See has cautioned

Bishops to exercise some restraints on the practice."[59] McClunn failed to specify what caution the Holy See had issued, but he clearly indicated that the diocese as a whole gave little sign of how it would adapt to the council.

Ireton seems often to have followed the advice of McClunn, who had a doctorate in canon law and became a stickler on a number of canonical niceties other than the liturgy. In the fall of 1957, John J. Lynch, S.J., a member of the Japanese vice-province of the Jesuits, was studying at Georgetown, but lived with Scannell in Annandale to save money on room and board. Ireton's problem was that canon law stated that only Rome could allow a religious to live outside his community for more than six months. Scannell had praised Lynch to McClunn and remarked that the only expense to the parish was the cost of gasoline and "toast" for breakfast.[60] McClunn responded that Ireton wanted to know if Lynch's provincial superior had the authority to allow him to reside outside a religious community.[61]

Scannell then wrote Lynch's superior in Japan, Father Pedro Arrupe, S.J., and enclosed a copy of McClunn's letter. Arrupe, in turn, wrote the provincial superior of the Maryland province, William Mahoney, forwarding a copy of McClunn's letter. In January 1958, Mahoney informed Ireton that he approved of the arrangement for Lynch to reside outside a community and had the authority of a canon lawyer at Woodstock College that no indult from Rome was necessary. He, furthermore, had Lynch's assurance that he could leave Annandale by the end of the month.[62] Arrupe, a medical doctor who had witnessed the dropping of the atomic bomb on Nagasaki and who later became the superior general of the Society of Jesus, must have been mystified at the canonical scruples of the bishop of Richmond and his chancellor.

In many instances, it was difficult to determine who governed the diocese, McClunn or Ireton. Ireton was growing older and declining in health. During his frequent absences, McClunn virtually ran the diocese. But Ireton's episcopate was coming to an end. He had just confirmed twenty-five students at Marymount School in Arlington on April 18, 1958, when he fell. Admitted to Georgetown University Hospital, he died on April 27. The next day, the consultors met in Richmond, elected Hodges as administrator, and recommended that Archbishop Francis P. Keough of Baltimore celebrate the funeral Mass and Bishop John J. Russell of Charleston preach the eulogy.[63]

On May 1, three archbishops, twelve bishops, and two abbots attended the funeral Mass in the cathedral.[64] For the 1,300 people gathered in the cathedral, had they known it, one era was ending and another beginning, for they had just listened to the sermon of the next bishop of Richmond.

Ireton had begun his episcopate under the tragic circumstances of Brennan's stroke at a time when the country and Virginia were still in the midst of the Depression. He lamented at the time that more people were leaving Virginia than were entering it. By the time of his death, the war had permanently changed the face of his diocese, the northern part of which was then burgeoning with newcomers. Much of the diocese's response to this rapid expansion had been independent of Ireton. But there was one area in which, if he did not take the lead, he at least accepted the leadership of others—the movement toward racial justice in his diocese upon which his successor, Russell, would build.

CHAPTER 26

African Americans in the Diocese of Richmond from World War I to Integration

African American Catholics are now an integral part of the diocese of Richmond, but this was not always the case. While they were always affected by events in the diocese at large, their story is different. Bishop John J. Keane and especially Bishop Augustine van de Vyver had begun to focus on urban schools as the means of evangelizing Virginia's Blacks, so few of whom were Catholic. Denis O'Connell would encourage the expansion of that work that remained exclusively in the hand of the Josephites until his successor, Andrew Brennan, established the first parish for Blacks staffed by a priest of the diocese. Peter L. Ireton increased the number of diocesan parishes for African Americans and also introduced the Redemptorists to engage in the work. But gradually, especially after World War II, Virginia Catholics would move toward integration. Ireton, in fact, led the way by desegregating diocesan schools on the eve of the Supreme Court's Brown decision.

JOSEPHITE WORK UNDER O'CONNELL

Funding for work among African Americans remained meager. Catholics who were otherwise generous in their charity restricted their gifts for this apostolate. In 1901, van de Vyver told Joseph Anciaux, S.S.J., in Lynchburg: "*Do not visit* and *do not write* to Mrs. [Thomas Fortune] Ryan, New York. She will not give to colored work."[1] Unfortunately, the annual collections for the Commission on Indian and Negro Missions continued in the 1920s to amount to less than one cent a year per Catholic. In 1907, the American bishops, under pressure from Pius X, had formed the Catholic Board for Mission Work Among the Colored People to raise funds to supplement the annual collections. In 1924, the board's director in New York, John E. Burke, made a special appeal to wealthy Catholics, but found he could count "on the fingers and toes" those who responded.[2] The diocese of Richmond reflected the national situation.

In 1915, the Josephites opened St. Joseph's Church in Alexandria. Since the first pastor, Joseph Kelly, was a friend of Katherine Drexel and had other important Philadelphia connections, he originally expected to be self-supporting,[3] but soon found himself short of funds. In 1917, O'Connell tried to transfer a grant from the Church Extension Society to a new Black mission in Newport News, only to learn that Extension gave money only to poor white missions, since Black missions received funds from the Commission on Indian and Negro Missions.[4] On occasion, tension arose even between the Josephites in regard to the allocation of commission funds. In 1913, Joseph Waring in Norfolk thought St. Joseph's in Richmond could well "take care of itself from other sources" and should therefore "waive all claims to the Indian and Negro fund and give Lynchburg and Norfolk a chance to build up."[5]

Despite financial restraints, education remained a hallmark of the Josephite churches. In the fall of 1914, O'Connell sent a gift for a school to St. Joseph's in Norfolk to supplement what the parish received from the commission. James Williams, the secretary of the parish, responded that "we feel and know that your heart and mind have always been with our people throughout your entire jurisdiction, and that you have always done whatever you could to make us good Catholics and good citizens." "The building which you have given us," he went on, "will be the avenue of furthering the advancement along educational and social lines." Waring, he reported, "has worked and is working hard and faithfully in this city where practically speaking Catholicism has been unknown among our people, but he is persuading us from one end of the city to the other that the Catholic Church is the place for us."[6]

In the summer of 1918, O'Connell submitted his report to the commission on the diocese's work among Virginia Blacks. Out of a total Virginia population of 2,500,000, only 42,500 were Catholic. Of the 450,000 Blacks in the state, only 1,600 were Catholic. In the previous year, however, 266 adults and 99 children had been baptized. If missions were included, the diocese then had eleven churches for Black Catholics in Richmond, Norfolk, Lynchburg, Alexandria, Columbia, Cartersville, Jarratt, Keswick, Rock Castle, Jefferson, and State Farm. The pastor of St. Joseph's church in Petersburg, moreover, permitted the use of the church for Black Catholics between the Masses. The diocese then had twelve schools for African Americans. Those in Richmond, Norfolk, and Rock Castle were the largest, with 289, 250, and 300 students respectively. The other schools at Lynchburg, Alexandria, Columbia, Jarratt, and Keswick had fewer than one hundred students each. Columbia had the lowest number, thirty-eight, and had only one teacher, Lydia Elizabeth Nicholas, who would later draw Ireton's attention. In addition, Richmond also had St. Joseph's kindergarten and Holy Innocents orphanage.

Seven priests were then engaged in exclusive work with African Americans, with the Josephites having two priests in Richmond and one in Alexandria, Norfolk, and Lynchburg. At Rock Castle, there were two Holy Ghost Fathers. O'Connell also cited the exodus of African Americans from the South to the North, a pattern that would continue until the mid-1930s. While rural areas had lost the most, St. Joseph's in Richmond lost 20 percent of its congregation. At the same time, the war doubled the Black population in Portsmouth and Petersburg. On one issue, O'Connell seemed to be in agreement with van de Vyver—the need to focus on cities, which meant opening more urban schools.[7]

While schools remained the principal means of outreach to the Black community, in the summer of 1919 Vincent Warren in Norfolk completed a social hall, which had "become already the most attractive place in the city for the better class of colored people."[8] In the fall of 1919, meanwhile, the Josephites opened a new mission in Newport News, as a forerunner to a school and church. O'Connell had also purchased property in Portsmouth, whose Black population was approaching the 40,000 of Norfolk. By this time, he was shifting his focus to establish secondary education, then largely under non-Catholic auspices. As he told the commission, "you can see that if we are to hold our children and keep their faith active we must be able to give them what they can get so easily elsewhere."[9] Throughout his episcopate, O'Connell made salaries for lay teachers the main item in the budget he submitted to the commission.

By 1922, O'Connell was confident about the wisdom of concentrating on cities, where "the interest of the negro in things Catholic is aroused and held by attractive churches and schools which rival with the churches of other denominations and with the public." Whereas Jarratt's Station had been abandoned as a Black mission and was now a "mixed" mission attended from Petersburg, St. Augustine's chapel in Richmond, formerly all white, was now a growing Black parish, soon to be in need of a school. In Richmond, moreover, the van de Vyver School of St. Joseph's had now opened a high school and a new School of Manual Training with trades and a commercial department. In Norfolk, the school was so successful that over one hundred applicants had to be turned away the previous year. In Alexandria, O'Connell wrote, two members of the Oblate Sisters of Providence, an African-American order founded in Baltimore in 1829, came over from Washington without pay to provide "great help to the struggling little parish in Alexandria where our resources are scantiest."[10]

The next year, O'Connell struck the same chord. Joseph B. Glenn, pastor of St. Joseph's in Richmond, thought the city was the metropolitan center of Virginia and the Carolinas and should have a high school that was a showpiece. Warren in Norfolk noted that "with scarcely any Catholics we endeavor to create a congregation through our school." His parish had increased from 215 in 1916 to 625 in 1923; of this number, 350 were converts.[11] In Richmond, Norfolk, and Alexandria, the pattern was virtually identical. The parishes opened high schools to compete with the local public ones and to preserve the faith of young Black Catholics. Their grammar schools educated predominantly Protestant children, but the enrollment in the high schools was almost exclusively Catholic.[12] O'Connell's successors, Brennan and Ireton, would continue this policy of focusing on education.

Not everyone was pleased with the Josephite success in educating Blacks. At a parish picnic in 1926, a car full of Klansmen drove up and kidnapped Father Warren. After driving him around for a while, however, they released him unharmed. But, if they hoped to scare him or the African Americans off from education, they failed. Appearing none the worse for wear, Warren reported a short time later that "from the Princess Anne section (where we met the Klan) a distance of 25 miles from the school, we have this year 25 pupils who make the trip daily; and not one of them a Catholic as yet. Before the manifestation of the Klan animosity we had only one from there. It is from this section that we had to refuse so many applicants."[13]

In 1927, Bishop Brennan, O'Connell's successor, called schools the "principal hope for the future." The van de Vyver school complex had made an impact. "Never before," Brennan wrote, "has Richmond been so immune from bigotry as it is today." But in Norfolk, the situation was different. St. Joseph's school had been condemned by the fire department and had to turn away 200 students. In Alexandria, St. Joseph's Church had had a school for nine years with eighty-five students in eight grades. Out of the total Black population of 4,000, however, only 161 were Catholic.[14]

In regard to educational work, St. Emma's and St. Francis de Sales continued to represent one of Virginia's premier endeavors. On October 24, 1928, Dennis Cardinal Dougherty of Philadelphia agreed to dedicate the new chapel at St. Emma's.[15] Bishops William Hafey of Raleigh, Patrick J. Barry of St. Augustine, Richard O. Gerow of Natchez, and Emmett M. Walsh of Charleston agreed to come.[16] Although Bishop Brennan and these other prelates openly promoted education for Black Americans, they were not so progressive in seeking Black vocations to the priesthood.

THE QUESTION OF A BLACK PRIEST FOR RICHMOND

Late in December 1921, O'Connell received a letter from Peter Jenser, provincial of the Divine Word Fathers, describing the education of Black seminarians. Jenser was convinced that an African-American clergy was necessary, if African Americans were to be converted. With considerable prescience, he said, "The race problem has become a troublesome one and may lead to a crisis" for which he thought "the best solution would be to make the negro CATHOLIC. It is his birthright as much as ours, of which he has been too long deprived."[17] Unfortunately, O'Connell left no record of his response.

In 1927, however, William L. Lane, a graduate of St. Emma's at Rock Castle and at that time a seminarian at St. Vincent's Archabbey in Latrobe, applied to Bishop Brennan to study for Richmond. Brennan turned him down, but Lane was accepted by Bishop Joseph

Schrembs of Cleveland. Two years later, however, Schrembs notified the young man that Cleveland would have no need for him. Lane again wrote Brennan to say that, although the bishop's original reply in 1927 "was in the negative, . . . it was so encouraging because it seemed as tho you went further to wish me God's blessing and your interest in a Race clergy among my people."[18] Brennan once again, however, rejected his application. Lane, nevertheless, found the bishop's letter "encouraging to read, even tho you cannot see the way clear just now to accept me for work in your diocese, that you are interested in the question of a race clergy. I feel certain that once the members of the American Hierarchy become interested in the matter, the beginning of a solution will be at hand."[19]

In October 1930, Lane took his case to Archbishop Pietro Fumasoni-Biondi, the apostolic delegate, and had Dr. Thomas Wyatt Turner of the Hampton Institute also write the delegate on his behalf. Fumasoni-Biondi then interceded with Archbishop John T. McNicholas, O.P., of Cincinnati, who finally agreed to accept Lane on trial in his seminary, Mount St. Mary's of the West. That plan also failed, and finally Lane completed his theological studies at Latrobe for Archbishop Pius Downing of Trinidad. He was ordained in New York in 1933.[20] Lane would later pass through the diocese and make a series of proposals for work with African Americans. His rejection by Brennan as well as northern bishops, however, indicates that racism was not limited to the diocese of Richmond and the South.

The diocese may not yet have been ready to ordain an African American priest, but that did not prevent one of Richmond's seminarians in Rome from proposing one. Vincent Waters was completing his final year of theology in November 1931, when he wrote Brennan that he had met a Black student, who had been rejected by the Society of the Most Holy Trinity and was then studying at his own expense in Rome. Waters thought him to be

> a very promising young fellow, quite cultured, speaks English perfectly without any dialect and seems to be fired with zeal to do something among his own people in the United States. Personally I believe he will have little trouble getting under the Propagation of the Faith and into the Urban College but if he continues in his present mind he will be anxious to get into some southern diocese in the States during the next year or so. Should you be interested in him I could give you more particulars."[21]

Apparently, however, Brennan was not interested in even a Roman-trained Black seminarian. For some years to come, Virginia's Black Catholics would be served by white priests.

WORK OF DIOCESAN PRIESTS WITH AFRICAN AMERICANS: OUR LADY OF VICTORY

The concern for Virginia's African Americans was not limited to the Josephites. Early in 1930, Harold Nott, whose older brother, Walter, was the director of Catholic Charities, was then studying in Rome. He informed Bishop Brennan that he had offered a novena in honor of the bishop's recent silver jubilee "for the conversion of the negroes in our diocese." He added that he and Bernard Moore, another Richmond seminarian, had often discussed "the possible conversion of those poor souls and have both expressed a hope that you will find work for us to do among them. We feel that we can do much good among them as we have been brought up in their midst."[22]

Neither Nott nor Moore would be assigned as priests specifically to work with African Americans, but in 1931 Brennan did open the first parish for Black Catholics under a diocesan priest. Nicholas Habets, an alumnus of Fribourg who had served in Fairfax, established Our Lady of Victory in Portsmouth, property for which O'Connell had earlier purchased. In February 1931, he reported that "the more I am in this work, the better I like it but also the better I see your guided wisdom in refraining and limiting my activity to this place alone."[23] By September 1932, in the midst of the Depression, his parishioners had increased from twenty to eighty-four; he had baptized twenty adults and one child; and his school, staffed by three Daughters of Charity, had three grades with 140 students, of whom only fifteen were Catholic.[24] Habets was following the Josephite strategy of using schools as vehicles for evangelization.

Habets was determined that his parishioners be considered an integral of the Catholic community. On November 27–29, 1933, the Daughters of Charity held a triduum in honor of Catherine Labouré, a member of their congregation in France who had recently been beatified. The celebration began with the rosary, a sermon, and solemn benediction at Sacred Heart Church in Norfolk. On the following days, there were ceremonies at St. Paul's Church in Portsmouth and St. Mary's Church in Norfolk, where Bishop Brennan officiated. All of these parishes were staffed by the Daughters of Charity, and an invitation was "extended to all the people of Norfolk and Portsmouth to participate and share in the special graces to be bestowed on this occasion."[25] But here was where harmony ended.

Habets had not attended the celebration and received a reprimand from Bishop Brennan. He explained that, after the first planning meeting of the daughters, Sister Madeleine, D.C., from Our Lady of Victory refused to attend another when she learned that their parishioners were excluded from the celebration. Habets had declined an invitation to be the celebrant of the solemn benediction at St. Paul's, because he had no connection with the parish. He would have consented to have a role in the Pontifical High Mass at St. Mary's, he told the bishop, "but no function was offered me." Warren had been invited, he observed, but "they had not to fear an influx of colored participants as his school is not staffed by the Daughters of Charity." As part of the celebration, there were "pilgrimages," but, he added, "the fear was imminent that a Negro parade would follow the Lily-white pilgrimage. They said there would be no room. Of course there was no room as it was planned to fill the churches otherwise."[26]

Habets went on to give his reactions to the racist attitudes among the clergy and religious. "If our priests and religious take that attitude and believe in time-serving and are opportunists in this color-question," he stated, "then we must not be surprised at the hostile attitude of the lay people who call white people worshiping in colored churches 'Irish niggers' or say that the Sisters bring a shame upon their holy habit by teaching 'Black lips' or that those Sisters have been missioned to a colored school to expiate some crime committed in their community." Far from being an isolated incident, he asserted, "priests have expressed themselves many a time adverse to this missionary endeavour. Even from the beginning we had to cope with it." In June 1931, the sisters had wanted to put on a show for the children at St. Joseph's Academy in Portsmouth, only to be turned down. They then obtained permission from the superior of the asylum in Norfolk, but Father F. Joseph Magri, the pastor in Portsmouth, saw them on the way and attempted to have Edward Brosnan, pastor of St. Mary's, stop them. Habets concluded that he hoped his explanation would assuage "the surprise" the bishop had "expressed at my absence."[27]

How accurate Habets was in his assessment of the attitudes of the other clergy is difficult to assess. He himself remained at Our Lady of

Victory until 1952, when he became the second pastor of Star of the Sea in Virginia Beach and was replaced in Portsmouth by Albert F. Pereira. In the meantime, as will be seen, Ireton also established St. Augustine's in Richmond as a Black parish, staffed by a diocesan priest, R. Dixon Beattie.

JOSEPHITE WORK DURING THE DEPRESSION

Meanwhile, although the Depression caused revenues from the Commission for Indian and Negro Missions to diminish, Josephite work continued to expand. In September 1932, Glenn reported that St. Joseph's in Richmond then had 672 parishioners, with its missions in Columbia and Cartersville having a total of sixteen. Over the year, he had baptized ninety people, including seventy-one adult converts. Schools, however, still remained a prime focus, with 636 as a total enrollment, of whom fifty-eight were then in Columbia. His schools were staffed by eleven sisters and two lay teachers, and his night school had five lay teachers. But it was difficult to provide exact statistics for his parish, he said, because unemployment caused the people constantly to move.[28]

In Alexandria, Kelly informed Brennan that his parishioners then numbered 184, but they too were feeling the effects of the Depression. Although many were trained mechanics, they had to accept positions as unskilled workers. Moreover, he stated, "the wage rate among the colored is much lower than the rate given to whites for the same kind of work performed." He had, nevertheless, opened his new school in October 1931, with eighty-nine students, of whom one-third were Protestant.[29] For the remainder of the 1930s, the Black Catholic population slowly increased, but a significant pattern emerged. In 1933, there were 70 girls and 38 boys in Richmond's van de Vyver high school, and 183 girls and 159 boys in the grammar school. Education in Richmond's African American community seemed to be more desirable for girls than for boys. Glenn also commented that the Church was drawing converts from the professional classes that "will soon establish for us a leadership in the Community." Those who frequented his school, moreover, were the children of Protestant ministers and public-school teachers, as a result of which Glenn reported, "the voice of bigotry is no longer heard among us; on the contrary many are the signs of respect and esteem shown us constantly by our non-Catholic Negro brethren."[30] The annual reports from the Josephites to the bishop for preparation of the appeal for funds from the commission on Indian and Negro Missions provide a year-by-year account of work among Black Virginians. Unfortunately, Warren's reports for Norfolk do not exist, but, from those that are extant, especially Glenn's for Richmond, the pattern continued of a gradual increase in Black parishioners, with girls outnumbering boys in school enrollment.

Early in 1937, Ireton, then the coadjutor of Richmond, sought to gain information on the number of Black Catholics in non-Black parishes.[31] The response was disappointing. Few parishes had any Black parishioners, and many had none.[32] In January 1940, at the request of the apostolic delegate, Ireton took a census of the Black Catholics in the diocese. There were at the time 2,090 in the six parishes for Black Catholics: St. Joseph's and St. Augustine's, in Richmond, St. Joseph's in Norfolk, St. Joseph's in Alexandria, Our Lady of Victory in Portsmouth, and Holy Family, about to be opened in Petersburg. In addition, there were 225 attending other parishes.[33] After over seventy years of outreach to the African-American community, the diocese of Richmond had still reached only a small minority.

The work of the diocese among Black Catholics was further hampered by its perennial lack of priests. Early in 1939, Father William Lane, who had earlier applied for and been rejected by the diocese, gave a mission in Portsmouth and discovered thirty Catholic students at the Hampton Institute. He recommended more missions at Black parishes and a chaplain for the institute. He also seems again to have offered his services to the diocese. Ireton acknowledged the need for more missions but pointed out that the situation of the students at the Hampton Institute was similar to that of white students at other colleges in the state. "There are," he wrote, "a hundred and fifty or more students at the College of William and Mary with no resident priest at Williamsburg" and "there is almost an equal number in Lexington, at Washington and Lee and Virginia Military Institute, and likewise no resident priest." Granted that the diocese was strapped for funds as well as personnel, he concluded that he could not hold out hope for Lane to work in the diocese.[34] The time still had not come for Richmond to break the color barrier in regard to its clergy.

During World War II, however, the diocese increased its work with African Americans, as Ireton opened more parishes for them. It was a policy of separate but equal that his successor would reverse. The war, moreover, would have a direct effect on the status of African Americans within American society.

FIRST RUMBLINGS OF RACIAL JUSTICE

On November 1, 1939, Pope Pius XII addressed *Sertum laetitiae* to the American hierarchy on the occasion of the one hundred and fiftieth anniversary of the naming of John Carroll as the first American bishop. Commending the progress of the Church and its implementation of social teaching, the pope particularly noted:

> We confess that We feel a special paternal affection, which is certainly inspired by heaven, for the Negro people dwelling among you; for in the field of religion and education We know they need special care and comfort and are very deserving of it. We therefore invoke an abundance of heavenly blessing and We pray success for those whose generous zeal is devoted to their welfare.[35]

Later in November, after the annual meeting of the hierarchy, Samuel A. Stritch, then archbishop of Milwaukee and chairman of the administrative board of the NCWC, and Emmett M. Walsh, bishop of Charleston and chairman of the NCWC committee on lay organizations, addressed a letter to Dr. Thomas Wyatt Turner, chairman of the biology department at Hampton Institute and president of the Federation of Colored Catholics. They commended him for his report on the Federation's work in "helping to right the social wrongs of our brothers by promoting a wider and deeper knowledge and practice of Christian social justice and charity." Quoting Pius XII's statement on African Americans, they concluded that "it were a sham Christianity were we to try to exclude from the embrace of justice any man, or to make our charity narrower than the outstretched arms of Christ on Calvary."[36] In view of Turner's prominence as Virginia's most outstanding Black Catholic, it is curious that there is no extant correspondence between him and any bishop of Richmond. Regardless of the lack of such documentation, however, the diocese seemed to take to heart the words of Pius XII and the letter from Stritch and Walsh.

Despite the distractions of the war, the diocese of Richmond took the first steps toward racial equality in the early 1940s. It actively participated in the Catholic Committee on the South and in the nascent movement for interracial justice.

THE CATHOLIC COMMITTEE ON THE SOUTH AND PAUL WILLIAMS

In 1936, Howard W. Odum of the University of North Carolina published his *Southern Regions of the United States.* It was an indictment of the South, which contained 61 percent of the eroded land in the nation and whose wages and income lagged between 30 and 50 percent behind the rest of the nation. In 1938, President Franklin Roosevelt called the region the nation's worst economic problem. The president's concern gave rise to the Southern Conference for Human Welfare, a biracial organization that anticipated the later civil rights movement. Because the conference also welcomed Marxist radicals, however, Paul D. Williams, a young Catholic layman of Richmond and active member of St. Paul's parish, decided to organize the Catholic Committee on the South (CCS). His job as a traveling representative of a publishing company took him throughout most of the South, where he made friends with clergy and lay leaders alike. He first discussed his proposals with Monsignor John A. Ryan, director of the Social Action Department of the NCWC, and his assistant, Father Raymond McGowan. Ryan suggested that Williams organize a Southern program for the National Social Action Congress to be held on June 12–14, 1939, in Cleveland.[37]

At the congress, Williams arranged for two forums, one on the Industrial South and the other on the Agricultural South. The entire congress heard Bishop Gerald O'Hara of Savannah deliver the ringing words: "You have heard President Roosevelt say the South is the country's No. 1 economic problem. Let me say to you that the South is the Church's No. 1 religious opportunity." O'Hara based his optimistic assessment on the increase in converts and interest on the part of state universities in Catholic social teaching.[38] Ireton joined O'Hara, Williams, and Father T. James McNamara in forming the nucleus of the new organization, the CCS.

At its first convention in Atlanta, in April 1940, the CCS established five departments: Industrial, Rural, Education, Negro, and

Youth. As the executive secretary, Williams made sure the CCS had representatives at meetings of other Southern reform groups, such as the Southern Cooperative Region Meeting and the Virginia Interracial Convention. His purpose was to inform the people of the South, where the Church constituted such a small minority, of Catholic teaching and help break down prejudice.[39] Increasingly, the CCS focused its attention on racism.

In April 1942, Richmond hosted the third convention of the CCS. The chairman for the convention was Thomas E. O'Connell, pastor of St. Paul's Church in Richmond, who later became an outspoken advocate of racial equality. In preparation, Williams asked Ireton to enlist the support of Archbishop Joseph F. Rummel of New Orleans and Bishops William L. Adrian of Nashville, Daniel F. Desmond of Alexandria, Louisiana, Emmet M. Walsh of Charleston, Jules B. Jeanmard of Lafayette, Mississippi, and Francis W. Howard of Covington, Kentucky.[40] Ireton urged all the priests of the diocese to attend the convention, which he substituted for that year's annual clergy conference.[41] In addition, the school superintendents of all the southern dioceses would hold their annual meeting in conjunction with the convention.

Ireton, in the meantime, invited Henry Wallace, vice president of the United States, to address the convention. He pointed out that "there is the danger that ugly radicalism might be the sequel to a brutal economic colonialism." While Wallace declined the invitation, Frances Perkins, secretary of labor, was part of a panel on "Labor and Industry and Family Life in the South." The convention heard addresses from Archbishop Samuel Stritch, who had been transferred to Chicago, Dr. Frank Graham, president of the University of North Carolina and a member of the War Labor Board, Howard Odum, and Father Francis J. Haas, a leading labor mediator.[42] Another panel treated the topic of "The Negro in National Defense." The participants included Thomas W. Turner and L. R. Reynolds, director of the Virginia Commission on Interracial Cooperation. After the panel discussion, Father Edward Murphy, dean of philosophy at Xavier University in New Orleans, stated that "to be anti-Semitic or anti-Negro is to be anti-Christian" and urged Catholics to join the Urban League and the NAACP. The CCS then gave its second annual award to Mother Katherine Drexel, whose Sisters of the Blessed Sacrament continued to operate St. Francis de Sales High School at Rock Castle—the first award had gone to George Washington Carver the previous year. According to one participant, the public took little notice that the assembly at the award ceremony was integrated.[43] Governor Colgate Darden also addressed the meeting and declared that "the Catholic Church stands today, as it has stood for centuries, like a rock in a wasting world." He predicted that once peace came, the Church would "play a magnificent part in bringing back to exhausted and weary people" an opportunity for "a finer and a cleaner and a better life."[44]

Unfortunately, the CCS was always hampered by financial restraints. In 1943, Williams resigned as executive secretary, frustrated at the lack of funding that forced him to withdraw the CCS from membership in agencies such as the Southern Governors Conference, the Southern Policy Committee, and the Southern Conference on Race Relations. In his letter of resignation, however, he urged that in the postwar South the CCS should align itself with the progressive, regional thinkers and combat the opportunists, such as the communists and socialists. Anticommunism became a hallmark for the CCS as it was for most American Catholics. Yet the committee continued to promote the rights of labor in the South and became more outspoken in calling for desegregation. At its convention in Columbia, South Carolina, in 1951, it passed a resolution calling for "ultimate integration." The committee's support of unions and desegregation set it apart from most white Southerners, but its strong anticommunism protected it from being attacked. The Columbia convention, however, was the high-water mark of the committee. It held its last convention in Richmond in April 1953, when it passed no resolutions but issued a statement written by the Southern bishops. Bishop John J. Russell of Charleston was the episcopal chairman, and he authorized the various departments to publish workshop ideas and suggestions, but these were not to be considered official statements unless they had the approval of the Board of Governors.[45]

While the CCS ceased to exist as a cohesive regional force within the Church by 1954, Williams's pioneering work in Richmond helped create an atmosphere for the diocese to move toward desegregation and prepare it for later participation in the civil rights movement. He was, moreover, also active in developing interracial work in Richmond.

INTERRACIAL WORK IN THE DIOCESE OF RICHMOND

On April 18, 1941, the Virginia Commission on Interracial Cooperation held its twenty-second annual conference in Richmond at St.

Paul's Episcopal Church. R. L. Reynolds, the director of the commission, enlisted the assistance of Williams and Vincent Waters, the chancellor, to have Father John T. Gillard, S.S.J., a noted writer on interracial justice, participate.[46] Invited to respond to a paper on training African Americans for industry,[47] Gillard readily agreed and pointed to the problem that the Catholic Committee on the South was beginning to address. In Baltimore, he noted, builders would not hire Negroes because they were not in unions, and unions would not admit them because they were not officially trained. "We got two union brick-layers on the Notre Dame [of Maryland] library building," he continued, "but the white union men quit. So there you are. In the meantime the Communists are making strides among the Negroes."[48] Waters, meanwhile, asked Reynolds to invite other priests.[49] As a result, both Nicholas Habets, pastor of Our Lady of Victory in Portsmouth, and James Albert, S.S.J., pastor of St. Joseph's in Norfolk, were on the program.

Asking Albert to explain the work of the Josephites, Waters pointed out the significance of the invitation, for "this year is the first time we as Catholics have been asked to participate in the Conference and of course we have not been given any of the principal addresses but our time will come and I figure we should not waste all our thunder this year on some secondary place in the program. A short report will make a better impression." Gillard would respond to one of the formal papers, he continued, and Reynolds wanted Albert on the program to enlist his interest in starting a commission on interracial cooperation in Norfolk.[50]

Catholic participation in the annual convention of the Virginia Commission on Interracial Cooperation seems to have been the occasion formally to launch a standing committee on Catholic Interracial Cooperation, which held its second annual meeting in Richmond on February 11, 1942.[51] The guiding forces were again Williams and Waters. By late 1943, just before he left the office of chancellor to become head of the mission band, Waters had also organized a number of interracial roundtable discussion groups.[52]

New Parishes for African Americans

Although Ireton was noted for delegating administrative duties to his subordinates, he took a personal interest in the welfare of Virginia's

African Americans. Early in 1937, he had already asked his priests to provide him with statistics on the number of Black Catholics in white parishes.[53] Three years later, he informed his clergy that there were a total of 902 Black families in the diocese with 73 in white parishes.[54] He now set about to increase those numbers. His work drew the favorable attention of the national board of Indian and Negro Missions which on several occasions gave him more than his requested allotment of $4,000, sometimes as much as $15,000, to be used at his own discretion.[55] These funds he used for new Black parishes. Late in 1941, he invited the Redemptorists to the diocese to take over St. Augustine's in Richmond, founded in 1937, and to establish an additional mission early in 1942. He also planned to open Black parishes in Newport News, Roanoke, and Lynchburg.[56] Two years later, however, Father Cornelius Hoffman, C.Ss.R., at St. Augustine's had still not established a new mission in Richmond, but had selected Church Hill as the site for what became Holy Rosary.[57] In 1945, the Redemptorists had begun a St. Alphonsus mission in Newport News, and the Oblates of Mary Immaculate had started Holy Family Church in Petersburg. In the meantime, Our Lady of Victory in Portsmouth had 309 parishioners with 430 students enrolled in its grammar and high schools.[58] While other orders assisted in this work among Black Catholics, notably the Holy Ghost Fathers who staffed both Rock Castle and the new parish of Our Lady Queen of Peace in Arlington, the Redemptorists would take on most of the responsibility for new parishes.

In June 1946, the Redemptorists founded a parish for Black Catholics in Roanoke. Maurice J. McDonald, C.Ss.R., a former Army chaplain, the first pastor, purchased a home to use for a rectory and chapel. Because he signed the contract on October 15, the feast of St. Gerard Majella, a Redemptorist, he chose that saint as the patron of the parish.[59] Less than a year later, a group of Catholics in nearby Salem petitioned Ireton for a church. In April 1948, the Redemptorists now had charge of both the Black and white people in that town. Temporarily they used facilities of Roanoke College until they transported an old Army chapel from Durham, North Carolina, to become the Chapel of Our Lady of Perpetual Help. From the beginning, there was no segregated seating.[60] Salem continued to be a mission of St. Gerard's until it became an independent parish in 1963.

Late in April 1948, Ireton instructed Robert Hickman, the chancellor, to compile the records of the work with African-American parishes with particular attention to the number of converts. The result of Hickman's survey was the list below of converts for 1947, with the total number of converts from the date of the beginning of each parish or the earliest date at which records were available.

Church	Converts in 1947	Total conversions
St. Joseph's, Richmond	16	1896 – 1947 = 2,234
St. Joseph's, Norfolk	30	1897 – 1947 = 1,693
St. Joseph's, Alexandria	16	1916 – 47 = 265
Our Lady of Victory, Portsmouth	23	1930 – 47 = 325
Holy Family, Petersburg	12	1940 – 47 = 59
Queen of Peace, Arlington	8	1945 – 47 = 12
St. Augustine's, Richmond	12	1935 – 47 = 104
St. Alphonsus, Newport News	6	1944 – 47 = 26
St. Gerard's, Roanoke	3	1946 – 47 = 3
St. Francis de Sales, Lynchburg	0	1908 – 47 = 45[61]

By 1951, the Redemptorists extended their work farther north in the Shenandoah Valley when they took over the missions of Holy Infant in Elkton and Our Lady of the Valley in Luray, neither of which was for African Americans. In August 1953 they established another mission for Black Catholics in Charlottesville, St. Margaret Mary. They purchased a Methodist church which they then renovated. Raymond Schantz, C.SS.R., former assistant at St. Alphonsus in Newport News, was named pastor and resided temporarily at Holy Comforter.[62] St. Margaret Mary would be short-lived, but even in the beginning there were tensions. In September 1954, Raymond Govern, C.SS.R., the superior in Elkton, petitioned Ireton to allow Schantz to have a second Mass at St. Margaret Mary.[63] Justin McClunn, the chancellor, replied that, since the church drew only about sixty-five people on Sunday, only forty of whom were Black, he saw no need for a second Mass.[64] In December 1955, Bishop Joseph Hodges, the auxiliary, dedicated the renovated church, next to which a house had been purchased to serve as a rectory and social center.[65]

In 1950, Ireton had recruited missionary Sisters of Verona, Italy, to work with the Redemptorists at St. Augustine's and Church Hill in Richmond.[66] Three years later, the sisters joined the Redemptorists in

Roanoke.[67] In 1953, the Church Hill community formally became Holy Rosary parish, though it would not have a permanent church for another decade. For the previous two years, the people had met for worship in the home of Mr. and Mrs. George Pollard. The Redemptorists at St. Augustine had, meanwhile, established a mission of St. Gerard in South Richmond in a former Baptist church.[68]

THE DIOCESE MOVES TOWARD INTEGRATION

Despite some advance in work among Black Virginians, however, early in 1944 *The Catholic Virginian* addressed the racial prejudice that still existed among Catholics. Noting the work of many priests and nuns among African Americans, the paper reported that "we have a number of white Catholics in this diocese who by coldness, discourtesy and unfairness towards Negroes are making them distrust and dislike the faith these so-called Catholics profess. Such Catholics are on the devil's side, doing *his* work. The question is: Which side are you on?"[69] But the tide was beginning to turn. In February 1948, Father Thomas E. O'Connell of St. Paul's in Richmond joined several other religious leaders to speak before the Virginia House Courts of the Justice Committee which was then considering five bills that would end segregation in meetings between races and in transportation. He noted that the Holy Name Society had already held an integrated convention in Richmond in October 1947, when white and Black Catholics went to Mass, met, and ate together. But, he noted, "we were violating the laws of Virginia." Now, he was having difficulty in finding a location for the next year's convention because of state laws. For O'Connell, "no true American can defend these barriers, since colored men and women were called upon to defend America and risk their lives in defense of a common flag. They, therefore, have a right to the fundamental liberties symbolized in that flag."[70]

In the meantime, Ireton mirrored the concerns of the rest of the hierarchy about communist infiltration in some African-American groups. In July 1947, Archbishop James Francis A. McIntyre, the coadjutor of New York, and later archbishop of Los Angeles, wrote to the hierarchy that he was "informed that the United Negro and Allied Veterans of America is a Communist Front Organization, working almost exclusively among Negro veterans of World War II, endeavoring to prove that the Negro veterans of the South are being discriminated against and are unable to obtain Government applications to apply for their terminal leave pay." The Catholic War Veterans offered to furnish the necessary application blanks for this pay, and, in this way, "the Church may be able to help combat and counteract the dangers of this un-American organization which uses these blanks as a foil to enlist the Negro veterans in the Communist party." Ireton simply turned McIntyre's letter over to Robert Hickman, his chancellor, who changed the wording slightly and forwarded it to every pastor over the bishop's signature.[71]

While anticommunism was a hallmark of the Church and the Catholic Committee on the South in the postwar years, others also saw this danger. As an attorney for the NAACP in the 1950s, Thurgood Marshall, later a Supreme Court Justice, was passing on information to the FBI about possible communist infiltration of Black organizations.[72]

Although it would be some years before Virginia was integrated, the diocese helped prepare the way early in 1949 by actively participating in the voter registration drive of the National Association for the Advancement of Colored People (NAACP). W. Lester Banks of the Virginia NAACP had written Ireton asking his "cooperation, support and guidance" in the campaign.[73] Ireton urged his Black parishes to join in the endeavor. In a letter to all their pastors, he quoted Banks's letter, which pointed out that, while in 1947 Virginia's Black population was estimated to be 693,728 of whom 350,000 were over 21, the voting age, only 50,000 "had met the first requirements of First Class Citizenship, i.e. payment of three consecutive years of poll taxes." In cooperation with the Voters League, the NAACP was launching a campaign to increase that number to 100,000 by 1949. To qualify, the potential voters would have to pay the poll taxes, register, and then vote in every election. Moreover, they should "join the NAACP to help secure equal protection under the Constitution of the United States for all, regardless of color, race or creed." Ireton informed the pastors that each parish would receive a chart with the names of those who had become registered voters, to be hung in the church vestibule.[74]

Ireton also supported the campaign in 1950 led by Henry L. Caravati to promote a memorial at the birthplace of Booker T. Washington. Introducing Caravati to Archbishops John J. Mitty of San Francisco and McIntyre of Los Angeles, he noted the campaign had "the back-ing of all who are interested in the welfare of the colored."[75]

One of Ireton's most significant actions to further race relations was his obtaining for Mrs. Lydia Elizabeth Nicholas the papal medal *pro ecclesia et pontifice.* He may actually have considered her for the honor as early as 1937. At least that was when he first met her and wrote to her. In a moving account of her life, she noted that her maiden name was O'Hare and her mother's maiden name was Burke, "both Irish names, so at home they used to call us 'Smoked Irish.' You see they were slaves [in Louisville, Kentucky] but belonged to good Catholic slave holders who saw that they were well reared in the Faith." She had been born in Mechanicsburg, Ohio, where "we were the only colored Catholics in the place we attended, St. Michael's Church. It is to these good Catholic people that I owe everything." In 1905, Father Charles Hannigan, S.S.J., had recruited her to teach in the one-room school in Columbia.[76]

Whatever may have been the context of her original correspon-dence with Ireton in 1937, fourteen years later she became the first woman in Virginia to receive the papal medal, in acknowledgment of her forty-six years of service as a teacher in Columbia. She accepted the award at the commencement ceremony at the parochial school of St. Joseph's Church on June 5, 1951.[77] Father Carroll Dozier, diocesan director of the Propagation of the Faith, preached. On July 2, Ireton expressed his gratitude for the award to Monsignor Giovanni Battista Montini, substitute secretary of state to Pius XII, who later became Pope Paul VI. "Our secular press and the Negro press carried unusual publicity in recognition of the honor conferred," he wrote; "the Catho-lic diocesan papers in every section of the country featured the event; for an EVENT the occasion was."[78]

By far the most dramatic of Ireton's actions in regard to African Americans, however, was his decision to integrate the Catholic schools. As early as January 1951, the Catholic Committee on the South, at its meeting in Columbia, South Carolina, had called for integration.[79] In March 1953, Archbishop Joseph F. Rummel of New Orleans pub-lished a pastoral letter prohibiting racial discrimination in churches and diocesan organizations. In June of that year, Vincent Waters, by then the bishop of Raleigh, banned segregated churches and pews.[80] But Ireton was the first bishop in the South to integrate his schools.

On May 7, 1954, shortly before the Supreme Court's Brown deci-sion, Ireton addressed the First Friday Club in Richmond on the question of integration. According to some sources, he chose his topic only in the car on his way to the meeting. He said Catholics should accept the court's decision when it came, but he added a more spiritual argument. Since the van de Vyver High School would soon close, he noted that there would no longer be a Catholic school for Richmond's African Americans. Yet, he continued, Catholic parents had an obligation to provide Catholic education. "Consequently," he declared, "we Catholics have the obligation of attempting to provide a Catholic education for them in the Catholic high schools of Richmond." He also reported that on April 30 the pastors who made up the board of Norfolk Catholic High School had already resolved that, if St. Joseph's High School for black students in Norfolk remained open, Norfolk Catholic would not admit any black students, because it "would be an injustice to St. Joseph's High School." If, however, St. Joseph's closed to make way for a proposed development project, "then any Catholic colored graduate of the eighth grade living within the area serviced by the high school will be admitted."[81] His statement was published a week later in *The Catholic Virginian,* from which *The Richmond News-Leader* picked it up and published it on the front page.[82] The secular newspaper further noted that the Catholic desegregation plan would go into effect in the fall regardless of the Supreme Court's pending decision.[83]

As he implemented Ireton's decision, Monsignor J. Louis Flaherty, the diocesan superintendent of schools, stated it was "in accord with Christian principles," a statement that received national acclaim.[84] In Richmond, thirteen black students from St. Joseph's parochial school were admitted to the Catholic high schools.[85] Other sections of the diocese immediately heeded Ireton's call for integration. In the fall of 1954, Flaherty reported that thirteen black students were already enrolled in three schools in Roanoke and between forty and sixty were attending the Catholic schools in the Arlington-Falls Church area.[86] *The Southern School News,* which monitored school desegregation in the South, quoted Flaherty as saying that integration "has worked out magnificently, without a ripple of discontent." He noted, however, that several white children did not return to the integrated schools. But the paper pointed out that there were only thirty-nine black students out of a total of 3,527 enrolled in four high schools and six elementary schools, with the highest ratio being six black students out of an enrollment of 138.[87] By the end of the academic year 1954–55, the *News* reported that the diocese then had sixty black students enrolled in fourteen elementary and high schools and that only fourteen white children in seven schools had been withdrawn by their parents.[88]

In 1955, the board of Norfolk Catholic, with Ireton's approval, voted to accept black students in the fall and issued a statement of confidence "that present pupils will recall the handicaps under which many of the newer pupils shall have labored, that any violation of the virtues of Charity and Justice is a serious breach of Christian morality, and that all will cooperate for the benefit of the high school."[89] Within the context of Virginia at the time, it was a bold decision. In 1956, the General Assembly held a special session to consider a bill withholding funds from local school systems that had integrated public schools. Addressing a joint committee of the Senate and House of Delegates, Adele Clark presented a resolution of the Richmond Diocesan Council of Catholic Women, of which she was an official, and reminded the legislators that the Virginia constitution provided for free public schools.[90]

In 1957, under the direction of Senator Harry F. Byrd, the state's Democratic boss, Virginia adopted a policy of "massive resistance." The legislature passed laws to circumvent the Brown decision. If Virginia's public schools were forced to integrate, they would be closed to all, and the state would support individual students in segregated, "private" schools. Some Catholics favored this stratagem. The journalistic spearhead of the movement was James Jackson Kilpatrick, Jr., editorial page editor of *The Richmond News Leader*. A convert to Catholicism, he had received instructions from Father Thomas E. O'Connell, a pioneer voice for integration, but would later leave the Church over the issue of integration. In 1955, he began calling for "interposition," that is for Virginia and other Southern states to interpose their sovereignty against the Federal government.[91]

Virginia's "massive resistance" drew the attention of the national Catholic press. Commenting on it in *America,* on September 20, 1958, Wilfrid Parsons, S.J., reminded his readers that "incidentally, Virginia's Catholic schools have been desegregated since early in May 1954, two weeks before the Supreme Court's decision, by decree of the late Bishop Peter L. Ireton."[92] By February 1959, Virginia's "massive resistance" was over. Both federal and state courts had declared its laws against integration unconstitutional, but Virginia still had a long way to go. Danville made the *New York Times* on May 21, 1960, when it closed its public library rather than allow African Americans to enter—the library opened again on September 12, but removed all chairs, so that patrons, black and white, could only take books out![93]

In 1958, Ireton had died, but his successor, John J. Russell, found the groundwork already laid for a forthright campaign for racial equality. He would take a different approach, closing many of the Black parishes Ireton had founded. In retrospect, however, the new era had already dawned in Richmond. On May 27, 1956, Father Theophilus Brown, O.S.B., had said his first Mass at St. Joseph's, with both Bishop Ireton and Bishop Waters in attendance. A native of Richmond and convert, Brown was the first parishioner of St. Joseph's to be ordained a priest, though not for the diocese, but for St. John's Abbey in Collegeville, Minnesota, where he served until coming to Mary Mother of the Church Abbey in Richmond.[94] He symbolized the long quest of Virginia's Black Catholics for equality within the Church they loved and served.

PART IV

The Shaping
of Contemporary
Virginia Catholicism

In 1958, John J. Russell, bishop of Charleston, was transferred to Richmond. His new diocese was vastly different from what it had been only two decades earlier and it would change still more during his episcopate. Peacetime prosperity, government jobs, the automobile, and air-conditioning continued to bring people pouring into the state.

Russell himself in some ways symbolized the change in Virginia Catholicism from its Southern roots to part of the megalopolis emerging in the eastern part of the state. Hardly had he taken office when Pius XII died and the new pope, John XXIII, announced the Second Vatican Council. As the diocese of Richmond was changing through in-migration from other parts of the country, the universal Church now underwent one of its most dramatic transitions in recent history. For Russell, like many other American bishops, the council was a school of theology. Before it opened, he established a permanent ecumenical commission. To implement the council's decrees when it was over, he held the fourth diocesan synod. But Virginia Catholicism now played a different role in the life of the Commonwealth. In the name of integration and racial justice, Russell closed many of the Black parishes Ireton had opened so their parishioners could attend existing white parishes. Although only one religious priest and no diocesan ones from Virginia took part in the civil rights march in Selma, he supported those who did. In his efforts to recruit Virginians to the priesthood, he did what his predecessors had only hoped to do and opened a minor seminary, St. John Vianney. The seminary's closing in 1978 was a sign that the Church universally and in Virginia was changing.

Virginia's Catholic population continued to grow. These new-comers, particularly Catholic ones, were primarily beneficiaries of the GI Bill of Rights that enabled veterans in unprecedented numbers to get a college education. They settled first in the northern Virginia sub-urbs of Washington, and later in the Norfolk area. In some ways, they represented a sharp break from Virginia's Catholic past, for in the areas from which they came in the northeast and Midwest Catholicism had a more visible presence and less of a tradition of accommodation between Catholics and Protestants. Yet in other ways, they represented continuity with that earlier tradition, for the experience of the elec-tion of John Kennedy and Vatican II seemed to signal acceptance of Catholics in American society and a new Catholic embrace of American culture. The difficulty was that that culture was no longer dominantly Protestant but increasingly secular.

The 1960s saw an unprecedented number of new parishes opened in northern Virginia. The next decade began to witness similar growth, particularly in Virginia Beach. Suburban Catholicism in Virginia be-came more the norm than the exception. With it, however, arose two problems. First, religion was in danger of becoming a private matter, relegated to home and family, but divorced from the public forum. Second, these newcomers were mobile. Not only did they commute to work and choose the parish they wished to attend, but few could trace their Virginia ancestry back two or three generations; some might not remain in the state long enough to produce even one generation. The Church began to face a well-educated, middle-class population with little corporate memory of, much less identification with, a histori-cal past. What began to develop were two expressions of Catholicism, the one rooted in Virginia's past and the other imported. Further com-plicating the issue was that the diocese of Richmond, one of the oldest in the country, was still not producing its own native vocations and depended heavily on priests recruited elsewhere.

Regardless of ideology or other issues, however, in 1974 the new diocese of Arlington was established, and the diocesan boundaries of Richmond and Wheeling were realigned to coincide with state lines. Both dioceses face similar problems of building upon the legacy of Virginia Catholicism's accommodation with its culture, while pre-serving the Catholic doctrine of the Church as the Mystical Body of Christ, visibly inserted into human history.

CHAPTER 27

John J. Russell, the Council, and Integration, 1958–1968

On November 9, 1960, the body of Bishop John McGill was solemnly transferred from the crypt of the old cathedral, St. Peter's, to the Cathedral of the Sacred Heart. The Sons of Confederate Veterans and the Daughters of the Confederacy accompanied the body of Richmond's Civil War bishop to its new resting place. Bishop John J. Russell celebrated Mass and preached on McGill's loyalty to the Confederacy.[1] It was a ceremony fraught with symbolism. The reinternment of Richmond's Confederate bishop marked the internment of Virginia Catholicism as part of the Old South. McGill had defended slavery; Russell would call not only for integration but also the civil rights of African Americans. As the second bishop of Richmond to attend an ecumenical council, Russell would play much more of a role at that assembly than his predecessor almost a century earlier. Vatican II, moreover, had far more of a pastoral effect on the diocese than Vatican I. Russell diligently implemented the council both by holding the Fourth Diocesan Synod and by engaging in ecumenical dialogue and cooperating with other denominations in working for civil rights. That implementation, however, forms the backdrop for the conclusion of this history, for historians tread on dangerous ground when they attempt to give an assessment of events in which many of the principals are still alive.

JOHN J. RUSSELL

On September 30, 1958, John J. Russell was installed as Richmond's tenth bishop. Born in Baltimore in 1897, he was raised in St. Ann's parish, where Ireton had been pastor. After secondary and higher education in Baltimore, he went to the North American College, where he was ordained on July 8, 1923, by his uncle, Bishop William T. Russell of Charleston. In 1947, with the formal division of the archdioceses of Baltimore and Washington, Russell remained in Washington as pastor of St. Patrick's and director of Catholic Charities under Archbishop Patrick J. O'Boyle. He was pastor of Nativity in 1950, when he was named bishop of Charleston. He was consecrated on March 14 by Archbishop Cicognani, the apostolic delegate, assisted by O'Boyle and Bishop John M. McNamara, auxiliary of Washington. At his installation in Richmond eight years later, Archbishop Francis P. Keough, as metropolitan, presided.[2] For the second time in a row, Richmond had a bishop from Baltimore.

In the beginning, Russell gave no sign that he would make any major innovations. Like other bishops, he saw communism as the major threat to the Church and nation. When Nikita Khrushchev visited the United States in September 1959, he ordered special prayers for the success of the visit, although he remarked that "Khrushchev's hands are crimsoned with the blood of our fellow Christians."[3] He also made changes in the diocesan administration. In June 1960, he named Justin McClunn, the chancellor, pastor of St. Paul's in Richmond to replace Thomas E. O'Connell who had been there since 1924. The new chancellor was Ernest Unterkoefler.[4] But Russell came to office at a period of transition in both the Church and the nation.

ELECTION OF JOHN XXIII AND PREPARATIONS FOR THE SECOND VATICAN COUNCIL

On October 9, 1958, Pope Pius XII died. On October 25, the cardinals began a three-day conclave to elect his successor. The Roman Curia, whose members dominated the college of cardinals, were clearly not as unified as the world may have believed. On the twelfth ballot, the electors finally settled on a "compromise candidate," the seventy-seven-year-old Angelo Cardinal Roncalli, patriarch of Venice, who took the name John XXIII. A compromise he may have been, but he soon electrified the Church by announcing on January 25, 1959, the Feast of the Conversion of St. Paul, that he was summoning an ecumenical council, the first one since 1870 and only the second in the history of the Church in the United States.

The American hierarchy was ill-prepared theologically for a council. The issue of religious liberty, so dear to Gibbons, Keane, and O'Connell was in dispute. Its leading theologian, John Courtney Murray, S.J., of Woodstock College in Maryland, remained under a cloud of suspicion. American Catholic biblical scholars were under attack, and the faculty of the Catholic University of America was divided on a series of issues. As the day for the opening of the council, October 11, 1962, drew near, Murray was not among the theologians invited to attend. As he himself put it, he was "disinvited" by conservative forces in Rome and Archbishop Egidio Vagnozzi, the apostolic delegate in the United States. He would, however, become an official theologian of the council from the second through the fourth and final sessions, through the intervention of Cardinal Spellman of New York.[5] Russell was uninvolved in these national disputes, but he did make his contribution to the preparation for the council.

In his "vota," or suggestions for the council's agenda, Russell indicated he was aware of the changing Church. He recommended that the lay apostolate be explained in light of the distinction between the character conferred by baptism and confirmation and that given in holy orders. He further proposed that the council continue the discussion begun at Vatican I in regard to papal infallibility, especially in regard to the authority of "encyclicals and other documents." On two points in particular, he anticipated some of the major work of the council. First, he argued that "the recitation of the Divine Office in the vernacular" would enhance "the spiritual life of priests" and be useful "in the preaching and instruction of the faithful." Second, he stated: "In a question of highest importance, the principles of total war ought to be judged and explained for the sake of the direction, information, and education of peoples and nations about nuclear explosions and the terrible and virtually universal destruction that would result from them."[6] He thus anticipated one of the key documents of the council, "The Church in the Modern World," which addressed such issues as the arms race.

By the time the council opened, the American Church was euphoric. In November 1960, the United States had elected its first Catholic president, John F. Kennedy. The bad memories of the Al Smith campaign of 1928 were laid to rest, and Catholics thought they had at last been accepted as Americans. The Catholic population of the diocese of Richmond continued to grow. A special census in July 1960 indicated that Catholics in the diocese now numbered 201,844, far above the estimate of 167,019 given in the 1960 *Official Catholic Directory*.[7] Russell would represent a far more important diocese at Vatican II than McGill had at Vatican I.

Both ordinaries and auxiliary bishops were to take part in the council. In May 1961, however, Bishop Hodges had been named coadjutor of Wheeling, where he succeeded as bishop in November 1962. In February 1962, Unterkoefler became Richmond's second auxiliary in history and was consecrated in Richmond by Archbishop Vagnozzi, assisted by Hodges and Bishop Vincent Waters of Raleigh. He and Russell would both attend the council.

Even before the council had opened, Russell began taking steps to implement two of its purposes, liturgical reform and the promotion of Christian unity. In less than a year and a half in office, he reversed Ireton's policy toward the liturgy. At the consultors' meeting on February 22, 1960, he announced that, on the following day, Father Walter J. Schmitz, S.S., of the Theological College at the Catholic University would address the clergy conference on "Lay Participation in the Mass." By the fall, he hoped to inaugurate lay participation throughout the diocese, and to implement it he appointed a committee consisting of Hodges as chairman, Louis Flaherty, Carroll Dozier, Chester Michael, Thomas Scannell, Walter Herbert, W. Rosser Muir, and Thomas Caroluzza.[8] Less than a year later, he named Dozier chairman of the commission to replace Hodges, who had gone to Wheeling.[9] It was but one step in the rise of the pastor of Christ the King to diocesan and national prominence.

On January 9, 1962, Russell proposed to the consultors a "program for co-operating with Pope John XXIII in promoting Church Unity." In addition to calling for prayers at all Masses during the "Church Unity Octave," January 18–25, and for prayers from January 25 until the opening of the council, he established a "Commission for Church Unity."[10] Richmond thus became the second diocese to establish an ecumenical commission—Archbishop Lawrence Shehan in Baltimore, Russell's classmate from boyhood, had preceded him by less than a week and liked to say it was easy for him to build on the work of his "predecessor," meaning Gibbons.[11] In Richmond, Russell, too, was building on the work of his predecessor, for Ireton had formed a commission for interdenominational cooperation twenty-five years before.

In the days before the council, Russell took further steps to promote ecumenism. He actively worked with other denominations to promote racial justice, but also fostered dialogue and understanding between Christians and Jews. In May 1962, Bishop John Wright of Pittsburgh informed Unterkoefler of the success of a retreat in Covington, Kentucky, for non-Catholic clergy under the auspices of the National Catholic Laymen's Retreat Conference. Unterkoefler was asked to select Protestant ministers to attend a second retreat at Loyola Retreat House, Faulkner, Maryland, conducted by the pioneer ecumenist, Gustave Weigel, S.J., of Woodstock College.[12] Unterkoefler complied by inviting Reverend Edward Meeks Gregory of St. Mark's Episcopal Church in Richmond, later affectionately known as "Pope Gregory," and Reverend A. Ronald Merrix of Monumental Episcopal Church in Richmond.[13]

Richmond's promotion of dialogue included participation of laity and clergy in interreligious discussion. In April 1962, for example, Russell approved the plan of the Council of Catholic Women of Annandale to sponsor a discussion at St. Michael's Church with the pastors of the local Lutheran and Presbyterian churches.[14] That summer, he invited all the priests of the diocese to attend a session in Richmond conducted by Father Thomas Stransky, C.S.P., at that time the only American on the Secretariat for Promoting Christian Unity, the special group John XXIII had created for ecumenical relations under the presidency of Augustin Cardinal Bea, S.J., a biblical scholar.[15] In January 1963, between sessions of the council, Russell became the first Catholic bishop to address the annual meeting of the Episcopal diocese of Virginia.[16] In June 1965, Richmond became the first diocese to promulgate detailed directives for both clergy and laity concerning ecumenical relations.

On October 11, 1962, the council opened. For Russell and many American bishops, it was a learning experience. Once in Rome, he took up residence in the Grand Hotel with several other bishops, including Unterkoefler, Lawrence Shehan of Baltimore, John Carberry, then bishop of Lafayette, Indiana, and later archbishop of St. Louis and a cardinal. Shehan brought with him Monsignor Porter White, a canonist, for the first session, and added Father James Laubacher, former rector of St. Mary's Seminary, for subsequent ones.[17] The informal discussions at the hotel after the official meetings of the council became a theological seminar. For perhaps the first time since leaving the seminary, Russell and many bishops were discussing theological issues. During the first session of the council, however, neither Russell nor Unterkoefler made any interventions. But they were absorbing their lessons.

ELECTION OF PAUL VI AND THE
CONTINUATION OF THE COUNCIL

On June 3, 1963, the period when Russell was actively engaged in promoting civil rights, John XXIII died after a prolonged bout with cancer. On June 21, the cardinals, a substantially different body than the one that had assembled in 1958, almost immediately turned to Giovanni Battista Cardinal Montini, archbishop of Milan, the first cardinal John had named. Paul VI would see the council through to its completion.

One of Montini's key interventions during the first session had been on the nature of the Church. On October 30, 1963, during the second session, Russell made his own contribution to this issue on the council floor. He proposed that the draft document on the Church treat the holiness of the Church before "the vocation of the faithful to holiness," since the Church also contained sinners. He explained his position:

> The Church is holy because it is the Body of Christ. Its author is God. It is consecrated to God who is peculiarly present to it and in it. The proper work of the Church is salvation, the union of man with God in Christ, the communication of grace through the Sacraments, through preaching the Word and through the presence of Christ in it.
>
> Finally, just as Christ Himself in His holy humanity was an instrument joined to divinity for sanctifying men, so the Church, as the true continuation of Christ in the world is the salutary instrument of the faithful and their union with God.[18]

He ended his speech with the customary "Dixi," that is, "I have spoken." He later told newsmen in Richmond: "It sounds like 'Dixie,' but I didn't let out a rebel yell."[19]

Later on in the council, Russell was the spokesman for 150 bishops in a brief intervention in favor of priests using the vernacular in the recitation of the breviary, which he had already recommended in his vota.[20] On December 8, 1965, the council ended. Among the decrees promulgated that day was the Declaration on Religious Liberty. The American position, so long held suspect, was now part of official Church teaching. The same day, Russell's friend, Lawrence Shehan of Baltimore, recently named the second cardinal of the nation's oldest see, was absent from the council. Paul VI had named him legate to go to Istanbul to remove the excommunication of Patriarch Athenagoras's predecessor, issued in 1054. A new era was dawning in the Church.

IMPLEMENTING THE COUNCIL: THE FOURTH SYNOD OF RICHMOND

In the meantime, in December 1964, Unterkoefler had become bishop of Charleston, bringing to three the ordinaries of other dioceses who had been priests of Richmond, but leaving Russell bereft of an auxiliary for the second time in less than four years. In August 1966, Monsignor Louis Flaherty, former superintendent of schools and then pastor of St. Andrew's in Roanoke, was named auxiliary and rector of the cathedral—in 1967, he was transferred to St. Paul's in Richmond and later to Blessed Sacrament in Norfolk. In the meantime, Walter F. Sullivan, previously director of the marriage tribunal, became chancellor. Also active were Monsignor John J. McMahon, director of Catholic Charities, and Richard J. Burke, superintendent of schools, who, eight years later, would become the first chancellor of the new diocese of Arlington.[21] These were the principal members of the diocesan curia as Russell presided over the Fourth Synod of the diocese, the first one since 1933.

On March 4, 1963, between the first and second sessions of the council, Russell announced that he would hold a synod at the end of the council. In preparation, he established a Central Preparatory Commission, modeled on that of the ecumenical council and consisting of the chairmen of five committees that would treat the clergy, the laity, the teaching authority of the Church, the sacraments and sacred liturgy, and the temporal goods of the Church. Beginning on April 1, 1963, each committee was to meet at least once a month, except in the summer, until its work was completed. In addition, the diocesan councils of men and women were to act in advisory capacities; the laity in general was invited to submit their views to the boards of the two councils.[22] The synod and preparation for it were to be instruments for educating the diocese about the teaching of the council.

For more than three and a half years, the various committees met, with input from the laity. In convoking the synod to meet at the cathedral on the afternoon of December 5, 1966, Russell invited all the diocesan and religious priests engaged in pastoral ministry and the newly established Diocesan Pastoral Council to participate.[23] On the eve of its convocation, he urged as many of the religious and laity as possible to attend. But, he noted, "in these changing times, it will probably be necessary to have another synod in a few years."[24]

The tone of the synod was noticeably different from the previous one held in 1933. The statutes were arranged in five sections: I. The People of God; II. The Worship of God in Christ; III. Proclaiming and Hearing the Word of God; IV. Promoting Christian Unity; and V. Caring for Material Goods. The first section provided for "A Pastoral Council composed of priests, Religious and laymen," "a Senate of Priests . . . to give effective assistance to the Bishop in the government of the diocese," and "a Parish Advisory Board . . . [to] advise the pastor 'in all matters that pertain to the temporal and spiritual good of the parish.'"[25]

Reflecting the work Russell and his priests had already done in integration and civil rights, the synod declared that "priests . . . should promote genuine concern for the poor, the sick, and the victims of prejudice and discrimination,"[26] but were "strictly [to] avoid . . . any activity in secular politics, and any public acts or statements which manifest partisan political views."[27]

Although the synod recognized the right of the laity to form their own organizations, "provided they maintain the proper relationship to Church authorities," it also decreed that "no Catholic shall be excluded from any Catholic organization because of race, color or national origin."[28] Implementing the council's norms for the liturgy, however, the synod illustrated the limits of Russell's openness to the new. "At special Masses for youth," there could be "approved folk hymns . . . sung to the accompaniment of organ or guitar," but "electrically amplified guitars and other unapproved musical instruments may not be used."[29]

The synod also mirrored Russell's goals for education in the diocese. While it called for Newman Clubs "at every secular college in the diocese,"[30] it encouraged parents to "send their children to Catholic schools—elementary school, high school and college."[31] It also legislated that ecumenism pervade the curriculum of the seminary and all private and diocesan schools, that "clergy of other religions" be invited to Catholic institutions to explain their beliefs, and that students tour other churches and synagogues. The junior clergy exams, given every year for five years after ordination, were to "include the ecumenical viewpoint and ecumenical subjects," and ecumenism should be part of the days of recollection held monthly in each deanery and of the annual clergy retreats. The synod, moreover, encouraged "informal conversations with the clergy of other religious bodies" and training in ecumenism for teachers in both Catholic schools and the Confraternity of Christian Doctrine. Cooperation with other individuals and groups on civic matters, long a characteristic of Virginia Catholicism, now became a synod statute.[32]

But the synod also seemed to see clouds of disagreement forming on the horizon. It decreed that "Catholics should give support and leadership to civic, state, and federal programs and legislation which deal with social justice and welfare as long as these programs are in keeping with Catholic moral principles and social teaching."[33] Within a few years support of government programs and ecumenical cooperation would be endangered by the legalization of abortion.

In many ways, the synod simply formalized what the diocese had already been doing for some time in regard to issues like civic cooperation with other groups. But in its implementation of liturgical reform and provision for lay involvement in church administration, it reflected the diocese's response to Vatican II.

St. John Vianney Seminary

Russell had made education one of his principal concerns. Early in his episcopate, he sought to realize one of the long-standing desires of several of his predecessors—the founding of a seminary. The occasion was the closing of the high school seminary at St. Bernard's in Alabama and the acceptance of only five Richmond candidates at St. Charles in Catonsville, Maryland. In light of these developments "and because the Holy See has strongly urged that every Diocese have its own minor seminary," Russell announced to his consultors, on September 1, 1959, that he would start a preparatory seminary the following year.

It would be under the direction of the diocesan clergy. The diocese had already procured a forty-acre tract on the James River, twelve miles from the cathedral on River Road. The consultors then voted to name the seminary "St. John Vianney." When asked for suggestions on the rector, Govaert proposed George Gormley, the former director of vocations, but Hodges prevailed with his nomination of Chester Michael.[34]

On September 20, 1960, the seminary opened with seventy-seven students, under Michael as rector and Carl J. Naro as vice-rector. By 1962, it had 154 students, of whom 45 left before going to the major seminary.[35] There then followed a series of rectors, Louis Flaherty (1963–65), Gabriel T. Maioriello (1965–68), Thomas F. Shreve (1968–74), and John Leonard (1974–78).

By 1967, however, the future of the seminary became embroiled with the plans for a Central Catholic High School in Richmond. At a meeting of the board of pastors of the proposed school, scheduled to open in 1969, Russell reported that none of the congregations of women contacted could staff the institution. Walter Sullivan then proposed that St. Patrick's High School be retained for girls and that St. John Vianney become a preparatory school for boys and accept day students. Although the board unanimously accepted this proposal,[36] it was not implemented. By the academic year 1971–72 the seminary enrolled 101 students, of whom 23 graduated. By 1973, however, the consultors recommended that the institution be closed.[37] The seminary, however, continued until 1978, when, despite its high enrollment, it was closed, partially because of the financial burden on the diocese.

HIGH SCHOOLS

Aside from the seminary, however, Russell had other educational plans. In February 1960, he informed his consultors that he hoped to establish three new high schools in Alexandria, Annandale, and Norfolk. Only one of these, Bishop Ireton High School for boys in Alexandria under the Oblates of St. Francis de Sales, ever opened. The other two fell victim to the decline in religious vocations and the inability or unwillingness of the Catholic population to support schools staffed by laypeople. The first of these two was a school for girls in

Annandale on property that Scannell had purchased to be staffed jointly by the Immaculate Heart of Mary Sisters, the Precious Blood Sisters, and the Bernardine Sisters. The second involved a more complicated arrangement. Ireton had given the Religious of the Sacred Heart of Mary an option on twenty acres in Norfolk for them to open a high school. The sisters, however, asked to exchange that property for thirteen acres in Fairfax County, where they would open a private school for girls in 1963. Although they would then be willing to staff a diocesan school for girls in Norfolk, that plan never materialized. But Norfolk Catholic at this time was planning on expanding its facilities to accommodate more students.[38]

Across Hampton Roads, the diocese took over the parish high school of St. Vincent de Paul in Newport News. Founded in 1903 through the generosity of Thomas Fortune Ryan, it had become coeducational in 1930 when the Xaverian Brothers closed the boys school. In 1960, Russell opened the school to all students on the Peninsula and, in 1966, renamed it Peninsula Catholic High School.[39] In 1965, he also announced that a new Central Catholic High School for Richmond would open on twenty-two acres in Henrico County.[40] These plans, too, had to be abandoned, partly because the property acquired had been condemned to make way for Interstate 64 and partly because the diocese failed to engender financial support for the project. Many Catholic parents in Virginia and elsewhere chose to send their children to the public schools. It was a trend that would have ramifications for the future education of Virginia Catholics. Although Russell had to abandon his plans for three of the high schools he proposed, he was more successful in completing one other long-term goal of his predecessor.

St. Mary's Hospital, Richmond

As early as 1921, Bishop O'Connell had investigated the possibility of having the Sisters of Mercy staff a hospital in Richmond. In 1929, Brennan had actually purchased property for a hospital.[41] Then, in 1937, Ireton had Father Thomas E. Mitchell, director of Catholic Charities, conduct a survey for a Catholic hospital in Richmond. While Mitchell concluded that Richmond had a sufficient number of hospitals, he stated there was still need for a Catholic one.[42] In

October 1939 a committee report recommended that, because group medical plans had increased hospitalization over the past two years, a Catholic hospital would be "a powerful factor in the elimination of religious prejudice and in the salvation of souls."[43] Here the matter rested for two years.

In March 1941, Ireton asked the Franciscan Sisters of Allegheny, Pennsylvania, if they would be interested in opening a hospital in Richmond. Brennan, he continued, had already purchased a site. He then reported the two surveys he had commissioned in 1937 and 1939.[44] Unfortunately, Ireton did not retain any reply to his query. In October 1944, however, he expressed annoyance at a physician for telling the Richmond Hospital Service Corporation that the diocese had the "hope or intent sooner or later" to open a hospital. He wanted his plans kept confidential, since he had not yet procured a site.[45] Just what happened to the site Brennan had purchased, he did not say, but, by the fall of 1945, he had selected a site, only to learn it would not sustain the eight-story building he planned.[46]

In the meantime, Ireton purchased property on Monument Avenue but developed no further plans. On September 1, 1959, Russell informed his consultors that he was proceeding with a hospital. "Few cities this size in our country," he commented, "are without a Catholic Hospital." At the urging of the Catholic Physicians Guild, he had hired a consultant who reported the need for a 150 bed hospital.[47] By October, he had arranged for the Sisters of Bon Secours to staff the new hospital.[48] Almost two years later, he announced that it would be named "St. Mary's Hospital."[49]

Meanwhile, the hospital received a benefaction. On February 23, 1962, Mrs. Florence H. Lawler, chair of the board and treasurer of the Union Life Insurance Company in Richmond, died in Florida, leaving a substantial amount for the hospital in her will.[50] On January 9, 1966, after almost three years of construction, Lawrence Cardinal Shehan of Baltimore presided at the dedication of the new building. The cardinal, Russell, and six other bishops then dedicated each floor.[51]

Systematic Fund-Raising

Construction of the hospital and of the new seminary, in addition to parish indebtedness, led Russell in 1959 to engage the services of the Community Counselling Services of New York to inaugurate what became an annual event, the Diocesan Development Fund. The strategy was one that became commonplace. Dividing the diocese into five regions, the campaign first targeted more affluent potential donors for advanced gifts before the campaign officially began in early October. Next, solicitors would seek "memorial gifts" of $360 or more from slightly less affluent people. Finally, they would approach the remainder of the parishioners for a pledge of $120 over two years.[52] Funding for the hospital was to come exclusively from parishes in the Richmond area. The goal for the first drive was set at $4,500,000. At its conclusion in December, the drive had realized $6,378,556.[53] The following year, the diocese set a goal of $550,000 to purchase sites for new parishes and buildings, pay for the education of seminarians, defray the cost of maintenance of the seminary, and provide for other diocesan projects. Again the contributions exceeded the goal, by more than $333,000. Richmond's Catholics, many of whom were newcomers, were generous. From the new fund, the diocese purchased property for the projected new St. Mary's parish in Richmond and St. Nicholas parish in Virginia Beach, as well as other sites. The following year, the diocese sought $550,000 and obtained $751,574. The funds were to be allocated to the education of seminarians and, as in the previous year, to the purchase of new sites.[54] These new pieces of property were made necessary by the continued development of the suburbs of northern Virginia and Virginia Beach. But Russell would be remembered not only for the parishes he opened but also for those he closed, as he moved the diocese further along to full integration.

BISHOP RUSSELL AND THE INTEGRATION OF PARISHES

In November 1958, less than two months after taking office in Richmond, Russell attended the annual meeting of the hierarchy in Washington. The bishops issued a ringing condemnation of segregation that "in itself and by its very nature imposes a stigma of inferiority upon the segregated people." The old legal doctrine of "separate but equal," they declared, could not be reconciled "with the Christian view of man's nature and rights" as articulated by Pius XII. "Negro citizens," they continued,

wish an education that does not carry with it any stigma of inferiority. They wish economic advancement based on merit and skill.

They wish their rights as American citizens. They wish acceptance based upon proved ability and achievement. No one who truly loves God's children will deny them this opportunity.

With a warning about the future, they concluded: "we hope and earnestly pray that responsible and soberminded Americans of all religious faiths, in all areas of our land, will seize the mantle of leadership from the agitator and the racist. It is vital that we act now and act decisively. All must act quietly, courageously, and prayerfully before it is too late."[55]

Although Russell was not one of the drafters of the statement, he made its words his own. He gradually shifted Ireton's approach to pastoral care of African Americans by closing some of the parishes Ireton opened and making territorial ones of others. In this, he was motivated by the desire for racial integration, but sometimes he ran counter to the desires of some Black Catholics.[56]

In 1959, he made his first report to the national committee for Indian and Negro Missions. Of all the Black parishes, only St. Joseph's in Norfolk was without debt, and its buildings were in desperate need of repair. St. Gerard's maternity home in Richmond, however, had influence throughout the state and served Black women in North Carolina, Maryland, and the District of Columbia. Still, the number of Black converts remained small.[57] A year later, however, he said that a recent census indicated there were 1,000 more Black Catholics in the diocese than had been previously known. But, for the first time, he noted another problem. Although Black children had been admitted to parochial and high schools in most areas, he still had to provide separate schools and churches for Black Catholics, "because the vast majority of them prefer to have their own facilities."[58]

In the meantime, the buildings of St. Joseph's in Norfolk had to be demolished to make way for the city's plans for urban renewal. Russell had the Josephites move to St. Mary's, the city's original parish nearby, which would serve all the people within the territory, most of whom were Black.[59] But his efforts at integration met resistance, not from white Catholics, he informed the national committee in 1961, but from Black Catholics, the "majority" of whom "do not seem eager to integrate in schools. It is also necessary to maintain thirteen churches for their use." One of these churches was Holy Rosary in Richmond. In the planning stage since the 1940s, it was now the fastest growing Black parish.[60] In 1962, the parish began building a church to replace the multipurpose hall it had been using. Unfortunately, because of the neighborhood, Russell commented, it would be "practically a segregated church."[61]

In northern Virginia, Russell made Our Lady Queen of Peace in Arlington a territorial parish in 1963.[62] Two years later, he closed Our Lady of Victory in Portsmouth, long suffering from debt, and the parishioners were transferred to the territorial parishes in the vicinity.[63] By 1967, he had closed St. Margaret Mary in Charlottesville, whose parishioners would now attend Holy Comforter, and St. Gerard's in Richmond, whose people would go to Sacred Heart in South Richmond.[64]

While Russell was intent on ending racially segregated parishes, he recognized the desires of the people themselves for separate schools.[65] In 1965, St. Joseph's in Richmond had received a grant from the Ford Foundation to conduct evening classes for adults to assist them in getting jobs.[66] The oldest parish for Black Catholics in the diocese, founded in 1884, seemed to be thriving. Three years later, however, a special committee of the council of priests, an independent study conducted by the Josephites, and the Franciscan Sisters of Mill Hill who operated St. Joseph's elementary school, still called the van de Vyver School, all agreed that the church and school should be closed. Russell then formed a committee, chaired by Monsignor Walter F. Sullivan, the chancellor, to make final recommendations. In December 1968, this committee then met with the parishioners, all of whom expressed their acquiescence in closing the parish, but feared being accepted in the territorial parishes. The committee made two recommendations. First, the pastor of the parish to which St. Joseph's former parishioners would now go should visit each new family or parishioner and then draft a letter to welcome them. Second, each parish was to hold an open house to welcome the newcomers. On June 1, 1969, St. Joseph's formally came to an end. Russell's reasoning sounded feasible. Eighty-five percent of the 516 parishioners lived outside the immediate vicinity and in the territories of thirteen other parishes, as did 95 percent of the 235 students.[67]

But the closing occurred simultaneously with the rise of Black consciousness and may have deprived the diocese of an important outreach to the African-American community, even though the buildings of the parish were subsequently used for a diocesan-sponsored community center, until the school burned in 1973. Since the church building also had many structural weaknesses, it and other buildings were demolished. The bishop then transferred the financial assets to Holy Rosary to build a child-care center. He sent the stained glass windows to St. John's Church in Woodstock, then under construction.

By 1970, other institutions that Ireton founded for Black Catholics were also closed. St. Augustine's, the mother church of Holy Rosary in Richmond, was included among the condemned buildings in the city's redevelopment of the Fulton area. St. Alphonsus in Newport News and its mission near Hampton Institute, Blessed Martin de Porres, and Holy Family in Petersburg were sold. Diocesan clergy took over Holy Rosary, and the Redemptorists now confined themselves to their retreat house in Hampton and the neighboring parish of St. Joseph.

In addition, rising costs, shrinking enrollments, and the availability of integrated schools led to the closing of two other pioneering institutions, St. Francis de Sales School for girls in 1970, and St. Emma's for boys in 1972. The Holy Ghost Fathers temporarily remained to take care of St. Edward's, the chapel of St. Emma's, and St. Catherine's in Cartersville.[68]

In a period of thirty years, the diocese had made remarkable progress in the work with African Americans. From interracial justice, it had moved to integration. In the process, it had shifted from a policy under Ireton of establishing Black parishes to one under Russell of making all parishes territorial, although this meant that in some cases, such as St. Mary's in Norfolk and Holy Rosary in Richmond, the parishes would be in neighborhoods that were predominantly Black.

The Diocese of Richmond and Civil Rights

By the middle 1960s, Russell had already taken leadership in other areas of racial justice. At this time, of course, Vatican II was in session, and its deliberations on the role of the Church in society seem to have shaped his approach to this most pressing of American problems. Russell used the periods between the sessions personally to promote racial justice. In June 1963, he joined 250 religious leaders at President Kennedy's invitation for a meeting at the White House, which led to the formation of a national interfaith committee, chaired by J. Irvin

Miller, president of the National Council of Churches.[69] In July, he followed the lead of Archbishop Patrick O'Boyle of Washington in issuing a pastoral letter on civil rights. He had it read in all the churches and published in *The Catholic Virginian.* He began by stating that "it is appropriate and important at this critical time to remind our good Catholic people of their obligation regarding fraternal charity and racial justice." He went on to quote John XXIII's encyclical *Pacem in Terris,* issued the previous April, in which the pope called for the "establishment of a civic order in which the rights and duties are ever more sincerely and effectively acknowledged." He cited Paul VI's statement to President Kennedy that "We are ever mindful in our prayers of the efforts to insure to all your citizens the equal benefits of citizenship which have as their foundation the equality of all men because of their dignity as persons and children of God." Russell reminded his people that the bishops of the United States had already addressed the question of discrimination in November 1958.

Russell then addressed the specific situation in the diocese. Although diocesan institutions and organizations had been integrated, "now the time has come when our Negro brethren are seeking their full rights as citizens," for which Catholics of the diocese "must apply Christian principles to present conditions and in our daily living practice what Christ teaches through His church." He concluded with the plea: "Let us Catholics in union with our fellow citizens of other faiths work for the cause of racial justice in Christian charity."[70] His letter was not only an implementation of the national interfaith committee's work but also a practical application of ecumenism then being discussed at the council.

Remarking to O'Boyle that "imitation is the sincerest flattery", he sent him a copy of his pastoral. During the clergy retreat, he continued, he had urged all his priests to join the clergy of other denominations in working toward racial justice and charity. In Richmond, he reported, the restaurants, theaters, ball park, and the Mosque, a civic auditorium, were already desegregated, but "Danville, Virginia is our trouble spot in the State and we have there only a one man parish and a new pastor," Carl J. Naro.[71]

Danville was indeed a "trouble spot." In July 1963, Dorothy Day, founder of the Catholic Worker movement, went to Danville to participate in demonstrations and speak for integration. This prompted a complaint from Dr. D. L. Arey, a member of the city government, whose wife was a Catholic.[72] In his reply, Russell admitted he knew nothing of Day's going to Danville until he heard reports of her taking part. While he acknowledged that "she certainly does not represent the Catholic Church in Danville," he enclosed a copy of his pastoral letter.[73] While some people complained of this new Catholic activism, Russell's pastoral letter drew praise from a wide variety of religious leaders and the endorsement of the Richmond Area Ministers' Association.[74]

The diocese of Richmond was placing itself decidedly on the side of integration and the civil rights movement. On August 28, 1963, Father John J. McMahon, moderator of the Catholic Interracial Council of Richmond, headed a delegation of seventy to take part in the Civil Rights March from the Washington Monument to the Lincoln Memorial. From Northern Virginia, 130 members and friends of the Catholic Interracial Council of Northern Virginia first attended special Masses before boarding buses to take them to the march.[75] With Catholic Interracial councils already in place in Richmond and northern Virginia, moreover, in May 1964 Russell called for establishing one in Tidewater.[76]

Monsignor Carroll Dozier, dean of the Tidewater Deanery and pastor of Christ the King in Norfolk, bristled at the veiled charge that, because his deanery did not have a Catholic Interracial Council, it was not working for racial justice. Because he suspected "the lines of communication to you are not open," he outlined for Russell the work of his deanery. As a result of the work of the deanery's pastors, all the parochial schools were integrated, as was Norfolk Catholic High School. Since "the place of [Our Lady of] Victory has been legislated out of existence," "territorial limits [were] set to St. Mary's Bowers Hill, so that there is not a soul who does not belong to a definite parish." The deanery's Council of Catholic Women had, moreover, continued its work in education for racial justice.

Dozier enclosed for Russell a recent newspaper article about De Paul Hospital. A Black youth leader had recently charged that Norfolk's hospitals remained segregated, but a member of the Citizens Advisory Committee personally undertook an investigation of De Paul Hospital to find that all but one ward was integrated, and that one was soon to be turned into an integrated ward for poor patients. Dozier further reported that as recently as May 15, one of Norfolk Catholic High School's few Black students, Kenneth McDaniel of St. Mary's parish, had been elected student council president. He had himself spoken at the annual Communion Breakfast of St. Mary's Sodality at which a Black woman was installed as president. He "spoke on the joint place of Pacem in Terris and the Constitution of the Liturgy in relation to spiritual life as the source of community life and made a special plea for them [the Sodality] to come join in this work of the Church." He concluded by saying, "Honestly, Bishop, I do not know what a Catholic Interracial Council can add to the present picture." While he preferred "some activation of the Diocesan Council of Men, which had "no solid mass support," he promised his "support for the Catholic Interracial Council, if you see fit."[77] Whether Tidewater was to have an interracial council made little difference. Its clergy were solidly behind the civil rights movement.

Throughout the diocese, Russell promoted fair housing. In Charlottesville, he joined Father Michael, the pastor of Holy Comforter, in opening a low-cost housing project. Early in 1965, meanwhile, Russell became actively involved in an ecumenical promotion of fair housing in northern Virginia, an issue in which Scannell had been a leader since the late 1950s.[78] In January, the bishop met with the priests of northern Virginia at Bishop Ireton High School to discuss the campaign for fair housing jointly conducted by the diocese, the Council of Churches of Greater Washington, and the Jewish Community Council of greater Washington. Coordinating these efforts, Rabbi Noah Golinkin invited Stewart Udall, the secretary of the interior, to attend a convocation on fair housing on February 11. He noted that Russell and Rev. David G. Colwell, president of the Council of Churches of Greater Washington, would be present.[79] On Sunday, February 14, over 15,000 Catholics, Protestants, and Jews signed a Fair Housing Statement. Over 1,000 Catholics then engaged in a house-to-house canvass on March 5 and 7 to gain additional signatures. The results were then given to bankers, home builders, apartment owners, and real estate brokers as proof that Northern Virginians wanted racially integrated neighborhoods.[80] Russell himself congratulated the director of the Northern Virginia Interracial Council for its success in gaining 40,000 signatures in this door-to-door canvass.[81]

But of all the events of Russell's episcopate, perhaps the March on Selma best revealed his support for racial justice and his ambiguity on the means to attain it. Early in March, 1965, he sent the NAACP a donation for the defense of 3,400 African Americans facing charges stemming from the voter registration drive led by Martin Luther King, Jr.[82] On April 2, *The Catholic Virginian* published an NCWC news story on the march in which many priests and nuns participated.[83] Although Father John McMahon and three Virginia laymen had been invited to go by the National Catholic Conference for Interracial Justice, Father William Stickle, O.P., of St. Thomas Church in Charlottesville was the only Virginia priest to participate.[84] Russell, nevertheless, received letters in opposition to the march. Arthur Leman, president of Southwest Oilfield Products, in Houston, and the John Walthall League, protested that these priests and nuns were present at Selma contrary to the authority of Archbishop Thomas J. Toolen of Mobile but with the permission of some bishops.[85]

Russell's response was forthright. He noted that the priests, nuns, and laypeople, "who took part in demonstrations in Alabama, are citizens of the United States." They had been instrumental in helping Black citizens gain their rights to register and vote. Furthermore, he continued, "The Negroes waited a hundred years and failed to receive these rights until they began to demonstrate. I would not want Catholics to remain entirely aloof from a movement to secure the rights of a minority." In regard to Leman's charge that Catholic participants were disobeying Toolen, like Russell a Baltimorean, he flatly denied that they were "disobeying Divine authority in the Church." Finally, he expressed the hope that Blacks would gain the right to vote in Alabama and, "if so, we can be proud that some of our fellow members of the Church had a part in that achievement."[86]

By the summer, Russell informed his pastors in a letter to be read at all Masses that the diocese would "no longer tolerate discriminatory hiring practices among firms and individuals with which it does business." He urged parishioners to adopt the same policy in their businesses.[87] He had also established the Office of Economic Opportunity under the direction of Sister Mary Thomasine, M.S.B.T., to coordinate the diocese's efforts to cooperate with the Federal government's war against poverty. Between January and March 1966, each deanery sponsored meetings to assess the needs of their areas and to enlist the aid of the laity in the program. Russell made attendance of clergy obligatory at these meetings, to which religious and laity were also invited.[88] It may well have been because the diocese already had an Office of Economic Opportunity that Russell's consultors rejected the national program, "Project Equality," as redundant and made Richmond the first diocese not to join the national program.[89]

INTEGRATION OF THE KNIGHTS OF COLUMBUS

While Russell had achieved statewide prominence for his stance for integration, he still had the problem of integrating other Catholic organizations, notably the Knights of Columbus. In November 1963, J. Michael Kelleher, Deputy Grand Knight for Virginia, complained to him about newspaper coverage of the failure of the Knights to accept Black members. He noted that the bishop had spoken at various times of his "interest in social justice" and, at the Clergy night sponsored by the Richmond council, "you said we should take colored people into our membership 'but that I do not expect you to do this tomorrow.'" While the Knights had taken this seriously, the Richmond *Times-Dispatch* and *News Leader* reported the strong criticism of the organization by Father McMahon. As Kelleher interpreted McMahon's comments,

> Catholic gentlemen were attacked without any prior notice whatsoever to my knowledge. Until this time I, as State Deputy, cannot remember him asking the Knights of Columbus to accept any particular colored man's application. We cannot understand why any problem can not be solved among us instead of by the public. Should Father McMahon be comparing the Knights of Columbus with an organization that is not in the favor of Catholic priests, we have no alternative but to feel his statement unjustified.

He went on to note that invitations were extended at two churches to Catholic men without reference to race and he knew of no survey indicating Knights opposed integration.[90]

Russell was intent on more than having the Knights of Columbus admit "Negro Catholics." The law in Virginia stated that fraternal beneficiary associations that admitted black and white members were not to be licensed to do business in the state. In January 1964, the bishop, therefore, sought the legal opinion of Luke E. Hart, formerly the Supreme Advocate and, at that time, the Supreme Grand Knight in New Haven, in regard to whether the law endangered the rights of

Knights to do business if Negroes were admitted. Russell wanted to work either to repeal the law or provide a test case in the courts. If he decided on a test case, he wanted to know "could we count upon your legal staff supporting us?" In his evaluation, the problem arose from the fact that five or six men could blackball a candidate because of color or race. Such action, he believed, was reprehensible, and he proposed a solution that, while not a canonical sanction, would embarrass the Catholic fraternal organization:

> I would feel that in this day and age, I could not condone such a variance from Catholic teaching and would feel it necessary to refuse to appoint Chaplains or to recognize the Knights of Columbus as a Catholic association. Thereby I would be penalizing a large majority who would be willing to adhere to Catholic principles and accept the Negro member.

He concluded by enclosing a copy of the Code of Virginia.[91]

Russell's request added to the pressure on Hart and the Knights of Columbus for their racial policies. Hart, never enthusiastic for integration, defended the "blackball" system of which the bishop complained, until a well-publicized incident occurred in Chicago in November 1963. A council of the order had rejected a Black candidate who was a graduate of Notre Dame. Six officers of the council resigned in protest. Bishop Cletus F. O'Donnell, auxiliary of Chicago, and the archdiocesan Interracial Council condemned the "blackball" system.[92]

While Russell was putting pressure on the Knights locally and nationally, he succeeded in maintaining cordial relations with the Knights individually, although he once refused them a dispensation from the Friday abstinence when they held their annual convention in Norfolk in 1966. They could have Mass in the hotel, he said, but "I believe our brother Knights of the Norfolk area would feel very hurt if a dispensation were given so that the Knights could eat meat in the city where one finds the finest seafood in all the world, which will be enjoyed so much that we will not gain much merit by abstaining from meat, so abstain we will."[93] Russell's approach had been one of gentle, yet firm, persuasion. But he was prepared to take stronger action.

In June 1966, Russell spoke before an assembly of Knights in Richmond. While he praised their campaign against pornography, he chastised them for having no Black members. As a result, he stated that he would no longer attend any functions involving councils of the Knights that were not integrated. He further urged that councils should actively recruit Black members.[94] In August 1966, he followed this with a letter to the Knights of Columbus chaplains, stating his reluctance to appoint chaplains to "any Councils which had not admitted into their ranks qualified Catholics of the Negro race." He granted that, in some areas of the diocese, recruitment of African-American Catholics was difficult, so "I was then asked in appointing Chaplains to urge them to assist the Grand Knights in a recruitment of new members into the Order, disregarding race, thus the Chaplains particularly would seek Negro prospects so that the Councils would not seem to fail to practice what the Church teaches." He now placed the onus of recruiting black members on the chaplains.[95] By the summer of 1967, his policy seems to have borne fruit. He reappointed Paul D. Jenkins as chaplain of the Richmond council, because he had "served well in that capacity, especially with regard to accepting Negro members into membership."[96]

The work of the diocese for racial justice and integration was due to several factors, not the least of which were the new people coming into the state from elsewhere, for whom segregation simply made no sense. This was especially true for members of the armed services that had been integrated since the Truman administration. But the success of the Catholic efforts can be attributed to the influence of Russell, who was to shepherd an ever growing flock through the years following Vatican II.

CHAPTER 28

"The Storied Land
of Power Mower and
Charcoal Cookout"

At the same time that Bishop Russell was working for the integration of his parishes, his diocese was undergoing increased suburbanization, especially in northern Virginia and Virginia Beach and to a lesser extent in Richmond itself. But the suburbs brought with them a vastly different lifestyle than that which had confronted the diocese and the American Church in the past. Suburban Catholics were affluent and well educated. They no longer walked to their neighborhood church that a generation before provided religious as well as ethnic identity. They were blending in with mainstream American culture. The criteria for finding a site for a suburban parish was similar to that for a shopping center. Both now needed space for a parking lot. Both had to be near a major artery, though not necessarily an Interstate. Neither was primarily concerned with access by public transportation.[1]

When addressing the national convention of Catholic Charities in New York in 1960, Russell referred to the suburbs as "the storied land of power mower and charcoal cookout."[2] That "storied land" in northern Virginia would lead in 1974 to the establishment of the new diocese of Arlington.

EXPANSION IN NORTHERN VIRGINIA

The Catholic population of northern Virginia continued to explode in the 1960s. As early as April 1959, Russell brought to the attention of his consultors that the school at St. Michael's in Annandale had become so overcrowded that he recommended establishing a new parish of St. Bernadette's in Springfield, for which the diocese had already purchased property.[3] Only a few months later, Our Lady of Angels in Woodbridge, formerly a mission of All Saints in Manassas, became a parish staffed by the Stigmatine Fathers.[4] To the west in the Shenandoah Valley, the Capuchins were closing their seminary in Staunton but agreed to take over St. John's Mission in Woodstock, subsequently renamed St. John Bosco.[5] In February 1960, Russell informed his consultors that in the previous year the diocese had purchased property in Broyhill Park, Braddock Road, Franconia, Springfield, and two sites in Burke, all in Fairfax County. These new properties did not include those already purchased by parishes.[6]

New parishes arose in northern Virginia in rapid succession as Interstates 95, 66, and 495, the Capital Beltway, not only opened the area to new settlement but also changed the way people commuted to their jobs. While this is not the place to tell in detail the story of the founding of each of these parishes, a mere listing of them, tedious though it may appear, illustrates the rapid growth of the region. Fairfax and Arlington Counties and Alexandria, the closest regions to Washington, experienced the first major growth. In Fairfax, St. Michael's in Annandale had already split to form St. Bernadette's in 1959. The territory was further divided into the new parishes of Holy Spirit (1964) and St. Ambrose (1966). Elsewhere in Fairfax, there followed St. Luke's in McLean (1961), St. Philip's in Falls Church (1962), St. Mark's in Vienna (1965), St. Timothy in Chantilly (1965), St. Thomas à Becket in Reston (1970), Christ the Redeemer in Sterling (1972), and Church of the Nativity in Burke (1973). The area immediately around Alexandria was also growing. In 1963, Queen of the Apostles was founded, followed in rapid succession by Good Shepherd in 1965, St. Lawrence in Franconia in 1967, and, further south on I 95, Holy Family in Dale City in 1970. Still further south in Stafford County, St. William of York opened in 1971, on property adjacent to the Brent family cemetery purchased by Bishop O'Connell in the 1920s.

Although most of this new growth was centered on the Washington suburbs, people were starting to move further away from the major urban center. In 1967, St. John's in Leesburg, Loudon County, was split to form St. Francis de Sales in Purcellville, staffed by the

Capuchins until 1997. Far to the east in Lancaster County at the confluence of the Chesapeake Bay and the Rappahannock River, St. Francis de Sales in Kilmarnock, long a mission, became a separate parish in 1966. Yet more growth would occur after the establishment of the diocese of Arlington in 1974.

DEVELOPMENT OF OTHER REGIONS OF VIRGINIA

With the opening of the Hampton Roads bridge-tunnel, the area beyond Norfolk to Virginia Beach began a rapid expansion, particularly in the 1970s. Nicholas Habets, pastor of Star of the Sea since 1950, opened a mission on property purchased by the diocese. In 1962, he moved there to found a new parish, St. Nicholas. After a hiatus of several years, other parishes rapidly followed: Resurrection in Portsmouth (1971) and Ascension in Virginia Beach (1972).

In the 1960s, the Richmond area, too, was developing, especially to the west and southwest of the city. In 1959, St. Edward the Confessor was separated from Sacred Heart in South Richmond, followed in 1973 by St. Augustine's. In 1962, St. Mary's was divided from St. Bridget's. Both St. Mary's and St. Augustine's took the names of parishes in the city that had been closed. But only in the 1980s would Richmond experience the rapid growth that already characterized northern Virginia and the Hampton Roads-Virginia Beach area.

The establishment of at least one new parish, however, illustrated the changes besetting the church. In 1962, Charlottesville had only one parish, Holy Comforter. By that time, William A. Stickle, O.P., in charge of the Catholic Center of the University of Virginia, estimated that of the 1,000 graduates that year, one-tenth were Catholic. In a circular letter, he announced his plan "to provide a Chapel for appropriate sacramental ministrations and a Center for competent instruction."[7] Early in 1963, he broke ground for St. Thomas Aquinas Church.[8]

The new parish was unique in the diocese. It was to be "personal," analogous to a "national parish," and intended for students, faculty, and staff of the university, regardless of the territory within which they resided. A difficulty arose, however, because, in 1960, Holy Comforter had finally opened a parochial school, staffed by Dominican Sisters of Adrian, Michigan. Originally, Stickle and Joseph Wingler, Holy Comforter's pastor, reached a financial agreement on the relationship between the two parishes. The Holy Comforter school would serve both parishes, and Stickle agreed to pay the full cost of tuition, estimated to be $230 per year for each child.[9] Within a few years, however, Stickle said he could no longer pay this amount.

In 1969, the diocesan Pastoral Council, established at the Fourth Diocesan Synod, now functioned for the first time as a mediating body in the Charlottesville dispute.[10] A year later, however, the agreement on the school was moot, as the Adrian Dominicans were forced to withdraw, and the school was closed. The vocation crisis was becoming manifest among religious women. Despite the recommendation of the synod of 1966 that Catholic parents send their sons and daughters to Catholic colleges and universities, moreover, Catholics began increasingly to attend Virginia's public institutions.

The Catholic population in Virginia continued to grow between 1965 and 1968, when it took a downturn. This may have been an effect of the escalation of the Vietnam War on military families, as service personnel left the diocese and their dependents returned to their home states. Whatever the cause, the table below illustrates the sudden decline in the number of Catholics, infant baptisms, and conversions:

	Catholics	Infant baptisms	Converts
1965	229,961	7,592	1,052
1966	253,280	7,313	1,179
1967	253,223	7,271	1,157
1968	257,727	6,833	1,045
1969	236,256	3,683	516[11]
1970	241,697	6,328	785[12]

The number of marriages likewise dramatically declined, from 2,439 in 1968 to 1,310 in 1969. As had been the case in the 1950s, the majority of these marriages were mixed.

While there could be other explanations for this sudden drop in the Catholic population after such a steady increase, the 1960s were tumultuous times. They began with the euphoria of the election of Kennedy and Vatican II. They passed through the assassinations of John Kennedy, Martin Luther King, and Robert Kennedy and witnessed growing Catholic objection to the unpopular war in Vietnam.

Nineteen sixty-eight was a watershed. In that year, Paul VI issued his encyclical *Humanae Vitae* that dashed the hopes of those who hoped for a change in the Church's teaching on artificial contraception. Although the diocese of Richmond would not experience the same upheaval in reaction to the encyclical that occurred in Washington and elsewhere, acceptance of authority in State or Church would never again be the same. These events, together with the dramatic increase in the northern Virginia population, formed the backdrop for the division of the diocese.

MOVEMENT TOWARD ESTABLISHING
THE DIOCESE OF ARLINGTON

On October 20, 1970, Walter F. Sullivan, then forty-two years old, chancellor and rector of the cathedral, was named auxiliary bishop. For the only time in its history, the diocese had two auxiliaries, Sullivan and Louis Flaherty. Born in Washington, Sullivan was ordained in 1953, and served as assistant pastor of St. Andrew's in Roanoke and St. Mary Star of the Sea in Fort Monroe, before pursuing studies in canon law at the Catholic University in 1958. On December 1, 1970, he was consecrated by Russell and two of Richmond's previous auxiliaries, Hodges of Wheeling and Unterkoefler of Charleston. Lawrence Cardinal Shehan, archbishop of Baltimore, presided. Dozier, the pastor of Christ the King in Norfolk, read Paul VI's official bull designating Sullivan a bishop. Dozier himself had just been named the first bishop of Memphis.[13]

Dozier was a Richmond native. After his ordination in Rome in 1937, he served as assistant in several parishes, and then as director for the Propagation of the Faith from 1945 until he was named administrator and then pastor of Christ the King in Norfolk in 1953. Largely responsible for the development of parishes in the Norfolk area, he was popular with his fellow priests, who elected him the first president of the diocesan Council of Priests in 1967. On January 6, 1971, he was consecrated in Memphis.[14]

On December 1, 1972, Bishop Russell reached his seventy-fifth birthday and submitted his resignation, made mandatory by Paul VI. For the first time, Richmond had an active retired bishop. In April 1973, Sullivan was named administrator. On June 6, 1974, he became

Richmond's eleventh bishop. At the same time, the Holy See announced that a new diocese would be established in Arlington. For two months, Sullivan was bishop of Richmond with the territory designated by the Seventh Provincial Council of Baltimore in 1849. On August 13, 1974, Thomas J. Welsh, auxiliary bishop of Philadelphia, was officially installed as the first bishop of the new diocese of Arlington in what was now the Cathedral of St. Thomas More. The new diocese included the area north of the Rappahannock River, with a line extending westward along county boundaries to West Virginia. Moreover, the Vatican finally determined to realign diocesan lines to coincide with the state boundaries, as Bishop Whelan of Wheeling had first proposed in 1872 and as Bishop Kain had requested to Gibbons' chagrin in 1875. The eight West Virginia counties, formerly in the diocese of Richmond, now became part of the diocese of Wheeling. Richmond took over the southwestern counties that were formerly part of Wheeling. It also received the Virginia counties on the eastern shore, Northampton and Accomack on the Delmarva Peninsula, formerly part of the diocese of Wilmington, now made more accessible by the completion of the Chesapeake Bay Bridge-Tunnel.

OVERVIEW OF THE GROWTH OF THE DIOCESE OF RICHMOND, 1974–1997

With the new configuration of the diocese of Richmond, it returned to a situation analogous to what had existed at the time Ireton came. It now had two urban centers, Hampton Roads and Richmond, but it again had a vast rural territory, stretching, as it had before 1850, to Kentucky and Tennessee. In 1974, the pastors in the principal towns still had to cover huge distances. In this, they were like their predecessors of the mid-nineteenth century, but at least they had cars and better highways. For the most part, the new territory added to Richmond from Wheeling still consisted of missions, and more would be added.

The principal growth of the diocese of Richmond after 1974 would be in the Virginia Beach area, which by 1997 had ten parishes, one of which, St. Matthews, had earlier been founded in the Berkley section of Norfolk but had built a new church on property in Virginia Beach. Other development occurred along Interstates 64 and 95. The diocese of Arlington continued to spread along Interstates 95, 66, and 495.

Even before the split of the diocese, however, Richmond lost two parishes for other reasons. In 1966, St. Elias in Roanoke and St. Anthony in Richmond were transferred to the jurisdiction of the new eparchy or diocese of St. Maron. Virginia would continue to attract few Oriental Rite Catholics, but by 1972 Melkite Catholics laid the foundations for the Church of the Holy Transfiguration in McLean. Ukrainian Catholics also had missions in Manassas and Richmond, served on Sundays from Silver Spring. In February 1972, Ruthenian Catholics established the Church of the Epiphany of Our Lord in Annandale, part of the Byzantine eparchy of Passaic. By 1996, the eparchy established two more parishes in Virginia, Ascension of Our Lord in Williamsburg and Our Lady of Perpetual Help in Virginia Beach.

While Virginia had never been the home for large numbers of immigrants, both the dioceses of Arlington and Richmond were becoming home to Hispanics, principally from Central America and the Carribean, and also to Vietnamese, Koreans, and other Asians. While these newcomers made Virginia into a pale reflection of the ethnic diversity of northeastern and midwestern cities, Virginia's principal Catholic growth continued to come from natural increase or from migration from other states.

In 1999, the major part of Virginia's Catholic population continued to reside in the diocese of Arlington, where Catholics numbered 338,128, or 15 percent of the total population of 2,228,575. The Diocese of Richmond, in contrast, covered more territory, with a larger overall population of 4,507,819 of whom only 191,051, about 4 percent, were Catholic.[15] Altogether, only 7 percent of Virginians are Catholic. Of all the counties in Virginia, only Arlington, Fairfax, and Prince William have Catholic populations exceeding 25 percent.[16] Some Virginia counties, like Highland, where Amadeus van Ingelgem labored in the early part of the century, still have neither a resident priest nor a church.

CONCLUSION

The story of Virginia Catholicism is that of a minority group carving out its own space amid a Protestant majority. In the colonial period, the penal laws severely restricted Catholic settlement, though the Brent family managed to thrive in Virginia's Northern Neck. The first

Irish who came in the nineteenth century were members of either the professional or mercantile classes. They sought to establish themselves in the prevailing society and served as a nucleus for later Irish workers and German settlers in Richmond. Virginia Catholics developed a distinctive lifestyle, adhering to Catholic belief and practices in private but cooperating with other denominations in civic affairs in public. With the exception of the Know-Nothing campaign of the 1850s, the Ku Klux Klan in the 1920s, and the Al Smith election in 1928, Virginia's Catholics were generally accepted. But that acceptance came at a cost; too often, they embraced the cultural mores of the majority, including racism that was only slowly eradicated in the 1950s.

The development of Virginia Catholicism depended largely on transportation. In the nineteenth century, railroad workers flowed into the state and settled along the lines they constructed. The diocese responded by establishing parishes along the same railroad lines. But the years after World War II brought a new form of transportation and the need for a new response from the diocese. The automobile dramatically changed how and where people lived. With that came a change in the role religion played in their lives. As their place of residence was now removed from the workplace, so religion became part of their private lives. In only one generation, from 1940 to 1960, Virginia's Catholic population had shifted from concentration in the urban centers of Norfolk, Alexandria, Richmond, and Roanoke to groups composed mainly of newcomers living in the suburbs of Northern Virginia and the Norfolk region, areas that had come into being as the result of highways and the Interstate system. The new parishes built to accommodate this new population symbolized the changing role religion played in people's lives. The parking lot replaced the schoolyard. Each family could now get in its car, drive to a parking place at the church, attend Mass, and then get back in the car to drive home, without necessarily even meeting their fellow worshipers. Community now became something to be built rather than an expression of commonality that flowed from a neighborhood or Catholic identity within a town or village.

The Catholic Church is primarily the People of God. Parishes and dioceses are established only because of the people who live there. Virginia's story has in the past too often concentrated on the Norfolk trustees who were extreme in their demands for lay rights but did bring the diocese of Richmond into being, albeit too soon. Forgotten have been the thousands of laypeople who laid the first foundations for parishes, people like Mrs. Dornin, who gathered children into her home for instruction in Lynchburg in the 1930s, or Richard McSherry and his descendants in Martinsburg. Unfortunately, the names of many of these lay founders are lost to history. These Catholics in the nineteenth century depended largely on Irish and later Belgian and Dutch priests to serve them. Some of the early Irish priests were inept or worse. But many were dedicated missionaries who contributed from their own wealth to build up the Church. Even as Virginia was going through its suburban revolution, it would still depend heavily on priests from outside the diocese. By design or necessity, moreover, parishes particularly in the diocese of Richmond, were staffed by a single priest, reflecting either the frontier experience of a century earlier or adaptation to Vatican II.[17]

The bishops who served the diocese in many ways reflected the changing needs of their people. Throughout the nineteenth century, they were to a greater or lesser extent itinerant missionaries, who expected from their priests what they demanded of themselves. Whelan and McGill were stern administrators who did not hesitate to remove errant priests. Gibbons coupled pastoral dedication with personal ambition. Keane, perhaps the most spiritual of Richmond's bishops, was a stickler for detail but took the first concrete steps to work with African Americans. Van de Vyver devoted himself exclusively to his diocese, was well loved by his people and priests, but revealed little of his personality.

In the twentieth century, the bishops reflected a people in transition. O'Connell was at the end of his career when he became bishop, but he presided over the first expansion of the diocese, as a result of World War I. Brennan had ambitious plans for modeling his diocese on those of the northeast, but he failed to leave a lasting mark on the diocese because of the Depression and the stroke that disabled him. Ireton sought to carry out many of Brennan's administrative plans and took the first major step toward integration in the diocese, but he seems to have followed the example of more prominent bishops elsewhere of being satisfied to leave details of administration to his subordinates. Russell virtually embodied the transition of Virginia Catholicism from the Old South to the New. He was determined to integrate all diocesan institutions and took seriously the lessons he learned at the Vatican Council.

The story of the diocese of Richmond and of Virginia Catholicism, of course, does not end with 1974 or the present. It is ongoing. Virginia Catholicism has developed from its origins in the nineteenth century, but its future development will result more from its more recent history since World War II than from the period when its members were generally a poor minority struggling to be accepted in a frequently hostile environment.

AAB, Archives of the Archdiocese of Baltimore
AACL, Archives of the American College, Louvain
AAHC, Archives of All Hallows College, Drumcondra, Ireland
AANY, Archives of the Archdiocese of New York
ADA, Archives of the Diocese of Arlington
ADC, Archives of the Diocese of Charleston
ADR, Archives of the Diocese of Richmond
ADW, Archives of the Diocese of Wheeling
ADS, Archives of the Diocese of Savannah
AIC, Archives of the Irish College, Rome
AKC, Archives of the Knights of Columbus
AMP, Archives of the Maryland Province of the Society of Jesus,
        Georgetown University
AMSM, Archives of Mt. St. Mary's Seminary and College, Emmitsburg, Md.
APF, Archives of the Congregation of Propaganda Fide, Rome
  ACTA=Acta della congregazione
  Lettere=Lettere et Decreti
  SCAmerCent=Scritture referite nei congressi, America Centrale
  SCIrlanda=Scritture referite nei congressi, Irlanda
  SOCG-Scritture originale referite nelle congregazioni generali
ASBS, Archives of the Sisters of the Blessed Sacrament
ASJPH, Archives of St. Joseph's Mother House of the Daughters of Charity,
        Emmitsburg, Md.
ASPF, Archives of the Society for the Propagation of the Faith

ASSJ, Archives of the Society of St. Joseph, Baltimore
ASV, Archivio Segreto Vaticano
  SS=Segreteria di Stato
  DAUS=Delegazione Apostolica degli Stati Uniti
SAB, Sulpician Archives, Baltimore

1. Catholicism in Colonial Virginia

1. Paul E. Hoffman, *A New Andalucia and a Way to the Orient: The American Southeast during the Sixteenth Century* (Baton Rouge: Louisiana State University Press, 1990), cited in David J. Weber, *The Spanish Frontier in North America* (New Haven: Yale University Press, 1992), pp. 36–37.

2. Clifford M. Lewis, S.J., and Albert J. Loomie, S.J., *The Spanish Jesuit Mission in Virginia: 1570–1572* (Chapel Hill: University of North Carolina Press, 1953), pp. 15–24.

3. Ibid., 28–42.

4. Ibid., 45–49.

5. Ibid., 49–62. For the most recent account of this abortive mission, see Thomas C. Parramore, *Norfolk: The First Four Centuries* (Charlottesville: University Press of Virginia, 1994), pp. 1–12.

6. Lewis and Loomie, pp. 58–62.

7. Warren M. Billings, *Jamestown and the Founding of the Nation* (Gettysburg: Thomas Publications, n.d.), pp. 31–32.

8. William Waller Hening, *The Statutes-at-Large, Being a Collection of All the Laws of Virginia (1619–1792)*, 7 vols. (New York, 1823), I, 268–69, quoted in Peter Guilday, *The Catholic Church in Virginia (1815–1822)* (New York: The United States Catholic Historical Society, 1924), p. xvii.

9. *Researches of the American Catholic Historical Society*, 19 (1908), 36.

10. Reuben Gold Thwaites, ed., *The Jesuit Relations and Allied Documents*, 73 vols. (Cleveland: Burrows Brothers, 1897), 4, 11–12.

11. Ibid., 33.

12. Josef Metzler, O.M.I., "Der älteste Bericht über Nordamerika im Propaganda-Archiv: Virginia 1625," *Neue Zeitschrift für Missionswissenschaft*, 25 (1969), 29–37.

13. On Calvert's attempt to found a colony in Ferryland, see R. J. Lahey, "The Role of Religion in Lord Baltimore's Colonial Enterprise," *Maryland Historical Magazine,* 72 (Winter 1977), 492–511, and "Avalon: Lord Baltimore's Colony in Newfoundland," in G. M. Story, ed., *Early European Settlement and Exploitation in Atlantic Canada* (St. John's, Newfoundland: Memorial University of Newfoundland, 1982), pp. 115–37.

14. *Researches of the American Catholic Historical Society,* 19 (1902), 26–27. The report was signed by Samuel Mathewes, John Potts, Roger Smyth, and U. Claybourne.

15. Thomas Hughes, S.J., *History of the Society of Jesus in North America: Colonial and Federal* (London: Longmans, Green, 1908), *Text,* I, 199–200. Hughes bases his conjecture about a priest ministering to Lady Baltimore and possibly some Irish exiles on two manuscripts in the archives of the Maryland Province of the Society of Jesus, but these date from the mid-nineteenth century. See also Martin I. J. Griffin, "Catholics in Colonial Virginia," *Records of the American Catholic Historical Society,* 22 (1911), 89–90.

16. On the role of property in relation to religious liberty, see my "Property and Religious Liberty in Colonial Maryland Catholic Thought," *Catholic Historical Review,* 72 (1986), 573–600.

17. Hughes, *History, Text,* p. 279; *Documents,* I–I, 101.

18. Edward D. Neill, *History of the Virginia Company of London,* cited in Griffin, "Catholics," pp. 90–91.

19. Hughes, *History, Documents,* I–I, 102.

20. John Tracy Ellis, ed., *Documents of American Catholic History,* 3 vols. (Wilmington, Del.: Michael Glazier, 1987), I, 98–99.

21. Hughes, *History, Documents,* I-I, 112.

22. Ibid., 31.

23. Hening, *The Statutes-at-Large,* I, 268–69. A year later, after the arrival of some Puritan ministers, the assembly declared that "For the preservation of the puritie of doctrine and unitie of the church, It is enacted that all ministers whatsoever which shall reside in the colony are to be conformable to the orders and constitutions of the Church of England and the laws therein established and not otherwise to be admitted to teach or preach publickly or privatly, And that the Gov. and Counsel do take care that all nonconformists upon notice of them shall be compelled to depart the colony with all convenience." See Charles Campbell, *History of the Colony and Ancient Dominion of Virginia* (Richmond, 1847).

24. Thwaites, *Jesuit Relations,* 31: 99.

25. Hughes, *History, Documents,* I–I, 36.

26. Bruce Steiner, "The Catholic Brents of Colonial Virginia: An Instance of Practical Toleration," *The Virginia Magazine of History and Biography,* 70 (Oct., 1962), 387–94.

27. Hughes, *History, Documents,* I–I, 131.

28. Hening, *Statutes-at-Large,* II, 48.

29. Edmund Sears Morgan, *Virginians at Home; Family Life in the Eighteenth Century* (Charlottesville, Dominion Books, 1963), pp. 81–82.

30. Quoted in Steiner, "Catholic Brents," p. 398.

31. Steiner, "Catholic Brents," pp. 399–405. While the brief reign of James II marked the zenith of any Brent's political influence, it is an exaggeration to suggest that Lord Howard was a Catholic and replaced Protestants with Catholics in other offices; see Richard L. Morton, *Colonial Virginia* (Chapel Hill: University of North Carolina Press, 1960), I, 316. Morton may have been influenced by Protestant fears in the election of 1960 to find Catholics denying Protestant liberties in the 1680s.

32. Hughes, *History, Text,* II, 158.

33. Hughes, *History, Documents,* I–I, 140.

34. Hughes, *History, Text,* II, 158.

35. *Researches of the American Catholic Historical Society,* 22 (1905), 233.

36. Fogarty, "Property and Religion," pp. 385–86.

37. Hening, *Statutes-at-Large,* III, 298.

38. Ibid., 172.

39. John Pendleton Kennedy, ed., *Journals of the House of Burgesses of Virginia, 1761–1765* (Richmond, 1907), pp. 125–30, cited in Steiner, "Catholic Brents," pp. 408–9.

40. Quoted in John Gilmary Shea, *History of the Catholic Church in the United States,* 4 vols. (New York: D. H. McBride, 1886), 1:408–9.

41. Hening, *Statutes-at-Large,* VI, 338.

42. For Maryland's act disarming Catholics and then taxing them double for not serving in the militia, see Fogarty, "Property and Religious Liberty," pp. 593–98.

43. Challoner to Christopher Stonor, Sept. 14, 1756, in Ellis, ed., *Documents,* I, 124–25.

44. Ibid., 136.

45. *American Catholic Historical Researches,* 8 (1891), 186–87.

46. Ibid., 141–42.

47. Ellis, *Documents,* I, 142.

48. Robert Fountain Beattie, "The Beginnings of Catholicity in Virginia," M.A. thesis, St. Mary's Seminary, Baltimore, 1929, p. 42.

49. For Propaganda's negotiations with the United States through France, see Peter Guilday, *The Life and Times of John Carroll, Archbishop of Baltimore (1735–1815)* (New York: America Press, 1922), pp. 178–201.

50. Ellis, *Documents,* I, 148.

51. Steiner, "Catholic Brents," pp. 404–9.

52. "Catholics in Virginia 1743–49," *American Catholic Historical Researches,* 21 (1904), 154–55.

53. Ellis, *Documents,* I, 150.

54. Henry Steele Commager, ed., *Documents of American History* (New York: Appleton-Century-Crofts, 1962) p. 126.

2. Post-Revolutionary Virginia Catholicism

1. John Tracy Ellis, ed., *Documents of American Catholic History,* 3 vols. (Wilmington, Del.: Michael Glazier, 1987), I, 163–67.

2. Christopher J. Kauffman, *Tradition and Transformation in Catholic Culture: The Priests of Saint Sulpice in the United States from 1791 to the Present* (New York: Macmillan, 1988), pp. 38–42.

3. Carroll to Plowden, Baltimore, Sept. 3, 1791, in Thomas O. Hanley, S.J., ed., *The John Carroll Papers,* 3 vols. (Notre Dame: The University of Notre Dame Press, 1976), I, 516.

4. Richard Shaw, *John Dubois: Founding Father* (Yonkers: U.S. Catholic Historical Society, 1983), pp. 11–18.

5. Ibid., 19–20.

6. Dubois to Fitzgerald, Richmond, Nov. 1, 1791, in Mary M. Meline and Edward F. X. McSweeny, *The Story of the Mountain: Mount St. Mary's College and Seminary, Emmitsburg, Maryland* 2 vols. (Emmitsburg, Md.: *The Weekly Chronicle,* 1911), I, 6.

7. *The Virginia Gazette,* Dec. 28, 1791, in Shaw, *Dubois,* p. 22.

8. Shaw, *Dubois,* p. 21.

9. Ibid., 24.

10. Ibid., 26.

11. AAB, 3R6, Cahill to Carroll, Hagerstown, Jan. 24, 1795.

12. Thomas W. Spalding, *The Premier See: A History of the Archdiocese of Baltimore, 1789–1989* (Baltimore: The Johns Hopkins University Press, 1989), p. 43.

13. A. L. Marshall, *Adam Livingston, the Wizard Clip, The Voice: An Historical Account* (Kearneysville, W. Va.: Livingston Publications, 1978), pp. 12–20.

14. Ibid., 22–48. For Gallitzin, see also Sarah H. Brownson, *Life of Demetrius Augustine Gallitzin, Prince and Priest* (New York: Fr. Pustet, 1873), pp. 101–6.

15. St. Joseph's Church, Martinsburg, W. Va., "History of St. Joseph's Church," MS for the centennial of the present church, 1950, p. 2.

16. Thomas R. Bevan, *200 Years: A History of the Catholic Community of the Frederick Valley* (Frederick: Da-Mark, Associates, 1977), pp. 12–14.

17. *St. Mary's: 200 Years for Christ, 1795–1995* (Alexandria: St. Mary's Catholic Church, 1995), pp. 6–7.

18. Ibid., 12–17.

19. Brother John McElroy, S.J., from Georgetown came to help him move and is erroneously included on some lists of priests who served in Richmond, but his ordination occurred only later. Though he played a minor role later in the history of Virginia Catholicism, he founded St. John's parish in Frederick where the Jesuits established their novitiate from which they visited neighboring parts of Virginia. He also founded Boston College.

20. A. M. Keiley, "Memorandum of the History of the Catholic Church, Richmond, Va.," *Proceedings of the Fourth Annual Convention of the Catholic Benevolent Union of the State of Virginia, held in the City of Norfolk, Virginia, on the 10th, 11th and 12th of June, 1874, with Appendix* (Norfolk, Va: Virginian Book and Job Print, 1874), p. 5.

21. AAB, 13D4, Baxter to Marechal, Richmond, June 13, 1818.

22. AAB, 13D6, Baxter to Marechal, Richmond, July 4, 1818.

23. *Makers of Richmond, 1737–1860: An exhibition of portraits, November 16, 1948 through January 2, 1949* (Richmond, Va.: The Valentine Museum, 1948), pp. 36–37.

24. AAB, 13D7, Baxter to Marechal, Georgetown, Aug. 3, 1818. For the agreement Neale had made with the Jesuits, see Spalding, *The Premier See,* pp. 70–73.

25. AAB, 13E12, Baxter to Marechal, Richmond, Mar. 2, 1819.

26. Thomas E. Buckley, S.J., "After Disestablishment: Thomas Jefferson's Wall of Separation in Antebellum Virginia," *Journal of Southern History,* 61 (Aug. 1995), 445–80, and especially p. 454 for the Gallego case.

27. AAB, 13E14, Baxter to Marechal, Richmond, Mar. 9, 1819.

28. AAB, 13E15, Baxter to Marechal, Georgetown, Mar. 21, 1819.

29. AAB, 13E18, Baxter to Marechal, Georgetown, May 31, 1919.

30. AAB, 13E19, Baxter to Marechal, Richmond, June 10, 1819.

31. AAB, 13F22, Baxter to Marechal, Richmond, Aug. 31, 1819; 13 F23: Baxter to Marechal, Richmond, Sept. 4, 1819. Later, Baxter prepared a pastoral letter for Marechal to issue on Egan, but it is unclear if it was ever published; see AAB, 13H41.

32. AAB, 13F24, Baxter to Marechal, Richmond, Sept. 22, 1819; see also 13 G25: Baxter to Marechal, Richmond, Sept. 21, 1819.

33. AAB, 13G27, Baxter to Marechal, Richmond, Oct. 1, 1819.

34. AAB, 13G29, Baxter to Marechal, Georgetown, Oct. 28, 1819; 13 G31: Baxter to Marechal, Georgetown, Dec. 6, 1819.

35. AAB, 13G33, Baxter to Marechal, Georgetown, April 12, 1820.

36. AAB, 13H34, Baxter to Marechal, Georgetown, May 7, 1820.

37. AAB, 18M11, Mahony to Marechal, Richmond, Oct. 5, 1820.

38. AAB, 13G27, Baxter to Marechal, Richmond, Oct. 1, 1819. On this dispute, see Spalding, *The Premier See,* pp. 84–85, 90–91.

39. AAB, 13H36, Baxter to Marechal, Georgetown, Nov. 26, 1820. For Baxter, see Robert Emmett Curran, S.J., *The Bicentennial History of Georgetown University: From Academy to University, 1789–1889* (Washington, D.C.: Georgetown University Press, 1993), pp. 81, 83, 84, 86, 90, 93, 96, 97, 356 n.59, and 357 n.73.

40. AAB, 13F21, Baxter to Marechal, Richmond, Aug. 21, 1819.

41. Oliveira Fernandez, *Letter addressed to the Most Reverend Leonard Neale, Archbishop of Baltimore, by a Member of the Roman Catholic Congregation of Norfolk, in Virginia* (Norfolk, 1816), cited in Peter Guilday, *The Catholic Church in Virginia (1815–1822)* (New York: The United States Catholic Historical Society, 1924), p. xxiv.

42. Neale to William Plume and Trustees of Norfolk, Washington, June 25, 1799, in Hanley, *John Carroll Papers,* II, 270. Although this is published as a letter of Carroll's, the reference to his having been in Norfolk and his residence in Washington makes it clear that it was written by Neale. John Gilmary Shea, *History of the Catholic Church in the United States,* 4 vols. (New York: D. H. McBride, 1888), II, 492 correctly identifies the author.

43. The first marriage recorded in the Norfolk records with Lacy as witness was on Nov. 20, 1802; see George Holbert Tucker, *Abstracts from Norfolk City Marriage Bonds (1797–1850) and Other Genealogical Date* (n.p.: William H. Delaney, 1934), p. 16. See also Carroll to Lacy, in Hanley, *John Carroll Papers,* II, 393, where Carroll told Lacy he would soon receive another assignment.

44. Shea, *History,* II, 166.

45. Carroll to Rossiter, April 30, 1802, in Hanley, *John Carroll Papers,* II, 386–387. See also Carroll to Rossiter, May 5, 1802, ibid., 388–90.

46. Oliveira Fernandez, *Letter*, pp. 39–41, in Guilday, *Virginia*, pp. xxiv–xxv.

47. Guilday, *Virginia*, pp. xxv–xxvi, xxxi–xxxii.

48. Ibid., xxxii–xxxiv.

49. Ibid., xxxiv–xxxv. He is listed as officiating at marriages, only from April 22 to July 12; see Tucker, pp. 61–63.

50. AAB, 12G5, Lucas to Neale, Norfolk, Feb. 8, 1816, in: Guilday, *Virginia*, p. 11.

51. Ibid.

52. AAB, 12R2, Neale to Lucas, Georgetown, Mar. 6, 1816. This and copies of Neale's other letters to Lucas are under this number. Text is given in ibid., 12–13.

53. For an analysis of the thought of the trustees, especially Oliveira Fernandez, see Patrick W. Carey, *People, Priests, and Prelates: Ecclesiastical Democracy and the Tensions of Trusteeism* (Notre Dame: University of Notre Dame Press, 1987), pp. 163, 178–79, 186–87, 236–37, 246–47.

54. Ibid., 181–89.

55. Guilday, *Virginia*, pp. 32–38.

56. AAB, 18E2, Lucas to Marechal, Norfolk, June 23, 1817; 18 E3, Lucas to Marechal, Norfolk, July 17, 1817.

57. Guilday, *Virginia*, pp. 39–40.

3. Richmond Becomes a Diocese, 1820

1. Peter Guilday, *The Catholic Church in Virginia (1815–1822)* (New York: The United States Catholic Historical Society, 1924), pp. 45–59.

2. Ibid., 60–61.

3. APF, Lettere, 298 (1817), 540v–542v: Litta to Oliveira Fernandez, Sept. 20, 1870.

4. APF, Udienze, 55, fols. 711r, 713r, 745r, 747r, 748r, 950rv, 951rv; see also Carey, pp. 246–47.

5. Ibid., 543r–544v, Litta to Marechal, Sept. 20, 1817.

6. Ibid., 298, 544–545rv., secretary to Marechal, Rome, Sept. 20, 1817.

7. APF, ACTA, 184 (1821), 577–579v: Somaglia Ponenza; 580–585v: Sommario.

8. Given in Guilday, *Virginia*, pp. 80–82.

9. AAB, Marechal Letterbook, Marechal to Litta, Baltimore, June 26, 1818.

10. Ibid., Marechal to Litta, Baltimore, October 16, 1818; this is also translated and published in John Tracy Ellis, ed., *Documents of American Catholic History*, 3 vols. (Wilmington, Del.: Michael Glazier, 1987), I, 202–20.

11. Guilday, *Virginia*, p. 87.

12. See ibid., 93–101.

13. Ibid., 104–6.

14. AAB, Marechal Letterbook, Marechal to Connolly, June 4, 1819.

15. Ibid., Marechal to Carbry, June 7, 1819.

16. Ellis, *Documents*, I, 220–23.

17. APF, SCAmerCent, IV, 447r–448r, Marechal to Litta, Baltimore, June 16, 1819.

18. Ibid., 495rv–496r, Marechal to Litta, Baltimore, July 30, 1819.

19. Ellis, *Documents,* I, 220–27. Ellis has abbreviated both documents.

20. APF, Lettere, 300, 624v–626v, Propaganda to Marechal, Rome, Sept. 11, 1819.

21. Ibid., 301, 452rv–453r, June 25, 1820.

22. Taylor to Marechal, Rome, July 8, 1820, in Guilday, *Virginia,* p. 126.

23. APF, Lettere, 301, 532v–535r, Litta to Kelly, Rome, July 22, 1820.

24. Guilday, *Virginia,* p. 129.

25. APF, Lettere, 301, 854rv–855r, Propaganda to Kelly, Rome, Nov. 11, 1820. See also Guilday, pp. 129–30.

26. APF, Lettere, 301, 856v–858v, Fontana to Marechal, Rome, Nov. 11, 1820.

27. Ibid., 861r–863r, Fontana to Norfolk congregation, Rome, Nov. 22, 1820.

28. See Guilday, *Virginia,* p. 134.

29. APF, SCAmerCent, VII, 157rv–158r, Marechal to Litta, Baltimore, Jan. 22, 1821.

30. AAB, 18I43, Lucas to Marechal, Norfolk, Jan. 21, 1821.

31. AAB, 18I45, Lucas to Marechal, Norfolk, Feb. 8, 1821.

32. AAB, 18M12, Mahony to Marechal, Richmond, Mar. 12, 1821.

33. AAB, 18J53, Lucas to Marechal, Norfolk, May 17, 1821.

34. Guilday, *Virginia,* pp. 136–44.

35. In ibid., p. 148.

36. APF, Letterc, 302, fols. 319 a–c, Fontana to Marechal, July 21, 1821.

37. Ibid., f. 346 a, Propaganda to Kelly, Rome, Aug. 4, 1821.

38. AAB, 18J60, Lucas to Marechal, Norfolk, Aug 9, 1821.

39. Patrick Carey, "John F. O. Fernandez: Enlightened Lay Catholic Reformer, 1815–11820," *The Review of Politics,* 43 (Jan. 1981), 112–29.

40. APF, Lettere, 302, 491rv–492rv, Fontana to Marechal, Rome, Oct. 5, 1821.

41. Annabelle M. Melville, *Louis William DuBourg: Bishop of Louisiana and the Floridas, Bishop of Montauban, and Archbishop of Besançon, 1766–1833* (Chicago: Loyola University Press, 1986), II, 668.

42. APF, Lettere, 302, f.499, Fontana to DuBourg, Rome, Oct. 3, 1821.

43. Ibid., 501r, Fontana to Connolly, Rome, Oct. 3, 1821.

44. Ibid., 499v–500r, Fontana to Connolly, vicar general of Waterford, Rome, Oct. 3, 1821.

45. Ibid., 188v–190v, Fontana to Kelly, Rome, Mar. 9, 1822. On February 9, the pope had approved the transfer; ibid., 303, 51rv, Decree of Propaganda, Jan. 28, 1822.

46. Given in Guilday, *Virginia,* pp. 154–55.

47. APF, SCIrlanda, 23 (1820–1822), 721–23: Kelly to Fontana, Waterford, Sept. 4, 1822.

48. *St. Mary's: 200 Years for Christ, 1795–1995* (Alexandria: St. Mary's Catholic Church, 1995), pp. 22–23.

49. AAB, Marechal Letterbook, Dzierozynski to Fairclough, Georgetown, Oct. 13, 1819 (copy).

50. AAB, 19W5, Plessis to Marechal, Quebec, Feb. 7, 1821.

51. APF, SCAmerCent, IV, 675r–676: Marechal to Plessis of Quebec, Baltimore, n.d.

52. Fontana to Plessis, Nov. 17, 1821, in Guilday, *Virginia,* pp. 150–51.

4. A Diocese without a Bishop, 1821–1841

1. AAB, 21D3, Walsh to Marechal, Richmond, December 16, 1822
2. AAB, 21D4, Walsh to Marechal, Richmond, December 30, 1822
3. AAB, 21D6, Walsh to Marechal, Richmond, Feb. 23, 1823.
4. AAB, 16S8, Fitzpatrick to Marechal, Newtown, Aug. 21, 1821; 16S9: Fitzpatrick to Marechal, Petersburg, April 1, 1823.
5. AAB, 16S9 1, Marechal to Fitzpatrick, Baltimore, April 5, 1823.
6. AAB, 16S12, Fitzpatrick to Marechal, Petersburg, June 10, 1823.
7. AAB, 22J17, Chevallié, Burke, Cullen, and Gardiner to Marechal, Richmond, June 21, 1824.
8. AAB,15N5, Delany to Marechal, Norfolk, July 7, 1824.
9. AAB, 15N6, Delany to Marechal, Richmond, July 29, 1824.
10. AAB, 15N7, Delany to Marechal, Norfolk, Nov. 17, 1824.
11. A. M. Keiley, "Memorandum of the History of the Catholic Church, Richmond, Va.," *Proceedings of the Fourth Annual Convention of the Catholic Benevolent Union of the State of Virginia, held in the City of Norfolk, Virginia, on the 10th, 11th and 12th of June, 1874, with Appendix* (Norfolk: Virginian Book and Job Print, 1874), p. 7.
12. AAB, 17K7, Hore to Marechal, Richmond, May 1, 1826.
13. AAB, 17K9, Hore to Marechal, Sept. 18, 1827.
14. AAB, 15N15, Delany to Marechal, Norfolk, Oct. 21, 1827.
15. AAB, 23J6, Thomas Hore to ? and Whitfield, Richmond, April 15, 1828.
16. AAB, 23J1, Hoerner to Whitfield, Richmond, June 10, 1828.
17. AAB, 23J2, Hoerner to Marechal, Richmond, Aug. 14, 1828.
18. Keiley, "Richmond," p. 7.
19. AAB, 23J2a, Hoerner to Whitfield, Richmond, July 29, 1829.
20. AAB, 23AN4, Van Horsigh to Whitfield, Norfolk, July 22, 1830.
21. Keiley, p. 7.
22. Clarence V. Joerndt, *St. Ignatius, Hickory, and Its Missions* (Baltimore, 1972), pp. 385–93, has brief biographical sketches of both Todrig and O'Brien.
23. APF, ACTA, 197, 92–93r, Whitfield to Propaganda, Baltimore, June 14, 1832.
24. AAB, 23P4, O'Brien to Whitfield, Richmond, July 3, 1832.
25. Thomas Spalding, *The Premier See: A History of the Archdiocese of Baltimore, 1789–1989* (Baltimore: The Johns Hopkins University Press, 1989), p. 110.
26. AAB, 23P5, O'Brien to Whitfield, Richmond, Feb. 19, 1833.
27. ADR, O'Brien to Whitfield, Richmond, Aug. 13, 1833.
28. ADR, Deed of Lot 630, Gallego's executor to O'Brien, recorded in the court of Hustings, Sept. 2, 1833.
29. APF, ACTA, 197 (1834), Sala ponenza on II Prov. Baltimore, March 1834, 85.
30. Ibid., 88v.
31. AAB, 24 7, O'Brien to Eccleston, Richmond, April 9, 1834.
32. *The Richmond Enquirer,* May 27, 1834, p. 3.
33. Archives of Georgetown University, Mulledy, Sermon preached on May 25, 1833 [*sic*], "The day of the consecration of the church of St. Peter in G. Street."
34. AAB, 23P6, O'Brien to Whitfield, Richmond, July 14, 1834.

35. Baptismal Records, St. Peter's Church, Richmond. The baptisms of Letitia and Lavalette are recorded on a loose piece of paper, inserted into the record with no date given.

36. See below, p. ooo.

37. Ibid., July 4, 1851.

38. Ray Allen Billington,, *The Protestant Crusade: 1800–1860: A Study of the Origins of American Nativism* (Chicago: Quadrangle Books, 1964),

39. ASJPH, Richmond, Va, St. Joseph's Asylum and School.

40. ASJPH, "Richmond Villa," quoted in Sister Bernadette Armiger, "The History of the Hospital Work of the Daughters of Charity of St. Vincent de Paul in the Eastern Province of the United States: 1823–1860," MS thesis in Nursing Education, Catholic University of America, Washington, D.C., 1947, p. 18.

41. Linda Singleton-Driscoll, "The Dooley Women of Richmond," unpublished MS, Maymount Foundation, 1979, pp. 1–6. The first recorded baptism of a Dooley child is that of James; Baptismal Records of St. Peter's Church, Richmond, Feb. 28, 1841.

42. *The Richmond Enquirer*, Sept. 4, 1835.

43. AAB, 17K3, Hore to Marechal, Norfolk, Feb. 6, 1823.

44. AAB, 15N2, Delany to Marechal, Norfolk, Oct. 1, 1823.

45. AAB, 15N3, Delany to Marechal, Norfolk, Nov. 26, 1823.

46. AAB, 15N4, Delany to Marechal, Norfolk, April 19, 1824.

47. AAB, 15N8, Delany to Marechal, Norfolk, April 6, 1825.

48. AAB, 15N9, Delany to Marechal, Norfolk, June 8, 1825.

49. AAB, 15N10, Delany to Marechal, Norfolk, June 25, 1825.

50. AAB, 15N11, Delany to Marechal, Norfolk, Sept. 1, 1825.

51. AAB, 15N13, Delany to Marechal, Norfolk, Jan. 25, 1826.

52. AAB, 15N14, Delany to Marechal, Norfolk, Oct. 5, 1826.

53. AAB, 21A2, Van Horsigh to Marechal, Norfolk, Oct. 13, 1826.

54. AAB, 21A3, Van Horsigh to Marechal, Norfolk, May 20, 1827.

55. AAB, 23A N4, Van Horsigh to Whitfield, Norfolk, July 22, 1830.

56. James Henry Bailey, *A History of the Diocese of Richmond: The Formative Years* (Richmond: The Chancery Office, 1956), pp. 74–77.

57. Virginia Bernadette Griffin, *The Golden Jubilee of the Church of St. Paul, with a Resume of Catholic History in the City of Portsmouth, Virginia* (Portsmouth, 1955), p. 12

58. AAB, 23J7, Van Horsigh to Whitfield, Norfolk, Nov. 20, 1832.

59. AAB, 23E1, Delany to Whitfield, Norfolk, Sept. 17, 1834

60. AAB, 23J5, James Herron to Whitfield, Norfolk, Oct. 8, 1834.

61. AMSM, de Lacy to Butler, Norfolk, Jan. 19, 1835.

62. Ibid., de Lacy to Butler, Norfolk, Sept. 6, 1835.

63. Mary M. Meline and Edward F.X. McSweeny, *The Story of the Mountain: Mount St. Mary's College and Seminary, Emmitsburg, Maryland,* 2 vols. (Emmitsburg: *The Weekly Chronicle,* 1911), I, 307, 313, 314, 324

64. AMSM, Hitzelberger to John McCaffrey, Norfolk, May 15, 1838.

65. ASJPH, Norfolk School; Bailey, *Richmond*, pp. 76–77.

66. ASJPH, Norfolk, St. Mary's Asylum & School.

67. Michael Glennon, "Reminiscences of Catholic Boyhood," paper read before the Emerald Literary Association, Nov. 17, 1893, p. 3.

68. For a provocative parallel for Michigan, see Leslie Woodcock Tentler, "'God's Representatives in Our Midst': Toward a History of the Catholic Diocesan Clergy in the United States," *Church History,* 67 (June 1998), 326–38.

69. Robert Emmett Curran, S.J., *The Bicentennial History of Georgetown University* (Washington, D.C.: Georgetown University Press, 1993), I, 107–12.

70. AAB, 18M13, Mahony to Marechal, Leetown, Mar. 29, 1823.

71. AAB, 18M16, Mahony to Marechal, Leetown, Nov. 3, 1824.

72. AAB, 18M16 1/, Richard McSherry, Robert Boone, and John Piet to Marechal, Martinsburg, Jan. 23, 1826. For a description of the fight see, AAB, 18M16 2/: Catherine Ann and Annastasia McSherry to Marechal, Martinsburg, Feb. 4, 1826; Catherine McSherry was Richard McSherry's sister-in-law, who said she was not aware of Father Mahony's drinking and admitted there was some provocation, but asked for Mahony's recall.

73. AAB, 18M17, Mahony to Marechal, Winchester, Feb. 8, 1826.

74. AAB, Nicholas Fitzsimmons to Marechal, Winchester, Feb. 25, 1826.

75. AAB, 18M18, Mahony to Marechal, Frederick, Aug. 20, 1826.

76. George F. O'Dwyer, *The Irish Catholic Genesis of Lowell* (Lowell, 1920; reissued, 1981), p. 59. In 1836, Mahony became pastor of St. Augustine's Church in South Boston where he died in 1839.

77. Meline and McSweeny, *The Story of the Mountain,* I, 205, 219.

78. AAB, 23AE2, Gildea to Whitfield, Martinsburg, Sept. 18, 1830.

79. AAB, 23AE3, Gildea to Whitfield, Martinsburg, Feb. 24, 1831.

80. AAB, 23I4 Gildea to Whitfield, Martinsburg, June 8, 1831.

81. AAB, 23I2 Gildea to Whitfield, Martinsburg, Oct. 21, 1832.

82. AAB, 23I3 Gildea to Whitfield, Harpers Ferry, April 2, 1833.

83. AAB, 23K1 Jamison to Whitfield, Martinsburg, April 30, 1834.

84. AAB, 23I4 Gildea to Whitfield, n.p., n.d. [1834?].

85. John F. Stover, *History of the Baltimore and Ohio Railroad* (West Lafayette: Purdue University Press, 1987), p. 39.

86. AAB, 23K2, Jamison to Whitfield, Martinsburg, July 8, 1834.

87. Spalding, *The Premier See,* pp. 137, 139.

88. *The United States Catholic Almanac; or, Laity's Directory, for the year 1835* (Baltimore: James Myres, 1835), p. 64.

89. AAB, 26N2, Whelan to Eccleston, Harpers Ferry, Dec. 26, 1836.

90. Mary J. Oates, C.S.J., "Catholic Female Academies on the Frontier," *U.S. Catholic Historian,* 12 (Fall 1994), 121–36, especially p. 131.

91. ASJPH, Martinsburg, St. Joseph's School.

5. RICHARD VINCENT WHELAN, SECOND BISHOP OF RICHMOND, 1841–1850

1. APF, ACTA, 203 (1840), 370: Fransoni Ponenza.

2. Pastoral Letter, Mar. 22, 1841, *New York Freeman's Journal,* quoted in John Gilmary Shea, *A History of the Catholic Church within the Limits of the United States,* 4 vols (New York: John G. Shea, 1890), III, 576–77.

3. AANY, Whelan to Hughes, Norfolk, June 19, 1841.

4. AANY, Whelan to Hughes, St. Vincent's Seminary, Jan. 24, 1843.

5. Stafford Poole, C.M., "Ad Cleri Disciplinam: The Vincentian Seminary Apostolate in the United States," in John E. Rybolt, C.M., ed., *The American Vincentians: A Popular History of the Congregation of the Missions in the United States, 1815–1987* (Brooklyn: New City Press, 1988), p. 102.

6. AANY, Whelan to Hughes, Richmond, July 29, 1841.

7. Henry F. Parke, "Some Notes on the Rise and Spread of the Catholic Missions in Virginia: A.D. 1774–1850," *Research*, 1 (Mar. 1943), 9.

8. Ibid., 8.

9. AANY, Whelan to Hughes, Richmond, April 14, 1842.

10. AANY, Whelan to Hughes, Richmond, Nov. 6, 1842.

11. Keiley, "Memorandum" (cited n. 11, chap 4.), p. 9.

12. AMSM, Moran to Butler, New York, July 14, 1836; Walsh to McCaffrey, Brooklyn, Nov. 13, 1839. Fox had taught school in Ireland before coming to the United States. He studied at Mt. St. Mary's and then taught school in Vincennes.

13. AANY, Whelan to Hughes, Richmond, Jan. 24, 1843.

14. See p. 87.

15. Kevin Condon, C.M., *The Missionary College of All Hallows: 1842–1891* (Dublin: All Hallows College, 1986), p. 61. Only the bishops in Indiana and Hartford responded positively.

16. AAHC, Whelan to Hand, Richmond, Mar. 30, 1843; Whelan to Hand, Richmond, Feb. 27, 1844.

17. AAHC, Whelan to Hand, Richmond, Oct. 23, 1845.

18. AAHC, Whelan to Hand, Richmond, Oct. 12, 1846.

19. AAHC, Whelan to Woodlock, Wheeling, Nov. 9, 1847.

20. Parke, "Missions of Virginia," pp. 9, 29.

21. Whelan to Mrs. Floyd, Richmond Feb. 24, 1843.

22. ADR, Whelan to Mrs. Floyd, Richmond, May 9, 1843.

23. ADR, Fox to Mrs. Floyd, Norfolk, Aug. 13, 1844.

24. ADR, Hughes to Mrs. Floyd, New York, Jan. 8, 1845.

25. ADR, Father John Donelan to O'Brien, Washington, Mar. 10, 1846; O'Brien to Mrs. Floyd, Richmond, Mar. 13, 1846.

26. ADR, Whelan to Mrs. Floyd, Richmond, May 8, 1845.

27. Baptismal Records of St. Peter's Church, Richmond, Va., May 26, 1836. Although O'Brien did not specify that these baptisms occurred in Lynchburg, the number of children baptized and the presence of the Dornins makes Lynchburg the logical site. Moreover, Michael and Mary Connell, who later show up in Lynchburg records, also had a child baptized on this occasion.

28. Jean M. Daniel, "Marie Rosalie Boudar Dornin," MS, n.d., Holy Cross Church, Lynchburg, Va.

29. Grace Walsh, *The Catholic Church in Lynchburg, 1829–1936* (Lynchburg: Coleman & Bradley Printers, 1936), pp. 13–14.

30. AANY, Whelan to Hughes, Richmond, April 14, 1842.

31. Parke, "Missions of Virginia," pp. 13–14.

32. Baptismal Records of Holy Cross Church, Lynchburg, Va.

33. *The Catholic Almanac for 1847* (Baltimore: F. Lucas, Jr., 1847), p. 177.

34. ADR, Fox to Mrs. Johnston, Lynchburg, Nov. 14, 1848.

35. Baptismal Records, Holy Cross Church, Lynchburg, Va., Aug. 5 and Aug. 25, 1850.

36. See, for example, Baptismal Records, Lynchburg, Oct. 29 and Dec. 18, 1850.

37. Baptismal Records, St. Francis of Assisi Church, Staunton, Va.

38. AAB, 23J4, Hoerner to Whitfield, Wheeling, Nov. 4, 1833.

39. AAB, 32J3, Whelan to Kenrick, Richmond, Mar 16, 1846.

40. AMP, 215P10, Whelan to Verhaegen, Wheeling, Aug. 23, 1846.

41. ASPF, Whelan to commission, Baltimore, Mar. 5, 1848.

42. *Centenary of the Convent of the Visitation, Mount de Chantal, Wheeling, West Virginia, 1848–1948*, n.p., n.d. There is no pagination.

43. AMP, 216K10, Whelan to Brocard, Wheeling, Aug. 19, 1848.

44. AMP, 216F17, Whelan to Brocard, Wheeling, Oct. 25, 1848.

45. AMP, 217T8, Whelan to Brocard, Wheeling, Feb. 25, 1849.

46. AMP, 217F11, Whelan to Brocard, Wheeling, Nov. 15, 1849.

47. AMP, 217F9, Whelan to Brocard, Wheeling, Nov. 22, 1849.

48. AMP, 218P4, Whelan to provincial, Wheeling, Aug. 26, 1850.

49. AAHC, B. 87, Richmond, # 2, 1850–1857: Talty to Woodlock, Martinsburg, Jan. 25, 1851.

50. Baptismal Records, St. Peter's Church, Feb. 24, 1838.

51. Robert J. Brennan, O.S.B., *A History of St. Mary's Church, Richmond, Virginia* (Richmond, 1962), p. 1.

52. Ibid. 2.

53. AMP, 217, Braun to Brocard, Nov. 13, 1848.

54. AMP, 217T5a, O'Brien to Brocard, Richmond, Feb. 19, 1849.

55. AMP, 218S1, Timothy O'Brien to ?, Richmond, June 3, 1850.

56. AMP, 218, Pallhuber to Brocard, Richmond, July 5, 1850.

57. AMP, 218, Joseph Bapst, Joseph Heirholzer and others to provincial of Jesuits, Richmond, July 18, 1850.

58. Brennan, p. 2.

59. AMP, 218P19, Whelan to Heirholzer and others, Wheeling, Aug. 4, 1850.

60. AMP, 218R5, Joseph Heirholzer, H. Schafer, and others to Brocard, Aug. 15, 1850.

61. See pp. 104–8.

62. AMP, McGill to Brocard, Richmond, Dec. 17, 1850.

63. AMP, Agreement between McGill and Brocard, Dec. 15, 1851.

64. Brennan, pp. 2–3.

6. Division of Richmond and Wheeling, 1850: John McGill, Richmond's Third Bishop

1. APF, SOCG, 972, 39–44.

2. On this point, see my Introduction, in Gerald P. Fogarty, S.J., ed., *Patterns of Episcopal Leadership* (New York: Macmillan, 1989), pp. xxiv–xxv, and my "Relations between the Church in the United States and the Holy See," *The Jurist*, 52 (1992), 215–16.

3. APF, SOCG, 972, 66rv–67rv.

4. APF, ACTA, 212 (1849–50), 432–439v: Fransoni Ponenza, June, 1850; 437–438rv: inserted in the above, General congregation, June 10, 1850; 440–446r: osservazioni, letter of Cullen, Dec. 10, 1849; 499–462v: Sommario; 463–464v. The section pertaining to Richmond is 437 and 455.

5. Clyde F. Crews, *An American Holy Land: A History of the Archdiocese of Louisville* (Wilmington, Del.: Michael Glazier, 1987), pp. 122–23, 130, 166, 168.

6. APF, SOCG, 970, 610rv–613, Eccleston to Propaganda, Baltimore, May 15, 1848; 246: 614rv-615rv, Purcell to Propaganda, Cinn., May 14, 1848.

7. APF, ACTA, 211, 163r–168r, General Congregation, April 3, 1848.

8. ADR, Lamy to McGill, Covington, Ky., Oct. 26, 1850.

9. ADR, Whelan to McGill, Wheeling, Jan. 10, 1851.

10. AAHC, B. 87, Richmond, # 2, 1850–1857: Talty to Woodlock, Martinsburg, Jan. 25, 1851.

11. AMP, McGill to Brocard, Richmond, Dec. 17, 1850.

12. ADR, Whelan to McGill, Wheeling, Dec. 18, 1850.

13. ADR, Kenrick to McGill, Philadelphia, Dec. 19, 1850.

14. ADR, John Purcell and R. H. Gallagher Petition, Dec. 21, 1850.

15. ADR, Whelan to McGill, Wheeling, Jan. 18, 1851.

16. ADR, "A Statement of facts relating to the conditions of matters at Richmond and Petersburg with respect to claims of Rev. T. O'Brien." This seems to have been McGill's petition to the commission established by the First Plenary Council in May, 1852.

17. Under the chairmanship of Bishop Michael Portier of Mobile, the committee consisted of Reynolds of Charleston, Amadeus Rappe of Cleveland, Whelan, Peter Paul Lefevere, coadjutor and administrator of Detroit, and John Martin Henni of Milwaukee, who arrived, however, after the matter was closed. Two of the bishops, Whelan and Reynolds, could be expected to be on McGill's side.

18. ADR, "A Statement of facts relating to the condition of matters at Richmond and Petersburg with respect to claims of Rev. T. O'Brien."

19. ADR, Report of the Committee of Grievances on claims of Rev. T. O'Brien against the congregation and Diocese of Richmond, Va., submitted to the national council and approved. May 15, 1852.

20. ADR, O'Brien to Lynch, secretary of the council, Lowell, May 17, 1852.

21. ADR, Fitzpatrick to McGill, Boston, Sept. 21, 1852.

22. ADR, O'Brien to McGill, Lowell, Sept. 22, 1852.

23. Clarence V. Joerndt, *St. Ignatius, Hickory, and Its Missions* (Baltimore: Publication Press, 1972), p. 391; Brian C. Mitchell, *The Paddy Camps: The Irish of Lowell: 1821–61* (Urbana and Chicago: University of Illinois Press, 1988), pp. 123–24, 138–39.

24. *Acta et Decreta Sacrorum Conciliorum Recentiorum: Collectio Lacensis* (Freiburg im Br., 1875), 3, 40–42.

25. APF, SOCG, 974, 78r, Eccleston to Prop. Baltimore, May 12, 1845.

26. APF, SOCG, 974, 67r, Kenrick, O'Connor, and McGill to Propaganda, Baltimore, April 26, 1851.

27. Ibid., 71rv, O'Connor and McGill to Prop., Baltimore, Apr. 27, 1851.

28. APF, SOCG, 974, 92r, Blanc to Propaganda, New Orleans, May 27, 1851.

29. ADR, Whelan to McGill, Wheeling, May 16, 1851.

30. ADR, Reynolds to McGill, Raleigh, May 20, 1851.

31. APF, SOCG, 974, 94rv–95rb, McGill to Prop., Richmond, May 28, 1851.

32. Ibid. 96rv: Reynolds to Prefect, Charleston, June 13, 1851.

33. McGill to Fransoni, Richmond, Jan. 2, 1852, quoted in Michael J. Curley, C.Ss.R., *Bishop John Neumann, C.Ss.R.: Fourth Bishop of Philadelphia* (Philadelphia: Bishop Neumann Center, 1952), p. 171

34. APF, SOCG, 977, 534r–540r, Kenrick to Propaganda, Baltimore, Oct 1, 1852.

35. ASPF, McGill to Propagation, Richmond, Nov. 2, 1852.

36. In fact, the only letter of his in the archives pertains to his opinion against allowing the Trappist monastery at New Melleray in Iowa to become an Abbey— that abbots wore miters, he thought, caused confusion among the people. See APF, SOCG, 977, 591rv, McGill to Propaganda, Rome, Dec. 13, 1852.

37. ADR, Ives to Convention of Episcopal Church, Rome, Dec. 22, 1852 (copy). Ives went to New York where he taught in the diocesan seminary. Later that year, Father John Early, S.J., in Baltimore founded a Relief Society to provide financial assistance to Protestant clergymen who converted to the Catholic Church.

38. ADR, F. P. Kenrick to McGill, New Orleans, Aug. 2, 1852.

39. ADR, F. P. Kenrick to McGill, Baltimore, Sept. 6, 1852.

40. AIC, O'Keefe to Kirby, Norfolk, May 31, 1854; ADR, O'Keefe to Gibbons, Norfolk, July 30, 1874.

41. ADR, Kenrick to McGill, Baltimore, July 6, 1853.

42. AIC, O'Keefe to Kirby, Norfolk, May 31, 1854.

43. AIC, McGill to Kirby, New York, Nov. 19, 1854.

44. AIC, O'Keefe to Kirby, Norfolk, May 20, 1856.

45. AIC, O'Keefe to Kirby, Norfolk, July 8, 1857.

46. AIC, O'Keefe to Kirby, Norfolk, June 6, 1860 and, written on the same sheet, McGill to Kirby, Richmond, May 8, 1860.

47. ADR, McGill, "A Record for things to be noted regarding the diocess," p. 21, Apr. 28, 1862.

48. AMP, Box 73, 220, Michael Tueffer to Brocard, Feb. 6, 1852.

49. ADR, Keiley to McGill, Petersburg, July 12, 1852.

50. ADR, R. Fust [?] to McGill, Petersburg, Sept. 29, 1855.

51. ADR, McGill to A. L. Hitzelberger, Dec. 17, 1855.

52. Quoted in James H., Bailey, *A Century of Catholicism in Historic Petersburg: A History of Saint Joseph's Parish, Petersburg* (n.p., n.d.), p. 15.

53. ADR, Mulvey to McGill, Lynchburg, Feast of St. Thomas the Apostle, n.d.

54. ADR, Keiley to McGill, Petersburg, April 10, 1860.

7. The Diocese on the Eve of the Civil War

1. In 1851, Mother Seton's Sisters of Charity merged with the French congregation of the Daughters of Charity, whose distinctive cornette Whelan thought less appropriate for an American apostolate than the earlier "widow's weeds"; AAB, 32J4, Whelan to Kenrick, Wheeling, Nov. 19, 1851.

2. APF, ACTA, 215 (1853), 184–210, Fornari Ponenza, June, 1853, 208v–211v and Sommario, 239–40: Kenrick to Prefect, Baltimore, Oct. 4, 1852.

3. APF, SOCG, 981, 1022r–1027v, Kenrick and suffragans to Propaganda, Baltimore, May 12, 1855.

4. ADR, Stonestreet to McGill, Georgetown College, Aug. 2, 1856.

5. AMP, 224E7, McGill to Stonestreet, Richmond, Aug. 3, 1856.

6. APF, ACTA, 220 (1856), Barnabò Ponenza, 463–64.

7. ADR, O'Keefe to McGill, Norfolk, May 15, 1855.

8. James F. Connelly, *The Visit of Archbishop Gaetano Bedini to the United States of America (June, 1853–February, 1854* (Rome: Università Gregoriana Editrice, 1960).

9. Philip Morrison Rice, "The Know-Nothing Party in Virginia, 1854–1856," *Virginia Magazine of History and Biography,* 55 (1947), 61–65. The most recent study is John David Bladek, "'Virginia is Middle Ground': The Know-Nothing Party and the Virginia Gubernatorial Election of 1855," *The Virginia Magazine of History and Biography,* 106 (Winter 1998), 35–70.

10. Mason to Rives, Selma, Va., Nov. 23, 1852, William C. Rives MSS, Library of Congress. For providing me with this citation and those in notes 14, 15, and 24 below, I am grateful to Michael Holt.

11. John Tyler to Robert Tyler, July 17, 1854, in Lyon G. Tyler, *The Letters and Times of the Tylers* (Richmond and Williamsburg, 1884–1896), II, 513, quoted in Rice, "Know-Nothing Party," p. 65.

12. Rice, "Know-Nothing Party," pp. 66–67.

13. AIC, McGill to Kirby, New York, Nov. 19, 1854.

14. Rives to Shirrard, Castle Hill, Jan. 2, 1855; Shirrard to Rives, Winchester, Jan. 16, 1855, Rives MSS, Library of Congress.

15. Rives to W. M. Burwell, Castle Hill, Mar. 19, 1855; Rives MSS, Library of Congress.

16. University of Virginia, Alderman Library, Special Collections, 1486, Box 1: Benjamin Johnson Barbour to W. D. Blair, Jan. 29, 1855.

17. Quoted in Rice, "Know-Nothing Party," pp. 70–71.

18. Quoted in James Henry Bailey, *A History of the Diocese of Richmond: The Formative Years* (Richmond: Chancery Office, 1956), p. 115.

19. Bladek, "Know-Nothing Party," 52, 54. For Norfolk, see Thomas C. Parramore, *Norfolk: The First Four Centuries* (Charlottesville: University Press of Virginia, 1994), pp. 180–81.

20. Josephine M. Bunkley, *The testimony of an escaped novice from the Sisterhood of St. Joseph, Emmittsburg, Maryland, the Mother-house of the Sisters of Charity in the United States* (New York, Harper & Brothers, 1855). For the best treatment of such stories of runaway nuns, see Ray Allen Billington, *The Protestant Crusade: A Study of the Origins of American Nativism, 1800–1860* (Chicago: Quadrangle Books, 1964).

21. Parramore, p. 181.

22. *The Southside Democrat,* May 22, 1855, p. 2.

23. Rice, "Know-Nothing Party," pp. 73–75.

24. Nathan Sargent to Richard Yates, Washington, May 31, 1855, Richard Yates MSS, Illinois Sate Historical Library.

25. See Stephanie Wilkinson, "A Novel Defense: Fictional Defenses of American Catholicism, 1824–1869"; Ph.D. dissertation, Department of Religious Studies, University of Virginia, 1997, pp. 94–101.

26. Quoted in Rice, "Know-Nothing Party," p. 160.

27. Quoted ibid., 162.

28. *Richmond Enquirer,* Sept. 14, 1855.

29. Quoted in Parramore, p. 180.

30. *Richmond Whig and Public Advertiser,* Sept. 11, 1855.

31. Ibid., Sept. 14, 1855.

32. Ibid., Sept. 18, 1855.

33. ADR, Mulvey to McGill, Lynchburg, Sept. 24, 1855.

34. Rice, "Know-Nothing Party," 165–67.

35. Unsigned, "Chaplain Matthew O'Keefe of Mahone's Brigade," *Southern Historical Society Papers,* 35 (1907), 180. The entry is dated Towson, Md., January 28, 1906, and was probably written by one of the associate priests at the Immaculate Conception Church, which O'Keefe later founded in that Baltimore suburb.

36. ASJPH, notes on founding of St. Vincent's Hospital, Norfolk, n.d.

37. ASJPH, "Notes on the Yellow Fever epidemic," n.d., no author.

38. AIC, O'Keefe to Kirby, Norfolk, Sept. 19, 1855.

39. ADR, Kenrick to McGill, Baltimore, Nov. 21, 1857.

40. Sister Bernadette Arminger, D.C., "The History of the Hospital Work of the Daughters of Charity of St. Vincent De Paul in the Eastern Province of the United States: 1823–1860," M.S. thesis, Catholic University of America School of Nursing Education, 1947, p. 86.

41. AAB, Kenrick Letterbook, p. 84: Kenrick to Herron, Baltimore, July 12, 1855.

42. ASJPH, Notes of Sister Bernard Boyle.

43. ASJPH, Behan to Burlando, Norfolk, Oct. 22, 1855.

44. ASJPH, notes on Miss Anne Herron, attached to "Yellow Fever in Norfolk, 1855."

45. ASJPH, Act to incorporate St. Vincent's Hospital.

46. John Farina, *An American Experience of God: The Spirituality of Isaac Hecker* (New York: Paulist Press, 1981), p. 104.

47. Richmond *Daily Dispatch,* Dec. 10, 1856, p. 2. McGill's diary says that Miss Herron had presented the painting of the Crucifixion and Queen Amélie, wife of Louis Philippe of France, had given one of the Assumption. See Bailey, *Richmond,* p. 121.

48. Cornelius M. Buckley, S.J., trans., *A Frenchman, A Chaplain, A Rebel: The War Letters of Pere Louis-Hippolyte Gache, S.J.* (Chicago: Loyola University Press, 1981), pp. 62–63.

49. AIC, 1983: O'Keefe to Kirby, Norfolk, July 8, 1857.

50. ADR, McGill, "Record," pp. 13–14: Oct. 2–10, 1858.

51. Virginia Bernadette Griffin, *Golden Jubilee: St. Paul's Catholic Church, Portsmouth, Virginia,* (Portsmouth, 1955), pp. 17–18.

52. *Synodus Dioecesana Richmondensis Prima, A.D. 1856 celebrata* (n.p., n.d.), pp. 3–5. Sears left the Jesuit novitiate in Frederick, Md., on Jan. 13, 1852; AMP, Dimissi, p. 12.

53. Ibid., 5.

54. Ibid., 10–11, no. XV.

55. ADR, R. McSherry to McGill, Martinsburg, May 7, 1856.

56. ADR, McGill, "Record," p. 4.

57. AAHC, McGill to Woodlock, Richmond, May 15, 1856.

58. AAHC, McGill to Woodlock, Richmond, Aug. 12, 1856.

59. Wyndham Notes, St. Joseph's Church, Martinsburg, W. Va.

60. AAHC, 19. Teeling to Woodlock, Richmond, Sept. 16, 1856.

61. *Shepherdstown Register,* May 16, 1857, St. Joseph's Church, Martinsburg, W. Va.

62. Kevin Condon, C.M., *The Missionary College of All Hallows, 1842–1891* (Dublin: All Hallows College, 1986), p. 197.

63. *Staunton Spectator and General Advertiser,* Dec. 16, 1857.

64. ADR, copy of the deposition of Thomas Honeyhan and Michael B. McAleer filed in the Clerk's Office of Augusta County.

65. ADR, Kenrick to McGill, Baltimore, Dec. 29, 1857.

66. ADR, Downey to McGill, Staunton, April 17, 1858.

67. Elizabeth Dabney Coleman, "The Blue Ridge Tunnel," *Virginia Cavalcade,* I (Summer 1951), 22–27; Staunton *News Leader,* Jan. 21, 1973, p. 23. For Downey's trials, see Hampton H. Hairfield, Jr., Elizabeth M. Hairfield, and James F. Smith, *A History of St. Francis of Assisi Parish, Staunton, Virginia, Celebrating 150 Years: 1845–1995* (Bridgewater, Va.: Good Printers, 1995), pp. 10–11.

68. ADR, Quaestiones in Concilio Baltimorensi IX discutiendae.

69. On this form of discipline, see Gerald P. Fogarty, S.J., *The Vatican and the American Hierarchy from 1870 to 1965* (Collegeville: Michael Glazier, 1985), pp. 14–15.

70. ADR, Downey to McGill, Staunton, May 17, 1859.

71. ADR, Kenrick to McGill, Baltimore, June 20, 1859.

72. See pp. 187–88.

73. ADR, McGill, "Record," Sept. 11, 1855.

74. Thomas Joseph Peterman, *The Cutting Edge: The Life of Thomas A. Becker* (Devon, Pa., William T. Cooke, 1982), pp. 8–10.

75. ADR, McGill to Prefect of Propaganda, Richmond, Dec. 3, 1856.

76. See pp. 177–78.

77. ADR, McGill, "Record."

78. ADR, McGill, "Record," p. 15:

79. ADR, McGill, "Record."

80. ADR, McGill, "Record," p. 23. Unfortunately, while McGill said he received Weed into the Church in June 1858, he did not give the date of his ordination.

81. Baptismal Records of St. Peter's Church, Richmond, Va., June 29, 1858; ADR, Sister Mary Charles Weed to Gibbons, Tuscaloosa, Nov. 30, 1872. See also Buckley, *Gache,* pp. 205, 261. For providing me with information on Weed's ministry in the Episcopal Church, I am grateful to Professor David Holmes of the College of William and Mary.

82. Given in Bailey, *Richmond,* pp. 127–28.

83. APF, Acta, 222 (1858), 324–334v, Altieri Ponenza, July 1858 on 8 Prov. Balto.

84. ADR, F. P. Kenrick to McGill, Baltimore, Oct. 1, 1858; F. P. Kenrick to McGill, Baltimore, Oct. 20, 1858; McGill, "Record," p. 14: Oct. 1, 1858. The rescript was dated Aug. 15, 1858.

85. AMP, 74, Bixio to Provincial, Alexandria, July 18, 1854.

86. AMP, 222 M8, John E. Blox to provincial, Dec. 12, 1854.

87. ADR, McGill, "Record," p. 12: June 27, 1857.

88. Ibid., p. 16: Mar. 20, 1859.

89. Ibid., p. 12: Sept. 19, 1858.

90. Ibid., p. 19.

91. Ibid., p. 21: Oct. 20, 1821.

92. *St. Mary Star of the Sea, Fort Monroe, Virginia: 1860–1985* (n.p., n.d.), p. 7.

93. ARD, McGill, "Record," p. 19.

94. Ibid., p. 17: June 12, 1859, Pentecost Sunday.

95. Quoted in *Acta et Decreta Concilii Plenarii Baltimorensis Tertii* (Baltimore: John Murphy & Co., 1886), no. 83, p. 44.

96. ADR, Costello to McGill, Harpers Ferry, Aug. 27, 1859.

97. Lee A. Wallace, Jr., and Detmar H. Finke, "Montgomery Guard," *Military Collector and Historian* (Fall 1958), 69.

98. AAHC, Costello to Harrington, Harpers Ferry, Feb. 11, 1860.

99. "Early Records of Saint Peter's Parish, Harpers Ferry, West Virginia," no pagination.

100. See, for examples, Baptismal Records, St. Paul's Church, Portsmouth, Sept. 7, 1846; Oct. 13, 1850; Sept. 26, 1852; June 6, 1858.

101. Hairfield, et al., *St. Francis of Assisi*, p. 8.

102. Tax rolls for 1859, copy in Maymont, Dooley family papers.

8. The Civil War: Virginia's Catholics Rally to the Cause

1. ADR, F. P. Kenrick to McGill, Baltimore, Jan. 3, 1860; F. P. Kenrick to McGill, Baltimore, Jan. 23, 1860. McGill seems to have proposed Peter Joseph Lavialle, a French-born priest of Louisville. Archbishop Kenrick preferred the appointment of A. A. Pellicer, a native of St. Augustine, but noted that Bishop Lynch of Charleston named James Corcoran, a theologian in his diocese, in first place. Bishop Spalding of Louisville agreed that Corcoran would be his first choice, were he not "too indolent." Like Kenrick, he thought "a southern man should be preferred," for "any other would be likely to die soon"; ADR, M. L. Spalding to McGill, Louisville, Feb. 3, 1860. In the fall of 1860, the Holy See named Lavialle, who was McGill's choice, but he later declined.

2. ADR, Kenrick to McGill, Baltimore, Sept. 24, 1860.

3. ADR, McGill, Will, Nov. 16, 1860.

4. ADR, F. P. Kenrick to McGill, Baltimore, Dec. 1, 1860.

5. James Henry Bailey, *A History of the Diocese of Richmond: The Formative Years* (Richmond: Chancery Office, 1956), p. 144.

6. ASPF, McGill to Society, Richmond, Feb. 5, 1861.

7. ADR, Kenrick to McGill, Baltimore, Feb. 14, 1861. On Verot's pamphlet, see John Peter Marschall, "Francis Patrick Kenrick, 1851–1863: The Baltimore Years," Ph.D. dissertation, The Catholic University of America, 1965, pp. 348–50.

8. Quoted in Bruce Catton, *The Coming Fury* (Garden City: Doubleday, 1961), p. 331.

9. Ibid., pp. 341–44.

10. ADR, Lynch to McGill, Charleston, Feb. 28, 1858.

11. AAB, Whelan to Kenrick, Wheeling, April 28, 1861.

12. AANY, Whelan to Hughes, Wheeling, May 3, 1861.

13. John R. G. Hassard, *Life of the Most Reverend John Hughes, D.D., First Archbishop of New York* (New York: D. Appleton and Company, 1866), p. 439.

14. Gibbons, "My Memories," p. 165, quoted in Marschall, "Kenrick," p. 352.

15. APF, SCAmerCent, 20, 213–14, Kenrick to Barnabò, Baltimore, May 19, 1863.

16. Kenrick to Spalding, Baltimore, May 4, 1861, quoted in Marschall, "Kenrick," p. 352.

17. Ibid, pp. 363–64.

18. *The Daily Dispatch,* April 22, 1861, quoted in Bailey, *Richmond,* p. 144. For Becker's problems, see pp. 177–78.

19. ADC, McGill to Lynch, Richmond, April 25, 1861.

20. Ibid., McGill to Lynch, Richmond, May 15, 1861.

21. Quoted in Joseph T. Durkin, S.J., ed., *John Dooley, Confederate Soldier: His War Journal* (Washington, D.C.: Georgetown University Press, 1945), p. 1.

22. Robert Emmett Curran, S.J., *The Bicentennial History of Georgetown University* (Washington, D.C.: Georgetown University Press, 1993), I, 222–24.

23. ADR, Records of the Young Catholic Friends Society, founded Dec. 30, 1855.

24. Richmond *Daily Dispatch,* Jan. 4, 1855.

25. Richard J. Sommers, *Richmond Redeemed: The Siege of Petersburg* (Garden City: Doubleday, 1981), 101–4.

26. For his military service, see Lee A. Wallace, *A Guide to Virginia Military Organizations, 1861–1865* (Lynchburg, 1986), p. 127. Richmond *Daily Dispatch,* Feb. 21, 1883, p. 1.

27. Bailey, *Richmond,* p. 145.

28. Lee A. Wallace, Jr., *1st Virginia Infantry,* 3d ed. (Lynchburg: H. E. Howard, 1985), pp. 15–16.

29. Ibid., p. 146.

30. Gregg David Kimball, "Place and Perception: Richmond in Late Antebellum Richmond," Ph.D. dissertation, Department of History, University of Virginia, 1997, pp. 342–43.

31. Ibid., 339–40.

32. ASSJ, Charles J. Crowley, *Brother Alfred Wakeham, Josephite* (St. Augustine, Fla., n.d.), pp. 5–6.

33. Benjamin H. Trask, *The 9th Virginia Infantry Regiment* (Lynchburg: H. E. Hammond, 1984).

34. Thomas M. Lacina and William C. Thomas, *A History of Sacred Heart Parish* (Boyce, Va.: Carr Publishing Co., 1953), pp. 80–81. On Mosby's unit, see Hugh C. Keen and Horace Mewborn, *43rd Battalion Virginia Cavalry: Mosby's Command* (Lynchburg: H. E. Howard, 1993), pp. 295, 355.

35. Kevin H. Siepel *Rebel: The Life and Times of John Singleton Mosby* (New York: St. Martin's Press, 1983), p. 1983. Interview with Mrs. Marian Ralph, Beattie's granddaughter, July 27, 1998.

36. William D. Henderson, *The 12th Virginia Infantry Regiment* (Lynchburg: H.E. Hammond, 1984); James M. Bailey, "The Family and Background of Anthony M. Keiley" (Petersburg), *Progress-Index,* May 25, 1947, p. 4.

37. *Progress-Index,* May 18, 1947, p. 4.

38. Daniel, "Marie Rosalie Boudar Dornin." See also Robert H. Moore, II, *Chew's Ashby, Shoemaker's Lynchburg and the Newton Artillery* (Lynchburg: H. E. Howard, 1995), p. 112.

39. William M. Glasgow, *Northern Virginia's Own: The 17th Virginia Infantry Regiment, Confederate States Army* (Alexandria, Va.: Gobill Press, 1989), pp. 28–29, 100; Lee A. Wallace, *17th Virginia Infantry* (Lynchburg: H. E. Howard, 1990), p. 8; *St. Mary's: 200 Years for Christ, 1795–1995* (Alexandria, Va.: St. Mary's Catholic Church, 1995), pp. 40–41.

40. ADC, J. P. O'Connell to Lynch, Columbia, S.C., June 24, 1861.

41. See pp. 177–78.

42. ADR, Lynch to McGill, Charleston, Aug. 23, 1861.

43. "St. Mary's Church and Residence, Alexandria, Virginia," *Woodstock Letters,* 14 (1885), 253.

44. University of Virginia, Alderman Library, Special Collections, Diary of Z. Lee Gilmer of Charlottesville, Co. B, 19th Virginia Regiment, Dec. 9, 1861.

45. Cornelius M. Buckley, S.J., trans., *A Frenchman, A Chaplain, A Rebel: The War Letters of Pere Louis-Hippolyte Gache, S.J.* (Chicago: Loyola University Press, 1981), p. 52.

46. Ibid., pp. 60 & 62.

47. Ibid., p. 77

48. "Chaplain Matthew O'Keefe of Mahone's Brigade," *Southern Historical Society Papers,* 35 (1907), 176.

49. Buckley, *Gache,* p. 68.

50. For providing me with this information, I am grateful to Emmett Curran of Georgetown University.

51. Buckley, *Gache,* pp. 74–75.

52. Ibid., p. 95.

53. Ibid., 121.

54. "A Year with the Army of the Potomac: Diary of the Reverend Father Tissot, S.J., Military Chaplain," *Historical Records and Studies,* 3 (1903), 76–78.

55. Ibid., 78.

56. Joseph T. Durkin, S.J., ed., *Confederate Chaplain: A War Journal of Rev. James B. Sheeran, C.Ss.R, 14th Louisiana, C.S.A.* (Milwaukee: Bruce, 1960), p. 2.

57. Ibid., 78–79.

58. Ibid., 79–80.

59. Tissot to *Etudes,* Fredericksburg, Jan. 27, 1863, in "L'Apostolat catholique aux Etats-Unis pendant la guerre," *Etudes,* new series, 2 (1863), 864.

60. Ibid., 80–81.

61. Ibid., 81–82.

62. "L'Apostolat catholique," 862.

63. See p. 138.

64. Parish Records of St. Mary's Church, Alexandria, Va.

65. Parish Records of St. Francis of Assisi, Staunton, Va.

66. Gache to Ph. de Carrièr, near Yorktown, Jan. 17, 1862, in Buckley, *Gache*, p. 92.

67. Peter Tissot to *Etudes*, Frederick, April, 1862, "Lettre d'un autre Père de la Compagnie de Jésus," *Annales de la Propagation de la Foi*, 35 (1863), 284.

68. Bixio also baptized several times at St. Peter's in July; see Baptismal Records of St. Peter's Church, Richmond, Va., July 20, 23, 1862.

69. Ray and Barbara Freson, eds., *St. Mary's Parish, Fairfax, Va., 1858–1983* (Fairfax: 1983), p. 16.

70. Durkin, *Sheeran*, pp. 101–2

71. Ibid., 99.

72. AMP, 58 T3, ASM [?] to "dear friend," Richmond Feb. 10, 1865.

73. St. Francis of Assisi Baptismal Records, Staunton, Va.

74. Archives of the California Province of the Society of Jesus, Summarium Vitae, P. Josephus Bixio, March 1, 1889.

75. Buckley, *Gache*, p. 99.

76. Father Gerald McKevitt, S.J., of Santa Clara University obtained this information for me.

77. Durkin, *Sheeran*, pp. 98–156.

78. Richard Shaw, *Dagger John: The Unquiet Life and Times of Archbishop John Hughes of New York* (New York: Paulist Press, 1977), pp. 361–69. See also Iver Bernstein, *The New York City Draft Riots: Their Significance for American Society and Politics in the Age of the Civil War* (New York: Oxford University Press, 1990), p. 62, for Hughes's role.

79. Philip Tucker, "Confederate Secret Agent in Ireland: Father John B. Bannon and His Irish Mission, 1863–1864," *Journal of Confederate History*, V (1990), 55–65.

80. Ibid., 69–74.

81. Ibid., 74–85.

82. Sister M. Anne Francis Campbell, O.L.M., "Bishop England's Sisterhood, 1829–1929," Ph.D. dissertation, History Department, St. Louis University, 1968, p. 136.

83. David C. R. Heisser, "Bishop Lynch's Civil War Pamphlet on Slavery," *Catholic Historical Review*, 84 (Oct. 1998), 681–96.

9. Nursing on the Battlefield and a Diocese Divided by War

1. Virginius Dabney, *Virginia: The New Dominion* (Garden City: Doubleday, 1971), p. 360.

2. Sister Zoe Hickey, "The Daughters of Charity of St. Vincent de Paul in the Civil War," M.A. thesis, The Catholic University of America, pp. 20–21. Hickey places the date at which the sisters took over the general hospital as July 26, whereas Angela Heath, "Annals of the War," gives June 26.

3. ASJPH, "Annals of the War," pp. 58–59.

4. Ibid., 60.

5. Ibid., 62.

6. Ibid., 52–57.

7. ASJPH, anonymous, "Portsmouth and Norfolk, Va," p. 53.

8. ASJPH, 7–5–1–2, nos. 482–483: Kenrick to Burlando, Baltimore, Dec. 17, 1861.

9. ASJPH, 7–5–1–2, nos. 484–86: Marshall, Dyer, Norris, Caulfield, and Burlando to Dix, Emmitsburg, Dec. 20, 1861 (copy).

10. Ibid.

11. ASJPH, "Annals of the War," p. 66.

12. Ibid., 67.

13. Buckley, *Gache*, p. 146.

14. Ibid., 147.

15. Ibid., p. 190.

16. Ibid., 176–77.

17. Ibid., 177–80, 186.

18. Ibid., 210

19. Ibid., 214.

20. Sister M. Anne Francis Campbell, O.L.M., "Bishop England's Sisterhood, 1829–1929," Ph.D. dissertation, History Department, St. Louis University, 1968, pp. 96–103.

21. ADC, McGill to Lynch, Richmond, May 24 and 31, 1862.

22. Campbell, "Bishop England's Sisterhood," pp. 106–8. See Dorothy H. Bodell, *Montgomery White Sulphur Springs: A history of the resort, hospital, cemeteries, markers, and monument* (Blacksburg, Va.: Pocahontas Press, 1993), pp. 28–29.

23. ADC, 27P5, Sister M. De Sales to Lynch, Aug. 27, 1862, quoted in Campbell, "Bishop England's Sisterhood," pp. 112–13.

24. Ibid., 114.

25. Campbell, "Bishop England's Sisterhood," pp. 114, 116–17.

26. ADC, 28K3, Drs. Isaac White, W. H. Keffer, and M. E. Daughtry to Dr. Samuel Moore, Montgomery White Sulphur Springs, Jan. 9, 1863, quoted in ibid., p. 118. The one contract physician who did not sign the protest was named Williams.

27. Campbell, "Bishop England's Sisterhood," pp. 118–19.

28. Ibid., pp. 119–20.

29. ADC, 28R7, O'Connell to Lynch, Montgomery White Sulphur Springs, Mar. 6, 1863.

30. ADC, 28S3, O'Connell to Lynch, Montgomery White Sulphur Springs, March 14, 1863.

31. ADC, 29A6, O'Connell to Lynch, Columbia, May 22, 1863.

32. Lynch to Northrop, April 18, 1863, quoted in Campbell, "Bishop England's Sisterhood," p. 122.

33. Ibid.

34. Sister M. De Sales to Brennan, Sept. 14, 1863, quoted in ibid., 134.

35. See p. 163.

36. Quoted ibid., 138–39. See also Bodell, *Montgomery White Sulphur Springs*, p. 32.

37. Bodell, p. 34.

38. Campbell, "Bishop England's Sisterhood," p. 219.

39. Ibid., 227–28.

40. Hickey, p. 29.

41. ADC, McGill to Lynch, Richmond, Sept. 2 1862. For Hughes's sermon, see Richard Shaw, *Dagger John: The Unquiet Life and Times of Archbishop John Hughes of New York* (New York: Paulist Press, 1977), p. 354.

42. AAB, 29M6, O'Keefe to Kenrick, Norfolk, Mar. 19 [1863]; 29M5, O'Keefe to Kenrick, Norfolk, Feb. 9, 1863.

43. *St. Joseph's Parish Church, Martinsburg, West Virginia* (n.p., 1969), no pagination.

44. APF, SCAmerCent, 20: 149–50, Becker to Barnabò, Martinsburg, Mar. 12, 1863.

45. Ibid., 316–19, Becker to Barnabò, Baltimore, July 8, 1863.

46. bid., 213–14, Kenrick to Propaganda, May 19, 1863. On Becker's imprisonment, see Joseph Peterman, *The Cutting Edge: The Life of Thomas A. Becker* (Devon, Pa.: William T. Cooke, 1982), 49–52.

47. APF, SCAmerCent, 20, 316–19, Becker to Prefect, Baltimore, July 8, 1863.

48. Thomas W. Spalding, *Martin John Spalding: American Churchman* (Washington, D.C.: The Catholic University Press, 1973), pp. 148–49.

49. APF, SOCG, 991, 265r-266v: McGill to Barnabò, Richmond, Confederate States of North America, July 22, 1863.

50. ADC, McGill to Lynch, Richmond, July 23, 1863.

51. Spalding, *Spalding*, pp. 148–50.

52. AAB, 35G11, McGill to Spalding, Richmond, Oct. 15, 1864.

53. AAB, 35G10, McGill to Spalding, Richmond, Nov. 23, 1864.

54. AAB, 35G13, McGill to Spalding, Richmond, Jan 7, 1865.

55. Ibid., enclosure.

56. Spalding, *Spalding*, p. 165.

57. AAB, 35G14, McGill to Spalding, Richmond, Feb. 17, 1865.

58. AAB, Spalding Letterbook, I, p. 83, Spalding to McGill, Baltimore, March 24, 1865, quoted in Spalding, *Spalding*, p. 165. The original of this letter is not in ADR.

59. ADR, St. Peter's Announcements, pp. 164–65.

60. Ibid., July 6, 1862, p. 165.

61. Ibid., Dec. 21, 1862, pp. 190–91.

62. Ibid., June 4, 1863, p. 215.

63. Buckley, *Gache*, 159–60.

64. Quoted in ibid., 166.

65. Michael B. Chesson, "Harlots or Heroines? A New Look at the Richmond Bread Riot," *The Virginia Magazine of History and Biography*, 92 (April 1984), 149.

66. Durkin, *Dooley*, pp. 106–7.

67. Curran, *Georgetown*, p. 240.

68. See ADR, St. Peter's Announcements, June 26, 1864, p. 181, Oct. 16, 1864, p. 295.

69. "A Virginia Confederate" [Anthony J. Keiley], *In Vinculis; or, The Prisoner of War, being, The Experience of a Rebel in Two Federal Pens, interspersed with reminiscences of the late war; anecdotes of Southern Generals, etc.* (Petersburg, Va.: "Daily Index" Office, 1866), p. 37.

70. Ibid., 42.

71. Ibid., 166.

72. ADR, St. Peter's Announcements, Sept. 11, 1864, pp. 289–91.

73. Ibid, Feb. 26, 1865, p. 311.

74. AMP, McMullen to ?, Richmond, Feb. 10, 1865.

75. Gache to Carrière, Charleston, July 18, 1865, in Buckley, *Gache*, pp. 220–21.

76. ADR, St. Peter's Announcements, April 9, 1865, pp. 318–19.

77. Buckley, *Gache*, pp. 221–23.

78. Durkin, *Dooley*, p. 208.

79. Abram J. Ryan, "C.S.A.," Abram J. Ryan, *Poems: Patriotic, Religious, Miscellaneous* (New York: P. J. Kenedy & Sons, 1896), p. 241.

80. APF, SCAmerCent, 21, 42r–44rv, McGill to Barnabò, Richmond, n.d.

81. ADW, Historical Data, Wytheville, 1942.

82. Ray and Barbara Freson, eds., *St. Mary's Parish, Fairfax, Va, 1858–1983* (Fairfax, Va., 1983), pp. 15–16.

83. Baptismal Records, St. Joseph's Church, Martinsburg, Sept. 25, 1864, contains an entry signed by Becker.

84. Henry Kyd Douglas, *I Rode with Stonewall* (Chapel Hill: University of North Carolina Press, 1940), pp. 336–39. See also *St. Joseph's Parish Church* (n.p., 1969), no pagination.

85. APF, SCAmerCent, 21, 42r–44rv, McGill to Barnabò, Richmond, n.d.

86. See pp. 195–96.

87. Ibid.

88. ADR, Downey to McGill, Staunton, Oct. 24, 1865.

89. U.S. Census, 1870, Augusta Co., Va., p. 187. He also had real estate valued at $2,500 and personal estate valued at $150. This was a substantial decrease from 1860, when he was listed as a "Catholic priest," with real estate valued at $3,000 and personal estate valued at $3,500; U.S. Census, 1860, Augusta Co., Va., p. 757.

90. Randall M. Miller, "Catholic Religion, Irish Ethnicity, and the Civil War," in Randall M. Miller, Harry S. Stout, and Charles Reagan Wilson, eds., *Religion and the American Civil War* (New York: Oxford University Press, 1998), pp. 261–96.

10. The Diocese Faces Reconstruction

1. John McGill, *Our Faith, The Victory; or, a Comprehensive View of The Principal Doctrines of The Christian Religion* (Richmond: J. W. Randolph, 1865), pp. 66–67.

2. Ibid., 70–71.

3. Ibid., 73.

4. Ibid., 38–40.

5. Ibid., v.

6. AAB, 35G14, McGill to Spalding, Richmond, Feb. 17, 1865.

7. AAB, 35G16, McGill to Spalding, Richmond, Sept. 1865.

8. ADR, Spalding to McGill, Baltimore, Ascension Thursday [May 5], 1865. See also Thomas W. Spalding, *the Premier See: A History of the Archdiocese of Baltimore, 1789–1989* (Baltimore: The Johns Hopkins University Press, 1989), p. 188.

9. AAB, 35G16, McGill to Spalding, Richmond, Sept. 1865.

10. APF, SCAmerCent, 21, 42r–44rv, McGill to Barnabò, Richmond, n.d.

11. Ibid.

12. Ibid.

13. APF, SCAmerCent, 21, 222r–223r, Becker to Propaganda, Richmond, April 25, 1866.

14. Spalding to McCloskey, Baltimore, Oct. 9, 1865, quoted in Spalding, *Premier See*, pp. 189–90.

15. AAB, 39A-D5, minutes of extraordinary session, p. 5, quoted in Cyprian Davis, O.S.B., *The History of Black Catholics in the United States* (New York: Crossroad, 1990), p. 119.

16. Ibid., pp. 119–20.

17. *Concilii Plenarii Baltimorensis II., in Ecclesia Metropolitana Baltimorensis, a Die VII. ad Diem XXI. Octobris, A.D., MDCCCLXVI, Habiti, et a Sede Apostolica Recogniti, Acta et Decreta* (Baltimore: John Murphy, 1868), no. 484, p. 244.

18. Ibid., no. 485.

19. Ibid., no. 487.

20. Ibid., no. 488, p. 246.

21. Ibid., nos. 489–90, pp. 246–47.

22. Ibid., no. 491, p. 247.

23. Ibid., no. 50, p. 41.

24. AAB, 35 G17, McGill to Spalding, Richmond, Nov. 13, 1865.

25. AAHC, Teeling to Woodlock, Richmond, April 6, 1859. Teeling makes only a passing reference to the forthcoming ordination of Becker in Rome and of an unnamed student who was studying under him.

26. *Sadliers' Catholic Directory, Almanac, and Ordo for the Year of Our Lord 1870*, pp. 266–67.

27. *Sadliers' Catholic Directory, Almanac, and Ordo for the Year of Our Lord 1877*, pp. 347–49.

28. Leslie Woodcock Tentler, "'God's Representatives in Our Midst': Toward a History of the Catholic Diocesan Clergy in the United States," *Church History*, 67 (June 1998), 338–42.

29. ADR, Diocesan Diary of McGill, Gibbons, and Keane.

30. AAHC, McGill to Woodlock, Richmond, Dec. 10, 1866.

31. AAHC, McGill to Fortune, Richmond, Sept. 9, 1868. See also Kevin Condon, C.M., *The Missionary College of All Hallows, 1842–1891* (Dublin: All Hallows College, 1986), p. 293.

32. AAB, 35G18, McGill to Spalding, Richmond, Dec. 18, 1865.

33. ADR, apportionment of Behan legacy, March 23, 1868. See also AAHC, 24. McGill to Woodlock, Richmond, July 22, 1863; 25. McGill to Woodlock, Richmond, Dec. 10, 1866; 27. McGill to Fortune, Aug. 7, 1867.

34. Richard E. Cross and Eugene L. Zoeller, *The Story of the American College,* extract from *The American College Bulletin* (1957), p. 14.

35. ADR, Pulsers to Keane, Louvain, Aug. 6, 1879. See also John D. Sauter, *The American College of Louvain (1857–1898).* (Louvain: Bibliothèque de l'université bureaux du recueil, 1959), p. 129, where he says McGill became a patron between 1863 and 1870.

36. Annemarie Kasteel, *Francis Janssens, 1843–1897: A Dutch-American Prelate* (Lafayette: University of Southwestern Louisiana, 1992), p. 39.

37. AAHC, McGill to Fortune, All Hallows College, Aug. 7, 1867.

38. A. M. Keiley, "Memorandum of the History of the Catholic Church, Richmond, Va.," *Proceedings of the Fourth Annual Convention of the Catholic Benevolent Union of the State of Virginia, held in the City of Norfolk, Virginia, on the 10th, 11th and 12th of June, 1874, with Appendix* (Norfolk, Va.: Virginian Book and Job Print, 1874), p. 16.

39. Robert J. Brennan, O.S.B., *A History of St. Mary's Church, Richmond, Virginia* (Richmond, 1962), p. 7; "Community History" of Benedictine Sisters, n.p., n.d., p. 16.

40. Walker Goller, "John Lancaster Spalding's Religious Anthropology: An American Catholic Understanding of the Human Person," Ph.D. dissertation, Toronto School of Theology, 1994, p. 364.

41. APF, SOCG, 994, 832r-v, 836, Bishops of the United States to Propaganda, Baltimore, Oct. 20, 1866.

42. Ibid., 827r, Bishops of the United States to Propaganda, Baltimore, Oct. 1866.

43. Ibid., 997rv–1000rv, Spalding to Propaganda, Rome, June 24, 1867.

44. John Tracy Ellis, *The Life of James Cardinal Gibbons, Archbishop of Baltimore: 1834–1921*, 2 vols. (Milwaukee: Bruce, 1952), I, 69–70.

45. Joseph P. O'Grady, "Anthony M. Keiley (1832–1905): Virginia's Catholic Politician," *Catholic Historical Review*, 54 (Jan. 1969), 624–25.

46. See p. 206.

47. Jack P. Maddex, Jr., *The Virginia Conservatives: 1867–1879* (Chapel Hill: University of North Carolina Press, 1970), pp. 55, 57.

48. Ibid., 57–59. See also Virginius Dabney, *Virginia: The New Dominion* (Garden City: Doubleday, 1971), p. 367–68.

49. *Richmond Dispatch,* June 13, 1868.

50. On Colfax as an active member of the Know-Nothings, see Willard H. Smith, *Schuyler Colfax; the Changing Fortunes of a Political Idol* (Indianapolis, Indiana Historical Bureau, 1952), pp. 54–60, 298–300.

51. Ibid., 627–28. See also Michael B. Chesson, *Richmond After the War: 1865–1890* (Richmond: Virginia State Library, 1981), p. 114.

52. ADR, Record Book of St. Vincent de Paul Society, St. Peter's Church.

53. *Richmond Dispatch,* Jan. 3, 1871.

54. Ibid., Jan. 13, 1871.

55. Ibid., 626–29.

56. James Henry Bailey, *A History of the Diocese of Richmond: The Formative Years* (Richmond: Chancery Office, 1956), p. 147.

57. AAB, Gibbons Diary, Dec. 18, 1876.

58. Chesson, *Richmond,* pp. 11 and 121.

59. Shank, "Raw Materials on the History of Norfolk-Portsmouth Newspapers," MS, Sargeant Memorial Room, Norfolk Public Library, pp. 133–34, 352.

60. Thomas C. Parramore, *Norfolk: The First Four Centuries* (Charlottesville: University Press of Virginia, 1994), pp. 242–52.

61. *Encyclopedia of Virginia Biography,* p. 246; Maymont Foundation: Handbook for Maymont Volunteers," pp. 36–38; and Mary Lynn Bayliss, "Will the Real Major Dooley Please Stand Up!" *The Richmond Quarterly,* 14 (Fall 1991), 31–34.

62. Linda Singleton-Driscoll, "The Dooley Women of Richmond," MS, Maymont Foundation, 1979.

63. Chesson, *Richmond,* p. 121.

64. Ibid., 177. See ADR, Diocesan Diary, p. 121: Jan. 7, 1883.

65. Cemetery Records, St. Mary's Church, Wytheville, Va.

66. AANY, McGill to McCloskey, Richmond, June 14, 1869.

67. Other members of the "Accademia" included Isaac Hecker, Richard Burtsell, and Edward McGlynn, who was later excommunicated. In addition to their support for Radical Reconstruction, they also discussed such ecclesiastical issues as papal infallibility, a vernacular liturgy, and a married clergy. See Robert Emmett Curran, *Michael Augustine Corrigan and the Shaping of Conservative Catholicism in America, 1878–1902* (New York: Arno Press, 1978), pp. 171–72, 175. Farrell himself later left money for the founding of a parish for African Americans in New York, St. Benedict the Moor.

68. James Hennesey, S.J., *The First Council of the Vatican: The American Experience* (New York: Herder and Herder, 1963), pp. 159, 169, 230.

69. AAB, 36A N18, McGill to Spalding, Paris, May 18, 1870.

70. Hennesey, *First Council of the Vatican,* pp. 135–40, 159–65, 180–86, 253–54.

71. Baptismal Records, St. Mary's Church, Fredericksburg.

72. Ibid., p. 68: Mar. 1, 1896 was his first recorded baptism.

73. Kevin H. Siepel, *Rebel: The Life and Times of John Singleton Mosby* (New York: St. Martin's Press, 1983), pp. 5–6, 176.

74. Janssens, Books of Sermons, quoted in Kasteel, *Janssens,* pp. 37–38.

75. ASJPH, personnel card gives date of baptism as Mar. 28, 1869, while Kasteel, *Janssens,* p. 38, gives July 25, 1869, as the date of baptism for the first two sisters.

76. Siepel, *Mosby,* p. 194.

77. ADA, Mosby file: Mrs. Stuart Mosby Coleman to Vincent Waters, Warrenton, Mar. 25, 1941; photocopy of Father Gill's report that he buried Mosby on May 30, 1916.

78. *Sadlier's Catholic Directory, Almanac, and Ordo for the Year of Our Lord 1872* (New York: D. & J. Sadlier, 1872), pp. 335–36.

79. Ibid., 336–37.

80. APF, SOCG, 999, 647–49: Becker to Barnabò, Wilmington, Jan. 22, 1872.

11. JAMES GIBBONS, FOURTH BISHOP OF RICHMOND, 1872–1877

1. APF, SOCG, 999, 651–652, Spalding to Barnabò, Baltimore, Feb. 6, 1872. The letter was written in Becker's hand, but was sworn to by Thomas Foley, Spalding's former chancellor and then coadjutor bishop of Chicago.

2. Ibid., 650, Becker to Barnabò, Baltimore, Feb. 6, 1872.

3. ARD, McGill, last will and testament, May 29, 1866.

4. ADR, Edward L. Ryan to Kaup, Richmond, Dec. 10, 1924. The letter refers specifically to the Gallego property, but the situation would apply to any other property included in McGill's will.

5. APF, SOCG, 999, 618r–619v, Spalding to Propaganda, Baltimore, Nov. 27, 1868.

6. Ibid., 621r, Becker to Barnabò, N.Y., Feb. 24, 1872.

7. Ibid., 631r–632r, Gibbons to Barnabò, Richmond, Feb. 15, 1872.

8. Ibid., 633–634: Whelan to Barnabò, Wheeling, Feb. 14, 1872.

9. Ibid., 624–625v: Persico to Barnabò, Baltimore Feb. 13, 1872.

10. Ibid., 653–654: Persico to Barnabò, Savannah, March 1, 1872.

11. Ibid., 629rv, Verot to Barnabò, St. Augustine, Feb. 26, 1872.

12. APF, Acta, 238 (1872), 313–319, De Luca Ponenza, July 1872, on Baltimore and Richmond.

13. *Catholic Mirror,* Oct. 26, 1872, quoted in John Tracy Ellis, *The Life of James Cardinal Gibbons: Archbishop of Baltimore, 1834–1921,* 2 vols. (Milwaukee: Bruce, 1952), I, 120–21.

14. ADR, Sister M. Charles [Weed], Ursuline Convent, Tuscaloosa, Ala., Feast of St. Andrew, [1872].

15. Ellis, *Gibbons,* I, 121–22.

16. ADR, O'Keefe to Gibbons, Norfolk, Mar. 23, 1872.

17. AAB, Gibbons Diary, Dec. 28, 1874. Gibbons seems to have remained on good terms with Keiley, inasmuch as he dedicated his new church in New Castle, Del.; see ibid., May 30, 1876.

18. Gerald P. Fogarty, S.J., *The Vatican and the Americanist Crisis: Denis J. O'Connell, American Agent in Rome, 1885–1903* (Rome: Università Gregoriana Editrice, 1974), pp. 6–8.

19. ASSJ, Diary of Canon Benoit, trip to the United States, Jan. 6, 1875–June 8, 1875.

20. Ellis, *Gibbons,* I, 124–25.

21. Ellis, *Gibbons,* I, 125–26; Fogarty, *O'Connell,* pp. 11–12.

22. AAHC, 35, Gibbons to Fortune, Richmond, Sept. 12, 1872.

23. AAHC, 37, Gibbons to Fortune, Richmond, June 23, 1873. But see 38, Brady to Fortune, Portsmouth, Dec. 19, 1873; 39, Gibbons to Fortune, April 2, 1874, where Gibbons asks for Irish recruits.

24. AAB, Gibbons Diary, April 23–25, 1873.

25. AAB, Gibbons Diary, June 20, 1874.

26. *Sadlier's Catholic Directory, Almanac, and Ordo, for the Year of our Lord 1877* (New York: D. & J. Sadlier, 1877), p. 349.

27. M[atthew]. O'Keefe, *The Key to True Christianity: Being a Series of Letters addressed to Rev. J. D. Blackwell* (Philadelphia: William P. Kildare, 1874).

28. ADR, Foley to Gibbons, Chicago, March 26, 1874.

29. Records of St. Mary's Parish, May, 19, 1875. William Manchester, *American Caesar* (Boston: Little, Brown, 1978), p. 38. Manchester, unfortunately, does not mention the fact that a Catholic priest officiated at the wedding.

30. Ellis, *Gibbons,* I, 130–31.

31. ADR, O'Keefe to Gibbons, Montreal, Aug. 28, 1874.

32. James Cardinal Gibbons, *The Faith of Our Fathers: Being a Plain Exposition and Vindication of the Church Founded by Our Lord Jesus Christ* (110th ed.; New York: P. J. Kennedy & Sons, 1917), vii.

33. Ellis, *Gibbons*, I, 145–51.

34. Gibbons, *Faith of Our Fathers*, p. 100.

35. Ibid., 101.

36. Ibid., 102.

37. Ibid., 108.

38. ADR, P. J. O'Keefe to Gibbons, Martinsburg, Sept. 6, 1872. George Brent to Gibbons, Martinsburg, Jan. 5, 1874. Brent listed the claims against O'Keefe.

39. AAB, Gibbons Diary, p. 52, Jan. 12, 1874. Thomas Kelly from St. Patrick's in Richmond went to Martinsburg. John Doherty from Warrenton went to St. Patrick's, and Patrick Hasty was assigned to Warrenton.

40. ADR, Becker to Matthew O'Keefe, Wilmington, March 23, 1874.

41. ADR, O'Keefe to Becker, Norfolk, March 25, 1874.

42. ADR, Becker to Gibbons, Wilmington, Del., March 28, 1874.

43. ADR, O'Keefe to Gibbons, Norfolk, April 6, 1874.

44. Ellis, *Gibbons*, I, 130. On McMaster's role in fighting for priests' rights, see Gerald P. Fogarty, S.J., *The Vatican and the American Hierarchy from 1870 to 1965* (Stuttgart: Anton Hiersemann, Verlag, 1982; Wilmington, Del.: Michael Glazier, 1985), p. 15.

45. AAB, Gibbons Diary, April 10, 21, 1874. See also Ellis, *Gibbons*, I, 129–30.

46. ADR, Foley to Gibbons, Chicago, April 22, 1874.

47. AAB, 41 S4: Gibbons to Bayley, Richmond, April 23, 1874.

48. ADR, P. J. O'Keefe to Gibbons, Macon, Ga., Nov. 15, 1874.

49. ADR, Bayley to Gibbons, Baltimore, Nov. 24, 1874.

50. At the same time that O'Keefe was appealing for a trial, Gibbons received from a parishioner in Martinsburg a final accounting that O'Keefe had incurred a debt at the church for $1,921.82; ADR, Thomas J. Kelly to Gibbons, Martinsburg, Nov. 17, 1874.

51. AAB, Gibbons Diary, Nov. 5, 1877, p. 66.

52. See pp. 237–39.

53. Stephen J. Ochs, *Desegregating the Altar: The Josephites and the Struggle for Black Priests, 1871–1960* (Baton Rouge: Louisiana State University Press, 1990), pp. 43–44.

54. Archives of the Archdiocese of Westminster, Diary of Herbert Vaughan, v. 1/32, p. 37.

55. Ibid., p. 38.

56. ADR, Edward H. Welsh, S.J., to Gibbons, Boston College, Jan. 30, 1874. Welsh was also one of the first incorporators of Boston College.

57. ASSJ, Diary of Benoit, cb6–92.

58. Ibid., 95–96.

59. Ibid., 97.

60. Quoted in Ellis, *Gibbons*, I, 144.

61. AAB, Gibbons Diary, June 7, 1876.

62. AAB, Gibbons Diary, Nov. 8–12, 1872.

63. ADR, Diocesan Diary, p. 93: Sept. 14, 1879; Archives of Georgetown University, Jesuit Community House Diary, Sept. 13–14, 1879.

64. AAB, Gibbons Diary, Jan. 6, 1874.

65. ADR, Brother Patrick to Gibbons, New York, Nov. 22, 1872.

66. AAB, Gibbons Diary, Sept. 28, 1873; Keiley, p. 17. See also ADR, Brother Patrick to Gibbons, New York, Nov. 22, 1872.

67. Gibbons to Purcell, Richmond, Nov. 30, 1872, quoted in Ellis, *Gibbons,* I, p. 123.

68. AAB, Gibbons Diary, Apr. 22, 1875.

69. Ibid., Feb. 1, 1876. The Sisters were Mary Elizabeth Roche, Loretto Dinkgreve, Eugenia Reeder, Mary Simeon Manot, and Gertrude Dolan; ASJPH, personnel lists.

70. ADR, Sister Placida Fitzgerald to Gibbons, Abingdon, Sept. 16, 1875.

71. *Sadlier's Catholic Directory, Almanac, and Ordo, for the Year of Our Lord 1877* (New York: D. & J. Sadlier, 1877), pp. 349–50.

72. AAB, Gibbons Diary, Oct. 14, 1873.

73. AAB, Gibbons Diary, Mar. 30, 1874; see Ellis, *Gibbons,* I, 133.

74. AAB, An Act to incorporate "The Little Sisters of the Poor," bound in Gibbons Diary, Apr. 21, 1874. The first incorporators were Sisters Sidonie Joseph (Lucie Debroucker), Marie des Apôtres (Marie Agnes Laiané), Sainte Enna (Marie Reardon), and Saint Patrick (Eliza Carmody), together with Anna Maria Cowardin and Sara Anne Robinson.

75. AAB, Gibbons Diary, Oct. 13, 1874.

76. AAB, Gibbons, Diary, Jan. 3, 1877.

77. ADR, Boniface Wimmer to Gibbons, St. Vincent's, Westmoreland, Pa., May 16, 1872.

78. ADR, Bishops' Diary, p. 92: July 7, 1879.

79. AAB, Gibbons Diary, July 26, 1875.

80. AAB, Gibbons Diary, March 25, 1876.

81. ADR, Joseph P. O'Connell to Gibbons, Charlotte, Jan. 27, 1873; APF, Lettere, 369, 241v, Propaganda to Gibbons, Rome, June 23, 1873.

82. AAB, Gibbons Diary, May 19, 1873.

83. ADR, O'Kane to Gibbons, Alexandria, May 29, 1873.

84. ADR, O'Kane to Gibbons, Alexandria, Sept. 12, 1873; O'Kane to Gibbons, Alexandria, Sept. 15, 1873.

85. ADR, O'Kane to Gibbons, Alexandria, Dec. 10, 1873.

86. AAB, Gibbons Diary, Oct. 18, 1874; ADR, O'Kane to Gibbons, Alexandria, Sept. 1, 1874.

87. AAB, Gibbons Diary, May 3–4, 1873.

88. ARD, petition of St. Mary's parish, Fairfax, July 28, 1873.

89. AAB, Gibbons Diary, Dec. 1, 1872.

90. Ibid., Feb. 14, 1873.

91. ADR, Foley to Gibbons, Chicago, March 26, 1874.

92. ADR, Wilson to Gibbons, Petersburg, March 3, 1874.

93. AAB, 41S6: Gibbons to Bayley, Richmond, Oct. 22, 1874.

94. Missions were a Catholic answer to Protestant revivalism. A team of priests, usually members of a religious order, would visit a parish for two weeks

and preach a series of fiery sermons each night, with separate weeks set aside for men and women. Afterwards, the priests would hear confessions, thus giving parishioners the opportunity of confessing to a priest other than their pastor. The purpose was to win back fallen away Catholics and possibly to convert Protestants. In some instances, a mission would be given when a parish first began, and then every two years thereafter. See Jay P. Dolan, *Catholic Revivalism: The American Experience, 1830–1900* (Notre Dame: University of Notre Dame Press, 1978).

95. AAB, Gibbons Diary, Apr. 25, 1874.

96. Ibid., May 14–12, 1874.

97. Ibid., April 3–4, 1875.

98. Ibid., Oct. 17, 1975.

99. AAB, 41S10: Gibbons to Bayley, Richmond, Nov. 5, 1875.

12. GIBBONS ACHIEVES NATIONAL RECOGNITION

1. John Tracy Ellis, "James Gibbons of Baltimore," in Gerald P. Fogarty, S.J., ed., *Patterns of Episcopal Leadership* (New York: Macmillan, 1989), pp. 123–25.

2. APF, Collegi esteri, no. 7, Americano Lovanio, 1858–1892, I, 1093r–1098r, Edmond Dumont, vice rector to Propaganda Louvain, Dec. 20, 1872.

3. Quoted in Annemarie Kasteel, *Francis Janssens, 1843–1897: A Dutch-American Prelate* (Lafayette: University of Southwestern Louisiana, 1992), p. 60.

4. ADR, Pulsers to Keane, Louvain, Feb. 24 and Aug. 6, 1879.

5. Archives of the Archdiocese of New Orleans, Becker to Janssens, Wilmington, Jan. 9, 1873.

6. APF, Collegi esteri, no. 7, Americano Lovanio, 1858–1892, I, 1107r, Becker to Pulsers, Wilmington, Jan. 1873.

7. Ibid., 1106v, Janssens to Pulsers, Richmond, Jan. 9, 1873.

8. Ibid., 1105rv–1106rv, Gibbons to J.J. Pulsers, pro-rector, Richmond, Jan. 10, 1873.

9. Pulsers to Elder, Feb. 6, 1873, quoted in Kasteel, *Janssens,* p. 60.

10. Gibbons to Elder, March 13, 1873, quoted in Kasteel, *Janssens,* p. 62.

11. APF, Lettere, 369 (1873), 185rv, Propaganda to Giacomo Cattani, nuncio to Brussels, Rome, May 19, 1873.

12. Kasteel, *Janssens,* p. 63.

13. Bayley to Janssens, Baltimore, July 5, 1873, quoted in John Tracy Ellis, *The Life of James Cardinal Gibbons, Archbishop of Baltimore: 1834–1921,* 2 vols. (Milwaukee: Bruce, 1952), I, 124.

14. APF, SCAmerCent, 24, fols.964rv–965rv, Bayley to Propaganda, Baltimore, July 25, 1873.

15. APF, Lettere, 369, 446r, Propaganda to Bayley, Rome, Aug. 27, 1873.

16. Quoted in Kasteel, *Janssens,* p. 65.

17. APF, Lettere, 369, 558rv, Propaganda to Janssens, Rome, Nov. 18, 1873. See Kasteel, *Janssens,* pp. 64–65, for a different chronology of Janssens' refusal.

18. AAB, 41S2, Gibbons to Bayley, Richmond, March 2, 1874.

19. AAB, Gibbons Diary, July 10, 1874.

20. Bayley to Gibbons, Madison, N.J., July 14, 1874, quoted in Ellis, *Gibbons,* I, 135.

21. AAB, 41S5, Gibbons to Bayley, Richmond, July 22, 1874.

22. AAB, 41S5, Gibbons to Bayley, Richmond, July 22, 1874.

23. AAB, Gibbons Diary, July 2–19, 1874.

24. ADR, O'Keefe to Gibbons, Norfolk, July 30, 1874.

25. Gibbons to Bayley, Richmond, April 12, 1875, quoted in Ellis, *Gibbons,* I, 138.

26. Gibbons to Bayley, Richmond, March 2, 1875, quoted in ibid., 137.

27. AAB, Gibbons Diary, April 27, June 17, 1875.

28. AAB, Gibbons Diary, May 23, 1875.

29. Ibid., April 27, 1873.

30. AAB, 72U6, Kain to Franchi, Wheeling, Nov. [?], 1875 (copy).

31. AAB, 72U6, Franchi to Gibbons, Rome, Dec. 20, 1875.

32. AAB, Gibbons Diary, Jan. 25, 1876.

33. AAB, 40G2, Gibbons to Bayley, Richmond, Jan. 26, 1876.

34. AAB, Gibbons Diary, Feb. 1, 1876.

35. AAB, 40G4, Gibbons to Bayley, Richmond, March 25, 1876.

36. AAB, 72V8, Kain to Gibbons, Wheeling, April 7, 1876.

37. APF, Acta, 245 (1877), Franchi Ponenza, April, 1877, 55v–60r; cf. Ellis, *Gibbons,* I, 157.

38. Ibid., 60r–61v.

39. AAB, 73B2, O'Connell to Gibbons, Rome, May 3, 1877.

40. AAB 73B8, O'Connell to Gibbons, Rome, May 27, 1877; see Gerald P. Fogarty, S.J., *The Vatican and the Americanist Crisis: Denis J. O'Connell, American Agent in Rome, 1885–1903* (Rome: Università Gregoriana Editrice, 1974), p. 14.

41. AAB, 73E5, Janssens to Gibbons, Tilburg, Aug. 27, 1877, quoted in Ellis, *Gibbons,* I, 159.

42. Ellis, *Gibbons,* I, 159.

43. Quoted in ibid., 160.

44. Ibid., 161.

45. Keiley to Gibbons, Richmond, Oct. 31, 1877, quoted in ibid., 162.

46. ADR, O'Keefe to Gibbons, Norfolk, May 17, 1877. See also O'Keefe to Gibbons, Norfolk, Saturday, the 4th [May 4, 1877].

47. Ellis, *Gibbons,* I, 161–62.

48. Ibid., 132.

49. Fogarty, *O'Connell,* pp. 16–30. For the instruction on clerical discipline, see pp. 254–55.

13. JOHN J. KEANE: RICHMOND'S FIFTH BISHOP, 1878–1888

1. APF, Acta, 246 (1878), 95–96, 105, Franchi Ponenza.

2. Ibid., 96v–105.

3. ADR, Diocesan Diary, Aug. 22 and Sept. 11, 1878.

4. ADR, Diocesan Diary, p. 83, Mar. 18, 1879.

5. Ibid., p. 99; Jan. 6, 1880; Richmond *Dispatch,* Jan. 7, 1880.

6. Ibid., p. 102, Apr. 25, 1880.

7. Ibid., p. 112, Oct. 16, 1881.

8. ADR, Diocesan Diary, Sept. 11, 1878.

9. *Acta Sanctae Sedis* 12 (1878), 88–89.

10. ADR, Diocesan Diary, Dec., 1878.

11. ADR, J. P. Hagan to Keane, Winchester, Feb. 9, 1880.

12. ADR, Diocesan Diary, p. 90: June 21, 1879; agreement between Keane and Xaverian Brothers, Sept. 27, 1881.

13. Ibid., p. 113: June 18, 1882.

14. ADR, Annual Meetings, Aug. 26, 1887, p. 52.

15. John Tracy Ellis, *The Life of James Cardinal Gibbons, Archbishop of Baltimore: 1834–1921,* 2 vols. (Milwaukee: Bruce, 1952), I, 186.

16. ADR, Simeoni to Keane, Rome, Nov. 23, 1878.

17. ADR, Joseph Mullen to Keane, Wytheville, Sept. 24, 1878.

18. ADR, Diocesan Diary, p. 77. O'Kane in Alexandria received faculties for any Jesuit. The Jesuit superiors in Frederick and Port Tobacco, in southern Maryland, received faculties for sick calls in Virginia. The pastor in Westernport, Md., received them for Virginia missions he regularly attended.

19. ADR, Mark S. Gross to Keane, Wilmington, N.C., July 16, 1878.

20. ADR, Gross to Keane, Wilmington, N.C., Feb. 6, 1879.

21. ADR, Simeoni to Keane, Rome, Feb. 6, 1879.

22. ADR, Gross to Keane, Wilmington, N.C., Sept. 16, 1879.

23. ADR, Simeoni to Keane, Rome, March 10, 1880.

24. ADR, Gross to Keane, Baltimore, April 6, 1880.

25. Ellis, *Gibbons,* I, 186, n.

26. AAB, 76D3, Keane to Gibbons, Fredericksburg, Sept. 5, 1880.

27. ADR, Diocesan Diary, p. 106, Nov. 24, 1880.

28. ADR, Diocesan Diary, p. 108, Feb. 15, 1881; Keane added his comment later.

29. Ellis, *Gibbons,* I, 186, n. Gibbons was sometimes cryptic in his diary entries, on which Ellis relied and therefore presumed that the *terna* of December 1880 was for North Carolina, whereas it was probably for Richmond in the event that Propaganda accepted Keane's resignation and transfer to North Carolina. The *terna* of May 1881 was for North Carolina. In 1883, Patrick Lynch of Charleston died, so Northrup was translated to the diocese of Charleston, but retained administration of North Carolina. In 1888, Leo Haid, O.S.B., abbot of Belmont Abbey, was named vicar apostolic. After his death in 1924, the Holy See elevated the vicariate apostolic into the diocese of Raleigh.

30. AAB, 74F6, Keane to Gibbons, Richmond, Dec. 23, 1878.

31. ADR, Elder to Keane, Natchez, April 5, 1880.

32. Annemarie Kasteel, *Francis Janssens, 1843–1897: A Dutch-American Prelate* (Lafayette: University of Southwestern Louisiana, 1992), p. 78.

33. Keane to Elder, Richmond, Oct. 23, 1879, quoted in ibid., 79.

34. ADR, Diocesan Diary, p. 108, Feb. 15, 1881.

35. AAB, 75Q10, Janssens to Gibbons, Richmond, Feb. 22, 1881; 75R1, Janssens to Gibbons, Richmond, March 1, 1881; 75U1, Janssens to Gibbons, Richmond, April 2, 1881.

36. Kasteel, *Janssens,* pp. 82–87.

37. ADR, Diocesan Diary, June 6, 1881.

38. ADR, Pulsers to Keane, Louvain, Feb. 24, 1879.

39. ADR, Pulsers to Keane, Louvain, Aug. 6, 1879.

40. ADR, Pulsers to Keane, Uden, Holland, Sept. 27, 1879.

41. ADR, Diocesan Diary, p. 101, Apr. 22, 1880.

42. Ibid., p. 138, Dec., 1885.

43. Ibid., 139, Jan., 1886.

44. ADR, Minutes of the Annual Meeting of the Clergy of the Diocese of Richmond, pp. 14.

45. Ibid., Mar. 22, 1883, pp. 28–29. The corporal is the cloth on which the priest places the host and chalice during Mass; the burse is a flat case, of the same color and material as the other vestments, in which the corporal is placed when not in use.

46. Ibid., Apr. 5, 1882, pp. 15–18.

47. Ibid., 19–30.

48. Ibid., 31–40.

49. Ibid., 41–46.

50. Ibid., 47–48.

51. ADR, Diocesan Diary, p. 144.

52. See pp. 293–97.

53. ADR, Minutes of the Annual Meeting of the Clergy of the Diocese of Richmond, p. 50.

54. ADR, Annual Meeting, Aug. 26, 1887, pp. 49–53.

55. Quoted in Joseph P. Chinnici, O.F.M., ed., *Devotion to the Holy Spirit in American Catholicism* (New York: Paulist Press, 1985), p. 42.

56. Given in ibid., 93–114.

57. ADR, Fitzsimmons to Keane, Keyser, Feb. 9, 1880.

58. ADR., J. R. Hagan to Keane, Winchester, Feb. 9, 1880.

59. ADR, Diocesan Diary, p. 101, n.d., but placed after entry for April 11, 1880.

60. Ibid., pp. 106–7, Nov. 24, 1880.

61. ADR, E. B. Brady to Keane, Hampton, Feb. 12, 1884.

62. ADR, A. P. Doyle to Keane, Baltimore, April 24, 1884.

63. Chinnici, *Devotion,* pp. 46–47.

14. Pastoral Life during Keane's Episcopate

1. ADR, J. P. Hagan to Keane, Winchester, Feb. 9, 1880.

2. ADR, van de Vyver to Keane, Harper's Ferry, June 9, 1879.

3. See p. 255.

4. ADR, Diocesan Diary, p. 116, Feb. 15, 1882; p. 123, Oct. 7, 1882; p. 129, Sept. 7, 1882.

5. AAB, 77H8, Keane to Gibbons, Rome, June 25, 1883.

6. AAB, 77H7, O'Connell to Gibbons, Winchester, June 21, 1883.

7. The only other reference to the family's Catholicism is a letter from McKeefry, who visited Mrs. Holmes about her son's relationship with a young women; see ADR, McKeefry to Keane, Staunton, Feb. 7, 1877.

8. ADR, McKeefry to Keane, Staunton, June 21, 1880.

9. ADR, McVerry to Keane, Staunton, June 23, 1880.

10. ADR, Richard Wakeham to Keane, Ellicott City, Feb. 12, 1884.

11. ASSJ, Charles J. Crowley, *Brother Alfred Wakeham, Josephite* (St. Augustine, Fla., n.d.), no pagination.

12. ADR, H. M. Meade to Keane, Milnes, Page Co., Aug. 13, 1882.

13. ADR, H. M. Meade to Keane, October 26, 1882. Brophy then told Keane that the committee would call on the Roanoke Land and Improvement Company to find out what ground could be obtained; ADR, S. M. Brophy, Keane to Roanoke, Oct. 28, 1882.

14. Margaret Maier Cochener, *On the Hill: St. Andrew's Parish, Roanoke, Virginia, a History of St. Andrew's Parish, November 1882–August, 1989* (n.p., 1989), p. 7, citing *The Roanoke Leader* for Nov. 2 and 16, 1882.

15. ADR, Lynch to O'Connell, Danville, Nov. 26, 1914.

16. Cochener, p. 5.

17. Ibid. 8.

18. ADR, Lynch to Keane, Lexington, Oct. 30, 1884.

19. Cochener, pp. 12–13.

20. Ibid., 16–17.

21. ADR, Lynch to O'Connell, Danville, Jan. 13, 1914.

22. ADR, Records, May 15, 1886, pp. 141–42.

23. Ibid., Aug. 27, 31, 1886, pp. 146–47.

24. Ibid., n.d., p. 154.

25. Cochener, pp. 18–19.

26. Ibid., 26–35.

27. ADR, Lynch to O'Connell, Danville, May 17, 1913, Jan. 13, 1914, and Nov. 26, 1914.

28. ADR, O'Sullivan to Gibbons, Westernport, Md., Jan 10, 1873.

29. ADR, O'Sullivan to Gibbons, Westernport, Md., March 13, 1874, enclosing E. F. Baldwin to Jeremiah O'Sullivan, Baltimore, March 8, 1874.

30. AAB, Gibbons Diary, July 2, 1874.

31. ADR, O'Sullivan to Gibbons, Westernport, Md., Feb. 10, 1875.

32. AAB, Gibbons Diary, Aug. 22, 1875.

33. *Church of the Assumption, Keyser, West Virginia: Centennial Celebration, 1874–1974* (n.p., n.d.), p. 11.

34. ADR, Diocesan Diary, p. 75, Sept. 9, 1878.

35. ADR, Fitzsimmons to Keane, Keyser, Nov. 27, 1878.

36. ADR, Fitzsimmons to Keane, Keyser, Jan. 16, 1879.

37. ADR, Diocesan Diary, p. 103: Aug. 4, 1880.

38. AAB, 76F10, Keane to Gibbons, Harpers Ferry, Oct. 11, 1881.

39. ADR, Eugene P. Mahony to Keane, Keyser, n.d.; Loughlin to Mahony, Brooklyn, Feb. 26, 1882.

40. ADR, Diocesan Diary, p. 103, Dec. 23, 1882.

41. Ibid., p. 108, Apr. 7, 1881.

42. ADR, McKeefry to Keane, Martinsburg, Feb. 23, 1883.

43. ADR, Sister Euphemia to Keane, Emmitsburg, Feb. 27, 1883.

44. ADR, Diocesan Diary, p. 125, Nov. 25, 1883.

45. James P. Shannon, *Catholic Colonization on the Western Frontier* (New Haven: Yale University Press, 1957), pp. 220–22.

46. ADR, Diocesan Diary, p. 68, July 1, 1878.

47. Shannon, *Colonization,* p. 223.

48. ADR, Diocesan Diary, p. 94, Oct. 1–2, 1879.

49. Habets to Griffin, Keileyville, Oct. 15, 1870, quoted in Shannon, *Colonization,* p. 229.

50. ADR, Diocesan Diary, p. 95, Dec. 20, 1879.

51. Shannon, *Colonization,* pp. 231–32.

52. Archives of the American Catholic Historical Society of Philadelphia, Griffin Papers, Habets to Griffin, Richmond, Aug. 19, 1880.

53. ADR, Diocesan Diary, p. 107, Dec. 19, 1880.

54. ADR, Petitioners of Keileyville Colony, Barnesville, Jan. 28, 1883.

55. Gerald T. Gilliam, "The Catholic Colony at Barnesville," *The Southsider,* 12 (1993), 36–46.

56. ADR, Diocesan Diary, Jan. 5, 1879. See also AAB, 74I5, Keane to Gibbons, Richmond, Feb. 5, 1879.

57. Patrick Henry Ahern, *The Life of John J. Keane: Educator and Archbishop, 1839–1918* (Milwaukee: Bruce, 1955), p. 42.

58. ADR, Diocesan Diary, p. 91, June 1879.

59. Michael B. Chesson, *Richmond After the War: 1865–1890* (Richmond: Virginia State Library, 1981), p. 202.

60. Quoted in Ahern, *Keane,* p. 43.

61. ADR, Diocesan Diary, p. 125, Nov. 25, 1883.

62. ADR, le Verdiere to Keane, Propagation, Paris, June 19, 1883, and June 12, 1884.

63. ADR, Benoit to Keane, n.p., Nov. 11, 1884.

64. ADR, Diocesan Diary, p. 133, Jan. 6, 1884.

65. Ibid., Jan. 25–Feb. 8, 1884.

66. Stephen J. Ochs, *Desegregating the Altar: The Josephites and the Struggle for Black Priests: 1871–1960* (Baton Rouge: Louisiana State University Press, 1990), p. 58.

67. ADR, Annual Meetings, Apr. 10, 1884, p. 40.

68. Ibid., Apr. 2, 1885, p. 44.

69. ADR, Diocesan Diary, pp. 133–34, Apr. 12 and May 5, 1885.

70. Ibid., p. 136, Nov. 22, 1885.

71. ASSJ, 10–H-15, Keane to Slattery, Richmond, Oct. 21, 1886.

72. Ochs, *Desegregating the Altar,* pp. 59–60.

73. Ibid., 62–63.

74. ADR, Diocesan Diary, p. 144, Aug. 18, 1886.

75. ASSJ, 10–2–2, Slattery to Gibbons, Richmond, Oct. 23, 1886.

76. Mary J. Oates, *The Catholic Philanthropic Tradition in America* (Bloomington: Indiana University Press, 1995), p. 62.

77. ADR, Diocesan Diary, p. 151.

78. ADR, le Verdiere to Keane, Paris, June 19, 1883, and June 12, 1884.

79. ADR, Diocesan Diary, p. 132.

15. RICHMOND: A DIOCESE IN TRANSITION, 1883–1888

1. AAB, 77H8, Keane to Gibbons, June 25, 1883. For the background to the Third Plenary Council, see Gerald P. Fogarty, S.J., *The Vatican and the American Hierarchy from 1870 to 1965* (Stuttgart: Anton Hiersemann, Verlag, 1982; Wilmington, Del.: Michael Glazier, 1985), pp. 27–29.

2. Ibid., pp. 29–31.

3. AANY, Edes to Corrigan, Rome, Jan. 8, 1884.

4. Fogarty, *The Vatican and the American Hierarchy*, p. 33.

5. Ibid., 33–35.

6. ADR, Diocesan Diary, p. 132.

7. ADR, Diocesan Diary, p. 135, June 27, 1885.

8. Gerald P. Fogarty, S.J., *The Vatican and the Americanist Crisis: Denis J. O'Connell, American Agent in Rome, 1885–1903* (Rome: Università Gregoriana Editrice, 1974), pp. 63–73.

9. ADR, Keane to O'Connell, Richmond, May 20, 1886. See also Patrick Henry Ahern, *The Life of John J. Keane: Educator and Archbishop, 1839–1918* (Milwaukee: Bruce, 1955), pp. 62–63.

10. John Tracy Ellis, *The Life of James Cardinal Gibbons, Archbishop of Baltimore: 1834–1921*, 2 vols. (Milwaukee: Bruce, 1952), I, 302; ADR, Diocesan Diary, p. 143, June 30, 1886.

11. ADR, Diocesan Diary, p. 143, June 18, 1886.

12. See Gerald P. Fogarty, S.J., "Diocesan Structure and Governance in the United States," in James K. Mallett, ed., *The Ministry of Governance* (Washington, D.C.: Canon Law Society of America), pp. 33–34.

13. ADR, T. Shahan to Tearney, Hartford, Oct. 18, 1888.

14. Edward L. Ayers, *The Promise of the New South: Life After Reconstruction* (New York: Oxford University Press, 1992), p. 216.

15. Ahern, *Keane*, pp. 66–67.

16. Fogarty, *Vatican and the American Hierarchy*, pp. 87–88.

17. Ibid., pp. 46–47.

18. Ibid., 45–49.

19. Ahern, *Keane*, p. 76.

20. Keane to Manning, Rome, Feb. 28, 1887, quoted in Ahern, *Keane*, p. 74. Unfortunately, the Manning Papers are not currently available in the archdiocese of Westminster.

21. AAB, 82Q1, Keane to Gibbons, May 14, 1887, quoted in Ahern, *Keane*, pp. 74–75.

22. Fogarty, *Vatican and the American Hierarchy*, pp. 89–92.

23. Ahern, *Keane*, pp. 80–81. See ADR, Diocesan Diary, p. 148, June 17, 1887.

24. ADR, Diocesan Diary, p. 148, June 17, 1887.

25. Ibid, quoted in Ahern, *Keane*, p. 84.

26. ADR, Diocesan Diary, p. 83, Jan. 20, 1879.

27. ADR, J. C. Carroll to Keane, Norfolk, Jan. 8, 1879.

28. ADR, McGurk to Keane, Loyola College, Baltimore, Jan 9, 1879.

29. AAB, 81K7, O'Keefe to Keane, Norfolk, July 3, 1886 (copy).

30. ADR, Diocesan Diary, p. 83, Jan. 20, 1879.

31. ADR, Mother Euphemia to Keane, St. Joseph's, March 17, 1879.

32. ADR, Diocesan Diary, p. 89, May 30, 1879.

33. ADR, R. Devereux Doyle to Keane, Norfolk, April 5, 1879.

34. ADR, O'Keefe to Keane, Norfolk, May 6, 1879; AAB, 81K7, O'Keefe to Keane, Norfolk, July 3, 1886 (copy).

35. ADR, O'Keefe to Keane, Norfolk, Jan. 18, 1882.

36. ADR, O'Keefe to Keane, Norfolk, March 30, 1885.

37. ADR, Keane to O'Keefe, Richmond, Jan. 3, 1886 (copy).

38. ADR, O'Keefe to Keane, Norfolk, Jan. 8, 1886.

39. Ibid., Keane's notation.

40. AAB, 80C6, Keane to Gibbons, Richmond, Jan. 16, 1886.

41. ADR, O'Keefe to Keane, Norfolk, May 31, 1886.

42. AAB, 81K7, O'Keefe to Keane, Norfolk, July 3, 1886 (copy).

43. ADR, Keane to O'Keefe, Fortress Monroe, July 16, 1886 (copy also sent to Gibbons).

44. ADR, Gibbons to Keane, Baltimore, July 22, 1886.

45. ADR, Keane to Gibbons, Fortress Monroe, July 25, 1886 (copy).

46. ADR, D. J. O'Connell to Keane, Rome, Aug. 22, 1886.

47. AAB, 83B9, Keane to Gibbons, Richmond, July 12, 1887.

48. *Baltimore Sun*, editorial Jan. 29, 1906, p. 6.

49. Ibid., Feb. 1, 1906, p. 14

50. Ahern, *Keane*, pp. 85–85.

51. AAB, 84Y2, Keane to Gibbons, Notre Dame, Aug. 29, 1888.

52. ADR, Diocesan Diary, list inserted between pp. 150 and 151.

53. Ibid., p. 154.

54. Ibid., pp. 155–56.

55. *Sadlier's Catholic Directory*, 1890, pp. 348–49.

16. Augustine van de Vyver: Pastoral Life in the Diocese of Richmond, 1889–1911

1. AAB, 84P6, Van de Vyver to Gibbons, Richmond, June 14, 1888.

2. AAB, 84R3, Keane to Gibbons, Richmond, July 3, 1888.

3. Gerald P. Fogarty, S.J. *The Vatican and the Americanist Crisis: Denis J. O'Connell, American Agent in Rome, 1885–1903* (Rome: Università Gregoriana Editrice, 1974), pp. 108–9.

4. APF, ACTA, 258 (1888), 585–596r, Mazzella Ponenza on Richmond, Dec. 1888.

5. Quoted in Fogarty, *O'Connell*, p. 112.

6. AAB, Gibbons Diary, Feb. 12, 1889.

7. Keane to Gibbons, Fulda, Apr. 5, 1889, quoted in Patrick Henry Ahern, *The Life of John J. Keane: Educator and Archbishop, 1839–1918* (Milwaukee: Bruce, 1955) p. 86.

8. ADR, Keane to O'Connell, Liverpool, Apr. 27, 1889.

9. Louis Smet, "The Rt. Rev. Augustine Van de Vyver, Bishop of Richmond, Va. (1889–1911)," *The American College Bulletin,* 10 (July 1912), 93.

10. APF, ACTA, 259 (1889), 364–70: Mazzella Ponenza, May 1889.

11. AAB, 86C12, O'Connell to Gibbons, June 14, 1889, quoted in Fogarty, *O'Connell,* p. 113.

12. AAB, 86B11, van de Vyver to Gibbons, Richmond, June 6, 1889.

13. AAB, 86D8, van de Vyver to Gibbons, Richmond, June 27, 1889.

14. AAB, 86E5, van de Vyver to Gibbons, Richmond, July 8, 1889.

15. Smet, "Van de Vyver," 94.

16. Fogarty, *O'Connell,* pp. 117–18.

17. AAB, 86L12, van de Vyver to Gibbons, Richmond, Sept. 12, 1889.

18. For a summary of this, Gerald P. Fogarty, S.J., *The Vatican and the American Hierarchy from 1870 to 1965* (Stuttgart: Anton Hiersemann, Verlag, 1982; Wilmington, Del: Michael Glazier, 1985), pp. 65–85.

19. AAB, 90K1, van de Vyver to Gibbons, Richmond, Oct. 15, 1892.

20. Fogarty, *Vatican and the American Hierarchy,* pp. 115–29.

21. Ibid., 103–14.

22. AAB, 91E 2, van de Vyver to Gibbons, Richmond, Feb. 7, 1893.

23. Fogarty, *Vatican and the American Hierarchy,* pp. 130–32.

24. Ibid., 139–40.

25. Ibid., 143–89.

26. *American College Bulletin,* II (1903), 85–86.

27. Ibid., III (1904), 36.

28. Ibid., XXXII, *Jubilee Number, 1854–1932,* List of Alumni.

29. John A. K. Donovan, "The Light of His Life: being the biography of Amadeus Joseph van Ingelgem, a Virginia Missionary," manuscript, Falls Church, Virginia, 1937, pp. 1–54.

30. Anonymous, "Our Friends on the Mission," *The American College Bulletin,* III (1905), 117–119.

31. Donovan, "van Ingelgem," pp. 55–90.

32. Joseph Hergesheimer, *Mountain Blood* (New York: Alfred Knopf, 1915), pp. 12–13, 104–9.

33. Ibid., 106–18.

34. *American College Bulletin,* X (1912), 29.

35. *The Golden Jubilee of the Original Stone Church: 1902–1952: St. James Church, Falls Church, Virginia* (n.p., n.d.)

36. ADA, Tearney to van de Vyver, West End, Va., Oct. 16, 1908.

37. "Commemorating the Centennial of St. Vincent de Paul Church, Newport News, Virginia, 1881–1981," pp. 14–18. William O. Foss, *The United States Navy in Hampton Roads* (Norfolk/Virginia Beach: The Donning Company, 1984), p. 48.

38. "The Story of Sacred Heart Parish," pp. 1–2.

39. ASJPH, Southgate Leigh, M.D. to Lennon, n.d. [but approximately Dec. 8, 1896]; Sister Isidore Kenny to Lennon, Norfolk, Dec. 8, 1916.

40. Beverley R. Tucker, "George Ben Johnston: An Appreciation," *Bulletin of the Medical College of Virginia,* 13 (Dec. 1916), 8.

41. ADR, van de Vyver Papers, copy of contract between Medical College of Virginia and Sisters of Mercy, Newberne, N.C., May 25, 1893.

42. Jodi Koste, Archivist, Virginia Commonwealth University, to author, July 17, 1990.

43. ASJPH, St Vincent's Hospital.

44. ADR, Konicek to van de Vyver, Petersburg, Nov. 14, 1905.

45. Victor C. DeClercq, C.I.C.M., *The Catholic Church in the Alleghany Highlands around 1882* (n.p., 1982), p. 25.

46. *St. Joseph's Catholic Church: 1889–1989* (n.p., 1989), pp. 4–9.

47. DeClercq, p. 7.

48. Aloysius Plaisance, O.S.B., to author, Cullman, Ala., July 10, 1990.

49. ADW, First Report of Wytheville, Va., 1869–1873.

50. *Saint Anne's Catholic Church and School, Bristol, Virginia* (n.p., 1990), pp. 5–8.

51. Cecilia Kelly and Julia Dennehy, "A History of the Catholic Church in Southwest Virginia and Norton," in *50 Years: St. Anthony Catholic Church, 1938–1988, pp. 4–5,* (n.p., 1988).

52. "St. Elizabeth Roman Catholic Church," mimeographed page, May 1988.

17. Benefactors of the Diocese

1. ASSJ, "Mission Work" (1890), p. 7.

2. Ibid., (1891), p. 22.

3. Ibid., (1896), pp. 9–18.

4. Ibid., (1897), pp. 9–18.

5. ASSJ, *The Colored Harvest,* 3 (Oct. 1901), 261.

6. Quoted in Stephen J. Ochs, *Desegregating the Altar: The Josephites and the Struggle for Black Priests, 1871–1960* (Baton Rouge: Louisiana State University Press, 1990), p. 126.

7. Quoted in Mary J. Oates, *The Catholic Philanthropic Tradition in America* (Bloomington: Indiana University Press, 1995), p. 63.

8. Cyprian Davis, *The History of Black Catholics in the United States* (New York: Crossroad, 1990), p. 197.

9. Ibid., 127.

10. ASSJ, Parish Annual Report by year, St. Francis, Lynchburg.

11. ASSJ, *The Colored Harvest,* 25 (Oct.-Nov. 1937), 1.

12. *Richmond Times,* Apr. 14, 1902, p. 6.

13. Quoted in Earle A. Newman, S.S.J., "Wales R. Tyrrell, dedicated Black Catholic layman," *The Josephite Harvest,* 81 (Spring 1979), 10–11.

14. Ochs, *Desegregating the Altar,* pp. 72–73.

15. Ibid., 79.

16. ASBS, van de Vyver to Katherine Drexel, Richmond, Aug. 26, 1891.

17. Ibid., Sept. 2, 1891.

18. Ibid., Sept. 19, 1891, and Sept. 25, 1891.

19. ASBS, van de Vyver to Mother Katherine, Richmond, April 25, 1892; attached is her draft of a response.

20. Ochs, *Desegregating the Altar,* pp. 82–85.

21. Sister Consuela Marie Duffy, S.B.S., *Katharine Drexel: A Biography* (Cornwells Heights, Pa.: Mother Katharine Drexel Guild, 1965), pp. 199–202.

22. ASBS, van de Vyver to Mother Katherine, Richmond, June 16, 1894.

23. Ibid., July 21, 1894.

24. Quoted in Ronald O. Pessner, Jr., "The St. Emma Military Academy: A Catholic Response to African-American Missions and Industrial Education," B.A. thesis, University of Virginia, Department of History, 1992, p. 47.

25. Ibid., 48–49.

26. ASBS, Van de Vyver to Mother Katherine, Richmond, Apr. 19, 1898.

27. Ibid., July 18, 1898.

28. Ibid., Feb. 24, 1899.

29. Ibid., Mar. 9, 1899.

30. *Catholic Directory* (1900), p. 261.

31. Patricia Lynch, S.B.S., MS, "History of the Blessed Sacrament Sisters," chapter 3, "Early Boarding Schools," pp. 6–7.

32. Nessa Theresa Baskerville Johnson, *A Special Pilgrimage: A History of Black Catholics in Richmond* (Richmond: Diocese of Richmond, 1978), p. 47.

33. Duffy, *Katharine Drexel,* pp. 208–9.

34. Lynch, "Early Boarding Schools," pp. 12–14.

35. Sister Marie Barat Smith, S.B.S., "A History of St. Emma's Military Academy and St. Francis de Sales High School," Master's thesis, Catholic University of America, Washington, D.C., 1949, pp. 11–12.

36. Ibid., 29–30.

37. ADR, Drexel to van de Vyver, Maud, Pa., Apr. 2, 4, and 10, 1910.

38. ASSJ, *The Colored Harvest,* 3 (Oct. 1900), 197–99.

39. Dom Paschal Baumstein, O.S.B., *My Lord of Belmont: A Biography of Leo Haid* (Herald House, 1985), pp. 141–62. Baumstein also recounts the origin of the property, a bequest of Sister Baptista Linton of the Georgetown Visitation Convent, and the failure of the Benedictines to get ownership in fee simple.

40. *Catholic Directory,* 1900, pp. 460–61; *Catholic Directory,* 1908, pp. 550–51.

41. Sister M. Helen Johnston, O.S.B., *The Fruit of His Works: A History of the Benedictine Sisters of St. Benedict's Convent, Bristow, Prince William County, Virginia* (Bristow: Linton Hall Press, 1954), pp. 51–53.

42. Ibid., 87–94; see also "Community History" of the Benedictine Sisters of Virginia. *Catholic Directory,* 1900, p. 461.

43. Francis Joseph Magri, *The Catholic Church in the City and Diocese of Richmond* (Richmond: Whittet & Shepperson, Printers, 1905), pp. 125–26.

44. Ibid., pp. 137–38.

45. Richmond *Times-Dispatch,* June 4, 1903, quoted in ibid., 21–22.

46. Ibid., 24.

47. Ibid., 19.

48. Ibid., 28–29.

49. ADR, Falconio to van de Vyver, Washington, Apr. 13, 1904.

50. *Catholic Directory for 1908,* pp. 552–53.

51. Annemarie Kasteel, *Francis Janssens, 1843–1897: A Dutch-American Prelate* (Lafayette: University of Southwestern Louisiana, 1992), p. 373.

52. AAB, 102 M2, Gibbons to Falconio, Baltimore, Aug. 9, 1905.

53. ADR, Gotti to Falconio, Rome, May 7, 1908, copy attached to Falconio to van de Vyver, Washington, May 20, 1908.

54. *The American College Bulletin,* 6 (April 1908), 111–12, and Louis Smet, "Rt. Rev. Augustine Van de Vyver, Bishop of Richmond, Va. (1889–1911)," ibid., 10 (July, 1912), 97.

55. ADR, Falconio to Van de Vyver, Washington, May 20, 1908.

56. Ibid., July 3, 1908.

57. *The American College Bulletin,* 6 (Oct. 1908), 165–66.

58. Gerald P. Fogarty, S.J., *The Vatican and the Americanist Crisis: Denis J. O'Connell, American Agent in Rome, 1885–1903* (Rome: Università Gregoriana Editrice, 1974), pp. 308–9.

59. J. De Becker, *The American College Bulletin* 10 (Jan. 1912), 1–2.

18. Denis O'Connell as Bishop:
The Diocese and Virginia Culture, 1911–1926

1. ASV, DAUS, IV, no. 121 (Richmond), 4, Falconio to De Lai, Washington, Oct. 17, 1911 (copy).

2. Ibid., 6, Falconio to Gibbons, Washington, Oct. 23, 1911 (copy).

3. James P. Gaffey, *Citizen of No Mean City: Archbishop Patrick Riordan of San Francisco (1841–1914)* (Washington: Consortium Books, 1976), pp. 411–412.

4. ASV, DAUS, IV, no. 121 (Richmond), 4, 7–8, O'Connell to Falconio, Washington, Oct. 19, 1911; 9–10, O'Connell to Falconio, Washington, Oct. 19, 1911.

5. Ibid., Riordan to Gibbons, San Francisco, Oct. 21, 1911 (copy).

6. Gerald P. Fogarty, S.J., *The Vatican and the Americanist Crisis: Denis J. O'Connell, American Agent in Rome, 1885–1903* (Rome: Università Gregoriana Editrice, 1974), p. 310. For this vote, see AAB, 109 U1, Minutes of the Consultors' Meeting, Nov. 15, 1911; and 109 U6: Minutes of the Meeting of the Bishops of the Province to Select Candidates for the See of Richmond, Nov. 22, 1911. In 1908, Pius X reorganized the curia and transferred the American Church from Propaganda, the missionary congregation, to the Consistorial Congregation, renamed the Congregation of Bishops after Vatican II. Unfortunately, the archives of this congregation are closed to research. What do exist for the American Church are the files of the Apostolic Delegation in Washington that were sent to the Vatican Archives. These are open up to 1922.

7. Ibid., 30–40, Cerretti to De Lai, Washington, Nov. 30, 1911 (copy).

8. ASV, DAUS, IV, no. 121 (Richmond), 16, Ternae, Nov. 21, 1911. In presenting the "Notulae" to Bonaventura Cerretti, Gibbons said that Budds was not on the bishops' list, but was born in Charleston; ibid., 18, Gibbons to Cerretti, Nov. 24, 1911.

9. Ibid., 20r–v, Stadelman to Cerretti, Rock Castle, Nov. 27, 1911; 21r, Meyer to Cerretti, Richmond, Nov. 27, 1911.

10. Ibid., 22r–v, Doyle to Cerretti, Washington, Nov. 27, 1911.

11. On this episode and O'Connell's alienation of the faculty, see Gerald P. Fogarty, *American Catholic Biblical Scholarship: A History from the Early Republic to Vatican II* (San Francisco: Harper & Row, 1989), pp. 96–119.

12. Ibid., 24, Merry del Val to Cerretti, Jan. 19, 1912; 25, Cerretti to Gibbons, [Jan 19, 1912]; 26, Cerretti to O'Connell [Jan. 19, 1922].

13. Ibid., 27, O'Connell to Cerretti, San Francisco, n.d.

14. Ibid., 28r, Gibbons to Cerretti, Baltimore, Jan 19, 1912.

15. Fogarty, *O'Connell*, pp. 309–10.

16. Quoted in John Tracy Ellis, *The Life of James Cardinal Gibbons, Archbishop of Baltimore: 1834–1921*, 2 vols. (Milwaukee: Bruce, 1952), II, 444.

17. Archives of the Archdiocese of Boston, Denis O'Connell to William O'Connell, Richmond, Nov. 8, 1922.

18. Fogarty, *O'Connell*, p. 78.

19. ADR, Julius Pohl to O'Connell, Bristow, July 16, 1913.

20. ADA, Smet to Kaup, Warrenton, March 5, 1914.

21. ADR, Leo Haid to O'Connell, Belmont, N.C., March 30, 1914.

22. ADR, Consultors' Book, April 9, 1914, pp. 12–13.

23. ADA, Smet to Kaup, Warrenton, April 28, 1914. Smet wrote two letters on this date. In the first, he described the boundaries of his missions.

24. ADR, O'Grady to O'Connell, Washington, Aug. 25, 1922; Fumasoni-Biondi to O'Connell, Washington, April 4, 1923.

25. ADR, Haid to O'Connell, Belmont, April 20, 1916.

26. ADR, M. Kivlighan to O'Connell, Staunton, July 5 and 14, 1917.

27. ADR, Benedictine College to Catholics of Richmond, July 20, 1918.

28. ADR, O'Connell to Kaup, Richmond, Aug. 2, 1918.

29. Johnston, *History of the Benedictine Sisters* (cited n. 41, chap 17), pp. 114–15. Moore himself was somewhat of a visionary with a fascinating career. He began as a Paulist and received an M.D. from the Johns Hopkins University and a Ph.D. He then taught psychology at the Catholic University. In World War I, he served in the army as a doctor, not as a chaplain. After flirting briefly with the possibility of being incardinated as a priest in Richmond, he entered the Benedictines and was one of the founders of St. Anselm's in Washington. He later left the Benedictines to become the first Carthusian in the United States.

30. ADR, Mark Cassidy, O.S.B., to O'Connell, Richmond, June 4, 1918.

31. ADR, Thomas Vernon Moore to O'Connell, St. Paul's College, Washington, Pentecost, 1919 and May 1, 1920.

32. Johnston, *Benedictine Sisters*, p. 115.

33. ADR, Condensed report of schools in Richmond, 1924.

34. ADR, van den Wildenberg to O'Connell, Fribourg, Oct. 23, 1914.

35. ADR, Chidwick to O'Connell, Dunwoodie, Dec. 12, 1912.

36. ADR, O'Connell to Hoban, Richmond, July 19, 1913.

37. ADR, Byrne to O'Connell, Rome, Nov. 27, 1921.

38. See Fogarty, *American Catholic Biblical Scholarship*, pp. 162, 168, 169.

39. Frank Parater, "My Last Will," archives of the North American College, Rome.

40. ADR, Charles A. O'Hern to O'Connell, Rome, Feb. 9, 1920.

41. Robert F. McNamara, *The American College in Rome: 1855–1955* (Rochester: The Christopher Press, 1956), pp. 467–70, tells the story of Parater's death and its effect on the college.

42. William O. Foss, *The United States Navy in Hampton Roads* (Norfolk/Virginia Beach: The Donning Company, 1984), pp. 66–67.

43. Ellis, *Gibbons,* II, 234, 241–42.

44. ADR, Lewis O'Hern to O'Connell, Washington, May 30, 1917.

45. ADR, O'Hern to O'Connell, Washington, June 5, 1917; Daniels to O'Hern, Washington, June 1, 1917.

46. Clifford Merrill Drury, *The History of the Chaplain Corps, United States Navy* (Washington, D.C.: U.S. Government Printing Office, n.d.), I, 166.

47. ADR, James A. Flaherty to O'Connell, New Haven, June 15, 1917, enclosing circular letter, Flaherty to "Dear Sir and Brother," New Haven, June 12, 1917.

48. ADR, James A. Flaherty to Grand Knight of Richmond, New Haven, June 30, 1917. See also in ADR, John T. Axton, Col., U.S.A., annual report, War Dept. Chief of Chaplains, Aug. 18, 1921, which stated that the number of Catholic and Lutheran chaplains were lower than the proportion in the Army of their respective denominations. Of 185 chaplains, forty-two were Catholic, the highest of any denomination, with the Episcopalians being second with forty-one.

49. ADR, Dillon E. Mapother to O'Connell, Washington, Nov. 30, 1917, three letters, sending checks for chaplains in Camp Lee, Jamestown, and Portsmouth.

50. ADR, Hoker to O'Connell, Washington, July 17, 1918.

51. Foss, *The United States Navy,* p. 75.

52. ADR, Joseph Pastorelli, O.P., to O'Connell, Marine Camp, Quantico, Feb. 10, 1918.

53. ADR, G. K. Roper to O'Connell, Richmond, Nov. 8, 1918.

54. ADR, Muldoon to O'Connell, New York, Nov. 14, 1918.

55. ADR, Baecher to O'Connell, Norfolk, May 29, 1918.

56. Foss, *The United States Navy,* p. 80.

57. *St. Mary Star of the Sea: 1860–1985* (n.p., n.d.), p. 9.

58. Timothy Michael Dolan, *"Some Seed Fell on Good Ground": The Life of Edwin V. O'Hara* (Washington: Catholic University of America Press, 1992), pp. 41–46; Christopher J. Kauffman, *Faith and Fraternalism: The History of the Knights of Columbus,* revised ed. (New York: Simon & Schuster, 1992), pp. 297–301. For the origins of the second Klan, see John Higham, *Strangers in the Land: Patterns of American Nativism 1860–1925* (New York: Atheneum, 1965), pp. 285–99.

59. ADR, John J. Blake to O'Connell, Richmond, June 16, 1920.

60. ADR, Blake to O'Connell, Richmond, Jan. 5, 1922; Blake to Board of Directors, Knights of Columbus, Richmond, Jan. 5, 1922 (copy).

61. ADR, Magri to O'Connell, Portsmouth, May 7, 1922.

62. Ibid., March 14, 1924.

63. AKC, *Bridgewater Times,* April 18, 1924.

64. Ibid.

65. Kauffman, *Faith and Fraternalism,* pp. 182–86.

66. AKC, Meredith to McGinley, Harrisonburg, May 2, 1924.

67. AKC, *Bridgewater Times,* May 2, 1924.

68. AKC, McGinley to Meredith, New Haven, May 8, 1924.

69. AKC, William J. Maher to McGinley, Clarksville, July 1, 1924. Maher was from Petersburg and was a state highway inspector. John E. Milan to McGinley, Norfolk, Aug. 16, 1924; Hart to Milan, St. Louis, Aug. 20, 1924 (copy).

70. *New York Times,* Nov. 2, 1925.

71. Ibid.

72. AKC, Conaty to McGinley, Richmond, Nov. 9, 1925; Conaty to Hart, Richmond, Nov. 23, 1925; Hart to Conaty, n.p. Nov. 25, 1925 (copy); D. J. Callahan to Conaty, Washington, Nov. 30, 1925; Hart to Conaty, n.p., Dec. 2, 1925 (copy); Conaty to Hart, Richmond, Dec. 10, 1925; Callahan to Hart, Washington, Dec. 14, 1925; Hart to Conaty, n.p., Dec. 15, 1925 (copy); Hart to Callahan, n.p. Dec. 15, 1925 (copy); Conaty to Hart, Richmond, Dec. 19, 1925; S. L. Kelley to Callahan, Richmond, Feb. 17, 1926; Callahan to Hart, Washington, Feb. 18, 1926.

73. *Richmond Times-Dispatch,* May 26, 1925.

74. Ibid., June 9, 1925.

75. John T. Kneebone, "'It Must be a Hoax:' Protest, Cultural Pride, and Richmond's Columbus Statue," *Virginia Cavalcade,* 42 (Autumn 1992), 84–95.

19. Virginia's First Suburban Growth, 1915–1924

1. See Kenneth T. Jackson, *Crabgrass Frontier: The Suburbanization of the United States* (New York: Oxford University Press, 1985), pp. 103–37.

2. Unfortunately, the O'Connell papers in ADR contain no information on these two parishes.

3. "History of St. Paul Catholic Church, Richmond, Va.," Section One and Two; MS, archives of St. Paul's Church.

4. Ibid. For the later activities of Williams and O'Connell, see pp. 502–5, 508.

5. "Souvenir Booklet of the History of St. Elizabeth's Church, Richmond, Va.: 1923–1965," no pagination.

6. James A. Verrecchia, Ann Augherton, and Michael Bates, *Saint Agnes Catholic Church, Arlington, Virginia: A Fiftieth Anniversary History, 1936–1986* (n.p., n.d.). The booklet is not paginated.

7. ADR, Lackey to O'Connell, Clarendon [Arlington], June 22, 1918.

8. Ibid., Feb. 5, 1919.

9. Ibid.

10. See ibid., June 22, 1919.

11. ADR, John F. Cavanaugh et al. to O'Connell, n.p. [Clarendon] June 1, 1923.

12. ADR, Lackey to O'Connell, Clarendon, May 31, 1922.

13. John A.K. Donovan, "The Light of His Life: being the biography of Amadeus Joseph van Ingelgem, a Virginia Missionary," manuscript, Falls Church, Virginia, 1937, pp. 125–26.

14. van Ingelgem to Mercier, Falls Church, Dec. 18, 1912, given in ibid., pp. 130–31.

15. Ibid., p. 164.

16. Archives of the Archdiocese of Mechlin, J. C. Neeter to "Votre Excellence," New York, 24 Froise, 1919.

17. Roger Aubert, "Cardinal Mercier's Visit to America in the Autumn of 1919," in Nelson H. Minnich, Robert B. Eno, S.S., and Robert F. Trisco, eds., *Studies in Catholic History in Honor of John Tracy Ellis* (Wilmington, Del.: Michael Glazier, 1985), p. 332.

18. ADR, Cuevas to O'Connell, West Falls Church, April 16, 1919.

19. ADR, van Ingelgem to O'Connell, West Falls Church, May 30, 1919.

20. Jeanne Rodriques and William Hammond, *St. Mary's Fairfax Station: the beginnings and growth of a community* (n.p., n.d.), p. 27; Ray and Barbara Freson, *St. Mary's Parish, Fairfax, Va.: 1858–1983* (Fairfax: Colorcraft Litho, 1983), p. 23.

21. ADR, Cuevas to O'Connell, West Falls Church, July 2, 1919.

22. Ibid., July 18, 1919.

23. Freson, p. 23.

24. ADR, Winston to O'Connell, Warrenton, Nov. 23, 1921.

25. ADR, Ibid., Nov. 26, 1921.

26. ADR, van Ingelgem to O'Connell, West Falls Church, Nov. 28, 1921.

27. ADR, De Gryse to O'Connell, Charlottesville, Dec. 2, 1921.

28. Ibid., Dec. 11, 1921.

29. ADR, Van Ingelgem to O'Connell, Falls Church, Nov. 30, 1921.

30. ADR, I. V. McGlone to T. A. Rankin, New York, June 4, 1913.

31. ADR, Rankin to O'Connell, Lynchburg, July 15, 1913.

32. ADR, O'Connell to Gill, Richmond, Dec. 12, 1914.

33. ADR, Ryan to O'Connell, Oak Ridge, April 23, 1917.

34. ADR, Ryan to O'Connell, New York, Feb. 13, 1919.

35. ADR, Rankin to Ryan, Charlottesville, Jan. 3, 1920.

36. ADR, Ryan to O'Connell, New York, Jan. 6, 1920 (copy).

37. ADR, O'Connell to Ryan, Richmond, Dec. 1, 1923 (copy or draft).

38. ADR, Cuevas to O'Connell, Fairfax, Aug. 4, 1922.

39. Freson, pp. 24–25.

40. ADR, Blenk to O'Connell, New Orleans, Aug. 5, 1912.

41. ADR, van Ingelgem to O'Connell, West Falls Church, April 23, 1924. See also ADR, Mother M. Hilda to O'Connell, April 1, 1924.

42. Mother Maria Alma, I.H.M., *Sisters, Servants of the Immaculate Heart of Mary: 1845–1967* (Lancaster, Pa.: The Dolphin Press, 1967), pp. 272, 339–40; Sister M. St.Michel, IHM, to author, Mar. 23, 1999; Mother M. Claudia, interview with author, Mar. 15, 1991.

43. ADR, Mrs. M.R. Sullivan, Mrs. Frank Hill and Miss Virginia R. Burke to O'Connell, Alexandria, Dec. 2, 1912.

44. ADR, Sally Teagan to O'Connell, Alexandria, Apr. 24, 1913.

45. *St. Rita's Parish, Alexandria, Virginia: 1924–1974* (Hackensack, N.J.: Custombook, 1974), pp. 4–5.

46. ADR, P.J. Conlon to O'Connell, Washington, May 2, 1914.

47. *St. Rita's Parish*, p. 6.

48. ADR, Smet to O'Connell [or Kaup], Alexandria, Aug. 6, 1916.

49. Ibid., Oct. 25, 1916.

50. Ibid., May 29, 1924.

51. After four years in Kilmarnock, John was assigned to St. Peter's in Richmond until 1932 when he became pastor of St. John's in Leesburg. He was pastor of

Fort Monroe from 1940 to 1950, when he went to St. Andrew's, where he died as pastor emeritus in 1969. After several assignments in the diocese, Michael succeeded his brother as pastor in Leesburg, where he remained until going to St. Louis in Groveton in 1951. In 1959, he became administrator of Sacred Heart in Hot Springs; he died in 1963.

52. *St. Mary's: 200 Years for Christ, 1795–1995* (Alexandria: St. Mary's Catholic Church), p. 182.

53. ADR, Smet to O'Connell, Alexandria, Mar. 16, 1916.

54. Ibid., Dec. 27, 1918.

55. ADR, Smet to O'Connell, Richmond, May 9, 1919.

56. ADR, R. D. McGowan to O'Connell, Washington, Oct. 4, 1919.

57. ADR, Smet to O'Connell, Alexandria, Oct. 10, 1919.

58. ADR, William Caleb Brown to O'Connell, Richmond, June 28, 1924.

59. ADR, Smet to O'Connell, Alexandria, July 24, 1924.

60. ADA, Quinn to McClunn, sometime before Dec. 1, 1949; McClunn to Quinn, Richmond, Dec. 1, 1949.

61. ADR, van de Vyver, J. B. Gleeson to Miss Ward, Virginia Beach, Aug. 31, 1909; Julia Ward to van Ingelgem, White Sulphur Springs, W.Va., Sept. 2, 1909.

62. ASJPH, 64, Sr. Pauline Strabel to Mother Margaret O'Keefe, Norfolk, Nov. 27, 1917.

63. ADR, Post to O'Connell, Virginia Beach, Feb. 23, 1914.

64. ADR, Doherty to O'Connell, Norfolk, Feb. 24, 1914; W. Esby Smith to O'Connell, Virginia Beach, Feb. 26, 1914. Smith was the representative of the Catholics.

65. ADR, Doherty to O'Connell, Newport News, Feb. 26, 1914.

66. ADR, James S. Groves to O'Connell, Norfolk, April 7, 1914.

67. ADR, Post to O'Connell, Virginia Beach, April 14, 1914.

68. Ibid., April 20, 1924.

69. ADR, Groves to O'Connell, Norfolk, April 23, 1914.

70. ADR, Groves to Post, Norfolk, April 23, 1914 (original and copy).

71. ADR, Post to O'Connell, Virginia Beach, April 25, 1914.

72. ADR, John A. Baecher to O'Connell, Norfolk, July 28, 1917.

73. Thomas J. Wertenbaker, *Norfolk: Historic Southern Port,* 2d revised edition (Durham: Duke University Press, 1962), p. 295.

74. ADR, Baecher to O'Connell, Norfolk, Nov. 4, 1916.

75. ADR, Baecher to O'Connell, Norfolk, Jan. 3, 1917; Jan. 13, 1917; Feb. 1, 1917; Norfolk, Feb. 19, 1917.

76. ADR, Kealey to O'Connell, Norfolk, Aug. 19, 1919.

77. ADR, Kealey to O'Connell, Ocean View, Sept. 16, 1919; Kealey to O'Connell, Ocean View, Sept. 22, 1919.

78. ADR, Kealey to O'Connell, Ocean View, Oct. 24, 1919.

79. Ibid., Oct. 30, 1919.

80. Ibid., May 12, 1920.

81. ADR, Thomas E. Waters to O'Connell, Norfolk, July 2, 1919.

82. See ADR, Baecher to O'Connell, Norfolk, Jan. 19, 1921.

83. Ryan to O'Connell, Norfolk, Nov. 4, 1919.

84. ADR, Waters to O'Connell, Norfolk, Nov. 6, 1919.

85. Ibid., Mar. 10, 1921. Waters enclosed a map and the exact details of the parish boundaries, which O'Connell approved on Mar. 18.

86. ADR, Kealey to O'Connell, Ocean View, Mar. 8, 1921; O'Farrell to O'Connell, Norfolk, Sept. 20, 1923; Waters, O'Farrell, Ryan, to O'Connell, Norfolk, Sept. 19, 1923.

87. ADR, Baecher to O'Connell, Norfolk, Mar. 20, 1924; May 15, 1924.

88. ADR, Kealey to O'Connell, Ocean View, Dec. 21, 1923.

89. ADR, O'Farrell to O'Connell, Norfolk, May 26, 1924.

90. ADR, *Norfolk Ledger Dispatch*, Sept. 9, 1924, and *Norfolk Pilot*, Sept. 9, 1924.

91. ADR, Philip Brennan to O'Connell, Norfolk, May 6, 1920.

92. ADR, Philip Brennan to Brennan, Virginia Beach, Apr. 5, 1929.

20. EVANGELIZATION IN THE COUNTRY AND CITY

1. ADR, Doyle to O'Connell, Washington, June 3, 1912.

2. ADR, Thomas E. Waters to O'Connell, Newport News, June 10, 1912.

3. ADR, McMullen to O'Connell, Cumberland, Md., Nov. 10, 1917.

4. Ibid., Jan 8, 1918.

5. ADR, Haier to O'Connell, Petersburg, Jan. 20, 1918.

6. ADR, McMullen to O'Connell, Cumberland, Feb. 2, 1918.

7. ADR, Brosnan, memo on Crewe, April 15, 1918.

8. *Official Catholic Directory for 1930*, p. 565.

9. Anna Louise Haley, *Our Lady of Nazareth Parish: 1914–86, Roanoke, Virginia* (Roanoke, 1986), pp. 5–17.

10. ADR, de Gryse to O'Connell, Staunton, Sept. 8, 1916.

11. Ibid., April 26, 1920.

12. See pp. 362–63.

13. ADR, Rankin to O'Connell, Winchester, Sept. 28, 1921.

14. Ibid.

15. ADR, Meredith to O'Connell, Philadelphia, Oct. 3, 1921.

16. See pp. 353–54.

17. ADR, O'Connell to de Lai, Mar. 26, 1913 (copy in French).

18. ADR, J. de Becker to O'Connell, Louvain, May 4, 1913.

19. Gerald P. Fogarty, S.J., *The Vatican and the American Hierarchy from 1870 to 1965* (Stuttgart: Anton Hiersemann, Verlag, 1982; Wilmington, Del.: Michael Glazier, 1985), pp. 61–64.

20. Salem T. Sanyour, "St. Anthony's Maronite Catholic Church, 1895–1960," MS in St. Anthony's Maronite Church, Richmond, VA.

21. ADR, Dyer to O'Farrell, Baltimore, Mar. 18, 1914.

22. ADR, list of faculties given to Tarbey; John Ireland to Abdalla Terbai, St. Paul, May 18, 1911; Hoban to Tarbey, Mar. 19, 1913.

23. ADR, O'Farrell, V. G., to Syrian Catholics of Richmond, Aug. 14, 1915.

24. ADR, Brennan, chancellor of Scranton, to whom it may concern, Feb. 3, 1915.

25. AAB, B1537, Brennan to Curley, Richmond, March 1, 1929.

26. ADR, Elias Pierre Hoyek, Maronite Patriarch, Jan. 10, 1916.

27. ADR, Rabil to O'Connell, Roanoke, n.d., but prior to July 13, 1917, with O'Connell's approval and notes, July 13, 1917.

28. *The Catholic Virginian*, 38, no. 18 (Feb. 28, 1964), p. 15.

29. ADR, W. Dowhovych to O'Connell, Philadelphia, Jan. 16, 1913. On Ortynsky's position, see Fogarty, *Vatican and the American Hierarchy*, p. 184n.

30. ADR, Orun to Kaup, Curtis Bay, Feb. 27, 1913.

31. ADR, van den Wildenberg to Kaup, Fribourg, June 10, 1914.

32. ADR, Brennan to Fumasoni-Biondi, Richmond, Nov. 28, 1931 (copy); Fumasoni-Biondi to Brennan, Washington, Nov. 17, 1931.

33. ADR, Pyznar to O'Connell, Baltimore, Apr. 10, 1913.

34. ADR, Kaup to Pyznar, Richmond, Apr. 30, 1913 (copy).

35. ADR, Pyznar to O'Connell, Baltimore, May 23, 1913.

36. ADR, Pyznar and O'Connell, draft of agreement, undated and unsigned, 1913.

37. ADR, Fitzgerald to O'Connell, West Point, Jan. 30, 1918.

38. Ibid., Feb. 8, 1918.

39. Notes on Gloucester for the fiftieth anniversary of the mission, p. 2.

40. ADR, Jakubowski to O'Connell, West Point, Oct. 8, 1918; Sept. 1, 1919; Sept. 5, 1919; Dec. 18, 1919.

41. ADR, G. W. Fitzgerald to O'Connell, West Point, April 19, 1920.

42. ADR, Jakubowski to O'Connell, West Point, June 11, 1924.

43. ADR, Schrembs to O'Connell, Cleveland, June 25, 1923.

44. ADR, Magri to O'Connell, Portsmouth, July 5, 1923.

45. ADR, Magri to O'Connell, Lynchburg, July 25, 1923; Budny to O'Connell, Cleveland, July 17, 1923.

46. ADR, Parishioners to O'Connell, Bowers Hill, Nov. 18, 1923.

47. ADR, II. Olszewski to Magri, New Cumberland, W. Va., Nov. 20, 1923.

48. ADR, Magri to O'Connell, Portsmouth, Nov. 22, 1923.

49. See Anthony J. Kuzniewski, *Faith & Fatherland: The Polish Church War in Wisconsin, 1896–1918* (Notre Dame: University of Notre Dame Press, 1980), pp. 122–28.

50. ADR, Janusz to O'Connell, Bowers Hill, April 5, 1924.

51. ADR, P. J. Monahan to Magri, Portsmouth, April 11, 1924.

52. ADR, Magri to Brennan, Portsmouth, Nov. 24, 1931; Blackburn to Brennan, Suffolk, Dec. 18, 1931.

53. ADR, Blackburn to Brennan, Suffolk, Jan. 8, 1932.

54. ADR, Bowers Hill parishioners to Brennan, Aug. 25, 1932.

55. ADR, Sept. 25, 1933, Bowers Hill petition.

56. ADR, Magri to Brennan, Portsmouth, Oct. 12, 1933.

57. ADR, Magri to O'Connell, Portsmouth, Apr. 24, 1918; Donahoe to O'Connell, Portsmouth, July 18, 1916.

58. *The Virginia Knight*, 3, no. 5 (Mar. 1928), 23.

59. Charles M. Caravati, *Major Dooley* (Richmond, 1978), pp. 58–59.

60. Quoted in Caravati, p. 65.

61. See pp. 418–21.

62. ADR, Alice Dooley to O'Connell, Richmond, April 6, 1924.

63. Linda Singleton-Driscoll, "The Dooley Women," pp. 9–13.

64. AAB, O190, O'Connell to Curley, Richmond, March 3, 1925.

65. ADR, Kaup to de Lai [?], Richmond, Feb. 6, 1926 (draft or copy).

66. ADR, Vincent to Kaup, Belmont, March 19, 1926.

67. ADR, Fumasoni-Biondi to O'Connell, Washington, April 3, 1926; de Lai to Kaup, Rome, April 23, 1926.

68. ADR, Fumasoni-Biondi to Kaup, Washington, May 13, 1926.

21. Bishop Andrew Brennan and Civic Life in Virginia, 1926–1934

1. ADR, Fumasoni-Biondi to Hoban, Washington, May 22, 1926.

2. Unfortunately, the archives of the Congregation of Bishops, as the Consistorial Congregation is now called, are not open to research. The archives of the apostolic delegation fall under the direct suervision of the Vatican Secret Archives but are not available after 1922.

3. John P. Gallagher, *A Century of History: The Diocese of Scranton: 1868–1968* (Scranton: Diocese of Scranton, 1968), pp. 314–316.

4. ADR, Eugene Burke to Brennan, Rome, July 22, 1926.

5. ADR, James J. McAndrews to Brennan, Emmitsburg, Dec. 4, 1926.

6. The bulls arrived two days later; see ADR, Fumasoni-Biondi to Brennan, Washington, Dec. 18, 1926. For a description of the installation, see F. Joseph Magri, "Installation of Rt. Rev. Andrew J. Brennan, D.D., Eighth Bishop of Richmond," *The Virginia Knight*, 2 (Feb. 1927), pp. 1–6, 26–27.

7. "In Memoriam: Denis J. O'Connell," *The Virginia Knight*, 2 (Jan. 1927), 1; F. Joseph Magri, "Death and Burial with Character Study of Most Rev. Dennis [*sic*] J. O'Connell, D.D., Archbishop of Mariamne, Syria, Formerly Bishop of Richmond," ibid., 2–7.

8. ADR, Mazzoni to Brennan, Rome, Feb. 6, 1928.

9. ADR, Brennan to Cardinal Lega, Richmond, n.d.

10. ADR, Curley to Brennan, Baltimore, Dec. 24, 1926.

11. ADR, Curley to Kaup, Baltimore, Feb. 21, 1927.

12. ADR, Consultors' Book, June 28, 1928.

13. Ibid., Dec. 27, 1929.

14. ADR, Brennan to Pius XI, Richmond, June 27, 1930.

15. *Synodus Dioecesana Richmondiensis Tertia celebrata die decima sexta mensis Februarii Anno Domini MCMXXXIII, preside Illustrissimo ac Reverendissimo Domino Episcopo Andrea Iacobo Brennan* (Diocese of Richmond, 1933), p. 76.

16. ADR, James T. McEntyre to Brennan, Dunwoodie, Oct. 4, 1927.

17. ADR, Fenlon to Brennan, Baltimore, Oct. 7, 1927.

18. ADR, John D. Wheeler, S.J., to Brennan, Worcester, Mass., Feb. 18, 1933; Fenlon to Brennan, St. Mary's Baltimore, Feb. 21, 1933.

19. ADR, Fumasoni-Biondi to Brennan, Washington, June 1, 1928.

20. ADR, Brennan to Cardinal Perosi, Richmond, Mar. 1, 1929 (copy).

21. ADR, Brennan to Priests, Richmond, Mar. 18, 1929.

22. ADR, Fox to Brennan, Holy Cross, July 21, 1931.

23. ADR, Moore to Brennan, Rome, Dec. 5, 1933.

24. Interview with Monsignor Thomas Scannell, Sept. 8, 1995.

25. ADR, Brennan to priests, Richmond, Mar. 18, 1929.

26. ADR, Brennan to clergy, Apr. 9, 1930.

27. See pp. 495–97.

28. ADR, Louis Smet to Brennan, Louvain, June 19, 1931.

29. ADR, William A. Gill to Kaup, Fort Monroe, Aug. 3, 1926.

30. ADR, McConnell to Brennan, Berkeley Springs, Aug. 13, 1932.

31. ADR, Findlay to Brennan, Wytheville, Aug. 24, 1931, and Lynchburg, Sept. 20, 1931.

32. ADR, van den Wildenberg to Brennan, Fribourg, Nov. 28, 1931.

33. ADR, Halbleib to O'Connell, Danville, June 5, 1924.

34. ADR, Halbleib to Brennan, Richmond, n.d.; Halbleib to Blackburn, S. Richmond, June 2, 1932.

35. ADR, Brennan to Halbleib, Richmond June 7, 1932.

36. ADR, Fumasoni-Biondi to Brennan, Washington, June 10, 1932.

37. ADR, Brennan to Halbleib, Richmond, June 11, 1932.

38. Ibid.

39. ADR, Halbleib to Brennan, Richmond, Aug. 15, 1932.

40. ADR, Halbleib to Brennan, Sept. 12, 15, 17, 1932; Brennan to Halbleib, Richmond, Sept. 24, 1932 (copy).

41. ADR, Blackburn to Brennan, Suffolk, Oct. 1, 1933.

42. ADR, Consultors' Book, Feb. 28, 1928: p. 12.

43. Ibid., May 21, 1929, p. 24.

44. ADR, Smet to Brennan, Louvain, April 27, 1931.

45. ADR, Brennan to clergy, July 25, 1928.

46. Virginius Dabney, *Dry Messiah: The Life of Bishop Cannon* (New York: Alfred A. Knopf, 1949), pp. 173–89.

47. *The Virginia Knight,* 3 (Sept. 3, 1928), 8.

48. Ibid., (Oct. 1928), 7.

49. Ibid., 8.

50. Ibid., (Nov. 1928), 8–9.

51. William Winston, "Where do we go from here?" *ibid.*, 4 (Feb. 1929), 1.

52. Ibid.

53. "Laymen's League of Virginia," ibid., 16.

54. "The Catholic Laymen's League," ibid., 7–8.

55. *The Catholic Virginian,* 7 (Dec. 1931), p. 29.

56. John E. Milan, "Catholic Laymen's League," ibid. (Mar. 1929), 12.

57. Ibid.

58. Ibid., 50.

59. *The Virginia Knight,* 5 (April 1930), p. 2; 6 (Dec. 1930), p. 21.

60. ADR, Fumasoni-Biondi to Brennan, Washington, Jan. 19, 1931.

61. Quoted in William M. Halsey, *The Survival of American Innocence: Catholicism in an Era of Disillusionment, 1920-1940* (Notre Dame: University of Notre Dame Press, 1980), p. 51.

62. Quoted in James Hennesey, S.J., *American Catholics: A History of the Roman Catholic Community in the United States* (New York: Oxford University Press, 1981), p. 253.

63. *Virginia Knight,* 5 (Nov. 1929), 2, 47.

64. ADR, Walter J. Nott to Brennan, Richmond, Apr. 27, 1931; Anne Randolph Archer to Brennan, Richmond, June 28, 1931.

65. See, for example, *Arlington Catholic Herald,* Sept. 19, 1996, p. 12.

66. ADR, Goodwin to Brennan, Williamsburg, June 10, 1931.

67. ADR, Burke to Brennan, Washington, June 27, 1931.

68. ADR, Goodwin to Brennan, Williamsburg, July 6, 1931.

69. ADR, Richard B. Washington to Brennan, Charlottesville, Sept. 28, 1931.

70. ADR, Burke to Brennan, Washington, Nov. 8, 1931.

71. ADR, S. O. Bland to Brennan, Washington, Nov. 25, 1931; S. O. Bland to Brennan, Washington, Dec. 26, 1931.

72. ADR, Pollard to Brennan, Richmond, Aug. 30, 1932.

73. ADR, Fumasoni-Biondi to Brennan, Washington, Sept. 23, 1932.

74. Ibid., Sept. 29, 1932.

75. Gerald P. Fogarty, S.J., *The Vatican and the American Hierarchy from 1870 to 1965* (Wilmington, Del.: Michael Glazier, 1985), pp. 131–32, 140–41, 354–55.

76. ADR, Washington to Brennan, Hot Springs, July 17, Aug. 24, 1932.

77. Ibid., Feb. 11, 1932.

78. Ibid., Dec. 5 and 27, 1932.

79. ADR, Benjamin Bland to Brennan, Toano, Jan. 30, 1931. Bland was the pastor.

80. ADR, Joseph D. Hebert to Brennan, Roanoke, Jan. 31, 1931.

81. Robert I. Gannon, *The Cardinal Spellman Story* (Garden City: Doubleday, 1962), pp. 72–73.

82. ADR, *Southern Churchman,* Richmond, Mar. 7, 1931 (reprint).

83. ADR, George S. Tarry to Brennan, Randolph-Macon College, Jan. 26, 1933.

84. ADR, "Ecumenical Commission," John A. MacLean to Brennan, Richmond, Feb. 3, 1933.

85. *The Catholic Virginian,* 11, no. 3 (Jan. 1936), p. 5.

86. ADR, Consultors' Book, p. 62, Dec. 17, 1935.

87. ADR, Frierson to Brennan, Winston-Salem, Dec. 31, 1935.

88. ADR, Gill to Frierson, Jan. 8, 1936.

89. *The Catholic Virginian,* 11, no. 5 (Mar. 1936), p. 36.

22. SOCIAL OUTREACH AND THE DEPRESSION

1. ADR, Smet to O'Connell, Alexandria, Sept. 10, 1910.

2. Dorothy M. Brown and Elizabeth McKeown, *The Poor Belong to Us: Catholic Charities and American Welfare* (Cambridge: Harvard University Press, 1997), pp. 1–7.

3. Archives of Catholic Charities, Richmond, Marie Leahy, "A Brief Outline of the Origins of the Bureau of Catholic Charities," n.d., prepared for Father Thomas E. Mitchell, later director of Catholic Charities, pp. 1–4.

4. Brown and McKeown, pp. 6–7.

5. Archives of Catholic Charities, Richmond, "Bureau of Catholic Charities, 1926," pp. 1–2, 11.

6. Ibid., Thomas E. Mitchell, "Survey of the Bureau of Catholic Charities: 1925–1937," p. 5.

7. ADR, Kaup to John W. Moore, Oct. 29,1926.

8. Mitchell, p. 7.

9. ADR, Legh Page to Kaup, Richmond, July 31, 1929. The inscription is given in Charles M. Caravati, *Major Dooley* (Richmond, 1978), p. 67.

10. Mitchell, pp. 6–7.

11. ADR, Morrell to Brennan, n.p., Oct. 1, 1931.

12. ADR, Morrell to Dear Father, n.p., Oct. 23, 1931.

13. ADR, Wehrle to Brennan, Bismarck, July 14, 1931.

14. ADR, Griffin to Brennan, Springfield, Ill., Oct. 23, 1931.

15. ADR, Gerow to Brennan, Natchez, Oct. 31, 1931; Curley to Brennan, Baltimore, Oct. 31, 1931.

16. ADR, McNicholas to Brennan, Norwood, Oct. 22, 1931.

17. ADR, FitzMaurice to Brennan, Wilmington, Nov. 3, 1931.

18. ADR, L. D. Morrell to Brennan, Philadelphia, Nov. 5, 1931.

19. ADR, L. D. Morrell to Brennan, Torresdale [Philadelphia], Nov. 13, 1931.

20. ADR, Fumasoni-Biondi to Brennan, Washington, Nov. 16, 1931.

21. ADR, Cantwell to Brennan, Los Angeles, Nov. 21, 1931.

22. ADR, C. E. Byrne to Brennan, Galveston, Dec. 24, 1931.

23. ADR, Katherine Drexel to Brennan, Cornwells Heights, Pa., June 23, 1932.

24. ADR, Smet to Brennan, Louvain, July 13, 1933.

25. ADR, Brennan to people, Richmond, Dec. 15, 1931.

26. Mitchell, pp. 8–9. C. Joseph Nuesse, *The Catholic University of America: A Centennial History* (Washington, D.C.: The Catholic University of America Press, 1990), p. 309.

27. ADR, Baecher to O'Connell, Norfolk, Dec. 29, 1918.

28. ADR, Brennan to Waters, Virginia Beach, June 8, 1937.

29. ADR, file "Barry Robinson Industrial School," Brother Paul to Brennan, Baltimore, Oct. 21, 1927; Consultors' Book, Feb. 28, 1928, p. 14.

30. ADR, Koch to Brennan, Latrobe, Sept. 7, 1933.

31. In a form letter sent to all pastors before the annual Christmas collection for Catholic Charities in 1932, Brennan announced that the diocesan consultors had recommended a parish assessment rather than voluntary collections for charity. He noted that at the time the Bureau of Catholic Charities was budgeted to receive $4,000 for the coming year, part of which went to the support of boys at St. Mary's Industrial School. See ADR, Brennan to "Reverend Dear Father," Richmond, Dec. 13, 1932.

32. ADR, Mitchell to John A. Baecher, May 24, 1933.

33. ADR, Ireton to Baecher, June 2, 1944; Baecher to Ireton, Norfolk, May 29, 1944.

34. *Virginian-Pilot,* Dec. 7, 1973.

35. ADR, Consultors' Book, Sept. 28, 1927, p. 9.

36. *The Virginia Knight,* 5, no. 12 (Oct., 1930), 1, 34.

37. *The Virginia Gazette*, Sept. 26, 1908. On Mrs. Wright, see ibid., Feb. 19, 1914. For providing me with copies of *The Virginia Gazette* and for other information below, I am indebted to Julia Woodbridge Oxrieder of Williamsburg.

38. Ibid., Oct. 7, 1932, p. 1.

39. *Virginia Gazette*, July 4, 1912.

40. *The Flat Hat*, Dec. 14, 1923, p. 5.

41. Félix D. Almaraz, "Biography of Carlos Eduardo Castañeda," MS, chap. 2, pp. 70–71, 114–15. For sending me a copy of this study, I am grateful to Dr. Almaraz, professor of history at the University of Texas in San Antonio. For the early officers and members of the Gibbons Club, see *Colonial Echo* (1924), p. 275 and (1925), p. 180.

42. *The Virginia Gazette*, Oct. 7, 1932, p. 1.

43. *The Flat Hat*, quoted in *The Virginia Gazette*, Oct. 28, 1932, p. 2.

44. ADR, Strahan to Ireton, Washington, Nov. 24, 1936.

45. ADR, Consultors' Book, Mar. 22, 1938, p. 72.

46. Ibid., Sept. 19, 1939, p. 76.

47. ADR, H.R. Pratt to Brennan, Charlottesville, Apr. 7, 1931.

48. ADR, Brochtrup to Brennan, Charlottesville, Feb. 17, 1932.

49. Ibid., Feb. 26, 1932.

50. ADR, H.R. Pratt to Brennan, Charlottesville, April 11, 1932.

51. ADR, Brochtrup to Brennan, Charlottesville, May 17, 1932.

52. ADR, Ross to Brennan, Champaign, Ill., Sept. 21, 1931.

53. John E. Lynch, C.S.P., "A Conflict of Values, a Confusion of Laws: The Case of John Elliott Ross," *Journal of Paulist Studies*, 4 (1995–96), 1–14.

54. Fred Baumgartner, "History of Saint Mary's Parish," n.p., n.d. (1988).

55. ADR, Swint to Brennan, Wheeling, Dec. 5, 1931.

56. ADR, Gilsenan to "Dear Friend," Roanoke, Dec. 29, 1931.

57. ADR, Gilsenan to Swint, Roanoke, Jan. 10, 1932 (copy).

58. ADR, Swint to Gilsenan, Wheeling, Jan. 12, 1932.

59. ADR, Martin to Brennan, Roanoke, Jan. 7, Jan. 10, and Mar. 21, 1931.

60. ADR, Joseph P. Mitchell to Brennan, Roanoke, Feb. 5, 1931. See also Patrick Francis Timon to Brennan, Roanoke, May 16, 1931.

61. ADR, Frances Raymond to Brennan, Roanoke, Aug. 27, 1931.

62. *The Catholic Virginian*, 7, no. 3 (Jan. 1932), 12–13, 48.

63. *The Catholic Virginian*, 6, no. 3 (Jan. 1931), pp. 4–5, 36–37.

64. ADR, Magri to Brennan, Portsmouth, Nov. 22, 1931.

65. *The Official Catholic Directory, Anno Domini 1940* (New York: P. J. Kennedy & Sons, 1940), pp. 526–27, lists no schools for Keyser and Ridgeley in West Virginia or for Danville and Winchester in Virginia.

66. William E. Leuchtenburg, *Franklin D. Roosevelt and the New Deal: 1932–1940* (New York: Harper & Row, 1963), pp. 18–19.

67. ADR, Father Patrick Burke to Brennan, Oracle, Arizona, July 29, 1932; Leo A. Gill to Burke, n.p., Aug. 4, 1932.

68. ADR, Burke to Gill, Oracle, Arizona, Aug. 8, 1932.

69. ADR, Edward J. Grier to Brennan, Ottumwa, Iowa, July 5, 1934.

70. ADR, Rankin to Brennan, Alexandria, Aug. 19, 1933.

71. ADR, Kelly to Brennan, Alexandria, Sept. 1, 1933.

72. ADR, Rankin to Brennan, Alexandria, Sept. 10, 1933; Tearney to Rankin, Lynchburg, Sept 9, 1933; Rankin to Brennan, Sept. 14, 1933; Rankin to Brennan, Alexandria, Sept. 17, 1933.

73. ADR, Curran to Brennan, Clarendon, Oct. 9, 1933.

74. ADR, Brennan to Brennan, Virginia Beach, Jan. 22, 1933.

75. ADR, Gallagher to Brennan, Staunton, April 4, 1933.

76. ADR, Burke to Brennan, Sept. 12, 1933.

77. ADR, Stephens to Brennan, Richmond, Sept. 21, 1933.

78. ADR, Consultors' Book, Sept. 26, 1933, p. 54. For a recent study of some of these CCC camps in Virginia, see Patrick Clancy, "Conserving the Youth: The Civilian Conservation Corps Experience in the Shenandoah National Park," *The Virginia Magazine of History and Biography*, 105 (Autumn 1997), 439–70. While Clancy does not explicitly treat the issue of providing chaplains for the camps, he does note some of the tension that developed when young men from the rural South encountered other young men from the industrialized and urban North, many of whom were Catholic.

79. ADR, Tearney to Brennan, Oct. 31, 1933.

80. ADR, Kiefer to Brennan, Danville, Dec. 13, 1933.

81. ADR, Martin to Brennan, Roanoke, Dec. 19, 1933.

82. ADR, Consultors' Book, Dec. 19, 1933, p. 56.

83. Ibid., Feb. 20, 1934, p. 58.

84. ADR, Schmidhausen to Ircton, Norfolk, Feb. 9, 1939.

85. ADR, Statistics, Mar. 3, 1937.

86. ADR, Joseph Brennan to Ireton, Danville, Nov. 20, 1938.

87. ADR, Waters to Brennan, Nov. 21, 1938.

23. Peter L. Ireton as Coadjutor, 1935–1940

1. ADR, Acta Diocesis Richmondicnsis, note added on Oct. 1, 1941, to entry of Feb. 26, 1934.

2. ADR, Cicognani to Ireton, July 27, 1935.

3. Notes of Msgr. John Hannon, July 17, 1999.

4. ADR, Cardinal Rossi, Consistorial Decree, Sept. 23, 1935.

5. ADR, Consultors' Book, p. 60, Nov. 7, 1935.

6. ADR, Acta Diocesis Richmondiensis, note added to entry of Feb. 26, 1934, on Oct. 1, 1941.

7. Hannon notes, July 17, 1999.

8. AAB, I169: Curley to Ireton, Baltimore, Nov. 23 and 30, 1935.

9. ADR, Acta Diocesis Richmondiensis, Ireton, "Financial Report of the Diocese of Richmond as of March–June 1937: A Statement," June 21, 1939, inserted after Feb. 26, 1934.

10. ADR, Brennan, power of attorney to Ireton, Feb. 29, 1936.

11. Ireton's note on ADR, Stritch to Hickman, Chicago, July 3, 1943.

12. Timothy Michael Dolan, *"Some Seed Fell on Good Ground": The Life of Edwin V. O'Hara* (Washington, D.C.: Catholic University of America Press, 1992), pp. 126–55.

13. ADR, Ireton to clergy, Oct. 28, 1936.

14. *The Catholic Virginian,* 12, no. 1 (Nov. 1936), p. 12.

15. ADR, Ireton to priests, Jan 12, 1937.

16. *The Catholic Virginian,* 12, no. 3 (Jan. 1937), p. 10.

17. *The Catholic Virginian,* 12, no. 7 (May 1937), p. 10; ADR, Jan. 27, 1938, May 3, 1939: flyers for Sheen lectures at Mosque; Sheen to Ireton, Washington, Jan. 20, 1940, setting date for April 10, 1940.

18. ADR, Martin to Ireton, Roanoke, May 8, 1941.

19. ADR, leaflet for open forum sponsored by Catholic Business and Professional Club and Ireton, Nov. 17, 1939, John Marshall Hotel.

20. ADR, Ireton to Dear Friend, April 1, 1940.

21. ADR, Ireton to clergy, Mar. 8, 1938.

22. ADR, Statistics, 1935–53.

23. ADR, Ireton, "The Diocese of Richmond," submitted to the American Catholic Missions Board, July 1, 1936.

24. Debra Campbell, "David Goldstein and the Rise of the Catholic Campaigners for Christ," *The Catholic Historical Review,* 72 (Jan. 1986), 33–50.

25. ADR, David Goldstein to Brennan, Mobile, Mar. 23, 1933; Toolen to Goldstein, Mobile, April 1, 1933; and Goldstein to Brennan, Montgomery, Ala., April 3, 1933.

26. ADR, Goldstein to Brennan, Rome, Ga., April 14, 1933.

27. ADR, Goldstein to Brennan, Ashville, N.C., May 10, 1933.

28. Campbell, "Goldstein," p. 46.

29. *The Pilot,* Aug. 5, 1933.

30. Goldstein Papers, Boston College, Goldstein to Dolans, Norfolk, July 1, 1933.

31. *The Pilot,* Aug. 5, 1933.

32. ADR, Goldstein to Brennan, Lincoln, Neb., Aug. 22, 1933.

33. ADR, Goldstein to Stephens, Washington, Mar. 9, 1938; Goldstein to Ireton, Mar. 13, 1938.

34. ADR, Ireton to priests, Mar. 18, 1937.

35. ADR, Remke to Ireland, Mar. 30, 1937.

36. ADR, Ireton to Father Ignatius Remke and people of St. Mary's, April 20, 1937.

37. ADR, Remke to Ireton, May 19, 1937.

38. ADR, Ireton to Remke, May 20, 1937.

39. ADR, Remke to Ireton, May 21, 1937.

40. ADR, Ireton to clergy and laity, Sept. 1, 1937.

41. ADR, Ireton to Waters, Scranton, Sept. 5, 1937.

42. ADR, Ireton, sermon, Sept. 12, 1937.

43. ADR, Stephens to Waters, South Boston, "Saturday Night," 1939.

44. ADR, paper read at annual convention, Mar. 22, 1938.

45. *The Catholic Virginian,* 14, no. 5 (Mar. 1939), pp. 10–11, 27.

46. ADR, Ireton, Sept. 15, 1953, circular letter.

47. ADR, Ireton to Waters, June 1, 1943.

48. ADR, Ireton to General William R. Dear, Sept. 7, 1943. Dear was the commander of Camp Pickett, where the band had held a mission with the assistance of the officers.

49. ADR, Ireton to Joseph Hirsch, Mar. 28, 1945.

50. ADR, account of Father Thomas, attached to Waters to Ireton, Richmond, Aug. 11, 1942 (copy).

51. ADR, Ireton to Sister Teresa of Jesus, Mar. 6, 1940 (copy).

52. In the 1950s, Carroll Dozier was one of the diocesan officials who made visitations of the group and found difficulties, including the *Time* article that was published on September 17, 1951. See also ADR, Ireton to Sister Teresa, Richmond, Sept. 28, 1951; and Sister Teresa to Ireton, Danville, Sept. 23, 1951. Justin McClunn continued to attempt to work with them well into the 1960s.

53. ADR, Ireton to Magri, Sept. 23, 1938, circular letter to consultors.

54. ADR, Consultors' Meetings, May 3, 1939, p. 74.

55. [Edward J. Stephens], *One Hundred and Fifty Years for Christ: 1795–1945: St. Mary's Church, Alexandria, Virginia* (Alexandria, 1945), p. 45.

56. ADR, Consultors' Meetings, Dec. 14, 1937, pp. 70–70bis.

57. Interview with Monsignor Scannell, Sept. 8, 1995.

58. ADR, Ireton to Carmody, May 26, 1937 (copy).

59. ADR, Carmody to Brennan, New Haven, May 28, 1937.

60. ADR, Gilsenan to Ireton, Roanoke, Oct. 3, 1937.

61. ADR, Ireton to priests, June 1, 1937.

62. Gerald P. Fogarty, S.J., *The Vatican and the American Hierarchy from 1870 to 1965* (Stuttgart: Anton Hiersemann, Verlag, 1982; Wilmington, Del.: Michael Glazier, 1985), pp. 230–36. Since the Mexican Revolution had begun in 1911, it had become increasingly anticlerical. Although the NCWC negotiated a modus vivendi with the Mexican government in 1928 that allowed Mexican bishops to return from exile in the United States and permitted limited public worship, persecution again broke out in 1932, and some bishops returned to their American exile. In 1935, President Lazaro Cardenas returned to the modus vivendi.

63. Virginius Dabney, *Dry Messiah: The Life of Bishop Cannon* (New York: Alfred A. Knopf, 1949), p. 182.

64. Spalding, *The Premier See*, pp. 251–352.

65. Hugh J. Nolan, ed., *Pastoral Letters of the United States Catholic Bishops*, 4 vols. (Washington, D.C.: National Conference of Catholic Bishops, 1984), 1: 416.

66. ADR, Ireton to priests and laity, Jan. 12, 1938.

67. ADR, O'Shea to Taylor, New York, Mar. 16, 1938.

68. ADR, O'Shea to Waters, New York, Mar. 19, 1938; Waters to Francis Talbot, S.J., Richmond, Jan. 25, 1939 (copy).

69. ADR, Michael Fox to Ireton, Jacksonville, Fla. Jan. 3, 1939.

70. ADR, Waters to Fox, Jan. 9, 1939.

71. ADR, Stephens to Ireton, Atlanta, Jan. 9, 1939.

24. Virginia's Catholics in War and Peace

1. ADR, Irving May, president, and Edward N. Calish, rabbi, to Ireton, Richmond, Feb. 10, 1939.

2. ADR, T. Rupert Coleman to Ireton, Richmond, Feb. 11, 1939.

3. ADR, Smet to Ireton, Louvain, July 21, 1937; Ireton to Smet, n.p., n.d.; Smet to Ireton, Beveren-Waas, April 19, 1940.

4. ADR, William H. Beach, American Consul, to "Monseigneur Fritow [*sic*], Bishop of Richmond," Antwerp, Aug. 27, 1940.

5. Gerald P. Fogarty, S.J., *The Vatican and the American Hierarchy from 1870 to 1965* (Stuttgart: Anton Hiersemann, Verlag, 1982; Wilmington, Del.: Michael Glazier, 1985), pp. 262–64.

6. AAB, I170: Ireton to Curley, Richmond, Oct. 14, 1939.

7. ADR, memorandum from George Waring, N.Y., n.d.

8. ADR, Ireton to senators and representatives, Richmond, July 27, 1940 (copy); Waters to deans, Richmond, July 30, 1940 (copy).

9. ADR, Ireton to clergy, Oct. 31, 1940.

10. *The Catholic Virginian*, 16, no. 5 (Mar. 1941), p. 19.

11. Ibid., 16, no. 10 (Aug. 1941), p. 21.

12. ADR, Strahan to Ireton, Ft. Kamehameha, Dec. 22, 1941.

13. ADR, Strahan to Rankin, Ft. Kamehameha, Feb. 12, 1942.

14. Interview with Monsignor Thomas Scannell, Sept. 8, 1995.

15. *The Catholic Virginian*, 16, no. 9 (July 1941), p. 21; 17, no. 10 (Aug. 1942), p. 24; no 12 (Nov. 1942), p. 23; 18, no. 2 (Dec. 1942), p. 38; no. 6 (Apr. 1943), p. 33; no. 7 (May 1943), p. 29; no. 9 (Aug. 1943), p. 23; 19, no. 3 (Jan. 1943), pp. 6, 23; no. 9 (July 1944), p. 19. For providing these references, I am grateful to Dr. James H. Bailey.

16. Ibid., 20, no. 4 (Feb. 1945), p. 20.

17. *New York Times*, Mar. 26, 1942, 17:3.

18. ADR, Ireton to Senator McCarran, May 1, 1942 (copy).

19. ADR, Byrd to Ireton, May, 1942.

20. ADR, Ireton to clergy, Richmond, May 11, 1942.

21. ADR, Ireton to Harold Nott, Aug. 30, 1942 (copy).

22. ADR, Catholic Theater Guild. Interview with Fritz Campbell, August 3, 1998.

23. Hannon notes, July 17, 1999.

24. ADR, Mission Helpers: Ireton to Teresita, Dec. 3, 1942; Mother Teresita to Ireton, Towson, Dec. 9, 1942.

25. ADR, Missionary Servants of the Most Blessed Trinity: Ireton to Dougherty, April 1, 1943; Ireton to Mother Mary of the Incarnate Word, April 1, 1943; Mother Mary to Ireton, Mar. 29, 1943.

26. Ibid., census of the cathedral, July 1, 1944.

27. Richmond *News Leader*, June 14, 1947.

28. ADR, Missionary Servants of the Most Blessed Trinity: Ireton to Mother Mary Francis, July 3, 1948; Mary Francis to Ireton, Philadelphia, June 18, 1948; Ireton to Mary Francis, May 21, 1949; Mary Francis to Ireton, May 27, 1949; Ireton to Mother Mary Francis, May 28, 1949.

29. ADR, Mission Helpers: Ireton to Teresita, Jan. 24, 1943; Teresita to Ireton, Apr. 23, 1943; Ireton to Teresita, Apr. 26, 1943; Teresita to Ireton, Oct. 13, 1943; Ireton to Teresita, Oct. 15, 1943.

30. Ibid., agreement between Mother M. Constance and Ireton, July 10, 1950.

31. ADR, Baecher to Ireton, May 29, 1944.

32. ADR, Ireton to Baecher, June 2, 1944.

33. *The Catholic Virginian*, 18, no. 9 (July 1942), p. 26.

34. ADR, Cicognani to Ireton, Washington, Sept. 23, 1943.

35. ADR, Cicognani to Hickman, Washington, Oct. 1, 1943; Hickman to Cicognani, Oct. 7, 1943.

36. ADR, Cicognani to Hickman, Washington, Oct. 8, 1943.

37. On July 26, 1943, Mussolini had resigned as premier. The new government of Marshall Pietro Badoglio began making overtures to Washington through the Vatican to declare Rome an open city. On September 11, Badoglio and Roosevelt jointly announced Italy's surrender. In the meantime, Enrico Galeazzi, a close friend of Pius XII and Archbishop Francis Spellman, arrived on a special mission to discuss, among other things, prisoners of war. See Fogarty, *Vatican and the American Hierarchy,* pp. 298–304.

38. ADR, Ireton to Cicognani, Nov. 25, 1943.

39. ADR, Cicognani to Ireton, Washington, Nov. 29, 1943.

40. ADR, Ireton to Cicognani, Mar. 15, 1944.

41. ADR, Cicognani to Ireton, Washington, Apr. 6, 1944.

42. *The Catholic Virginian,* 19, no. 6 (Apr. 1944), pp. 20–21.

43. ADR, Strahan to Ireton, Aliceville, Ala., June 21, 1943.

44. ADR, Findlay to Ireton, Roanoke, Feb. 25, 1945.

45. ADR, Father Denis, O.S.B., to Ireton, Rock Castle, Feb. 23, 1945.

46. ADR, Brochtrup to Ireton, Petersburg, Sept. 23, 1944.

47. *St. Mary's: 200 Years for Christ, 1795–1995* (Alexandria, Va.: St. Mary's Catholic Church, 1995), pp. 99–101.

48. *The Catholic Virginian,* 17, no. 1 (Nov. 1941), pp. 30–31.

49. Ibid., 17, no. 2 (Dec. 1941), pp. 31–32.

50. Ibid., 17, no. 5 (March, 1942), pp. 21–24.

51. Ibid., 17, no. 12 (Oct. 1942), p. 38.

52. ADR, Habets to Ireton, Portsmouth, June 22, 1943.

53. *Norfolk News Index,* Feb. 22, 1940.

54. ASJPH, Box 11–14–1–2, De Paul Hospital.

55. Eric D. Kohler, "To the Further Ends of the Earth: Baptized Jewish Physicians in the Third Reich," MS, p. 10.

56. Fogarty, *The Vatican and the American Hierarchy,* p. 312.

57. ADR, Montini to bishops, Vatican, Feb. 26, 1945.

58. *The Catholic Virginian,* 20, no. 12 (Oct. 1945), p. 21.

59. Ibid., no. 8 (June 1945), pp. 3, 44–45.

60. For providing this information, I am grateful to Dr. James H. Bailey.

61. ADR, Ireton to Cicognani, Richmond, June 25, 1947 (copy).

62. Interview with Monsignor William V. Sullivan, former pastor of St. Peter's, July 27, 1998.

63. ADR, Ireton to Women of Diocese, Feb. 4, 1946.

64. ADR, William B. Ball to McClunn, Harrisburg, Aug. 23, 1961; Unterkoefler to Ball, Aug 24, 1961. Unterkoefler had just replaced McClunn as chancellor.

65. ADR, McClunn to W. E. Garnett, July 17, 1952.

66. Ibid., Aug. 19, 1952.

67. AAHC, McClunn to Purcell, Richmond, July 29, 1956.

68. *The Catholic Virginian,* 23, no. 21 (Mar. 19, 1948), p. 1; no. 35 (June 25, 1948), p. 1; no. 51 (Oct. 15, 1948), p. 3.

69. Ibid., 24, no. 19 (Mar. 11, 1949), p. 1.

70. Ibid., 24, no. 38 (July 22, 1949), p. 1.

71. Ibid., 25, no. 15 (Feb. 3, 1950), p. 1.

72. Ibid., 26, no. 21 (Mar. 23, 1951), p. 1.

73. ADR, MS, Alexandria, n.d., but placed under March 1946.

74. These figures are derived from *The Official Catholic Directory* for the years 1940 to 1955.

75. ADR, Emmett P. Gallagher to Waters, Staunton, Nov. 21, 1942; Waters to Gallagher, Nov. 24, 1942.

76. ADR, Acta Diocesis Richmondiensis, p. 151, June 4, 1949.

77. ADR, Ireton to Weedon, June 22, 1949.

78. ADR, *Brooklyn Tablet,* Feb. 24, 1945, attached to Calish to Ireton, Richmond, Mar. 7, 1945.

79. ADR, Edward Calish to Ireton, Richmond, Mar. 7, 1945.

80. ADR, Ireton to Calish, Richmond, Mar. 9, 1945 (copy).

81. Fogarty, *Vatican and the American Hierarchy,* pp. 353–59.

82. ADR, R. B. Montgomery, president of Lynchburg College, and Clarence Wagner to Ireton, Richmond, Jan. 9, 1946.

83. ADR, Thomas D. Hinton to Ireton, Washington, Dec. 21, 1948.

84. Ibid., Jan. 24, 1950.

85. ADR, John M. Fulmer to Ireton, Petersburg, Jan. 18, 1951.

86. ADR, Ireton to Spellman, Richmond, Dec. 29, 1950 (copy).

25. The Postwar Population Explosion Hits Virginia

1. ADR, Statistics, 1935–53.

2. ADR, Ireton to people, April 8, 1946.

3. ADR, Ireton to people of Richmond, Mar. 13, 1951.

4. *The Catholic Virginian,* 28, no. 27 (May 8, 1953), 1, 13.

5. Ibid., 29, no. 24 (April 16, 1954), 1.

6. ADR, Ireton to people of Richmond, Mar. 28, 1955.

7. ADR, Ireton to O'Brien, July 29, 1946 (copy).

8. *History of St. Patrick's Parish: Celebrating Eightieth Anniversary, 1873–1953, of the Old Church and Dedication of New Church* (Lexington: 1953), pp. 31–35.

9. ADR, Dieltiens to Ireton, Arlington, Oct. 25, 1946. Victor C. DeClercq, C.I.C.M., *Missionhurst—C.I.C.M. in the U.S.A.: 1944–1949* (Arlington, Va.: Missionhurst, 1986), pp. 41–43, 57–60.

10. ADR, "Seminaries/Missionhurst."

11. *The Catholic Virginian,* 20 (Sept. 1945), 3, 30–31.

12. Ibid., 29 (April 30, 1954), 2; (Oct. 1, 1954), 5.

13. Ibid., 32 (June 21, 1957), 1.

14. Ibid., 25 (June 30, 1950), 1; 26 (Nov. 24, 1950), 1; 27 (Sept. 5, 1952); ADR, Seminaries/Berryville/Trappists.

15. *Our Lady Queen of Peace, Arlington, Virginia, 40th Anniversary of the Dedication of the Church* (Arlington, 1987), p. 1.

16. *St. Ann Church, Arlington, Virginia: 40th Anniversary of Dedication of New Parish Buildings* (Arlington, 1987), p. 1.

17. *Dedication Mass: St. Joseph's Catholic Church, Herndon Virginia* (n.p., 1987), pp. 4–5.

18. ADA, McClunn to Benton T. Boogher, Richmond, Apr. 1, 1954 (copy).

19. *St. Mary's: 200 Years for Christ, 1795–1995* (Alexandria: St. Mary's Catholic Church, 1995), pp. 70–71.

20. ADR, Stephens to Ireton, Alexandria, Aug. 26, 1953.

21. Interview with Monsignor Thomas P. Scannell, Sept. 8, 1995.

22. *Our Lady of the Angels: 1959–1984* (n.p.: 1984), p. 1.

23. *Joy is the Spirit of God in the Midst of Men: Twenty-Five Years of Love and Faith* (n.p., 1973), pp. 12–13.

24. *Dedication Ceremony, St. Joseph Catholic Church, Hampton, Virginia,* June 26, 1983, pp. 16–17.

25. *Our Lady of Mount Carmel Church: Early History* (n.p., 1978), pp. 1–3.

26. *The Catholic Virginian,* 30, no. 30 (May 20, 1955), p. 1; no. 37 (July 8, 1955), p. 3.

27. *The Church of St. Gregory the Great, 1957–1982* (Hackensack, N.J.: Custombook, 1982), pp. 8–10.

28. See pp. 506–8.

29. "History of Our Lady of Lourdes Church," enclosed with Richard Dollard to Walter F. Sullivan, Richmond, Dec. 6, 1988.

30. Bess Revene, "A Reminiscence."

31. *The Catholic Virginian,* 22, no. 34 (June 27, 1947), p. 1; no. 45 (Sept. 5, 1947), p. 1.; 25, no. 24 (April 7, 1950), p. 3.

32. *The Catholic Virginian,* 30, no. 14 (Jan. 28, 1955), p. 1.

33. Ibid., 30, no. 35 (Junc 24, 1955), p. 1.

34. Interview with Monsignor Thomas P. Scannell, Sept. 8, 1995.

35. ADR, Sister Anne Robb, D.C., to Marcus K. West [1972?].

36. ADR, Hospitals: Portsmouth, Maryview. *The Catholic Virginian,* 20, no. 8 (June, 1945).

37. *The Catholic Virginian,* 27, no. 22 (April 4, 1952), p. 1; no. 23 (April 11, 1952), p. 3; no. 33 (June 20, 1952), p. 1.

38. Ibid., 26, no. 11 (Jan. 12, 1951), p. 1; no. 14 (Feb. 2, 1951), p. 1; 29, no. 22 (April 2, 1954), pp. 1, 6. See also ADR, Hospitals: Martinsburg, Kings Daughters, for the correspondence on this episode.

39. ADR, Hospitals, Potomac Valley, Keyser, W. Va.

40. Gerald P. Fogarty, S.J., *The Vatican and the American Hierarchy from 1870 to 1965* (Stuttgart: Anton Hiersemann, Verlag, 1982; Wilmington, Del.: Michael Glazier, 1985), p. 364.

41. *The Catholic Virginian,* 29, no. 29 (May 21, 1954), 16.

42. Fogarty, *The Vatican and the American Hierarchy,* pp. 379–81.

43. ADR, Ireton to Pius XII, Oct. 11, 1946 (copy). See also Ireton to Jepson, Oct. 15, 1946 (copy), with attachments of pastors urging the definition.

44. James M. O'Toole, "'The final Jewel in Mary's Crown': American Responses to the Definition of the Assumption," *U.S. Catholic Historian,* 14 (Fall 1996), 83–98.

45. See pp. 510–12.

46. See p. 510.

47. ADR, Marian Year. honors. See also Ireton to Cicognani, Jan. 7, 1954.

48. ADR, McClunn, "Regulations and Recommendations for the Observance of the Marian Year," Nov. 3, 1953.

49. *The Catholic Virginian,* 29, no. 51 (Oct. 15, 1954).

50. ADR, Ireton, "Report on Marian Year Activities in the Diocese of Richmond."

51. *The Catholic Virginian,* 32, no. 3 (Nov. 16, 1956), p. 1; no. 4 (Dec. 7, 1956), p. 1.

52. ADR, Spellman sermon, pp. 1–3.

53. Ibid., 4, 7.

54. Ibid., 10–23.

55. ADW, *Bristol Herald Courier,* April 15, 1952.

56. *The Catholic Virginian,* 32, no. 6 (Dec. 7, 1956), pp. 1, 4; no. 8 (Dec. 21, 1956), p. 1.

57. ADR, Ireton to priests, Dec. 6, 1957.

58. ADR, Mrs. Kenneth M. Sullivan to Ireton, Alexandria, Jan. 17, 1958.

59. ADR, McClunn to Mrs. Sullivan, Jan. 21, 1958 (copy).

60. ADR, Scannell to McClunn, Annandale, [Dec. 9, 1957?].

61. ADR, McClunn to Scannell, Dec. 11, 1957 (copy); Ireton to John J. Lynch, S.J., Dec. 19, 1957 (copy).

62. ADR, Mahoney to Ireton, Baltimore, Jan. 20, 1958.

63. ADR, Consultors' meeting, Apr. 28, 1958.

64. *The Catholic Virginian,* 33, no. 28 (May 9, 1958), pp. 1–3.

26. African Americans in the Diocese of Richmond
from World War I to Integration

1. ASSJ, 17–A-38, van de Vyver to Anciaux, Sept. 21, 1901, quoted in Mary J. Oates, *The Catholic Philanthropic Tradition in America* (Bloomington: Indiana University Press, 1995), p. 63.

2. John E. Burke, "Parochialism and the Missions," *Our Colored Missions,* 10 (Jan., 1924), 3, quoted in ibid.

3. ADR, McCarthy to O'Connell, Baltimore, June 21, 1915.

4. ADR, Ledvina to O'Connell, Church Extension, Chicago, July 18, 1917.

5. ADR, Waring to O'Connell, Norfolk, Jan. 2, 1913.

6. ADR, Williams to O'Connell, Norfolk, Oct. 10, 1914.

7. ADR, O'Connell, application for aid, Commission for the Catholic Missions among the Colored People and the Indians, Aug. 15, 1918.

8. ADR, Warren to O'Connell, Norfolk, July 11, 1919.

9. ADR, O'Connell to Dyer, Richmond, Aug. 20, 1919 (copy).

10. ADR, O'Connell, report to Commission on Indian and Negro Missions, Aug. 15, 1922.

11. ADR, O'Connell, report [Indian and Negro Missions], n.d. [August 1923].

12. ADR, Report for Indian and Negro Missions, Oct. 24, 1924.

13. ADR, Brennan, report to the Commission on Indian and Colored Missions, 1927.

14. Ibid.

15. ADR, Dougherty to Brennan, Philadelphia, Sept. 27, 1928.

16. ADR, William Hafey to Brennan, Raleigh, Oct. 3, 1928; Emmett M. Walsh to Brennan, Charleston, Oct. 10, 1928; Acta Diocesis Richmondiensis, Oct. 24, 1929.

17. ADR, Jenser to O'Connell, Techny, Ill., Dec. 15, 1921.

18. ADR, Lane to Brennan, Beatty, Pa., Oct. 9, 1929.

19. ADR, Lane to Brennan, Latrobe, Pa., Jan. 22, 1930.

20. Stephen J. Ochs, *Desegregating the Altar: The Josephites and the Struggle for Black Priests, 1871–1960* (Baton Rouge: Louisiana State University Press, 1990), pp. 314–17.

21. ADR, Waters to Brennan, Rome, Nov. 1, 1931.

22. ADR, Nott to Brennan, Rome, Jan. 26, 1930.

23. ADR, Habets to Brennan, Portsmouth, Feb. 19, 1931.

24. ADR, Habets to Brennan, Portsmouth, Sept. 1, 1932. He also noted that at the beginning of the 1931–32 school year he had 185 students.

25. *The Catholic Virginian,* Nov. 1933, p. 29.

26. ADR, Habets to Brennan, Portsmouth, Dec. 30, 1933.

27. Ibid.

28. ADR, Glenn to Brennan, Richmond, Sept., 1932.

29. ADR, Kelly to Brennan, Alexandria, Sept. 1, 1932.

30. ADR, Glenn to Brennan, Richmond, Sept. 21, 1933.

31. ADR, Ireton, Ireton to priests, Feb. 3, 1937.

32. ADR, reports collected under Mar. 3, 1937.

33. ADR, Ireton to clergy, Jan. 18, 1940; attached is census for March 1940.

34. ADR, Ireton to Father William Lane, Feb. 19, 1939.

35. Given in John Tracy Ellis, ed., *Documents of American Catholic History,* 3 vols. (Wilmington, Del.: Michael Glazier, 1987), 2, 632.

36. Raphael M. Huber, ed., *Our Bishops Speak* (Milwaukee: Bruce, 1952), p. 178.

37. Katherine Martensen, "Region, Religion, and Social Action: The Catholic Committee on the South, 1939–1956," *The Catholic Historical Review,* 68 (April 1982), 250–51.

38. Wilfrid Parsons, "The Congress at Cleveland," *Columbia,* 19 (Aug. 1939), 2, quoted in Martensen, p. 252.

39. Martensen, pp. 253–54.

40. ADR, Williams to Ireton, Richmond, Feb. 10, 1942.

41. ADR, Ireton to clergy, Mar. 30, 1942.

42. ADR, Ireton to Henry Wallace, Jan. 16, 1942 (copy). Wallace's response is not extant.

43. Martensen, p. 254. *The Catholic Virginian,* May, 1942, pp. 20, 22–25.

44. ADR, clipping attached to file on convention.

45. Martensen, pp. 256–63.

46. ADR, L. R. Reynolds to Waters, April 24, 1941.

47. ADR, Waters to Gillard, Mar. 25, 1941 (copy).

48. ADR, Gillard to Waters, Baltimore, Mar. 28, 1941.

49. ADR, Waters to Reynolds, Mar. 31, 1941 (copy).

50. ADR, Waters to James Albert, April 11, 1941 (copy).

51. ADR, Waters to Habets, Feb. 4, 1942 (copy).

52. ASSJ, "Mission Work" (Jan. 1944), 13–14.

53. ADR, Ireton to priests, Feb. 3, 1937. Attached to this letter were the responses of the priests throughout the diocese, together with the statistics of the black parishes.

54. ADR, Ireton to clergy, Jan. 18, 1940 (copy).

55. For example, in 1941, 1947, and 1951, he received, in addition to the $4,000 grant, $2,000, $15,000, and $12,000, respectively. See ADR, J. B. Tennelly to Ireton, Washington, Nov. 14, 1941; Nov. 17, 1947; and Nov. 16, 1951.

56. ASSJ, "Mission Work" (Jan. 1942), pp. 17–18.

57. Ibid. (Jan. 1944), 13–14.

58. Ibid. (Jan. 1945), 11–12.

59. Anna Louise Haley, *The St. Gerard Story* (Roanoke, 1981), pp. 4–6.

60. Anna Louise Haley, "Roanoke Catholic Churches," *Journal of the Roanoke Valley Historical Society,* 12, no. 2 (1988), 52–54.

61. ADR, Ireton to Dear Father, Richmond, April 29, 1948. In his response, Hickman noted that records for some years were missing.

62. *The Catholic Virginian,* 28, no. 41 (Aug. 14, 1953), p. 1

63. ADR, Govern to Ireton, Elkton, Sept. 9, 1954.

64. ADR, McClunn to Govern, Sept. 14, 1954 (copy).

65. *The Catholic Virginian,* 31, no. 8 (Dec. 23, 1955), p. 3.

66. ASSJ, "Mission Work" (Jan. 1951), 11–14.

67. Ibid. (Jan. 1954), 7–12.

68. Nessa Theresa Baskerville Johnson, *A Special Pilgrimage: A History of Black Catholics in Richmond* (Richmond: Diocese of Richmond, 1978), pp. 49–51.

69. *The Catholic Virginian,* 19 (Feb. 1944), p. 7.

70. Ibid. (Mar. 5, 1948), p. 1. In this endeavor, O'Connell joined Rabbi Nathan Kollin, Mrs. Henry W. Decker, member of the Richmond School Board and a spokesperson for First Baptist Church and the YWCA, Dr. E. T. Thompson of Union Theological Seminary, and Dr. Theodore F. Adams, pastor of First Baptist Church.

71. ADR, McIntyre to Ireton, New York, July 28, 1947.

72. *Washington Post,* Dec. 3, 1996, A.2.

73. ADR, Banks to Ireton, Richmond, March 10, 1949.

74. ADR, Hickman to Thomas V. Cantwell, S.S.J, n.p., March 14, 1949.

75. ADR, Ireton to McIntyre, San Francisco, Feb. 6, 1950 (copy); Ireton to Mitty, n.p., Feb. 6, 1950 (copy).

76. ADR, Nicholas to Ireton, Columbia, Jan. 13, 1937.

77. ADR, Ireton to Nicholas, May 25, 1951.

78. ADR, Ireton to Montini, July 2, 1951. Among the Catholic press reports preserved in ADR are: *Our Sunday Visitor,* June 17, 1951, and *Brooklyn Tablet,* June 16, 1951.

79. ADR, Catholic Committee on the South, meeting, Columbia, S.C., Jan. 22–24, 1951.

80. Martensen, p. 264.

81. *The Catholic Virginian,* May 14, 1954, p. 1. For information about how Ireton chose his topic, I am grateful to Msgr. Thomas Shreve.

82. *The Richmond News Leader,* May 13, 1954, p. 1.

83. Ibid., May 14, 1954, p. 21. See also *Richmond Times-Dispatch,* May 14, 1954, p. 3.

84. *America,* 91 (July 10, 1954), 378.

85. ASSJ, "Mission Work" (Jan. 1955), 12–13.

86. ASSJ, "Our Colored Missions," 40 (Oct. 1954), 150.

87. *Southern School News,* 1, no. 2 (Oct. 1, 1954), 14.

88. Cited in *The Catholic Virginian,* 30, no. 35 (June 24, 1955), 1, 16.

89. *The Catholic Virginian,* April 8, 1955, p. 16.

90. *The Catholic Virginian,* 31, no. 45 (Sept. 7, 1956), 3.

91. Benjamin Muse, *Virginia's Massive Resistance* (Bloomington: Indiana University Press, 1961), pp. 20–21. Information on O'Connell giving Kilpatrick instructions was provided by Charles E. Mahon, editor of *The Catholic Virginian.*

92. Wilfrid Parsons, "Washington Front," *America,* 99 (Sept. 20, 1958), 637.

93. Harold C. Gardiner, "National Library Week—For All?" *America,* 105 (April 15, 1961), 150.

94. Johnson, *A Special Pilgrimage,* p. 58.

27. JOHN J. RUSSELL, THE COUNCIL, AND INTEGRATION, 1958–1968

1. *The Catholic Virginian,* 36 (Nov. 18, 1960), 1.

2. Ibid., 33 (Sept. 26, 1958), p. 1.

3. Ibid., 34 (Sept. 11, 1959), 1.

4. Ibid., 35 (June 17, 1960), 1.

5. For the confusion among Americans on the eve of the council, see my *American Catholic Biblical Scholarship: A History from the Early Republic to Vatican II* (San Francisco: Harper & Row, 1989), pp. 281–322.

6. Russell vota, April 16, 1960, *Acta et Documenta Concilio Oecumenico Vaticano II Apparando,* series I, vol. II, part VI (Vatican: Typis Polyglottis Vaticanis, 1960), p. 416.

7. *The Catholic Virginian,* 35 (July 15, 1960), p. 1.

8. ADR, Consultors' Meeting, Feb. 22, 1960.

9. *The Catholic Virginian,* 36 (June 9, 1961), 1.

10. ADR, Consultors, Jan. 9, 1962.

11. Thomas W. Spalding, *The Premier See: A History of the Archdiocese of Baltimore, 1789–1989* (Baltimore: The Johns Hopkins University Press, 1989), p. 420.

12. ADR, Wright to Unterkoefler, Covington, May 21, 1962.

13. ADR, Unterkoefler to Father Thomas Middendorf, May 25, 1962 (copy). Middendorf was the executive secretary of the Laymen's Retreat Conference.

14. ADR, Mrs. Josephine Wendt to Unterkoefler, Annandale, April 1, 1962; J. L. Flaherty to Unterkoefler, St. Luke, McLean, April 12, 1962; Unterkoefler to Flaherty, April 16, 1962.

15. ADR, Russell to priests, July 20, 1962.

16. *The Catholic Virginian,* 38 (Jan. 24, 1963), 9.

17. William Sullivan to author, Richmond, Aug. 4, 1998.

18. Vincent A. Yzermans, *American Participation in the Second Vatican Council* (New York: Sheed and Ward, 1967), pp. 40–41.

19. Virginius Dabney, "The Bishop Russell Story," *Virginia Record,* Sept. 1967, p. 13.

20. Yzermans, p. 140.

21. *The Catholic Virginian,* 42 (Aug. 22, 1966), p. 1.

22. ADR, Russell to priests, Richmond, Mar. 6, 1963; *The Catholic Virginian,* 38 (Mar. 15, 1963), p. 1.

23. *The Catholic Virginian,* 42 (Nov. 11, 1966), p. 1.

24. Ibid., 42 (Dec. 2, 1966), p. 1.

25. *Fourth Synod of the Diocese of Richmond, Celebrated by The Most Rev. John J. Russell, Bishop of Richmond, Together with The Clergy, Religious and Laity of the Diocese,* December 5, 1966, nos. 3–5, p. 1.

26. Ibid., no. 15, p. 4.

27. Ibid., no. 16, p. 4.

28. Ibid., no. 67, p. 15.

29. Ibid., no. 126, p. 27.

30. Ibid., no. 199, p. 42.

31. Ibid., no. 206, p. 43.

32. Ibid., nos. 223–33, pp. 47–50.

33. Ibid., no. 238, p. 51.

34. ADR, Consultors' Meeting, Sept. 1, 1959.

35. ADR, St. John Vianney, history and statistics.

36. ADR, Central Catholic High School, minutes of board of pastors, Oct. 13, 1967.

37. ADR, St. John Vianney, 1970–74.

38. ADR, Consultors' Meeting, Feb. 22, 1960.

39. ADR, Peninsular Catholic, Newport News.

40. ADR, Cathedral Central Catholic High School.

41. ADR, Consultors' Meetings, p. 22, Mar. 27, 1929.

42. ADR, File: Physicians, Catholic Guild of, Survey for Catholic Hospital in Richmond, Jan. 1937–Oct. 1939; Mitchell to Dr. Fred Fletcher, Richmond, Mar. 18, 1937.

43. Ibid., committee report, Oct. 31, 1939.

44. ADR, Ireton to Mother Jean Marie, O.S.F., Mar. 28, 1941 (copy).

45. ADR, Ireton to Dr. William Bickers, Oct. 26, 1944 (copy).

46. ADR, memo on Catholic hospital, Oct. 9, 1945; Michael McInerney, O.S.B., to Ireton, Belmont, N.C., Dec. 8, 1945. McInerney was the consulting architect. The proposed site was the Hood property on Ladies Mile Rd.

47. ADR, Consultors' Meeting, Sept. 1, 1959.

48. *The Catholic Virginian,* 34, no. 50 (Oct. 9, 1959), p. 1.

49. Ibid., 36 (May 26, 1961), p. 1.

50. Ibid., 36 (Mar. 9, 1962), p. 1.

51. Ibid., 41 (Jan. 7, 1966), pp. 1, 16.

52. ADR, Consultors' Meeting, Sept. 1, 1959.

53. *The Catholic Virginian*, 35, no. 7 (Dec. 11, 1959), p. 1.

54. Ibid., 37 (Feb. 16, 1962), p. 1; no. 25 (Apr. 20, 1962), p. 1; 38, no. 25 (Apr. 19, 1963), p. 1.

55. Hugh J. Nolan, ed., *Pastoral Letters of the United States Catholic Bishops* (Washington, D.C.: United States Catholic Conference, 1983), II, 201–6.

56. For a study of the movement toward racial integration in the North, see John T. McGreevy, *Parish Boundaries: The Catholic Encounter with Race in the Twentieth-Century Urban North* (Chicago: University of Chicago Press, 1996), especially pp. 79–248. For a Boston parallel to the establishment of a Black parish in the 1940s and its subsequent closing, see William C. Leonard, "A Parish for Black Catholics of Boston," *Catholic Historical Review*, 83 (Jan. 1977), 44–68.

57. ASSJ, "Our Indian and Negro Missions" (Jan. 1960), 7–12.

58. ASSJ, "Our Indian and Negro Missions" (Jan. 1961), 13–14.

59. *The Catholic Virginian*, 36, no. 28 (May 12, 1961), p. 8.

60. ASSJ, "Our Indian and Negro Missions" (Jan. 1962), 7–12.

61. Ibid., (Jan. 1963), 7–10.

62. Ibid., (Jan. 1964), 7–20.

63. Ibid., (Jan. 1966), 7–11.

64. Ibid., (Jan. 1968), 12–14.

65. For a poignant reflection on this period, see Nessa Theresa Baskerville Johnson, *A Special Pilgrimage: A History of Black Catholics in Richmond* (Richmond: Diocese of Richmond, 1978), pp. 54–56.

66. ASSJ, "Our Indian and Negro Missions," (Jan. 1966), 7–11.

67. *The Catholic Virginian*, 44 (Feb. 7, 1969), pp. 1, 6.

68. Ibid., 47 (May 5, 1972), p. 3.

69. Ibid., 38 (June 28, 1963), p. 3.

70. Ibid., (July 12, 1963), p. 1.

71. ADR, Russell to O'Boyle, July 11, 1963 (copy).

72. ADR, Arey to Russell, Danville, July 18, 1963.

73. ADR, Russell to Arey, July 22, 1963 (copy).

74. *The Catholic Virginian*, 38, no. 38 (July 19, 1963), p. 18.

75. Ibid., (Sept. 6, 1963), p. 4.

76. ADR, Russell to Deanery of Tidewater, May 14, 1964.

77. ADR, Dozier to Russell, Norfolk, May 18, 1964, with enclosure of newspaper clipping.

78. Scannell interview, Sept. 8, 1995.

79. ADR, Rabbi Noah Golinkin to Stewart Udall, Arlington, Feb. 1, 1965 (copy).

80. *The Catholic Virginian*, 40 (Mar. 5, 1965), p. 5.

81. ADR, Russell to Joseph S. Wholey, Mar. 22, 1965 (copy).

82. ADR, Russell to Allan Knight Chalmers, Mar. 3, 1965 (copy).

83. *The Catholic Virginian*, April 2, 1965, pp. 1, 12.

84. Archives of Marquette University, Mathew Ahmann to McMahon, Chicago, Mar. 19, 1965 (telegram). Ahmann was the executive director of the conference and also sent telegrams to Joseph S. Wholey of Arlington, Jack D. Etz of Richmond, and John B. Jonak of Portsmouth. McMahon had left Richmond and the

telegram could not be delivered to him until Sunday, Mar. 21, the day the march was to begin. For providing me with this information, I am grateful to Gregory Hite.

85. ADR, Arthur Leman to Russell, Houston, April 6, 1965.

86. ADR, Russell to Leman, April 12, 1965 (copy).

87. ADR, Russell to pastors, Aug. 31, 1965 (copy), published in *The Catholic Virginian*, 40 (Sept. 3, 1965), p. 1.

88. *The Catholic Virginian*, 41 (Jan. 14, 1966), pp. 1, 17.

89. ADR, Thomas H. Gibbons to McMahon, Chicago, May 24, 1966.

90. ADR, Kelleher to Russell, Richmond, Nov. 29, 1963.

91. ADR, Russell to Luke E. Hart, Jan. 7, 1964.

92. Christopher J. Kauffman, *Faith and Fraternalism: The History of the Knights of Columbus*, rev. ed. (New York: Simon & Schuster, 1992), pp. 396–97.

93. ADR, Russell to John B. Bowden, Richmond, Mar. 16, 1966.

94. *The Catholic Virginian*, 41, no. 34 (June 24, 1966), p. 3.

95. ADR, Russell to Knights of Columbus Chaplains, Richmond, Aug. 29, 1966.

96. ADR, Russell to John F. Barrett, July 5, 1967.

28. "The Storied Land of Power Mower and Cookout"

1. For a provocative parallel to the choice for a site of a suburban parish, see Lizabeth Cohen, "From Town Center to Shopping Center: The Reconfiguration of Community Marketplaces in Postwar America," *American Historical Review*, 101 (Oct. 1996), 1050–81, and Kenneth T. Jackson, "All the World's a Mall: Reflections on the Social and Economic Consequences of the American Shopping Center," ibid., 1111–21.

2. Quoted in Thomas W. Spalding, *The Premier See: A History of the Archdiocese of Baltimore, 1789–1989* (Baltimore: The Johns Hopkins University Press, 1989), p. 397.

3. ADR, Consultors' Meeting, Apr. 14, 1959.

4. ADR, Consultors' Meeting, Sept. 1, 1959.

5. Ibid.

6. ADR, Consultors' Meeting, Feb. 22, 1960.

7. ADR, St. Thomas, Stickle to "Dear Friends," Charlottesville, June 1962.

8. Ibid., Stickle to friends, Charlottesville, January 1963.

9. Ibid., Financial Agreement between Holy Comforter and St. Thomas Aquinas.

10. *The Catholic Virginian*, 44 (Mar. 14, 1969), 1, 14.

11. ADR, Annual Reports, 1965–69.

12. *Official Catholic Directory, 1971*, p. 695.

13. *The Catholic Virginian*, 45 (Oct. 30, 1970), 1; 46 (Dec. 4, 1979), 1; and (Dec. 11, 1970), 1.

14. Ibid., 46 (Nov. 20, 1970), 1.

15. *Official Catholic Directory, 1996*, pp. 39, 931.

16. Martin B. Bradley, Norman M. Green, Jr., Dale E. Jones, Mac Lynn, and Lou McNeil, *Churches and Church Membership in the United States, 1990* (Atlanta:

Glenmary Research Center, 1992), pp. 396–409. Fairfax led with a Catholic population of 41 percent, followed by Prince William with 29 percent and Arlington with 25 percent. Loudon was then up to 23.7 percent and would continue to grow.

17. Leslie Woodcock Tentler, "'God's Representatives in Our Midst': Toward a History of the Catholic Diocesan Clergy in the United States," *Church History,* 67 (June 1998), 346–49.

BIBLIOGRAPHY

I. Sources

A. Archives and Manuscript Collections

Archives of the American Catholic Historical Society of Philadelphia, Griffin Papers
Archives of the Archdiocese of Baltimore
Archives of the American College, Louvain
Archives of All Hallows College, Drumcondra, Ireland
Archives of the Archdiocese of New York
Archives of the Diocese of Arlington
Archives of the Diocese of Charleston
Archives of the Diocese of Richmond
Archives of the Diocese of Wheeling
Archives of the Diocese of Savannah
Archives of the Irish College, Rome
Archives of the Knights of Columbus, New Haven
Archives of the Maryland Province of the Society of Jesus, Georgetown University
Archives of Mt. St. Mary's Seminary and College, Emmitsburg, Md.
Archives of the Congregation of Propaganda Fide, Rome
Archives of the Sisters of the Blessed Sacrament, Bensalem, Pa.
Archives of St. Joseph's Mother House of the Daughters of Charity, Emmitsburg, Md.
Archives of the Society for the Propagation of the Faith (microfilm)
Archives of the Society of St. Joseph, Baltimore
Archivio Segreto Vaticano
Jones Memorial Library, Lynchburg, Va.
Maymont Foundation, Richmond
Sargeant Memorial Room, Norfolk Public Library
Special Collections, Alderman Library, University of Virginia

623

Sulpician Archives, Baltimore
Virginia Historical Society, Richmond, Va.
Virginia State Library, Richmond, Va.

B. Printed Sources

Acta et Decreta Concilii Plenarii Baltimorensis Tertii. Baltimore: John Murphy, 1886.
Buckley, Cornelius M., S.J., trans. *A Frenchman, A Chaplain, A Rebel: The War Letters of Pere Louis-Hippolyte Gache, S.J.* Chicago: Loyola University Press, 1981.
Commager, Henry Steele, ed. *Documents of American History.* New York: Appleton-Century-Crofts, 1962.
Concilii Plenarii Baltimorensis II., in Ecclesia Metropolitana Baltimorensis, a Die VII. ad Diem XXI. Octobris, A.D., MDCCCLXVI, Habiti, et a Sede Apostolica Recogniti, Acta et Decreta. Baltimore: John Murphy, 1868.
Douglas, Henry Kyd. *I Rode with Stonewall.* Chapel Hill: University of North Carolina Press, 1940.
Durkin, Joseph T., S.J., ed. *Confederate Chaplain: A War Journal of Rev. James B. Sheeran, C.Ss.R, 14th Louisiana, C.S.A.* Milwaukee: Bruce, 1960.
Durkin, Joseph T., S.J., ed. *John Dooley, Confederate Soldier: His War Journal.* Washington, D.C.: Georgetown University Press, 1945.
Ellis, John Tracy, ed. *Documents of American Catholic History.* 3 vols. Wilmington, Del.: Michael Glazier, 1987.
Fernandez, Oliveiria. *Letter addressed to the Most Reverend Leonard Neale, Archbishop of Baltimore, by a Member of the Roman Catholic Congregation of Norfolk, in Virginia.* Norfolk, 1816.
Gazeau, F. "L'Apostolat catholique aux États-unis, pendant la guerre." *Études religieuses* I (1862), 807–30.
Gibbons, James Cardinal. *The Faith of Our Fathers: Being a Plain Exposition and Vindication of the Church Founded by Our Lord Jesus Christ.* 110th ed. New York: P. J. Kennedy & Sons, 1917.
Hanley, Thomas O., S.J., ed. *The John Carroll Papers.* 3 vols. Note Dame: The University of Notre Dame Press, 1976.
Hening, William Waller, *The Statutes-at-large, Being a Collection of All the Laws of Virginia (1619–1792).* 7 vols. New York, 1823.
[Keiley, Anthony J.], "A Virginia Confederate." *In Vinculis; or, The Prisoner of War, being, The Experience of a Rebel in Two Federal Pens, interspersed with reminiscences of the late war; anecdotes of Southern Generals, etc.* Petersburg, Va.: "Daily Index" Office, 1866.
Kennedy, John Pendleton, ed. *Journals of the House of Burgesses of Virginia, 1761–1765.* Richmond, 1907.
King, Terence, S.J. "Letters of Civil War Chaplains." *Woodstock Letters* 43 (1914), 24–34, 168–80.
McGill, John. *Our Faith, The Victory; or, a Comprehensive View of The Principal Doctrines of The Christian Religion.* Richmond: J. W. Randolph, 1865.
Metzler, Josef, O.M.I. "Der älteste Bericht über Nordamerika im Propaganda-Archiv: Virginia 1625." *Neue Zeitschrift für Missionswissenschaft* 25 (1969), 29–37.

O'Hagan, Joseph B., S.J. "Chaplains During the Civil War," *Woodstock Letters* 15 (1886), 111–14.

O'Keefe, Matthew. *The Key to True Christianity: Being a Series of Letters addressed to Rev. J. D. Blackwell.* Philadelphia: William P. Kildare, 1874.

Synodus Dioecesana Richmondensis Prima, A.D. 1856 celebrata. n.p., n.d.

Synodus Dioecesana Richmondiensis Tertia celebrata die decima sexta mensis Februarii Anno Domini MCMXXXIII, preside Illustrissimo ac Reverendissimo Domino Episcopo Andrea Iacobo Brennan (Diocese of Richmond, 1933).

Fourth Synod of the Diocese of Richmond, Celebrated by The Most Rev. John J. Russell, Bishop of Richmond, Together with The Clergy, Religious and Laity of the Diocese, December 5, 1966.

Thwaites, Reuben Gold, ed. *Jesuit Relations and Allied Documents.* 73 vols. Cleveland: Burrows, 1896–1901.

Tissot, Peter. "A Year with the Army of the Potomac: Diary of the Reverend Father Tissot, S.J., Military Chaplain." *Historical Records and Studies* 3 (1903), 42–87.

Tissot, Peter. "Missions des États-unis." *Annales de la Propagation de la Foi,* 35 (1863), 278–87.

Toulemont, P. "L'Apostolat catholique aux États-unis, pendant la guerre." *Études religieuses* II (1863), 862–87.

II. Secondary Works

A. Books

Alma, Mother Maria. *Sisters, Servants of the Immaculate Heart of Mary: 1845–1967.* Lancaster: The Dolphin Press, 1967.

Ayers, Edward L. *The Promise of the New South: Life After Reconstruction.* New York: Oxford University Press, 1992.

Bailey, James H. *A Century of Catholicism in Historic Petersburg: A History of Saint Joseph's Parish, Petersburg.* Petersburg, n.d.

Bailey, James Henry. *A History of the Diocese of Richmond: The Formative Years.* Richmond: Chancery Office, 1956.

Baumstein, Dom Paschal, O.S.B. *My Lord of Belmont: A Biography of Leo Haid.* Herald House, 1985.

Billings, Warren M. *Jamestown and the Founding of the Nation.* Gettysburg: Thomas Publications, n.d.

Bernstein, Iver. *The New York City Draft Riots: Their Significance for American Society and Politics in the Age of the Civil War.* New York: Oxford University Press, 1990.

Billington, Ray Allen. *The Protestant Crusade: 1800–1860: A Study of the Origins of American Nativism.* Chicago: Quadrangle Books, 1964.

Bodell, Dorothy H. *Montgomery White Sulphur Springs: A history of the resort, hospital, cemeteries, markers, and monument.* Blacksburg: Pocahontas Press, 1993.

Brownson, Sarah H. *Life of Demetrius Augustine Gallitzin, Prince and Priest.* New York: Fr. Pustet, 1873.

Bunkley, Josephine M. *The testimony of an escaped novice from the Sisterhood of St. Joseph, Emmittsburg, Maryland, the Mother-house of the Sisters Charity in the United States.* New York: Harper & Brothers, 1855.

Campbell, Charles. *History of the Colony and Ancient Dominion of Virginia.* Richmond, 1847.

Carey, Patrick W. *People, Priests, and Prelates: Ecclesiastical Democracy and the Tensions of Trusteeism.* Notre Dame: University of Notre Dame Press, 1987.

Catton, Bruce. *The Coming Fury.* Garden City: Doubleday, 1961.

Chesson, Michael B. *Richmond after the War: 1865–1890.* Richmond, Virginia State Library, 1981.

Chinnici, Joseph P., O.F.M., ed. *Devotion to the Holy Spirit in American Catholicism.* New York: Paulist Press, 1985.

Condon, Kevin, C.M. *The Missionary College of All Hallows, 1842–1891.* Dublin: All Hallows College, 1986.

Connelly, James F. *The Visit of Archbishop Gaetano Bedini to the United States of America (June, 1853–February, 1854).* Rome: Università Gregoriana Editrice, 1960.

Crowley, Charles J. *Brother Alfred Wakeham, Josephite.* St. Augustine, Fla., n.d.

Crews, Clyde F. *An American Holy Land: A History of the Archdiocese of Louisville.* Wilmington, Del.: Michael Glazier, 1987.

Curley, Michael J., C.Ss.R. *Bishop John Neumann, C.Ss.R.: Fourth Bishop of Philadelphia.* Philadelphia: Bishop Neumann Center, 1952.

Curran, Robert Emmett, S.J. *The Bicentennial History of Georgetown University.* Washington, D.C.: Georgetown University Press, 1993.

Dabney, Virginius. *Dry Messiah: The Life of Bishop Cannon.* New York: Alfred A. Knopf, 1949.

Dabney, Virginius. *Virginia: The New Dominion.* Garden City: Doubleday, 1971.

Davis, Cyprian, O.S.B. *The History of Black Catholics in the United States.* New York: Crossroad, 1990.

Dolan, Jay P. *Catholic Revivalism: The American Experience, 1830–1900.* Notre Dame: University of Notre Dame Press, 1978.

Ellis, John Tracy. *The Life of James Cardinal Gibbons, Archbishop of Baltimore: 1834–1921.* 2 vols. Milwaukee: Bruce, 1952.

Farina, John. *An American Experience of God: The Spirituality of Isaac Hecker.* New York: Paulist Press, 1981.

Fogarty, Gerald P., S.J. *American Catholic Biblical Scholarship: A History from the Early Republic to Vatican II.* San Francisco: Harper & Row, 1989.

Fogarty, Gerald P., S.J. *The Vatican and the American Hierarchy from 1870 to 1965.* Stuttgart: Anton Hiersemann Verlag, 1982; Wilmington, Del.: Michael Glazier, 1985.

Fogarty, Gerald P., S.J. *The Vatican and the Americanist Crisis: Denis J. O'Connell, American Agent in Rome, 1885–1903.* Rome: Università Gregoriana Editrice, 1974.

Foss, William O. *The United States Navy in Hampton Roads.* Norfolk/Virginia Beach: The Donning Company, 1984.

Guilday, Peter. *The Catholic Church in Virginia (1815–1822).* New York: The United States Catholic Historical Society, 1924.

Hassard, John G. *Life of the Most Reverend John Hughes, D.D., First Archbishop of New York*. New York: D. Appleton, 1866.

Henderson, William D. *The 12th Virginia Infantry Regiment*. Lynchburg: H. E. Howard, 1984.

Hennesey, James, S.J. *The First Council of the Vatican: The American Experience*. New York: Herder and Herder, 1963.

Hergesheimer, Joseph. *Mountain Blood*. New York: Alfred Knopf, 1915.

Hughes, Thomas, S.J. *History of the Society of Jesus in North America: Colonial and Federal*. 2 vols. London: Longmans, Green, 1908.

Johnston, Sister M. Helen, O.S.B. *The Fruit of His Works: A History of the Benedictine Sisters of St. Benedict's Convent, Bristow, Prince William County, Virginia*. Bristow: Linton Hall Press, 1954.

Kasteel, Annemarie. *Francis Janssens, 1843–1897: A Dutch-American Prelate*. Lafayette: University of Southwestern Louisiana, 1992.

Kaufmann, Christopher J. *Faith and Fraternalism: The History of the Knights of Columbus*. Rev. ed. New York: Simon & Schuster, 1992.

Kaufmann, Christopher J. *Tradition and Transformation in Catholic Culture: The Priests of Saint Sulpice in the United States from 1791 to the Present*. New York: Macmillan, 1988.

Keen, Hugh C., and Horace Mewborn. *43rd Battalion Virginia Cavalry: Mosby's Command*. Lynchburg: H. E. Howard, 1993.

Keiley, A. M. "Memorandum of the History of the Catholic Church, Richmond, Va." *Proceedings of the Fourth Annual Convention of the Catholic Benevolent Union of the State of Virginia, held in the City of Norfolk, Virginia, on the 10th, 11th and 12th of June, 1874, with Appendix*. Norfolk: Virginian Book and Job Print, 1874.

Lewis, Clifford M., S.J., and Albert J. Loomie, S.J. *The Spanish Jesuit Mission in Virginia: 1570–1572*. Chapel Hill: University of North Carolina Press, 1953.

Maddex, Jack P., Jr., *The Virginia Conservatives: 1867–1879*. Chapel Hill: University of North Carolina Press, 1970.

Manchester, William. *American Caesar*. Boston: Little, Brown, 1978.

Marshall, A. L. *Adam Livingston, the Wizard Clip, The Voice: An Historical Account*. Kearneysville, W. Va.: Livingston Publications, 1978.

Meline, Mary, M., and Edward F. X. McSweeney. *The Story of the Mountain: Mount St. Mary's College and Seminary, Emmitsburg, Maryland*. 2 vols.; Emmitsburg: The Weekly Chronicle, 1911.

Melville, Annabelle M. *Louis William DuBourg: Bishop of Louisiana and the Floridas, Bishop of Montauban, and Archbishop of Besançon, 1766–1833*. 2 vols. Chicago: Loyola University Press, 1986.

Mitchell, Brian C. *The Paddy Camps: The Irish of Lowell: 1821–61*. Urbana and Chicago: University of Illinois Press, 1988.

Moore, Robert H., II. *Chew's Ashby, Shoemaker's Lynchburg and the Newton Artillery*. Lynchburg: H. E. Howard, 1995.

Morgan, Edmund Sears. *Virginians at Home; Family Life in the Eighteenth Century*. Charlottesville: Dominion Books, 1963.

Morton, Richard L. *Colonial Virginia*. 2 vols. Chapel Hill: University of North Carolina Press, 1960.

Oates, Mary J. *The Catholic Philanthropic Tradition in America*. Bloomington: Indiana University Press, 1995.

Ochs, Stephen J. *Desegregating the Altar: The Josephites and the Struggle for Black Priests, 1871–1960*. Baton Rouge: Louisiana State University Press, 1990.

O'Dwyer, George F. *The Irish Catholic Genesis of Lowell*. Lowell, 1920; reissued, 1981.

Parramore, Thomas C. *Norfolk: The First Four Centuries*. Charlottesville: University Press of Virginia, 1994.

Peterman, Thomas Joseph. *The Cutting Edge: The Life of Thomas A. Becker*. Devon, Pa.: William T. Cooke, 1982.

Reilly, John T. *Collections and Recollections in the Life and Times of Cardinal Gibbons*. 2 vols. Martinsburg: Herald Print, 1892–93.

Sauter, John D., *The American College of Louvain (1857–1898)*. Louvain: Bibliothèque de l'université bureaux du recueil, 1959.

Shannon, James P. *Catholic Colonization on the Western Frontier*. New Haven: Yale University Press, 1957.

Shaw, Richard. *Dagger John: The Unquiet Life and Times of Archbishop John Hughes of New York*. New York: Paulist Press, 1977.

Shaw, Richard. *John Dubois: Founding Father*. Yonkers: U.S. Catholic Historical Society, 1983.

Shea, John Gilmary. *History of the Catholic Church in the United States*. 4 vols. New York: D. H. McBride, 1886.

Siepel, Kevin H. *Rebel: The Life and Times of John Singleton Mosby*. New York: St. Martin's Press, 1983.

Smith, Willard H. *Schuyler Colfax; the Changing Fortunes of a Political Idol*. Indianapolis: Indiana Historical Bureau, 1952.

Spalding, Thomas W. *Martin John Spalding: American Churchman*. Washington, D.C.: The Catholic University Press, 1973.

Spalding, Thomas W. *The Premier See: A History of the Archdiocese of Baltimore, 1789–1989*. Baltimore: The Johns Hopkins University Press, 1989.

Stover, John F. *History of the Baltimore and Ohio Railroad*. West Lafayette: Purdue University Press, 1987.

Trask, Benjamin H. *The 9th Virginia Infantry Regiment*. Lynchburg: H. E. Howard, 1984.

Tucker, George Holbert. *Abstracts from Norfolk City Marriage Bonds (1797–1850) and Other Genealogical Data*. Norfolk: William H. Delaney, 1934.

Valentine Museum. *Makers of Richmond, 1737–1860: An exhibition of portraits, November 16, 1948 through January 2, 1949*. Richmond: The Valentine Museum, 1948.

Wallace, Lee A. *A Guide to Virginia Military Organizations, 1861–1865*. Lynchburg: H. E. Howard, 1986.

Wallace, Lee A., *1st Virginia Infantry*. 3d ed.; Lynchburg: H. E. Howard, 1985.

Weber, David, J. *The Spanish Frontier in North America*. New Haven: Yale University Press, 1992.

B. Articles and Contributions to Books

Anonymous. "Our Friends on the Mission." *The American College Bulletin* III (1905), 117–20.

"Chaplain Matthew O'Keefe of Mahone's Brigade." *Southern Historical Society Papers* 35 (1907), 180.

Bailey, James M. "The Family and Background of Anthony M. Keiley" (Petersburg). *Progress-Index*, May 25, 1947, p. 4.

Bayliss, Mary Lynn. "Will the Real Major Dooley Please Stand Up!" *The Richmond Quarterly* 14 (Fall 1991), 31–34.

Bladek, John David. "'Virginia Is Middle Ground:' The Know Nothing Party and the Virginia Gubernatorial Election of 1855." *The Virginia Magazine of History and Biography* 106 (Winter 1998), 35–70.

Buckley, Thomas E., S.J. "After Disestablishment: Thomas Jefferson's Wall of Separation in Antebellum Virginia." *Journal of Southern History* 61 (Aug. 1995), 445–80.

Carey, Patrick. "John F. O. Fernandez: Enlightened Lay Catholic Reformer, 1815–1820." *The Review of Politics* 43 (Jan. 1981), 112–29.

Chesson, Michael B. "Harlots or Heroines? A New Look at the Richmond Bread Riot." *The Virginia Magazine of History and Biography* 92 (Apr. 1984), 131–75.

Coleman, Elizabeth Dabney. "The Blue Ridge Tunnel." *Virginia Cavalcade* I (Summer 1951), 22–27.

Cross, Richard E., and Eugene L. Zoeller. *The Story of the American College*, extract from *The American College Bulletin* (1957), p. 14.

De Becker, J. "The Right Reverend Augustine Van de Vyver, Bishop of Richmond." *The American College Bulletin* 10 (Jan. 1912), 1–6.

Ellis, John Tracy. "James Gibbons of Baltimore." In Gerald P. Fogarty, S.J., ed. *Patterns of Episcopal Leadership.* New York: Macmillan, 1989.

Fogarty, Gerald P., S.J. "Diocesan Structure and Governance in the United States." In James K. Mallett, ed., *The Ministry of Governance.* Washington, D.C.: Canon Law Society of America, 1986.

Fogarty, Gerald P., S.J. "Property and Religious Liberty in Colonial Maryland Catholic Thought," *Catholic Historical Review* 72 (1986), 573–600.

Gilliam, Gerald T., "The Catholic Colony at Barnesville." *The Southsider* 12 (1993), 36–46.

Glennon, Michael. "Reminiscences of Catholic Boyhood." Paper read before the Emerald Literary Association, Nov. 17, 1893.

Griffin, Martin I. J. "Catholics in Colonial Virginia." *Records of the American Catholic Historical Society* 22 (1911), 89–90.

Heisser, David C. R. "Bishop Lynch's Civil War Pamphlet on Slavery." *Catholic Historical Review* 84 (Oct. 1998), 681–96.

Lahey, R. J. The Role of Religion in Lord Baltimore's Colonial Enterprise." *Maryland Historical Magazine* 72 (Winter 1977), 492–511.

Lahey, Raymond. "Avalon: Lord Baltimore's Colony in Newfoundland." In G. M. Story, ed. *Early European Settlement and Exploitation in Atlantic Canada*

(St. John's, Newfoundland: Memorial University of Newfoundland, 1982), pp. 115–37.

O'Grady, Joseph P. "Anthony M. Keiley (1832–1905): Virginia's Catholic Politician." *Catholic Historical Review* 54 (Jan. 1969), 624–25.

Parke, Henry F. "Some Notes on the Rise and Spread of the Catholic Missions in Virginia: A.D. 1774–1850." *Research* 1 (Mar. 1943).

Poole, Stafford, C. M. "Ad Cleri Disciplinam: The Vincentian Seminary Apostolate in the United States." In John E. Rybolt, C.M., ed. *The American Vincentians: A Popular History of the Congregation of the Missions in the United States, 1815–1987* (Brooklyn: New City Press, 1988).

Rice, Phillip Morrison. "The Know-Nothing Party in Virginia, 1854–1856." *Virginia Magazine of History and Biography* 55 (1947), 61–75; 159–69.

Smet, Louis. "The Rt. Rev. Augustine Van de Vyver, Bishop of Richmond, Va. (1889–1911)." *The American College Bulletin* 10 (July 1912), 88–100.

Steiner, Bruce. "The Catholic Brents of Colonial Virginia: An Instance of Practical Toleration." *The Virginia Magazine of History and Biography* 70 (Oct. 1962), 387–94.

Tucker, Beverly R. "George Ben Johnston: An Appreciation." *Bulletin of the Medical College of Virginia* 13 (Dec. 1916), 3–24.

Tucker, Philip. "Confederate Secret Agent in Ireland: Father John B. Bannon and His Irish Mission, 1863–1864." *Journal of Confederate History* V (1990), 55–65.

Wallace, Lee A., Jr., and Detmar H. Finke. "Montgomery Guard." *Military Collector and Historian* (Fall 1958), 69.

C. Manuscripts

Anonymous. "St. Elizabeth Roman Catholic Church." Mimeographed page, May, 1988.

Arminger, Sister Bernadette, D.C. "The History of the Hospital Work of the Daughters of Charity of St. Vincent De Paul in the Eastern Province of the United States: 1823–1860," M.S. thesis, Catholic University of America School of Nursing Education, 1947.

Beattie, Robert Fountain, "The Beginnings of Catholicity in Virginia." M.A. thesis, St. Mary's Seminary, Baltimore, 1929.

Campbell, Sister M. Anne Francis, O.L.M. "Bishop England's Sisterhood, 1829–1929." Ph.D. dissertation, History Department, St. Louis University, 1968.

Coleman, Elizabeth Dabney. "The Story of the Virginia Central Railroad: 1850–1860." Ph.D. dissertation, Corcoran Department of History, University of Virginia, 1957.

Donovan, John A. K. "The Light of His Life: being the biography of Amadeus Joseph van Ingelgem, a Virginia Missionary." Manuscript, Falls Church, Virginia, 1937.

Goller, Walker. "John Lancaster Spalding's Religious Anthropology: An American Catholic Understanding of the Human Person." Ph.D. dissertation, Toronto School of Theology, 1994.

Hickey, Sister Zoe, "The Daughters of Charity of St. Vincent de Paul in the Civil War." M.A. thesis, The Catholic University of America.

Kimball, Gregg David. "Place and Perception: Richmond in Late Antebellum America." Ph.D. dissertation, Department of History, University of Virginia, 1997.

Marschall, John Peter. "Francis Patrick Kenrick, 1851–1863: The Baltimore Years." Ph.D. dissertation, The Catholic University of America, 1965.

Pessner, Ronald O. "The St. Emma Military Academy: A Catholic Response to African-American Missions and Industrial Education." B.A. thesis, Corcoran Department of History, University of Virginia, 1992.

Shank, Joseph E. "Raw Materials on the History of Norfolk-Portsmouth Newspapers." Manuscript, Sargeant Memorial Room, Norfolk Public Library.

Singleton-Driscoll, Linda. "The Dooley Women of Richmond." Manuscript, Maymont Foundation, 1979.

Wilkinson, Stephanie. "A Novel Defense: Fictional Defenses of American Catholicism, 1824–1869." Ph.D. dissertation, Department of Religious Studies, University of Virginia, 1997.

D. Parish Histories and Local Studies

Anonymous. "Commemorating the Centennial of St. Vincent de Paul Church, Newport News, Virginia, 1881–1981."

Anonymous. *Centenary of the Convent of the Visitation, Mount de Chantal, Wheeling, West Virginia, 1848–1948* (n.p., n.d.).

Anonymous. *Church of the Assumption, Keyser, West Virginia: Centennial Celebration, 1874–1974* (n.p., n.d.), p. 11.

Anonymous. *Saint Anne's Catholic Church and School, Bristol, Virginia* (n.p., 1990).

Anonymous. *St. Joseph's Catholic Church: 1889–1989* (Clifton Forge, 1989).

Anonymous. *St. Joseph's Parish Church, Martinsburg, West Virginia* (n.p., 1969).

Anonymous. *St. Mary's: 200 Years for Christ, 1795–1995* (Alexandria: St. Mary's Catholic Church, 1995).

Anonymous. *The Golden Jubilee of the Original Stone Church: 1902–1952: St. James Church, Falls Church, Virginia* (n.p., n.d.).

Bevan, Thomas R. *200 Years: A History of the Catholic Community of the Frederick Valley* (Frederick: Da-Mark, Associates, 1977), pp. 12–14.

Brennan, Robert J., O.S.B. *A History of St. Mary's Church, Richmond, Virginia* (Richmond, 1962).

Cochener, Margaret Maier. *On the Hill: St. Andrew's Parish, Roanoke, Virginia, a History of St. Andrew's Parish, November 1882–August, 1989* (n.p., 1989), p. 7.

DeClercq, Victor C., C.I.C.M. *The Catholic Church in the Alleghany Highlands around 1882* (n.p., 1982), p. 25.

Freson, Ray and Barbara, eds. *St. Mary's Parish, Fairfax, Va., 1858–1983* (Fairfax, Va., 1983).

Griffin, Virginia Bernadette. *Golden Jubilee: St. Paul's Catholic Church, Portsmouth* (Portsmouth, 1955).

Hairfield, Hampton H., Jr., and Elizabeth M., and James F. Smith, *A History of St. Francis of Assisi Parish, Staunton, Virginia, Celebrating 150 Years: 1845–1995* (Bridgewater, Va.: Good Printers, 1995).

Haley, Anna Louise. *Our Lady of Nazareth Parish: 1914–86, Roanoke, Virginia.* Roanoke, 1986.

Haley, Anna Louise. *The St. Gerard Story.* Roanoke, 1981.

Joerndt, Clarence V. *St. Ignatius, Hickory, and Its Missions* (Baltimore: Publication Press, 1972).

Kelly, Cecilia, and Julia Dennehy. "A History of the Catholic Church in Southwest Virginia and Norton." In *50 Years: St. Anthony Catholic Church, 1938–1988* (n.p., 1988).

Lacina, Thomas H., and William C. Thomas. *A History of Sacred Heart Parish* (Boyce, Va.: Carr Publishing, 1953).

Walsh, Grace. *The Catholic Church in Lynchburg, 1829–1936.* Lynchburg: Coleman & Bradley Printers, 1936.